DATE DUE

FE - 1 '10			

DEMCO 38-296

THE MILTON CROSS
NEW ENCYCLOPEDIA OF
THE GREAT COMPOSERS
AND THEIR MUSIC

THE MILTON CROSS

New Encyclopedia

of the Great Composers

and Their Music

MILTON CROSS

AND

DAVID EWEN

Revised and Expanded

VOLUME ONE

GARDEN CITY, NEW YORK

DOUBLEDAY & COMPANY, INC.

Library of Congress Catalog Card Number 70–87097
Copyright © 1953, 1962, 1969 by Doubleday & Company, Inc.

Foreword

This is a book for the music lover, an attempt to gather within the confines of two volumes all the information he needs on every facet of serious music.

Basically it is about the foremost composers of the past and present (sixty-seven in number) and their music. Here will be found exhaustive biographies of each of the giant figures tapping the latest musicological findings—a detailed story of each one's life together with a personal portrait, an evaluation of his place in musical history and his contribution to it, and an analysis of his most important works in every branch of musical composition (symphonic, operatic, choral, vocal, chamber music, and so forth). Where a composer's music introduces or develops a major trend, technique, or style in music history, that trend, technique, or style is explained.

We feel that this is the first time that a popular work has attempted to provide so much about so many composers and so many of their works within such comparatively limited confines.

Yet we could not stop there. An intelligent understanding of the great composers and their music demands other information on the part of the perceptive music lover. Consequently, to set the stage for these composers, we have prefaced their section with a brief history of music before Bach. And to clarify the evolution of the musical art beginning with Bach, and the role played by the composers in that evolution, we have followed this section with a brief history of music since 1750.

Two volumes which must discuss in such detail the greatest masters of all time, together with analysis of so many of their significant compositions, obviously cannot include as many composers of our own times as the editors would have liked. Those most representative of the twentieth century have been included. But it was necessary to fill out the picture of what is happening in our own day. And so, ending Part Three, we have presented a panorama of the evolution and development of modern musical techniques and trends since 1900, and followed it with a survey of the avant-garde movement that has swept through the world of music since the middle 1950s.

Other sections provide still more information essential to a mature appreciation of music: a glossary of basic terms in music; a dictionary of musical forms; a study of the anatomy of the symphony orchestra. We also felt that the music lover would find useful a list of basic works for the record library (with recommended recordings) and a select bibliography of books in the English language that are readily available in large bookstores and major libraries.

DAVID EWEN
MILTON CROSS

Contents

VOLUME I

PART ONE   *Before Bach*   1

PART TWO   *The Composers and Their Music*   13

Johann Sebastian Bach • 15
Samuel Barber • 43
Béla Bartók • 52
Ludwig van Beethoven • 65
Alban Berg • 106
Hector Berlioz • 116
Georges Bizet • 132
Ernest Bloch • 141
Alexander Borodin • 153
Johannes Brahms • 163
Benjamin Britten • 193
Anton Bruckner • 210
Frédéric Chopin • 223
Aaron Copland • 242
Claude Debussy • 255
Frederick Delius • 279
Gaetano Donizetti • 290
Antonín Dvořák • 299
Sir Edward Elgar • 318
Manuel de Falla • 330

Gabriel Fauré • 343
César Franck • 352
George Gershwin • 365
Christoph Willibald Gluck • 384
Charles Gounod • 396
Edvard Grieg • 405
George Frideric Handel • 421
Howard Hanson • 447
Roy Harris •455
Joseph Haydn • 468
Paul Hindemith • 497
Arthur Honegger • 516
Aram Khatchaturian • 526
Zoltán Kodály • 533
Franz Liszt • 543
Gustav Mahler • 561
Jules Massenet • 577
Felix Mendelssohn • 585
Gian Carlo Menotti • 606
Giacomo Meyerbeer • 618

Contents

VOLUME II

Darius Milhaud • 627
Wolfgang Amadeus Mozart • 639
Modest Mussorgsky • 682
Serge Prokofiev • 699
Giacomo Puccini • 720
Sergei Rachmaninoff • 739
Maurice Ravel • 754
Ottorino Respighi • 773
Nicholas Rimsky-Korsakov • 780
Gioacchino Rossini • 797
Camille Saint-Saëns • 813
Arnold Schoenberg • 829
Franz Schubert • 851
Robert Schumann • 882

Alexander Scriabin • 906
Dmitri Shostakovich • 919
Jean Sibelius • 940
Bedřich Smetana • 957
Richard Strauss • 968
Igor Stravinsky • 996
Peter Ilitch Tchaikovsky • 1025
Ralph Vaughan Williams • 1054
Giuseppe Verdi • 1070
Richard Wagner • 1095
Sir William Walton • 1136
Karl Maria von Weber • 1148
Hugo Wolf • 1161

PART THREE   *A Brief History of Music Since
Bach*   1171

PART FOUR   *Basic Works for the Record Library*
(With Recommended Recordings)   1183

PART FIVE   *The Anatomy of the Symphony
Orchestra*   1193

PART SIX   *A Dictionary of Musical Forms*   1199

PART SEVEN   *A Glossary of Basic Musical Terms*   1215

PART EIGHT   *A Select Bibliography*   1233

Index   1251

THE MILTON CROSS
NEW ENCYCLOPEDIA OF
THE GREAT COMPOSERS
AND THEIR MUSIC

Part One

BEFORE BACH

BEFORE BACH

Chronologically, as well as alphabetically, Johann Sebastian Bach is the first composer in the gallery of great composers found in the next section. But there were eminent composers before Bach's day who wrote much distinguished music. They are not included in this volume because both the composers and their music are now somewhat esoteric and are not basic to the concert experiences of the average music lover. But it is illuminating to trace, even briefly, the growth of the musical art up to the time of Bach and to point to those composers and those musical works which made Bach and his successors possible.

I

The first important period in musical history was the polyphonic period, which emphasized the simultaneous performance of several equally important melodies. The number of melodies ("parts") ranged from four to eight, the most usual being four or five. The music was for unaccompanied ("*a cappella*") voices. Its focal point was the Catholic Church.

The Gothic period, roughly from 1200 to 1450, was the first era in polyphonic music.

The earliest of the polyphonic forms was the organum.* This was developed in France, mostly by the choirmaster of Notre Dame, Magister Leoninus (twelfth century). Another form was the conductus, a manner perfected by Magister Perotinus (twelfth century), who was also responsible for the early development of notation.

All this early polyphonic music is known as the *Ars Antiqua* (*The Ancient Art*). In or about 1320 there appeared a book by Philippe de Vitry called *Ars Nova* (*The New Art*). This book clarified a new rhythmic procedure: duple time. There next came

---

* The organum, and other musical forms mentioned in this section—conductus, oratorio, cantata, modrigal, concerto grosso, toccata, passacaglia, fugue, and so forth —are explained in Part VI. All other musical terms are defined in Part VII.

about a new age for polyphonic music, known as that of the *Ars Nova,* in which a new concept of rhythm and melody was realized. One of the leading masters of this new style was Guillaume de Machaut (c.1300–77). With him we find the earliest evolution of such important polyphonic forms as the Mass and the motet. When the *Ars Nova* passed from France to Italy, the madrigal was born.

Polyphonic music now underwent a vital transformation, which was achieved by several important schools of composers. The first of these schools was the Flemish (or Netherlands). Its founder was Guillaume Dufay (1400–74), and later significant members included Jean de Okeghem (c.1430–95), Josquin des Prés (c.1445–1521), Jacob Arcadelt (c.1514–70), and Orlando de Lasso (1532–94). With this group, technique and mechanics of contrapuntal writing were combined for the first time with attention to musical idea and beauty of musical sound.

A second school was the Venetian, its principal composers including Giovanni Gabrieli (1557–1612) and Adrian Willaert (sixteenth century). Greater richness in the polyphonic texture is found in the music of the Venetians. This is due largely to the fact that they wrote for several choirs at once (the choirs being placed in different parts of the church), thereby developing the technique of antiphony.

A third major school was the Roman, and its dean was the greatest church composer of his generation, Giovanni Pierluigi da Palestrina (c.1525–94). As choirmaster of the S. Maria Maggiore in Rome, he wrote some of his finest works, including the celebrated *Missa Papae Marcelli,* in memory of Marcellus II, which helped bring about a reform in Italian church music. This Mass established Palestrina as one of the leading composers in Rome and became the prototype for all later Masses. Palestrina wrote many other Masses as well as motets, madrigals, Magnificats, psalms, and so forth (about one thousand works in all). No one before him had brought to polyphonic music such a devotional character, such spiritual beauty, nobility of expression, and majesty of thought. He is the greatest master before Bach.

The Spanish-born composer Tomás Luis de Victoria (c.1548–1611) was a product of this Roman school, as he was Palestrina's pupil and as most of his works were written and published in Rome. To the style and technique of Palestrina, Victoria brought a mysticism and a vividness of color, a force and drama that are of Spanish rather than Italian origin.

But polyphonic music was not confined exclusively to the church. In the sixteenth century, secular polyphonic music came into being. It was livelier and more rhythmic than its liturgical counterpart. The madrigal was one of these early secular forms. It was born and developed in Italy by such masters as Orazio Vecchi (1550–1605) and Carlo Gesualdo (1560–1613). The madrigal achieved structural perfection with Claudio Monteverdi (1567–1643), who will be discussed in a later paragraph in connection with the opera. Among Monteverdi's most important innovations within the madrigal form were the inclusion of elaborate solos and the occasional substitution of accompanied numbers for *a cappella* ones.

An amateur musician, Nicholas Yonge (died 1619), is believed to have brought the madrigal from Italy to England, and it was in England that this form achieved its greatest significance. In 1588 Yonge published a volume of fifty-seven madrigals which included not only the best examples of the Italian style, but also two numbers by an English composer, William Byrd (1543–1623). It was with Byrd that the English madrigal came into being. The golden age of the English madrigal was not slow in arriving: with Thomas Morley (1557–1603), composer of "Now Is the Month of Maying" and "Sing We and Chant It"; with Orlando Gibbons (1583–1625), who wrote "The Silver Swan"; with John Wilbye (1574–1638), whose many madrigals included the well-loved "Adieu, Sweet Amaryllis"; and with the last of the great madrigalists, Henry Purcell (1659–95). In the twentieth century, the English madrigal was rediscovered and presented in new settings by Ralph Vaughan Williams (1872–1958).

II

In the seventeenth century, the Baroque style dominated every facet of art. This style was characterized by its grandiose effects and highly ornamented details within elaborate structures and designs.

In music, the Baroque period brought about the following developments: (1) the birth of new forms of secular and liturgical music, the most important of which were the opera and the oratorio; (2)

the rise and development of instrumental music, which assumed a status equal to that of choral music; (3) the emergence of a "new music" (*"Nuove musiche"*)—the homophonic style, which stressed the single melody with harmonic accompaniment, as opposed to polyphony.

Opera was created by a group of dilettantes (known as the *"camerata"*) in Florence in the closing years of the sixteenth century. Inspired by the spirit of the Renaissance, this group aspired to revive the glory of ancient Greek drama through the union of plays on classical subjects with music. But the music of the period—polyphony—was poorly suited for dramatic purposes. The *camerata* had to evolve a new musical style, modeled after speech (so that the text might be intelligible) and intended for a single voice. Thus the monodic style—recitative, or declamation—came into being. Jacopo Peri (1561–1633), a member of the *camerata,* wrote a work in 1594 called *Dafne,* which he designated as a *"dramma per musica."* This was the first work in history to be set to music *throughout,* and consequently it can be regarded as the first opera. With Peri and his immediate successor, Giulio Caccini (c.1546–1618), the *dramma per musica* was amorphous in form, consisting of a sequence of dull recitatives only infrequently interrupted by a brief chorus or ballet. The accompanying orchestra was primitive, consisting primarily of lutes and a harpsichord. There was no attempt to bring dramatic force into the musical writing; and there was little emotion or feeling.

The *dramma per musica* originated in Florence, but it was developed into an art form in Venice. The Venetian school in opera was created by one of the giant figures in the early history of music, Claudio Monteverdi.

Monteverdi had written and published several volumes of madrigals when he heard a performance of Peri's *dramma per musica* and became enthusiastic about the new form. The marriage of the Duke of Mantua's son to the Infanta of Savoy, in 1607, led him to write a work in a similar vein. It was his operatic masterpiece—and the work generally credited with being the first masterwork in operatic music—*Orfeo,* produced in Mantua on February 24, 1607. In 1613 Monteverdi became *Maestro di cappella* at the St. Mark's Cathedral in Venice, where he remained for many years, writing and producing his later operas, which included *Il Combattimento di Tancredi e*

Clorinda and *L'Incoronazione di Poppea*. As the most famous opera composer of the day, he made Venice the center of operatic activity. Consequently it was in Venice that the first public opera house was opened, in 1637, the San Cassiano Theater.

He was always the fearless experimenter, always the seeker after new idioms and techniques. Singlehanded, he changed the destiny of the then primitive *dramma per musica*. In his hands, the stilted and expressionless declamation of Peri and Caccini became flexible and filled with emotional force. He brought the human element into the musical theater. So highly developed and so filled with lyric beauty were some of his recitatives that it can be said with justification that Monteverdi was the first to arrive at the writing of an aria. He was also the first to introduce into opera ensemble numbers—duets, trios, and so forth—as well as instrumental passages. And the orchestra—greatly extended to include violins, violas of all kinds, harp, flute, cornet, and so forth, as well as lutes and harpsichords—now became an important element of the musical theater; and for that orchestra Monteverdi created all sorts of new instrumental devices, such as the pizzicato and the tremolo, in order to make his music more expressive.

We find the word "opera" used for the first time in Venice, and it was used by Monteverdi's immediate successor, Pietro Francesco Cavalli (1602–76). Cavalli referred to his first dramatico-musical work, *Le Nozze di Teti* (1639), as an *"opera-scenica"* and not as a *"dramma per musica."*

Some of the traditions of Italian opera were first set and popularized in Naples, which soon succeeded Venice as an operatic center. The leader of this new school was Alessandro Scarlatti (1660–1725), father of Domenico Scarlatti, famous as a composer of harpsichord sonatas. Alessandro Scarlatti's many operas, presented in Naples, exerted a profound influence on all his contemporaries, who imitated him. With Scarlatti several important innovations appear: one is the *da capo* aria, with which the aria form is greatly extended and developed; another is the so-called Italian overture. With Scarlatti, the orchestra was given increasing importance, and ensemble and choral singing were greatly amplified.

The operatic style as evolved in Naples dominated the entire world of opera for more than a generation. Outside of Italy, as well as in it, Italian opera as written by the Neapolitans was in vogue; Italian opera was a reigning favorite in the courts and theaters of Germany, France, and England. But the first tentative efforts to break with the Italian style are already to be discerned in those countries. In Germany, Heinrich Schütz (1585–1672) wrote an opera, *Dafne,* in 1627. As the first opera in the German language, it must be considered one of the cornerstones on which a Germanic opera was later to be erected. In France, a Florentine opera composer, Jean Baptiste Lully (1632–87) laid the foundations of French opera— as director of and composer for the Paris Opéra—by placing increased emphasis on the dramatic element, glorifying the ballet, and introducing the French, or Lully, Overture. In England, English opera was evolved by Henry Purcell with *Dido and Aeneas,* whose melodies are reminiscent of English airs and ballads and whose choral numbers were sometimes derived from madrigals. Purcell also contributed to opera greater expressiveness and realism than it had known previously.

Perhaps the most significant change in church music during the Baroque period was the conversion from *a cappella* choral music to music in larger forms calling for recitatives, solos, duets, accompaniment by orchestra, and orchestral interludes.

Three major forms made their appearance: the oratorio, the Passion, and the cantata.

The oratorio was created late in the sixteenth century by Filippo Neri, founder of the Congregation of the Oratorians, which met in the oratory of San Girolamo della Carità Church in Rome. St. Filippo Neri felt that the Bible could be more appealing and inspiring to the younger members of his order if parts were set to music. He engaged composers to make such settings and had them performed each day during the services following his sermon. The settings came to be known as "oratorios" after the place (the oratory) in which they were heard.

But these settings were oratorios in name only. The first important creator of the oratorio was a member of the Florentine *camerata,* Emilio del Cavalieri (c.1550–1602). Cavalieri brought the declamatory style of the *Nuove musiche* to the liturgical text. In this style he wrote a work called *La Rappresentazione di anima e di corpo,* first heard in Rome in 1600. It required the use of soloists, chorus, and two orchestras. Although the solo numbers were all in the declamatory style, the choral pages were naïve, and the work as a whole lacked cohesion, *La Rappresentazione* was the first work to suggest what the oratorio form would become.

Impressive development took place with Giacomo Carissimi (1605–74). Carissimi produced a large variety of oratorios—*Job, David and Jonathan, Lucifer, Jephtha,* and so forth—in which we find an enriched lyricism and harmony, a deeper dramatic feeling, and a greater understanding of the function of the orchestra. Polyphonic writing, however, was not abandoned. Carissimi made such immense strides that he brought the form of the oratorio to its highest development before Handel. Handel admired Carissimi greatly, studied his works, was profoundly influenced by him, and at times even imitated him.

Carissimi was also the creator of the church cantata. He recognized that certain churches did not have the facilities to present oratorios. He decided to evolve a work in a similar vein, but more modest, economical, and requiring smaller forces. The church cantata was further developed by Dietrich Buxtehude (1637–1707) and reached its peak with Johann Sebastian Bach; after Bach it passed out of general use.

The Passion—the Easter story according to the Gospels, presented in a dramatico-musical form—had been an established institution in the church for centuries. The first important Passions are found in the Flemish and Roman polyphonic schools of the fifteenth century. They were motets in form—entirely polyphonic and exclusively for *a cappella* voices. In the seventeenth century the Passion was affected by the development of the oratorio. Solos, choral numbers, and recitatives were interpolated into the Passion. During the Reformation in Germany, the German language often supplanted Latin in rendering Passions (as well as Masses and motets). At the same time a new kind of religious song for unaccompanied voices came into being: the chorale, in the singing of which the congregation would join.

Heinrich Schütz was one of the most important composers of the Passion before Bach's time. Having come into contact with the *Nuove musiche* style in Italy and having himself written a *dramma per musica,* Schütz was able to bring to the music of the Passion some of the innovations of the new style: accompanied recitatives; the aria; and, most important of all, an increased feeling for drama.

III

The first instrumental music was for the organ. Early contrapuntists such as Giovanni Gabrieli (1557–1612) and Jan Sweelinck (1562–1621) wrote for the organ as they did for the human voice, without recognizing the salient fact that instrumental style calls for variety of color and nuance and flexibility of rhythm not required in vocal music.

The first important composer who realized such an instrumental style, and consequently the first of the great organ composers, was Girolamo Frescobaldi (1583–1643). Frescobaldi crystallized some of the major organ forms, such as the toccata, the fugue, and the partita. These and other forms—passacaglia, chorale-prelude, chaconne, fantasia, and so forth—reached an advanced stage of technical and artistic development with Buxtehude.

Simultaneous with this development of organ music came the growth of music for other instruments. One of the earliest instrumental forms was the canzona, a piece in the polyphonic style. As early as 1600, Giovanni Gabrieli wrote canzoni for a quartet or double quartet of musical instruments. Once again, as was the case with the first pieces for organ, we have a tendency to imitate vocal music. Before long, however, the instrumental concept came into being.

The word "sonata" now comes into use, as a piece of music to be "sounded," or played, by instruments—not to be confused with the later sonata—and usually built around a solo instrument (or group of instruments) and an accompaniment. The first important sonatas were in the so-called *sonata da chiesa* form, forerunner of the later sonata. A second kind was the *sonata da camera,* made up of a group of dances, and predecessor of the suite.

The first master of the *sonata da chiesa* was Arcangelo Corelli (1653–1713), the greatest violin virtuoso of his time and the first great composer for that instrument. Corelli produced two epoch-making works. In one of these (Op. 6) the foundation of the concerto grosso was built. Corelli evolved a style of concerto grosso writing that remained a model for his contemporaries and successors. He wrote with such a richness of musical ideas, such an elastic lyricism, such effective contrasts of light and shade, and such skill in the interplay of solo groups and orchestra that the concerto grosso became at once a flexible medium for instrumental writing. His concerti grossi, widely heard and widely distributed in publication, had an enormous influence on his entire generation and made possible the appearance of Handel's concerti grossi and Bach's Brandenburg Concertos. As the Corelli concerto grosso pitted a small group of instruments against a larger orchestral body, it can also be regarded as the ancestor of the concerto for solo instrument and orchestra.

Corelli's other epoch-making work was his Op. 5, in which twelve sonatas for violin and accompanying bass were gathered. While these Corelli works are not sonatas in the accepted meaning of that form, they did help produce that genre by establishing a definite style of violin writing and extending the technique of violin playing. It was through Corelli's influence that instrumental music started to flower in England, France, and Germany, for such composers as Henry Purcell, François Couperin-le-Grand (1688–1773), and Georg Telemann (1681–1767) openly expressed their indebtedness to the Italian master in the writing of their own chamber music works.

Further development of instrumental music in general, and the concerto in particular, took place with Antonio Vivaldi (c.1678–1741). He went a step beyond Corelli in establishing the concerto form as we know it today, giving it both clarity of design and solidity of structure. Vivaldi taught his contemporaries how to write a singing melody and produce a poetic lyricism. He showed the way toward contrasts of thematic ideas as well as toward their development—basic tools of all later instrumental composers. He was one of the first great exponents of program music. We know how profound his influence was on Johann Sebastian Bach—how Bach used to copy out these Vivaldi concertos and transcribe many of them for different instruments. And we also know that the Bach concertos for solo instruments and orchestra consistently reveal the effect that Vivaldi's music had had on him.

It was not long after Corelli published his first opus that the first sonata for a solo piano (or, more accurately, for the ancestor of the piano, the clavier) was written. The composer was Johann Kuhnau (1660–1722), who in 1695 published a set of piano pieces called *Frische Klavier Früchte*. This publication was an important event in musical history for two reasons: It represented one of the earliest attempts to write seriously for a keyboard instrument other than the organ; and six of the pieces in this set were designated for the first time as sonatas. François Couperin-le-Grand, often described as the "father of French keyboard music," brought increasing articulateness to keyboard writing. Couperin was the first composer to understand the harpsichord and to realize its potentialities. In 1716 he issued a treatise on the science of harpsichord playing in which keyboard style was painstakingly analyzed; this analysis had a profound impact on Bach's development as a composer of clavier music. Couperin also wrote and published four volumes of *Piéces de clavecin,* between 1713 and 1730, in which theory was translated into practice. Nothing up to that time could compare with these pieces for resourcefulness of technique, aptness of musical expression, effectiveness of atmosphere, and successful transmutation into tone of pictures, suggestions, customs, incidents, and objects.

Couperin wrote numerous pieces for the harpsichord, but no sonatas. The next major composer of piano sonatas, after Kuhnau, was Domenico Scarlatti (1685–1757), son of Alessandro. Domenico was a famous virtuoso of the harpsichord whose technique was so phenomenal that some of his contemporaries believed he was "possessed of the devil." He wrote many operas and large church works; but his fame rests exclusively on his many sonatas for the harpsichord, which are still frequently performed. He made the harpsichord speak a fresher and more varied language than heretofore. His gamut was wide. In his sonatas we find wit, grace, drama, whimsey, and infectious beauty. He had variety of rhythm and increasing richness of harmony. He introduced new techniques of playing the harpsichord—runs, arpeggios, and crossing of hands. But the development of the technique of playing the harpsichord is only an incidental contribution; his sonatas have survived because they are a vibrant and living art.

We are now at the threshold of Johann Sebastian Bach.

Part Two

THE COMPOSERS AND THEIR MUSIC

Johann Sebastian Bach

"The most stupendous miracle in all music."

WAGNER

BORN: Eisenach, Thuringia, March 21, 1685.

DIED: Leipzig, Germany, July 28, 1750.

MAJOR WORKS: *Chamber Music*—6 sonatas for violin and clavier; 3 sonatas for unaccompanied violin; 3 partitas for unaccompanied violin; 6 sonatas (or suites) for unaccompanied cello; 3 sonatas for cello and clavier; 3 sonatas for flute and clavier; 4 trio sonatas; The Musical Offering. *Choral Music*—295 church cantatas; over 20 secular cantatas; 3 oratorios; 2 Magnificats; 4 small Masses; 4 motets; 5 Sanctuses; 2 Psalms; 2 Passions (St. John, St. Matthew), *Clavier Music*—6 English Suites; 6 French Suites; partitas; The Art of the Fugue; Chromatic Fantasy and Fugue; Goldberg Variations; Inventions; Italian Concerto; Little Clavier Book of Anna Magdalena Bach; The Well-Tempered Clavier. *Orchestral Music*—6 Brandenburg Concertos; 4 suites (or overtures), concertos for various solo instruments and orchestra. *Organ Music*—Chorale preludes, fantasias, fugues, preludes, toccatas; Little Organ Book; Passacaglia and Fugue in C minor. *Vocal Music*—5 songs in the Anna Magdalena Bach Notenbuch including "Bist du bei mir" and "Komm süsser Tod."

HIS LIFE

On one of the rare occasions when Bach appraised his own life's work he remarked simply, "I worked hard." No composer worked harder. The volume of his music is staggering in its proportions. It took the Bach Gesellschaft forty-six years to gather and publish all his music, and when the job was finished it filled sixty huge volumes. It has been said that a present-day copyist, writing out all the parts as Bach did, would require seventy years for this task alone. And yet Bach wrote all this music while fulfilling many other chores: those of organist, conductor, musical director of church services, and even teacher to a class of boys.

If all his life Bach worked hard to earn his salary, he was no less industrious in trying to enrich the storehouse of his musical knowledge. He had had in boyhood and youth comparatively little systematic training under professional guidance. What he learned had to be acquired by hearing, absorbing, copying, transcribing, imitating, and experimenting—but always experimenting. The hunger to learn was insatiable. It sent him many different times on large and sometimes arduous journeys on foot to hear the music of his celebrated contemporaries. It made him willing to copy down the music of other composers, or to transcribe it for other instruments, so that, in the process, he might assimilate its technique.

Two anecdotes, one out of his boyhood and the other out of his old age, illustrate this indefatigable striving to learn. As a boy of nine he copied an entire library of instrumental music to which his brother, Johann Christoph (for some unexplained reason), had denied him access. For this task he used only the late hours of night, when his brother was asleep, and the moonlight was his only illumination. He almost ruined his eyesight, only to have the fruit of his hard work confiscated and destroyed by his brother.

In the closing year of his life he created *The Art of the Fugue,* his last work. It was a vast and complicated attempt to demonstrate the many different ways of treating a given theme in the fugal style. Because the work, when published, gave no indication of the instrument for which Bach had intended it, a good case can be built for the accepted theory that Bach never intended it for performance at all; that the old master, at the dusk of his career, was testing himself for what he knew about the science of the fugue and perhaps trying to uncover such technical problems as he still had to solve.

When he said, "I worked hard," he was evaluating himself as he saw himself. It is doubtful if he ever considered himself anything more than an industrious artisan, doing his daily chores to the best of his ability. We never find him speaking of works produced in a fever of inspiration (which Beethoven, referring to his own case, once described as a *"raptus"*). Nor do we find him inspired by the kind of holy dedication to art which motivated, say, Wagner.

He never entertained the suspicion that he might be a genius. Certainly his children never thought of him as such. Karl Philipp Emanuel Bach spoke of him condescendingly as "that old peruke"; once, when pressed for information about his father, all he could say was that Johann Sebastian had been "musical director to several courts and in the end cantor of Leipzig." Wilhelm Friedemann Bach thought so little of his father's music that he sold some of his works for ten cents apiece and negligently lost others.

Yet this hard-working man, so little appreciated by himself, his children, his contemporaries, and even his immediate successors, was one of the geniuses of music. And if you should be one of those who consider him *the* greatest composer of them all, you would find yourself in good company indeed.

Seven generations of Bachs were professional musicians. At one time, early in the eighteenth century, thirty Bachs held organ posts in Germany. It has also been recorded that in the town of Erfurt anybody who was a reputable musician was automatically referred to as a "Bach."

Johann Sebastian's father was a fine performer on the violin and viola, a musician highly respected in Eisenach. Both he and his wife Elisabeth died when Johann was ten years old. The boy went to Ordurf to live with his twenty-four-year-old brother, Johann Christoph, a church organist. Johann Christoph gave the boy some training at the harpsichord—grudgingly, we are told. Peeved that he had another mouth to feed, Johann Christoph treated the intruder with severe discipline untempered by either kindness or sympathy.

A position as choirboy at St. Michael's Church in Lüneburg freed him from his brother's tyranny after five years. Now that his environment was more favorable to the study of music, Johann Sebastian gave himself up to every possible musical pursuit. He studied (and with almost savage intensity) the organ, clavichord, violin, and composition. He buried himself in the church library, memorizing every musical score within reach. This lust for music made him tramp several times the thirty-mile distance to Hamburg to hear the greatest organist of the day, Jan Adams Reinken; he also walked the sixty miles to Celle to attend performances of French music, which he was hearing for the first time.

When he was nineteen he became church organist at Arnstadt. At Lübeck, Dietrich Buxtehude (1637–1707), the celebrated composer and organist, gave organ concerts and arranged a weekly evening of instrumental music. In his second year at Arnstadt, Bach asked for, and received, a month's leave of absence to visit Lübeck and hear Buxtehude. So preoccupied did Bach become with the exciting musical activities there that he remained not one month, but three. The prolonged absence displeased the Arnstadt authorities. They were even more upset when their organist, no doubt remembering the way the great Buxtehude played, began to confuse the churchgoers by interpolating elaborate improvisations into the chorales. Still another point of contention is found in the recorded minutes of a meeting of the church board: "To make protest on his having recently allowed the stranger maiden to show herself and to make music in the church." The "stranger maiden" thus referred to was Bach's cousin, Maria Barbara, with whom he was in love.

Bach was not reluctant to exchange his Arnstadt post for a similar one at the St. Blasius Church in Mühlhausen in 1707. His personal needs were taken care of by his salary of eight-five gulden a year, supplemented by "three measures of corn, two trusses of wood, and six trusses of faggots" a year. In addition he had recently inherited a legacy of fifty gulden from his maternal uncle. He was now able to marry Maria Barbara, which he did at the village of Dornheim, a short distance from Arnstadt, on October 17, 1707.

He did not stay long at Mühlhausen. Once again he met opposition to the kind of music he wanted to make. A cantata, *Gott ist mein König,* written for the municipal council's festival service and introduced on February 4, 1708, was too new and original to be comprehended. In 1708, therefore, Bach left Mühlhausen to become church organist and chamber musician at the Ducal Chapel in Weimar.

This was his first major appointment, and he held it for nine years. Bach now devoted himself mainly to the writing of music for the organ, producing what is probably the greatest contribution to organ literature ever made by a single man. He also distinguished himself as a performer both in Weimar and on annual tours in nearby cities. When, in 1714, the Prince of Hesse heard him perform a brilliant pedal passage, he spontaneously took off his jeweled ring and presented it to him. By 1717 Bach was generally regarded as one of the greatest organists of his day. It happened that both he and France's greatest organist, Louis Marchand, were in Dresden at the same time in 1717. The question as to which of the two was the greater performer inspired a contest: Each was to play a different piece of music at sight before a discriminating jury. The day and hour of the contest was arranged. But at the zero hour Marchand refused to make an appearance, admitting defeat by default. It is said that on that very morning he had heard Bach limber up his fingers at the church organ, and what he had heard had convinced him that retreat was the better part of valor.

Even more impressive was the reaction of the venerable organist Reinken when he heard Bach improvise for half an hour on a chorale theme. "I thought," Reinken told him, "this art was dead, but I see it still lives in you."

It cannot be said that in Weimar Bach received the honor he deserved, in spite of his great reputation as an organist, and even though in 1714 he had been elevated to the position of Konzertmeister. To his fellow townspeople he was a simple, humble, hard-working musician, of a station no higher than the local cobbler or tailor. His employer, the Duke of Weimar, also underrated him. When an appointment for Kapellmeister was open, the duke bypassed Bach and selected somebody else. Bach, therefore, was receptive to a call from Prince Leopold of Anhalt to become Kapellmeister at Cöthen. The Duke of Weimar, however, refused to relieve him of his post, his personal vanity piqued at the thought that Bach would prefer working for somebody else. Bach expressed his discontent vociferously. What happened after that was recorded by the court secretary, Theodor Benedict Bormann: "The sixth of November, the Konzertmeister and organist Bach, until now in office, was sent to jail because of his obstinacy in trying to obtain his dismissal by force. He was freed on the second of December after being notified of his disgrace."

Finally, Bach was given his release. In his new position as Kapellmeister and director of chamber music at Cöthen, Bach was required to lead an orchestra of eighteen players in concerts of orchestral and chamber compositions. He was also expected to write new music for these performances. The very nature of his post sent him in a new direction creatively. The organ period was for the most part over. Bach now wrote numerous works for solo instruments and for chamber orchestra, including concertos, suites, sonatas, and compositions for clavier.

Bach's wife—who had borne him seven children, four of whom survived—died in 1720. One year later, on December 3, 1721, he married again. His choice was Anna Magdalena Wülken, the twenty-one-year-old daughter of the town trumpeter. Besides bearing him thirteen children, Anna Magdalena cultivated her own musical interests. To further her study of the clavier Bach wrote charming educational pieces (which have been gathered in *The Little Clavier Book of Anna Magdalena Bach*), the Inventions, and the French and English Suites.

The six years spent in Cöthen was a time of contentment as well as productivity. "There," Bach said, "I had an amiable prince who knew and loved music and I thought that I should end my days with him." But then the prince married Princess Bernburg, a frivolous and pleasure-loving young lady who hated music. The marriage brought about a change of musical values at court. The serious and the artistic were now shunned. In such a scheme of things Bach, of course, had no place. Besides, he had long felt a nostalgia for the church, where his musical career had begun. He gave expression to this feeling by writing several church cantatas and the *Passion According to St. John*—almost as if in anticipation of the last, and monumental, creative epoch that lay ahead for him.

Learning that the post of cantor in Leipzig had been vacated by the death of Johann Kuhnau (1660–1722), Bach did not hesitate to apply for it. He had to undergo several trials to prove his ability. He sent his *Passion According to St. John* as a sample of his gifts for writing church music. On February 7, 1722, he came to Leipzig to conduct one of his own church cantatas. Apparently, he passed all tests with flying colors. He was officially accepted on

May 5, 1722. For the next twenty-seven years, up to the time of his death, he remained in Leipzig.

His activities were many and varied. As cantor he had to teach a boy's class in Latin, and had to train singers and instrumentalists. He also had to play the organ and write the music for, and organize and direct the musical activities at, the two leading churches in Leipzig—St. Peter's and the New Church. He was required "whenever possible" to attend funeral processions, and he was forbidden to leave the city without the burgomaster's permission. For all these activities he was paid about $2500 a year, the bulk of his income coming from special fees for weddings, funerals, and so forth. Many another musician would have found life difficult and the work artistically stultifying. Housed at the school proper, whose facilities had been allowed to run down to a point of decay, Bach had to accept the most dismal kind of living conditions: dark, constricted, cold, unsanitary. (The shockingly high death rate of his children—of the first eight born in Leipzig, six died—was attributed to this unhealthy environment, which was described as "a hotbed of disease.") His pupils were outright scoundrels whom no one tried to discipline; the singers and instrumentalists under him were for the most incompetent. Besides all this, Bach was in a continual feud with his rector, old Johann August Ernesti, who had long since lost control over the boys and who tried to show his authority by treating Bach contemptuously and humiliating him. And Bach was ever in conflict with the church officials and the town council, who resented his fierce independence, his strong will, and his intransigence. They did everything they could to obstruct him and at times even tried to defraud him.

And yet, petty annoyances, discomforts, even personal tragedy could not stem his industry. For the church services he wrote those wonderful works which are among his greatest compositions: the *Passion According to St. Matthew,* the Mass in B minor, cantatas, chorales, motets, and other towering masterworks in the literature of church music.

His face, says Albert Schweitzer, was that of a man "who has tasted of the bitterness of life. There is something fascinating in the harsh expression of these features. . . . Round the tightly compressed lips run the hard lines of an inflexible obstinacy. . . . In . . . other portraits, the severity is often softened by a touch of easy good nature. Even the shortsighted eyes look out upon the world from their half-closed lids with a certain friendliness that is not even negated by the heavy eyebrows arched above them. The face cannot be called beautiful. The nose is too massive for that, and the underjaw too prominent."

He lived but to worship God and to write music. It was a circumscribed sphere for a great creative artist, but it was enough for him. All his life he had lived in a restricted area, restricted not only geographically but also culturally. He knew almost nothing of the other arts. His reading tastes were plebeian (confined mostly to the field of theology). His ugly scrawl, his ungrammatical German and confused diction, all betrayed an uneducated mind. This amazing paradox of a low cultural level set against unequaled musical ability tempted Ernest Newman to confess that "truly, we have as yet barely the glimmer of an understanding of what the musical faculty is, and how it works."

In 1747 Bach visited Potsdam, where his son Karl Philipp Emanuel was serving as Kapellmeister for Frederick the Great. The story goes that when Bach arrived, Frederick the Great was about to play the flute with his orchestra. Hearing the news, he exclaimed, "Gentlemen, old Bach is here!" He did not even permit Bach to change his clothes, but summoned him without delay. Bach tried out the pianos and organs in the palace with delight, playing a theme here, improvising a subject there, and on a third instrument extending a fragmentary idea into a fugue. Frederick the Great was astonished at this performance and flattered when Bach created a six-part fugue on one of his own melodies. Later on, back in Leipzig, Bach extended this six-part fugue on the king's theme into a major work comprising two fugues, several canons, and a concluding trio. He called it *The Musical Offering* and dispatched it to the king as a token of gratitude for the warm way in which he had been received.

Because of failing eyesight Bach was persuaded to undergo an operation performed by John Taylor, who had operated on Handel previously. It was a failure, and blindness resulted. Bach's health disintegrated to a point where paralysis left him a pathetic invalid. Just before his death his sight returned briefly. Grateful for the borrowed time, he worked feverishly at copying and revising parts of his last work, *The Art of the Fugue.*

The last piece of music he wrote was an organ chorale on the hymn "When We Are in Direst Need." Aware that he did not have much longer to live, he changed the title of the hymn to "I Will Appear Before Thy Throne." He died soon after, just before nine o'clock on the evening of July 28, 1750. He was buried in the churchyard of St. John in Leipzig. Since no identification was put on his grave its whereabouts was not pin-pointed for many years. In 1894, during excavations to extend the foundations of the church, three coffins were found, one of which contained remains definitely identified as Bach's. He was reburied in a sarcophagus underneath the church.

The century-old tradition that the Bachs were a family of musicians did not die with Johann Sebastian. The oldest son of Johann Sebastian and Maria Barbara was a distinguished composer of chamber and piano music. He was Wilhelm Friedemann Bach (1710–84), whose personalized style led to the development of *Empfindsamkeit,* or expressiveness, which led music away from Baroque objectivity and began endowing it with dramatic and emotional interest.

His brother, Karl Philipp Emanuel Bach (1714–88) was also an exponent of the *Empfindsamer Stil,* but his historical importance goes beyond this. The sonata form, still in infancy when he began to write symphonies and piano sonatas, was developed by him. Thus Karl Philipp Emanuel Bach was to become a significant transitionary figure between two great epochs in music history: the age of counterpoint, which his father had brought to a magnificent culmination; and the age of homophony and the sonata. Both Haydn and Mozart knew the piano sonatas of Karl Philipp Emanuel and expressed their indebtedness to them. "For what I know," Haydn confessed, "I have to thank Karl Philipp Emanuel Bach." Mozart said, "He is the father, and we his children." Bach's dramatized writing and expressive moods affected and influenced the young Beethoven.

It was this Bach who established the convention of three movements for a sonata or symphony (two fast movements separated by a slow one); who, in the first movement, suggested a two-theme technique, a basic element of the sonata form; who, in the slow movement, realized the lyric character of homophonic music.

John Christian Bach (1735–82), youngest son of Johann Sebastian and Anna Magdalena, also wrote delightful symphonies, concertos, and sonatas, as well as operas. Because of his long residence in

England, where for many years he served as music master to Queen Charlotte, he is known as the "English Bach."

HIS MUSIC

Johann Sebastian Bach was more or less forgotten by the music world at large soon after his death, and his music was forgotten with him. For more than half a century, it was Karl Philipp Emanuel or John Christian who were considered the greatest of Bachs. The reasons for this are not difficult to discover. For one thing, almost nothing was known about Johann Sebastian's music. Only nine or ten of his compositions were printed during his lifetime and nothing else for half a century after his death. In addition to this, Johann Sebastian came at the end of an epoch in musical history: polyphony, which emphasized the deployment of several melodies simultaneously, each equally important. After Bach came the age of homophony, which stressed the single melody and its accompaniment. Because Bach's music was essentially the product of an old era rather than the new one, many of his contemporaries regarded him as stuffy and old-fashioned, while his successors were inclined to consider him obsolescent. Little was thought of his music. Soon after his death a bundle of his cantatas sold for forty dollars; the engraving plates of *The Art of the Fugue* went as scrap metal; the catalogue of the musical library of the Margrave of Brandenburg did not even bother to list the Brandenburg Concertos, each of which was valued at approximately ten cents; some Bach manuscripts were even used as wrapping paper by Leipzig butchers and other merchants.

For about seventy-five years after Bach's death, little of his music was published or performed. The turning point came in 1829 with a Berlin revival of the *Passion According to St. Matthew* under Felix Mendelssohn. The grandeur of this music gave the world its first indication of the powers of the long-neglected master. Four years later came a performance of the *Passion According to St. John,* one more step in the rediscovery of Bach. By 1850 awareness of Bach's greatness encouraged the formation of the Bach Gesellschaft for the purpose of gathering and publishing all of his works. This project, which took fifty years for completion, was the final evidence

that the music of the old Leipzig cantor was a mine yielding inexhaustible treasures.

Bach wrote music in every known form except the opera (though
some of his secular cantatas, such as *Phoebus and Pan,* are occasionally presented in an operatic version). He invented no new
forms and created no new style or idiom. But to the old forms
and styles and idioms he brought an emotional expressiveness, a
nobility of thinking, a majesty of concept, a spaciousness of design
which were unique. So completely had he exhausted both the technical and aesthetic possibilities of polyphony that by necessity the
composers who followed him had to set off in an altogether new
direction.

"Bach bestrode the whole world of the music of his day," once
wrote Ernest Newman in a newspaper article.

The music of the half century that followed him, indeed, rich as it was in
new achievements, has often the air of having gone back to the nursery
after having become, with him, a grown man. There is nothing in the
epoch of 1750–1800 to compare with the farflung luxuriance of Bach's melody . . . or the intensity of his harmony, or the way he could force the
most complex polyphony into the service of the profoundest emotional expression, of the freedom and variety of musical speech to which he could
attain even while he fettered himself with seemingly the most crabbed of
forms. . . . Within these forms he could indulge himself to his heart's content in the sounding of the very depths of the human soul; no other contemporary instrumental form, for instance, would have afforded him such
opportunities both for intensity and spaciousness of poetic expression as
that of the organ chorale prelude; it is safe to say that in these works of
his alone there is hardly an emotion that is not expressed, and that with a
poignancy that remains undiminished even after three generations of post-
Tristan developments.

But we find in Bach's music not only the ultimate technical development and the fullest artistic expression of an existing musical
style. We also find in him prophetic suggestions of things to come.
Although he did not himself evolve the concept of a single melody
set against a harmonic accompaniment, he did succeed in increasing
the expressiveness of lyric writing. When we listen to some of the
slow movements of his instrumental works, or to an occasional aria

of his church music, we come upon a lyric style that belongs to the new age and not to the old.

ANALYTICAL NOTES

Chamber Music. At Cöthen, between 1718 and 1723, Bach completed a library of music for solo violin, for violin and clavier, for solo cello, and for cello and clavier. Three, for unaccompanied violin, are designated as sonatas, since each of the movements (usually four in number) bears a tempo indication, with the first and third movements slow, and the second and fourth movements fast. Three more for unaccompanied violin are called partitas, made up as they are of such dance movements as allemande, courante, sarabande, minuet, gigue, and so forth. Three sonatas are for cello and clavier, while six works for unaccompanied cello are termed suites, the term "suite" being used by the composer interchangeably with "partita."

Two sections from the violin solo partitas have become celebrated apart from their context. One is the opening prelude of the Partita in E major. This music derives its effect through its motor energy, the momentum created by the first electifying measures never relaxing until the end of the movement. How effective this music is can be gauged by the number of times it has been transcribed: for orchestra (by Lucien Cailliet, Sir Henry J. Wood, Leopold Stokowski, Pick-Mangiagalli, among others); for violin and piano (Robert Schumann, Fritz Kreisler); for piano solo (Rachmaninoff); for guitar solo (Segovia). Bach's partiality for it became evident when he presented it in orchestral dress in his church cantata No. 29, *Wir danken dir, Gott* (1731). The American composer Lukas Foss used it in 1966—in an *avant-garde* idiom—as the basis of *Phorion,* a composition utilizing electronic sounds as well as formal instruments.

Even more famous a movement from one of these solo violin partitas in the Chaconne, one of the most majestic pieces of music created for the instrument. It appears as the closing movement of Partita No. 2 in D minor, and opens with a spacious and noble subject in full chords. This is followed by thirty-one variations, remarkable for variety of feeling, mood, and color. Bach here brought such a wealth of harmonic and polyphonic writing and instrumental timbres to the four strings of the violin that the effect is at times almost orchestral. The Chaconne has been adapted for orchestra by Leopold Stokowski. Other transcriptions include these for solo piano (Busoni), piano left hand (Brahms), and guitar (Segovia). Mendelssohn wrote for it a piano accompaniment.

In many of the partitas and sonatas, whether for violin or for cello, whether unaccompanied or with clavier, Bach's remarkable skill at polyphony is in evidence: for example, the complex fugue that opens the first unaccompanied Sonata in C major for Violin, or the third movement of the Sonata No. 3 in A major for Violin and Clavier. In other works, Bach's gift for spinning wonderful melodies in anticipation of a homophonic style is revealed: for example, in the exalted pages of the adagio and andante movements of the first two sonatas for cello and clavier, in G major and D major.

The Musical Offering (*Das musikalische Opfer*) is Bach's last chamber music work. It is based on the subject provided him by King Frederick II in Potsdam for extemporaneous fugal treatment when the master visited the court in 1747. In Potsdam, Bach had improvised a three-part fugue on the king's theme, and followed it with a six-part fugue on a subject of his own. Later on, the king's theme became the source of a trio sonata for flute, violin, and thorough bass, and ten instrumental canons intended for an unspecified instrumental ensemble.

The entire composition is in polyphonic style and in the key of C minor. It opens with a three-part fugue and three canons. After that comes a four-movement trio sonata. Five more canons follow, while the entire composition concludes with a six-part fugue.

Choral Music. The Church was the focal point of Bach's life. He was a deeply religious man, serving his Master humbly. The books he read were on theological subjects; the only subject outside of music in which he might have had a claim to authority is the Bible. It is, therefore, easy to understand why religious subjects should have stimulated his musical imagination above all others. He drew from them his most ambitious, his most sublime concepts. Whether writing a simple and popular chorale (which, in his day, was the music of the masses) or an immense setting of the death of Christ, he interpreted the infinite; as Charles Sanford Terry said of him, "he saw the heavens opened and was prophetically oracular."

Perhaps no greater service has been performed by recorded music than the release on disks of Bach's church cantatas. Before the record industry tapped this rich vein, these works were virtually unknown. Today, the most famous of these cantatas, and a good many less famous as well, have become basic to the listening experiences of sophisticated music lovers. By virtue of these recordings the general music public has come to recognize what many Bach scholars have long maintained: that these cantatas are a seemingly inexhaustible storehouse of treasures; that in no medium did Bach pour forth so much exalted music; and that if he had written nothing else, this literature would still have placed him with the greatest polyphonic composers of all time.

It is believed that Bach wrote some three hundred church cantatas. Only two thirds have survived. While his first cantata came in 1714 (*Wie schön leuchtet der Morgenstern*), and while several master-works appeared during the Weimar period, the bulk of Bach's church cantata writing was done in Leipzig between 1723 and 1744 when he created over 250 of such works.

These cantatas were intended for the Sunday and Saint Day services. Apparently Bach wrote enough works to satisfy the needs of a five-year church cycle, since 295 such works are required if none is repeated. Bach's cantatas vary in length, the shorter taking about twelve minutes, while the longest last as much as forty minutes. Texts are taken from hymns, from the Bible, or are suggested by some scriptural lesson of that day. In general, the structure comprises an opening and closing chorus, the closing one being a chorale. Between them come recitatives and arias, and with them sometimes vocal duets, trios, instrumental episodes, and accompanied chorales. Most Bach cantatas are scored for solo voices, chorus, and orchestra, but a few are for a single voice and orchestra: for example, *Jauchzet Gott in allen Landen* (1731), for soprano and orchestra, or *Ich habe genug* (1731), for basso and orchestra. When only a single voice and orchestra is used the cantata usually consists of alternating recitatives and arias.

In his earliest cantatas, there are as yet no recitatives nor da capo arias, the melodic numbers being rhythmed melodies, or ariosos. Generally, these early cantatas comprise just a few simple ariosos for voice and orchestra and several choral numbers. In this group we find *Aus der Tiefe* (1707), a five-movement composition for tenor and basso solos, chorus, and orchestra, with Psalm 130 as text. Three movements are for chorus. To the two solo-voice movements, Bach used a sixteenth-century hymn, "Herr Jesu Christ, du höchstes gut" as contrapuntal background.

After 1710, Bach began employing recitatives, and combined ariosos with fully extended melodies within the da capo structure. Now orchestral accompaniments begin to assume importance in providing dramatic or emotional interest or in illuminating text. Now, too, the chorale is used for the closing section. In such a style is *Nun Komm, der Heiden Heiland* (1714), intended for the first Sunday after Advent, and based on Christ's words from Revelation ("See thou, see thou, I stand before the door and knock thereon").

In Leipzig, Bach produced an average of a cantata a month. He now developed the "chorale cantata," where hymn material is used as text. The first such masterwork is *Christ lag in Todesbanden* (1724), for solo voices, chorus, and orchestra, performed on Easter Sunday. This is the only Bach cantata where the hymn melody ("Christ ist erstanden" from the twelfth century) recurs in every number, and where the verses (words by Martin Luther) are used exclusively. The opening fourteen-measure sinfonia is pervaded with the sorrow of death, but the seven verses that follow are an affirmation of life. These verses are for chorus, for soprano and alto duet, for tenor solo, for chorus, for bass solo, for soprano and tenor duet, and for chorus (chorale).

Wachet auf! (1731), for solo voices, chorus, and orchestra, is also famous. The hymn used here is "Wachet auf!" by Philipp Nicolai, published in 1599. The text, taken from the Gospels, relates the parable of the wise and foolish virgins who make ready the lamps for the Bridegroom. The parable is narrated in the first two verses. The remaining parts sing the praises of God and the heavenly hosts.

With some of Bach's church cantatas, parts have become more celebrated than the whole, having become popularized through transcriptions. "Jesu, Joy of Man's Desiring" is the tenth number of *Herz und Mund und Tat und Leben* (1716). There the flowing chorale over accompanying triplets is set to the words *"Jesu bleibt meine Freunde."* This melody has become familiar in various guises: in an orchestral transcription by Lucien Cailliet; and as a composition for solo piano (Myra Hess), for organ (E. Power Biggs), and solo voice and piano (Hess).

The opening sinfonia (or arioso) for strings and oboe obbligato from *Ich steh' mit einem Fuss im Grabe* is also better known than the cantata of which it is the preface. This pastoral music portrays the steps leading to the grave. A descending adagio motive receives prominent treatment, with several variants found in the bass.

The closest that Bach came to writing opera was in his secular cantatas, some of which have enough of a plot structure to permit them to be staged. Actually, of course, they were all intended for concert performance. Their interest lies in that they reveal the non-religious side of Bach's personality: the man who enjoyed a good glass of wine and his pipe, and the man who had a healthy respect for money and station in life.

One of these works is the *Coffee Cantata* 1732—*Schweigt stille, plaudert nicht*. This is a "domestic comedy" in ten sections discussing the pros and cons of drinking coffee while describing how Lieschen has become addicted to that drink. Another cantata concerns itself with taxes and tax collectors. It is the *Peasant Cantata* (1742)—*Mer hahn en neue Oberkeet*—celebrating in twenty-four sections the choice of Karl Heinrich von Dieskau as Lord of the Manor. The work ends with a choral admonishment to the people to forget all about taxes and go off to the inn for song and wine.

A similar satirical attitude is found in *Phoebus and Pan* (1732)—*Der Streit zwischen Phoebus und Pan*. This treats the old Greek legend of the song contest between Phoebus and Apollo in mocking tones. Bach here permits himself the luxury of chuckling over the sanctimonious and ponderous attitudes adopted by some composers when they wrote operas.

Descriptive rather than humorous or satrical is the famous *Wedding Cantata* (1720)—*Weichet nur, betrübte Schatten*. The text tells about the coming of spring and the death of winter. Much of Bach's music has a bucolic or pastoral identity. Pastoral, too, is the celebrated excerpt from still another secular cantata, *Was mir behagt* (1716). This excerpt is remarkable for its tranquil beauty: *"Schafe können sicher weiden,"* or "Sheep Shall Safely Graze"—a poignant soprano aria accompanied by two flutes. Sir John Barbirolli and Sir William Walton each transcribed it for orchestra. Percy Grainger adapted it for solo piano; Mary Howe, for two pianos; and E. Power Biggs, for organ.

The *Christmas* (*Weihnachts*) *Oratorio* (1734) is just a stringing together of six church cantatas, each heard at one of the six church services between Christmas and Epiphany. An Evangelist (tenor) serves as a unifying factor by narrating in recitatives the story of Christ's birth as detailed in the Gospels of Matthew and Luke. The rest of the work consists of a series of what Michael Hauptmann has described as "lyrical meditations," presented in ariosos, arias, and choral numbers. Hauptmann also notes that a good deal of the power and expressiveness of this work springs from the "brilliance of Bach's orchestra, with high D trumpets, tympani, choirs of flutes and oboes." The only instrumental passage to be found in the entire work happens to be its most familiar excerpt. It is the pastorale, or "shepherd music," in the key of G major, scored for flutes, oboes, strings, and organ accompaniment. This serene, beatific music announces the birth of Christ. In the chorale with which the oratorio ends, the main melody of the pastorale is recalled following each line of the concluding hymn.

The *Easter Oratorio* (1736)—*Kommt, eilet und laufet*—is the only Bach work which can accurately be designated as an oratorio. This is no longer just a number of church cantatas assembled into a single mold, but a major work, an integrated and unified composition based throughout on a biblical text. The story of the Resurrection unfolds in the recitatives, while arias and ariosos interpret and underline the emotional content. Two contrasting instrumental sections open the oratorio, the initial one, a sinfonia in D major, joyous and ebullient music in which trumpets and tympani are prominent; this is followed by a more reflective orchestral episode, an adagio in the relative minor. The narrative is then begun with "*Kommt, eilet und laufet,*" a duet of Peter and John in which they learn of Christ's resurrection. After that we get ten lyrical sections, some reaching altitudes of poignancy and eloquence, such as Peter's lullaby "*Sanfte soll mein Todeskummer*" and Mary Magdalene's aria "*Saget, saget mir geschwinde.*" A paean to the glory of the Lord, "*Preis und Dank,*" brings the oratorio to an exultant conclusion.

The crown of Bach's church music is the *Passion According to St. John,* the *Passion According to St. Matthew,* and the *Mass in*

B minor. These are among the most epical musical works ever conceived.

The Passion is an oratorio; but its text always concerns the final suffering of Christ. It had been the custom for centuries to perform Passion music during Holy Week. With the great German contrapuntist Heinrich Schütz (1585–1672), the Passion acquired the form and character it was henceforth to possess. Schütz Passions were the models studied, admired, and emulated by Bach. The music assimilated dramatic choruses, recitatives, and expressive arias from Italian opera—thus becoming dramatic as well as religious. The text, while drawn from different Gospels, had a similarity of treatment. The Narrator (tenor) tells the story. When he comes to the words of one character—say, Jesus, St. Paul, the Evangelist, Pontius Pilate, Judas, etc.—that character takes over and speaks for himself in recitatives and arias. (Sometimes one singer assumes different parts at different times.) The chorus, usually representing the crowd, is given passages of great dramatic impact. But throughout the Passion simple and devout chorales are interpolated, serving as a kind of commentary on what is taking place; the congregation usually joined in singing them.

Bach greatly extended the structure of the Passion. He used immense musical forces. He shaped his music to such dimensions that his Passions require several hours for performance. And he interpreted the biblical text with a reverence and compassion, and at other times with a power, rarely found in the music of his predecessors or contemporaries.

The *Passion According to St. John* came first (1723). Most of it was written while Bach was still at Cöthen. He completed it soon after taking over the office of cantor in Leipzig, where he conducted the *première* performance in 1723, probably on Good Friday. The text was prepared by Heinrich Brockes, who took his material mostly from the eighteenth and nineteenth chapters of St. John.

Generally speaking, the *St. John* is more theatrical than the monumental *Passion According to St. Matthew* which followed it. The spine of the earlier work is the recitative, which is often charged with strong dramatic feeling as it tells of Christ's arrest, trial, and crucifixion. Most of these recitatives are consigned to the Evangelist (tenor). After a narrative passage comes an aria or arioso to reflect the emotional response the narrative has inspired. Some of these pages of lyricism rank with Bach's most sublime conceptions, namely the celebrated aria for contralto with viola da gamba obbligato, *"Es ist vollbracht,"* and the no less moving aria for basso with two viole d'amore as obbligato, *"Betrachte, meine Seel'."* Other telling pages in this score rise to climaxes of immense theatrical effect. Stirring choruses of the crowd are stressed in the avenging cry of the mob, *"Kreuzige!"* and the horrifying voices of fanaticism, *"Wäre dieser nicht ein Übelthäter."* Radiant chorales provide a welcome emotional contrast, soaring to peaks of eloquence in the music that brings the *Passion* to its end, *"Ach Herr, lass dein' lieb' Engelein am letzten End'."*

The *Passion According to St. Matthew* came six years later, its first performance taking place at the St. Thomas Church in Leipzig on April 15, 1729, the composer conducting. On the whole, this is a more reverent, spiritual, and contemplative work than the *Passion According to St. John.* It has two contrasting sections. The first is tender and introspective; the second, dramatic and tragic. The story of the *Passion* is derived from the Gospels (the twenty-sixth and twenty-seventh chapters of St. Matthew), with supplementary material by Christian Friedrich Henrici, a postal clerk. It unfolds without a lapse of continuity, and is interpreted in music that is now realistic, now psychological, now emotional, now devotional. The emphasis is always on the suffering of Christ and the tragedy of the betrayal; Bach speaks with humility, adoration, and immense sorrow. Pages such as the aria for alto *"Buss' und Reu',"* the aria for alto with violin obbligato, *"Erbarme dich,"* and the poignant aria for soprano *"Aus Liebe will mein Heiland sterben"* achieve a poignancy that stabs the heart. Nor is there in all music a moment of elegiac tenderness to surpass the closing chorus, *"Wir setzen uns mit Tränen nieder."*

Bach's approach to the *St. Matthew* was clearly more reverent than that to *St. John,* as can be seen in his treatment of Christ's recitatives. In *St. John* they are no different from the others, all being accompanied by chords on a keyboard instrument. In *St. Matthew,* however, the words of Christ—and His alone—are spoken against an incandescent background of instrumental music which has been likened to a halo; thus Christ's words are sharply set apart from the recitatives of all the other characters.

The *Mass in B minor* is unique among Bach's towering masterworks in that a Protestant is here writing a service belonging to the Catholic Church. In view of the fact that the Mass is Bach's greatest work—and one of the greatest in all music—it may come as a surprise that it was something of a patchwork creation. The first two parts were written as an independent composition in 1733 and dispatched by Bach to Augustus III of Saxony in an effort to gain the honorary title of "Court Composer." Five years later Bach added other parts, using materials he had developed in earlier works. But if there is any lack of cohesion in form or in integration of style, this fact has surely eluded several generations of zealous admirers. The Mass was never performed during Bach's lifetime. The *première* took place almost a century after Bach died, the first part on February 20, 1834, and the second on February 12, 1835, and both in Berlin.

The Mass is a more objective work than the *Passion According to St. Matthew*. In the *Passion* we hear the personal expression of a devout Christian, who does not inject a personal or human element when he writes the Mass. Instead, Bach here is building a mighty structure to the greater glory of God.

The Mass is in twenty-four sections, including fifteen choruses, six sections for solo voices, and three duets. The preponderance of choral music is significant; so is the sublimity of the music Bach wrote in this medium. Beginning with the majestic *Kyrie* (which seems to beg the Redeemer for mercy from the very depths of the believer's soul), to the concluding paean of thanksgiving, *Dona nobis pacem,* the choral music is as awe-inspiring as a cathedral. It is for chorus that Bach wrote his most eloquent music in the Mass, just as in the more personal *St. Matthew Passion* his eloquence is found principally in arias. The greatest of these choruses include the joyous, five-part *Gloria,* the *Qui tollis peccata mundi* and *Crucifixus,* with their overwhelming pathos, the mighty six-part *Sanctus,* and the overpowering *Credo.* The most effective arias include the *Laudamus te,* for mezzo soprano, the spiritual *Benedictus,* for tenor against the poignant background provided by a solo violin, and the tender *Agnus Dei,* for contralto. The Mass is concluded with a prayer for peace, *Dona nobis pacem*.

The literature of Bach's church music also includes two Magnificats and five unaccompanied motets. Of the former, that in D major (1723) is the one deserving of consideration. Based on a text from St.

Luke (1:46–55)—the words of the Blessed Virgin when she learns from the Angel she is to become the mother of Christ—this is joyous, exalted music, whose exultant mood is established without preliminaries in the opening five-part chorus, *Magnificat anima mea Dominum*. Structurally, this is just an extended cantata, comprising twelve sections, including arias, duets, choral numbers, and so forth.

Of Bach's four unaccompanied motets, *Jesu, meine Freude* (1723) is the most significant. Since compositions for unaccompanied choruses were infrequent in Bach's day, belonging to an earlier polyphonic era, this work holds a unique place in Bach's literature. It is a five-part *a cappella* chorus in eleven sections. Six verses of a chorale alternate with five numbers using as text the eighth chapter of the Epistle to the Romans. Opening and closing sections are chorales, each using the same music, though for a different text.

Clavier Music. "Clavier" is the generic term for stringed keyboard instruments that in Bach's time included the harpsichord (also known as the cembalo) and the clavichord. Today all such music is most often played on the piano. Of course, the piano as we know it was unknown when Bach was alive. The instruments for which he wrote were the ancestors of the piano. Their tone was thinner than that of the present-day piano, incapable of being sustained; the sound these instruments produced was crisp and metallic.

Bach's best-known clavier works were written during the Cöthen period. Many of them had specific functional purposes: for example, the two- and three-part inventions collected in the *Little Clavier Book of Anna Magdalena Bach* (1720), intended as educational tools for Bach's wife and children.

The Art of the Fugue (1750)—*Die Kunst der Fuge*—also had a specific functional purpose: to demonstrate all the artistic and technical possibilities of which the fugue form was capable. Bach completed this vast project when his life was drawing to a close. It was almost as if he wanted to give a final demonstration of his own powers at polyphonic writing. He took a subject in D minor and then subjected it to every possible treatment of which the fugal technique was capable. The result was a monumental work comprising sixteen fugues, two canons, two fugues for two claviers, and a final fugue which his death kept him from completing. Except for the two fugues for two claviers, Bach did not designate for what instrument or instruments he was planning this fugal exercise. It is altogether possible that Bach had intended the work merely as a practical treatise and did not expect to have it played. Nevertheless, this composition has been heard on the concert stage and in recordings in various versions: most often on piano or harpsichord; sometimes in transcriptions for orchestra (Wolfgang Graeser, Paul Graener, Hans T. David), string quartet (Roy Harris in collaboration with M. D. Herter Norton), two pianos (Erwin Schwebsh), and organ (E. Power Biggs).

The Chromatic Fantasy and Fugue in D minor (1724) acquired its name from the chromatic modulations appearing in the fantasy and the chromatic character of the theme of the three-part fugue. It begins with a dramatic recitative and continues with the fantasia section, in which Bach makes electrifying use of runs and arpeggios. The fugue that follows has, by contrast, an austere personality, but it rises to an overpowering climax.

The English Suites and the French Suites (1722–25) were written to further the keyboard education of Bach's wife, but they have artistic and aesthetic as well as pedagogic interest. The French Suite derived its name from the fact that it was written in the style of such French composers as François Couperin (1668–1773) and was usually in the graceful and delicate vein identified with French music. On the other hand, the English suite was more grave and sedate in character, which may be the reason (though nobody is sure) that it is called "English." Bach wrote six compositions in each group. The English Suites open with a prelude, the French Suites with an allemande. The rest of the movements in both sets are in dance structures (courante, sarabande, gigue, and so forth).

The so-called *Goldberg* Variations in G major (1742)—or more officially *Aria with Thirty Variations*—may with full justification be entitled Bach's *The Art of the Variation*. This elaborate work, consisting of thirty variations on a stately sixteen-measure sarabande theme, was actually meant by the composer to serve as a soporific. Count von Kayserling, Russian envoy to Saxony, suffered from insomnia. He found relief in the clavier performances of Johann Gottlieb Goldberg. Count von Kayserling commissioned Bach to write a peaceful work especially for those nocturnal sleep-inducing concerts. Bach felt that an extended series of variations on a tranquil melody would fit the bill. The composition ends with a final recall of the serene sarabande melody.

The Italian Concerto in F major (1735)—*Concerto nach Italienische Gusto*—departs from the usual concept of a concerto in that it is for solo clavier, and is not accompanied by orchestra. Bach here was creating a piece of music in a form and style popularized by such Italian masters as Corelli. The two outer movements are vigorous and muscular. The middle movement is a soaring aria.

Bach wrote six partitas for clavier (1731). All these compositions are basically suites, in that they are made up of dance movements. Bach referred to these compositions as "galanteries composed for the mental recreation of art lovers." The Partita No. 3 in A minor is unusual in that it combines dance movements with two humorous episodes, a scherzo and a burlesca. The Partita No. 4 in D major boasts music of nobility and grandeur in the sarabande. The Partita in No. 5 G major maintains a tranquil mood throughout most of the movements.

In writing *The Well-Tempered Clavier* (1722–44)—*Das Wohl-tempierte Clavier*—Bach once again wanted to create music that would help his wife and children learn to play the keyboard instruments. The word "tempered" means "tuned." Bach wanted to show how music could be written effectively for a "well-tuned clavier." In short, Bach was championing a new way of tuning keyed instruments—the way with which we today are familiar.

This subject of old and new tuning is a highly complex one, not easily reducible to the layman's vocabulary. But it is possible to give a general idea of the problems involved. Before Bach the tuning method was influenced solely by correct acoustics. Such enharmonic notes as F-sharp and G-flat, or C-sharp and D-flat, had different pitches in those days, pitches they no longer possess. In the original key of C major, this way of tuning made for effective and acoustically true music. But as a performer progressed further and further away from the key of C major, he became more and more out of tune. Another difficulty in those days was that modulation from one key to another was extremely troublesome. Then there arose a theorist, Andreas Werckmeister, who hit on the happy idea of dividing the octave into twelve equal notes (called "equal temperament"). Each key could then be approximately in tune, the discrepancy of pitch being distributed equally among all the twelve notes and hardly perceptible to the ear. This new method of tuning meant that every key was now equally in tune. Composers could now easily transpose from one key to another, while a group of players could play together in tune more easily than theretofore. Bach advocated this new system. To demonstrate its practicability he wrote forty-eight preludes and fugues in this tuning, with two preludes and fugues in each of the twelve major and twelve minor keys. Bach not only produced functional music—whose influence on the technical development of music cannot be overestimated—but also a work of art of great aesthetic significance.

The Well-Tempered Clavier comprises two volumes of preludes and fugues. There are twenty-four such works in each volume. Bach completed the first volume in 1722, and the second one twenty-two years later.

Orchestral Music. The six Brandenburg Concertos for orchestra (1721) have acquired their name from the Margrave of Brandenburg, a collector of concerto music. He commissioned them from Bach in or about 1720. Each concerto is for a different group of solo instruments (with the exception of the third concerto, which has no solo instruments; in this concerto the orchestra is divided into three distinct groups). In the manner of the Italian composers of the concerto grosso, Bach used the solo instruments either in unison with or in contrast against the orchestra. What was often only a formal procedure with the Italians became, with Bach, the means for achieving a most ingenious contrapuntal network of instrumental voices. Albert Schweitzer considers these concertos "the purest products of Bach's polyphonic style" because the orchestra, unlike the organ or the piano, "permits him absolute freedom in the leading and grouping of the obbligato voices."

Generally speaking, these concertos follow the three-movement pattern of the Italian concerto grosso: a vigorous first movement, a lyrical second, an impetuous and sometimes lighthearted third. There are, however, two exceptions. In the first concerto, in F major, a minuet appears as a fourth and final movement. The third concerto, in G major, has only two fast movements, separated by two slow chords; but it is here the practice of some conductors to interpolate a slow movement from one of Bach's other works.

One of the most popular of these works is the Brandenburg Concerto No. 2 in F major. Here the solo group is a quartet of high-pitched instruments: trumpet, flute, oboe, and violin. The finest part of this concerto is the middle movement, in which flute, oboe, and violin intertwine their voices in a discourse of radiant beauty, accompanied only by cellos and cembalo. This slow movement stands between two robust ones. The first is built out of a stout theme, around which the solo instruments (particularly the trumpet) weave fascinating arabesques. In the concluding movement the trumpet, in high register, is used throughout with brilliant virtuoso effect.

The middle-movement andante of the fourth concerto, in G major, has surpassing nobility and elegance. (Bach transcribed this orchestral concerto as a clavier concerto, in F major.) In the fifth concerto, in D major, there is an extended first-movement cadenza for harpsichord in which the instrument acquires altogether new and significant character in Baroque music. The sixth concerto, in B-flat major, is unusual for its scoring, dispensing as it does with the violins and including a viola da gamba in the orchestration.

Bach wrote four suites for orchestra (1717–50), of which only two are in the permanent repertory. The Suite No. 2 in B minor, is scored for flute and strings. A three-part overture (two slow sections separated by a fugue) prefaces five old dances: rondo, sarabande, bourrée, polonaise, and minuet. The rondo is gay; the sarabande, slow and stately; the bourrée, polonaise, and minuet, all light and infectious. These dances are followed by a concluding movement called "Badinerie," which is a merry caprice or trifle.

The Suite No. 3 in D major—for two oboes, three trumpets, drums, strings, and cembalo—opens with a two-section overture, the first part being dignified and courtly and the second a fugue in brisk tempo. This is followed by a movement unorthodox for a classical suite: a lyrical section called "Air," for first and second violins, violas, and cembalo. This is one of Bach's most eloquent melodic flights. A yearning, soulful song for the first violins (enmeshed inextricably with a second melody, in the second violins) moves against an accompanying figure by violas and cembalo. This air is even more familiar as the Air for the G string, a transcription for violin and piano by August Wilhelmj. Four vivacious dances follow the air: two gavottes, bourrée, and gigue.

Bach also wrote many concertos for an individual instrument, or several solo instruments, and orchestra. These are not concertos in the present-day acceptance of this term, as virtuoso music for an individual instrument with orchestral accompaniment. Rather, they carry on the concerto grosso technique of the Brandenburg Concertos. The soloist is used as an integral part of the orchestra in much the same way that the solo groups are used in the Brandenburg Concertos.

Bach was the first composer to write concertos for the piano (or, strictly speaking, the ancestors of the piano: the clavichord and the harpsichord, or cembalo) and orchestra. There are seven such concertos in existence. Strange to say, these works are usually transcriptions of other compositions, a few originating as violin concertos. The three piano concertos heard most often today are: No. 1, in D minor, No. 4, in A major, and No. 5, in F minor (c.1730).

One of the finest of this trio of concertos is the first one, in D minor (sometimes also heard as a violin concerto). The solo instrument is often used for filigree work, with the most exquisite effect. The robust six-bar theme, heard at the opening of the concerto in unison orchestra, and the spacious melody for strings that begins the second movement are orchestral backgrounds to which the soloist provides soaring melodic flights and piquant, decorative passage work. Soloist and orchestra weave a contrapuntal fabric.

Two Bach concertos for solo violin and orchestra have survived: the Concerto in A minor and the Concerto in E major (1717–23). As Bach often wrote music to be played interchangeably by either the violin or the piano, obviously the artistic procedure remained the same for each instrument. Stylistically the traditions of the concerto grosso are maintained. The outer movements are robust (a single theme usually dominating the first one). The middle part is lyrical. And, as in the piano concertos, the principal themes are often heard in the orchestra while the solo instrument is heard contrapuntally in intriguing figurations. These figurations are sometimes fragmentary, but usually extended and sinuous.

Fine as these two concertos for the violin are, they must occupy a position secondary to the consistently inspired Concerto in D minor for Two Violins and Orchestra (the so-called "Double Concerto"). Like the other concertos for solo instruments and orchestra, this one was written at Cöthen, between 1717 and 1723. Here Bach's consummate fugal technique is the means with which to project music of the most dramatic and expressive character. In the first movement the second violin is heard in unison with the orchestra in a proud and vigorous three-bar theme which progresses to a second idea as the first violin enters contrapuntally with the original theme. In the same way a melody of spiritual beauty is spun fugally by the two solo instruments in the slow movement. The concluding movement begins with whirlwind motion, which is temporarily arrested by a sensitive and haunting melody; the treatment throughout remains contrapuntal.

Bach was the first composer to write concertos for two pianos and orchestra. He wrote two: No. 1, in C minor, and No. 2, in C major (1727–36). Between 1730 and 1733 he completed two concertos for three claviers and orchestra; No. 1, in D minor, and No. 2, in C major. As an outgrowth of the concerto grosso, all these works give greater emphasis on collaboration than on contest. In the three-piano concerto in C major, for example, the trio of solo instruments are partners in a mutual artistic endeavor. In the first movement the solo instruments and orchestra are one in the presentation of the robust main theme. After that, each takes turns both in elaborating this material or embellishing it. And in the second movement, the soulful song first heard in strings over harmonies in the pianos is immediately assumed by the pianos to accompany the strings. This give-and-take proceeds throughout the work.

Bach's Concerto in A minor for Four Pianos and Orchestra (1730–33) is a transcription of a concerto by Vivaldi. Bach changes the key (from B minor), fills out the harmonic structure in the solo instruments, and adds one measure in the finale.

The Concerto in D minor for Violin, Oboe, and Orchestra (1730–33) is an adaptation of Bach's Concerto in C minor for Two Pianos and Orchestra.

Organ Music. Bach's organ works came in the Weimar period of his life, his first great creative phase (1708–17). This music reached exclusively into the past. The organ forms he used had been inherited from his predecessors, principally Frescobaldi (1583–1643) and Buxtehude (1637–1707). These forms included the passacaglia and chaconne, both old dance forms and both characterized structurally by a series of variations on an ever recurring theme in the bass. There was the toccata, a showpiece marked by brilliant passage work in which the organist could exhibit his virtuosity. There was the fantasia, which, as its name suggests, was free in form, allowing the composer to expand his ideas in an almost improvisational manner. There was the chorale-prelude, which combined traits of both the toccata and the fantasia: In a free form, a given theme was amplified in a virtuoso manner. Bach produced forty-six such compositions in his *Orgelbüchlein (Little Organ Book)*. There was the fugue, a subtle and often intricate network of contrapuntal voices on a single brief theme, one voice following another at carefully measured intervals.

In whatever organ form he wrote Bach blended science with poetry, technique with emotion, virtuosity with grandeur and nobility of thought, and in a way nobody before him had approached. Too often, in the hands of Bach's predecessors, these forms had been mere technical exercises. But with Bach they became the channel through which he transmitted great and moving art.

Some of the most famous of Bach's works for the organ have become familiar to present-day concertgoers in transcriptions for orchestra: the Passacaglia and Fugue in C minor; Toccata and Fugue in D minor; Fantasia and Fugue in G minor; Toccata in C major.

Samuel Barber

"He is a lyric poet . . . aloof from the swirling currents in which many of his colleagues are immersed."

NATHAN BRODER

BORN: West Chester, Pennsylvania, March 9, 1910.
DIED: New York, January 23, 1981.
MAJOR WORKS: *Ballets*—Medea; Souvenirs. *Chamber Music*—Dover Beach, for soprano and string quartet; Cello Sonata; String Quartet; Summer Music; Two-Violin Sonata. *Choral Music*—A Stopwatch and an Ordnance Map; Reincarnations; Prayers of Kierkegaard; The Lovers. *Operas*—Vanessa; Antony and Cleopatra. *Orchestral Music*—2 symphonies; Adagio for Strings; Essays Nos. 1 and 2; Violin Concerto; Capricorn Concerto; Cello Concerto; Medea; Knoxville: Summer of 1915, for soprano and orchestra; Medea's Meditation and Dance of Vengeance; Dei Natali; Piano Concerto; Fadography of a Yestern Scene. *Piano Music*—Sonata; Souvenirs. *Vocal Music*—Hermit Songs; Mélodies passagères; Despite and Still; individual songs for voice and piano.

HIS LIFE

Music was an integral part of the Barber household. Samuel Barber's mother was an excellent pianist. Whenever her sister paid a visit the living room would be the scene of music-making of the first order, for the sister was none other than Louise Homer, the celebrated contralto of the Metropolitan Opera, one of the leading figures of America's Golden Age of opera. That Samuel should develop into a musician, and an outstanding one, was therefore more or less taken for granted in the Barber family.

When he was six years old he began studying the piano with William Hatton Green, a Leschetizky pupil. A year later he wrote his first composition, a sentimental piano piece called *Sadness,* the manuscript copy of which he still has. In his twelfth year he became organist in the local church. A dispute arose when the choirmaster insisted that he hold a fermata not indicated in the music; Barber, faithful to the composer, stubbornly refused to do it and was summarily dismissed.

He next became a charter pupil of the Curtis Institute of Music (while attending high school, from which he was graduated in 1926). At Curtis, between 1924 and 1932, he studied the piano with Isabella Vengerova, voice with Emilio de Gogorza, and composition with Rosario Scalero. In 1928, he received the $1500 Bearns Award of Columbia University for the first time, for a violin sonata. This was one of several honors soon to come his way now, others being the American Prix de Rome in 1935, and the Pulitzer Traveling Fellowship in 1935 and 1936. During this period he completed several works testifying to his flowering creative gifts. The most notable were: *Dover Beach,* for soprano and string quartet, heard in New York on March 5, 1933; *The School for Scandal* Overture, with which he received the Bearns Award a second time and which was first performed in Philadelphia on August 30, 1933; and *Music for a Scene from Shelley,* introduced by the New York Philharmonic Orchestra under Werner Janssen on March 24, 1935.

Winning both a Pulitzer Traveling Fellowship and the American Prix de Rome in 1935 enabled Barber to go to Europe for some unusual experiences. He gave several lieder recitals in Vienna (for he had been trained as a singer at the Curtis Institute), then made his debut as a conductor under dramatic circumstances. He was invited to direct a concert at the Workers' Theater, in the workers' apartment-development in Vienna, at a time when the air was electric with labor threats to the Dollfuss regime. Indeed, the day after his concert an uprising of workers did take place. Only then did Barber discover that under the stage on which he had been conducting was a cache of arms and ammunition.

During a brief stay at Lake Maggiore he decided to realize a lifelong ambition to meet Arturo Toscanini, whose summer home was nearby. Timidly he rang the bell and inquired if he could possibly speak to Mrs. Toscanini; he had been instructed that the only route to the maestro was by way of his wife. The word came back that, unforunately, Mrs. Toscanini was not at home. Would he care to see the maestro instead? It was an experience he has never forgotten. When they grew tired of talking about music Toscanini led Barber to the piano where, together, they went through the entire score of Monteverdi's *Orfeo,* singing the individual roles and joining in the choruses.

In Italy, Barber produced an important work, the Symphony in One Movement, which the Augusteo Orchestra under Bernardino Molinari introduced in Rome on December 13, 1936. Five weeks later the symphony was performed in the United States by the Cleveland Orchestra under Artur Rodzinski, and during the summer of 1937 it was heard at the Salzburg Festival in Austria, also under Rodzinski, the first time the work of an American was heard at the festival. Barber later revised this symphony, and the new version was presented on February 8, 1944, with Bruno Walter conducting the Philadelphia Orchestra.

Upon Barber's return to the United States he became a member of the faculty at the Curtis Institute. There during the next few years he taught orchestration and conducting. Significant performances now brought him into the limelight. On November 5, 1938, Toscanini directed the NBC Symphony in *première* performances of the Adagio for Strings and Essay for Orchestra No. 1. (These were the first American works performed by Toscanini and the NBC Symphony.) Albert Spalding introduced the Concerto for Violin and Orchestra with the Philadelphia Orchestra in 1941, and one year later Bruno Walter conducted the New York Philharmonic Orchestra in the first performance of the Essay for Orchestra No. 2.

One year after Pearl Harbor, Barber joined the Armed Forces and was assigned to the Army Air Corps. While in uniform he completed his Second Symphony, which he had been commissioned to write in honor of the Air Force and which Serge Koussevitzky and the Boston Symphony introduced on March 3, 1944. The work was then transmitted by short-wave broadcast throughout the free world by the Office of War Information. Originally realistically descriptive of air flight, the symphony was subsequently revised to eliminate programmatic connotations, the new version heard first in Philadelphia in 1948. Meanwhile, Barber's Concerto for Cello and Orchestra was given by Raya Garbousova and the Boston Symphony under Koussevitzky in 1946 to become the recipient of the New York Music Critics Circle Award.

Following his separation from the Air Force, Barber secluded himself in Mount Kisco, New York, in his rambling Scandinavian-like home which he named "Capricorn," and which he shared with Gian Carlo Menotti, the opera composer. There Barber worked upon several ambitious works, the earlier ones under a Guggenheim Fellowship which he had received in 1945. Two of these works are of particular significance. One was Barber's first ballet, *Medea,* written for Martha Graham on a Ditson Fund commission; under its original title of *The Serpent Heart* it was produced in New York on May 10, 1946. Another major achievement of the 1940s was Barber's Piano Sonata in E-flat minor, commissioned with funds by Irving Berlin and Richard Rodgers to help celebrate the twenty-fifth anniversary of the League of Composers. Vladimir Horowitz played it in 1950.

Together with the important symphonic and choral music that Barber produced in the years that followed (including his Concerto for Piano and Orchestra in 1962, for which he received the Pulitzer Prize in music a second time) there came his first opera—*Vanessa,* libretto by Gian Carlo Menotti. The Metropolitan Opera produced it on January 15, 1958. It received the Pulitzer Prize in music and became the first American opera to be featured at the Salzburg Festival in Austria. *Vanessa* was so well received in New York that it was kept in the Metropolitan Opera repertory a second season, and then was revived in 1964–65 (the only American opera to be performed at the Metropolitan Opera for three seasons). He revised it in 1974. His second opera, *Antony and Cleopatra,* was commissioned by the Metropolitan Opera to open its new auditorium at the Lincoln Center for the Performing Arts. Lavishly produced as befitting such an august occasion—with staging by Zeffirelli—*Antony and Cleopatra* was seen on September 16, 1966. Possibly because the overdressed costuming, cumbersome scenery and last minute staging problems tended to obscure some of the eloquent moments in Barber's score, *Antony and Cleopatra* was a failure and it was dropped from the repertory after that season. But it stood up far better after Barber had revised his score and it had been revived at the Juilliard School of Music on February 9, 1975.

"Capricorn" was sold in 1973. Until his death, Barber lived in an apartment on East 72nd Street in New York and, during vacations, a small chalet at Santa Cristina in the Italian Dolomites.

His biographer, Nathan Broder, has described Barber as "withdrawn and rather cold, though urbane, when with people he does not know well." When not working, Barber enjoyed taking long walks in the woods, reading, and traveling. He was impatient with parlor games and had no interest in games of chance. Inept in mechanics he had never even learned to operate a phonograph.

Describing Barber's working habits, Broder adds: "He attaches great importance to his thematic material, and the search of the right themes is often painful and long drawn out, with many discarded along the way. When he is engaged in such a search he is usually in a bad temper and wanders about, silent and melancholy. . . . Once satisfactory themes are found, his mood changes immediately to one of gaiety and exhilaration."

HIS MUSIC

One of the two basic influences molding Barber's style was great literature. All his life he was a passionate reader; his response to books was sensitive, cultured, discriminating. This interest—his greatest one outside of music—inevitably gave direction to his composing. Many of his works were inspired by literary subjects: the source of his *Dover Beach* was a work by Matthew Arnold; the celebrated play of Sheridan inspired the early overture, *The School for Scandal;* the poetry of Shelley, *Music for a Scene from Shelley;* a poem by James Agee, *Knoxville: Summer of 1915.* Shakespeare was the source for his opera, *Antony and Cleopatra.* Lyrics by Stephen Spender, Emily Dickinson, William Butler Yeats, James Joyce, and A. E. Housman provided words for songs and choral works. His Essays for Orchestra, Nos. 1, 2, and 3, translated a literary form, the essay, into musical terms. Love of literature not only gave Barber his subject matter, texts, and forms; it also made him more disposed to poetic ideas and moods than to musically cerebral ones.

The second basic influence on Barber's style was his fascination with the singing voice, first acquired through listening to his famous aunt, then cultivated through his own study of the voice. This was probably the source of the warm and tender and truly vocal lyricism of his finest works, in which the melodic element is ever given precedence over the rhythmic or the harmonic. In these works, which are those most readily accepted by his audience, Barber's search for beauty—beauty of form as well as sound—has produced sensitive melody, rich-sounding harmonies, expressive counterpoint, delicate atmosphere, and refined moods.

ANALYTICAL NOTES

Opera. *Vanessa* (1958) is an opera of commanding importance. The melodramatic and at times neurotic text by Gian Carlo Menotti—penetrating for its psychological insight into female characterization and compelling for its dark moods and somber atmosphere—is set in a Scandinavian country in 1905. The plot is a morbid love triangle involving Vanessa, Anatol (son of Vanessa's dead lover), and Vanessa's niece, Erika. Vanessa has been waiting twenty years for her lover to return. He never does, for he is dead. But in his place comes his son, Anatol. After Anatol has seduced Vanessa's niece, Erika, he marries Vanessa and takes her off with him. Erika is now left alone in the grim baronial manor to wait for her love the way Vanessa had done these many years.

Though dissonance and atonality serve Barber to project the high tensions involving his characters, and the funereal mood surrounding them, his writing is generally Romantic in feeling and lyrical in style; and in the orchestra, it has symphonic breadth. The music ranges from bravura duets and sentimental arias of the Italian school to dramatic writing with the majestic sweep of a Wagner. Notable lyrical pages include the enchanting waltz of the old doctor in the first act, "Under the Willow Tree," and Vanessa's second-act song, "Our Arms Entwined." The theatrical impact is never permitted to lag, in spite of the many moments of melodic eloquence, rising to a climax of unforgettable emotional power in the final scene with the five-part fugue "To Leave, To Break, To Find, To Keep."

Orchestral Music. In its revised, and now definitive, version the Symphony in One Movement in E minor, is really a four-movement symphony in capsule form. The work begins with an allegro "movement" in miniature, in which the symphony's three principal themes are stated. The first, announced in the full orchestra, is followed by a more lyrical second theme in the violas and English horn; a swirling, rising passage in the strings builds to the closing theme, played by the full orchestra. After these themes are developed, the first theme reappears in quickened tempo to serve as the basis of a scherzo "movement." The second theme now comes back in a more leisurely tempo, first in an oboe solo against a low, sustained background of strings, then with increasing sonority as the strings take up the melody and the other orchestral choirs are added. A crescendo in the full orchestra leads to the finale: a brief and stately passacaglia built on the first theme, here played by the cellos and basses. The other two themes of the symphony are reintroduced by the woodwinds and upper strings over the bass melody; the brass enter with a final statement of the first theme; and the passacaglia becomes a dramatic summation of the work.

Barber's Second Symphony is in a stylistically different vein from his other early orchestral works. Here we find dissonance and rhythmic momentum rather than melody; energy and motion instead of poetic moods. Inspired by Barber's association with the Army Air Corps, which had commissioned him to write the symphony, it evokes sights and sounds familiar to pilots. In the course of the second movement, a dreamy nocturne, the staccato sounds of a radio beam interrupt the tranquil mood—the sounds being reproduced electronically upon an instrument manufactured for this composition. The third movement opens with a rapidly cascading figure in the strings, representing an airplane spinning to earth. In 1947, Barber revised the symphony, eliminating all the tonal references to airplanes.

Barber has written concertos for the violin, for the cello, for the piano. The Piano Concerto, written in 1962, is one of his masterworks. It was performed for the first time on September 24, 1962, by John Browning and the Boston Symphony Orchestra under Erich Leinsdorf at the Lincoln Center for the Performing Arts during the opening week festivities.

Three principal thoughts dominate the opening movement. One is declamatory, while the other two are rhythmic. In the second movement, a song unfolds first in flute, then in solo piano, and after that in muted strings. The finale is brought in with several resounding chords in the orchestra. Several themes are then superimposed on an ostinato bass figure in the piano. Two contrasting sections are contributed by clarinet solo and by three flutes, muted trombones, and harp.

Barber's most frequently heard orchestral compositions are the three shorter pieces which he wrote early in his career and with which he achieved his first significant success. All are in a poetic vein. The Adagio for Strings (which had originated as the slow movement of the String Quartet in B minor before Barber transcribed it) is constructed entirely out of a single theme, lyrical and emotional, heard at the very beginning in the violins. The theme is taken up by other groups of strings before a stirring climax is reached. This theme returns quietly, after a brief pause, to conclude the work on the note of serenity with which it began.

The Essays for Orchestra Nos. 1 and 2 develop reflective ideas in much the same way the literary form does. Several subjects are expounded briefly, then amplified, correlated, and brought to their logical conclusion. The first Essay opens softly with an expansive melody for violins that grows in volume and intensity until, at the melodic peak, the horns are added, playing a fragment of the violin melody. The strings then drop out and the horns alone are heard in a short martial episode, the second subject of the Essay. The third is a contrasting scherzo-like, transparent subject shared by strings and flutes.

In the second Essay, completed five years later, the first subject is announced by solo flute, the second in the violas, and the third in the brass. The last of these is developed fugally and carried toward an impressive climax. The main theme is then repeated loudly before the Essay ends with a coda in which the third theme is passingly recalled by the basses.

From his score to the ballet *Medea* (which he had written and which was produced in 1946), Barber extracted material for two effective orchestral compositions. One was a suite prepared in 1947; the other, a tone poem entitled *Medea's Meditation and Dance of Vengeance,* was completed in 1955. The ballet, with choreography by Martha Graham, was based on the legend of Medea and Jason—but only loosely. As the composer has explained, the story was not treated literally, but the characters were used "to project psychological states of jealousy and vengeance which are timeless." The orchestral suite was planned to follow the form of a Greek tragedy. It opens with the

"*Parados,*" in which the characters appear. This is followed by a reflective "*Choros,*" commenting on the action to come. Two contrasting dances are now presented, the fresh and simple one of the princess, and the heroic one of Jason. A second "*Choros*" is the transition to "Medea's Dance of Vengeance." After that the menacing "*Kantikos Agonias*" tells of Medea's terrible crime. The suite ends with an "*Exodos*" in which are combined the different themes of the principal characters.

The tone poem *Medea's Meditation and Dance of Death* is a revision and a rescoring for a larger orchestra of one of the sections of this suite, similarly entitled.

Barber wrote *Fadograph of a Yestern Scene* on a commission from the Alcoa Company for the opening of Heinz Hall for the Performing Arts in Pittsburgh on September 10, 1971. The title comes from a line in James Joyce's *Finnegan's Wake.* The composition is a short, tranquil and sensitive mood picture in an impressionistic vein.

Piano Music. The Piano Sonata in E-flat major, which Barber completed in 1949—and which Vladimir Horowitz introduced in New York City on January 23, 1950—is one of its composer's major works. Its large four-movement design (most of it conceived along classical lines) is the mold into which Barber poured energetic ideas dramatized by harmonic and rhythmic idioms. Nevertheless, a strong lyrical element is not wanting, and is most expressive and most deeply moving in the third-movement adagio mesto. The fourth and concluding movement is a fugue of monumental design. Harriet Johnson, the critic of the New York *Post,* described the sonata as a whole aptly when she said that it "encompasses realism and fantasy, conflict and resolution, poetry and power."

Béla Bartók

"His pagan barbarity, his explosive and angrily defiant melancholy, his demoniacal instinct . . . these are all echoes . . . of the thousand-year-old Hungarian psyche."

EMIL HARASZTI

BORN: Nagyszentmiklós, Hungary, March 25, 1881.
DIED: New York City, September 26, 1945.
MAJOR WORKS: *Ballets*—The Wooden Prince; The Miraculous Mandarin. *Chamber Music*—6 string quartets; 2 violin sonatas; Sonata for Solo Violin. *Choral Music*—Cantata profana. *Opera*—Bluebeard's Castle. *Orchestral Music*—3 piano concertos; 2 violin concertos; 2 rhapsodies for violin and orchestra (also for violin and piano), Music for Strings, Percussion, and Celesta; Divertimento for String Orchestra; Concerto for Orchestra; Viola Concerto (completed and orchestrated by Tibor Serly). *Piano Music*—Allegro barbaro; Mikrokosmos.

HIS LIFE

While still living in Hungary, Bartók told an interviewer that he had been born not once but twice.

The second time took place in 1904, in the town of Kibed, in the Maros-Torda region of Hungary. An eighteen-year-old servant girl was cleaning his room, singing as she worked. Her song with its unusual progressions and exotic melody fascinated Bartók. He had never heard a tune quite like it. She could not tell him where the melody came from or who wrote it. All she knew was that her mother had sung it to her, that it was popular in the region where she had been raised as a child, that many other melodies like this one were known and sung there.

Ever an avid hunter after musical knowledge, Bartók felt that he had come upon the scent of some new information. He decided to visit not only the setting of his servant's childhood but other places in Hungary remote from city life. He would listen to and study the indigenous song and dance of every locality he visited.

He made that first trip in 1905, terminating it only because his funds ran out. That experience (some of whose findings he gathered in his first publication, Twenty Hungarian Folksongs, released in December of 1906) was like the discovery of a vast continent. Here was a veritable treasure house of song and dance, unknown not only to the rest of the world, but even to sophisticated Hungarian musicians. Bartók now dedicated himself to uncover this music. During the next eight years he traveled extensively throughout Hungary, Romania, and Slovakia (sometimes in the company of a fellow musician, Zoltán Kodály), taking down on paper, or on phonograph records, all the songs he heard, more than six thousand of them. Later on he saw to it that they were published. Thus he made known an immense library of Hungarian folk music, far different in style and character from that music which had been thought of as the only native Hungarian music. Up to then, the outside world had considered the sentimental, sinuous, decorative melodies of the gypsy as the authentic music of the Hungarian people. Brahms thought so when he wrote his celebrated dances, and so did Liszt in his even more popular rhapsodies. But the music Bartók discovered was different in style and technique. The melody was severe, patterned after the rise and ebb, the inflection, of Hungarian speech; the rhythms were irregular; the tonality reached back to the modes of the church. It was a savage music: intense, passionate, strong, and uninhibited. Nothing quite like it could be found anywhere else.

"The genuine Hungarian peasant music," Bartók wrote, "was all but unknown at that time. . . . In the most valuable part of it, the oldest Hungarian peasant melodies, the material was at last discovered that was destined to serve as the foundation for a renaissance of Hungarian art music." In that renaissance he was destined to become a primal force. Thenceforth he was not satisfied with merely writing music; from then on he had to write *Hungarian* music.

In short, he was a far different composer after 1905, when he first came upon this folk music, than he had been before. For this reason he considered he had been (artistically at any rate) born anew.

His actual birth took place in 1881 in the small town of Nagyszent-miklós, in Transylvania, where Hungarian, Romanian, and Slavic elements merge. He was a sickly child, suffering from a bronchial condition that made it impossible for him to play with other children. He became a self-contained, introspective child who sought diversion in reading and in music. His father, director of the School of Agriculture and a fine amateur musician, died when Béla was only eight. The family responsibilities were assumed by the mother. Not only did she support her children, but she attended personally to their education. She was Bartók's first piano teacher and saw him reveal unmistakable signs of talent. When he was nine he wrote his first piano piece (a waltz), and a year or so after that, on May 1, 1892, he made his first public appearance as a pianist.

In 1893, to give her son an opportunity to develop his talent in a way that could not be done in a provincial town, she accepted a teaching position in Pressburg (now Bratislava, Czechoslovakia). There László Erkel taught him the piano and encouraged him in his creative attempts, which were then imitative of Brahms. (An early two-movement violin concerto was later adapted into the first of his mature works, the *Two Portraits for Orchestra*.) From 1899 to 1903 Bartók studied with Thomán and Koessler at the Liszt Academy in Budapest. For a while he was more active as pianist than as composer, making several successful appearances at the Academy and at the Royal Hall. Hearing Richard Strauss's *Thus Spake Zarathustra* led him first to study Strauss's tone poems intensively, and then to imitate him in his own composition. *Kossuth*—a tone poem strongly influenced by Strauss's *A Hero's Life*—was introduced in Budapest on January 13, 1904, and soon after that was successfully performed in Manchester, England, under the direction of Hans Richter. He had now found his artistic goal in national music, stimulated as he was by a revival of interest in Hungarian culture that was then taking place in his country. He had still to find the means of achieving a truly national idiom in music. The means came to him between the years of 1905 and 1913 with the discovery of Hungarian folk music and the collection of over six thousand native melodies. Meanwhile, after leaving the Academy in 1903, he earned his living, such as it was, by playing the piano, teaching, and making musical arrangements. In 1907 he was appointed a teacher of the piano at the Liszt Academy, a post he held for the next thirty years. One of his students there was a fourteen-year-old girl, Márta Ziegler, to whom Bartók dedicated several piano compositions. They were married in 1909, and in 1910 a son, Béla, was born to them.

The production of musical works was his major activity, second only to that of exploring Hungarian folk music. And the creator was profoundly influenced by the explorer, as Bartók began assimilating many elements of Hungarian folk song and dance. Thus his writing became increasingly complex and individual, discouraging popular acceptance. There were always those ready to admire and respect him, for his technical mastery, scholarship, and articulateness were beyond question. But the general public just did not care for his music; its performances were far less frequent than those of lesser composers. Yet from time to time he did enjoy a measure of success—with the opera *Bluebeard's Castle* when it was introduced in Budapest on May 24, 1918; also with his Second Piano Concerto, which he played in Frankfurt, Germany, on January 23, 1933, Hans Rosbaud conducting.

He visited the United States for the first time in 1927; his trip was financed by the Baldwin Piano Company. For ten weeks he assisted in performances of his important works. Wherever he appeared he was greeted respectfully, but the enthusiasm was at best restrained.

Nor was the attitude toward Bartók much different when he returned to the United States thirteen years later—even though in the interim he had completed such major works as his Fifth and Sixth String Quartets (1934, 1939), the Music for Strings, Percussion, and Celesta (1936), the Second Violin Concerto (1938), and the Divertimento for String Orchestra (1939). His return to America was made early in 1940 for some concert appearances. Then later the same year, as a refugee from war-torn Europe, he decided to make New York his permanent home. A research grant in folk music at Columbia University provided him with a modest income ($3000 a year) which he could supplement with fees from concert appearances and lectures.

He came to America with his second wife—the former Ditta Pásztory, a concert pianist whom he had married in 1923 (the year he divorced his first wife, Marta)—and their son, Peter. They made their home in a modest apartment near Columbia University. As long as Bartók retained his research grant he did not have serious financial problems, since his wants and needs were modest. But the grant was terminated at the end of 1942, and from then on he was in a continual struggle to make ends meet—an appalling situation for which his fierce pride would not allow alleviation through loans or gifts. Strange to say, in view of Bartók's world prestige, he and his music were not in great demand. The critics were ready to concede him the position of first importance among Hungarian composers; the musicologists paid tribute to his monumental contributions to musical folklore; his few ardent admirers insisted that he was one of the most original and forceful musical figures of our generation. But the habitué of the concert hall remained cold toward him, and performances of Bartók's works remained infrequent.

That his music was not getting heard was not the sole thing to depress him. He could not be happy in a foreign land where he had to struggle with a strange language and habituate himself to new customs. He missed his own country, language, and people sorely. In addition to all this, his health was deteriorating. Always a small, slight, and fragile man, he was at times reduced from his normal weight of 115 pounds to under 90. His body was being ravaged by an almost continuous fever that defied diagnosis, and the pains in his joints were often so acute as to make walking difficult. "The doctors don't know the real cause of my illness," he wrote to a friend on June 28, 1943, "and consequently can't treat and cure it. They are groping about in a darkness, trying desperately to invent the most extraordinary hypotheses. But all of that is of no avail."

In spite of all these forces that seemed to combine for the express purpose of destroying him, he remained a man of fanatical will, a spirit that could not be defeated. Those of us who had an opportunity to meet him and talk to him during his last years were struck by the contradiction between the frail vessel that was the physical man and the indestructible and heroic spirit that represented the inner man, the creative artist. Nothing could tamper with his intellectual curiosity which made him so *au courant* with politics, science, literature, philosophy. And nothing could crush the creative powers that had made this slight, little man such a giant in twentieth-century music.

Out of illness and frustration sprang some of the greatest music Bartók was to write.

Only the fact that the American Society of Composers, Authors, and Publishers (ASCAP) stood ready to provide the necessary funds made it possible for Bartók to receive the hospitalization and medical care he needed. In the hospital he was visited by Serge Koussevitzky, who came to him with a commission from the Koussevitzky Music Foundation for a new orchestral work. Two other distinguished musicians came with commissions, Yehudi Menuhin and William Primrose.

For Koussevitzky, Bartók wrote his most famous symphonic composition, the Concerto for Orchestra. For Menuhin he produced the Sonata for Solo Violin, and for William Primrose he worked upon a viola concerto which he did not live to complete. In addition to these compositions, he also was deeply involved in the writing of his Third Piano Concerto.

Few incidents in contemporary music so demonstrate the strength of the creative force as the spectacle of Bartók racing with death to finish his last two masterworks: the Concerto No. 3 for Piano, and the Concerto for Viola and Orchestra. His body was wasting away; his voice was almost gone; he was often in terrible pain. He did not have to be told that he was dying. Only one thing mattered to him any longer. He had to finish his two concertos.

Time was running out; he knew it. He worked feverishly, defying fatigue and pain. He devised all sorts of short cuts to save time. He had his son, Peter, sit at his bedside and mark in for him all the necessary technical details on the manuscript paper so that he might use his energy only for writing down the music. He even hastily improvised a shorthand technique so that whole passages could be compressed into one or two symbols, and whole chords could be designated with a single stroke. There was no time for erasing; corrections had to be hurriedly grafted onto the original.

He completed all but the last seventeen bars of his piano concerto. Pathetically enough, he knew that he had written his swan song. After the stenographic markings of the last few bars he put the Hungarian word *"vege"* ("the end")—the first time he had done this in one of his manuscripts. He had come to the end of his lifework as well as his concerto.

The Viola Concerto consisted almost entirely of the stenographic signs and symbols Bartók had devised. The monumental task of decoding the work went to Bartók's friend Tibor Serly, who described the formidable problems that faced him:

First there was the problem of deciphering the manuscript itself. Bartók wrote his sketches on odd, loose sheets of music paper that happened to be on hand at the moment, some of which had parts of other sketches already on them. Bits of material that came to his mind were jotted down without regard for their sequence. The pages were not numbered nor the separation of the movements indicated. . . . The next problem involved the matter of completing harmonies and other adornments which he had reduced to a form of "shorthand" known only to close associates. . . . Finally, except for Bartók's statement that "the orchestration will be rather transparent," there were virtually no indications of its instrumentation. Strangely, this part presented the least difficulty, for the voice leadings and contrapuntal lines upon which the background is composed were clearly indicated in the manuscript.

If he lived long enough to bring his last two concertos to an advanced stage, he also lived long enough to see audiences, which had so long rejected him, respond sympathetically. The *première* of the Concerto for Orchestra by the Boston Symphony Orchestra on December 1, 1944, inspired an ovation, his first in many years, the only one he himself experienced in America.

With the liberation of Hungary in 1945, Bartók was invited to return to his native land. He planned to do so. But leukemia (the disease that was destroying him) took its final toll. Bartók died in New York on September 26, 1945. One of the last things he said was to his doctor: "The trouble is that I have to go with so much to say."

He did not live to know that most of his major works were so soon to win acceptance. Within a few months after his death there were forty-eight important performances of his larger works—twenty-five of them in the months of January and February of 1946. These included the *première* of his Concerto No. 3 for Piano and Orchestra on February 8, 1946, in Philadelphia. In the span of two years several all-inclusive Bartók cycles were performed in several different cities. In 1949, the Juilliard String Quartet presented all six Bartók string quartets in New York—an event that proved once and for all that here was the most significant contribution to chamber music made in the twentieth century. In 1951, the New York City Ballet produced *The Miraculous Mandarin,* and in 1952 the New York City Opera offered *Bluebeard's Castle.* Virtually everything Bartók had written has since become available in recordings, with his most celebrated works procurable in several different performances.

HIS MUSIC

Bela Bartók belongs with those composers of the past and present who drew their inspiration from the folk music of their native lands to realize a national art: composers like Mussorgsky and Rimsky-Korsakov in Russia, Smetana in Bohemia, Albéniz (1860–1909) and Manuel de Falla in Spain, Georges Enesco (1881–1955) in Romania.

The appropriate use of folk-song material [Bartók once wrote] is not, of course, limited to the sporadic introduction or imitation of these old melodies, or to the arbitrary thematic use of them in works of foreign or international tendencies. It is rather a matter of absorbing the means of musical expression hidden in the treasury of folk tunes, just as the most subtle possibilities of any language are assimilated. It is necessary for the composer to command this musical language so completely that it becomes the natural expression of his own musical ideas.

Bartók was not speaking theoretically; he was talking about himself. He never copied, imitated, or quoted. What he did was to absorb so completely all the essential traits of Hungarian folk music that these became an inextricable part of his own musical thinking. Once and for all he renounced his former romantic tendencies, the lip service he had been paying to Liszt and Richard Strauss. His style now became more austere and personal: discordant, rhythmically barbaric, intense, dynamic. The first two string quartets, the early rhapsodies, and such pieces for the piano as *Allegro barbaro* and *Bear Dance* were not only rhythmically and harmonically complicated, but were decidedly unpleasant to listen to. Philip Hale, hearing the *Bear Dance* in 1912, reported that the "composer was regarded with certain indulgence by the audience as, if not stark mad, certainly an eccentric person."

The identifying mannerisms of Hungarian folk song and dance became as well the traits of his writing: the disposition toward the use of church modes; the abrupt and shifting accents; the declamatory lyric line; the barbaric rhythms; and the free tonality. But these are only the bricks, the mortar, and the stone. With them Bartók proceeded to build a monument to national art.

In his last works Bartók simplified his idiom and structure and permitted an infusion of deep feeling and humanity into his writing. In his Concerto for Orchestra and in his Third Piano Concerto (the last works he was able to finish) he speaks more with heart than with mind. And these are the reasons why these masterworks have gained such universal favor.

ANALYTICAL NOTES

Chamber Music. The six string quartets give us a *coup d'oeil* over the evolution of Bartók's style. To the first quartet (1907) there still clings some of the post-Romantic influence to which Bartók had been subjected before he had embarked upon his explorations in Hungarian folk music. Yet in its rhythmic strength and variety it already suggests that this folk music had begun to affect his writing. In the second quartet (1917) the full impact of his folk music studies is felt. This is music filled with abrupt, changing rhythms, and piercing, at times agonized, chords. An unusual structural feature of this work is that it ends with a funereal slow movement. With the third quartet (1927) Bartók deserts a unifying tonality. The thought is more concentrated here than in the earlier two quartets, the style harsher and more primitive, while the atonal writing at times suggests the twelve-tone technique. Contrapuntal writing, which was to be found in the two earlier quartets, here gives way to discordant harmonies and rapidly changing rhythms. Even greater objectivity and restraint—though with much less of a tendency to concentrate on sheer brutal strength—characterizes the fourth quartet (1928). The first and last movements are built from a germinal idea (a six-note phrase in the seventh bar of the first movement). Both movements are fiery and energetic, while three middle movements have a lighter texture. In the fifth quartet (1934) Bartók becomes simpler and more lyrical as he began to revert not only to tonality but, in the last movement, to polyphony, the climax of that finale being a fully developed fugue. The two slow movements are chorales. The interest in a unifying tonality, as well as in greater simplicity, becomes even more apparent in the sixth and last quartet (1939). Unification is achieved through the recurrence of a single theme in various transformations, or the suggestion of that theme, in each of the movements. The third movement has a sardonic, even burlesque, identity, while rich poetic thought, with overtones of melancholy, penetrate the writing of the finale.

Choral Music. Bartók's most important work for chorus is the *Cantata profana* (1930), for tenor, baritone, double mixed chorus, and orchestra. Here the composer uses the text of several Romanian folk songs telling the legend of nine sons transformed into stags. Their father pleads with them to come home and reassume a human form again, but they refuse to do so, having found happiness in the freedom of the forests. The cantata is in three sections. The first describes how the sons are changed into stags; the second is the father's plea for the sons to come home; and in the third part the entire legend is reviewed by the chorus. Stylistically, Bartók's music is characterized by its imitation of peasant folk songs, and structurally, by the use of such forms as aria, canon, fugue, and cadenza.

Orchestral Music. The Concerto for Orchestra was the first composition (other than a transcription) which Bartók completed after making the United States his home during World War II. It was also his last exclusively orchestral composition. Its success was immediate, and it has become the composer's most frequently performed, most widely recorded, and most admired work for orchestra.

It has five movements, alternating between sad and optimistic feelings; the first and last movements are in the traditional sonata form (with clearly defined exposition, development, and recapitulation), while the middle ones are built out of a consecutive series of short sections.

The first movement is suffused with melancholy, both principal themes being expressions of severe pessimism. The first theme is heard at once in the lower strings; the second appears in the flute, and then is taken over by the trumpet. A note of levity appears in the second movement, which Bartók subtitled "The Game of Couples." Five couples are represented by five different pairs of wind instruments in five subjects. The pairs of winds appear in the following order: bassoons, oboes, clarinets, flutes, and muted trumpets. Separating each of the five musical subjects is a short chorale for the brass.

The third movement is elegiac; its thematic material is derived from the first theme of the first movement. Then there is an intermezzo, lighter in mood and texture than the music that precedes it. The concerto concludes with a Hungarian rondo which is vital and energetic; this is victory over defeat and pessimism. The development section of this finale is a fugue.

Two other exclusively orchestral compositions have had wide circulation: the Music for Strings, Percussion, and Celesta (1936) and the Divertimento for String Orchestra (1939). In the first of these, the string orchestra comprises two string quartets. They are combined in the first movement, and treated independently in the other three. In the first movement the first theme is presented quietly by violas, accompanied by percussion; it then receives fugal treatment. The second movement offers the first string group in the initial theme with the second group replying with a second subject. The third movement is for the most part dreamy music with the character of a nocturne. The finale has the vitality of a peasant dance.

The Divertimento opens with energetic music that has a good deal of buoyancy to it. Much of the interest lies in the alternation of a syncopated rhythm with intriguing patterns in solo instruments. A haunting melody rises from muted violins to become the heart of the second movement. The finale begins with lively music, and progresses to a secondary subject that is treated polyphonically. After a violin cadenza, the first subject is recalled, to be succeeded by a brief coda.

Bartók wrote three piano concertos. The first came in 1926. With the second (1931) Bartók achieved one of his greatest successes up to that time, performances taking place all over Europe following the world *première* in Frankfurt on the Main, Germany, on January 23, 1933. In the first movement Bartók dispenses with the strings. That movement opens with a trumpet motive, the preface to the first theme discussed by the solo piano. The solo instrument is also the first to give the second subject its hearing. These two themes are elaborated contrapuntally in the development. In the second movement, a chorale-like melody in the strings precedes the arrival of the piano and the tympani in an exchange. A presto section, derived from the piano subject, comes midway in the movement. Then the music reverts to the quiet atmosphere and slow tempo of the opening. The finale is dramatized by exciting rhythms and a motor energy which engage both the solo piano and the tympani.

Bartók's Third Piano Concerto (1945) was his swan song, and he knew it. This may explain why this is one of Bartók's most deeply expressive compositions and one of his most personal documents. In fact, in few places had he expressed such an eloquence of thought, and such a serene spirit, as he did in the second-movement adagio religioso. The first movement is in sonata form. The nine-measure first subject, heard in solo piano, has a recognizable Hungarian identity. The secondary theme comprises two ideas (grazioso and scherzando); this, too, comes first in the piano. The finale, rondo in form, is consistently dashing, dependent for its attraction more on rhythmic vitality than on melodic appeal. Fugal episodes, however, contribute contrapuntal interest.

Of Bartók's two violin concertos, it is the second (1938) that has earned a rightful place with his most significant creations. The first movement, in sonata form, begins with a six-measure introduction. Solo violin then appears with the main theme. Some subsidiary ideas are then introduced before the broad, lyrical second theme is shared by the solo violin and the orchestra. Bartók has explained that this second theme, despite its pronounced tonality, gives a suggestion of the twelve-tone technique. The development section is in two sections, the first vigorous and lively, the second more lyrical. The second movement is in the form of theme and variations. Solo violin states the theme, which then undergoes six variations, some of which have an improvisatory character, and the last of which is in the form of a canon. The original theme then returns in the solo violin an octave higher than when first heard. The finale opens with a spirited Hungarian subject and continues with a secondary theme, both freely based on material from the first movement. To Mosco Carner, the finale as a whole is "an image of the opening Allegro, but an image reflected, as it were, in a distorting mirror, by which metaphor I mean to indicate the altered shape and character which the material of the first movement now takes on." Once again reminiscent of the first movement is the two-part format of the development. A brief cadenza for the solo instrument is found in the coda.

Piano Music. *Mikrokosmos* (1926–39) comprises 153 pieces for the piano, gathered in six volumes. The title means "Little World," and the pieces are intended to teach children piano technique, the contemporary idiom, and national styles. Most of the pieces pose and solve various technical problems such as "chord study," "staccato and legato," "divided arpeggios"; or provide studies in canonic writing, chromatic invention, modes, the five-tone and the whole-tone scale, and so on. A good many of the pieces introduce the child to contemporary idioms and techniques, as the student is made to play in the language of polytonal harmony or polyrhythm reduced to the simplest common denominator. Still other pieces afford the child an opportunity to become acquainted with various national idioms through Hungarian folk songs, peasant dances, Bulgarian rhythms, pieces in a Russian or Transylvanian style. Finally, these albums contain descriptive items that carry picturesque titles to give a clue to the programmatic intent of the music, such as "Buzzing," "Wrestling," "Village Joke," "Bagpipe," "From the Diary of a Fly," and "Jack in the Box."

Ludwig van Beethoven

"He was a Titan, wrestling with the Gods."

WAGNER

BORN: Bonn, Germany, December 16, 1770.
DIED: Vienna, March 26, 1827.
MAJOR WORKS: *Chamber Music*—16 string quartets; 10 violin
sonatas; 9 piano trios; 5 string trios; 5 cello sonatas; 4 piano
quartets; 3 string quintets; Septet; Grosse Fuge for string
quartet. *Choral Music*—Mass in C; Piano Fantasy; Christ on
the Mount of Olives; Missa Solemnis. *Opera*—Fidelio. *Orchestral Music*—9 symphonies; 5 piano concertos; Concerto for Violin
and Orchestra; Concerto for Violin, Piano, Cello, and Orchestra; 2 romances for violin and orchestra; Ah, Perfido!, for
voice and orchestra; Fidelio Overture, Leonore Overtures Nos.
1, 2, and 3; Coriolan Overture; Egmont Overture. *Piano Music*
—32 sonatas; Variations on a Waltz by Diabelli; Thirty-two
Variations. *Vocal Music*—An die ferne Geliebte; songs for voice
and piano including "Adelaide," "Andenken," "Die Ehre
Gottes," "Ich liebe dich," "In questa tomba oscura," "Nur wer
die Sehnsucht kennt."

HIS LIFE

Beethoven's birthplace, on the Bonngasse in the Rhine city of Bonn,
is today a museum to which the music lovers of the world come as
to a religious shrine. Here are kept many relics of his lifetime, in-

cluding his piano, which is roped off to keep visitors from touching it. The temptation to touch piano keys once played upon by Beethoven is, however, something which few can resist. One woman hurriedly played the eight notes of the first theme from the Fifth Symphony, then turned sheepishly to the scowling caretaker. "I suppose," she said, *"everybody* just wants to play on Beethoven's piano!" The caretaker answered, "Not *everybody*. Only last week we had a visitor who refused to put his hand on the instrument. He said he wasn't worthy of it. His name was Paderewski."

A biographer of Beethoven cannot altogether free himself from a similar feeling of humility and reverence toward his subject. There was once an eccentric conductor by the name of Jullien who had his own way of showing his worship. Each time he mounted the podium to perform a Beethoven work he would have a pair of kid gloves brought to him on a silver platter. While the audience waited he would put on these gloves with a great deal of ceremony and proceed to conduct the music—with a special jeweled baton.

Each one approaches Beethoven in his own way, though more usually with the simple veneration of a Paderewski than with the ostentation of a Jullien. There are few composers who inspire the kind of awe that makes Wagner speak of Beethoven as a "Titan" and leads Tchaikovsky to call him a "god." He inspires awe not only because of his stature as a composer, but also for his qualities as a man: his vision, sense of personal dignity, pride, idealism, and genuine heroism. Beethoven created some of the mightiest music conceived by man; he was also the central figure in a life-and-death struggle with destiny, from which he emerged triumphant.

He had an unhappy childhood. His father, Johann, a singer in the Electoral Chapel in Bonn, was a chronic drunkard who squandered the little he earned and who made his home sordid with drunken scenes. When the child Ludwig began to show an interest in music the drunkard was suddenly fired with ambition. Mozart had brought in a great deal of money as a child prodigy. Why not the young Beethoven also? Johann enlisted the services of his friend Tobias Pfeiffer to teach the boy the piano. With the tyranny of a despot, Johann kept his son at the piano hour after hour. There were times when Pfeiffer and Johann, arriving home late at night and drunk, would drag the boy out of his warm bed to make him practice until dawn. When there were mistakes—as there had to be when the boy grew tired and cold and sleepy—the blows would descend.

It was a sad childhood: poverty and drunkenness in the home; slavery at the piano until the muscles ached and the head swam with fatigue. There were blows for mistakes, but no kind word for a lesson well done. To make matters even worse, Beethoven had no friends, not even casual companions. He was an ugly boy, untidy in dress and appearance, clumsy in everything he did, extremely sensitive and shy. He was avoided by the children of his age, and he avoided them. Thus he never knew the meaning of childhood play. Whatever warmth entered his life came from his mother, whose tenderness compensated somewhat for the father's brutality. She was a patient, understanding, compassionate woman whom no one had ever seen smile. She no longer lived for herself, but for her children, and particularly for her oldest living son, Ludwig.

Ludwig van Beethoven made his concert debut in his eighth year (his father advertised that the boy was only six). He revealed talent, but not enough talent to arouse his audience. Johann's maneuvers were not proceeding according to plan. But music study continued. Beethoven's first important teacher was the court organist Christian Gottlob Neefe, who understood him, appreciated him, and knew how to nurse his growing talent. When he was eleven, Beethoven had his first publications, three piano sonatas. A year later he substituted for his teacher Neefe as court organist. One year after that he was appointed Neefe's assistant by the Elector Max Franz, filling this post so competently that there was talk of his replacing his master. He also served as "cembalist" at the court theater, assisting in the production of operas. Despite the lack of electrifying brilliance, of such exploits as characterized Mozart's childhood, the discerning could recognize maturing ability. His teacher saw it, at any rate, for in 1783 Neefe wrote: "If he goes on as he has begun, he will certainly become a second Mozart."

His talent attracted the interest of the Elector, who generously provided Beethoven with the funds to visit Vienna in 1787. There was good reason for Beethoven's desire to go there. It was a great center of music-making. It was the home of the great Mozart, a musician Beethoven admired profoundly. To play for Mozart, to get the master's opinion of his talent, was his major ambition.

In Vienna, Mozart listened politely to his playing but did not appear to be greatly impressed. "Now," young Beethoven said, "I will improvise." Here he showed imagination and originality. But Mozart withheld words of praise until Beethoven had passed the severest test of all: spontaneous improvisation on a given theme. Mozart gave the theme; Beethoven improvised. At last Mozart was convinced. "You will someday make a big noise in the world."

The news that his mother was dying of tuberculosis abruptly ended Beethoven's holiday after two months. He rushed back to Bonn in time to be at her side as she passed away. Her death was a shattering blow; he had lost the one person close to him, the one person who had given him tenderness and affection.

Her death made his life at home more difficult than ever. His father, now a hopeless drunkard, once had to be rescued from the hands of the police. His intemperate drinking brought about his dismissal from the Electoral Chapel, and it was Ludwig's responsibility to support and run the household and to see that his father kept out of trouble. To support the family Ludwig played the viola in a theater orchestra, gave lessons to children of the nobility, played the piano. He was also doing some composing—piano works which were not of any great consequence. However, people in Bonn began to speak well of his gifts and to prophesy a promising future for him. He made some good and powerful friends among the nobility: the Breunings, at whose home he got his first smattering of culture; Count Waldstein, later to become a patron, who was always ready with a sadly needed loan.

In 1790 a celebrated musician passed through Bonn en route to London. He was Joseph Haydn, of Vienna, considered by most of his contemporaries the greatest composer of his age. He stepped into the Bonn Cathedral to hear a new Mass by the young Beethoven. "He is a man of great talent," Haydn said. Evidently the great Haydn did not easily forget the impression this music had made on him. Returning to Vienna from London, he once again stopped off at Bonn to meet the young composer personally. Beethoven showed him some of his compositions. "You have great talent," Haydn told him. "You must come to Vienna to study with me." Count Waldstein, informed of Haydn's visit, agreed that Beethoven's place was in Vienna, studying with the master. He arranged for Beethoven's salary from the Elector to be continued during an indefinite leave of absence and sent the young man off with the following message: "You are going to Vienna in fulfillment of your wishes so long denied to you. Mozart's guardian angel still mourns and weeps over the death of his charge. He found a refuge in the inexhaustible Haydn, but no occupation with him. He wants through Haydn to form a union with another. Through assiduous diligence you shall receive Mozart's spirit from the hands of Haydn."

In November 1792 Beethoven came to Vienna for a second time, this time for good. Aware that life in a great city called for certain refinements, and eager to make a good impression on the nobility to whom he bore letters of introduction, he bought himself a wig, silk hose, fashionable boots, and a handsome coat. He looked clumsy in all this elegance, which, truth to tell, he soon discarded; and he behaved with the awkwardness and self-consciousness of a small-town boy. He looked much older than his twenty-two years. He was short, stocky, and compact, with a face leonine in strength but disfigured, pock-marked, and florid. Strength—crude and ungovernable strength—spoke through him. Few could sense that this was a new age arrived, the very spirit of the French Revolution, a greater, stronger, fiercer, nobler Figaro who had read Rousseau passionately and was a republican at heart.

He was determined to make his mark as a musician, determined to study and learn as never before. The firmly set jaw, assertive chin, flaming eyes announced silently that what he set out to do he would do successfully.

He became a pupil of Haydn. Strange to report, he did not do well. How, indeed, could the quiet, imperturbable Haydn—greatest spokesman of an age gone by—sit patiently and watch the untrammeled stormings of the younger man, whose talent he admired, but whose ungovernable genius he did not understand? Haydn was impatient with Beethoven's boorish manners and intolerant of the way the student broke the rules of harmony and form as freely as those of social behavior. Nor did Beethoven react more enthusiastically to his teacher. He found Haydn fussy, academic, too firmly rooted in tradition. Before long they parted ways.

Beethoven sought other teachers, Albrechtsberger of St. Stephen's Cathedral, and the celebrated Kapellmeister Salieri. But with these masters, too, he was an intractable pupil, and they could teach him little. "He has never learned anything," Albrechtsberger once remarked sadly, "and he can do nothing in decent style." Lesser men, more sympathetic and farsighted, proved more successful teachers, men like Ignaz Schuppanzigh, later the founder of a great string quartet, and Johann Schenk.

Meanwhile the doors to Vienna's leading nobility were opened by Count Waldstein's letters of introduction. Prince Lichnowsky, Prince Lobkowitz, and Baron van Swieten were among those who welcomed him. Prince Lichnowsky, who recognized Beethoven's genius and even felt in awe of it, invited him to live in his palace. In the salons of Vienna's great, Beethoven played and taught the piano and introduced his compositions. He did not lack for appreciation. This is a tribute to the musical perceptiveness of these noblemen, for though Beethoven was writing in the styles of Mozart and Haydn, he was already asserting independence in his use of form and harmony. Besides, crude in his manners, so sensitive that the slightest affront aroused his violent temper, so conscious of his powers that he considered himself the proud equal of these noblemen and did not hesitate to say so, Beethoven was not easy to get along with. Once he insulted the guests in the Lichnowsky music room because they spoke while he was playing for them. "I shall not perform before such swine!" he cried as he slammed the lid of the piano. The noblemen disregarded his ill-tempered remarks, tolerated his boorishness, and soothed his sensitive nature—because they admired his music so profoundly.

By 1793 Vienna knew that his powers of improvisation at the piano had few if any equals. Karl Czerny said: "Apart from the beauty and originality of the ideas, there was something extraordinary in the expression." And it was not long before he began to make his mark as well both as a composer and as a piano virtuoso. In March 1795 he made his first public appearances in Vienna, at two charity concerts. Besides introducing his new piano concerto (the Second, in B-flat major), he revealed himself to be, as one unidentified Viennese writer remarked, "the giant among pianoforte players."

By the end of the century he had made considerably more forward strides as composer by publishing a first set of trios, a number of piano sonatas, and the song, "Adelaide." He was beset by commissions. "I have more orders than I can execute. I have six or seven publishers for each one of my works, and could have more if I choose. No more bargaining! I name my terms and they pay."

On April 2, 1800, there took place in Vienna a concert for Beethoven's benefit in which two of his works were introduced: the Septet and the First Symphony. It cannot be said that Vienna, for all its enthusiasm for Beethoven, recognized the musical event as one of historic importance: the *première* of the first symphony by the one destined to become the greatest symphonist of all. The performance was inadequate. The music was regarded as too difficult by the orchestra, which performed lackadaisically. The critics were devastating. In the opinion of the critic for the *Allgemeiner Musikalische Zeitung* there was "too much use of wind instruments, so much so that the music sounded as if written for a military band rather than for orchestra." A Leipzig critic was even harsher, describing the work as "the confused explosions of the presumptuous effrontery of a young man."

Early in 1801 Beethoven began recognizing signs that he was growing deaf. Not to hear music any longer, not to hear that which he was putting down on paper—surely this was the bitterest of all fates to befall a musician! "Sorrowful resignation," Beethoven wrote at this time, "in this must I find refuge." Sensitive about his oncoming deafness, he tried pathetically to conceal it; but he had to give up playing the piano in public and he had to keep aloof from the society of all who were not intimate friends.

Deafness brought on a period of despair, a despair which he expressed in a remarkable document called the *Heiligenstadt Testament,* written in the Viennese suburb of Heiligenstadt in 1802 as an expression of his terrible anguish. "O ye men, who think or say that I am malevolent, stubborn, or misanthropic, how greatly do ye wrong me, you do not know the secret cause of my seeming"—so began the tortured self-revelation. "For me there can be no recreation in the society of my fellows, refined intercourse, mutual exchange of thought; only just as little as the greatest needs command may I mix with society. I must live like an exile," the document continued. And it ended: "O Providence—grant me at last but one day of pure joy—it is so long since really joy echoed in my heart—O when—O when, O Divine One—shall I feel it again in the temple of nature and man—Never? No—O that would be too hard!"

Deafness sent him to composing music with a fever and passion he had not known before. Removed from the society of people, he sought communion with the spirit. Deaf to the sounds of music, he sought to put down the turbulent and majestic sounds he heard within him.

One masterpiece after another came from him: the *Waldstein, Appassionata,* and *Moonlight* Sonatas for the piano; the *Eroica* Symphony; the *Kreutzer* Sonata, for violin and piano.

He created one other remarkable document, the letter to the "Immortal Beloved," found in a secret drawer after his death. He was often in love—his "love affairs" were usually of brief duration; the objects of his love were invariably young, beautiful women of high station, generally out of his reach. Many of them have been identified. One was Giulietta Guicciardi, to whom he dedicated the *Moonlight* Sonata. Another was her cousin, Therese von Brunswick, inspiration for the *Appassionata* Sonata. A third was the fifteen-year-old Therese Malfatti. A fourth was the poetess Bettina Brentano, friend of Goethe. Which of these was Beethoven's "Immortal Beloved"? The riddle has never been solved; we do not even know the date on which he wrote his flaming letter. It may well have been written not to any one woman, but to all womankind; or it may have been written to a woman who existed only in his disturbed imagination and dreams. In any case, few love letters are composed of such tortured distress, of such emotional intensity. "What tearful longings after you—you—my life—my all!—farewell. Oh, continue to love me, never misjudge the faithful heart of your beloved L.—— Ever yours—Ever mine—Ever each other's——"

As his deafness increased he grew more irritable, scornful, sensitive, petulant, and irascible. His friend Ferdinand Ries has recorded how at a noonday meal at a Viennese tavern, the Silver Swan, Beethoven threw a dish of meat and gravy at a waiter who brought him the wrong order. An innocent incident might cause a rupture with the closest friend. From Hummel he became estranged because he misinterpreted a casual remark and would permit no explanation to heal the breach. He drove away one of his dearest friends, Stephan von Breuning, for a mere trifle, and he did this after von Breuning had nursed him through a serious illness.

More and more he required those around him to believe as unquestioningly in him as he did himself. "With men who do not believe in me . . . I cannot and will not associate," he once told Prince Lobkowitz. He *did* find such men, who clung to him, understood him, bore with him. They came back after each of his storms ready to give him their unselfish friendship. There were Prince Lobkowitz, Countess Erdödy, and—most important of all—

Archduke Rudolph, who could be tolerant even to his republican views. They loved him, tended to him as if he were a helpless child. They were also generous: in 1809 they arranged a decent annual pension for him.

A vivid word picture by Romain Rolland enables us to see Beethoven with the eyes of his friends:

He was short and thick set, broad shouldered and of athletic build. A big face, ruddy in complexion, except towards the end of his life, when his color became sickly. . . . He had a massive and rugged forehead, extremely black and extraordinarily thick hair. . . . His eyes shone with prodigious force. . . . Small and very deep set, they flashed fiercely in moments of passion or warmth, and dilated in a peculiar way under the influence of inspiration, reflecting his thoughts with a marvelous exactness. . . . His nose was short and broad with nostrils of a lion; the mouth, refined, with the lower lip somewhat prominent. He had very strong jaws, which could easily break nuts; a large indentation in his chin imparted a curious irregularity to the face. "He had a charming smile," said Moscheles, "and in conversation a manner often lovable and inviting confidence; on the other hand his laugh was most disagreeable, loud, discordant and strident"—the laugh of a man unused to happiness. His usual expression was one of melancholy. . . . His face would frequently become suddenly transfigured, maybe in the access of sudden inspiration, which seized him at random, even in the street, filling the passers-by with amazement, or it might be when great thoughts came to him suddenly, when seated at the piano. "The muscles of his face would stand out, his veins would swell; his wild eyes would become doubly terrible. His lips trembled, he had the manner of a wizard controlling the demons which he had invoked."

Withdrawing more and more from the society of men, Beethoven found solace in nature and in composition. He worked hard on his music—sketching, writing, revising, but always revising. To bring to life what he heard in his mind was a Herculean task to which he gave himself unsparingly. "With whom need I be afraid of measuring my strength?" he once asked proudly. He knew he was opening up new horizons with works like the Fifth and Seventh Symphonies, the *Emperor* Concerto, the three *Rasoumovsky* String Quartets. And his contemporaries recognized him as the greatest composer of the age. During the Congress of Vienna, when Europe's nobility and royalty streamed to Vienna to restore order to Europe after the Napoleonic wars, Beethoven was the object of attention and admiration. Men of the highest station vied with one another to meet him and entertain him.

After 1812 Beethoven's genius entered a five-year period of quiescence. He wrote little, and what he wrote was without the old power and immensity. But beginning with the *Hammerklavier* Sonata in B-flat major, in 1818, the giant, so long held in check, stirred again. There now came the last productive period of his life. In some respects it was the greatest of all. This was the period in which a spiritual radiance rare even for him entered his music, the period of the Ninth Symphony, the *Missa Solemnis,* the last piano sonatas, and the last string quartets.

Spiritual concepts were not all that concerned him during this period. At the same time that he was producing his last masterworks he was also occupied with expensive and sordid court quarrels to gain the guardianship of his nephew, Karl. The suit finally succeeded in 1820, but was hardly worth the effort it had cost. The nephew was a lazy, dissolute fellow who piled up immense debts and—adding insult to injury—regarded his uncle with mild contempt. The years 1820–26, during which Beethoven strove pathetically to reform his nephew and to win his love, were years of continual crisis, climaxed by Karl's futile effort to commit suicide. At last Beethoven was relieved of his burden when Karl found a niche for himself in the army.

On May 7, 1824, in Vienna, Beethoven appeared at a public concert for the last time. The occasion was the *première* of his latest, and last, symphony—the Ninth. Michael Umlauf was the conductor. Beethoven was seated on the platform with the orchestra players, beating time with the music. The audience was most enthusiastic, though the symphony was none too well performed. "Never in my life," recorded Schindler, Beethoven's friend and biographer, "did I hear such frenetic . . . applause. Once the second movement . . . was completely interrupted by applause—and there was a demand for a repetition."

In the final movement there took place an episode which surely must have brought tears to many an eye. The symphony ended. But Beethoven, stone-deaf, had heard nothing, and, mentally, being several measures off, continued to beat time with his hands. He was completely oblivious of the tumult of the audience acclaiming his symphony. At last, the contralto soloist, Caroline Unger, walked over to the master and gently turned him around to the demonstrative audience. "His turning around," remarked Sir George Grove, "and the sudden conviction thereby forced on everybody that he had not done so before because *he could not hear what was going on,* acted like an electric shock on all present. A volcanic explosion of sympathy and admiration followed which was repeated again and again, and seemed as if it would never end."

In 1826, while visiting his brother, Beethoven caught cold. Pneumonia set in; and after that, jaundice and dropsy. Confined to his bed as an invalid, Beethoven was cheered by gifts from different parts of Europe: a complete edition of Handel; a cash gift of $500; a case of Rhine wine. But he was very sick, and he knew it. On March 23, 1827, he signed his will. A day later he submitted peacefully to the Last Sacraments. One day more and he lapsed into unconsciousness.

On March 26 the Viennese heavens were split with lightning and growled with thunder. It was almost as if the city were giving voice to grief. A peal of thunder rumbled in Beethoven's death room. Then Beethoven fell back, dead.

All Vienna mourned. The schools were closed; many people stayed away from work. Thousands lined the streets on March 29 to watch his body being carried to its final resting place (Franz Schubert was one of the torchbearers). And as they watched, they wept.

HIS MUSIC

It is sometimes said that the age produces the genius. This is undoubtedly true in the case of Beethoven. In no earlier era could he have asserted his creative ego so defiantly, broken so decisively with the past, and struck out in new directions with such independence. The spirit of the French Revolution had spread throughout Europe, stirring rebellion against established authority. Crowns toppled, traditions were shattered before the tidal wave of new ideas and the cry for political and intellectual freedom that stemmed from such philosophers of the "Enlightenment" as Rousseau and Voltaire.

In keeping with this new spirit, Beethoven shook loose from the constrictions of the classical form and style, smashing those structural dikes that would have checked the surge of his inspiration. Creative necessity drove him to venture into dissonance, free tonality, enlargement of instrumental resources. In the last phase of his life, when he adopted musical thinking and form that were iconoclastic, he proved himself a true disciple of Rousseau, whom he read avidly. Freedom, the right of the creative ego to assert itself unhampered, was a religion with him. When he filled his music with a profound humanity, he was the son of the French Revolution, the true democrat, who believed passionately in the equality of man and who identified himself with mankind's struggles. "I, too, am king," was his credo.

There are three clearly defined periods in Beethoven's creative evolution. In the first, roughly up to 1800, his compositions show the heavy hand of authority and the past. These works, which include the first two piano concertos and the first few piano sonatas, sound as if they belong to the age of Haydn and Mozart: Here are the classical forms and style with an eighteenth-century charm. But even in the music of this apprentice period we can detect an occasional gesture of impatience with tradition.

A shadow fell over Beethoven's second period: He had to face the fact that he was growing deaf. His music grew more intense, more personal; his forms more spacious; his harmonic and tonal writing more daring. "I am now making a fresh start," he wrote at this time, and proceeded to prove his point with masterworks like the *Eroica* Symphony and the *Appassionata* Sonata, considered by many to have heralded the birth of the Romantic era. Rules were radically altered, sometimes even dispensed with, to meet his artistic demands. Technique had to be extended. When Schuppanzigh came to him complaining that the violin part in one of the *Rasoumovsky* Quartets was too difficult for performance, Beethoven shouted, "Does *he* really suppose I think of his puling little fiddle when the spirit speaks to me and I compose something?" The structure of the symphony, concerto, sonata, and quartet had to be amplified to give his ideas *Lebensraum*. The harmonic vocabulary had to be enriched so that he could express feelings and ideas rarely before embraced by music. The poetic thought that Beethoven now brought to musical sound was something which nobody before him had realized in quite this way. As Paul Bekker put it: "Music is no longer sonority pure and simple. It contains abstract ideas. . . . The idea . . . determines the character of the work."

After 1817 Beethoven entered upon an altogether new phase. It was his last period, that of the Ninth Symphony, the *Missa Solemnis,* and the final quartets. The break with the past was sharper than ever before; Beethoven entered spheres of expression previously unknown to music. Within a new subtle and tenuous structural logic he expounds a language daring for its modulations, progressions, and harmonic vocabulary. His thematic material becomes immensely varied, fertile, unorthodox in presentation and treatment. At times his style becomes savage and brutal. At other times he arrives at a spirituality in which his resignation to fate is complete—and he has found true peace at last.

ANALYTICAL NOTES

Chamber Music. To know Beethoven only through his symphonies and piano sonatas, and to be unfamiliar with the sixteen string quartets, is to have an incomplete picture of the master's art. For his quartets embody his most intimate thoughts, his most personal confidences, his purest writing; and these quartets, even more than the symphonies and the piano sonatas, provide a key to his evolution as a composer.

Beethoven was to produce seventeen published works (trios, quintets, sonatas for solo instruments and piano, etc.) before completing his first string quartet. Perhaps his reluctance to write a quartet before he felt sure of his powers stemmed from his profound admiration for the quartet music of Haydn and Mozart, which was his model.

In the first six string quartets, Op. 18 (1800)—known as the *Lobkowitz* Quartets because they were dedicated to Prince Lobkowitz—we have a good deal of the neat proportions, stylistic elegance, propriety, and refinements of the Haydn quartets. Indeed, the reason why the second member of this Op. 18 group, the Quartet in G major, is known as *The Compliments* is because the first theme of the opening movement has such courtly grace. But from time to time, throughout Op. 18, it is Beethoven—and not Haydn or Mozart—who can be identified. Occasionally we find a brusqueness and strength not often encountered in Haydn, such as the vitality of the staccato octaves over a drone bass in the trio of the scherzo movement in the first quartet, in F major, or the sudden release of energy in the slow movement of the second quartet, or the uninhibited motor energy of the concluding presto of the third quartet, in D major. From time to time it is the future Beethoven who emerges in this music, even if yet only in dim outlines: the way in which a germinal theme (a two-bar motive) becomes the source of an extended elaboration in the first movement of the first quartet; the passionate, almost unruly temperament of the opening theme in the first movement of the fourth quartet, in C minor; or the gift at variation found in the slow movement of the fifth quartet, in A major. At times we also get emotional content, of a depth and an intensity, singularly Beethovian. The poignancy of the slow movement of the first quartet, and the *"La Malinconia"* movement of the sixth quartet, in B-flat major, sound a new expressive note for chamber music.

Six years after the *Lobkowitz* Quartets came another set, three in number this time, collectively published as Op. 59 and known as the *Rasoumovsky* Quartets. They were commissioned by Count Rasoumovsky, Russian ambassador to Austria. In these works the middle-period Beethoven, of the volatile moods, is reflected in music that is now agitated and frenetic, now of an almost religious ardor. The tendency to uncover new horizons for form, the impatience with structural limitations is no less marked in these quartets than in the symphonies and sonatas of this period.

Because these works were commissioned by a Russian, Beethoven incorporated a Russian theme in two of the three quartets: in the finale of the first quartet, in F major, and in the scherzo movement of the second quartet, in E minor (the latter Russian subject is later quoted by Mussorgsky in the Cornonation Scene of *Boris Godunov*). The first quartet is unusual in its architecture: All four movements are in the two-theme, three-section form usually reserved for the first movement of the classic sonata, symphony, and quartet. This work has been dubbed the *Cello* Quartet because that instrument is used so prominently. In the second quartet we have a molto adagio movement which is one of the most exalted pieces of music written by Beethoven, sometimes compared to a prayer. The third quartet, in C major, has such dramatic power and force that it has been called the *Hero* Quartet. The high point of this work is the fugue in the finale. The third movement, instead of being the expected scherzo, is a light-textured and delicate allegretto marked "Grazioso."

A little over three years after the *Rasoumovsky* Quartets came the String Quartet in E-flat major, Op. 74 (1809), and the F minor Quartet, Op. 95 (1810). These are the last quartets of Beethoven's middle creative period. The E-flat major Quartet has come to be known as the *Harp* because pizzicato arpeggios for the four strings in the first movement suggest the sound quality of that instrument. Otherwise, this quartet is distinctive for its beautiful adagio ma non troppo movement which finds contrast in the quixotic moods of the third-movement presto, with its remarkable rhythmic vitality.

The F major Quartet is identified as the *Serious* for its subdued emotion and austerity of mood. The first harsh measures of the opening allegro con brio project a grimness that pervades most of this movement. The ensuing allegretto (in place of the usual slow movement) remains the medium for sober reflections that often touch the mournful. Even the scherzo, where a greater lightness of heart might be expected, is often submerged under dark shadows. In the finale, however, a more optimistic attitude asserts itself, but only after some preliminary struggles.

The quartets that Beethoven wrote in 1824–26, the provocative "last quartets," are unique even for the Beethoven of the third period. Beginning with the Quartet in E-flat major, Op. 127, and including the Quartet in B-flat major, Op. 130, the C-sharp minor Quartet (Op. 131), the A minor Quartet (Op. 132), and the F major Quartet (Op. 135), we find a new Beethoven. Not even in the Ninth Symphony or the Piano Sonata in C minor (Op. 111) does he reach for such a mystic and spiritual plane, nor is he so emancipated from the constructions of form and accepted creative procedures.

The traditional way of developing themes is once and for all abandoned, as idea follows idea—and sometimes only fragments of ideas—now stated, now interrupted, now varied, now reconstituted. As Beethoven himself said, there was here an altogether new "manner of voice treatment" just as there was here an altogether new sense of form.

But what is most important in this music of the last period is that Beethoven's poetic expressiveness achieved a peace and radiance not found anywhere else among his works. This is a kind of peace such as we can never know. We are made aware, to use the description of J. W. N. Sullivan, of "a state of consciousness surpassing our own where our problems do not exist and to which our highest aspirations

. . . provide no key." The character Rampion, in Aldous Huxley's novel *Point Counter Point,* put it in still another way after listening to the Quartet in A minor (Op. 132). "It's the most perfect spiritual abstraction from reality I've known." And Huxley adds: "It was as though heaven had suddenly and impossibly become more heavenly, had passed from achieved perfection into perfection yet deeper and more absolute. The ineffable peace persisted; but it was no longer the peace of convalescence and passivity. It quivered, it was alive, it seemed to grow and intensify itself, it became an active calm, an almost passionate serenity. The miraculous paradox of eternal life and eternal repose was musically realized."

The mysticism and the spirituality which recur so continually in these last quartets are first encountered in the slow movement of the E-flat major Quartet where an exalted melody is transformed by five variations, in each of which it acquires a new personality. This is one of the longest slow movements encountered in any Beethoven quartet. In the B-flat major Quartet, Beethoven enlarges his structure to embrace six rather than the usual four movements. The two additional ones comprise a section "in the style of a German dance" (*"alla danza tedesca"*), and a second slow movement. The latter is a sixty-measure cavatina, over one of whose passages the composer scribbled the word "anguished"—a description which might well serve for the entire movement. The C-sharp minor Quartet is longer still, being made up of seven movements, beginning with a brooding, melancholy fugue that projects an atmosphere of awe and majesty that returns in two slow movements—the third-movement andante, a theme and variations, and the twenty-eight-measure adagio, one of Beethoven's most profound contemplations. In the A-minor Quartet, the slow movement once again is one of those rare spiritual utterances of which only Beethoven seemed capable. Over the molto adagio movement Beethoven placed the following verbal comment: "A sacred thanksgiving of a Convalescent to the Divinity, in the Lydian Mode." The music was the composer's hymn of gratitude, in modal style, for having recovered from a serious illness. The heart of this movement is a chorale that recurs several times and is continually contrasted with a more dynamic episode. Beethoven's last quartet, in F major, has been the subject of a good many questions and arguments. The reason for this is that over the slow movement Beethoven wrote the question: "Must it be?", while over the first theme of the ensuing episode he wrote his answer, "It must be!" The meaning of this verbal interpolation has been debated for a long time, the most logical answer being that it was Beethoven's realization that his life was drawing to a close and that he would never again write another quartet. This explanation is further substantiated by the fact that in his manuscript, following the closing measure, Beethoven added the following two words: "last quartet."

One other piece of quartet music belongs to this last period, the *Grosse Fuge,* Op. 133, written in 1825. It was originally intended by the composer as the last movement of the B-flat major Quartet, Op. 130, but the publishers considered the music so complex, so forbidding, so elusive in content that they prevailed on Beethoven to publish it separately and to produce a new movement for the quartet. Beethoven complied, and the new movement he produced for the B-flat major Quartet was the last piece of music he was destined to write. The *Grosse Fuge* opens with an "overture" in which the subject of the fugue is suggested. A single variation of this material follows. Only then does the fugue itself unfold. The composition ends on a note of triumph.

The two most often heard of Beethoven's nine piano trios are those in D major, Op. 70, No. 1, and in B-flat major, Op. 97. In the first of these (1808) we find recurrent tremolo piano chords that contribute a ghostly atmosphere. This is the reason why this work has been named *Geister,* or *Spirit.* This first movement as a whole is one of the most melancholy found in Beethoven's chamber music, and it is the most significant in the entire work. The B-flat major Trio (1811) was Beethoven's last piano trio, a work generally referred to as the *Archduke* by virtue of the fact that it was dedicated to the Archduke Rudolph. The principal thought in the first movement is an affecting *dolce* melody for the piano. A lively scherzo movement is then heard, taking the place usually reserved for the slow movement, which comes *after* the scherzo. That slow movement opens with a deeply religious subject which receives five variations. A coda, in recitative style, serves as transition to the gay finale, which enters without interruption.

Beethoven wrote ten sonatas for violin and piano. To some of them he added the illuminating comment that they were "for pianoforte with the accompaniment of the violin." He was trying to emphasize that the piano role in these sonatas was a major one. In his sonatas both instruments are equal partners in the projection of the music. The most famous of these works is the Sonata in A major, Op. 47, better known as the *Kreutzer* Sonata (1803). Its first and closing movements have the ungovernable temperament and passion which we associate with Beethoven's tempestuous nature. It is the dramatic character of this music that inspired Leo Tolstoy to write his story *The Kreutzer Sonata.* The slow movement contains a majestic melody which goes through a series of variations.

Among the earlier violin sonatas, those in F major, the *Spring,* Op. 24 (1801), and C minor, Op. 30, No. 2 (1802) are particular favorites. The *Spring* Sonata deserves its name: The music is consistently bucolic and sunny throughout the three movements, including the slow one, which is based on a simple, forthright melody that is almost like an aria from a Mozart opera.

The expressive character of the Sonata in C minor has tempted W. W. Cobbett to seek out hidden programmatic implications. He finds that the first movement is martial, pointing out that the second theme sounds like a bugle call. The finale, in his opinion, is a battle scene, while the eloquent second movement, an idyllic duet, is a "pause between two battles." Cobbett's explanation is that, upset by his unsuccessful love affair with Countess Giulietta Guicciardi, Beethoven sought escape from his emotional turmoil in patriotism and in nature.

Beethoven also wrote five sonatas for cello and piano. The finest and the most frequently heard is the Sonata in A major, Op. 69 (1809). The cello is here given importance equal to that of the piano, its independence established in the very opening bars with an unaccompanied theme which is a basic idea of the entire first movement. The second movement is a delightful scherzo, the main subject of which is, in the words of John N. Burk, the "merest wisp of a tune," the last two notes of which "continue in a dreamy ostinato and furnish the trio." There is no extended slow movement. A brief and singularly eloquent adagio serves as a kind of preface to the sprightly finale.

Choral Music. Beethoven's greatest work for chorus and orchestra is the monumental *Missa Solemnis,* which he wrote in the closing years of his life. He began sketching the music in 1818, intending to have it performed in honor of the installation of his friend, pupil, and patron, the Archduke Rudolph of Olmütz. But as he worked on, the structural proportions and the aesthetic aims of the work continually expanded. On the day of the ceremony, March 20, 1820, the *Missa Solemnis* was still three years from completion, and the music of Hummel and Haydn had to be substituted. Not until three years after that, in 1823, had Beethoven brought his own work to completion. Beethoven knew the measure of the music he had just written; he was to refer to it as his most accomplished work. And he was not overestimating it. It has since been acknowledged to be the greatest religious work since Bach's Mass in B minor.

When he had finished writing the music, Beethoven inscribed on the manuscript the following words: *"Von Herzen—möge es wieder zu Herzen gehen!"* ("From the heart—may it go to the heart!") The expenditure of emotion seems to have been enormous. Those who saw him while he was in the process of creation reported that he appeared to be transfixed. At times he would cry out in agony as an idea came to him and he put it down on paper.

Though Beethoven was not a religious man in the formal meaning of the term, he seemed suddenly to have been aroused by religious excitation. He wrote in his notebook during this period: "God above all things! For it is an eternal providence which directs omnisciently the good and evil fortunes of human men. . . . Tranquilly will I submit myself to all vicissitudes and place my safe confidence in Thine unalterable goodness. O God! Be my rock, my life, forever my trust."

But God to Beethoven was someone quite different from what He was to Bach. And the *Missa Solemnis* is far different in character from the Mass in B minor. It is not religious humility that we find in Beethoven's music, the humility of the devout believer or the ecstasy of the worshiper. Instead we have the defiant pride of a man who believes that there is within him something of God. This music has strength and passion as well as radiance. When the chorus proclaims its belief in God in the powerful *Credo,* one feels that Beethoven is really promulgating his belief in the human spirit, in the godliness of the creative process. But when the passions are spent, when the pride and the defiance have been expressed, there come the heavenly pages of the *Benedictus* and the *Agnus Dei* to inform us that the spirit has found peace.

The Mass is in five large sections. There is a solemn orchestral introduction of twenty-two measures before the chorus enters with the moving *Kyrie eleison.* It is as though, in the words of Wasielewsky, "all humanity were joining in a universal liturgy." The next part is the *Gloria in excelsis,* which begins with a powerful theme stated now by one section of the chorus, now by another, until all voices join in unison in *in excelsis Deo.* The other portions of this section include the *Gratias agimus,* the *Qui tollis,* and the *Quoniam tu solus sanctus,* all three for quartet and chorus. The third section is the forceful *Credo,* which culminates in an overpowering fugue (*Et vitam venturi"*). A brief, slow orchestral prelude brings on the *Sanctus,* the fourth part, which contains the most spiritual music of the entire work, that of the *Benedictus,* in which the chorus is given an ethereal background by a solo violin. The *Agnus Dei,* the concluding section, maintains this high plane of eloquence with a beautiful melody started by the solo bass and continued by the other solo voices. With the *Dona nobis pacem* the music becomes turbulent and dynamic; Beethoven is not begging for peace, he is demanding it. But the awe and the grandeur and the serenity of the earlier pages return to bring the Mass to a peaceful conclusion.

Opera. Beethoven wrote only one opera, *Fidelio,* Op. 72 (1805), based on a French play by Bouilly called *Leonore,* adapted into a libretto by Joseph Sonnleithner. No other work, unless it be the *Missa Solemnis,* caused him such agony in composition; he rewrote one aria eighteen times. "This work," he once said, "has won me the martyr's crown." And no other work meant so much to him. The story of Florestan's unjust imprisonment and his ultimate release because of the devotion of his wife, Leonore, was much more to him than the love story of husband and wife and the trials that beset them. Florestan was the symbol of all the oppressed people of the world and Leonore the force of liberty that sets oppressed men free. Aroused and inspired by this theme, Beethoven wrote, within the established patterns of the opera form, some of his noblest music. Few operas contain music of such moving pathos as the chorus sung by the prisoners emerging from their cells into the garish light of day. Leonore's magnificent aria *"Abscheulicher! wo eilst du hin?"* is a defiant challenge to all oppressors of the free spirit; the somber introduction to the second act, followed by Florestan's gloomy description of his setting, is the musical expression of the man who has been unjustly put into bondage.

It is customary to use the so-called *Fidelio* Overture as the orchestral prelude to Act I. The overture begins with a brisk and loud four-measure passage for full orchestra followed by a stately theme for horns. The main portion of the overture consists of two principal melodies. The first is given by the horn and answered by the clarinets; the second appears in the strings. The overture ends with a presto section in which a phrase from the first theme is developed into a dramatic climax.

Though in the original libretto the entire first act takes place in the courtyard of the state prison near Seville, Spain, it is now habitual to divide this act into two different scenes. The first scene is set in the kitchen of the jailer, Rocco. Leonore, disguised as the boy Fidelio, comes to work for Rocco in the prison so that she may help save her husband from his unjust incarceration at the hands of his enemy, the prison governor, Pizarro. Rocco's daughter, Marcellina, is in love with Leonore (disguised as Fidelio), while Marcellina is loved by Jacquino, each of whom (together with Rocco) expresses his reaction to this curious situation in the beautiful quartet in canon style *"Mir ist so wunderbar!"* Pizarro arrives with the news that Don Fernando, the Prime Minister of Spain, is about to inspect the prison; Florestan must be murdered and his body disposed of before the arrival of the Minister. Overhearing this, Leonore gives voice to her tempestuous feelings in the aria *"Abscheulicher! wo eilst du hin?"*

The scene changes to the prison courtyard. The prisoners are filing out of their cells for a breath of air, blinded by the daylight sun. They sing a moving paean to freedom, *"O welche Lust!"* Eagerly does Leonore scan the faces of the prisoners for a sight of Florestan, but he is not among them.

In the first scene of Act II we are plunged into the depths of the prison, to the cell where Florestan is chained to the wall. He remembers happier days of freedom, *"In des Lebens Frühlingstagen,"* then frantically brings to mind a vision of his beloved wife, Leonore. She and Rocco now enter the cell, and though overwhelmed by the tragic plight of her husband she does not betray her true identity. Instead she helps Rocco dig a grave for Florestan. When Pizarro comes to kill his enemy, Leonore intervenes, reveals herself, and protects herself and her husband by menacing Pizarro with a pistol. At that moment the sound of trumpets announces the arrival of the Prime

Minister. Florestan is saved; he and his wife express their joy with an ecstatic duet, *"O namenlose Freude."*

With the lowering of the curtain, for a change of scene, the monumental music of the famous *Leonore* Overture No. 3 is heard. (The overture is analyzed under Orchestral Music.) The second scene returns to the courtyard of the state prison. The prisoners, who have been freed, emerge once again—and this time forever—into the bright light of the day. Leonore herself removes the chains from Florestan. As the evil Pizarro is arrested by the men of the Prime Minister, the liberated prisoners sing a hymn to Leonore, whose courage and fidelity made possible the saving of her beloved husband (*"Wer ein holdes Weib errungen"*).

Orchestral Music. The nine symphonies span twenty-three years of Beethoven's life and encompass a continent of symphonic development. It is a curious fact that, generally speaking, the odd-numbered symphonies are of epical cast, while the even-numbered ones are slighter of texture, and lighter in mood. The reason for this may very well be the necessity on Beethoven's part to find a breathing spell in a smaller and slighter effort after completing a giant project and before undertaking another such.

The Symphony No. 1 in C major, Op. 21 (1800), and the Symphony No. 2 in D major, Op. 36 (1802), are obviously derivative from Haydn and Mozart. The form is clearly defined. The melodies, presented simply and directly, are refined, pleasing, and of no great emotional depth. The main subject in the slow movement of the First Symphony even carries a recollection of the one in the slow movement of Mozart's Symphony in G minor. In the Second Symphony, the beautiful song in the slow movement, with its reverential overtones, is entirely Beethoven's, but even this music is a recognizable offspring of Mozartean classicism.

Yet there are some points of departure, too. In the third movement of each work Beethoven already shows an adventurous spirit. In the classical symphony the third movement was a minuet. Beethoven's First Symphony also has a "minuet"; but what we hear in this work is no longer a stately court dance but music of quicksilver movement, vigorous, lighthearted, with a touch of whimsey—a minuet in name only. In the Second Symphony Beethoven abandons even the name of minuet. The third movement of this symphony is a musical form of his own invention called the "scherzo," which literally means "a musical joke." Its three-quarter time and three-sectional form are carry-overs from the minuet, but there the similarity ends. Instead of a dignified dance, the third movement becomes a light, gay, and fanciful piece of music.

Beethoven was also adventurous in the use of tonality. The unorthodox opening of the First Symphony shocked the Viennese audience of the day. Who had ever heard of a symphony in C major which opened in F major and then progressed through the keys of A minor and G major before arriving at its basic tonality? Such music—which falls so pleasingly on our ears today accustomed as we are to more brazen audacities!—had a shocking, discordant effect in the year 1800, when classical symphonies began with chords in their basic keys. Shocking, too, to the audience of its day was the orchestration, which paid so much stress on the brass and tympani that one of the critics insisted that the music sounded as if it had been performed by a brass band.

Notwithstanding Beethoven's early tentative attempts to break down classical tradition, his first two symphonies remain music of the eighteenth century. It is with the Symphony No. 3 in E-flat major, Op. 55, the *Eroica,* completed in 1804, that Beethoven takes a giant step into the nineteenth century. It seems hard to believe that two such works as the Second Symphony and the *Eroica* were written within two years of each other. Compare the slight, formalized music of the Second with the towering majesty of the Third: a basilica stands side by side with a cathedral. The usually reserved Paul Henry Lang remarked that the *Eroica* is "one of the incomprehensible deeds in arts and letters, the greatest single step made by an individual composer in the history of the symphony and the history of music in general."

It was Beethoven himself who baptized the Third Symphony the *Eroica.* He had originally planned to dedicate it to Napoleon Bonaparte, whom he regarded as a champion of human freedom and the common man. The name "Bonaparte" appeared prominently on the title page of the manuscript over that of the composer. Then came the news that Napoleon had proclaimed himself emperor; that he, like the royalty he replaced, was motivated not by high ideals, but by personal vanity and ambition. "He is only an ordinary man after all," Beethoven cried out in disillusionment, "and he will turn tyrant." He

erased the name of Bonaparte from his manuscript and replaced it
with the simple word *"Eroica,"* dedicating his symphony now to
"the memory of a great man."

Beethoven intended no specific program for his music. He was giving his musical concept of a hero, not a military hero by any means,
but a hero of the spirit who carried to ultimate victory the banner
of some high mission. In expressing this heroic concept Beethoven,
the idealist, produced music which for grandeur, spaciousness, majesty,
eloquence, and sheer drama dwarfs any symphony that preceded it.

The epic character of the symphony becomes evident with the
first two abrupt, powerful chords. Then comes the first theme, in the
cellos, a simple four-bar melody. As it passes on to the different sections of the orchestra it gathers strength and erupts proudly and
defiantly in full orchestra. The second theme is a sequence of exquisite chords in the woodwinds and violins. The idyllic nature of
this passage suggests resignation, but the storm and stress are by no
means over. A climax is reached as the orchestra hurls one piercing
chord after another until there is only jarring dissonance. Then
comes a new melody, gentle and tender, in the woodwinds. So it goes
through the movement: turmoil alternating with repose. The concluding section, the coda, arrives as a kind of summation; the struggle
now assumes monumental proportions. "It is," commented Romain
Rolland, "the Grand Army of the soul that will not stop until it has
trampled the whole earth."

The second movement is a funeral march, the first ever to be incorporated into a symphony, though Beethoven had previously used
a funeral march in a piano sonata. Never had a composer evoked a
lament of such majesty. The violins introduce the death theme against
throbbing surges of anguish in the basses. This grows into a plaintive
melody for the strings. The death march is temporarily over. Now
comes a calm and introspective trio, almost as if the hero's past
accomplishments were being reviewed objectively. Against quivering
triplets in the violins, an elegiac song is heard in the flutes and
clarinets; after a brief emotional upheaval the song is finally unfolded in the violins with even greater poignancy. There is a short suggestion of the march theme again, and a powerful fugue emerges, its
vigorous theme first pronounced by the second violins. This is the
climax of the movement. The death theme returns, at last, in the first

violins—given by fits and starts, even as the voice breaks when the pain of grief grows intolerable.

After music of such intense feeling, the gay and brisk scherzo, with its middle section of hunting calls played by the horns, comes as a welcome relief. But in the finale the dramatic and emotional impact of the first movement returns. There is a tempestuous swell of orchestral sound. The principal theme is then plucked by the strings; this is the subject of a series of variations. (Beethoven had used this theme in several previous works.) The variations are climaxed by a fugal passage out of which comes a hymn for the woodwinds. It is as if the ultimate victory of the hero is being celebrated. Once again, as in the first movement, the two main themes are developed to titanic dimensions. The opening surge returns, and after a series of vital chords the symphony comes to a powerful conclusion.

After writing a symphony of such emotional ferment, Beethoven required a breathing spell. The Symphony No. 4 in B-flat major, Op. 60, written in 1806, is a gentle idyll. In style and structure it is nearer to the Second Symphony than to the *Eroica*. It makes no pretense at grandiloquence or sublimity. It is gentle, lovable, peaceful throughout. Two of its parts are particularly memorable. The first such arrives without delay. It is the opening adagio of the first movement that establishes and builds up an extraordinary tension and suspense with a descending string subject accompanied by a sustained B-flat in the winds. The second is the eloquent slow movement. "Such must be the song of the Archangel Michael as he contemplates the world's uprising to the threshold of the empyrean," Berlioz wrote of this music. "The being who wrote such a marvel of inspiration . . . was not a man." This song is first heard in the violins, and is then repeated by the woodwinds. The clarinets then interpolate an exalted thought of their own.

But the demoniac strength and passions of the *Eroica* return in the most famous of all Beethoven's symphonies: the Symphony No. 5 in C minor, Op. 67, completed in or about 1808.

The drama of the first movement is built up almost entirely out of the simple theme announced without preliminaries in strings and clarinets in unison. This theme—three eighth notes followed by a half note sustained by a fermata, repeated—is perhaps the most familiar one Beethoven ever wrote. People whistle it who have never heard the symphony or known the name of its composer. During

World War II it acquired political significance. In Morse code, three short dots and one dash—equivalent to the theme's three short notes and one long note—stand for *V*. The letter *V* having been used as a symbol for victory by nations subjugated by the Nazis, the Beethoven theme was now played, whistled, and scrawled on walls as an expression of defiance to Nazi tyranny.

This terse subject must have meant a good deal to Beethoven. He wrestled with it for years. Its embryo is found in his sketchbook as early as 1800. For a number of years after that his sketchbooks are filled with ways in which the theme could progress and the various guises it might assume. Now we encounter one version, now another. Again and again Beethoven changes, revises, refines, eliminates, adds —only to be still dissatisfied. The torment that went into this sustained creative effort is reflected in the way these sketches appear to the eye—scratched-out phrases, crossed-out notes, sloppily superimposed notes, all an ugly, angry mass of blots and blotches. The first movement of the Fifth Symphony is not the only place we encounter a four-note phrase in Beethoven. He had used it previously in the *Appassionata* Sonata for piano (1804) and again in the opening phrase of his *Piano* Concerto No. 4 (1806). Even after writing the Fifth Symphony, Beethoven was not through with this subject. It recurs in the String Quartet in E-flat major, Op. 74 (1809). In all instances the key is C minor.

It is doubtful if Beethoven ever actually interpreted this theme to mean "thus fate knocks at the door," as his friend Schindler recorded. But the restlessness of struggle is in the music of the first movement, and the immensity of that struggle might signify a tussle with destiny. With incomparable concentration Beethoven proceeded to build his entire movement out of the simple rhythmic phrase. It passes from one section of the orchestra to another, hardly changed melodically or rhythmically, accumulating power and drive all the way. The second theme, lyrical rather than rhythmic, which is shared by clarinets and flutes in conjunction with violins, is only incidental; notice how even here the basic opening theme is asserted insistently by the cellos and basses as a background to the melody.

In the melancholy and sedate second movement, two principal themes are subjected to variations. The first theme appears at the opening of the movement, in violas and cellos; it is a fully realized song. The song comes to its logical conclusion when, without transition, the second subject appears in clarinets and bassoons against triplets in the viola and plucked strings in the bass. The themes now stated, Beethoven proceeds to vary now one, now the other.

A theme, mysterious and foreboding, rises from the cellos and basses to open the third movement. This theme is played twice, following which the principal subject of the movement is enunciated proudly and loudly by the horns; it is significant that this theme has the same rhythmic pattern as the celebrated opening motive of the first movement. In the development, the mysterious ascending passage of the opening bars recurs as background material in the cellos and basses. The succeeding trio consists primarily of a fugal treatment of an onrushing, savage theme, begun in the basses, carried to the violas, then passed on to the second and first violins respectively. Never before had that clumsy member of the orchestra—the double bass—been given such virtuoso treatment. The trio over, the opening ascending motive is heard in the bassoons, punctuated by the clarinets' repeated quotation of the four notes of the main theme. This leads to a transitional section of overpowering effect: Against a quietly sustained "C" note in the violins, the kettledrums softly pound out the initial theme. The dynamics swell until, without a pause, the final movement bursts forth in all magnificence—a paean of joy, marchlike in character. The second main theme of the finale is no less triumphant: a proud hymn in the woodwinds, soon taken up by the first violins. The movement maintains this exultant mood to the very end.

The Symphony No. 6 in F major, Op. 68 (1808)—the *Pastoral*—was stimulated by Beethoven's great love of nature. It is the only one of his symphonies to have five movements in place of the traditional four. It is also the only Beethoven symphony which is programmatic, the titles of the movements providing the necessary clues. In the first movement, "The Awakening of Joyful Feelings upon Arrival in the Country," the exhilaration of first coming into the presence of nature finds voice in the buoyant theme for strings over a sustained pedal point with which the movement opens and which recurs throughout. The second movement, "The Brook," evokes a tranquil rustic scene, its main subject a theme in falling thirds in triplets. At the end of the movement the calls of the nightingale, cuckoo, and quail are imitated by the woodwinds. The third movement, "Village Festival," describes villagers and peasants in a scene of merrymaking, the principal melody being a peasant dance. In the trio section, a village band is amusingly caricatured. "The Storm" comes without warning (there is no break between the third and fourth movements) and descends with fury on the merrymakers. But the storm is soon over. A descending scale in the oboe (evoking the picture of a rainbow) and a shepherd's piping lead to the finale, "The Shepherd's Song." The song, first suggested by the clarinets, then taken up by the horns, and finally realized fully in the first violins, sounds a hymn of thanksgiving which dominates the movement.

The *Pastoral* Symphony was once again just a breathing spell. In the Symphony No. 7 in A major, Op. 92, completed four years later in 1812, we have music of the proportions and emotional sweep of the *Eroica* and the Fifth. The power generated throughout the Seventh Symphony is rhythmic; it accumulates force during the four movements until at last a kind of demoniac frenzy sets in. This emphasis on rhythm led Wagner to describe the symphony as an "apotheosis of the dance."

There is an extended slow introduction in which the basic melodic ideas are an ascending scale passage for the first violins and a berceuse type of melody in oboes and clarinets. The repetition of the single note "E" in the flute is allowed to evaporate; it is the transition to the main body of the movement. This "E," now expanding in volume, germinates into a lively main theme out of which the entire movement is constructed. The rhythmic drive set off by this theme is allowed to proceed unrestricted until the end of the movement.

There is no slow movement; its place is taken by a brisk allegretto in which the rhythm flows relentlessly. An opening chord sounds, and the cellos and basses intone a marchlike subject which, when completed, is taken up by the second violins, as the violas and cellos chant a melody in counterpoint. This contrapuntal treatment is elaborated into a sonorous climax, to be succeeded by a fugato section whose theme is initiated by the first violins. The middle section is built out of a sensitive lyric passage for clarinets and bassoons against triplets in the first violins.

The presto that follows is impetuous, as the full orchestra launches immediately into a sprightly and lighthearted idea which is then tossed about from one section of the orchestra to another. The trio is built out of a caressing melody for clarinets, bassoons, and horns. The two sections—the opening presto and its trio—are repeated.

The finale is one of Beethoven's most vigorous pieces of music. After the opening chords the orchestra plunges into a febrile dance; the theme is almost savage in its impetuousness. The volcanic energy continues unabated in an orgiastic outburst of rhythmic power.

The Symphony No. 8 in F major, Op. 93, completed in the same year as the Seventh, maintains the tradition that even-numbered symphonies be comparatively slight in form and content. It has, throughout the four movements, an infectious gaiety and the irrepressible high spirits of, in Wagner's description, "the games and caprices of a child." To maintain a consistent mood of levity Beethoven supplanted the customary slow movement with an allegretto scherzando in which a sprightly little theme in the violins and cellos is set against soft, but brisk, chords in the winds. It is often suggested that the even rhythm of these chords was meant to satirize the metronome, which Beethoven's friend Mälzel had recently invented. In the third movement Beethoven reverts to the minuet form he had utilized in his First and Fourth Symphonies.

In the monumental Symphony No. 9 in D minor, Op. 125—completed in 1824—Beethoven enlisted the collaboration of a chorus and vocal soloists for the finale. For almost a quarter of a century Beethoven had nursed the ambition of setting to music Schiller's "Ode to Joy," in which the composer's own ideal of the brotherhood of all mankind was voiced. The idea of incorporating it into a symphony first occurred to him in 1817, but he did not get around to the actual planning and writing of the work until six years after that, though sketches had appeared in his notebooks for several years. No symphony of his had taken so long to germinate; to the writing of no other symphony had he brought such a feeling of dedication, such effort, such expenditure of creative energy; and in no other symphony had he produced such an all-encompassing feeling of humanity, spirituality, and exaltation.

An atmosphere of awe is created immediately in the first sixteen measures as, against a shimmering background of tremolo second violins, the fragment of a theme is provocatively introduced by the first violins. The theme grows, swells, and at last (after sixteen bars) is fully projected in the orchestra—a proud affirmation of the spirit. What follows is a development of fabulous proportions, overwhelming in passion and intensity, alternating between the bitterness of struggle and the intoxication of victory. New ideas follow each other as part of this vast structure; a whole gamut of emotions is released. It is, as Richard Wagner wrote, "a struggle conceived in the greatest grandeur of the soul contending for happiness against the oppression of that inimical power which places itself between us and the joys of the earth." At the closing of the movement there is still another new thought: A funereal melody for oboe and clarinets begins softly and grows in sonority until it achieves shattering emotional effect. The first theme is hurled once again by full orchestra against the ominous roll of tympani, and the movement ends.

Beethoven changed the usual order of movements by employing a scherzo-like movement before the slow one. Marked "molto vivace," the second movement is an uninhibited expression of joy. The principal theme, a fleet staccato passage, is treated fugally, appearing first in the second violins, passing to the violas, then the cellos, and finally the first violins. Here all is lightning movement, rhythmic momentum. The middle section—the trio—is, by way of contrast, a hymnlike melody for oboes and clarinets followed by an upward-sweeping subject for the strings.

The adagio that succeeds this gaiety is surely one of the noblest movements in music. Such humanity, compassion, and lofty thought are found in its main melodies that Berlioz was led to say of them that "if my prose could only give an approximate idea of them, music would have found a rival in the written speech such as the greatest of poets himself would never succeed in putting against her." A reflective, melancholy melody in the first violins opens the movement. It is completely stated before the second theme—more resigned and peaceful, but also touched with otherworldly radiance—appears in the second violins and violas. The subsequent transformations of these two melodies reflect Beethoven's consummate skill in the art of variation.

After the grandiose utterances of the first three movements anything less than a culminating, exultant paean of joy for the human voice would have been anti-climactic. The orchestra has exhausted its articulateness; now the voice must carry on.

A piercing chord followed by a savage outburst of orchestral sound shatters completely the sustained serenity of the adagio. One by one, a main theme from each of the three earlier movements is briefly recalled; the orchestra is searching now for the appropriate melody with which to hymn the brotherhood of man. Each time a decisive recitative in the double basses rejects the theme. At last there appears an altogether new melody: The cellos and basses present it; the violas join in; the violins take it up. This, indeed, is an ode to joy! Once more there is a return to the angry surges of the opening bars. But they are summarily interrupted by the recitative of a solo baritone, with the following admonishment: "O Friends, no more these sounds continue. Let us raise a song of sympathy and gladness. O Joy, let us praise thee!"

The admonishment is heeded. Baritone solo, a vocal quartet, then full chorus now hymn Schiller's poetry:

> Praise to Joy the God descended
> Daughter of Elysium,
> Ray of mirth and rapture blended
> Goddess, to thy shrine we come.
> By thy magic is united
> What stern custom parted wide,
> All mankind are brothers plighted,
> Where thy gentle wings abide.

This ode to joy, and a subsequent dramatic exhortation by the chorus, "O Ye Millions I Embrace You," are repeated and varied until the joy—spiritual as well as physical—becomes unconfined and through it man becomes ennobled.

Beethoven's overtures are dramas in miniature. There are four overtures to the opera *Fidelio,* the most celebrated being the *Leonore* Overture No. 3. The Second *Leonore* Overture, Op. 72a, was actually the first to be written, and the one heard when the opera was first introduced. The Third *Leonore* Overture, Op. 72b, came next, as part of a drastic revision to which the opera was subjected for its first revival in Vienna in 1806. The *Leonore* Overture No. 1, Op. 138, is a condensation and simplification of the latter work, prepared for a projected Prague performance of *Fidelio* which did not materialize. The fourth is known as the *Fidelio* Overture, Op. 72c, rather than *Leonore* Overture No. 4. This composition, which uses material that is different from that found in the previous works, was written by Beethoven for the 1814 revival of the opera. Today it is a general practice, first established by Gustav Mahler, to use the *Fidelio* Overture as the opening prelude to the opera and the *Leonore* Overture No. 3 between the first and second scenes of Act II. An analysis of the *Fidelio* Overture will be found in the section devoted to the opera.

The *Leonore* Overture No. 3 is the greatest of the four, the very essence and crystallization of the drama. It opens with a majestic adagio. After some scale passages we hear the first principal theme in clarinet and bassoon, a quotation of Florestan's famous aria from Act II, *"In des Lebens Frühlingstagen."* The second theme, which arrives after an elaborate development and climax, appears first in the horns and is then echoed by first violins and flute. Once again a climax is evolved. There is now heard twice the offstage trumpet call (which in the opera announces the arrival of the Prime Minister, Don Fernando, and the imminent freeing of the unjustly imprisoned Florestan), each time answered by the theme of Leonore's song of thanks. The overture ends with a jubilant coda in which the joy of the liberated and the liberator is voiced exultantly.

The *Coriolan* Overture, Op. 62, written in 1807, was not meant to be a prelude to the Shakespeare tragedy, but to a drama by a German writer, Heinrich von Collin. After the cogent introductory chords of the first fourteen bars, the main theme is heard in the strings, descriptive of both the heroism and restlessness of Coriolanus. The softer and gentler qualities of Coriolanus are portrayed in the second theme, a beautiful melody for strings. The agitated development tells of the storm and stress of a hero's life, while the majestic coda speaks of his death. The overture ends with a restatement of the Coriolanus theme, fading away even as does the last breath of the hero.

In 1809 Beethoven wrote incidental music for *Egmont,* Op. 84, the historical play of Goethe. Only the overture is now heard frequently. The stirring theme in the violins with which it opens suggests the strength and nobility of Egmont, who fought so heroically to liberate the Netherlands from Spanish domination. The no less forceful and majestic second theme is also proclaimed by the strings. Once again, as in the *Coriolan* Overture, we have the depiction of turmoil and struggle in the development section. After a tempestuous climax the brilliant coda sounds a fanfare for full orchestra.

Beethoven wrote only one Concerto for Violin and Orchestra, in D major, Op. 61, (1806), but that one is among the greatest in the entire repertory. The two basic themes of the first movement are heard in the magnificent orchestral introduction, which opens with four drumbeats. The first theme is heard immediately in the woodwinds, and after some extension of this material, and a climactic outburst by the entire orchestra, the second theme appears, also in the woodwinds, to be taken up immediately by the violins. Another development and climax are heard before the solo instrument enters with ascending octaves. What follows is a monumental working out of the principal theme by both the solo instrument and the orchestra, with the soloist frequently providing decorative embroidery. In the second movement, a larghetto, the main melody is played by muted strings; the solo instrument then supplies filigree work around it. The second melody then is heard in the solo violin. After the first subject returns, plucked in the strings, the solo instrument once again adds trimmings, this time to the second subject.

The concluding movement, a rondo, opens with the presentation of a spirited main theme in the solo violin. After this theme is taken up by the full orchestra, a hunting call appears in the horns with decorations by the solo violin. This is a transitional passage. The development of the first theme unfolds, culminating in a repetition of the opening pages. A sentimental melody—the second principal idea of the movement—is now heard in the solo violin. But the original material returns, and after some development the soloist and orchestra bring the concerto to a resonant conclusion.

There are five concertos for piano and orchestra, of which the last two are towering masterworks. The first three follow the pattern of the Mozart concerto both as to structure and style. The virtuosity of the soloist is a paramount concern; the passage work for the piano is full of brilliant effects. Besides, there are the engaging lyricism, the eighteenth-century grace, and (in concluding movements) the Viennese gaity and ebullience which persistently remind the listener of Mozart.

The Piano Concerto No. 2 in B-flat major, Op. 19, was actually the first to be written (1795) and was second only in date of publication. What we today call the Piano Concerto No. 1 in C major, Op. 15, was completed in 1798, while the finest and most original of this trio of works, the Concerto No. 3 in C minor, Op. 37, came in 1800. In the Third Piano Concerto, we recognize the Mozart parentage. But the child is now beginning to acquire identifying traits of his own. The enlargement of orchestral writing, the increased dramatic power of some of the themes, and the occasional tendency to use the solo

instruments for expressive rather than virtuoso effects, all indicate
that Beethoven was beginning more and more to think for himself.

With the Piano Concerto No. 4 in G major, Op. 58, written in
1806, the piano concerto once and for all shakes itself loose from the
eighteenth century. Virtuosity no longer concerns Beethoven at all;
his artistic aim here, as in his symphonies and quartets, is the expression of deeply poetic and introspective thoughts. The very opening marks a new approach. No introductory chords here to attract
attention, no long preliminary orchestral preface to the theme! The
piano enters alone, presenting the first four measures of the first
theme. Then, and only then, does the orchestra take over with a
long symphonic discourse, developing the first theme before presenting the second principal subject in the strings. The enlargement
of these ideas, as they pass from solo instrument to orchestra, and the
recapitulation of the basic material, is charged with feeling and with
typically Beethovian grandeur and drama.

The second movement, largo, is one of the most moving and eloquent discourses in concerto literature. It consists of a dialogue between the solo instrument and the orchestra maintained on a plane
of uninterrupted sublimity. The orchestra speaks defiantly; the piano
answers with soft tones of resignation.

The figure [wrote William Foster Apthorp] continues at intervals in stern,
unchanging *forte* through about half the movement and then gradually dies
away. In the intervals of this harsh theme the piano as it were improvises
little scraps of the tenderest, sweetest harmony and melody, rising for a
moment into the wildest frenzied exultation after its enemy, the orchestra,
has been silenced by its soft pleading, then falling back into the hushed
sadness as the orchestra comes in once more with a whispered recollection
of its once so cruel phrase; saying as plainly as an orchestra can say it, "The
rest is silence."

In the concluding rondo the solo piano at once announces the first
theme. After the orchestra has taken this theme up, the piano introduces the second subject. Out of these two important melodies the
entire movement is constructed; and a spirit of reckless gaiety prevails throughout. The concerto ends with a brilliant coda in which
the tempo increases to a presto.

The Concerto No. 5 in E-flat major, Op. 73, the so-called *Emperor*
Concerto, was completed in 1809. The name "Emperor" appears to

have been bestowed on this work by a later publisher who felt that it was the most fitting descriptive title for a work of such majesty.

The concerto opens in an improvisational manner. After a loud orchestral chord the piano enters with music in a rhapsodic style. It is only then that the orchestra, in a magnificent hundred-bar exposition, unfolds the two main themes: The first is in the violins and after that the clarinets; the second, after a transition of four even notes, appears in the strings and is repeated by the horns. After a development of epical proportions, with emphasis on the first theme, the orchestra reaches an impressive climax. A brief pause, and the solo instrument embarks on the traditional cadenza, but with a difference. Custom had dictated until then that the cadenza be a spontaneous improvisation on the part of the performer. In this concerto Beethoven refuses to arrest the growth of his musical thinking; he provides the performer with a cadenza which maintains the dramatic and poetic nature of the work.

A simple, almost religious, chant for strings opens the second movement. The solo piano appears after this, to comment on it in an improvisatory manner without actually quoting the theme. Only when this introspective reflection has ended does the piano intone the melody with slight decoration, against plucked strings in the orchestra. Two bars before the end of the movement there is a warning of the principal subject soon to unfold in the concluding rondo, which arrives without interruption. As in the Fourth Concerto, the finale is spirited and jovial; both of its major themes are full of exuberance and motor energy.

In addition to his single concerto for the violin and his five concertos for the piano, Beethoven completed in 1805 the Concerto in C major for Piano, Violin, Cello, and Orchestra, Op. 56—the so-called *Triple* Concerto. Stylistically, it is closer to the first three piano concertos than it is to the two later ones, in spite of the year of its composition. Structurally it suggests the concerto grosso by using the three solo instruments as the concertino and the orchestra as the ripieno as prescribed by concerto grosso tradition. The two main themes of the first movement appear in the orchestral introduction. The simple melody of the slow movement is heard first in solo cello accompanied by the solo piano. The concluding movement (which comes without a break) is lively music highlighted by a polonaise-like tune presented first by the solo cello.

Piano Music. Several works in the piano repertory have been individually described as "the pianist's Bible." But none merits this description more than the thirty-two sonatas of Beethoven. They represent the cornerstone of piano sonata literature, if not all piano literature, and are as basic to the musical development of the pianist as the Shakespearean tragedies are to the study of literature.

The historic importance of these sonatas can hardly be overestimated. They brought a new concept of writing for the piano—a concept almost orchestral in approach—with enriched harmonic and dynamic resources. They extended the structures of the sonata form to huge dimensions; they realized a freedom of musical thinking, a mobility for musical ideas. Most important of all, they brought to piano music a new flood of emotional feeling.

Beethoven's first three piano sonatas (Op. 2), written in 1795, were dedicated to Joseph Haydn. Without slavishly copying the old master's style, they are nevertheless the fruits of the Haydn era in their respect for the classical form and in the pleasing grace, rather than Beethovian expressiveness, of the melodic ideas. But this Beethovian expressiveness is, of course, not long in revealing itself. In the slow movement of the Sonata in D major (Op. 10, No. 3), written in 1798, the tragic element is pronounced. Romain Rolland described this music as a "sovereign meditation" in which "the full grandeur of Beethoven's soul is for the first time revealed." Tragedy develops from poignancy to passion in the opening measures of the Sonata in C minor, Op. 13 (1798), better known as the *Pathétique*. The chromatic shifting chords in this opening *grave* section speak of an anguish which in the ensuing allegro molto becomes a titanic struggle. Serenity, however, falls like a welcome benediction in the slow movement (adagio cantabile). The *Pathétique* is the first of the great Beethoven sonatas, and one might even say it is the first *modern* piano sonata. The writing is *pianistic*—that is, in its dynamics and colors it could not have been written for the harpsichord or clavichord, as most of the sonatas before this could have been. The working out of the thematic material is on an elaborate scale unknown before this. And the four movements have a kind of subtle spiritual affinity to one another which makes a unity of the whole work.

Beethoven's Sonata in A-flat major, Op. 26 (1801), is unusual in that the slow movement is a funeral march, the first time such a thing happened to a piano sonata. (This is three years before Beethoven interpolated a funeral march into a symphony, the *Eroica*.) This music has been transcribed for orchestra and for brass band, the latter arrangement heard from time to time at funeral processions.

The Sonata in A-flat major came in the same year as the so-called *Moonlight* Sonata, the Sonata in C-sharp minor, Op. 27, No. 2 (1801). The *Moonlight* name was coined by a critic named Rellstab, who seemed to see in the placid first movement a picture of the moonlight streaming over ocean waves. Beethoven himself designated the work as *Sonata quasi una fantasia* ("A sonata somewhat like a fantasia"). This is because the first movement, instead of being in the usual sonata form, is an adagio sostenuto built from a romantic melody over triplets in the bass; also because of the freedom with which the themes throughout the composition are developed. The sonata form, neglected in the first movement, appears in the turbulent finale. Midway in the sonata stands a graceful and delicate allegretto.

The Sonata in D major, Op. 28 (1801), is now identified as the *Pastoral,* a name given it not by the composer but by the publisher, Cranz. The serene or bucolic quality that gives the music its pastoral character is found mostly in the first and fourth movements. The two middle movements have a different quality and personality. The second is sober and reflective, while the third, dominated by a waltzlike subject, has the kind of "unbuttoned humor" which Beethoven often reserved for his scherzos.

The Sonata in D minor, Op. 31, No. 2 (1802), is for the most part passionate and agitated. Before the storm breaks out in the first movement we hear an introductory largo only a measure and a half long. The slow movement relaxes the tension of the preceding movement, a tension which returns in the finale, whose triplets and sextuplets create dramatic impact, while the rhythmic pulse of its main theme suggests to one annotator the canter of a horse. When Schindler inquired from Beethoven the programmatic intent of this music, the master is supposed to have said: "Read Shakespeare's *Tempest.*" If it is true that this is what Beethoven said—and Schindler, unfortunately, cannot always be relied upon—then what the master had in mind was more the title of the Shakespeare play than its content.

The *Waldstein* Sonata in C major, and the *Appassionata* Sonata in

F minor (Op. 53 and Op. 57, respectively) belong in the middle period, when Beethoven produced some of his most celebrated masterworks. Both compositions were written in 1804, the year of stress when the full impact of his tragic deafness had been met. If the *Pathétique* represents the first grief-stricken realization that he was growing deaf, then the *Waldstein* and the *Appassionata* can be said to voice Beethoven's defiance of fate, his grim determination to meet his destiny and meet it courageously. ("I shall seize fate by the throat," he said; "it shall certainly never overcome me.") The *Waldstein* derived its name from the fact that it was dedicated to Count Waldstein. The name *Appassionata* was invented by the publisher Cranz to describe the passionate emotions of this music.

The first movement of the *Waldstein* is an unleashing of demoniac forces before they come to rest on a chorale-like second theme. This movement and the finale both have an epic-like character both as to structure and content. The slow movement Beethoven originally wrote for this sonata seemed out of place in a work of such heroic proportions. Beethoven removed it (later publishing it as a separate piece under the title of *Andante favori,* Op. 170). He replaced it with a three-part movement that plumbs the depths of emotion.

In the first movement of the *Appassionata* we hear the four-note phrase which the composer would later use in the first movement of his Fifth Symphony and which has come to be identified as the "fate motive." Here, as in the symphony, this subject is in C minor. The slow movement represents a theme (in simple chords) and its variations, the hymnlike theme returning after the variations have been concluded. Dynamic chords set the stage for the passions and energy of the finale, which temporarily are dissipated with a quiet, religious-like theme in the minor mode.

The last sonata of Beethoven's middle period is that in E-flat major, Op. 81a (1809). Its bears a title which the composer himself fixed to it: *Farewell, Absence, and Return*—in German, *Das Lebewohl, Die Abwesenheit, Das Wiedersehen;* in French, *Les Adieux L'Absence, Le Retour.* Beethoven wrote this sonata for his patron and friend, Archduke Rudolph, who had left Vienna precipitously as soon as the invading French forces approached the city. The music was intended to express Beethoven's sorrow at seeing his friend depart and being separated from him, and to anticipate the joy of their reunion. Over the three-note motive with which the first movement opens Beethoven scrawled the word "Farewell." This is the motto theme from which not only the movement but the entire sonata is built.

In the piano sonatas of his last period, Beethoven's writing acquired a new vein—that of mysticism and spirituality, such as are also encountered in his last string quartets. At the same time his form achieved a Gargantuan stature; his sonorities, harmonies, and contrapuntal texture approximated orchestral plenitude. The Sonata in A major, Op. 101 (1816), is the first of his last five sonatas. Here Beethoven continued a practice he had begun with two movements of his preceding *Les Adieux* Sonata, that of using German tempo markings together with Italian ones. Contrapuntal writing, with which Beethoven concerned himself more and more in his last sonatas, is encountered in the canonic imitations of the trio section of the second movement, and in the four-voiced fugue which comes toward the end of the sonata.

The most monumental in design among these last sonatas is the *Hammerklavier* in B-flat major, Op. 106, written in 1818. "It is as long as a symphony, as brilliant and as difficult as a concerto," is Robert Haven Schauffler's description. "It makes more strenuous demands upon the instrument, the performer, and the listener than any other composition of the master." *Hammerklavier* was the German word for the piano as distinguished from the harpsichord, since in the piano the sound is produced by the striking of the hammers, whereas in the harpsichord it comes from plucking. Beethoven used the designation *Hammerklavier* not only for this sonata, but for all his last sonatas, probably to emphasize the new sonorous and dynamic qualities of these works. The sonata opens with thunderous, defiant chords that set into motion music of power and strength; these chords are the germinal motive for the movement. Following the scherzo, there comes one of the longest slow movements in Beethoven's piano literature—music of utter anguish, expressed in shifting tonalities, discords, quixotic leaps from uppermost to lowest registers of the piano. The sonata ends with a three-voiced fugue.

The Sonata in E major, Op. 109 (1820), is the second of Beethoven's sonatas described by him as *"quasi una fantasia."* Here the reason is found in the fantasia-like character of the opening movement. This is Beethoven's only piano sonata to end with a slow movement

—a theme and variations. The Sonata in A-flat major, Op. 110 (1821), is more melodic than the others in this last group, the most affecting lyricism encountered in the slow movement. This sonata comes to a culminating climax in the finale with a fugue.

If the *Hammerklavier* is the greatest from the point of view of structure, the Sonata in C minor, Op. 111 (1822)—Beethoven's farewell to the sonata form—is the greatest in eloquence and profundity. In it we find the apotheosis of Beethoven's poetic style. It has only two movements: The first, in a free fugal style, brings up cosmic concepts never before realized in piano music; the second, a series of variations, traverses an immense gamut of introspective and philosophic thought.

Throughout his life, Beethoven produced a literature of piano music comprising forms other than sonatas: bagatelles, écossaises, minuets, rondos, waltzes. The most popular of these shorter items— particularly to piano students—is "Für Elise." This is a bagatelle, in A minor, Op. 173 (1810). Nobody knows who "Elise" in the title represents. Some authorities maintain that this name was put on the title page by a hurried copyist, but that the woman for whom Beethoven had intended the composition was Therese—Therese Malfatti, with whom Beethoven is believed to have been in love at the time.

But the most significant of Beethoven's piano works, outside the field of the sonata, is a set of variations which he poured into a monumental mold. The Thirty-three Variations in C major, Op. 120 (1823), is based on a trite waltz tune by Diabelli—a trifle, which the master used as the foundation stone for a cathedral. One of the curious features of this unusual work is that the last variation is in the style and tempo of a minuet—almost as if the master, in his last years, was paying a final obeisance to the age of Haydn and Mozart. But the minuet music soon lapses into the kind of amorphous writing with which Beethoven's last sonatas are associated. To Robert Schumann this progress from the minuet to Beethoven's own last style represented Beethoven's way of saying farewell forever to the piano. He never again wrote another note for his beloved instrument.

Vocal Music. Though Beethoven wrote a considerable amount of important music for voice—particularly in his opera, choral music, and the Ninth Symphony—he was not at ease in doing so, and his vocal writing is often ungrateful to his medium. Too often he tended to think in instrumental terms; too often he was impatient with the impediments placed upon him by the limitations of the human voice in his quest of poetic or dramatic expressiveness.

Nevertheless, Beethoven wrote an effective larger work for voice and orchestra and several notable songs. The larger work is *Ah, Perfido!*, Op. 65 (1796). The composer designated this composition as a *scena*, a *scena* being an extended concert work in which the dramatic interest of an operatic scene is maintained, even though it has no plot line or characterization to develop. Beethoven probably wrote *Ah, Perfido!* for the celebrated Bohemian singer Mme. Josephine Duschek, who introduced it in Leipzig in 1796. (Others maintain it was written for Countess Clari, to whom it is dedicated.) It is a miniature drama (author of text not known) beginning with an emotional and electrifying recitative. ("Ah, unfaithful deceiver! Cruel traitor! Dost thou leave me now?") The aria that follows is a poignant expression of grief. ("Say not the words of farewell, I implore thee. How shall I live without thee?")

Of the almost two hundred songs Beethoven wrote, the two most popular are "Adelaide," Op. 46 (1796), and "In questa tomba oscura," (1807). Both are dramatic, and both have the expansiveness of an opera aria or arietta. "Adelaide" (poem by Matthison) is an extended song in six divisions. "In questa tomba oscura" (text by G. Carpani) is atmospheric and moody, the setting of a poem in which an anguished person seeks the tranquillity of death and begs his beloved not to disturb his rest with her weeping.

Beethoven was also the composer of the first important song cycle in musical history: *An die ferne Geliebte* (*To the Distant Beloved*), text by A. Jeitteles, written in 1816. This cycle is made up of six songs, the melody of the first one being repeated in the last. The text describes the emotional reactions of a poet who looks down from a mountain peak into the valley where his beloved lives. He yearns to be with her; he calls upon clouds, the brook, and the breezes to carry to her his message of love; he contrasts the joy of birds with his own pain at being separated from his beloved. In the last song the poet submits his sheaf of verses to the woman he loves.

Alban Berg

"I am proud that [I was] . . . enabled to guide this great talent . . . toward the superb fulfillment of its individual potentialities, toward the greatest independence."

SCHOENBERG

BORN: Vienna, February 9, 1885.
DIED: Vienna, December 24, 1935.
MAJOR WORKS: *Chamber Music*—String Quartet; Chamber Concerto; Lyric Suite for String Quartet (three movements also for chamber orchestra). *Operas*—Wozzeck; Lulu (unfinished). *Orchestral Music*—Five Songs for Voice and Orchestra; Three Pieces for Orchestra; Der Wein, for soprano and orchestra; Violin Concerto. *Piano Music*—Sonata. *Vocal Music*—Four Songs; Canon; "Schliesse mir die Augen beide," two settings.

HIS LIFE

Until the middle 1950s, when the avant-garde virtually canonized Anton Webern, it was Alban Berg who was the most influential, the most frequently performed, and the most highly regarded composer of the twelve-tone school. But this universal admiration for Berg did not come easily. Berg, like his fellow twelve-tonalists, was years ahead of his time, and there is an inescapable penalty for the composer who speaks in the language of the future. Recognition came slowly to Berg and most of it came after his death. While he lived, and virtually up to the time of his death, he had to face misunderstanding, severe criticisms, and the derision of music audiences.

Yet he never doubted himself and his work, or the fact that eventually the world of music would embrace his music. He produced only a handful of major works, one of which (the opera *Lulu*) he did not live to complete. But almost everything he wrote, once he had hit his creative stride, is now treasured by discriminating music lovers. And one or two of his works occupy a class all their own. No opera since Debussy's *Pelléas et Mélisande* is now so highly esteemed by more people the world over than is *Wozzeck*. And few violin concertos in the twentieth century hold a rank equal to the one Berg wrote.

The youngest of four sons of a middle-class merchant of Bavarian extraction, Alban Berg was first given the conventional academic education. As a boy his main interest was books; the German classics and Romantic literature, the plays of Ibsen, and the prose and poetry of Oscar Wilde. It was a happy and well-adjusted boyhood, with winters spent in Vienna and summer vacations in a villa in Carinthia. When he was fifteen he was affected by a bronchial asthma which broke his health, and whose effects he would feel for the remainder of his life. To complicate matters further for him, his father died during this same period, leaving the family financially impoverished, and Alban emotionally depleted. It was now that Berg first turned to music, possibly as a haven; without the benefit of a single lesson he wrote some seventy compositions (mainly songs and pieces for the piano) which revealed the influence of Wagner and Mahler.

In his eighteenth year Berg suffered a nervous breakdown precipitated partly by an unhappy love affair and partly by his failure in school examinations. At one point he attempted suicide. His physical and mental rehabilitation was greatly helped a year later, in 1904, when he was introduced to and became a pupil of Arnold Schoenberg, the first time Berg was getting any formal instruction in music. "When I saw the compositions he showed me," Schoenberg later recalled, "I recognized at once that he had real talent." Berg remained Schoenberg's student for six years, the teacher proving an inexhaustible source of stimulation and inspiration. When in 1905 Berg became a government official to support himself, he devoted all his spare time to musical activities: working on his exercises, reading theoretical texts, experimenting with composition, laboring often late into the night and kept awake through continual drinking of strong tea. In 1908, a modest inheritance enabled Berg to give up his job and direct all his energies into study and composition. During the next two years he completed a piano sonata, Op. 1 (1908), the Four Songs, Op. 2 (1909), and his only string quartet, Op. 3 (1910).

Berg's studies with Schoenberg ended in 1910. A year later Berg married Helene Nahowski, with whom he set up a modest home in Vienna. Composition now dominated his life, as he began to free himself from the influences of Wagner and Mahler that had clung to his writing through Op. 3. The first composition he completed following his period of study with Schoenberg was also his first work to reveal an individuality and a freedom induced through atonal practices. That composition was the Five Songs for Voice and Orchestra, Op. 4 (1912), the setting of texts compiled from postcard messages which Peter Altenberg, the poet, had been sending to friends and enemies. Two of these songs were introduced in Vienna on March 31, 1913, at a concert devoted entirely to the music of Schoenberg and his disciples. This concert created one of the greatest uproars ever experienced in Vienna concert halls. First there was laughter; then hisses; then outraged cries. At length an actual riot broke out and the police had to be called. The critics expressed themselves with equal violence. One of them, whose identity has not been disclosed, wrote: "We thought we knew all the discords which human ingenuity can devise, but here even the wisest can learn something. . . . These strange whimpers and sighs . . . can they be the birth pangs of a new art, these zoological expressions that would make the real menagerie seek cover with drooping tails and ears in their general disgust at nature's provision to them of such inadequate vocal talents? . . . They may be called 'Ultralists,' though by any other name they could by no means lose their fragrance."

The savage reaction of the public to his first performed work did not keep Berg from planning other works even more unconventional and iconoclastic. He completed two more before World War I: Four Pieces for Clarinet and Piano, Op. 5 (1913), and Three Pieces for Orchestra, Op. 6 (1914). Here Berg became increasingly interested in atonal procedures; but his former Romantic tendencies had not altogether been abandoned.

When World War I broke out, Berg tried joining the army, but was turned down for reasons of health. He served his country in the Ministry of War in a civilian capacity. He wrote no music during these years of war, but he was spending a good deal of thought planning an opera, the subject of which had interested him since 1914 when he had seen a production of *Woyzeck*, a drama by Georg Büchner. This grim play, which anticipated expressionist drama of a later age, seemed to him at once ideal material for an atonal opera. During the war he completed the preparation of a suitable libretto.

He did not begin writing the music until the war was over. By 1920 he had completed the basic score, and by 1921 the orchestration. Three excerpts were heard at the Frankfurt Music Festival in 1924. They aroused so much heated controversy—both pro and con—that the Berlin State Opera accepted the opera for its repertory. Formidable production difficulties necessitated 137 rehearsals before *Wozzeck* came before the footlights, on December 14, 1925. It created a sensation. The audience was aroused to loud and hostile demonstrations; and the critics poured fresh vitriol on the troubled scene. When Paul Zsorlich wrote in the *Deutsche Zeitung* that "I had the sensation of having been not in a public theater but in an insane asylum," he was expressing the majority opinion toward the new opera. (A minority report was submitted by H. H. Stuckenschmidt, who maintained that *Wozzeck* placed its composer "beside the most notable musico-dramatists of our time" and that the opera itself was "a meaningful event in the history of music drama.") For the next year or so, *Wozzeck* continued to inspire attack, and sometimes even riots, whenever it was performed. The situation grew out-of-hand at the National Theater in Prague on November 29, 1926; the municipal authorities had to step in and order the production withdrawn for the sake of public peace. The capacity of *Wozzeck* to arouse shock gave the opera, for all its complexity, box-office appeal. It was widely performed throughout Europe; in less than a decade it was seen 150 times in twenty-eight different European cities. Its American *première* was conducted in Philadelphia by Stokowski on March 19, 1931. By the time *Wozzeck* entered the repertory of the Metropolitan Opera on March 5, 1959, it was acknowledged by both public and critics to be one of the crowning masterworks in the operatic theater of the twentieth century.

Berg wrote only one opera after *Wozzeck*, and that was left unfinished at his death. It was *Lulu,* based on two tragedies by Frank Wedekind, its world *première* taking place after Berg's death, in Zurich on June 2, 1937. Between his two operas, Berg completed the writing of several significant concert works: the Concerto for Violin, Piano, and Thirteen Wind Instruments, Op. 13 (1924); the Lyric Suite, for String Quartet, Op. 15 (1926); *Der Wein,* Op. 16 (1929), a concert aria for soprano and orchestra based on three poems by Baudelaire; and the Concerto for Violin and Orchestra, Op. 20 (1935). The last of these works was introduced by Louis Krasner, the violinist who had commissioned it, in Barcelona, Spain, on April 19, 1936.

After 1932, Berg divided his year between his Viennese apartment and "Waldhaus," a villa on the Wörthersee in Carinthia where he spent his summers. His health was going from bad to worse, his energies sapped by his chronic bronchial condition. Financially he was also in a bad way since his income had been sharply curtailed from lack of performances and decreasing sale of his printed music following the rise of Nazism in Germany and Austria. Such was his poverty that on one occasion, when he was tormented with pain from an infected tooth, he did not have the price for a dentist. Something else threw a dark shadow over his life. His teacher, friend, and inspiration—Arnold Schoenberg—had become bitter at him because Berg had preferred staying on in Austria, even under the Nazi rule, rather than expatriate himself the way Schoenberg had done.

Two weeks before his death, Berg attended a performance of a suite from *Lulu* which took place in Vienna on December 11, 1935. He was mortally ill at the time, suffering from a poisoning of the blood brought about by the sting of a bee. Nevertheless he not only attended the concert, but even helped in preparing the performance at rehearsals. On December 19, he had to be given a blood transfusion. Two days later he had a hallucination that he was conducting a performance of *Lulu,* crying deliriously "Upbeat! Upbeat!" The end came on December 24, 1935. "I still remember," recalled one of his pupils, Leonard Marker, "that miserable, rainy, cold December day, the handful of friends, following a plain brown coffin at the little Catholic cemetery in Hietzing. No one seemed to realize that this was the end and that his warm voice would be heard no more."

Berg looked strikingly like Oscar Wilde, even to the way he used to part his hair. Despite the fact that he was frequently ill, and usually in pain, he was a person of considerable charm, good humor, and sensitivity. He cared little for city life. His usual recreation was to drive his battered old car through the countryside. He found his only real happiness apart from his music while on visits to the Austrian lake district of Carinthia where he spent several months each year. Other pet diversions included watching soccer games and going to the movies. Interestingly enough, he had a pronounced mystical bent, was a keen student of comparative religion, and believed fervently in the symbolism of numbers.

Leonard Marker tells us:

His surroundings when he worked were characteristic. He could not abide interruption. He would lock himself in his darkened room, with closed windows, even in the hot summertime, and would not allow himself to be summoned or disturbed for any reason on earth. . . . In his last days, his work room was hung on every side and every angle with tone rows of his designing, to be chosen from at need. These went into the composition of *Lulu.*

He had inordinate pride and faith in his work, but with them a sense of balance, as was proved when he said: "It is only when I compose that I believe myself to be Beethoven—but *not* after my composition is finished."

HIS MUSIC

Alban Berg belongs to the Schoenberg school of composition. His major works are in the atonal style, a style in which the melody and harmony are free to move in any direction without relation to a key center (or tonic). This often produces stark melodies, acrid dissonances, and strange transitions. There is a tendency toward anarchy in this method. It is for this reason that Schoenberg arrived at a disciplined technique called the twelve-tone system, or row (*see* Schoenberg). Berg, like his teacher Schoenberg and other members of the Schoenberg school, advanced from atonality to twelve-tonality (or dodecaphony). Berg's first composition in a strict twelve-tone technique is the Chamber Concerto of 1925. A twelve-tone row appears in parts of the Lyric Suite (1926) and becomes the basis of the Violin Concerto (1935) and *Lulu*. But Berg never completely freed himself from the Romantic element which had so characterized his earliest compositions. The Mahler influence can be detected in some parts of *Wozzeck;* in the Lyric Suite Berg was able to realize melodic expressiveness; and in his Violin Concerto he injected a compelling emotion into his precise language. This strong emotional and melodic interest in Berg is the reason why some critics have come to refer to him as the "Romanticist" of the Schoenberg school.

ANALYTICAL NOTES

Chamber Music. The Lyric Suite for String Quartet (1926), wears its title gracefully. This is music with deep subjective feelings and strong Romantic content. To the tempo markings of each of the six movements, the composer added a descriptive word to identify the emotional intent of his music: allegretto gioviale; andante amoroso; allegro misterioso; adagio appassionato; presto delirando; largo desolato. Thus the mood projected in each of the movements is, in turn, joyful, loving, mysterious, passionate, delirious, and desolate.

A twelve-tone row is encountered in the first movement, within the three forceful chords with which it opens. The joyousness in this section is found mainly in the principal subject. The second movement carries a reminder of the Viennese waltz, while the third movement, by contrast, is characterized by emotional disturbances. The fourth movement is the most lyrical in the work, and the fifth the most discordant. The composition ends with lugubrious music in which Berg quotes from the prelude to Wagner's *Tristan and Isolde*.

Berg transcribed the second, third, and fourth movements for chamber orchestra.

The Chamber Concerto, or Kammerkonzert, for Piano, Violin, and Thirteen Wind Instruments (1925) reveals Berg's lifelong interest in the symbolism of numbers. Berg wrote this composition as a birthday gift to Schoenberg. Recognizing that the twelve-tone school was dominated by a trinity (Schoenberg, Berg, and Webern), Berg constructed his work ever conscious of the number "three." It is in three movements; the instrumental body is composed of three groups (keyboard, strings, wind); three principal themes recur; the slow movement is in three-part song form; in the finale, earlier material is recalled in three combinations. The work is prefaced by an "Epigraphe" in which letters from the names of Schoenberg, Berg, and Webern become musical notes (in German notation) to create a musical anagram.

Operas. Berg's masterwork is the opera *Wozzeck*, Op. 7. (1921). The text, which Berg himself wrote based on the famous play *Woyzeck* by Georg Büchner, has for its main character a poor, downtrodden soldier named Wozzeck. He discovers that Marie, with whom he is in love, has been unfaithful to him. His rival is the Drum Major, who, adding insult to injury, beats Wozzeck soundly. Marie, out of pity for Wozzeck, consents to take a walk with him, during which—blind with rage and jealousy—Wozzeck murders her. He seeks escape from his guilt at a nearby inn through drink. Suddenly he remembers that he had left his murder weapon, a knife, at the scene of the crime. Finding it, he throws it into a pond. Then, in an attempt to recover it, he drowns in the water.

Wozzeck is unorthodox from many points of view. Instead of traditional arias, duets, or ensemble numbers, we have as the spine of the opera *Sprechstimme* (song-speech), in which the rhythm is free, the measures are of unequal length, and the voice swoops up or down to an indicated pitch. The vocal line, then, is severe to the point of being harrowing; an almost continuous shrieking recitative that helps build up the tension as the drama of murder and death progresses to its shattering climax. The formal orchestra is replaced by several ensembles, including a chamber orchestra, a restaurant orchestra of high-pitched violins, a military band; the formal instruments of the orchestra are supplemented by others less conventional, such as a bombardon (an obsolete kind of tuba), an accordion, and an out-of-tune upright piano.

The structure of the opera is also original. The three acts become the three parts of an A-B-A song form. The first act is called "Exposition" and is made up of such non-dramatic forms as passacaglia, rhapsody, suite, military march, cradle song, rondo. This is the part where Wozzeck's relation to his environment is described. The second act, entitled "Denouement," is a five-movement symphony (sonata, fantasia and fugue, largo, scherzo, rondo marziale). In this part Wozzeck's learns of Marie's infidelity. The concluding act, "Catastrophe," is built from five inventions. Here we encounter the murder of Marie and the death of Wozzeck.

Yet for all its unusual structure and style, *Wozzeck* is an opera whose impact on any audience is tremendous. If the ideal of opera—any opera—is the harmonious marriage of music and text, then *Wozzeck* must surely be said to have realized this ideal. Berg's music—or, if you prefer, Berg's sounds—interprets the subtlest nuances of characterization, catches the most fleeting mood or emotion of the text, mirrors with fantastic realism the conflicts of the play. Not all of those who have loudly acclaimed *Wozzeck* in its more recent performances are able to follow the complex train of Berg's musical thought; but they do know they have gone through a powerful and unforgettable experience in the musical theater.

Three excerpts (or "fragments," as they are sometimes designated) have become familiar through performances at symphony concerts. They contain some of the highlights of the opera. In the first, a military march (played in the opera offstage) reveals Marie's interest in the Drum Major. This is immediately followed by one of the most deeply moving episodes in the opera, the lullaby Marie sings to her son. The second excerpt is the music accompanying Marie's reading of the Bible when she finds a relationship between her own life and that of Mary Magdalene. The third excerpt is the music with which the opera ends. Marie is dead, but her little son, unaware of this tragedy, is playing on his hobbyhorse with the other children.

Berg labored on his second and last opera, *Lulu,* during his last seven years, completing two full acts, a part of a third and the finale. At its world *première* (Zurich, 1937) *Lulu* was given in its incomplete state. In 1953, in Germany, the third act was filled out with Wedekind's spoken dialogue (the textual source of the opera), the way in which *Lulu* was first given in the United States—at Santa Fe, New Mexico, in 1963. However, at the first Metropolitan Opera production (March 18, 1877), the musical score was filled out mainly with materials long withheld by Berg's widow.

Two plays by Frank Wedekind—*Erdgeist* and *Die Büchse der Pandora*—provided Berg with the material for his libretto. The heroine, Lulu, is a disreputable woman who goes from one man to the next, each of whom meets a tragic doom: one from suicide; another from heart attack; a third from murder. She eventually becomes a prostitute in London where she meets her own dismal end by means of disembowelment at the hands of Jack the Ripper, one of her customers. "She is a phenomenon of nature," is the way an unidentified Prague critic described her, "beyond good and evil . . . a heroine of four-dimensional power in her endurance and her suffering, destroying all that she magnetizes."

Where *Wozzeck* had depended on instrumental forms for its overall structure, *Lulu* makes use of vocal forms, such as aria, duet, trio, and various ensembles. The entire opera is based on the twelve-tone row heard in the opening measures. The twelve-tone technique leads to greater austerity of style, objectivity of expression, and concentration of thought than the idiom found in *Wozzeck*. Nevertheless, the opera does contain some emotionally charged scenes, among which are Lulu's Lied, the duet of Lulu and Alva in the second act, Alva's song of praise to Lulu's beauty, and the poignant closing episode in which Countess Geschwitz sings farewell to Lulu, "my angel."

A symphonic suite derived from the opera score is made up of five sections: Rondo; Ostinato; Song of Lulu; Variations; and Adagio.

Orchestral Music. Berg's finest work for orchestra, and his last completed composition in any form, is the Concerto for Violin and Orchestra (1935). Its inspiration was the death of a young girl, the daughter of Gustav Mahler's widow by a second marriage. Berg intended his concerto as a requiem "to an angel." In the first movement he described the character of the girl in music that is graceful and buoyant. One of the main melodies has the identity of an Alpine folk song, while another is in the style of a Viennese waltz. This movement opens with a series of open fifths—the interval of the fifth symbolizing the purity of the girl's soul. When the solo violin appears it presents the twelve-tone row on which the entire work is based. The second and concluding movement is tragic, speaking as it does of death and the deliverance of the soul. Death's struggle is suggested in a cadenza for the solo instrument; the deliverance of the soul, in a quotation from Bach's chorale *"Es ist genug,"* from the cantata *O Ewigkeit, du Donnerwort*. A number of variations on the chorale tune follows. The concerto ends as it had begun, with the open fifths.

Hector Berlioz

> "He is an immense nightingale, a lark as great as an eagle.
> . . . The music causes me to dream of fabulous empires
> filled with fabulous sins."
>
> HEINE

BORN: La Côte-Saint-André, December 11, 1803.
DIED: Paris, March 8, 1869.
MAJOR WORKS: *Choral Music*—Requiem; Romeo and Juliet,
dramatic symphony; The Damnation of Faust; Te Deum;
L'Enfance du Christ. *Operas*—Benvenuto Cellini; Les Troyens;
Beatrice and Benedict. *Orchestral Music*—Fantastic Symphony;
King Lear Overture; Rob Roy Overture; Roman Carnival Over-
ture; Harold in Italy; The Corsair Overture. *Vocal Music*—
Irish Songs; Les Nuits d'été.

HIS LIFE

To Théophile Gautier, the essence of the Romantic movement in
France was concentrated in three people: a poet, a painter, and a
musician. They were Victor Hugo, Eugène Delacroix, and Hector
Berlioz. Berlioz was the true Romantic not only in his music, but
also in his life. He lived as intensely, as individually, as turbulently,
and as expansively as he wrote. As a boy he was known to weep
copious tears while reading Virgil, and to express rapture at the
beauty of a Catholic church. One incident could come only from the

biography of an early nineteenth-century Romantic. As a boy of twelve Berlioz fell in love with a girl six years his senior, carrying on in a way to amuse his neighbors and embarrass the innocent object of his adoration. The love affair disintegrated quickly. Berlioz was to see her only once in the next fifty years. Yet in the closing years of his life, after having gone through two turbulent marriages, he sought her out. Now a white-haired woman of sixty-five, the mother of four grown children, she was to hear from Berlioz' lips—and with an amazement that can only be imagined—that she had been the only love of his life.

The excessive display of emotion, the fluctuations from ecstasy to melancholia, the sentimentality, the conflicts against misfortune (much of which was only imaginary), the deification of the ego, the eccentricities and attitudes—in short, the qualities that went into the making of the nineteenth-century Romantic—were all found in Berlioz.

His father was a small-town physician who did not have too great a sympathy for a musical career. He dismissed Hector's musical talent with indifference, planning instead on making his son a physician like himself. He personally tutored the boy in anatomy. Hector's mother also looked with considerable disfavor on her son's interest in music, since she was a religious woman who regarded the making of music and attendance at the theater as sinful practices. Nevertheless, Hector could not be deflected from music. His first vivid musical experiences came at his first Communion, in the singing of the Eucharist hymns by the church choir. As he later put it, "a new world of love and feeling" unfolded before him. Not long after this he found an old flageolet in his house; a means of producing musical sound had thus been put into his hands. It was not long before he began receiving lessons on the piano and guitar from local teachers. From textbooks he learned harmony and counterpoint, reading them in bed through half the night. The will to create soon asserted itself. He wrote some chamber music, which in 1819 he dispatched to a publisher. When it was rejected the composer destroyed his manuscript.

But his father's determination to make him a physician was inflexible. Hector was sent to Paris in October 1821 to study medicine. The first time he was called upon to dissect an animal he knew that medicine was not for him. He fled from the school, sick and horrified, and locked himself in his room. Despite this experience he continued bravely with his medical studies and actually received his Bachelor's degree in science in 1824.

But he had not abandoned music. He attended performances at the Paris Opéra and spent many hours in the Conservatory library studying musical scores. Hearing Gluck's opera *Iphigénie en Tauride* stirred him profoundly. Soon after this he heard a Beethoven symphony for the first time, and it was as if he had suddenly discovered a new world. He was now impatient to learn much more about this great and wonderful art that could yield a work like the Beethoven symphony. He went to Lesueur for additional study, and under that master's guidance wrote his first opera, *Estelle et Namorin.* Lesueur told him, "You will never be a doctor or a druggist, but a great composer, for you have genius."

But encouragement from other quarters was not forthcoming. A Mass written for the St. Roch Church, and performed there on December 28, 1823, was an outright failure. An attempt to enroll in the Conservatory was unsuccessful. But Berlioz remained undismayed. In the summer of 1824 he went home to announce to his father that he was through with medicine forever, that thenceforth he would concentrate on music. The session was stormy, but Berlioz held his ground; and he won the battle. His father promised to continue the allowance, but only on one condition: Berlioz must prove within a reasonable period of time that he had ability.

He now managed to get into the Paris Conservatory, supporting himself by teaching the guitar and singing in a theater chorus. For the next two years he was a pupil of Lesueur and Reicha. To prove his skill he arranged a second performance of his Mass on July 10, 1825, with funds borrowed from a friend. The work was now somewhat better received, especially by his friends, but it left him with a staggering debt. The necessity of paying off that debt made Father Berlioz more impatient than ever with his son's musical activities. To make matters worse, he knew that Hector had twice applied for the Prix de Rome and had been unsuccessful both times. At last Father Berlioz convinced himself that his son had neither ability nor ambition and summarily discontinued all support. Berlioz had to shift for himself as best he could.

It was at this time that he became involved in the tempestuous love affair of his life. In the fall of 1827 an English Shakespearean company came to Paris for a series of performances at the Odéon.

The role of Ophelia in *Hamlet* was enacted by an attractive artist by the name of Harriet Constance Smithson. Berlioz attended the performance and from his seat in the theater fell in love with the star. He left the theater with the anguish of one who knew that peace would never be his until he had realized his love. He tried to contact her—even though he could not speak her language, nor she his—but with no success. He deluged her with love letters which first startled and then terrified her; they went unanswered. By many devious means he tried to draw her attention to his musical skill. In deference to her Irish background, he wrote some Irish songs to texts by Thomas Moore. He arranged a special concert of his works at the Conservatory on May 26, 1828, just to impress her with his gifts. She did not even know that the concert had taken place. Finally he rented a room next to hers, only to discover with horror that she was going to leave Paris. Realizing reluctantly that his quest was proving futile, he tried to find solace in a love affair with a concert pianist, Camille Moke, to whom he actually became engaged. But there was neither peace nor escape.

Yet he found the time and energy to write his first two important works. The first of these, his Op. 1, was a cantata based on eight scenes from *Faust* (1829). With the ink hardly dry on his manuscript (later to become the core of his famous *The Damnation of Faust*) Berlioz wrote a second important work, stimulated and inspired by, and giving programmatic expression to, his unrequited *grande passion*. It was the *Fantastic* Symphony, introduced in Paris on December 5, 1830. Since Harriet Smithson was now back in Paris, Berlioz arranged that *première* expressly to attract the attention of his loved one and perhaps win her admiration. "Would the tidings of my success reach Miss Smithson in the intoxicating whirl of her own triumphs?" he asked. "Alas! I learned afterward that, absorbed in her own brilliant career, she never even heard of my name, my struggles, my concert, or my success!" The concert was a huge success. Franz Liszt, who was in the audience, was so profoundly impressed by what he heard that from that time on he became one of Berlioz' most devoted friends and admirers. But to Berlioz, whose restless eyes had searched every corner of the auditorium for a sight of Harriet Smithson, the concert had been a failure because she had not heard it.

Meanwhile, Berlioz had—at long last!—won the Prix de Rome, with the cantata *Sardanapale*. Introduced in October 1830, the cantata was so poorly performed that in a violent fit of anger the composer threw his score at the musicians. Thus Berlioz left for the Villa Medici in Rome, to spend the three years prescribed by the Prix de Rome. He was not happy there. He was uncomfortable under the rigid rules set for the young musicians; he disliked Italian food; he was intolerant of Italian music. Scandalous rumors about his betrothed, Camille Moke, aroused him to such a pitch of fury that he left Rome for Paris disguised as a lady's maid with the intention of killing both her and her lover. When he lost his disguise in Genoa and had to wait for another, his rage was suddenly dissipated. He sublimated his feelings by writing several orchestral works, then meekly returned to the Villa Medici.

He was back in Paris in 1832, without completing his three-year residence at the Villa Medici. Soon after his return he discovered that Harriet Smithson was back in the city. His love for her was once again aroused. Once again, on December 9, 1832, he arranged a performance of the *Fantastic* Symphony so that she might be able to hear it. She attended the concert with her sister. Berlioz, from his place by the tympani, immediately remarked her presence.

On entering her box in front of the stage [he wrote in his *Memoirs*] she found herself in the midst of an immense orchestra, and an object of interest to the whole room. So astonished was she at the unprecedented murmur of conversation of which she was plainly the object, that without being able to account to herself for it, she was filled with a kind of instinctive terror, which moved her powerfully. Habeneck was conducting. When I came in panting and sat down behind him, Miss Smithson, who until then had doubted whether she were not mistaken in the name at the head of the program, saw and recognized me. "It is the same," she said to herself. "Poor young man. No doubt he has forgotten me. I hope that he has." The symphony began and created a tremendous effect. This success and the passionate character of the work were bound to produce, and did in fact produce, an impression as profound as it was unlooked-for upon her.

Her suddenly awakened sympathy for Berlioz may have been caused by the profound effect that the symphony had had upon her, or by the extenuating circumstance that her popularity as an actress had waned and she was now suffering disastrous financial reverses. In any event it was no longer difficult for Berlioz to meet his beloved and to press his suit ardently. At one point Berlioz even tried to commit suicide in her presence to prove the intensity of his feelings for her. A feverish courtship followed. On October 3, 1833, they were married, at last, at the British Embassy.

It was not a happy marriage. Both of them were too temperamental and volatile to be at peace with one another. Besides this, they were poor, and Harriet (Berlioz liked to call her Henrietta) suffered the additional anguish of a star who has been eclipsed by other actresses. She became hotheaded, shrewish, even jealous. Their life was marked by intermittent tempests of outraged emotions. At last they decided to live apart (they were never divorced), Berlioz seeking consolation in a new love affair, with a singer, Marie Recio. But Berlioz never quite forgot his onetime ardor for Harriet. When, toward the end of her life, she became an invalid, he attended her with tenderness, even affection, despite the fact that to the very end she remained churlish and inflammable. She died on March 3, 1853. One year later Berlioz married Marie Recio—a marriage hardly more successful than the first.

The performance of the *Fantastic* Symphony that finally brought Berlioz and Harriet Smithson together was also responsible for bringing Berlioz an important benefactor. After that concert a lean, gaunt, cadaverous-looking gentleman with piercing eyes came to congratulate Berlioz, but also to commission him to write a new work. He was Niccolò Paganini (1782–1840), who had recently acquired a fine viola which he wished to play in public. Would Berlioz write a work expressly for him?

The work Berlioz finally wrote for Paganini was quite different from what the virtuoso had wanted and expected. It was no virtuoso music but a symphony with viola obbligato of deep poetic content: *Harold in Italy,* inspired by Byron's *Childe Harold's Pilgrimage.* When Paganini saw the sketches of the first movement he lost all interest in the work. Its first performance, which took place in Paris on November 23, 1834, was without the benefit of Paganini's collaboration. Paganini did not hear the work until December 16, 1838, when his reaction was overwhelmingly enthusiastic. He sent Berlioz the following message: "Beethoven is dead and Berlioz alone can revive him." And with the message came a gift of twenty thousand francs.

To Berlioz, whose financial situation up to then had been precarious, the gift meant a temporary respite from hack work and the writing of critiques for the *Journal des débats*. He could undertake the writing of several ambitious compositions: the Requiem, introduced in Paris on December 5, 1837; Berlioz' first opera, *Benvenuto Cellini,* a failure when seen at the Paris Opéra on September 10, 1838; and, most significantly, the dramatic symphony *Romeo and Juliet.* In the last-named work, Berlioz recalled musically his own tempestuous feelings when first he saw Harriet Smithson at the Odéon in the role of Juliet, an experience so overwhelming that all that night he had wandered dazed through the streets of Paris. The symphony was performed at the Conservatory on November 24, 1839, and was a huge success. One member of the audience was a young, struggling, and still unknown composer by the name of Richard Wagner, who marveled at the *"puissance"* of Berlioz' orchestral virtuosity. "The reckless boldness and severe precision . . . took me by storm and impetuously fanned the flame of my personal feeling for music and poetry."

In 1842 Berlioz visited Belgium and Germany to conduct several of his works. This was the first of many tours that brought him to Austria, England, even Russia, and which made him almost as familiar a figure abroad as he was in Paris. To his audiences, as to his friends and colleagues, his most impressive physical feature was his head, which once seen was not soon forgotten. Ferdinand Hiller described it as follows: "High forehead, precipitously overhanging the deep-set eyes; the great, curving hawk nose; the thin, finely-cut lips; the rather short chin; the enormous shock of light-brown hair, against the fantastic wealth of which the barber could do nothing." In a later generation, Romain Rolland contributed an additional description of Berlioz' appearance and personality: "He was of medium height, rather thin and angular in figure. . . . He had a deep voice, but his speech was halting, and often tremulous with emotion; he would speak passionately of what interested him, and at times be effusive in manner, but more often he was ungracious and reserved. . . . He was very restless, and inherited from his native land . . . the mountaineer's passion for walking and climbing, the love of a vagabond life, which remained with him nearly to his death."

During one of his tours, in 1846, he completed a project begun seventeen years earlier, the dramatic legend *The Damnation of Faust.* Its first performance at the Opéra-Comique in Paris, on December 6, 1846, was both poorly attended and poorly received, plunging him into a ten-thousand-franc debt. Meanwhile, in 1843, he published the *Traité de l'instrumentation,* one of the most significant treatises on instrumentation published up to that time.

The last years of Berlioz' life were unhappy. His second marriage was as unfortunate as the first, ending with Marie's death in 1862. Finally, his health had begun to deteriorate as he began suffering acutely from intestinal neuralgia. Notwithstanding such unhappy circumstances, he was able to write some of his sunniest music—music filled with laughter and mockery: the score to the opera *Beatrice and Benedict,* based on Shakespeare's *Much Ado About Nothing.* This was his last work. It was produced with outstanding success, under the composer's own direction, at Baden-Baden, Germany, on August 9, 1862.

Thereafter, Berlioz lived in seclusion in his apartment in Paris, exhausted physically and spiritually. The death of his only son, of yellow fever, in Havana in 1867, was the final blow. Berlioz died in Paris on March 8, 1869. His body was carried by Gounod, Ambroise Thomas, and other famous musicians to its final resting place in the Montmartre cemetery. The funeral march from his own *Symphonie funèbre et triomphale* was his requiem.

HIS MUSIC

When it is recalled that Berlioz was born when Beethoven and Haydn were still alive, and that he wrote his first major works before 1830, his role in musical development becomes clear. He was the first Romantic in music. In form and style he represents the first complete break with classical tradition, away from the strictly outlined structure to expansive and elastic ones, away from the pure and the objective in musical expression to the pictorial and the programmatic. He was the first to bring to music the Romantic's love for fantasy, his indulgence in emotional outbursts, his exploitation of literary subjects for musical treatment.

He was one of music's great innovators. Orchestration as we know it today, handled with virtuoso brilliance, can be said to have emerged with him. He often used Gargantuan forces, greater than any employed by any composer up to then, not because he was addicted to size, but because he was indefatigable in his quest for new sounds and colors. He was always trying out different combinations of instruments and always experimenting with new instruments. It is because of him that more than one instrument entered the orchestral family to stay there—for example, the harp and the English horn.

His use of rhythm was as daring as his instrumentation, emancipating music from its subservience to rhythms of two, four, and eight beats, and utilizing such a variety of rhythmic patterns, regular and irregular, that many of his contemporaries regarded him as eccentric in this direction.

And he was a pioneer in the writing of programmatic symphonic music, music following a literal program with vividness and realism. As Ernest Newman wrote: "All Berlioz' music, whether that of the painting of a scene or that of psychological probe—and he has achieved some marvels in the latter field—has the quality of controlled objectivity that is the antithesis of the northern ecstatic mystical swoon; it is the seeing of things as they appear and are, not as one would fain persuade oneself they are by calling in speculation and metaphysic to supplement the evidence of the eye." We have only to remember Liszt's enthusiasm for the *Symphonie fantastique* to realize how vital a role that work must have played in the evolution of the Liszt programmatic tone poem. And we have only to recall that the then unknown Wagner also admired Berlioz to suspect that Berlioz' use of the *idée fixe*—or the recurrent idea—might have given Wagner his first suggestion for the use of the *leitmotiv* technique.

It has been said that his skill was often greater than his inspiration. True! But while conceding that he usually relied more on his rhythmic virtuosity and his orchestral wizardry than on vigor and force of ideas (his melodic materials were usually second-rate) and that parts of his mammoth works are frequently better than the whole, we must also confess that his vehemence, boldness, immense originality, brilliance, and *puissance* more than make up for his weaknesses.

ANALYTICAL NOTES

Choral Music. Berlioz once remarked: "If I were threatened with the burning of all my works except one, it is for the Requiem that I would ask for mercy." A composer is not always partial to his best brain children, but the Requiem—*Grande Messe des Morts,* Op. 5 —written in 1837 is one of Berlioz' giant achievements. It is music of great dramatic power, as in the *Rex tremendae,* and sometimes of an awesome grandeur, as in *Dies irae* and *Tuba mirum.*

The work calls for giant vocal and instrumental forces. When first performed (at the Invalides in Paris in 1837), the chorus numbered four hundred and the orchestra one hundred and ten; in addition, the score called for several brass choirs, ranging in number from eight to fourteen. Four of them are heard in the *Dies irae* section, where they are distributed "at the four corners of the choral and instrumental mass" to announce the coming of Judgment Day.

L'Enfance du Christ (The Childhood of Christ), Op. 25 (1854), came seventeen years after the Requiem. Berlioz designated this work as a "dramatic trilogy," but actually it is an oratorio in three parts: "Herod's Dream," "The Flight into Egypt," and "The Arrival at Saïs." In the first part Herod orders the massacre of the children of Judea, and the angel brings warning to Joseph and Mary. In the second part shepherds come to bid farewell to the Holy Family, which has been warned by the angels to flee to Egypt. The concluding section describes how the Holy Family is rejected by the Roman citizens of Saïs and how it finally finds welcome among the Ishmaelites. To F. Bonavia, the general character of this oratorio is "essentially gentle, introspective and tender."

Orchestral Music. The *Symphonie fantastique* or *Fantastic* Symphony, in C major, Op. 14 (subtitled by the Composer "An Episode in the Life of an Artist") was Berlioz' first major work and to this day is his most popular work. It was completed in 1830 as his passionate protestation of love for Harriet Smithson. The image of Harriet Smithson is the *idée fixe*—or the recurrent idea—of the entire symphony. The musical theme of this *idée fixe* is heard in the opening allegro; it is a tender melody in the first violins and flute. This is the motto theme of the entire work. It recurs in each of the five movements, though frequently transformed in structure and filled with varied feelings.

Berlioz provided a detailed program for his symphony, prefacing it with the following explanatory paragraph:

A young musician of morbid sensibility and ardent imagination poisons himself with opium in a fit of amorous despair. The narcotic dose, too weak to result in death, plunges him into a heavy sleep accompanied by the strangest visions, during which his sensations, sentiments, and recollections are translated in his sick brain into musical thoughts and images. The beloved woman herself has become for him a melody, like a fixed idea, which he finds and hears everywhere.

Berlioz' detailed program for each of the five movements follows:

FIRST MOVEMENT: *Dreams, Passions*
He first recalls that uneasiness of soul, that *vague des passions,* those moments of causeless melancholy and joy, which he experienced before seeing her whom he loves; then the volcanic love with which she suddenly inspired him, his moments of delirious anguish, of jealous fury, his returns to loving tenderness, and his religious consolations.

The symphony begins with an introductory largo in which the main subject is an extended and passionate melody for the violins. The allegro section enters with a solo for the horn against a violin obbligato. After a series of sharply rhythmed chords, the motto theme is heard in unison flute and first violins. This theme appears and reappears throughout the movement, even as the image of the beloved haunts the consciousness of the artist. It is now heard dramatically in the flute and clarinet against surging violins; now passionately in the violas, cellos, and basses; now tenderly in the flutes, clarinets, and bassoons. The movement ends with a simple, religious statement of the motto in the violins.

SECOND MOVEMENT: *The Ball*
He sees his beloved at a ball, in the midst of the tumult of a brilliant fête.

After a tremolo in the strings, a buoyant waltz unfolds. After this waltz melody has been completely presented, the *idée fixe* emerges in flute and oboe. The original waltz section returns and is concluded brilliantly and vigorously by the full orchestra; the waltz theme surges in a dramatic upward flight from the basses to the cellos and violas and culminates in the highest registers of the violins.

THIRD MOVEMENT: *Scenes in the Country*

One summer evening in the country he hears two shepherds playing a *ranz-des-vaches* in alternate dialogue; this pastoral duet, the scene around him, the light rustling of the trees gently swayed by the breeze, some hopes he has recently conceived, all combine to restore an unwonted calm to his heart, and to impart a more cheerful coloring to his thoughts; but *she* appears once more, his heart stops beating, he is agitated with painful presentiments; if she were to betray him! . . . One of the shepherds resumes his artless melody, the other no longer answers him. The sun sets . . . the sound of distant thunder . . . solitude . . . silence. . . .

The music of the entire movement is for the most part pastoral and tranquil. We hear first an unaccompanied duet for English horn and oboe. After twenty bars the principal theme is delicately projected by flute and first violins—a theme which carries a reminiscence of the *idée fixe*. This theme is brought to a climax, after which a new theme appears in the woodwinds. The first subject returns in the violas, cellos, and bassoons against elaborate decorations by the violins. As cellos, basses, and bassoons present a third theme, the woodwinds suddenly bring up reminders of the motto subject. A loud and vigorous climax is achieved by the full orchestra, after which an altogether new idea is presented by the solo clarinet against plucked strings; this idea is repeated by the winds in unison. The motto theme is not abandoned; it appears once again in the woodwinds. The movement ends with the opening idyllic theme in the English horn accompanied by soft chords in the tympani.

FOURTH MOVEMENT: *The March to the Gallows*

He dreams that he has killed his beloved, that he is condemned to death, and led to execution. The procession advances to the tones of a march which is now somber and wild, now brilliant and solemn. The dull sound of the tread of heavy feet follows without transition. And the end, the fixed idea reappears for an instant, like a last love-thought interrupted by the fatal stroke.

A vigorous, fantastic march in full orchestra introduces this movement. Two other robust ideas follow, the first simultaneously in woodwinds and brass, the second alternately in brass and woodwinds. The three themes are worked out into a loud and dramatic climax. After a sudden pause the motto theme appears in a solo clarinet. A shattering chord from the full orchestra arrives as an interruption. The percussion then thunder a vital rhythm. The march theme returns briefly in broken chords to end this section.

FIFTH MOVEMENT: *Dream of the Witches' Sabbath*

He sees himself at a witches' Sabbath in the midst of a frightful group of ghosts, magicians, monsters of all sorts, who have come together for his obsequies. He hears strange noises, groans, ringing laughter, shrieks to which other shrieks seem to reply. The fixed idea again appears; but it has lost its noble and timid character; it has become an ignoble, trivial, and grotesque dance tune; it is she who comes to the witches' Sabbath. . . . Howlings of joy at her arrival . . . she takes part in the diabolic orgy. . . . Funeral knells, burlesque parody on the *Dies irae*. The witches' dance and the *Dies irae* are heard together.

An eerie atmosphere is set forth with tremolo chords in divided strings. The motto theme appears somewhat grotesque in the clarinets. After the motto theme is repeated by the woodwinds, the chiming of bells introduces a new section: a burlesque of the *Dies irae* in tubas and bassoons. A frenzied dance follows, presented fugally. A monumental climax is now reached, after which the *Dies irae* is played first by unison strings then loudly and majestically by the brass and woodwinds. The movement ends with demoniac energy and strident sounds.

La Damnation de Faust, or *The Damnation of Faust,* Op. 24 (1846), which the composer described as a "dramatic legend," has been presented both as an opera and as an oratorio. (Berlioz himself preferred the oratorio-type performance.) Scored for solo voices, chorus, and orchestra, it has four sections. Most concertgoers, however, know this work through three delightful orchestral excerpts:

"Minuet (or Dance) of the Will-o'-the-Wisps," "Dance of the Sylphs," and "Rakoczy (or Hungarian) March."

The minuet concludes the scene in which evil spirits and will-o'-the-wisps are evoked by Mephisto to surround the house of Marguerite. A delicate minuet theme for the woodwinds and brass opens this section. After some development there is a trio in which the strings, accompanied by the rest of the orchestra, present the main subject. After the minuet theme returns, a presto passage features a mocking and burlesque idea in piccolo, flute, and oboe. The minuet theme is heard twice after this; the second time it is interrupted after each phrase by loud chords in full orchestra.

The "Dance of the Sylphs" describes the dancing of the gnomes and sylphs who appear in Faust's dream, even as does the image of Marguerite. The entire movement, transparent and delicate, is built out of a graceful waltz melody played by the first violins against a background of droning cellos and basses.

The "Rakoczy March," or "Hungarian March," is based on a Hungarian folk theme that had caught Berlioz' fancy. He made its inclusion in the "dramatic legend" seem logical by having Faust wander in the fields of Hungary. In *The Damnation of Faust* it becomes a march of overpowering dramatic effect. It begins with a fanfare for trumpet utilizing the rhythm of the Rakoczy theme. The theme itself begins softly in the woodwinds against plucked strings; a countertheme follows in the strings to woodwind accompaniment. The melody and countersubject are worked out. A fragment of the Rakoczy theme now passes from one section of the orchestra to another, the volume increasing all the time until a mighty climax is reached. The Rakoczy melody is now heard triumphantly in full orchestra, punctuated by throbbing tympani and crashing cymbals.

Romeo and Juliet, Op. 17 (1839), is another expansive composition for solo voices, chorus, and orchestra best known to concertgoers through orchestral excerpts. *Romeo and Juliet* is a dramatic symphony made up of three large sections which, in turn, are divided into twelve segments. The first part describes the feud of the Capulets and Montagues, with the Prince demanding peace. In the second part, Romeo invades the ball at the palace of the Capulets where he sees and falls in love with Juliet. This is followed by the love music for the famous balcony scene, and the episode in which

Mercutio describes how the fairy queen, Mab, visited him in his sleep. The concluding section tells of the death of the lovers, a tragedy leading the Montagues and Capulets to end their hostilities and vow eternal friendship.

The orchestral excerpts performed most often are the "Love Music" and the "Queen Mab" scherzo, both found in the second of the three large sections into which the symphony is divided. The "Love Music" is an adaptation of the famous balcony scene. It is an intense and passionate love duet, with Romeo represented by the violas and cellos in unison, and Juliet by the oboes, flutes, and clarinets. Walter Damrosch once remarked that the music "reproduces the dialogue between Romeo and Juliet so vividly that you can almost understand the words." The "Love Music" is followed by the exquisite and scintillating "Queen Mab" scherzo with which the second section ends. Mercutio's famous description of Queen Mab becomes a gossamer-like piece of music, diaphanous and limpid on its orchestral texture and mercurial in its motion.

Le Carnaval romain, or the *Roman Carnival* Overture, Op. 9 (1844), was originally intended to serve as a prelude to Act II of Berlioz' opera *Benvenuto Cellini.* The composer decided to develop it into an independent symphonic work, while still utilizing materials from the opera. It begins with a dazzling theme for violins and violas, which has the rhythm and character of a saltarello, a sixteenth-century Roman dance usually in 6/8 time. After this theme is assumed by different sections of the orchestra, there is a brief pause. Trills of increasing sonority introduce a beautiful melody for the English horn, soon to be taken over by the violas with a contrapuntal countertheme first in flutes, then in cellos and violas. A dance melody is suddenly heard, first softly, then with increasing volume. The main section of the overture now begins, with a theme for strings which is fully developed. Earlier material returns: first the dance theme, then the beautiful melody, and after that the saltarello subject. The last of these ideas, developed and changed, brings the overture to its conclusion.

The overture to *Beatrice and Benedict* (1860–62) is one of Berlioz' rare excursions into comedy. *Beatrice and Benedict* was Berlioz' last composition, a two-act *opéra comique* whose text was based on Shakespeare's *Much Ado About Nothing.* Berlioz was a harassed man when he wrote this score, yet there is nothing in this music to suggest the unhappy circumstances under which it was written. The opera is consistently lighthearted and vivacious, now touched with mockery, now sparkling in its travesties and parodies. The overture is in a similarly light and infectious vein. It begins with an introduction highlighting a vivacious melody for the strings and woodwinds; this theme is lifted from the second-act duet of Beatrice and Benedict. A slow section follows where we hear a romantic song for horn and clarinets; this is the subject which, in the opera, reveals that Beatrice is really in love. The main body of the overture (allegro) is built from the subject first heard in the introduction, but it also introduces a new idea, a haunting tune for violins over woodwind harmonies. In the coda, the comic element is strongly accentuated.

Georges Bizet

"His music has the tang of sunny climates, their bracing air, their clearness. It voices a sensibility hitherto unknown to me."

NIETZSCHE

BORN: Paris, October 25, 1838.

DIED: Bougival, near Paris, June 3, 1875.

MAJOR WORKS: *Operas*—Les Pêcheurs de perles; La Jolie fille de Perth; Carmen. *Orchestral Music*—Symphony; Roma; L'Arlésienne, two suites (the second arranged by Ernest Guiraud); Patrie Overture; Petite Suite. *Piano Music*—Chants du Rhin; Jeux d'enfants, for piano duet (also for orchestra). *Vocal Music*—Songs for voice and piano including "Agnus Dei," "Chanson d'Avril," and "Ouvre ton coeur."

HIS LIFE

Bizet came from a family of musicians. His father was a singing teacher. His aunt, a fine pianist, was married to François Delsarte, a distinguished voice teacher. The boy Bizet soon revealed such a natural aptitude for music that he was entered in the Paris Conservatory when he was only nine years old, the youngest member in his class. He remained at the Conservatory nine years, studying piano with Marmontel, organ with Benoist, and composition with Jacques Halévy. The winning of awards for piano playing, fugue, and organ attested to his outstanding ability. When he was seventeen he wrote the Symphony in C major, which lay in discard until 1935 when it was discovered, performed, and accepted as a highly welcome addition to the Romantic symphonic repertory. Further evidence of his growing creative gifts came in the year of 1857 when, at the age of nineteen, he won the Prix de Rome for the cantata *Clovis et Clotilde* and the Prix Offenbach for a one-act opera, *Le Docteur Miracle*. The latter was successfully performed at the Bouffes Parisiens in that same year.

The three years Bizet spent in Italy as a result of winning the Prix de Rome were among the happiest of his life. He loved that country, the people, the language, the music. And he was productive. He completed a Te Deum for chorus (1858), an *opéra bouffe, Don Procopio* (1859), and a descriptive symphony with chorus, *Vasco da Gama* (1860).

Back in Paris, Bizet set out to carve a career as an opera composer. He succeeded in getting the Opéra-Comique to accept *La Guzla de l'Emir* (1862), a one-act *opéra comique*. But even before the first rehearsal he had a change of heart, refused to allow its performance, and subsequently destroyed the score. His next project was an opera with an oriental setting, *Les Pêcheurs de perles* (*The Pearl Fishers*), introduced at the Théâtre Lyrique on September 30, 1863. It was a failure. For it Bizet wrote the now famous tenor aria *"Je crois entendre encore."* This was followed by the opera *La Jolie fille de Perth* (1866), which received a favorable reaction from the critics when performed in Paris in 1867.

He became involved in an illicit romance with Céleste Mogador, an actress and courtesan, in 1863. He was sowing his wild oats, and he knew it. But by the fall of 1863 he was through with "parties and mistresses" and he announced his engagement to Geneviève Halévy, daughter of the famous composer of *La Juive*. Halévy violently opposed the marriage and saw to it that the engagement was broken off. But the romance did not die. Finally, on June 3, 1869, Bizet and Geneviève were married.

Bizet settled down to the humble existence of an unrecognized composer who supported himself mainly through hack work. He continued writing *opéra comiques—Grisélidis* (1870–71), *Djamileh* (1871), and *Don Rodrigue* (1873)—but to no avail; two of these he did not even bother to finish. "Since we are not wanted there,"

Camille Saint-Saëns told Bizet sadly—he was speaking about the French opera house—"let us take refuge in the concert hall." And Bizet replied just as sadly, "I *must* have a stage. Without it, I am nothing."

Despite this protest, Bizet did not altogether neglect orchestral music. Léon Carvalho, the new director of the Théâtre du Vaudeville, planned a performance of Daudet's *L'Arlésienne* as his inaugural production. He approached Bizet with the idea of writing incidental music for that offering. Bizet accepted and produced twenty-seven numbers. They were heard for the first time on October 1, 1872, and neither the play nor the music were well received. But later the same year Bizet extracted from his score four numbers for an orchestral suite which was introduced on November 10, 1872. It proved such a triumph that one of the movements had to be repeated, while the suite itself was performed again several times during the next three years. A second suite, also comprising four numbers, was subsequently prepared by Bizet's friend—Ernest Guiraud.

Two other Bizet works for orchestra were heard in quick succession. The Petite Suite (an orchestration of five pieces for piano duet, *Jeux d'enfants,* written in 1871) was introduced by the Colonne Orchestra in 1873, and one year after that the dramatic overture *Patrie* was performed by the Pasdeloup Orchestra. Both were only minor successes.

He was also working on a new opera which had been commissioned by the Opéra-Comique. He himself had selected the subject: Prosper Mérimée's hot-blooded story, *Carmen.* Two of Paris' leading librettists, Henri Meilhac and Ludovic Halévy, had prepared the libretto for him. *Carmen* was introduced at the Opéra-Comique on March 3, 1875.

The facts about the *première* of *Carmen* have so often been distorted that it is both interesting and illuminating to seek out the truth. The audience which attended the Opéra-Comique was, in truth, startled by what it saw and heard. There were many disturbing things about the new opera, both in the text and the music. To a nineteenth-century opera audience, the naturalism of *Carmen*— the sight, for example, of girls smoking on the stage—was a shock. So were the sensual story, the immoral episodes, and the lurid characterization of the heroine. Besides all this, patrons of the Opéra-Comique did not come to see the heroines of their operas die.

French operagoers, who were instinctively opposed to Wagner, had other grievances against the new work. They resented the Wagnerian tendencies, such as the use of leading motives, the closely knit texture of the opera as a whole, the symphonic character of the orchestral background. Students of Spanish music insisted that Bizet's attempt to re-create a national Spanish idiom lacked both authenticity and conviction.

Carmen, then, was shocking to some, objectionable to some, disappointing to some. But legend notwithstanding!—it was no failure. There was an enthusiastic response after the first act. This enthusiasm waned after the next two acts, but most of the critics regarded the new work with favor. It is, remarked the critic of *Le Courier de Paris,* "one of those works which redound to the credit of the musician." A few of Bizet's friends, including Vincent d'Indy, did not hesitate to describe it a masterpiece.

There is the testimony of the librettist, Ludovic Halévy, that "after the . . . *première* the performances went on, but not, as has been said, to empty houses; the receipts, on the contrary, were respectable, and generally in excess of those for the other works in the repertory." *Carmen* enjoyed a run of thirty-seven performances—a respectable figure when we take into account the fact that the opero was introduced comparatively late in the season. When the new season of the Opéra-Comique began, *Carmen* remained in the repertory, which most certainly would not have been the case if the opera had been the fiasco some writers have described. Besides, the publisher, Choudens, paid twenty-five thousand francs for the publication rights, which he most certainly would not have done if the opera had been a failure.

Legend, too, would have us believe that Bizet's death was caused by a broken heart. It was true that he died only three months after the *première* of *Carmen,* but the success or failure of his opera had nothing to do with it. For many years he had been suffering from an affliction of the throat, which may have been cancerous. Aggravation of this condition led to a heart attack and death.

HIS MUSIC

Bizet helped create the French lyric theater. Before his time French opera, successfully realized by Meyerbeer, was primarily a spectacle, melodramatic and emotional in content. With Gounod, economy, refinement, and sensitivity entered French opera. Bizet's contributions included: an enriched orchestration and harmonization; a unified texture; the *leitmotiv* treatment of the Wagnerian school combined with his own fine sense for rhythm; and a sensitive feeling for atmosphere. With Bizet the French opera became invested with power and passion, was charged with drama and filled with human feelings and conflicts.

Bizet's feeling for atmosphere is worthy of additional comment. His finest works are noteworthy for the rich and subtle way his music succeeds in evoking the background of the Orient (in *Les Pêcheurs de perles*), of Spain (in *Carmen*), and of the Provence (in the *L'Arlésienne* Suite). He had never visited any of these places. He had, at best, only a superficial knowledge of their music and dance and culture. Yet such was his rhythmic and instrumental virtuosity, and so sure were his instincts, that in translating his texts into music he always found the proper means with which to paint authentic local color.

ANALYTICAL NOTES

Opera. Any selection of the world's favorite operas must include *Carmen*. Its universal popularity is not difficult to explain. It is a vibrant play, varied in mood and feeling. The music is melodic, colorful in instrumentation, and exciting in its rhythms. There is the fascination of the exotic in its Spanish and gypsy backgrounds.

The brilliant prelude immediately sets the mood for the entire opera, a mood that is half festive and half ominous. The spirited opening melody for full orchestra (heard again in the last act to mark the preparations for the bullfight) introduces the rousing "Toreador Song." The opening melody returns, following which a song full of foreboding appears in the cellos against a tremolando of the strings; a motive from this melody is heard throughout the opera to warn of approaching doom. Then all is light and gay again.

The curtain rises on a street scene in Seville, in or about 1820. It is the noon hour, and the square is crowded with dragoons, townspeople, and the cigarette girls from the nearby factory enjoying a brief noonday respite. One of the last is the passionate and volatile gypsy girl Carmen, who sings coquettishly about love. This is the famous "Habanera" aria (*"L'amour est un oiseau rebelle"*), so called because it is written in the rhythm of the Cuban dance, the habanera. Actually Bizet borrowed not only the rhythm, but also the melody, appropriating the tune from "El Arreglito," a song by Sebastian Yradier (1809–65). Carmen makes flirtatious advances to the brigadier, Don José, who, in spite of himself, succumbs to her charm and magnetic appeal. He takes the flower she has thrown at him and conceals it in his bosom.

After Carmen and the other cigarette girls return to the factory, Don José's sweetheart, Micaëla, arrives, to bring him news of his mother (*"Parle-moi de ma mère"*). Don José and Micaëla then recall the happiness they once knew as children in their home town (*"Ma mère, je la vois"*). But neither the news from home nor the presence of his beloved can make Don José forget Carmen. Suddenly there is a hubbub. Carmen has stabbed one of the cigarette girls and is seized and bound by one of the soldiers. She is left to be guarded by Don José until a warrant for her arrest can be drawn up. She has lost none of her spirit or insolence, and she continues to taunt Don José by telling him that someday soon they will meet at the disreputable tavern of Lillas Pastia (Séguedille: *"Près des remparts de Séville"*). Now hopelessly in love with Carmen, Don José loosens the bonds that tie her hands and makes it possible for her to escape.

The second act opens with a brief prelude made up of melodic and contrapuntal embellishments of the even-rhythmed "Song of the Dragoons," which Don José sings offstage later in the act. The scene is the tavern of Lillas Pastia, haunt of gypsies, smugglers, and officers. The martial strains now assume the rhythmic garb of gypsy music. The colorful tavern is in festive mood ("Chanson bohème"). Suddenly the popular bullfighter Escamillo makes his entrance. He tells the admiring throng of the thrills and drama of his profession in what is probably one of the most celebrated baritone arias in all opera, the "Toreador Song." After he departs, Don José arrives, having escaped from prison—his punishment for having let Carmen go free. He is warmly welcomed by Carmen, who dances for him and urges him to renounce his uniform permanently and stay with her. Yielding, from Don José ardently, passionately, tells her what she has come to mean to him, of how he has nursed and saved the flower she had once thrown to him (*"La fleur que tu m'avais jetée"*). Now a helpless victim to Carmen, Don José attacks his commanding officer come to apprehend him, deserts his troops for good, and joins her and the other gypsies.

The third act is preceded by a brief orchestral interlude. After a few notes from the harp there is heard a sensitive night song in the flute. This brief moment of peace is shattered by a smuggler's march, which introduces a wild mountain scene in the lair of the gypsies. Don José is unhappy as a deserter and a collaborator with smugglers, but he is unable to leave Carmen. She now gets a quick glimpse of her future when she reads her own fortune in the cards (Card Song: *"En vain pour éviter"*). After the smugglers go off to ply their illicit trade, leaving Don José behind as a guard, Micaëla is seen approaching. As she stumbles over the crags she begs for heavenly protection (*"Je dis que rien ne m'épouvante"*). She is followed by Escamillo, who has come for Carmen. Only the precipitate return of the gypsies and the intervention of Carmen keep José from killing his hated rival. Before departing Escamillo invites all the gypsies to his next bullfight. It is then that Micaëla is discovered, timidly hiding behind the rocks. She has brought sad news: Don José's mother is dying. Torn between duty and passion, Don José finally decides to return home with Micaëla, but not before he has warned Carmen that he will return to her.

The prelude to the final act pulses with Spanish rhythms and is languorous with Spanish melodies. It is spirited, gay, abandoned music, but the oboe and other woodwinds sound ominous notes in the background. A crowd has gathered in the square for the bullfight. There is a parade, and after that dancing. But tragedy is about to descend. Haggard and drawn, Don José has come to beg Carmen to return to him; but she is now in love with Escamillo. When she brusquely pushes him aside and tries to enter the arena, he stabs her. Escamillo, emerging triumphant from the arena, finds her dead body on the ground. Near it is Don José, sobbing that he is the murderer.

Two points should be clarified about the score of *Carmen*. Bizet originally wrote it as an *opéra comique,* which means that it has spoken dialogue. It is still often performed this way in Paris. The adaptation with which American operagoers are familiar—recitatives replacing the spoken dialogue—was made by Ernest Guiraud. The ballet usually seen in the fourth act has been interpolated since

Bizet's time. The music for this dance sequence is derived from other Bizet works, notably the *L'Arlésienne* Suite.

Orchestral Music. The *L'Arlésienne* Suite No. 1, adapted by Bizet from his incidental music to the Daudet drama, is the composer's most famous orchestral work. It catches the flavor of the Daudet play, which is set in the Provençal city of Arles, through simulation of Provençal rhythms and folk songs.

It begins with a prelude whose melody, first heard in full orchestra, is a robust march adapted from an old Provençal *noël*. It undergoes several transformations of rhythm and tempo, then is permanently discarded. A delicate duet between saxophone and clarinet follows. After this the strings begin an impassioned song with which the movement ends.

The minuet is a brisk and sharply rhythmed melody in full orchestra; midway there is a trio, dominated by a bucolic theme for clarinet decorated by runs in the strings. After a brief interlude for flutes the bucolic theme returns.

The adagietto is a religious chant for the strings. This is followed by the closing movement, "Carillon," in which we hear imitated the tolling of carillon bells in the horns; against this is set a robust melody for the strings. By contrast there now follows an extended idyll for the flutes, later carried by the rest of the woodwinds, and finally taken up by the strings. The movement ends with the return of the carillon melody.

The *L'Arlésienne* Suite No. 2, adapted by Ernest Guiraud, is not heard frequently. It is also in four movements: pastorale, intermezzo, minuet, and farandole. The most interesting movements are the second and fourth. The second movement has deep religious feeling —so much so that the Latin liturgical text *Agnus Dei* has been used for this music to make a highly effective religious song. The finale begins with the march theme that opens the first movement of the first suite; this is followed by a lively melody for the flutes in the rhythm of the Provençal dance, the farandole. The section ends with both these subjects played simultaneously.

The now quite familiar Symphony in C major has had a curious history. Bizet wrote it when he was only seventeen, never had it performed during his lifetime, and in fact seemed to have forgotten having written it. No mention of it was ever made in Bizet's letters, so that even many Bizet authorities were completely unaware of its existence. The musicologist D. C. Parker found it in the archives of the Paris Conservatory and brought it to the attention of the conductor Felix Weingartner, who presented its world *première* in Basel, Switzerland, on February 25, 1935. It turned out to be a work of encompassing charm and emotional appeal, now characterized by Mozartean grace and lucidity, and now by Schubertian romanticism. The fact that this symphony, written in 1855, sounds so much like Schubert is remarkable because in 1855 very little of Schubert's orchestral music was known.

All four movements are so clear in form, so direct in appeal, and so assimilable in thematic material that no detailed analysis is required for their immediate appreciation. The symphony opens with a brisk, swiftly paced subject for orchestra; the second principal theme is lyrical and expressive. The second movement has a melancholy cast. It begins with an eight-measure introduction after which a poignant song is heard in the oboe accompanied by plucked strings. The third-movement scherzo has sprightliness and gaiety, its main subject returning in the trio slightly transformed. The good humor of the third movement is maintained in the fourth, in which three important ideas can be found: The first, which sets the finale into motion, is a vertiginous subject in sixteenths; the second is a march-like episode; the third is a lilting song for the violins.

The symphony was the inspiration for two ballets. One was *Le Palais de cristal,* which the Paris Opéra Ballet produced in 1947. More famous, however, is *Symphony in C,* a production of the Ballet Society of New York with choreography by George Balanchine, introduced in New York in 1948.

Ernest Bloch

"This music makes one feel as though an element that had remained unchanged throughout three thousand years, an element that is in every Jew and by which every Jew must know himself, and his descent, was caught up in it and fixed there."

PAUL ROSENFELD

BORN: Geneva, Switzerland, July 24, 1880.
DIED: Portland, Oregon, July 15, 1959.
MAJOR WORKS: *Chamber Music*—5 string quartets; 2 piano quintets; 2 violin sonatas; 2 sonatas for solo violin; 2 suites for solo cello; Suite for Viola and Piano (also for viola and orchestra); Baal Shem, for violin and piano. *Choral Music*—Sacred Service. *Operas*—Macbeth; Jézabel. *Orchestral Music*—2 concerti grossi; Symphony in C-sharp minor; Hiver-Printemps; Poèmes d'automne, for voice and orchestra; Three Psalms, for voice and orchestra; Schelomo; Israel Symphony; America; Helvetia; A Voice in the Wilderness; Evocations; Violin Concerto; Suite symphonique; Concerto symphonique, for piano and orchestra; Scherzo fantasque, for piano and orchestra; Suite hebraïque, for viola and orchestra; Sinfonia breve; Symphony for Trombone Solo and Orchestra; Symphony in E-flat; Suite modale, for flute solo and string orchestra. *Piano Music*—Sonata.

HIS LIFE

Ernest Bloch came from a family of bourgeois shopkeepers. His father, a merchant in Geneva, Switzerland, hoped his son would enter his business, but voiced no objection when Ernest chose music instead. Bloch's music study began when he was fourteen under Emile Jaques-Dalcroze (the creator of eurythmics) in solfeggio and Louis Rey in violin playing. It was not long before young Bloch started composing. The first results were an *Oriental* Symphony and an Andante for String Quartet, both completed when he was sixteen. One year later he went on to Brussels for additional music study at the Conservatory, with Eugène Ysaÿe, violin, and François Rasse, composition. His music study continued in Frankfurt on the Main, Germany, with Ivan Knorr, and was completed in Munich with Ludwig Thuille.

His studies ended, Bloch produced his first mature work, the Symphony in C-sharp minor, completed when he was twenty-two. Excerpts were heard in Basel in 1903. Every effort to gain a hearing for this symphony in its entirety, both in Germany and in France, proved futile. Discouragement, combined with the news that things were going badly in his father's shop, sent him back to Geneva to work there as bookkeeper and salesman. At the same time he settled down to domesticity by getting married on August 13, 1904. Music, filling the evening hours, was pursued as passionately as before. Within a few years he completed *Hiver-Printemps,* a tone poem (1904–5), and *Poèmes d'automne,* songs for mezzo soprano and orchestra (1906). He also gave weekly lectures on metaphysics at the University of Geneva.

Between 1904 and 1909 he worked on an opera, *Macbeth,* the libretto by Edmond Fleg adapted from the Shakespeare drama. It was accepted for performance not by one of Europe's minor theaters, but by the celebrated Opéra-Comique in Paris. The opera was introduced on November 30, 1910, and received a mixed reception, though one or two critics were rhapsodic in their praises. One of these was Romain Rolland, who had also been present when the complete Symphony in C-sharp minor was finally heard under the composer's direction in Geneva in 1910. "Your symphony is one of the most important works of the modern school," Rolland wrote Bloch. "I know of no work in which a richer, more vigorous, more passionate temperament makes itself felt. It is wonderful to think that it is an early work! If I had known of you at the time, I should have said to you: Do not trouble about criticism, or praise, or opinions from others. Do not let yourself be turned aside or led astray from yourself by anything whatsoever, either influence, advice, doubts, or anything else. Continue expressing yourself in the same way, freely and fully; I will answer for your becoming one of the masters of our time."

Rolland paid a visit to the composer at his Geneva home to give him additional encouragement. He was amazed to discover Bloch, a bookkeeper by trade, neck-high in business accounts and ledgers. Rolland did what he could to persuade Bloch to give up his job once and for all and to concentrate on music.

Between 1909 and 1910 Bloch conducted symphony concerts at Lausanne and Neuchâtel in Switzerland. After giving up business for good, he earned his living by teaching composition and aesthetics at the Geneva Conservatory. In his composition, he was no longer willing to continue along the Romantic lines of his symphony or to pursue the Impressionist tendencies of some of his other works. He was now fired with a new ambition: to write Hebrew music that would express and interpret the religion of his birth and his people. This Hebrew period, which began in 1912, yielded several major works: Two Psalms, for soprano and orchestra (1912–14); *Three Jewish Poems,* for orchestra, written in 1913 as a memorial to his father; Psalm 22, for baritone and orchestra (1914); *Schelomo,* a rhapsody for orchestra with cello obbligato (1916); and the *Israel* Symphony (1916).

In 1916, Bloch came to the United States as conductor of the visiting Maud Allen troupe. A coast-to-coast tour ended in bankruptcy and left Bloch stranded in a foreign land, without funds and with few friends. He made his home in a small, dark apartment in New York, supporting himself by teaching composition at the David Mannes School of Music. It was, quite naturally, a difficult period, though some of the leading musicians of the country came forward to help him—by arranging performances of his works. Karl Muck invited him to Boston to direct the Boston Symphony Orchestra in a program of his music. Stokowski did the same in

Philadelphia. Artur Bodanzky led an all-Bloch program in New York with the Society of Friends of Music. The Flonzaley Quartet performed his First String Quartet (1916). By 1919, when Bloch was awarded the $1000 Elizabeth Sprague Coolidge Prize for his Suite for Viola and Piano, his reputation in America was established.

From 1920–25 Bloch was director of the Cleveland Institute of Music, a period that saw the composition of such distinguished works as the Piano Quintet (1923), the *Baal Shem* Suite (1923), and the First Concerto Grosso (1925). In 1924, Bloch became an American citizen, and in 1927—now director of the San Francisco Conservatory—Bloch entered a rhapsody, *America,* in a national competition conducted by the journal *Musical America.* Submitted under a pen name, *America* was the unanimous choice of the judges. It won not only a cash award of $3000 but also simultaneous performances by several of the foremost symphony orchestras in the United States one day after the world *première* in New York on December 20, 1928.

An endowment from one of San Francisco's patrons enabled Bloch to give up his directorial post in 1931 and to devote himself entirely to composition. In a secluded corner of Switzerland—in Ticino, Roveredo—he worked on his *Sacred Service,* a large work for soloists, chorus, and orchestra, built around the text of the Sabbath morning prayers. The *Sacred Service* was introduced in Turin on January 12, 1934, the composer conducting.

In 1943, Bloch settled in a spacious, rambling cottage overlooking the Pacific Ocean, in Agate Beach, Oregon—his home for the rest of his life. For a time, he spent each summer teaching composition at the University of California at Berkeley, but then gave up all his outside activities to concentrate on composition. He proved more productive now than ever before in his life, in spite of the fact that he was suffering from cancer. He also found the time to restudy the scores of the masters, to read extensively, to take hikes in the mountains or relaxed walks on the beach, and to take photographs with his camera.

In 1954 he became the first composer to receive the top award from the New York Music Critics Circle in two categories: in chamber music for his Third String Quartet, and in orchestral music for his Second Concerto Grosso. His last compositions were two sonatas for solo violin which Yehudi Menuhin had commissioned him to write.

Bloch died of cancer in Portland, Oregon, on July 15, 1959, survived by his seventy-eight-year-old widow and their three children. Among the honors Bloch had gathered were an honorary membership in the Santa Cecilia Academy in Rome in 1929, a membership in and a gold medal from the American Academy of Arts and Letters in 1942, and his first award from the New York Music Critics Circle for his Second String Quartet in 1946.

HIS MUSIC

In his early works, culminating with *Macbeth* and the Symphony in C-sharp minor, Bloch combined Impressionist or Romantic writing with occasional intensity of expression, rhythmic vigor, and a sympathy for oriental intervals and vivid harmonic colors. The vigor, intensity, and oriental vividness are the traits of his later style, first crystallized during the Hebrew period. Bloch became a rhapsodist, inclining toward spacious forms and passionate statements. He did not copy so much as draw from Hebrew synagogical music and Jewish folk songs. Through the adoption of intervals, progressions, rhythm patterns, and colors found in actual Hebrew music he arrived at a style that was at times touched with mysticism, at other times filled with barbaric force; at times it was spiritual, and at other times almost pagan. It was music that interpreted the Jewish soul, "the complex, glowing, agitated soul," as he put it, "that I feel vibrating through the Bible . . . the freshness and naïveté of the Patriarchs, the violence of the prophetic Books; the Jew's savage love of justice; the despair of the Ecclesiastes; the sorrow and the immensity of the Book of Job; the sensuality of the Song of Songs." And he concluded: "It is all this that I endeavor to hear in myself, and to translate in my music; the sacred emotions of the race that slumber far down in our soul."

After 1923, Bloch no longer concentrated his creativity exclusively on Hebraic music, though from time to time he did write a composition of Hebraic content and interest. For the most part such titles as Concerto, Suite, Scherzo, Quartet, Quintet, Concerto Grosso, Symphony—which give no hint of the programmatic implications of the music—appeared among his works. Other compositions, bearing descriptive titles, had no racial interest. The epic rhapsody *America* was, of course, inspired by the land of his adoption, and *Helvetia* by the land of his birth. *A Voice in the Wilderness* was intended to speak of the unhappy destiny of all mankind.

To all intents and purposes, then, Bloch abandoned Hebrew music—that is, except for compositions where a Hebraic intent is indicated in titles like *Sacred Service* and the *Suite hebraïque,* for viola and orchestra (1952). But—and this is significant!—Hebrew music did not abandon him. The qualities that made his Hebraic works unique and significant are contained in his later works: in the slow movements, the brooding mysticism that always has a deeply religious quality; in the fast ones, a ferocity and passion in his rhythms and in the clipped phrases of his melodies. Thus, with inexorable logic, with conciseness, with high-minded purpose, his music passes from spiritual revelation to intense drama.

ANALYTICAL NOTES

Chamber Music. Bloch's five string quartets span almost forty years of his creative life. The first came in 1916 (its last movement being the first piece of music he wrote in the United States). This is a highly personal document in which the composer views the world around him, the peaceful world of visions and dreams he knew in Switzerland in the years preceding World War I, shattered by the turmoil and anguish of the war. The second quartet came in 1945, almost thirty years later. A good deal of the struggle and tenseness encountered in the first quartet have been replaced in the second by a spiritual uplift and an incandescence of speech which led Ernest Newman to compare it with the last quartets of Beethoven. In explaining the structure of his work, Newman said: "From an embryo in the second of the four movements there comes into being an entity which from that point onward moulds the whole quartet from the inside into a single organic substance." This embryo comes to full growth in the finale in the theme of the passacaglia and in the subject of the ensuing fugue.

The Second String Quartet was the recipient of the New York Music Critics Circle Award. And so was the Third String Quartet

(1951). While adhering to a basic classic structure, the Third String Quartet has greater objectivity in its writing, greater sobriety of expression, and greater economy in the use of materials than were encountered in the two earlier quartets. Here heights are soared to in the exalted slow movement, once again music in which Bloch yields to a Beethovian kind of "raptus." Bloch's last two quartets (1953, 1955) continue along the trend of the Third String Quartet in their compactness of structure, sparing thematic material, compression of writing, and depersonalization of style.

The Quintet for Piano and Strings, written in 1923, is one of the most consistently inspired pieces of music in the contemporary repertory of chamber music. Bloch originally planned this work in order to experiment with the artistic possibilities of quarter-tone music. Ornamentations built out of quarter-tone intervals appear sporadically in the first movement, usually to increase the tension, and are used with outstanding dramatic effect.

A unifying element of the work is the integrating use of a powerful theme, strongly suggestive of the *Dies irae,* heard in all three movements. It opens the quintet, thundered out in the piano against a shimmering background of quarter-tone music by the strings. The second principal theme of the first movement comes after a descending passage for the piano; it is a passage of incandescent and luminous beauty for the lower strings, soon taken up by the piano. This mood is shattered with the brusque return of the opening subject, which, as it passes from one instrument to another, is built up with overpowering effect. Intense and unrelieved gloom pervades the second movement. The strings present a melancholy melody against a persistent rhythmic background of the piano. The melody develops into a wail. The rhythm of a funeral march is now interpolated. The grief becomes unconfined and arrives at a climax of agony with outcries by the violins in high, piercing notes while the piano provides a morbid setting of dark chords. The first theme of the first movement returns to open the finale, played by all the instruments in a feverish outburst. The movement gains rhythmic momentum and primitive strength until an orgiastic eruption of sound takes place. The conflict is over. A tender song is heard in the viola, gentle and contemplative, which Bloch described as the peace that comes when man has learned to accept spiritual instead of material values. In this atmosphere of calm and resignation the quintet comes to a close.

Bloch produced several fine works for solo instrument and piano, including two violin sonatas (1920, 1924), two sonatas for solo violin (1958), three suites for solo cello (1958), the Suite for Viola and Piano, also scored for viola and orchestra (1919), and the *Baal Shem* Suite, for violin and piano (1923). The last of these is the one still heard most often. Its inspiration was a mystic named Baal Shem, who founded a new Hebraic sect in the eighteenth century: Hasidism. Hasidism believed in joy, redemption, religious ecstasy, and the essential goodness of all. The Hasid worshiped God ecstatically, frequently with rapturous song and frenetic dances.

Baal Shem consists of three characteristically Hasidic melodies. In the first movement, *"Vidui"* ("Contrition"), we have a plaintive song which interprets the emotions aroused by true repentance. In the second movement, *"Nigun"* ("Melody"), the free improvisation of a cantoral chant is simulated. This is followed by *"Simchas Torah,"* an uncontrolled expression of joy. *"Simchas Torah"* is one of the happiest of Jewish holidays, commemorating as it does the delivery of the Holy Torah to Moses. To the true Hasid this was an occasion for joy unconfined, and Bloch's music expresses this joy without inhibitions.

Choral Music. The *Sacred Service* (*Avodath Hakodesh*)—for baritone (cantor), mixed chorus, and orchestra, completed in 1933— is the most ambitious of all Bloch's compositions in a Hebrew style and with Hebrew content, and one of the few which is grounded deep in the soil of religious worship. It is a setting of the Sabbath morning service as practiced in American reform temples, with adherence to the order of the prayers in the liturgy. "The texts embody the essence of Israel's aspirations and its message to the world," the composer has explained. "Though Jewish in roots, this message seems to me above all a gift of Israel to the whole of mankind. It symbolizes for me more than a 'Jewish service,' for in its great simplicity and variety, it embodies a philosophy acceptable to all men."

In five sections, the *Sacred Service* is intended for performance without interruption. Brief orchestral preludes and interludes tie together the different vocal parts. These orchestral episodes are intended to replace the usual "responsive readings" during the service while providing the worshiper an opportunity for silent meditation. In the first such episode, the opening "Meditation," we encounter a motive in the mixolydian mode which recurs prominently throughout the composition.

Orchestral Music. *Schelomo,* a rhapsody for cello and orchestra, is one of Bloch's finest works. "Schelomo" refers to Solomon, the all-wise biblical king. Bloch's inspiration is said to have been a figure of Solomon created by the artist Catherine Barjanska, the wife of the cellist for whom Bloch wrote his rhapsody in 1916; the work is dedicated to her. The figure—showing the king "weary of life, weary of riches, weary of power," in Olin Downes's description— may be regarded as the key to the emotional content of the music.

The solo cello speaks for Solomon. "Now melodic and with moments of superb lyricism, now declamatory and with robustly dramatic lights and shades," wrote Guido M. Gatti in his definite analysis, "the cello lends itself to a reincarnation of Solomon in all his glory."

The rhapsody, which is free in form, opens with a declamation of the cello punctuated by chords in the woodwinds. A brooding discourse by the cello, unaccompanied, now leads to the first of two principal themes: a clipped, sharply rhythmic phase gently suggested by the strings before being proudly exclaimed by the horns and after that by the full orchestra. A long and tender monologue follows in the solo cello. The passionate outburst by the strings, with exclamations by the brass, becomes the climax of the first section. The cello, once again unaccompanied, brings on the second section, the main theme of which is a tortuous oriental melody heard in the bassoons and oboes, then in the solo cello. This theme is elaborately worked out both in the solo cello, sometimes with sensuous counterthemes given by the orchestra contrapuntally, and in the orchestra itself. Another sonorous climax is realized with a majestic statement for the brass against passionately surging strings. After the climax has subsided the cello enters upon an extended meditative soliloquy. The rhapsody ends with a return of the first theme in the brass, then in the solo cello, and finally in full orchestra.

A Voice in the Wilderness (1936) is another orchestral work by Bloch in which the cello is assigned obbligato status. But the cello here serves a different function from the one it had in *Schelomo*. In *A Voice in the Wilderness,* the cello appears as a commentator between each of six short movements to discuss briefly what had gone on before. Bloch described these six movements as "meditations," and the work as a whole was intended by him to describe "the apparently unhappy destiny of man." The six parts are played without interruption, one movement linking up with the next, "sometimes bound together," the composer explains, "by a barely perceptive thematic relationship or 'reminiscence,'" while always retaining a consistent defined character.

In the *Israel* Symphony, completed in 1916, Bloch had in mind the holiest of all Jewish holidays, the Day of Atonement. This is the day the Jew seeks atonement through grief and repentance. In his music Bloch tried to voice the immeasurable grief of a people despised and rejected.

Although it has only one movement the symphony is actually in three contrasting parts. It opens with a solemn introduction, the principal theme being an elegy in the solo horn, soon supplemented by oboe and viola. The second section is fiery, built out of a brusque and savage theme first heard in flutes, English horn, clarinet, and strings. The closing section is described by the composer as a "fresco of Hebrew struggle." At first it is disturbed and over-wrought as the full orchestra enters upon an agitated section. Then it becomes contrite and poignant; the woodwinds, violins, harp, and solo viola share a subdued song of prayer. Agitation is followed by tranquillity a second time. After a brief recollection of the introduction, the chorus enters with a humble prayer of atonement to God with which the symphony ends: "Adonai, my Elohim, O my Elohim! Alleluia, O my Elohim! Hear Thou my voice, my Elohim. Hear my prayer!"

The Concerto Grosso No. 1 (1925), for string orchestra and piano, another of Bloch's celebrated works, is far different in character from both *Schelomo* and the *Israel* Symphony. Its idiom is not Jewish but modern; its form is strictly classical rather than free, flexible, and rhapsodic. The origin of the concerto is interesting. At the Cleveland Institute of Music, where Bloch at the time was director, young students, eager to produce "modern music," vied with one another in breaking traditions. Bloch wrote his concerto to prove to them that even within a strictly classical form it was possible for a composer to arrive at a modern spirit through deployment of modern techniques in melody, harmony, and rhythm.

It is in four movements. The first, "Prelude," is built entirely from a brusque, sharply accented theme with which the concerto opens; a rhythmic momentum is maintained throughout the movement without relaxation. This is followed by a dirge. The choir of strings hymn a song of despair; the three-note motive which begins this melody is afterward reiterated throughout the movement, gaining an effect of overpowering grief through persistent repetition. Music lighter in heart follows. The third movement begins with a short and tender passage called "Pastorale" and continues with a group of vigorous rustic dances spiced with modern harmonies. The rhythmic variety of these dances is particularly interesting, utilizing the most modern of alternating meters and cross rhythms. The concerto ends with a powerfully constructed fugue, the thematic core of which is an epigrammatic subject, highly modern in spirit.

Almost two decades later, in 1952, Bloch completed a second concerto grosso, for string orchestra, which received the New York Music Critics Circle Award. Here, as in the earlier work, the tradition of concerto grosso writing is followed sometimes by alternating and at other times by combining a smaller group of instruments with the rest of the orchestra in the style of ripieno and concertino. A dramatic fugue follows a more tranquil maestoso section in the first movement. The second movement is lyric; the third is rhythmic; and the finale consists of four variations on a descending theme of chromatic construction.

Bloch wrote only one violin concerto. He began it in 1930, and did not complete it until 1938. A good deal of the first movement has a strong American Indian identity, which asserts itself without delay in the opening theme. The solo violin repeats it, as trumpets provide an answering "call motive" and the harp sustains a harmonic background. An expressive song for solo violin follows; this subsequently receives contrapuntal treatment through a countersubject in the woodwinds. Agitation follows, achieving a huge climax, and bringing the movement to a close with a dramatic coda. The second movement is primarily devoted to a diatonic melody in three-four harmony which flutes and bassoons share; a subsidiary thought is then introduced by the solo instrument. The finale is turbulent music in which the solo violin recalls the principal subject of the first movement.

Bloch's only piano concerto came one decade later, in 1948. He called it Concerto symphonique to point up the importance of the orchestra in the over-all scheme of things. The concerto is large in design, intense in expression, powerful in the working out of the thematic material. There is a dominating thought in the first movement: a unison motive heard first in solo piano, then repeated by the brass. The second movement is scherzo-like, a welcome contrast to the solemnity of the preceding movement and to the restlessness and questioning attitudes of the finale, which is for the most part built up from episodic statements.

Alexander Borodin

"He was an epic poet."

STASSOV

BORN: St. Petersburg, November 11, 1833.
DIED: St. Petersburg, February 27, 1887.
MAJOR WORKS: *Chamber Music*—2 string quartets; String
Sextet; Piano Quintet; Piano Trio; Flute Sonata; Cello Sonata.
Opera—Prince Igor. *Orchestral Music*—2 symphonies; In the
Steppes of Central Asia. *Vocal Music*—Songs for voice and
piano including "Full of Poison Are My Songs," "The Sea,"
"Sleeping Princess," and "Sunset."

HIS LIFE

The chemist Professor Zinin once told Borodin, "All roads are open
to you. But you must spend less time writing songs. I count on
you to succeed me, but you think of nothing but music. You make
a mistake hunting two hares at once."

Throughout Borodin's life science was a major preoccupation. The
importance of his research in the field of solidifying various aldehydes
was acknowledged and honored. He was also a graduate doctor and a
professor of chemistry.

In music he regarded himself as little better than an amateur. "I
am a Sunday composer who strives to remain obscure" was the way he
once described himself to Balakirev. Yet his musical achievements
were no less significant than those in science. He was destined to

write the first Russian music of national character acclaimed outside his own country.

He was the illegitimate son of Prince Luke Ghedeanov, a descendant of Caucasian royalty, and Avdotya Kleineke, of middle-class station, the wife of a physician. As was then the custom with children born out of wedlock, he was registered under the name of one of the Prince's serfs, Porfiry Borodin. He was only seven years old when his father died. He was brought up by his cultured, sensitive, and doting mother. Because he was a frail child—for a while it was believed that he had tuberculosis—he was not sent to any public school, but received his early academic training at home with a governess and private tutors. He was so completely under feminine influence (his only friend was his cousin, Maria) that he sometimes referred to himself as a girl.

He had a keen intelligence and a retentive memory, showing unusual aptitude for languages, the natural sciences, and music. His first vivid musical impression came from the band music that he heard from his window, played in a nearby barracks. Before long he developed a talking acquaintance with some of these band musicians and arranged with one of them to be taught to play the flute. He was ten when he wrote his first piece of music, a polka for piano, inspired by his love affair with a mature woman. His musical horizon was extended when he became friendly with Stchiglev, a boy hailed as a musical prodigy. Together they explored the world of classical music on the piano in four-hand arrangements. They attended orchestral concerts at Pavlovsk. Then, without outside assistance, they learned to play string instruments so that they might participate in chamber music performances. They would walk seven miles, even in inclement weather, for these musical meetings, to which they gave themselves with such passion that one session lasted twenty-four hours. Composition went hand in hand with these activities. When Borodin was fourteen he completed a concerto for flute and piano, and a string trio based on a theme from Meyerbeer's *Robert le Diable*.

For all his devotion to music he did not neglect science. He set up a laboratory in his room to pursue experiments in chemistry. In his seventeenth year he was enrolled in the Academy of Medicine and Surgery in St. Petersburg, where he specialized in botany and chemistry. There he soon attracted the interest and enthusiasm of Professor Zinin, who was thenceforth to take him under his wing.

Borodin was a brilliant student, carrying away honor after honor. In 1856 he was appointed assistant professor of pathology and therapeutics. Two years later he received a doctorate in chemistry. In 1859 he was sent abroad for a scientific mission.

A stay in Heidelberg proved as important to his musical development as to his scientific growth. He met a young and charming pianist, Catherine Protopopova, with whom he soon fell in love. She introduced him to the piano music of Chopin and Schumann. They attended many concerts, on one occasion making a trip to Mannheim to hear several Wagnerian operas. She kept his musical interests alive even while he was deeply involved in his chemistry studies.

Back in his native land Borodin married Catherine and settled in St. Petersburg in the apartment at the Academy of Medicine which was to be his home for the rest of his life. He proceeded to lead the dual life of scientist and musician. For a while, his progress in science outstripped his musical efforts. He wrote important papers and made a few significant researches in chemistry. He became a lecturer at the Petersburg Academy of Forestry and a professor at the Academy of Medicine. Music was a diversion—but a major one. The hours he could steal from science were spent in playing the piano and the cello, and in composing.

The boundary separating the musical amateur from the professional was soon crossed. The one most responsible for bringing this about was Mily Balakirev (1837–1910). When Borodin began studying with him, composition at once assumed a new importance for the pupil. Balakirev himself put it this way: "Until then, he . . . ascribed no importance to the impulse that drove him toward musical composition. I believe I was the first to tell him that composition was his real business." Under Balakirev's guidance, Borodin started work on his First Symphony. The writing went slowly, but the task absorbed him. "I heard him play portions," wrote Rimsky-Korsakov. "These delighted me. . . . But even in the midst of playing or talking, he would jump up all of a sudden and fly to his retorts and burners to make sure that all was well—filling the air, as he went about, with incredible sequences of sevenths and ninths, bellowed at the top of his voice."

In the writing of his symphony he was not only given technical guidance by his teacher, but his aesthetic ideas were also clarified by his friendship and conversations with composers like Mussorgsky,

Cui (1835–1918), and Rimsky-Korsakov. These men, together with Balakirev, were joined in a single mission: to create a truly national art in their composition. Borodin joined them in this ideal, thus completing that quintet which has since been baptized by musical history as the "Russian Five" or the "Mighty Five."

Borodin completed his First Symphony, the first of his works with a national character, in 1867. It was introduced on January 16, 1869, his public bow as a composer, at a concert of the Russian Musical Society, Balakirev conducting. Balakirev reported: "The first movement was coldly received, the scherzo very warmly, the composer being cheered and an encore called for. The last two movements went splendidly. At the end Borodin had to take several calls."

The warmth with which his First Symphony was received encouraged him to begin planning a second; but it was nine years before he was able to complete it. Meanwhile he produced some songs and the score for a farcical opera, *The Bogatyrs*—a *bogatyr* being a giant hero of ancient Russian epics. This opera was presented anonymously in 1867, then forgotten. In 1936 it was revived in Moscow and was quickly suppressed by the Soviet Government, which resented its mockery of Russian *mores*.

Ever hampered by his devotion to science, he could find little time for creative work. His energies were absorbed in the founding of medical courses for women, in which he also assisted as teacher, and of a free laboratory for impoverished science students. In 1877 he had to make an intensive tour of Germany, to inspect its laboratories preparatory to a reorganization of the laboratory in his own Academy. "I am never able to concentrate on composition," he once complained, "except during my summer holiday, or when some ailment compels me to keep to my rooms."

He was not able to finish his Second Symphony until 1876. When it was introduced, on March 10, 1877, under Napravnik, it was a complete failure, due partly to an inadequate performance and partly to some faulty writing for the wind instruments.

Slowly and laboriously Borodin produced a few other major works: the First String Quartet, in 1879; the tone poem *In the Steppes of Central Asia* in 1880; the Second String Quartet, a labor of seven years finally completed in 1885.

But the work that absorbed him, that sapped his energy and vitality, and that remained a challenge, was the folk opera *Prince Igor*.

He had been planning it as early as 1869, and then worked on it, on and off, for the rest of his life, sometimes in a concentrated and feverish burst of enthusiasm and effort, at other times allowing it to lie untouched for a few years. During the composition of the opera he remained indefatigable in his study of Russian history and folk music, to be certain that both his libretto and score would be authentic. The opera was never completed; that task was left to his friends Rimsky-Korsakov and Glazunov. And he was no longer alive when it was introduced at the St. Petersburg Opera on October 23, 1890.

Perhaps what most arrested the development of *Prince Igor* was a series of tragedies that struck him in the closing years of his life. His wife became chronically ill. Then he himself suffered a serious illness in 1884, which some diagnosed as cholera and from which he never actually recovered. After that came the death of his mother-in-law, to whom he was singularly attached. For periods he suffered through stifling mental depressions. Yet he kept on working, not only on his opera, but also on sketches for a third symphony.

During all those years, despite the excessive demands made upon him by science and music, he was a singularly gregarious soul who found the time for the society of people. His apartment always overflowed with visitors: students, relatives, friends, associates, strangers coming for a favor. Some came for a meal; others for a day; still others lingered on for indefinite periods. He did not mind these visits; on the contrary, he encouraged them. He always found an excuse to escape from his working table to join his guests in lively conversation while drinking enormous quantities of tea.

"Not even in his study did Alexander get any privacy," wrote Victor I. Seroff in *The Mighty Five*.

No one bothered to ask him whether he was busy, or to keep the door shut while he was working on scientific treatises which had to be copied and corrected and made ready for publication. The fact that his papers and books on the desk were submerged under gloves, sweaters, hats, and magazines which his visitors dropped there as they came in, or that his drawings, sketches for songs, and parts of his symphony were used . . . in the kitchen to cover jars of sour milk or line cat-boxes did not seem to worry him. . . . [His wife] Ekaterina had more than one thing wrong with her health. . . . She suffered from asthma . . . developed insomnia and roamed all night through the apartment stumbling over chairs and the bodies of sleeping guests who, like the cats, slept wherever they found a bed or a couch that could be turned into a bed, or just dozed on chairs in the corridor or on the stairs. She had long since turned day into night, and of course completely prevented any normal schedule on her husband's part. But Alexander loved her, and in order not to hurt her feelings he arranged his life as best he could. He never knew whether they had already had lunch or dinner, or whether they were going to have it, and if so at what time. Sometimes he ate two dinners, and sometimes just three soft-boiled eggs.

Seroff provides the following additional personal information:

Ekaterina did not like him to wash naked in the morning, to walk about the bathroom without any clothes on, or to use the face towel on his body. She told him to cut his nails, and not to sing aloud or whistle as he walked from one room to another, not to take such big bites while eating that he choked, not to put so much lemon in his tea, not to press it with his spoon. . . . Borodin's eyes were sensitive to light, and he could sleep only in a very dark room or by putting a piece of dark cloth over his eyes. Noise kept him awake and he liked to cover his ears with blankets, but Ekaterina insisted that he use only the sheet. However, she did not have much occasion to nag about his sleeping habits because either she was up when he went to sleep, or one of her relatives or visitors got ahead of him and took his bed. Then he would hunt up a pillow and an old blanket or heavy shawl and sleep either on the couch in his study or in the sitting room.

During the carnival of 1887 Borodin attended a dance at the Medical Academy, decked out in national costume. He was exceptionally gay, and even participated in the dancing and the merrymaking. Suddenly he collapsed. When his friends realized that he was not clowning they rushed to him, but it was too late; they found that he had died of a burst aneurism.

HIS MUSIC

As a member of that group of composers known as the "Russian Five" (*see* Rimsky-Korsakov), Borodin inevitably was influenced by, and helped foster, a national music, a music that sprang from the soil of Russian folk art and culture. Before he met Balakirev, Borodin wrote in the vein of the German Romantic composers, particularly in that of Mendelssohn.

With his First Symphony he became a *Russian* composer. The works he produced were few in number, but they are all successful realizations of the principles of "The Five." We have in each of them the pageant of a land and people—in music which is in heroic mold and Russian to the core. But Borodin differed from the other composers of "The Five" in that his writing was frequently more oriental than Slavic. His Georgian ancestry, so strongly suggested in his oriental eyes and manner, is also found in his sinuous and sensuous melodies, barbaric rhythms, and lavish instrumental colors.

ANALYTICAL NOTES

Chamber Music. The slow movement of Borodin's second string quartet, in D major (1885), is one of the most famous pieces in Russian chamber music. It has invaded the world of American popular music by way of the hit song "And This Is My Beloved," which Robert Wright and George Forrest wrote for the operetta *Kismet* in 1953, in a score based on Borodin's melodies. This slow movement is a "Notturno," or "Nocturne," in which a haunting twenty-four-measure melody in the cello is set against an accompaniment of broken chords. The melody is then dressed up with intriguing figurations and embellishments.

The "Nocturne" is the third movement. In the first movement, the first principal theme is originally stated by the cello, while the second subject is assigned to the first violin, accompanied by plucked strings. The second-movement scherzo has no trio section. It has an elfin grace and refinement that is almost Mendelssohnian; one of its intriguing thoughts is a waltz tune in the violins. In the finale, a slow recitative is the preface to a vivace section in which the two main themes become subjects for fugal treatment and whose heart is an extended, expressive melody.

Opera. *Prince Igor* is one of those operas that are talked and read about more often than they are heard and seen. The history book assigns to it a place of first significance among Russian folk operas, and Borodin authorities consider it one of this master's most important creations. Yet very few operagoers—outside the Soviet Union— have ever seen a performance; and those who have, generally find more interest in parts of the opera than in the whole. The opera lacks sustained dramatic interest both in text and music so that, apart from several musical episodes, splendiferous staging and costuming become the focal point of the production—rather than drama, characters, or the music.

Borodin worked on this opera many years, having first become interested in the subject of Prince Igor when Stassov brought him an outline of a libretto in 1869. Borodin later prepared his own libretto based on that outline. For two decades he worked on his score by fits and starts. He never lived to complete it, leaving behind numerous sketches and rough drafts which had to be assembled and completed by Rimsky-Korsakov and Alexander Glazunov. The opera was finally produced in St. Petersburg on November 4, 1890.

The main action takes place in the twelfth century when Russian troops, headed by Prince Igor, clash against the Polovtsi, a race of Central Asian Tartars ruled by Khan Konchak. The opera opens with a prologue in which Prince Igor's army goes off to attack the Polovtsi. By the end of the first act, the Russians have been soundly defeated. Prince Igor and his son are captured and brought to the camp of the Polovtsis where, as befitting their high station, they are feted with gala festivities. Since Igor's son has fallen in love with the daughter of Khan Konchak, he refuses to escape with his father. The opera ends with the Prince's triumphant return home.

Some of the most deeply moving vocal episodes are assigned to the chorus, notably the villagers' chorus ("We Come in Our Distress"), the girls' chorus ("The Prairie Flowereth"), and the peasants' chorus ("'Twas Not the Furious Tempest Wind"). One or two vocal pages have become popular, such as the tenor aria "Daytime Is Fading" and the baritone aria "No Sleep, No Rest."

Undoubtedly, the most celebrated excerpts from the opera are the *Polovtsian Dances,* a staple in symphonic literature. These dances occur at the end of the second act when Khan Konchak arranges a monumental feast and entertainment for his distinguished captives, Prince Igor and his son. In the opera these dances are accompanied by chorus, but at symphony concerts the chorus is usually omitted.

In the first dance a melody for flute and oboe brings on the introductory procession of the royal captives. This is followed by a dance of savage men: A gay clarinet tune is set against a descending phrase of four sharply accentuated notes; this tune is taken up by the orchestra. Then comes the dance of the boys indulging in simulated war games. A brusque syncopated theme for strings is punctuated with crashes of the cymbals. The music grows wilder and wilder. The war games are ended when the dance of young girls begins. A languorous oriental melody is shared by violins and cellos; it is as undulating as the motions of the bare bodies of the dancers. The last dance is a savage and impetuous outburst, as woodwinds begin a passionate and intense melody and strings take it up against a background of horns. The dance progresses to a whirlwind finish, with whirling passages for the strings, outcries in the brass, and a crash of the cymbals. The dancers are saluting their mighty leader, Khan Konchak.

Orchestral Music. The tone poem *In the Steppes of Central Asia* is Borodin's most integrated masterpiece, the only work of his which is of a single consistency. It is a miniature, to be sure, but an exquisitely perfect miniature. It was written in 1880 to accompany a *tableau vivant* commemorating the twenty-fifth anniversary of the reign of Alexander II.

Borodin provided the following descriptive analysis of his tone poem:

Through the silence of the steppes of Central Asia is heard the strain of a peaceful Russian song. Sounds of horses and camels come from the distance, approaching ever nearer, and with them the strains of a haunting Eastern melody. A caravan is crossing the desert escorted by Russian soldiers. It progresses on its long journey confident in the protection afforded it by the soldiers. The caravan disappears into the distant horizon. The song of the Russians blends with that of the Orientals in a common harmony, until both fade away from the plains.

The music follows this program literally. The "peaceful Russian song" is heard in the solo clarinet. Plucked strings then depict the tread of the animals. The "haunting Eastern melody" now rises in the English horn. A phrase for the woodwinds, and the Russian song is repeated by two horns, then erupts loudly with full orchestra. Clarinets and cellos, then the strings, recall the Eastern melody. The blending of the Russian and oriental themes is soon heard—the Russian theme in violins and flutes, and the oriental one in bassoons and horns. They fade away. The composition ends with the soft, sad tones of a solo flute and the disappearing voices of flute and violins.

Borodin wrote three symphonies, the third of which he never completed. Only the Symphony No. 2 in B minor, which took him six years to write, and which he completed in 1877, has achieved permanency in the repertory. It is an offshoot of the composer's folk opera *Prince Igor*. Because of its heroic and epic mood it has been nicknamed *"Bogatyrskaya,"* a *bogatyr* being, as we have previously remarked, a giant of ancient Russian epics. In it Borodin incorporated musical ideas he was planning for his opera. One critic, Gerald Abraham, goes so far as to believe that to Borodin, in despair of ever completing *Prince Igor,* the symphony was a substitute, "perhaps, in a sense, it was the *Igor* of his dreams."

Stassov disclosed the fact that Borodin actually wanted to picture feudal Russia in this music. Thus he made the first movement describe the gathering of ancient princes; the third, evoke the songs of the ancient Slav troubadours (*bayans*); the finale, re-create a hero's banquet made festive with the music of such ancient instruments as the *gusli* (a many-stringed zither) and the bamboo flute.

The music of the symphony, like that of *Prince Igor,* is for the most part of an oriental cast. The epic character of the first movement is achieved immediately with a powerful theme in unison strings, supported by bassoons and horns, which dominates this entire section. A vigorously propelled scherzo follows in which a powerful statement for brass and a syncopated idea for the strings are prominent. The trio section places emphasis on a haunting refrain for oboe. In the andante, a poignant troubadour melody is presented by the horn following an introductory passage for clarinets and harp. The brilliant finale enters without interruption, music full of savage strength and oriental splendor. It opens with a seventeen-measure introduction, after which the main subject is stated by full orchestra, with a contrasting subsidiary idea contributed by the clarinet.

Johannes Brahms

"In him converge all previous streams of tendency, not as into a pool, stagnant, passive, motionless, but as into a noble river that receives its tributary waters and bears them onward in larger and statelier volume."

W. H. HADOW

BORN: Hamburg, Germany, May 7, 1833.
DIED: Vienna, April 3, 1897.
MAJOR WORKS: *Chamber Music*—3 string quartets; 3 piano quartets; 3 piano trios; 3 violin sonatas; 2 string sextets; 2 string quintets; 2 cello sonatas; 2 clarinet sonatas; Piano Quintet; Clarinet Quintet; Clarinet Trio. *Choral Music*—A German Requiem; Rhapsody (Alto Rhapsody); Song of Fate; Song of the Fates; Song of Triumph. *Orchestral Music*—4 symphonies; 2 serenades; 2 piano concertos; Violin Concerto; Concerto for Violin, Cello, and Orchestra; Variations on a Theme by Haydn (also for two pianos unaccompanied); Academic Festival Overture; Tragic Overture; Hungarian Dances. *Piano Music*—3 sonatas; Variations on a Theme by Handel; Variations on a Theme by Paganini; ballades, capriccios, Hungarian dances, intermezzi, rhapsodies, waltzes. *Vocal Music*—Liebeslieder Waltzes; Neue Liebeslieder Waltzes; Zigeunerlieder; 4 ernste Gesänge; numerous individual songs for voice and piano including "An die Nachtigall," "Auf dem Kirchhofe," "Die Botschaft," "Erinnerung," "Immer leiser wird mein Schlummer,"

"Die Mainacht," "Sappische Ode," "Sonntag," "Ständchen,"
"Der Tod das ist die kühle Nacht," "Vergebliches Ständchen,"
"Verrat," "Von ewiger Liebe," and "Wiegenlied."

HIS LIFE

There is a common bond between Beethoven and the composer often
described as Beethoven's successor in symphonic music. It assigned
to both of them an equally unhappy childhood. The Brahms family
lived in poverty in a crowded tenement on the waterfront of Hamburg. Father Brahms was a mediocre musician (a double bass player
for the Hamburg Opera) and an indigent one. His wife, who was
slightly deformed, worked with the needle. What they earned together was hardly enough to feed and clothe their children ade-
quately. Johannes often went hungry. To make matters even worse
he often had to witness ugly scenes between his parents. They had
been incapable of getting along with each other almost from the day
of their marriage, incompatible as they were in age—she was seventeen years older—and in temperament.

Even in school Johannes found little peace. He disliked his studies
—French particularly—and he detested his teachers, who seemed to
delight in either teasing or torturing him. In short, the impressionable
years of childhood were spent in a setting hardly propitious for the
development of a world-famous composer.

It did not take long for Johannes to reveal his gift for music. As a
child he used to make up little melodies. As he knew nothing about
music, he invented a kind of musical notation enabling him to put
these tunes down on paper. Father Brahms, noticing his son's musical
interests, decided to nurse and develop them. He hired a local pianist,
Otto Cossel, to give the boy lessons. Johannes learned so quickly that
before long he was able to earn some sadly needed coins by playing
the piano in the disreputable taverns along the waterfront.

When he was ten years old Brahms was taught the piano by one
of the best music teachers in Hamburg, Eduard Marxsen. From then
on his development was rapid. He was able to give a piano recital
when he was only fourteen years old, his program including one of
his own pieces, a set of variations for the piano.

His intense poverty made it impossible for him to devote himself as completely to serious music as he would have liked. He was compelled to write hack compositions and make hack arrangements, sold to publishers for a few pennies a number. About one hundred and fifty of them appeared under such pen names as G. W. Marks and Karl Würth. He had to give piano lessons. He played the piano in saloons. The strain of all this work told: His health gave way. There might have been serious consequences if a relative had not taken him to the country for a period of enforced rest. With all this, serious composition was not neglected. He wrote some songs and piano pieces, and a piano trio, the last given a private performance in 1851.

In 1853 Brahms met the Hungarian violinist Eduard Reményi. This was one of the important moments in the composer's life. Impressed by Brahms's gifts, Reményi invited the young man to tour with him as an accompanist. This tour brought Brahms into personal contact with some of Germany's foremost musicians and won him powerful allies. In Hanover, for example, he met one of the most celebrated violinists and musical figures of the day, Joseph Joachim. Joachim had already heard tidings of a feat performed by Brahms in Celle: the piano was discovered at the last moment to be out of tune by a semitone; spontaneously Brahms transcribed all his accompaniments a semitone higher. This incident aroused Joachim's curiosity about the young man. Hearing Brahms play his own Sonata in C major for piano (1852–53) further confirmed for Joachim the extent of the young musician's talent. From then on Joachim was one of Brahms's most ardent admirers and sincerest friends.

At Weimar, Brahms visited Franz Liszt. Conscious of Liszt's reputation as pianist, Brahms diffidently declined the master's invitation to play for him. Instead he showed Liszt some of his compositions. Liszt tried them out on the piano and praised them. Then, perhaps as a reciprocal gift, Liszt proceeded to play for Brahms his own Sonata in B minor—only to discover midway that his audience had fallen asleep! This unfortunate episode upset Liszt only temporarily. When Brahms departed from Weimar, Liszt presented him with a cigarette case.

Brahms's next stop was Düsseldorf, where Robert and Clara Schumann lived. Brahms did not delay in paying his respects. Robert Schumann at first appeared impatient with his visitor, but generously, if also somewhat coldly, consented to listen to some of his music. The first few bars of Brahms's Sonata in C major sent Schumann scurrying into the kitchen for his wife. "Clara," Schumann cried, "you must come and hear music such as you've never heard before." The Schumanns now virtually adopted Brahms, had him live with them for three months, and gave him bountifully of their experience and wisdom.

It was Schumann who first recognized Brahms's genius. In an entry in his diary that is dated September 30, 1853, Schumann noted Brahms's initial visit, describing him as "a genius." Less than a month later, on October 28, he wrote his now celebrated article in the *Neue Zeitschrift für Musik,* singling out the unknown Brahms "to give the highest and most ideal expression to the tendencies of the times." Soon after this Schumann succeeded in interesting a publisher in Brahms's early piano works and, indirectly, helped procure an invitation to Brahms to appear as pianist at the Gewandhaus in Leipzig.

The bond that held Brahms and the Schumanns together was not only that of mutual admiration and respect, but also that of love. When, after he returned to Hamburg, Brahms received the terrifying news that Robert Schumann had lost his mind and was consigned to an asylum, he unhesitantly rushed to Düsseldorf to be with Clara during this critical period. He took an apartment above the Schumanns' and for the next two years gave of himself unsparingly. He was continually with Clara, to comfort her, to help take care of her children; he made periodic visits to the asylum to be with Robert. Brahms remained in Düsseldorf until Schumann's death, on July 29, 1856. The tenderness and affection which he had always felt for Clara could now ripen into undisguised love.

He was to love her for the next forty years. His letters to Clara were filled with the most ardent and tender sentiments. Throughout his life, and up to the time of her death, he reached for the warmth of her love with an almost desperate need. No less urgently did he rely on her musical judgment and counsel, which he respected profoundly.

Why two people who were so attracted to each other did not marry cannot readily be explained unless one takes into account Brahms's emotional maladjustment to all women. He could court them, flirt with them, and even fall in love with them (and they with him). But when the time for a decision neared he was filled with tortured doubts and fears. Clara Schumann was not the only one. Soon after Robert Schumann's death Brahms fell in love with Agathe von

Siebold, daughter of a professor in Göttingen. But when marriage was imminent Brahms fled, as if from a plague. "Fetters," he exclaimed, "I cannot wear!" He found relief by writing the String Sextet in G major (1865) to his beloved, explaining that in writing the music he had freed himself from his love.

There were still other women with whom he was in love: the singer Luise Dustmann; Elisabeth Herzogenberg (Stockhausen). But the pattern was invariable: ardent pursuit followed by precipitate flight. Few men appeared so suited for marriage as Brahms was, and few men fought it so relentlessly. He provided his own explanation: "When I entered my lonely chambers after . . . failures, they did not hurt me. But if I had been obliged to meet the questioning eyes of a wife and to tell her that once again I had failed—that I could not have endured." But it is obvious that Brahms was merely rationalizing. The answer is possibly more profound. He may have been impotent, as some have suggested. Sordid boyhood experiences in disreputable inns might have warped his personality and made any permanent relationship with a woman impossible. Or he may even have had a psychic fear of marriage itself. Whatever the answer, the fact remains that, for Brahms, love and desire often had to be sublimated in music.

In 1857 Brahms served as music master to the Prince of Lippe-Detmold. It was at this time that he wrote his first works for orchestra, two serenades, in D major (1857) and A major (1859), and the Concerto No. 1 for Piano and Orchestra (1854–58). The concerto was introduced in Hanover, on January 22, 1859, with Brahms playing the solo part and Joseph Joachim conducting the orchestra. It was a failure and continued to be a failure when it was repeated in Leipzig five days later. Brahms refused to be discouraged. "I believe," he wrote, "that this is one of the best things that could have happened. It forces one's thoughts to concentrate properly and enhances one's courage."

Between 1859–63 Brahms led a women's choir in Hamburg. Meanwhile, in 1862, he paid his first visit to Vienna. The manuscripts he brought to Julius Epstein so impressed the pianist that he arranged for Brahms to meet one of Vienna's most powerful musical figures, Joseph Hellmesberger, leader of a famous string quartet and concertmaster of the Vienna Philharmonic. After looking through Brahms's Piano Quartet in G minor (1861) Hellmesberger said,

"This is Beethoven's heir." On November 16 three members of the Hellmesberger Quartet, in collaboration with Brahms, introduced this work. The Viennese appeared to be more impressed with Brahms's ability as a pianist than with his talent as a composer. They found the quartet to be "gloomy, obscure, and ill-developed." A second concert, at which were heard the Piano Quartet in A major (1861–62), some lieder, and the Variations on a Theme by Handel (1861), aroused greater sympathy. "After the quartet had been received most favorably," Brahms wrote home, "I had an extraordinary success as a pianist. Every number met with the greatest applause."

Back in Hamburg, Brahms hoped to become musical director of the Philharmonic Society. When he failed to be appointed he decided to leave Germany and settle permanently in Vienna, where he had at least had a taste of success. For one year he conducted the Singakademie in Vienna, and between 1871 and 1875 he directed the orchestra of the famous Gesellschaft der Musikfreunde.

All the while he worked assiduously on major works. With one of these, *A German Requiem* (1857–68)—inspired by the death of his mother—he encountered his first important success. This came the first time that all but the fifth movement (yet to be written) was heard—in Bremen, on April 10, 1868, the composer conducting. The performance of the complete Requiem—in Leipzig, on February 18, 1869—was a greater triumph still.

His first important orchestral work came a few years later: the Variations on a Theme by Haydn (1873). When it was introduced in Vienna, on November 2, 1873, the critics were most enthusiastic. This may have encouraged Brahms to undertake an even more ambitious project, namely a symphony. "You will never know," he once said, "how the likes of us feel when we hear the tramp of a giant like Beethoven behind us." The shades of Beethoven hovered over Brahms —a deterrent to the writing of music in a form to which Beethoven had brought such grandeur. For years Brahms worked on the sketches of a symphony. At last, in 1876, he completed one. Three other symphonies followed between 1877–84.

He was now recognized as a master and, befitting a master, he was continually surrounded by disciples and admirers. Usually be spent one or two of the winter months traveling, making guest appearances as conductor and pianist. During the summer, when he did most of his composing, he would live outside of Vienna in the mountain and lake districts which he loved so dearly. The rest of the time he occupied the same humble, overcluttered, and atrociously furnished three-room apartment in the Karlsgasse in Vienna which was his home for a quarter of a century.

He was a simple man, who brewed his own coffee, ate at modest restaurants, always traveled third-class, and indulged in such simple pleasures as taking long solitary walks through Vienna, enjoying the society of intimate friends at the café, or playing with tin soldiers in the privacy of his living room. He was a man of strange contradictions. At times he was kind and solicitous and full of warm feelings. At other times his remarks were acidulous, his behavior was brusque and rude, his attitudes were callous. In his dress he was sloppy and unorthodox, wearing the same inexpensively priced clothing for many years; his desk and his closets were invariably in a state of chaos. But in intellectual and artistic matters he was meticulously ordered and disciplined, methodical in his working, reading, and writing habits. He could be calculating in business dealings and he was usually as parsimonious as a fishwife. Yet, on the other hand, he was ingenuous about the way he put his money to use, never knew how much he had, and often kept bundles of uncounted notes carelessly in his closet.

"He was broad-chested, of rather short stature, with a tendency to stoutness," wrote Sir George Henschel. "The healthy and rather ruddy color of his skin indicated a love of nature and a habit of being in the open air in all kinds of weather; his thick hair fell nearly down to his shoulders. His clothes and boots were not exactly of the latest pattern, nor did they fit particularly well, but his linen was spotless. What, however, struck me most was the kindliness of his eyes. They were of a light blue, wonderfully keen and bright, with now and then a roguish twinkle in them, and yet of almost childlike tenderness."

He worked hard, producing masterworks in every form of music except the opera. And his genius was recognized not only in Vienna but in the rest of Europe as well. In 1879 the degree of Doctor of Philosophy was conferred on him by the University of Breslau. In 1886 he was elected a member of the Berlin Academy of Arts and made a Knight of the Prussian Order for Merit. In 1889, Hamburg gave him the freedom of the city, while in 1890 he received the Order of Leopold from the Emperor of Austria. His earnings from his published works were so extensive that upon his death he left an estate of about $100,000.

He was attending the funeral of his beloved Clara Schumann, in 1896, when he caught cold. This infection aggravated the sickness from which he had been suffering a long time: cancer of the liver. Suddenly he became an old man. His friends sensed that he did not have long to live.

Brahms attended a concert for the last time on March 7, 1897, when Hans Richter directed a performance of his Fourth Symphony. The audience realized that it was probably looking at the master for the last time. The members of the orchestra rose to honor him when they saw him in the artists' box, and the audience followed suit. In her biography of Brahms, Florence May reported the scene that followed:

A storm of applause broke out at the end of the first movement, not to be quieted until the composer, coming to the front of the artists' box . . . showed himself to the audience. The demonstration was renewed after the second and third movements, and an extraordinary scene followed the conclusion of the work. The applauding, shouting house, its gaze riveted on the figure standing in the balcony, so familiar, and yet in its present aspect so strange, seemed unable to let him go. Tears ran down his cheeks as he stood there, shrunken in form, with lined countenance, strained expression, white hair hanging lank; and throughout the audience there was a feeling of a stifled sob, for each knew that they were saying farewell. Another outburst of applause, and yet another. One more acknowledgement from the master. Then Brahms and his Vienna were parted forever.

One month later, on April 3, he died. "All musical Vienna accompanied the great man to the grave," reported one of the newspapers, "and a stranger not knowing the man's greatness might have measured it by the number of prominent artists mingling in the immense assemblage of the funeral procession, and by the celebrated men and women who came from afar to pay their last honor to Brahms.'"

HIS MUSIC

In Vienna, where they always went in for cliques, intrigues, and aesthetic tugs of war, there were some who insisted on making Brahms the spearhead for musical reaction. These younger men, who marched under the banner of "the music of the future" and whose gods were Wagner and Liszt, had faith in only one kind of music, the new kind, and they were bitterly antagonistic to all other styles.

It is true that Brahms had no sympathy for the program music produced by Liszt and his imitators. And while he had a higher regard for Wagner than Wagnerites said he did, musical-dramatic writing on so grand a scale was foreign to his way of thinking. Brahms preferred an art that was pure, objective, and, above everything else, classical. Brahms was partial to polyphonic practice and he favored such Baroque structures as the serenade, the concerto grosso, variations, fugue, and passacaglia. Because his art was antithetical to that of Wagner and Liszt, because it appeared to look backward in time rather than forward, he was regarded by some as dull and old-fashioned.

Fortunately there were many who recognized his genius. These admirers—and they included some of Vienna's most influential musicians—realized that Brahms's pronounced classical bent was combined with Romanticism. If Brahms had the classicist's healthy respect for form and tradition, he did not neglect ardor and poetic expression. To a remarkable degree Brahms combined freedom of emotion and flexibility of thought with the discipline of structure. Those admirers of Brahms pointed to those fingerprints that identified so many of Brahms's masterworks: those sad or mellow melodies scored usually for the lower strings or for the woodwinds—melodies often irregular in length and just as often without an ending but allowing themselves to get absorbed into the contrapuntal texture; the Grecian nobility, serenity, and introspective calm of so many of Brahms's slow movements; Brahms's use of soaring strings in his passionate pronouncements, rising ecstatically over a throbbing rhythmic accompaniment; the tendency to side-step the binary structure for a series of motives or themes, or for fully developed songlike melodies that continually underwent variation and transformation; his interest not only in polyphony, in which he was a master second only to Bach, but also in polyrhythmic combinations and complex rhythmic patterns.

Brahms can be said to bear the same relation to his times that Bach did to his own. Each came at the end of an epoch: Bach was the culmination of the age of counterpoint, Brahms of the age of Romanticism. Each composer added little new to music in the way of structure, style, or idiom—Brahms even less than Bach. If Brahms had never lived, the course of musical evolution would have been unaltered. But both composers brought such richness of speech to an existing style, such increased flexibility to existing forms, such majesty and grandeur of expression to existing idioms, that in their works music becomes alive and vital.

ANALYTICAL NOTES

Chamber Music. Brahms's first important chamber music works came comparatively early in his career. The Piano Quartet in G minor (Op. 25) and the Piano Quartet in A major (Op. 26), with which he made his bow in Vienna, were both written in 1861, the composer's twenty-eighth year. They are still heard often. It was the first of these two works that led Joseph Hellmesberger to select its composer as "Beethoven's heir," a prophecy that Brahms was to fulfill not only through the quality and quantity of his chamber music but also through the important place his chamber music was to occupy in his creative output.

These two piano quartets differ on one major point: The first, in G minor, is built out of fully developed melodies; the second, in A major, is constructed out of themes that are generally episodic and epigrammatic. But while the first work is more interesting melodically, the second has a more convincing structural logic. Both works are motivated by passion and vitality in the fast movements and tenderness in the slow ones. The G minor Quartet is noteworthy for a scherzo that is both delicate and endowed with an air of mystery, a brooding second movement (called an intermezzo), and a finale that has the hot blood of the Hungarian folk dance. The A major Quartet also ends with music in the style of the Hungarian folk song and dance. The finest movement of the latter quartet, however, is the second, a poetic poco allegro in free rondo form that has the character of a nocturne.

Brahms wrote a third piano quartet three years after the first two: the Quartet in C minor (Op. 60). It is generally of lesser inspiration than its predecessors and more somber and dramatic in style, particularly in much of the first movement (which opens with an ominous subject in double octaves in the piano followed by a disturbed passage for strings), in the scherzo that follows it, and in the gloomy finale, which is in a contrapuntal style. The third-movement andante is a rapturous lyrical page whose basic melody is sustained in the high register of the cello; to Brahms's biographer Richard Specht, this melody represents Brahms's renunciation of love for Clara Schumann.

Renunciation of love was the inspiration for still another chamber music work, the String Sextet in G major (Op. 36), written in 1865. The lady in question here is Agathe von Siebold, and this is the reason why this composition has been subtitled *Agathe*. She enters into the first movement by means of the principal theme, which is constructed from notes spelling out her name: A-G-A-H (H, in German notation, representing B-flat)-E. Most of this composition is highly romantic, but romance yields to whimsical humor in parts of the second-movement scherzo, and to passion and intensity in the finale.

Three years after Brahms wrote this sextet, he created a chamber music work of the first order, one of the accepted masterworks in chamber music literature: the Piano Quintet, in F minor (Op. 34). Brahms arrived at the writing of this work by a circuitous route. He originally planned to write a string quintet, but his material did not lend itself for string treatment exclusively and he tried adapting it for two pianos. This was also an unsuccessful medium. He finally decided to combine a single piano with four strings.

The work is prolific with thematic subjects. The first movement, for example, has five fully developed themes. But the material is developed with such mastery and with such integration that there is never a feeling of profusion. Youthful vigor and optimism are the dominant traits of the entire work, though the second movement is in Brahms's recognizably reflective vein with occasional excursions into sensuous passages. The scherzo movement is interesting for its repeated contrasts in rhythm and tonality. The finale is long, complex, and somewhat amorphous in form; it is prefaced by a soulful introduction to the gay melody that becomes the principal subject.

In the closing years of his life Brahms produced another masterwork for a quintet of instruments: the Clarinet Quintet in B minor (Op. 115), written in 1891. This is one of several works written for the clarinetist Richard Mühlfeld. This work is at an opposite emotional pole from the Piano Quintet. Where the latter is mostly the im-

petuous music of youth, the Clarinet Quintet has the serenity and introspection of old age. The opening melody of the first movement,
the entire second movement with its poignant song for clarinet against
tremolo strings, and many pages of the last movement (a theme and
variations) have a restrained sadness. Even the scherzo, which makes
a pretense at good spirits, is subdued in feeling.

Still another remarkable chamber music work with clarinet (a companion to the Clarinet Quintet) is the Clarinet Trio in A minor (Op.
114), another fruit of the year of 1891. Like the quintet, this trio has
much about it that is elegiac and serene, much that has autumnal
beauty. The year of 1891 was in the twilight of the composer's life;
the shadows of old age hover over his writing. There is almost a
premonition of death in the lugubrious opening theme of the first
movement. What is unusual in this movement is that a contrasting
second theme is dispensed with, replaced by a canonic treatment of
the inversion of the opening theme. The funereal atmosphere of the
first movement pervades the slow movement as well. The third movement has somewhat greater sobriety than we usually encounter in
Brahms's scherzos. The ominous shadows that hovered in the first
two movements come back to darken the finale, much of which has
contrapuntal interest.

Brahms's last two chamber music compositions were two sonatas
for clarinet and piano (Op. 120). They are in the keys of F minor and
E-flat major, and both were written in 1894. The second of these
sonatas ends with a slow movement. Thus Brahms's final farewell
to chamber music comes with music of great gravity and earnestness.

Brahms approached the writing of the string quartet with the same
hesitancy and apprehension that he later brought to the symphony. He
began the sketches of the Quartet in C minor (Op. 51, No. 1) sixteen
years before he completed it in 1873. But once the first string quartet
was written Brahms proceeded, with his custom of producing works in
pairs, to do a second work in this form—the Quartet in A minor (Op.
51, No. 2). The first quartet is mostly somber; it has many pages
turbulent with struggle and suffering. Daniel Gregory Mason once
remarked that there is a single thematic idea unifying the entire work:
a brief rising motive "suggesting indomitable will" opposed to a
falling motive "of the tenderest sensibility." The thematic scheme
appears throughout the work.

The Quartet in A minor is more elegiac, more poetically expressive. Where the first quartet is somewhat heavy-handed, the second is graceful and buoyant. The tenderness of the two main themes of the first movement is characteristic of the second quartet's emotional temper. If there is a feeling of gloom in the second movement, it is dissipated with the arrival of a sensitive dialogue between first violin and cello. The minuet is diaphanous and graceful. Only in the finale do we confront the expected Brahmsian vigor. This finale is a dynamic Hungarian theme which receives six variations.

The Quartet in B-flat major in 1875 (Op. 67)—Brahms's last attempt at string quartet writing—has a prevailing air of good humor. An interesting hunting fanfare is the principal theme of the first movement. There is whimsey in much of this work, as in the second theme of the first movement and in the entire third movement. The gaiety is maintained in the finale, in which a carefree tune is the basis for eight variations.

Brahms's last chamber music composition exclusively for strings was the String Quintet in G major (Op. 111), in 1890. The opening of the first movement is strong, with a virile idea in the cello over an upper-string accompaniment. A transition in the violins brings a lyrical subject for the viola, to which violins and cellos contribute a rhythmic background. A third motive in this movement is a Viennese waltz tune. In the adagio that follows, tragedy replaces vigor and charm, the entire movement built around an ample melody presented by the first violin. A waltz melody, with which the scherzo opens, restores a modicum of levity. In the finale, gypsy fervor is found in an exciting subject for the viola (with which the movement opens) and in a subsequent fiery Hungarian dance tune.

Brahms wrote three trios for piano, violin, and cello. The Piano Trio in B major (Op. 8) was his first chamber music work, written in 1854 when he was only twenty-one. Thirty-seven years later Brahms revised it completely. In the new version the trio is a delightful blend of youthful freshness and a mature approach. The scherzo of the earlier version was permitted to stand as it was. But in the other three movements, Brahms retained the principal opening material but created new subsidiary ideas. Thus, in the first movement, for example, an austere melody written in 1890 provides contrast to the preceding romantic tune, from 1854. The slow movement introduces a new dramatized middle section to replace two extended episodes which Brahms had written for the first version.

The finest of Brahms's piano trios, and the one heard most frequently, is his last one, the Trio in C minor (Op. 101), composed in 1886. Here we have brusque and vigorous attitudes, as in the first movement (which is built primarily out of a robust four-note theme) and in the dramatic coda of the finale. But this vigor is contrasted with the gentleness of the slow movement, the second, and the elfin grace of the third.

Two of the three sonatas Brahms wrote for violin and piano have acquired identifying titles. The Sonata in G major (Op. 78), composed in 1879, is known as the *Rain* Sonata. There are two reasons for this. One is that Brahms quoted in this work his song "Regenlied." Another is that in the finale there is a repeated figure of sixteenth notes in the piano suggesting the fall of raindrops. An integrating element in this composition is the persistent use of a motto motive: the note "D" repeated three times, its initial appearance occurring in the opening theme of the first movement.

The Sonata in A major (Op. 100), composed in 1886, is called the *Thun* Sonata after the lake in Austria near which it was written. Actually, it is also less officially sometimes identified as the *Prize Song* Sonata since it opens with a theme strongly reminiscent of the opening phrase of the "Prize Song" from Wagner's *Die Meistersinger*. The Sonata in D minor (Op. 108), composed in 1888, has no sobriquet. But Richard Specht interprets the vehemence of the first movement, the restlessness of the closing presto, the reflectiveness of the slow movement, and the sobriety of the third as a many-sided character study of the famous pianist and conductor Hans von Bülow, to whom the work is dedicated.

The Sonata in F major for Cello and Piano (Op. 99), composed in 1886, is the second of two sonatas for cello. This is febrile music, even in the slow movement. Because of its restless and dramatic character this sonata has been christened by Walter Niemann as Brahms's *Appassionata* or *Pathétique* Sonata, in contrast to the Sonata in E minor for Cello and Piano, Op. 38 (1865), which Niemann considers as Brahms's *Elegiac* or *Pastoral*.

Choral Music. Brahms achieved the first major success of his career with *Ein deutsches Requiem,* or *A German Requiem* (Op. 45)—but this happened only when the work was heard more or less in its entirety. Before that, three sections were heard in Vienna, on December

1, 1867, and were hissed; but on that occasion the performance was far from satisfactory. A few months after that, on April 10, 1868, Brahms himself led a performance of his Requiem in Bremen. This time six sections were heard (Brahms did not complete a seventh until later that year) and it was a triumph. "Never had the cathedral been so full," wrote Albert Dietrich, who was present, "never had the enthusiasm been so great. The effect . . . was simply overwhelming and it at once became clear to the audience that *A German Requiem* ranked among the loftiest music ever given to the world."

Brahms called this work *A German Requiem* because in place of a liturgical Latin text he adapted one in German from the Lutheran Bible. Walter Niemann provided this pithy summary:

Blessed are they who mourn, for they shall be comforted. It is true that all flesh is as grass and all the glory of man like the flower of grass; it is true that every man must one day die. But death is not an eternal annihilation; the redeemed of the Lord shall obtain everlasting joy and gladness, and sorrow and sighing shall flee away. And, therefore, we say in the end: Blessed are the dead who die in the Lord from this time on. For death leads us into a better life; those who lead a God-fearing and upright life on earth, shall see their dear ones again in heaven, and rest from their care and labor, for their works follow them.

As this text indicates, *A German Requiem* speaks of hope and resignation rather than despair. Brahms's music is tender and greatly sorrowful, but in the main resigned. Thus the threnody that the chorus sings in dialogue with the orchestra in the first part, "Blessed are they that mourn," is music of serenity rather than grief. In the second section the tremendous emotional effect built up by the increasing sonority of the orchestra against throbbing beats of the tympani, to bring on the choral exclamation "For all flesh is as grass," is really a challenge. The dramatic apostrophe of the baritone and chorus in the third part, "Make me to know," has the strength of hope and assurance. There is longing and pity in the next two sections, "How lovely is thy dwelling," and "Ye that are sorrowful," the latter for soprano solo and chorus. But objectivity returns as the mystery of death is contemplated in "Here on earth," for baritone solo and chorus. The concluding section, "Blessed are the dead," begins with the pride of victory over death and ends with peace of mind and heart.

Brahms wrote two works for chorus and orchestra whose texts discuss the subject of Fate. One is the *Schicksalslied,* or *The Song of Fate,* Op. 54 (1868–71); the other, *Gesang der Parzen,* or *Song of the Fates,* Op. 89 (1882). *The Song of Fate* uses a text by Hölderlin which discusses the contrast between the struggles of life with the peace of eternal rest that comes with death. The work opens with an ethereal orchestral prelude. A description of the happy existence of Olympian gods follows, after which we get a picture of the agony of life on earth. The composition ends with a return of the opening prelude and the choral picture of Olympian happiness.

In *Song of the Fates,* Brahms sets a text by Goethe derived from the Greek tragedy *Iphigenia in Tauris.* The prelude establishes a mood of torment which continues in the dramatic chorus that follows, accompanied by a persistent drum motive. A dancelike episode brings relief, but only temporarily. The opening chorus, slightly altered, is heard again. The work ends on a note of consolation, with music that gently ebbs away into mysterious quiet.

The *Alto Rhapsody,* Op. 53 (1869)—or, more correctly, the Rhapsody for Alto Voice, Men's Chorus, and Orchestra—sets three of eleven verses from *Harzreise im Winter* by Goethe. Goethe's poems are somber, touched with the pathos of solitude. When Brahms set three of these poems to music in 1869 he too was a victim of despondency, largely due to an unhappy love affair. He translated the poems into music of darkness and despair. In the first two verses only the orchestra accompanies the voice; it is here that the gloom is deepest. But optimism penetrates through the last song. With the entry of the chorus, against a soft background of horns, the song of the alto is filled with hope; and the work ends in a kind of radiance.

Brahms wrote to his friend Dietrich concerning the *Alto Rhapsody:* "To you at least it may be gratifying that I do not always express myself in the frivolous ¾ time." In writing this way Brahms was assuming a familiar pose: flippancy toward one of his own works. For he had just completed a work in this "frivolous ¾ time"—the *Liebeslieder* Waltzes, Op. 52 (1869), for four voices and two pianos. These waltzes are surely lighthearted and infectious in the spirit of old Vienna. This "loosely bound wreath of songs," as Karl Geiringer referred to them, requires no analysis to be enjoyed at a single hearing. However, not even its ¾ time makes this work frivolous. But then, Brahms himself never really regarded the composition lightly. In 1870 he adapted eight of the waltzes for four voices and orchestra, and in 1874 he wrote a second set for four voices and piano, the *Neue Liebeslieder* Waltzes (Op. 65).

Orchestral Music. The *Variations on a Theme by Haydn*, Op. 56a (1873) was Brahms's first major work for orchestra alone. The only orchestral works he produced before this were two charming serenades —minor works compared to those by the older Brahms and works which even he regarded with a certain measure of condescension. With these variations, written when he was forty years old and in full maturity, he made his first serious attempt to invade the symphonic field. He produced a work which ranks high among his masterpieces.

It is the first example in musical literature of orchestral variations written as an independent creation, instead of as a part of some larger work. Actually there are two versions of this composition; the other is for two pianos, unaccompanied, Op. 56b. It is not known which came first, though the piano version was published and performed before the orchestral. Clara Schumann and Brahms performed it for a group of friends in August 1873, the year of its composition, a month before its orchestral counterpart was introduced by the Vienna Philharmonic.

The Haydn theme on which this work is based came from the second movement of a little-known divertimento. Since Haydn himself referred to the theme as "the Chorale St. Antoni," there has long existed serious doubt if it was original with him or borrowed from some anonymous source.

The work opens with the theme given by the wind instruments against a pizzicato background by cellos and double basses. Eight variations follow. In the first the violins present an embroidered version of the melody against a steady rhythmic background. An energetic variation follows, with the theme presented in altered form by clarinets and bassoons against a descending passage for strings. The third variation offers a lyrical adaptation of the melody in oboes and bassoons. In the fourth variation the theme becomes a song of sensuous beauty, given by oboes and horns against a descending passage in the violas. The fifth variation is fleet and diaphanous; a delicate subject in flutes, oboes, and bassoons appears against an accompaniment of violas and cellos. In variation six the music becomes martial; the theme, in martial rhythm, is found in horns and bassoons. In the seventh variation a magical effect is achieved when flutes and violins give an exquisite melody while violas and clarinets descend the scale in counterpoint. The final variation is gossamer music from first bar to last, with muted strings providing an atmosphere of mystery. We now come to the finale, which opens with a five-bar ground bass version of the Haydn theme. The bass theme is persistently repeated as harmonies are added by different parts of the orchestra. While this is taking place the rhythmic momentum increases and the sonority swells. At last the chorale returns in its original form in woodwinds and then is promulgated by the full orchestra. The work ends suddenly with a dramatic outburst by the entire orchestra.

The Symphony No. 1 in C minor, Op. 68, came three years after the Variations on a Theme by Haydn. It took Brahms more than twenty years to get around to the writing of a symphony and several more years to complete it. The symphony he finally did produce was described by Hans von Bülow as "Beethoven's Tenth Symphony" and by others as "the greatest first symphony in the history of music." He had, in short, emerged as the greatest symphonic composer since Beethoven.

The work is of epic proportions. Its thirty-seven-bar introduction is surely one of the sublime utterances in symphonic literature. The strings sweep upward in flight against a descending woodwind phrase; the inexorable single tone of "C" in the basses and tympani throbs in the background. The allegro proper begins with a sweeping subject for the violins. There is here an element of conflict, but a contrasting second theme, in the woodwinds, brings repose. These two major themes (and several subsidiary subjects) are worked out with a restlessness, dramatic struggle, and intensity of emotion in the vein of Beethoven—but the Beethoven of the *Eroica* and the Ninth Symphonies.

Then the battle is over. There comes the peace of the second movement, in which Brahms probes deeply within himself to seek out his most poetic thoughts. A melody simple as a folk song appears in the strings and bassoons. This is followed by an even more yearning song in the oboe. The strings now engage in a sensual outburst, as different voices weave in and out against a pulsating rhythm. The music now becomes ecstatic. But the serenity of the earlier measures soon returns. It appears first in an altogether new subject presented alternately by oboes and clarinets. Then the second theme is brought back by horn and solo violin.

The third movement—an allegretto instead of the customary scherzo—is consistently light and graceful. Without preliminaries the clarinet presents a pastoral theme. The middle section is of stronger fiber: The woodwinds present a robust phrase in 6/8 time which is answered by the strings. This interplay between the two sections continues until the earlier, and more graceful, material returns.

The concluding movement is the apogee of the entire symphony. The winds sound chromatic chords as a cry of anguish is heard in the violins. Plucked strings then introduce a mysterious atmosphere. The pace grows faster and faster until, at last, a song of triumph emerges in the horn and is repeated by the flute, against tremolos in the strings. This brings on the most famous theme of the work: the exultant song of joy (not unlike the song of joy in Beethoven's Ninth Symphony) in the strings. This song, and the countertheme which follows it, is given a development of Beethovian proportions, as other ideas are hastily interpolated. Earlier material is recalled with increasing power. After a recollection of the song of triumph (this time fortissimo in the orchestra) the symphony rushes to a dramatic conclusion with a breathless gait.

The Symphony No. 2 in D major, Op. 73, completed one year later, is of an entirely different character. The First was epic and essentially tragic. The Second is pastoral. Brahms planned, sketched, and wrote it in a benign, sunny little Austrian village lying comfortably in the lap of Wörthersee. The altogether unique personality of the Second Symphony must surely owe a huge debt to this lovely Carinthian spot. The music breathes the serenity, inner peace, quiet joy, and the gentle moods the composer must have experienced in that charming village. The Second is Brahms's *Pastoral* Symphony; its composer is a man in love with nature. This is precisely what Richard Specht meant when he described the work as a "serenade" and went on to say it is "suffused with the sunshine and warm winds playing on the water." This is also what Brahms's good friend Billroth emphasized when, trying out the new symphony for the first time at the piano, he exclaimed: "It is all rippling streams, blue sky, sunshine, and cool green shadows."

A three-note introduction in the cellos introduces the first principal theme (horns). Some transitional material follows, including a passionate outburst by the violins. An eloquent song now unfolds in the cellos and violas and is repeated by the flutes. All this material is extended and developed with intensity and breadth, following which the two basic themes return. A tranquil coda features a beautiful solo for the horn, and the movement ends serenely with a quiet sustained chord in the woodwinds.

The pastoral nature continues on into the second movement. The cellos offer a gentle and reflective melody which is soon taken up by horn, oboes, and flutes. The second theme, flutes and oboes, is in a similar lyrical vein. One other principal idea is presented: an expansive melody for the strings which is given passionate treatment. In the development of these three important subjects, the prevailing idyllic mood is never destroyed.

The third movement is more of an intermezzo than a scherzo. We hear the principal theme immediately in the woodwinds, the cellos providing a pizzicato accompaniment. Two trios follow, separated by a restatement of the main melody; each of these trios is actually a variant of the theme.

The concluding movement begins with a transparent melody for the strings. The full orchestra takes up this idea with vigor, leading directly to the second subject, which is a subdued theme for the woodwinds. Almost immediately a third theme is presented—a stately melody for the violins. These three themes are developed, altered, repeated, as an infectiously gay mood prevails. A jubilant statement of the opening phrase of the third theme brings the symphony to a vital conclusion.

The Symphony No. 3 in F major, Op. 90, which came six years after the Second, was described by Hans Richter, the conductor, as Brahms's *Eroica*. "It repeats neither the poignant song of Fate of the First, nor the joyful idyll of the Second. Its fundamental note is proud strength that rejoices in deeds."

The three loud chords for the winds with which the symphony opens provide a kind of motto theme that appears throughout the movement, sometimes as transitional material, sometimes as a background. The sweeping first theme that appears in the strings following these three chords is set against the three notes of the motto (cellos and basses). The second theme is a gentle subject first heard in the clarinet, and then in oboe and cello. As these two melodies are enlarged and varied, the motto repeatedly asserts itself, now briefly in the oboe, now in augmentation in the horn. The motto serves as the transition to the recapitulation section and is once again heard as a preface to the coda. The movement ends with the first theme.

A meditative chorale melody is given by the woodwinds in four-part harmony to start the second movement. It undergoes some elaboration before a second theme, in which the idyllic mood is maintained, emerges in the clarinet and bassoon. The violins soon engage in a passionate episode such as we often encounter in Brahms's music. Earlier material then returns, varied in rhythm and instrumentation, and sometimes with contrapuntal trimmings. There is another passionate outburst by the violins, after which a variation of the chorale theme brings the movement to a peaceful end.

The third movement has greater sobriety than we are accustomed to find in the third movements of the Brahms symphonies. We first hear a long, contemplative melody for the cellos, decorated by arpeggios in the other strings. The violins repeat this melody and then enter into a fanciful little dialogue with the cellos. A repetition of the opening song, this time by flute, oboe, and horn, brings on the second principal theme: a delicate subject in waltz time for the woodwinds. The earlier song returns, first in the oboe and after that in violins and cellos.

The first theme of the finale, given by strings and bassoons, is nebulous in texture and foreboding in character. A second theme, a solemn subject for strings and winds, is developed and then interrupted by an outburst in strings and woodwinds. The storm subsides momentarily; a stately melody is heard in the cellos and horns, and is then repeated by woodwinds and violins with increasing feeling. This and earlier material is now enlarged as the music passes from tender to feverish moods. But in the end there is resignation, as the first violins recall the motto theme that opened the symphony.

The Symphony No. 4 in E minor, Op. 98, was the composer's last, written in 1885. It is touched with that autumnal melancholy we so often find in the composer's last works. But it also has epic character. This combination of the epic and the melancholy gives credence to the belief that the symphony was inspired by a reading of Sophocles' *Oedipus.*

It begins immediately with the first theme, a melody for the violins divided into groups of two notes. After being fully presented the theme is treated more sensuously. The vital second theme is now presented by the woodwinds and horns; the second part of it is soon taken over by the cello and horns against a pizzicato setting by the violins and is then evolved into a soaring melodic flight in the upper register of the violins. The development concerns itself principally with the first theme and only incidentally with the second part of the second theme. An augmentation of the first four notes of the first theme brings on the recapitulation. All the earlier material is restated.

Two horns, reinforced in the second and third meassures by the woodwinds, announce the rhythmic pattern of the main theme of the second movement. The theme arrives in the fifth measure in the clarinets and bassoons, accompanied by pizzicato strings. After a sensuous passage for the strings, a brief transition leads to the second theme in the cellos, one of the composer's most inspired flights of lyricism. In the development the strings give prominence to both themes, frequently with enriched harmonies. The coda is constructed of the first theme.

Although the third movement is marked allegro giocoso, it is actually a scherzo—music that passes from gaiety to whimsey. The principal theme appears at once in full orchestra. The first violins then present the second theme. The development proceeds without digressing from this happy vein.

Brahms went to an old contrapuntal form for his last movement: the passacaglia. A passacaglia is a series of variations on a theme heard repeatedly in the bass. The ground bass of Brahms's passacaglia is heard in the brass and woodwinds. Thirty variations follow, built up with the dramatist's feeling for climax; the theme is sometimes presented as a melody, sometimes as an accompaniment, sometimes as a contrapuntal countertheme, and is sometimes made to pass hurriedly from one register to another. The composer's subtlety is such that it is frequently difficult to detect the theme or recognize all the variations. But, as Sir Donald Francis Tovey pointed out, "the listener need not worry as to whether he can trace the theme in the variations. If and where he can, that is well; but beauty is skin-deep, though it need bones to keep it in shape." What the listener should concern himself with is the force of the music and the sweep of the ideas, which are irresistible.

The *Akademische Ouverture,* or *Academic Festival* Overture, Op. 80, and the *Tragische Ouverture,* or *Tragic* Overture, Op. 81, came in the same year—1880. The former was written as a grateful acknowledgment of the honorary degree of Doctor of Philosophy conferred on the composer by the University of Breslau. With the academic life uppermost in mind, Brahms created an overture based on student songs, the most famous being "Gaudeamus Igitur," which comes as a climax to the work. The overture begins with a brisk introduction for strings, horns, bassoons, and drums. After a brief development the first student song is heard in the woodwinds and basses, "Wir hatten gebauet ein stattliches Haus." Another short development brings on the second student song in the second violins, "Der Landesvater." After a third development the third student song is heard in bassoons and clarinets, "Fuchslied." The closing section recalls these songs in a slightly varied form and is climaxed by the famous "Gaudeamus Igitur," powerfully presented by full orchestra.

Brahms never disclosed what tragedy he had in mind in writing the *Tragic* Overture, but its nobility and strength suggest a Greek drama. Some have seen in the music the struggle of a hero against fate, and its febrile nature strongly suggests a conflict. Two incisive chords introduce a restless and brooding theme in the strings. This theme receives a free and elaborate development in which the struggle assumes Herculean intensity. After the opening material is repeated in a slightly altered version, we hear the second major theme in the woodwinds, bringing with it a feeling of resignation. The music now alternates between struggle and resignation as both subjects are enlarged and varied with force and breadth. In the closing page the first subject returns triumphantly in the brass and strings, as if to emphasize the victorious resolution of the hero's struggle.

The Concerto in D major, Op. 77, is Brahms's only concerto for violin and orchestra. He wrote it in 1878 for his friend Joseph Joachim, whose advice and criticism were indispensable to the composer in the writing of this music. This is not virtuoso music, to exhibit the powers of the soloist, but music of symphonic character throughout. So concerned was Brahms with his artistic concept as a whole that in the energetic development of his ideas he often forgot the limitations of his solo instrument and wrote ungrateful passages. In the first and last movements there are brusque pages not usually negotiated successfully by a violin. In fact Hans von Bülow was once tempted to say of this work that Brahms had not written a concerto *for* the violin, but a concerto *against* the violin. But as was the case with Beethoven, who refused to keep a "puling fiddle" in mind when the spirit spoke to him, Brahms could not restrict the flow of his thought or hem in the turbulence of his emotions even when writing for the violin.

The concerto begins with a hundred-measure orchestral introduction. It contains the materials out of which the entire movement is constructed: the lyrical theme for cellos, violas, bassoons, and horns with which the concerto begins; the tender and expressive second theme which follows in the oboe, and subsequently in the violins, after the full orchestra has worked out the first subject. A robust marcato section in the strings introduces the soloist. He goes in for detailed passage work before repeating the first theme. The second theme now is heard in the flute and after that in the violins, with the soloist providing interesting embellishments. The working out of both themes is rhapsodical.

The second movement is an idyllic song, first encountered in the oboe (accompanied by the woodwinds and horns), then repeated by the solo instrument in a varied version. The solo instrument now presents a second soulful melody. The first theme later returns in the oboe against octaves in the violins. The soloist takes it up against pizzicato strings as the movement dies out.

The finale is a rondo in form; in style, it is a Hungarian dance. An exciting theme is first given by the soloist in double-stops, and is soon taken over by the entire orchestra. The second subject is just as forceful and spirited; it is heard in the solo instrument. The development of these two themes is often vigorous, even brusque. A brief cadenza brings on the concluding marchlike coda.

The Concerto No. 1 in D minor for Piano and Orchestra, Op. 15, was a fiasco when first introduced. Audiences thought the music too austere and gloomy. Time has proved that while this music surely evidences austerity, it also shows power and beauty. What we have here is the turmoil and passion of youth, for the concerto was completed in 1858, when Brahms was only twenty-three.

It opens with a stirring theme in the strings. Two introspective melodies, both given by the violins, follow. The mood is temporarily shattered by a return of the angry first subject. When the anger is spent the piano enters softly with a reflective theme. The piano then engages the first three themes before embarking on a new idea—a rhapsodic melody. But the essential mood of the movement is that of turmoil—so much so that it is believed to reflect Brahms's agitation on learning that his dear friend Robert Schumann had tried to commit suicide.

The inscription above the second movement suggests that this part of the concerto may have been inspired by Schumann's premature death in 1856: *"Benedictus qui venit in nomine Dei."* It is a deeply felt elegy. Muted strings and bassoons share a melody which speaks the pathos of a broken heart. The finale breaks the spell. The piano enters with an exuberant and spirited theme which sets the tone for the movement.

The Concerto No. 2 in B-flat major for Piano and Orchestra, Op. 83 (1881), is the fruit of Brahms's maturity, just as the First Piano Concerto is a product of his youth. And so, whereas the First Piano Concerto is mostly agitated and intense, the Second is sober, reflective, philosophical. It is a work of large structural dimensions; no other work in the literature of the concerto has such scope and stature. But to Brahms, who enjoyed being whimsical about his own works, it was "a tiny, tiny pianoforte concerto, with a tiny, tiny wisp of a scherzo."

The principal theme of the first movement is heard at once in the first horn. A passage from the piano leads to an orchestral exordium in which the first theme is fully projected by the entire orchestra, followed by the second theme in the violins. An octave passage in the piano leads to a repetition of the first theme. Both ideas are elaborated. An extended orchestral section brings on the development section, while the recapitulation is introduced with recollections of the opening horn subject. A long coda develops material heard originally in the first orchestral *tutti*.

The concerto is in four movements, instead of the traditional three, a second-movement scherzo being interpolated. The first theme of this scherzo is announced loudly by the solo piano and repeated by the full orchestra; a yearning second theme is given by the violins in the upper register. The second section of this movement approximates the traditional trio; it begins with a strongly accented theme in the violins.

The slow movement begins with a haunting melody for solo cello, a subject used by Brahms for his beautiful song "Immer leiser wird mein Schlummer." Other instruments quote this melody before passing it on to the solo instrument. A second important subject, equally poignant, appears in the piano and clarinet. After the original melody returns in the solo cello, a brief coda concludes the movement.

As was the case with the Violin Concerto, the Second Piano Concerto ends with Hungarian melodies and rhythms. The piano presents the principal subject of the finale. A second vigorous idea is assigned to the woodwinds and strings alternately. These two themes are worked out ardently, often with electrifying vigor.

The Concerto in A minor for Violin, Cello, and Orchestra, Op. 102, the so-called "Double Concerto," was Brahms's last concerto. It was completed in 1888. It is heard less often than his other works for solo instrument and orchestra and can be commented upon briefly. Here Brahms tried a nineteenth-century adaptation of the old concerto grosso form. The two solo instruments are used sometimes in conjunction with, sometimes in contrast to, the orchestra, in the style of the older form. Less consistently inspired and less well integrated than either the Violin Concerto or the Second Piano Concerto, it nevertheless has some remarkable pages, the most notable being the poetic and meditative music of the second movement. The first movement is more virile, though the strength of the first theme is tempered with the sweetness of the second. This first movement opens with an orchestral introduction which offers the strong first theme without preliminaries. A recitative for the cello (based on the concluding three notes of the orchestral introduction) becomes a bridge to the elegiac second theme, in the woodwinds. For the second movement, Brahms created one of those grandiloquent instrumental songs for which so many of his slow movements are famous. It is first played by the two solo instruments. Two new ideas enter midway in the movement, the first in woodwinds, and the second shared by the two solo instruments. In the finale, in rondo form, the main subject is an energetic Hungarian melody in the solo cello. Subsidiary material after that includes a motive in double stops for the solo cello, and a theme in double stops and triplets for the two solo instruments.

Piano Music. Brahms wrote three sonatas for the piano, all of them the works of youth. The one heard most often is the Sonata No. 3 in F minor (Op. 5), written in 1853, in his twentieth year; but this is, at best, a lesser Brahms. This sonata breaks structural tradition in that it consists of five movements: a third-movement scherzo and a fourth-movement intermezzo standing between an andante and the finale. The slow movement is perhaps the one that most strongly foreshadows the later Brahms in its sad, poetic lyricism. A quotation by

C. O. Sternau in the published score provides a clue to the emotional content of this music: "The twilight glimmers, by moonbeams lighted; two hearts are here in love united, and locked in blessed embrace." To the fourth-movement intermezzo, the composer appended the title of "Retrospect." This is not the kind of lighthanded music we encounter in so many of Brahms's later intermezzi; the mood is so funereal that this movement has been described by some critics as a funeral march.

Of Brahms's larger solo piano works the finest is the Variations on a Theme by Handel (Op. 24), written in 1861. Brahms took his theme from Handel's Suite in B-flat major, where it is also the subject for variations. It is interesting to contrast the variation techniques of these two masters. Handel merely dresses up the melody with decorative figures, or subjects rhythm or tempo to a slight alteration. With Brahms the method is more complex and subtle; in many of his transformations it is difficult to recognize the original idea. A turn of a phrase or a rhythmic pattern of the original melody sets him off to flights of fancy. Brahms called these variations "studies for the piano," but they are by no means technical excursions. The twenty-four variations, climaxed by a monumental fugue, may be an exercise, but mostly in creative imagination.

The Variations on a Theme by Paganini (Op. 35), written in 1863, is less impressive. This work consists of two sets of "studies," thirty-five in all. The theme is the famous melody of Paganini's Twenty-fourth Caprice, which was also used for purposes of variation by Serge Rachmaninoff in the Rhapsody on a Theme by Paganini. In contrasting this work with the Handel Variations, Ernest Hutcheson remarked that the latter was an "intellectual feat" while the former was "a technical tour de force." Hutcheson does point out, however, that the eleventh variation in the first set and the twelfth in the second set are a refreshing departure from the étude genre. It has been the custom of some pianists to use the best numbers of the two sets and delete the weaker ones, presenting the two sets as one.

Brahms's richest contribution to the literature for solo piano is found in the shorter forms. For technical mastery, lucidity of form, inevitability of construction, and variety and originality of emotional or dramatic expression, Brahms's shorter works for the piano have few rivals.

In the five ballades, Brahms tries to tell a story, though this does not mean that there is a specific program for each. The ballades are essentially pieces of absolute music, but filled either with dramatic outbursts or gentle reflections, so much so that the music appears to unfold a narrative. Four ballades are gathered in Op. 10 (1854). The dramatic vein is represented by the Ballade in D minor, Op. 10, No. 1, inspired by the Scottish ballad "Edward," and in the B minor, Op. 10, No. 3. A more reflective style is displayed in the Ballades in D major and B major, Nos. 2 and 4. The fifth ballade, in G minor, is found in Op. 119 as No. 4 (1893). This too has strong dramatic interest.

As the name implies, the capriccio (or "little caprice") is light and fanciful. Brahms wrote seven in this form, of which he was the inventor. Four are found in Op. 76 (1878) and three more in Op. 116 (1892). In the first group one of the most popular is the B minor, No. 2, where a glittering staccato subject is contrasted with an affecting lyrical one. In the second set, the G minor, No. 3, is of interest for its cross rhythms and the D minor, No. 1, for its bravura octave and chordal writing.

The three rhapsodies are in the Lisztian tradition of bold and heroic music within a spacious mold. Here we have, in Billroth's description, the "heaven-storming Johannes" instead of the philosophic and moody one. Two of these rhapsodies—in B minor and G minor—comprise Op. 79 (1879); a third, in E-flat major, appears as the fourth number in Op. 119 (1893). The last piece of music Brahms wrote for the piano, the E-flat major rhapsody, is also the only rhapsody touched with sadness.

The eighteen intermezzi are more personal and deeply felt than either the capriccios or the rhapsodies. The intermezzo is a flexible structure to which Brahms brought some of his more romantic moods. The first four, found in Op. 76 (1878), are of interest for their fresh, exuberant lyricism. Four more appear in Op. 116 (1892), three in Op. 117 (1892), four in Op. 118 (1893), and three in Op. 119 (1893). There is a touch of whimsey, at times even gaiety, in some of these (for example, the A minor, Op. 116, No. 2; the E minor, Op. 116, No. 5; and the E major, Op. 118, No. 6). Others have a stark intensity and a severity of line (F minor, Op. 118, No. 4; A major, Op. 118, No. 2). And the Intermezzo in E-flat minor, Op. 118, No. 6, has tragic overtones.

Among the shorter compositions, some of Brahms's lightest and most infectious moods and rhythms are captured in the four books of Hungarian Dances, for piano duet, which were written between 1869 and 1880, two books in each of these years. Brahms later adapted the first two books for solo piano, and the first, third, and tenth dances for orchestra. Various transcribers (among whom are Dvořák, Leopold Stokowski, Walter Goehr, Andreas Hallen, and Albert Parlow) have adapted all of the dances for orchestra. Joseph Joachim transcribed all the dances for violin and piano. These dances are actual Hungarian tunes to which Brahms had been introduced by the violinist Eduard Reményi, though given new life through energetic harmonizations. The fiery Dance No. 5 in F-sharp minor is among the most popular of Brahms's smaller works and even more famous in transcriptions for orchestra, and for the violin and piano, then in its original version. Dances No. 6 in D-flat major, No. 19 in B minor, and No. 21 in E minor are also extremely popular.

Similarly light and ingratiating in style, though more elegant in workmanship and material, are the sixteen Waltzes, Op. 39 (1865), originally written for piano duet. These are pieces in a true Viennese style—though more Schubertian than Straussian (Johann). They are all based on melodies original with Brahms. Most familiar is the Waltz No. 15 in A-flat major, of which an excellent and now famous transcription for violin and piano was made by David Hochstein. The closing waltz, in C-sharp minor, is a reflective piece of music in double counterpoint which Eduard Hanslick described as "a gracefully lulling air above an expressive middle part."

Vocal Music. Brahms is among the greatest composers of the German lied, in that royal line of lied creators that began with Schubert and continued with Schumann. Brahms wrote about two hundred songs for solo voice and piano. Some of his best-known and best-loved songs are in the lyrical, wistful, sentimental style of Schubert. In this manner we have the world-famous "Wiegenlied," or "Lullaby," Op. 49, No. 4 (1868); and such other melodic inspirations as "Immer leiser wird mein Schlummer," Op. 105, No. 2 (1886); "Vergebliches Ständchen," Op. 84, No. 4 (1881); "Die Mainacht," Op. 43, No. 2 (1868); and "Ständchen," Op. 106, No. 1 (1881). Also in this manner are some of the most beautiful love songs ever written, such as "Erinnerung," Op. 63, No. 2 (1874), and "Sonntag," Op. 47, No. 3 (1868).

In other songs Brahms gives us a preview of the lied in the hands of such later composers as Hugo Wolf and Richard Strauss. The song now becomes a miniature drama, with a melodic line that often approaches declamation and a piano accompaniment that has dramatic force and individuality. Brahms unfolds a mood or atmosphere or emotional conflict with wonderful effect, as in "Der Tod das ist die kühle Nacht," Op. 96, No. 1 (1886); "Verrat," Op. 105, No. 5 (1886); and the cycle *Vier ernste Gesänge,* Op. 121 (1896), four tragic and at times bitter songs with texts from the Bible; this song cycle was the penultimate of the composer's works, published in the last year of his life.

In "Gestillte Sehnsucht" and "Geistliches Wiegenlied," Op. 91 (1884), Brahms tried to restore the eighteenth-century aria with instrumental obbligato; both songs are for contralto with viola and piano.

Benjamin Britten

"The Model of a composer."

FRANCIS POULENC

BORN: Lowestoft, Suffolk, England, November 22, 1913.
DIED: Aldeburgh, England, December 4, 1976.
MAJOR WORKS: *Ballet*—The Prince of Pagodas. *Chamber Music*
—2 string quartets; Phantasy Quartet for Oboe, Viola, and
Cello; Six Metamorphoses After Ovid, for solo oboe; Sonata
for Cello and Piano; Suite for Solo Cello; Gemini Variations
for Piano Duet, Flute, and Violin. *Choral Music*—A Boy Was
Born; Hymn to St. Cecilia; A Ceremony of Carols; Saint
Nicolas; Spring Symphony; Cantata Academica; Missa Brevis;
Cantata Misericordium; A War Requiem; Voice of Today;
Children's Crusade. *Operas*—Peter Grimes; The Rape of Lu-
cretia; Albert Herring; Billy Budd; The Turn of the Screw; A
Midsummer Night's Dream; Curlew River, religious parable;
Crossing the River, religious opera; The Burning Fiery Furnace,
religious parable; The Prodigal Son, religious parable; Owen
Wingrave; Death in Venice. *Orchestral Music*—Variations on a
theme by Frank Bridge; Piano Concerto; Violin Concerto; Les
Illuminations, for high voice and string orchestra; Sinfonia da
Requiem; Prelude and Fugue; Scottish Ballad for Two Pianos
and Orchestra; Serenade for Tenor, Horn, and String Orchestra;
The Young Person's Guide to the Orchestra; Nocturne, for tenor
solo, seven obbligato instruments, and orchestra; Symphony for
Cello and Orchestra. *Vocal Music*—The Holy Sonnets of John
Donne; A Charm of Lullabies; Songs from the Chinese; Six
Hölderlin Fragments; Songs and Proverbs of Blake; Who Are
These Children?

HIS LIFE

If it were at all possible to make a computation of performances (live and recorded) commissions, honors, and other forms of recognition, Benjamin Britten might very well turn out to be the most successful composer of the twentieth century, with the possible exception of Stravinsky. The first performance of every new Britten work becomes a prize for which major musical organizations of the world compete; failing to capture it, they then try desperately to gain the privilege of a local *première*. Britten is the central and dominating figure of what is now one of England's most significant music festivals (at Aldeburgh), a further opportunity for him to present his music under the best possible auspices and before audiences come from far and wide to pay him homage. As one of his compatriots and colleagues once remarked, with more than just a touch of envy: "Britten has only to sneeze and it's immediately published, performed, and recorded."

How highly Britten is regarded in his own country was demonstrated when he became the only composer ever commissioned to write an opera for an English coronation (*Gloriana,* in 1953), once again, in 1965, when he was given the Order of Merit, and in June of 1976 when he recieved a life peerage, becoming Baron Britten of Aldeburgh. Honors have also come to him from other countries. In America he became in 1964 the first recipient of the Aspen Award of $30,000 for his contributions "to the advancement of the humanities."

His father was a dental surgeon, his mother an excellent amateur pianist and singer. "My parents' house directly faced the sea," he has written, "and my childhood was colored by the fierce storms that sometimes drove ships onto our coast and ate away whole stretches of the neighboring cliffs." The sea has left its impress on his two finest operas, *Peter Grimes* and *Billy Budd.* Britten has always remained partial to the sea. This is why he makes his home where he can see and smell it every day.

He was so extraordinarily precocious in music that his exploits inevitably invited comparison with those of the child Mozart. *"Pay pano,"* he would whimper when he was only two years old, which meant that he wanted to be taken to the piano. After his mother began teaching him, he monopolized the piano to such an extent that he was the despair of an older brother and two sisters who also wanted to play. In his seventh year he took scores of symphonies and operas to bed to read them with the open-eyed fascination children now usually reserve for comic books. Two years later he completed the writing of an oratorio and a string quartet. By the time he was sixteen he had produced a symphony, six quartets, ten piano sonatas, and many smaller works. It is interesting to remark that Britten thought well enough of some of the melodic material in these childhood efforts to use it in a comparatively mature work entitled *Simple Symphony,* completed in 1934.

Besides studying the piano, Britten began taking lessons on the viola when he was ten, with Audrey Alston. His academic education took place at South Lodge, a preparatory school. During this time, in 1926, he was Frank Bridge's pupil in composition. Frank Bridge (1879–1941) was an eminent English composer. His influence on Britten's early development was profound, as Britten himself readily confesses; and up to the time of his death Bridge remained the young man's friend and adviser.

For two years, beginning in 1928, Britten attended the Gresham School in Holt, Norfolk, where he was adept at mathematics, the sciences, cricket, and tennis. In 1930, a scholarship brought him to the Royal College of Music in London for his first intensive training in music. For three years he studied composition with John Ireland and piano with Arthur Benjamin and Harold Samuel. He was a remarkable pupil, continually amazing his teachers with his facility in learning his lessons and his instinctively correct judgment. The music he was writing, and the important places where it was getting performed, provided convincing testimony of his developing creative powers. His first works to receive major performances were the Phantasy Quartet and three two-part songs for women's voices on texts by Walter de la Mare. Both were introduced in London on December 12, 1932. In 1933, his first publication made an appearance, a Sinfonietta for Orchestra, which was performed in London on January 31, 1933.

Soon after leaving the Royal College of Music, Britten made further significant strides as composer with the choral variations *A Boy Was Born,* heard first in a radio broadcast over the BBC on February 23, 1934. During that same year, on April 5, his Phantasy Quartet for

Oboe and Strings represented England at the festival of the International Society for Contemporary Music at Florence.

His father's death compelled him to find ways and means of earning a living while he was working on his compositions. Between 1935 and 1939 he was employed at the Government Post Office Film Unit, where he wrote background or incidental music for sixteen documentary films. He also contributed several scores for commercially produced motion pictures, including *Love from a Stranger*.

On April 21, 1936, Britten was once again heard at a festival of the International Society for Contemporary Music, this time with his Suite for Violin and Piano, performed at Barcelona. His first major success, however, came with the Variations on a Theme by Frank Bridge, for orchestra, whose *première* performance was given at the Salzburg Festival in Austria on August 27, 1937. In a review of these variations for *Modern Music,* Aaron Copland wrote: "The piece is what we would call a knock-out." Following its *première* in London in 1938, and in the United States in 1939, the Variations went a long way in establishing Britten's reputation.

With war in Europe imminent, Britten—an ardent pacifist—decided to settle in the United States. He arrived in time to hear the American *première* of his Variations in New York. For six months he shared a Brooklyn apartment with the poet W. H. Auden. Living there proved a hectic affair: Poets, musicians, and theatrical people drifted in and out at all hours, not only using it as a convenient rendezvous, but frequently living there for extended periods. He had to find a quieter refuge if he expected to write any music. After a brief visit to California in 1941 he moved into a private house in Amityville, Long Island, where he remained three years.

Among the major works written during this extended stay in the United States were a violin concerto, a song cycle for high voice and orchestra to poems by Arthur Rimbaud (*Les Illuminations*), an opera (*Paul Bunyan*), and an important work for orchestra (*Sinfonia da Requiem*). The opera, libretto by W. H. Auden, was produced at Columbia University in May of 1941 and—as he put it—was "politely spat at." The Sinfonia had been commissioned by the Japanese Government to help celebrate the twenty-six-hundredth anniversary of the Japanese Imperial Dynasty, which rejected it in November 1940 on the grounds that it was "too Christian" in treatment (though the international situation was also a factor). It became instead a memorial to Britten's father. Introduced by the New York Philharmonic under John Barbirolli on March 29, 1941, it was a major success.

In 1942 Britten decided to go home. The war was going badly for England. The terrible blitz was inflicting havoc on his countrymen. He felt he had to do what he could toward furthering the war effort without sacrificing his pacifist ideals.

While awaiting passage to England he attended a performance of his Sinfonia da Requiem in Boston under Koussevitzky. The conductor approached him with the idea of writing a new opera. Britten confessed that both the theater and vocal music interested him greatly, that despite the failure of *Paul Bunyan* he was not unwilling to consider an opera project. Koussevitzky then gave him a commission through the Koussevitzky Music Foundation.

Back in England, Britten appeared before the Tribunal of Conscientious Objectors and was exempted from military duty. But he was ready to do his part out of uniform. He performed in hospitals, bomb-proof shelters, and bombed-out villages. During this period he worked on his new opera for the Koussevitzky Music Foundation. That opera—it was *Peter Grimes*—was introduced at the Sadler's Wells Theater in London on June 7, 1945. The theater was reopening after five years—having been closed by Nazi bombs in 1940. Resumption of activity by Sadler's Wells and the first *première* of an English opera in several years combined to make the performance of *Peter Grimes* an event of outstanding significance. Anticipation ran so high that there were some who doubted that the opera could possibly live up to expectations. Twenty-four hours before curtain time the queues sprouted in front of the theater. Long before the zero hour all tickets had been sold—not only for the *première,* but for all the performances scheduled. The notables of the music world were present, as well as correspondents from most of the great newspapers and syndicates of the world.

As the opera began, the excitement and tension mounted. The music was complex and subtle and harmonically modern, not the kind that can be fully appreciated at a single hearing. But its dramatic impact was so inescapable that the audience sat spellbound. The American writer Edmund Wilson, who had gone to that performance reluctantly, described his own reaction in *Europe Without*

Baedeker: "The opera seizes on you, possesses you, keeps you riveted to your seat during the action and keyed up during the intermissions, and drops you, purged and exhausted, at the end." Between each act a shower of bouquets descended on the stage from the gallery until the floor was carpeted with flowers. Then the opera was over. A thunderous five-minute ovation greeted the composer, and innumerable curtain calls were demanded from conductor and singers. "It is a milestone in modern opera," wrote the correspondent of the New York *Times*.

Peter Grimes brought to Britten international fame and a dominating position among English composers. In a short period it was heard more than a hundred times in most of the European countries, translated into eight languages. On August 6, 1946, it received its first American performance—in Tanglewood, in Lenox, Massachusetts, under the direction of Leonard Bernstein. On February 12, 1948, it was given by the Metropolitan Opera Association.

Britten's fame was further extended and his position further solidified during the next few years with the writing of three other fine operas: *The Rape of Lucretia, Albert Herring,* and *Billy Budd*. He produced fine works in other forms too, the most important being *The Young Person's Guide to the Orchestra,* the *Spring* Symphony, the cantata *Saint Nicolas,* and the Second String Quartet. Two of these works scored a major success. One was the *Spring* Symphony, for soloists, chorus, and orchestra. Commissioned by the Koussevitzky Music Foundation, it was introduced at the Holland Music Festival on July 14, 1949, and received a tremendous ovation. "The cheers of 3,000 persons who jammed Amsterdam's Concert Hall," reported Daniel L. Schorr in the New York *Times*, "showed that this was the great event of the festival." There was also an ovation when the *Spring* Symphony was heard in this country for the first time, at the Berkshire Music Festival at Tanglewood, under Serge Koussevitzky, on August 13 of the same year.

Two years after the *Spring* Symphony came *Billy Budd,* Britten's most ambitious opera since *Peter Grimes. Billy Budd* had been commissioned for the Festival of Britain and was introduced in conjunction with that festival on December 1, 1951, the composer conducting. It had been preceded by immense ballyhoo, as was perhaps to be expected of a work by England's foremost opera composer. *Billy Budd* was recognized as an important and original opera, even by those who expressed reservations on details. As Stephen Williams reported from London to the New York *Times:* "*Billy Budd* is a challenging, stimulating work of art quite able to stand on its own merits without a lot of hysterical ballyhoo." The original Covent Garden cast, conducted by Britten, brought *Billy Budd* to Paris on May 25, 1952, as a major attraction of the Exposition of Masterpieces of the Twentieth Century. In the same year it was introduced to the United States on the television screen over the NBC network. *Billy Budd* was followed by *Gloriana,* an opera about Elizabeth and Essex, which Britten wrote on a commission from the Crown for the coronation festivities in London in 1953; it was introduced at Covent Garden on June 8 of that year with Queen Elizabeth II attending.

From 1948 until his death, Britten's home was at Aldeburgh, in Suffolk, at the fringe of the sea that had come to mean so much to him. It is only twenty miles along the coast from the town where Britten was born. In Aldeburgh he occupied a spacious, impressive rose-colored brick manor equipped with an outdoor swimming pool which Britten used several times a day in warm weather. Swimming was only one of several forms of exercise that helped to keep him in trim. He habitually took long walks along the beach or in the country, usually dressed in baggy slacks and sweater, his hands in his pockets, his face tense with concentration. He also liked to play tennis and badminton. Another less strenuous form of relaxation came from driving his high-powered car at breakneck speeds.

His life followed a well-grooved pattern. Work at composition took place all morning in a crowded studio above the stage; exercise and relaxation in the afternoon; more work at composition following afternoon tea. Another musical activity besides composition absorbed Britten's energies a good part of each year: the planning and preparation of an annual festival at Aldeburgh. He had helped to create this festival in 1947 as a home for the English Opera Group which he then organized (and which he has since conducted in major music centers of the world), a group formed to present experimental chamber operas. Since then the Aldeburgh Festival, which takes place annually in June, has expanded its activities to embrace concerts, operas, lectures, art exhibits, poetry readings. To celebrate the twentieth anniversary of its founding, a new auditorium, the Snape Concert Hall, was dedicated in 1967 in the presence of Queen Elizabeth II. Through the years, Britten's music was a principal attraction of the festival—often world *premières* of important works—performances in which, to be sure, Britten involved himself deeply both as conductor and as pianist. In addition to his performing activities at Aldeburgh, Britten also made many appearances as pianist and conductor elsewhere, generally, though not exclusively, in the presentation of his own music. He made numerous appearances as piano accompanist for the English tenor Peter Pears in song recitals, their American debut having taken place on October 23, 1949.

From his Aldeburgh studio came significant compositions in all forms. Some commanding world attention were the opera *The Turn of the Screw,* based on Henry James, introduced at the Venice Festival on September 14, 1954; the ballet *The Prince of Pagodas,* first heard at Covent Garden on January 1, 1957; the opera *A Midsummer Night's Dream,* given at Aldeburgh on June 11, 1960; and the opera *Death in Venice,* based on Thomas Mann's novella, first heard at Aldeburgh on June 16, 1973.

One of the greatest successes Britten enjoyed since *Peter Grimes* came not from an opera but from a choral composition, *A War Requiem.* This is an eloquent expression of Britten's own anti-war sentiments whose text is partly based on the traditional Mass, and partly on poems by Wilfred Owen. Following its world *première* on May 30, 1962, at Coventry, England, *A War Requiem* was given a hearing the world over, its American *première* taking place at the Berkshire Music Festival on July 27, 1963. Everywhere it has been acclaimed as a monument in twentieth-century choral music; and there are some critics who look upon it as Britten's crowning masterwork. One of them, Irving Kolodin, in the *Saturday Review* regarded it as "a work more dramatic than any opera Britten has composed, rising through successive climaxes to a *Libera me Domine* which can best be described as a frenetic outcry, musically conveyed by resources hitherto unsuspected in the composer."

Without abandoning opera, Britten experimented successfully with a more intimate religious kind of stage-music medium, "church parables." His primary consideration in developing this musicodramatic form was primarily a practical one—to get more performances for his stage works. "What's the use of writing English operas when there are no English opera houses in which to perform them?" he asked. "On the other hand, almost every town, not to say village, has one of those old Gothic churches in which this form of writing can flourish and involve the local musicians as performers." With this in mind he wrote *Curlew River,* a medieval miracle play based on a Japanese Noh drama, and *The Burning Fiery Furnace* and *The Prodigal Son,* the latter two with their source in the Bible. All three were introduced at Aldeburgh, on June 13, 1964, June 9, 1966, and June 10, 1968 respectively.

During his last three years, Britten suffered from a severe heart condition. He returned to his home at Aldeburgh from the hospital three weeks before his death, to die there on December 4, 1976. "Thankfully," said his friend, Donald Mitchell, who was with him when he died, "the end was peaceful for him."

HIS MUSIC

Variety is the spice of his music. Although he is most famous for his dramatic works, he has also produced many symphonic, choral, vocal, and chamber music works. His style is as varied as his media. He can be modern and dissonant, as in many pages of *Peter Grimes* and *The Turn of the Screw,* and he can realize a medieval atmosphere as in *A Ceremony of Carols* and *Curlew River.* He can produce music full of regal pomp and circumstance, as in *Gloriana.* He can write with a most engaging simplicity and purity, as in *Simple Symphony* and his children's work, *Let's Make an Opera,* and then he can weave a complex polyphonic texture in his large choral works, such as *A War Requiem.* He can be romantic and poetic, as in the *Spring* Symphony, and witty and satirical, as in *Albert Herring.*

In short, the artistic work he is producing dictates his style. The salient point is that—regardless of what form he selects or the idiom he employs—he is always the master of his trade, writing with force, conviction, clarity, technical skill, and inspiration.

ANALYTICAL NOTES

Choral Music. Britten's two most ambitious works for chorus, solo voices, and orchestra are the *Spring* Symphony, Op. 44 (1949), and *A War Requiem,* Op. 66 (1962).

In the *Spring* Symphony (for soprano, tenor, mixed chorus, boys' chorus, and orchestra), Britten took fourteen poems about springtime and dressed them in music that has warmth and the character of Elizabethan madrigals. The fourteen numbers are gathered into four sections to simulate the four movements of a symphony. First there is an introduction, a setting of the sixteenth-century poem "Shine Out, Fair Sun, with All Your Heat." The first section has the expansive nature of an opening movement of a symphony. Five poems are here treated: "The Merry Cuckoo," by Edmund Spenser, for tenor and three muted trumpets; "Spring, the Sweet Spring," by Thomas Nashe, for mixed chorus and orchestra; "Driving Boy," by John Clare, and "When As the Rye," by George Peele, both for boys' chorus and orchestra; and "Morning Star," by John Milton, for mixed chorus, brass, and percussion.

The second section, which has the character of a slow movement, comprises three poems: "Welcome Maids of Honor," by Robert Herrick, for alto, woodwinds, and divided strings; "The Shower," by Henry Vaughan, for tenor solo and violins; and "Out on the Lawn," by W. H. Auden, for alto, chorus, winds, and percussion.

The third part has the quality of a scherzo. Like the preceding movement, it is built out of three poems: "When Will My May Come," by Richard Barnfield, for tenor solo with strings; "Fair as Fair," by George Peele, a duet for soprano and tenor with woodwinds and strings accompanying; and "Sound the Flute," by William Blake, for chorus and orchestra.

In the finale only two verses appear, and these are sung contrapuntally. The first, by Beaumont and Fletcher, is "London to Thee I Do Present," for full chorus and orchestra. This is set against "Summer Is Icumen In," the thirteenth-century English round, for boys' chorus.

A War Requiem was commissioned for a festival celebrating the consecration of the restored St. Michael's Cathedral at Coventry. Coventry, to be sure, is the Warwickshire town which was virtually obliterated by a Nazi air attack in November of 1940. This fact was very much on Britten's mind in writing *A War Requiem,* which he made a voice of his passionate pacificism. He prepared a text by taking part of his material from the traditional *Missa pro Defunctis* and part from poems by Wilfred Owen, a poet killed during World War I who was decorated with the Military Cross for bravery. Owen's lines were bitterly anti-war—a scathing indictment of the cruelty and the futility of mass murder. Some of Owen's lines appear in the published score as a motto: "My subject is War, and the pity of War. The Poetry is in the pity. All a poet can do today is warn."

In fashioning his text Britten follows a section of the Latin missal text with one of Owen's poems. For example, the work begins with the *Requiem aeternam* of the Mass and then continues with verses beginning with the line "What passing-bells for these who die as cattle?" In the second part, the text of the *Dies irae* alternates with verses beginning with the lines "Bugles sang, sadd'ning the evening air," "Out there, we've walked quite friendly up to Death," "Be slowly lifted up, thou long black arm," and "Move him, Move him into the sun." A good deal of the emotional impact of the composition as a whole springs from this unusual marriage of the ritual and the secular, of this juxtaposition of a part of the Mass with its solemn overtones and Owen's anti-war poems with their expression of protest and utter despair.

Britten calls upon three performing groups: the full chorus, orchestra, and soprano for the sections from the Mass; a boys' choir for parts of the Mass; a solo tenor, solo baritone, and a small chamber orchestra for Owen's verses, which are presented in recitative style.

Britten has also written a number of distinguished smaller works for chorus. The most famous is *A Ceremony of Carols,* Op. 28 (1942), scored for treble voices and harp obbligato. This composition begins with a procession in which the choristers march up the aisles of the church singing about Christ's birth. This is followed by nine medieval carols. The composition ends with a recession, in which the choristers leave the church, singing the same music they had presented in the opening procession.

Operas. Britten's chef-d'oeuvre is the work that made him world-famous—the opera *Peter Grimes,* Op. 33 (1945), based on George Crabbe's poem *The Borough,* which Montagu Slater adapted into a libretto. The subject of man's cruelty to man, of a human being victimized and destroyed by injustice and hate, was something close to Britten's heart. The central character is a fisherman, Peter Grimes, who is accused of having murdered his apprentice. Though he is proved innocent at the trial, he remains an object of suspicion among his townspeople. Their silent accusation makes him surly and ugly of mood, even to Ellen Orford, the woman with whom he is in love. He engages a new apprentice who is killed accidentally. The suspicious townspeople are now certain that Peter Grimes is a murderer. They descend on his lonely fishing hut with hate in their hearts. Rather than confront an angry mob he goes out to meet his death in the sea. "Grimes represents man against a narrow society," Britten has explained. "He is a little different; he has a little more imagination. You have to sense his pride and his helplessness."

This grim and relentless tragedy evoked from Britten music of overwhelming power. The stark fatalism is echoed in a score that is high-tensioned, realistic, surging with dramatic force. Yet other passages are poetic, sensitive, even tender. For, as F. Bonavia wrote, "Britten has found the right symbol for every situation."

His style is varied, now simple and lyrical (Ellen Orford's soliloquy at the end of the first scene) and now piercingly dissonant (the "Storm" interlude). It is filled with ingenious jigs and salty sea chanteys of naïve folk-song character and also with complex polyrhythmic choruses (the "Boar" scene in Act I). There is fully developed song (the trio in the second act) and there is a continuous flow of acrid song-speech. But varied though the means are, the result is a unified work of art, evoking the sea, the fishing town, the humble fishing folk—background for the relentless tragedy of a man crushed by an implacable fate.

Five orchestral interludes from *Peter Grimes* are sometimes performed at orchestral concerts. In the opera they are played with the curtain lowered and are remarkably effective in establishing a mood, etching a background, or suggesting conflicts to come. "Dawn" comes between the Prologue and Act I, to portray a fishing town alive with preparation for the day's activities. "The Storm," between the first and second scenes of the same act, re-creates the blind fury of a gale, probably symbolic of the equally blind fury of an angry mob. "Sunday Morning" prefaces Act II and is descriptive of the serenity of a fishing village echoing with the ringing of church bells. "Passacaglia" separates the two scenes of Act II, forewarning of the coming struggle between Grimes and the mob. "Moonlight," introducing Act III, once again brings up a picture of peace, as the village is bathed in darkness.

The Rape of Lucretia, Op. 57, which came in 1946, is as grimly realistic and as starkly tragic as its predecessor. But it is a more intimate opera of slighter proportions. There are only six characters, and the two so-called "choruses" consist of one man and one woman. The orchestra comprises merely twelve instruments. And Britten's writing is as lean and economical as his forces, usually lyrical (as in Tarquinius' lullaby that opens the second act, "Within this frail crucible"), often atmospheric or pictorial (as in the orchestral episode describing Tarquinius' horseback ride). The text, which Ronald Duncan adapted from André Obey's *Le Viol de Lucrèce,* concerns the seduction of Lucretia, wife of the Roman general Collatinus, by the Etruscan prince Tarquinius.

Britten's next opera, *Albert Herring,* Op. 39 (1947), was far different in style and approach. The text by Eric Crozier, a free adaptation of Maupassant's story "Le Rosier de Madame Husson," is unashamedly a broad farce. Albert Herring, selected King of the May because of his great virtue and chastity, becomes inebriated when a practical joker pours rum into his lemonade. He goes in search of pleasures he has so long denied himself. When his orange-blossom wreath is found trampled in the road the townsfolk believe him dead, and hymn his passing. But Albert Herring returns—dirty, disheveled, confused, but idyllically happy. This gay tale finds its counterpart in the score. Within the formal *opera buffa* structure of arias, recitatives, duets, and ensemble numbers, Britten has released music of wit, satire, broad burlesque, and even parody. One of the amusing moments in the score finds Britten quoting the love potion music from Wagner's *Tristan and Isolde,* at the point in the play where Albert Herring drinks his lemonade spiked with rum.

There is a great deal in *Billy Budd,* Op. 50 (1951), to remind us of *Peter Grimes.* Both operas have the large dimensions of grand opera and require large musical forces and elaborate stage sets. Both operas have the sea for a setting and make effective use of sea chanteys. The basic theme of both is man's suffering at the hands of tyrannical oppression and injustice.

Billy Budd is based on the celebrated story of Herman Melville, which E. M. Forster and Eric Rozier adapted into a libretto. The central character, Billy Budd, is a sailor on a British vessel during the war of England against France in the eighteenth century. Arousing the displeasure of John Claggart, the master-at-arms, Billy Budd becomes the victim of flagrant injustice when Claggart falsely accuses him of treason. In a fit of uncontrolled anger, Budd kills his accuser. For this he must pay with his life. But even the man who must pass sentence on him, Captain Vere, recognizes that injustice has been done.

Billy Budd is an unusual opera in several ways. It calls for an all-male cast, and must therefore sacrifice love interest in the drama and the lighter texture of female voices in the music. It avoids lyricism in favor of a brittle kind of recitative that can allow the action fluidity of movement; arias and ensemble numbers are reduced to a bare minimum. The orchestra is unorthodox, requiring pipes, drums, bugles (to portray the atmosphere aboard a ship), and the wail of a saxophone (to portray the brutality of some of the officers). At one point, immediately after Budd is condemned to die, the stage is entirely empty, while the orchestra takes over the dramatic action with disconnected triads; at another point the orchestra is completely dispensed with, as the opera ends with an unaccompanied monologue.

With *The Turn of the Screw,* Op. 54 (1954), Britten returns to the intimate style and modest dimensions of *The Rape of Lucretia.* In a prologue and sixteen scenes (divided into two acts), *The Turn of the Screw* calls for six voices and a chamber orchestra of fifteen players. However, the horror story by Henry James upon which it is based, adapted by Myfanwy Piper, calls for Britten's fullest resources as a composer, and he meets the challenge with the conviction and authority of a master. The story itself concerns two children, afflicted by an evil curse and haunted by two ghosts. Despite the protection of a neurotic governess, they finally meet a tragic doom. Britten's atmospheric and at times impressionistic writing, his subtle characterizations, and a telling ability to build up a climactic scene help to create a musical drama of overwhelming impact. An interesting musical innovation in the opera is the use of the theme-and-variations technique. Each scene is preceded by an orchestral episode, a variation of a twelve-note theme made up of fourths and thirds; these episodes serve as an orchestral commentary on the stage action.

A Midsummer Night's Dream, Op. 64 (1960), is once again in an ambitious design, summoning large musical forces and elaborate stage techniques. The adaptation of Shakespeare's play—made by the composer in collaboration with Peter Pears—keeps only half of the original. Nevertheless, all of Shakespeare's lines are kept intact (except for a single line of transition). The opera functions on three levels: the worlds of the fairies, the rustics, and the lovers. With his remarkable resiliency, Britten adapts his musical style for each with light-fingered, subtle episodes for the fairies, arioso-kind of recitatives reminiscent of Italian opera for the rustics, and a highly romantic idiom for the lovers. The music is always Britten's own. He made no attempt to re-create Shakespeare's times and background through simulation of old English folk songs and dances.

Orchestral Music. The *Variations on a Theme by Frank Bridge,* Op. 10 (1937), was Britten's first successful work, and it is still one of his finest compositions for the orchestra. The theme, which is the second of Bridge's *Three Idylls,* is heard in the first violins after a brief introduction of chords, trills, and runs. There are ten variations. The first, Adagio, consists of soft chords in the strings. A march follows, with the theme appearing sharply rhythmic in the lower strings. The basses take over the theme with plucked strings in the Romance, while in Aria Italiana it becomes a caricature of a Rossini aria. Two more caricatures follow: Bourrée Classique and Wiener Waltz. The theme is heard in unison strings tremolando in Moto Perpetuo. Two lyrical and emotional variations are now heard, entitled respectively Funeral March and Chant. The last variation consists of a fugue in which the entire exposition is in unison, with each group of the orchestra participating.

The *Sinfonia da Requiem*, Op. 20 (1940), became the composer's memorial to his father. Britten explains: "The Latin titles, indicating the mood and scheme of the work, derive from the Catholic Requiem Mass, though the relation of the Sinfonia to the Catholic ceremony, avowedly, is emotional rather than liturgical." The first movement is *Lacrymosa,* a slow funeral march. This is built out of three motives: The first, syncopated, is heard in the cellos and developed by solo bassoon; the second is a spacious melody for strings; the third comprises chords for flute and trombones set against an accompaniment by piano and harps. There is an impressive climax, based on the first theme, after which the second movement, *Dies irae* enters without pause. Flutes introduce the main subject, which develops into a series of dramatic climaxes. After the most impressive of these is dissipated the final section, *Requiem aeternam* is heard, once again without pause. A beautiful melody for flutes is heard against solo strings and harp. The lyrical character is sustained until the work ends quietly with a prolonged note for clarinet.

The Young Person's Guide to the Orchestra, Op. 34 (1945), is functional music for children. However, the musical treatment is so rich and varied that this orchestral work has often been heard at symphony concerts. The purpose here is to teach children the different instruments of the orchestra. This work was commissioned by the English Ministry of Education for an educational film, in which a spoken commentary is interpolated before each section to describe the instrument or instruments about to be heard. At concerts, the narrative is dispensed with.

Britten's scheme is a theme for variation, each variation built for a different instrument or group of instruments. The theme is taken from the rondeau of Henry Purcell's incidental music to *Abdelazar*. It is given by the full orchestra. Then choirs of the orchestra are introduced, first the woodwinds, followed by the brass, the strings, and the percussion. Once again the Purcell theme is heard in full orchestra. Thirteen variations on this theme present the instruments in the following sequence: flutes and piccolo; oboes; clarinets; bassoons; strings; violas; cellos; double basses; harp; French horns; trumpets; trombones; tympani and other percussion instruments. With the variations over, there begins a fugue in which the instruments return in the order in which they appeared in the variations. The composition ends with a final statement of the Purcell melody.

Britten has written two significant works for voice and orchestra. *Les Illuminations,* Op. 18 (1939), is for high voice and string orchestra. This is a setting of ten decadent prose poems of the symbolist poet Rimbaud. This composition was used for a one-act ballet, with choreography by Frederick Ashton, produced by the New York City Ballet in 1950.

The Serenade for Tenor, Horn, and String Orchestra Op. 31 (1943), sets to music poems by Tennyson, Blake, Cotton, Ben Jonson, and Keats. The work begins with a prologue for horn solo. Edward Sackville-West thus describes the context of the poems that follow: "The subject is Night and its prestigia, the lengthening shadow, the distant haze at sunset, the Baroque panoply of the starry sky, the heavy angles of sleep; but also the cloak of evil—the worm in the heart of the rose, the sense of sin in the heart of man. The whole sequence forms an elegy or Nocturnal (as Donne would have called it) reviewing the thoughts and images suitable to the evening." Following the presentation of the songs there comes an epilogue in which the horn solo heard in the prologue is sounded offstage.

Anton Bruckner

"It is no common mortal who speaks to us in this music."

LUDWIG SPEIDEL

BORN: Ansfelden, Austria, September 4, 1824.
DIED: Vienna, October 11, 1896.
MAJOR WORKS: *Chamber Music*—String Quintet in F major.
Choral Music—3 Masses; Requiem in D minor; Te Deum;
Ave Marias, cantatas, male choruses, hymns, offertories, and
psalms. *Orchestral Music*—9 symphonies (the ninth unfinished);
Overture in G minor.

HIS LIFE

A single star guided the course of Bruckner's life: Richard Wagner.
There was something decidedly neurotic about the younger man's
adoration and reverence for the master. Before he had met Wagner he
would stare for hours at him in silent adoration without having the
courage to approach him. On first meeting him, Bruckner insisted on
remaining in an erect, standing position throughout a long interview; to sit in the august presence of his personal god was unthinkable. After hearing *Parsifal* he fell on his knees before Wagner
and exclaimed, "Master—I worship you." And after Wagner's death
he never visited Bayreuth without paying attendance at Wagner's grave
and weeping.

Wagner was the source of his creative strength, his inspiration, the
touchstone of his own life and efforts. Wagner, the cause of his
exaltation was also to be—though indirectly—the reason for his greatest

suffering. The savage and frequently irresponsible battles fought in the name of Wagner in Vienna often victimized the innocent. Because Bruckner had identified himself so unmistakably with the Wagnerian cause, he became the object for the most violent attacks on the part of those powerful forces in Vienna bent on destroying Wagner and Wagnerism. Eventually the triumph of Wagner in Vienna was complete, creating an atmosphere in which Bruckner could be appraised without venom or prejudice; and, by the same token, eventually Bruckner came into his own.

He stemmed from a family of humble schoolteachers. It was for the teaching profession that he was trained, though an exceptional talent for music and a pronounced distaste for all other subjects were evident in him from childhood. He was playing the violin and composing tunes when he was only four. His talent impressed his cousin, who began teaching him to play the organ, together with composition and theory. In his thirteenth year, on the death of his father, Bruckner was sent to the secular music school of St. Florian as choirboy. There, for a period of four years, he received an intensive musical training. The original plan to make him a schoolteacher was not abandoned. After leaving St. Florian in 1840, Brucker took a ten-month course at the teachers' preparatory school in Linz. He assumed his first teaching position in the mountain village of Windhaag; his salary was about a dollar a month, and his duties included helping out in the fields in his spare time. He was not a very good teacher and he was negligent about his duties in the fields. Before long he was transferred to a smaller school, in nearby Kornsdorf.

Having passed all the examinations for a teaching license, Bruckner was recalled to St. Florian in 1845 to join the faculty of the music school. His official duties did not interfere with musical activity. He played the organ unceasingly, became a virtuoso of the first order, and developed a gift at improvisation which was later to command the admiration, and sometimes even the awe, of Europe's leading musicians. He also started composing in earnest, producing his first large and ambitious work, the Requiem in D minor, which was performed at St. Florian's on March 13, 1849.

By 1853 he had decided irrevocably to give up teaching for music. He settled in Vienna and began to study counterpoint with Simon Sechter. He was so conscientious in his application to study (for one lesson he arrived with a dozen notebooks filled with exercises) that

Sechter had to warn him not to overtax himself. "I never had a more serious pupil than you," the teacher added. Bruckner also worked hard on harmony, fugue, and thorough bass. At last he felt ready to submit to the severest trial a Viennese musician of that period could face: a test conducted by a commission comprising five outstanding musicians. The commission submitted to him a theme on which he improvised with such skill and inventiveness that Johann Herbeck, one of the judges, exclaimed, "He knows more than all of us together."

In 1856 Bruckner became organist at the Linz Cathedral, a post he held for a dozen years. While he lived in Linz he maintained contact with Vienna by regular visits. In 1860 he was appointed musical director of a Viennese choral society, with which organization he made his Vienna bow as a composer. On May 12, 1861, he directed the *première* of his Ave Maria, for seven-part chorus.

The year of 1863 was decisive in Bruckner's life. It was then that he heard for the first time a performance of a Wagnerian opera, *Tannhäuser*. Suddenly he became dissatisfied with his own work and sought the new expression and the drama he had encountered in Wagner's music. He did not abandon the writing of church music, but he now brought to it a new independence, a new romanticism, as well as traces of Wagnerian mannerisms. The first such work was the Mass in D major, which was introduced at the Linz Cathedral on November 20, 1864.

In 1865 he was one of the pilgrims to head for Munich to attend the world *première* of Wagner's *Tristan and Isolde*. With that experience his worship of Wagner became complete. He now met Wagner personally; one can hardly guess what inner conflict took place before he could bring himself face to face with the master! Timidly he showed Wagner the sketches of a first symphony. Wagner appeared to be impressed with both the symphony and the hero worship, and treated Bruckner with genuine warmth of feeling. Bruckner was so touched that he found it difficult to suppress tears of gratitude.

When he was appointed professor of counterpoint and organ at the Vienna Conservatory, in 1868, Bruckner made a permanent home for himself in the Austrian capital. For the rest of his life he was to occupy the some small three-room apartment, attended to by his conscientious maid, Kathi. Ever concerned over her master, she tried to keep him safe from visitors when she knew he was working; and she tried solicitously to nag him into doing his work in the mornings and reserving the night for sleep.

His first few years in Vienna formed a period of trial and humiliation. Attempts to get a performance for his Mass in F minor proved futile, on the grounds that it was "unsingable." He was more fortunate with the Symphony No. 1 in C minor, in that it was accepted for performance in Linz on May 9, 1868, but neither the audience nor the critics liked it. He had to pay eight months of his salary to hire the Vienna Philharmonic to play his long-neglected Mass in F minor in 1872, and almost a year's salary for a performance of his Symphony No. 2 in C minor in 1873. Despite these sacrifices the concerts did little to enhance his reputation. "I have been compelled to borrow money over and over again or accept the alternative of starvation," he complained in one of his letters.

With his Symphony No. 3 in D minor, which he dedicated to Wagner, Bruckner began to feel the full brunt of Viennese hostility. The anti-Wagner forces now found a logical victim on which to concentrate their attacks. The most indefatigable attacker was Vienna's powerful critic Eduard Hanslick, who described Bruckner's Second Symphony as "insatiable rhetoric." A leading official of the Conservatory solicitously advised Bruckner to throw his symphonies in "a trash basket" and to turn his talent to making piano arrangements! The Third Symphony, accepted by the Vienna Philharmonic, was discarded after a single rehearsal; all the musicians of the orchestra, with a single exception, were opposed to playing the work.

Later, on December 16, 1877, when the Third Symphony was performed in Vienna, it had to be conducted by the composer himself, as no one else wanted to do it. The directors of the Conservatory burst into audible laughter as the music was being played. Others in the audience began expressing their disapproval with loud jeers. Before long, so many people in the audience had left the auditorium in indignation that by the time the symphony was over there were only a handful left. When, after the concluding chord, Bruckner turned around to accept the applause, he saw, to his bewilderment, that there were only twenty-five people left in the large auditorium— seven of them in the parterre. He remained rooted to his platform in a daze, the tears streaming down his cheeks. As he stood there the musicians discreetly made their withdrawal from the stage. A few of the younger men ran up to him, one of them Gustav Mahler, to express their admiration. But Bruckner remained frozen in his place. At last he brushed aside his admirers with the brusque remark, in his peculiar Austrian dialect, *"Lasst mi aus, die Leut woll'n nix von mir wissen"*—"Let me go. The people don't want to know anything of me."

If he was attacked, it was not only because of his music and his allegiance to Wagner. There was something both ludicrous and revolting about him physically. His face was too large for the body, and he wore clothes absurdly too large for the frame. As he walked in the streets of Vienna—his ugly face tense, his eyes gleaming—he appeared almost a caricature of an artist or a mystic. He was the peasant in the great city, and he made no effort to disguise it, never abandoning his small-town wardrobe or his rural accent. Awkward and boorish in social behavior, naïve as a child, he often encouraged intolerant gibes. But even worse were his sickly humility, his perpetual self-debasement, his obsequiousness. He was always bowing and scraping—even to inferiors. A kind word or a generous act from others evoked from him a gratitude so effusive or tearful as to embarrass the benefactor. Impetuous, and extravagant in expressing his emotions, he often made himself a ridiculous figure. A Viennese critic by the name of Gehring referred to him, to his very face, as a "fool and a half." Far kinder was the remark of Rudolf Louis, who could not forget that this man was also kind and soft by nature, "A man of fine feelings might smile at Bruckner's appearance; he would not laugh at it."

Hatred and contempt surrounded Bruckner, and now the pro-Brahms clique took offense at him because he had criticized the Brahms symphonies unfavorably. The Vienna Philharmonic refused one work after another until, as a measure of self-protection, he swore he would never again submit to it another of his scores. His gaze grew more abstracted; the pathetic body became more bent and servile. Only God, Wagner, and his own music kept him alive. For he never lost faith in himself. Despite his defeats he kept on writing, confident in his creative power. "When God calls me to Him and asks me: 'Where is the talent which I have given you?' Then I shall hold out the rolled-up manuscript of my Te Deum and I know he will be a compassionate judge," he once said. And he felt the same way about his symphonies.

During the trying period in which his music was being rejected so ruthlessly he was also undergoing a series of emotional crises brought on by unsuccessful love affairs. Throughout his life he responded only to very young girls. When he was forty-three he loved a seventeen-year-old girl, Josephine Lang. Her parents' refusal to permit marriage was a blow to him. Thirteen years later he was again in love. On a visit to Oberammergau he met and succumbed to seventeen-year-old Marie Bartl. This time parental blessing was forthcoming. But the girl soon tired of the old, eccentric man and before long would not answer his passionate letters.

In old age he sought out his beloved of former years, Josephine Lang. Discovering that she was the mother of a fourteen-year-old girl he proceeded to fall in love with the daughter. He was humiliated to learn that nothing serious could come out of this affair. And when he was seventy he seriously entertained the idea of marrying a young chambermaid who had been solicitous about his health. Only her stout refusal to embrace his religion frustrated this plan.

Thus his lifelong search for the woman to share his life was never successful. But his equally feverish pursuit after recognition was to have a happier resolution. On February 20, 1881, Hans Richter directed the first performance of the Fourth Symphony in E-flat major. It was received with unqualified enthusiasm—the first time one of his symphonies was favorably accepted. The victory for which he had been waiting so long stirred him deeply. He was in tears as, after the performance, he humbly came to the conductor to express his gratitude. And with childlike ingenuousness he tried to speak what was in his heart by squeezing a Viennese coin into the conductor's hand! "Take it," he said, "and drink a pitcher of beer to my health." Hans Richter thenceforth wore that coin on his watch chain. It was, as he later recalled, "the memento of a day on which I wept."

Even greater enthusiasm greeted Bruckner's Seventh Symphony in E major when that work was introduced in Leipzig on December 30, 1884, under Artur Nikisch. An unnamed critic described Bruckner's reaction to the ovation he received: "One could see from the trembling of his lips, and the sparkling moisture in his eyes, how difficult it was for the old gentleman to suppress his deep emotion. His homely but honest countenance beamed with a warm inner happiness such as can appear only on the face of one who is too goodhearted to succumb to bitterness even under the pressure of the most disheartening circumstances. Having heard this work and now seeing him in person, we asked ourselves in amazement, 'How is it possible that he could remain so long unknown to us?'"

Other performances of the Seventh Symphony followed in rapid succession in several European cities: Hermann Levi conducted it in Munich; Felix Mottl, in Karlsruhe; Karl Muck, in Graz. "It is the most significant symphonic work since 1827," was Hermann Levi's sweeping verdict.

Meanwhile the death of Wagner, in 1883, was a major tragedy to him. He seemed to have had a prophetic warning of that catastrophe. "At one time," he later wrote, "I came home and was very sad. I thought to myself, it is impossible that the Master can live long, and then the Adagio came to my head." The adagio he speaks of is the slow movement, the funeral march, of his Seventh Symphony— one of the noblest pieces of music he was to write. Biographers who are none too exact chronologically have suggested that this threnody was actually inspired by Wagner's death; this of course could not be so, as it was written a year earlier.

Honor now followed honor for Bruckner. In 1891 he received an honorary doctorate from the University of Vienna. Soon after this he was given an imperial insignia by Emperor Franz Joseph. The story goes that the emperor was ready to grant the composer any reasonable request—a house, a pension. With characteristic humility and naïveté, Bruckner could make only one plea. Could the emperor prevail on the critic Hanslick to treat Bruckner's music less harshly in his reviews? But Bruckner did not require the emperor's intercession. On December 18, 1892, at the first performance of the Eighth Symphony in C minor, the Viennese public interceded for him when it booed Hanslick and sent him scurrying out of the auditorium. That performance proved a triumph for Bruckner in other ways too. The emperor sent a wreath to the concert hall, and after the performance contributed fifteen hundred florins to help get the symphony published. Another wreath came from the Wagner Verein, while Johann Strauss II sent a telegram of congratulations.

Less than two years late Bruckner's seventieth birthday became the occasion for celebration throughout all of Austria. After fifty years of the most intense struggle he had won his battle; but it had come none too soon.

On January 12, 1896, he attended a performance of his Te Deum. This was the last time he was to hear one of his works at a public concert. That summer he fell ill. He appeared to have recovered, and was hard at work on the sketches for the finale of his Ninth Symphony, when he complained of a chill. He was helped into bed and given a cup of tea. A few minutes later he was dead.

At the funeral services they played the slow movement of his Seventh Symphony; the requiem he had unconsciously written for Wagner had now become his own. Outside the church stood a man whom Vienna had set as his enemy—Johannes Brahms, now old and sick. For some mysterious reason he refused to enter the church, but he had to pay his last respects. He remained in the street for a while, whispered sadly to a friend "It is my turn soon," and left before the services were over. It is unfortunate that Bruckner could not have been a living witness to Brahms's presence at his funeral, for that surely would have appeared to him the crowning triumph of all.

HIS MUSIC

The Wagnerian imprint on Bruckner's music is unmistakable. Like Wagner, he had a weakness for vastness; his symphonies are of epical design, spacious and monumental. Like Wagner, Bruckner wanted to express sensuous and passionate feelings, to make Herculean leaps toward the grandiose and the sublime. Stylistic traits of harmony and orchestration that are identifiably Wagner's appear in Bruckner again and again; and, as if this were not enough, his symphonies even contain echoes and reminiscences of thematic material originating in the music dramas.

He was influenced and he imitated. This alone would have made Bruckner the provocative figure in music history that he has been— fiercely attacked and just as fiercely defended. But he had other palpable weaknesses. His symphonies are uneven in quality. Time and again he mistook expanse for grandeur, rhetoric for inspiration, declamation for eloquence. Never too critical of his own work, although he was continually revising, he could be tiringly long-winded. With justification he has been called the re-creator of the "baroque" in music—for he piles detail upon detail, and ornament upon ornament, until we often lose sight of his original thought.

And yet, for all his weaknesses, there is strength too. The mystic and the peasant in him speak in his music with often compelling effect. Some of the scherzos and finales of his symphonies are filled with the lusty peasant vigor of the Austrian folk dance; here we have a Bruckner who is infectious, full of spirit, ingratiating. But even finer are many of the slow movements, in which the mystic unfolds his revelations. Now, stripped of pomp and pretentiousness, his music unfolds vistas of beauty and serenity rarely encountered in symphonic literature. In these pages, as Lawrence Gilman once remarked so aptly, "there is a curious intimation of immortality." Gilman went on to say: "These pages are filled with amusing, consolatory tenderness, with a touch of that greatness of style which we sometimes get in the Elizabethans when they speak of death. . . ."

ANALYTICAL NOTES

Choral Music. The profoundly religious man speaks in Bruckner's choral music in the same way that the man who worshiped Wagner is heard in his later symphonies. It was through choral music that Bruckner first made his appearance as a composer—with compositions large and small in which a devout Christian speaks with reverence and humility, where religious ardor is often combined with a strong mysticism. Neville Cardus, in speaking of Bruckner's last two major sacred works—the Te Deum in C major (1884) and the Psalm CL (1892)—describes the composer as a "God-intoxicated man." This is also the Bruckner we encounter in his three Masses, the first of which, in D minor, came in 1864. The most distinguished of this trio of Masses is the third, in F minor (1868). Scored for solo voices, chorus, and orchestra—and divided into six sections—this composition has been identified as the "Grand Mass" because of its ambitious design and because of Bruckner's expansive symphonic style in writing for the orchestra. Here we find a fusion of Bruckner's strongly Romantic temperament with neomedieval tendencies. The music vibrates throughout with spiritual overtones, and on occasion—as in the *Et incarnatus est*—soars to altitudes of eloquence.

Orchestral Music. The first of Bruckner's symphonies to gain wide circulation was the Third in D minor (1878), the one he dedicated to Richard Wagner. Some of the orchestration reveals Wagner's influence (particularly the way Bruckner uses his brass instruments), and a melodic episode or two has a Wagnerian profile. But for the most part this is not a particularly Wagnerian composition. The opening subject of the first movement has two sections, the first heard in horn over tremolo strings, and the second presented loudly by the full orchestra. The subsidiary theme, which comes twenty-four measures later, is divided between the first violins and violas. In the development, a good deal of attention is given to a three-note motive with which the second theme opens, while the coda addresses itself mainly to the horn episode of the first theme. After a two-measure introduction, the slow movement opens with a stately melody. Later in the movement we also hear an effective chorale-like subject for the strings. The scherzo is characteristically Bruckner in that the main subject sounds like an Austrian peasant dance. The finale opens with a somber idea which is soon stated by full orchestra. For contrast, a lyrical passage for flute and clarinet in octaves comes later in the movement.

There are several different versions of this symphony, a fact that requires clarification. Bruckner completed the first one in 1873. Between 1876 and 1877 he revised it for its publication in 1878. Then between 1888 and 1889 he made further changes. It is the second version, the one published in 1878, that we hear most often today, though it is true that on occasion conductors present the 1889 revision.

The Symphony No. 4 in E-flat major, known as the *Romantic* Symphony, is the most assimilable of all Bruckner's symphonic works and consequently has proved to be the most popular. Bruckner himself provided the name *Romantic* two years after he had completed the work; he also drew up some kind of program for his music, a program whose unimportance can best be gauged by the composer's later confession that he had forgotten what he had in mind for the finale. The symphony was completed in 1874. When it was introduced in 1881 it was heard in an elaborately revised version, with an altogether new third movement.

There are two important unifying elements in the symphony. The first is the descending interval of a perfect fifth, with which the opening horn theme begins. This interval appears as part of the main theme of the second movement, in the hunting call of the scherzo, and throughout the last movement. The second element is a rhythmic pattern so often employed by the composer that it is known as the "Bruckner rhythm": two quarter notes followed by a triplet of three

quarter-notes in 4/4 time. The rhythm is first found in the second
main theme of the first movement, in full orchestra. This rhythm is
the spine of the hunting theme of the scherzo movement.

The symphony begins in an atmosphere of rustic beauty, as a
broad theme is heard in the horn against tremolando strings. After
this theme has been taken up by different members of the woodwind
family, the full orchestra announces a second subject, the one with
the "Bruckner rhythm." This idea is discussed for thirty-two measures, whereupon another basic theme is heard, divided between first
violins and violas. These three subjects undergo involved development. The movement ends with a majestic coda in which the opening
horn theme plays a prominent role.

The second movement opens with two measures of muted chords
in the strings, after which a melody of compelling beauty appears in
the cellos. After ten measures the woodwinds adopt the melody
against pizzicato basses. A chorale passage, suggestive of a religious
hymn, is then heard in the strings, a transition to the second principal
melody of the movement, a song for violas against a background of
plucked strings in violins and cellos. After a development of this
basic material a powerful climax is evoked when the third theme,
which had originated in the violas, is blaringly taken up by the brass
against a sweeping tide of sound in the violins. As the movement
draws to a close the music fades away with an expressive passage
for the strings, followed by soft phrases for horn, oboe, and clarinet.
A gentle rumbling of the kettledrums is the background; as the
movement ebbs, only the throb of the drums is heard.

The third movement, a scherzo, is music of the forest and the
hunt. A fanfare for horns is the core of its opening section. The
principal theme of the trio has the buoyancy and spirit of an Austrian
peasant dance; it is heard in flute and clarinet. After the trio the first
section returns in a somewhat concentrated form.

Bruckner utilizes his finale as a kind of summation of all that has
transpired; but new material is continually interpolated. We hear first
a sustained passage for woodwinds and horns against quivering strings.
An echo of the scherzo's hunting theme is brought up by the horns.
Then the principal theme of the movement is thunderingly proclaimed by full orchestra. This material is worked out, brought to a
climax, then allowed to subside until only a few soft pulsations of
the kettledrums are heard. After a pause a few introductory measures

bring on the second main new theme of the movement, played by flutes and clarinets in octaves with a countersubject in the violas; this theme has an emotional affinity to the melodies of the second movement. A powerful *tutti* passage for violins and brass leads to the development of all ideas already stated. A brilliant coda reaches the culminating point in full orchestra. The strings then return with a recollection of the third theme of the first movement. An elegiac melody appears in the horns against muted strings. The feeling now grows more poignant and intense as a crescendo evolves in full orchestra to bring the symphony to a close.

The Symphony No. 7 in E major (1883) is another of Bruckner's symphonies that has gained favor with concert audiences. The principal theme of the first movement appears first in the cellos and after that in the violins and woodwinds. It is built up with great power into a resounding climax. The second subject, a tranquil melody, is given by the oboe and clarinet. Both ideas are worked out freely, and often skillfully, as idyllic passages are contrasted with forceful ones. The slow movement is the finest section of the symphony and one of the most moving pages written by Bruckner. The main melody, which has organ-like sonorities, has a hymnlike character. It is followed by other lyrical ideas equally solemn and majestic. The scherzo begins with a lilting dance tune and continues with a more dramatic subject; the main idea of its trio is a pastoral tune for the first violins. The two principal themes of the finale are presented by the first violins. The finale has a heroic character, filled as it is with tempestuous moods, and it concludes with an overpowering coda.

The symphony with which Bruckner achieved his greatest success during his lifetime—the Symphony No. 8 in C minor (1886)—is also the last symphony he lived to complete. (He wrote only the first three movements of a Ninth Symphony, in D minor. When performed today it is sometimes the practice to use Bruckner's Te Deum as a finale.)

The Eighth Symphony begins in a questioning mood and progresses from that to unrest and agitation. But before the movement ends the music becomes a mighty lamentation in which the soft-spoken first theme (originally consigned to the lower strings) is transformed into a threnody for the oboe. The second-movement scherzo has robust, peasant good humor. The most eloquent movement is the third, an adagio—one of the longest as well as one of the most expressive movements found in any Bruckner symphony. First comes an exalted song on the G string for the first violins. Then follow two more affecting melodies, one in the cellos, the other in the tubas. For some reason never explained, Bruckner interpolates the rhythm of the "Siegfried motive" from Wagner's *Ring* before the movement ends. The finale opens with a ceremonious fanfare in D-flat. Several changes of key follow before the main subject in C minor is heard. There is a good deal of contrapuntal interest in this movement, as three basic ideas are presented and developed. When the symphony comes to an exultant conclusion, material from earlier movements is hurriedly remembered.

Frédéric Chopin

"He confided . . . those inexpressible sorrows to which the pious give vent in their communication with their Maker. What they never say except upon their knees, he said in his palpitating compositions."

LISZT

Born: Zelazowa Wola, near Warsaw, Poland, March 1, 1810.
Died: Paris, October 17, 1849.
Major Works: *Chamber Music*—Piano Trio in G minor; Cello Sonata in G minor. *Orchestral Music*—2 piano concertos; Variations on "Là ci darem," for piano and orchestra. *Piano Music* —55 mazurkas; 24 études; 24 preludes; 15 waltzes; 11 polonaises; 6 ballades; 4 impromptus; 4 scherzos; 3 sonatas; Barcarolle in F-sharp minor; Berceuse in D-flat; Tarantella in A-flat; écossaises, fantaisies, rondos; Rondo in C major, for two pianos. *Vocal Music*—17 Polish songs.

HIS LIFE

When Chopin left Poland in 1830 his teacher, Joseph Elsner, presented him with a silver urn containing some Polish earth. He did not want Chopin to forget the land of his birth. Though this little bit of earth was henceforth to be Chopin's only immediate contact with Poland, and it was buried with him when he died, he never did forget his native land. Poland was an integral part of him, both as man and as composer. There are some biographers who explain his deeply rooted melancholia as at least partially caused by the fact that he missed his country and his people so keenly. "I lie in bed and my eyes look over the fields," he wrote one day. "A big space before the windows. The soil of France. Far away under the Polish skies, I see the eyes of my mother. Tears unshed weigh heavily. 'Frédéric,' she said, 'thou wilt be a great musician; thy Poland will be proud of thee.'"

"Poland, Poland," wrote Georges Jean-Aubry, "how many nights has he held her to his heart. Yes, in the Majorca evenings, and the nights in Paris, amongst the ocean breezes which blew over the old convent, in the Baleares, amidst drawing-room talks and elegant women and all the little refinements dear to his sensitive taste, he thought but of Poland."

His strong national consciousness was not only a part of his emotional make-up. It also affected his art. As a boy he had been fascinated by the songs and dances of the Polish peasants; he felt an intimate bond with his folk art. Later he became an intensely national composer, who produced a vital Polish musical art and who was the first to incorporate successfully Slavic expression into the music of the Western world.

What Poland meant to Chopin, Chopin's music was, in turn, to mean to Poland. Few other composers wrote music so bound up with the history of their lands. In the last century, when Poland was under the domination of Czarist Russia, Chopin's music was the voice of hope to speak for Polish liberation among ardent nationalists. "All was forbidden us," recorded Paderewski in his autobiography, "the language and the faith of our fathers, our national dress, our songs, our poets. Chopin alone was not forbidden. . . . In him we could still find the living breath of all that was prohibited. . . . He gave all back to us, mingled with the prayers of broken hearts, the revolt of fettered souls, the pain of slavery, lost Freedom's ache, the cursing of tyrants, the exultant songs of victory."

When the Nazi hordes attacked Poland, in September 1939, Chopin's music once again became a national symbol, this time the symbol of resistance. It is now familiar how the *Revolutionary* Etude and other Chopin pieces were sounded day and night from the Warsaw radio, to buoy the spirits of a city savagely stricken by an uninterrupted rain of Nazi bombs. The last piece of music heard over the

Warsaw radio before the Nazis took over was by Chopin: The first eleven notes of the Polonaise in A major were played on the xylophone for the last time just before the city surrendered to the Nazis.

The greatest of all Polish composers, and the most Polish of all great composers, came from a mixed ancestry. (The date of Chopin's birth has long been accepted as February 22, 1810. But recent musicological research reveals that when he was baptized on April 23, 1810, a mistake of one week had been made when his date of birth had been recorded in the parish register. In all probability, then, Chopin was born on March 1.) His father was an Alsatian schoolteacher who settled in Poland and became a French tutor for the family of Countess Skarbek at Zelazowa Wola. There he fell in love with and married the Countess's lady in waiting, Justina Krzyzanowska, herself of Polish nobility. Chopin was their second child and first son. Soon after his birth the Chopin family moved on to Warsaw, where the father became a French professor at one of the *lycées* and later on opened up a boarding school of his own. The Chopin household was both harmonious and cultured. Thus Chopin's childhood was spent in a felicitous setting. He was a sensitive, imaginative, and happy child, with an infectious sense of humor, who indulged as eagerly in childish pranks and mimicry as in music, in which he demonstrated exceptional interest and talent from earliest childhood. He was continually found at the piano, trying to produce pleasing melodies and harmonies. When a melody was particularly beautiful he would suddenly burst into tears. A local fiddler, Adalbert Zwyny, began giving Chopin piano lessons when he was six years old and helped him put down his first ideas on paper. Such was Chopin's progress that when he was seven one of his compositions was published, a Polonaise in G minor. In his ninth year he made a public appearance as pianist at a charity concert in which he scored so great a success that immediately he became the pet of Warsaw society and a frequent visitor to the palaces and estates of nobility.

When he was fifteen, Chopin entered his father's school for academic studies. He now became a piano student of Josef Elsner, director of the Warsaw Conservatory. Between 1826 and 1829 Chopin was a full-time student with Elsner at the Conservatory. Elsner, destined to be Chopin's last teacher, was the kind of musician who could both respect and encourage the individuality of a pupil. He understood Chopin's sensitive and delicate temperament and catered to it. Instead of burdening Chopin with rules and laws he allowed the young boy to grow and develop freely in the direction in which his artistic nature sent him: free romantic expression. And it was largely due to Elsner's sympathy and understanding that Chopin was able to evolve a personal style of writing almost from the very beginning of his creative career—a style already thoroughly recognizable in the mazurkas, nocturnes, sonatas, and variations he was writing.

When his studies at the *lycée* ended in 1828, Chopin visited Berlin, whose musical life stimulated him greatly. His appetite for travel was whetted; Chopin began to nurse the ambition of visiting the musical capital of Europe, Vienna. The desire to leave Warsaw was intensified by a schoolboy love for Constantia Gladkowska, a singing student. He was too diffident to make his feelings known; instead he brooded. A change of scene seemed the logical prescription. When Chopin was graduated from the Conservatory in July of 1829 with highest honors, his father provided him with the necessary funds, and in the summer of 1829 he came to Vienna. He gave two highly successful concerts, on August 11 and 18, and found a publisher for one of his works: the Variations on Mozart's *"Là ci darem,"* for piano and orchestra.

This brief taste of success, and the exhilaration of life in Vienna, convinced him that he preferred living, working, and making his way in foreign capitals. Back in Warsaw he continued by turns to be bored with the city and agonized by his unrequited love. At last he decided to leave. On November 2, 1830, he left Warsaw. In the city of his birth a cantata was performed in his honor by its composer, his faithful and admiring teacher, Elsner. At the end of these festivities, Elsner presented Chopin with the aforementioned handful of Polish earth. "May you never forget your native land wherever you may go, nor cease to love it with a warm and faithful heart," Chopin was admonished.

In Vienna, Chopin gave two concerts—on April 4 and June 11. These were once again well received, but Chopin's attempts to land a publisher for his music were in vain. Still in Vienna, Chopin received the news that Poland had risen in revolt against Russian rule. His impulse was to rush back and fight for the liberation of his land—even as a bosom friend who had come with him to Vienna had done! But discretion proved the better part of valor. He hired a coach to take him to Warsaw, but en route he had a change of heart and instructed the driver to turn back. He now permitted himself to be convinced by his mother's argument that he was too frail to become a soldier. He remained in Vienna for six months, then went on into Germany. In Stuttgart, in July of 1831, he heard the news that Warsaw had been recaptured by the Russians. Inflamed by this news he expressed his loyalty and patriotic ardor in the only way he could, as he had long since given up the thought of fighting. He wrote a piece of music, the Etude in C minor (Op. 10, No. 12), now known as the *Revolutionary*.

From Germany, Chopin went on to Paris. He expected to stay a short while, for he was actually en route to London. But he stayed for the rest of his life. Through Luigi Cherubini (1760–1842), the Italian opera composer who was living permanently in Paris, to whom he had brought letters of introduction, Chopin was introduced (at the composer's Monday evening *salons*) to the leading musicians of Paris. They became interested in him and arranged for his debut in the French capital on February 26, 1832. This debut was not successful. Chopin's style of piano playing was too intimate and refined for Parisian tastes. Nor did they like his music much better. The powerful critic Fétis found in Chopin's works "too much luxuriance in modulations, and disorder in the linking of phrases." But a few discerning musicians knew they were in the presence of greatness and said so, and these included Felix Mendelssohn, Franz Liszt, Meyerbeer, and Ferdinand Hiller.

Chopin became so discouraged at the reaction to his performance that he decided to give up concert work and even entertained the thought of leaving France for America. A chance meeting with Prince Radziwill changed Chopin's destiny. Through the prince, Chopin was brought into the *salon* of Baron Jacques de Rothschild, where he played and triumphed. From then on Chopin was the darling of the French *salons*. He received munificent fees as teacher and as performer at intimate and exclusive social functions.

In the fashionable *salons* Chopin felt quite at home not only as artist but also as man. Though by nature he was usually reserved, self-centered, and highly moody, he changed character in the *salons*. He liked to mingle with the highborn and the rich; the company of beautiful women exhilarated him; he sought contact with the famous and the powerful, even Jews, though he was essentially anti-Semitic. Moving in a setting of wealth and luxury was a basic need. He was revolted by poverty. His highly fastidious and sensitive nature—which expressed itself in the quiet elegance of his dress, in the tasteful furnishing of his home, in his love for flowers, perfume, and *objets d'art*—wanted beauty around him all the time. "To tear Chopin away from so many *gâteries*," wrote George Sand, "to associate him with a simple, uniform, and constantly studious life, he who had been brought up on the knees of princesses, was to deprive him of that which made him live, of a factitious life, it is true. . . . In Paris he visited several *salons* every day, or he chose at least every evening a different one as a milieu. He had thus by turns twenty or thirty *salons* to intoxicate or charm with his presence."

Here is the way Chopin appeared to Liszt: "His glance was intelligent rather than dreamy; his soft, shrewd smile had no touch of bitterness. The fineness and transparency of his complexion charmed the eye, his fair hair was silky, his nose slightly aquiline, his movements well-bred, and his manners bore such an aristocratic stamp that one involuntarily treated him like a prince. His gestures were frequent and graceful. His voice was always toneless, and often indistinct; he was not very tall, and was slight of build."

He was now being honored not only as a performer but also as a composer. The exquisite piano pieces he was writing caught the fancy of the Parisian *salons*. The waltzes, nocturnes, études, polonaises, and mazurkas that Chopin played for them were loved for their sensitive and exquisite lyricism, romantic sentiment, and elegance of form. But little was it realized at the time that with these small pieces a new world was being opened for music. A true measure of the greatness of his music was to come later. Meanwhile, he was enjoying immense popularity. Publishers competed with one another to issue his latest works; the *salons* reverberated with enthusiasm whenever Chopin introduced a new piece.

In another respect his life was successful. His second great love was for Maria Wodzinska, the young and flighty daughter of a count. Chopin pursued her relentlessly, and she encouraged him. But her family refused to consider the possibility of marriage. Chopin had nothing to show for a second tortured love affair but a faded flower and a bundle of letters which for many years he kept carefully assembled in a package marked "My Sorrow." And with these a group of compositions he wrote for her, including the Waltz in A-flat major, Op. 69, No. 1.

But the *grande passion* of his life was yet to come. In the fall of 1836, at the *salon* of Liszt's mistress, Countess d'Agoult, Chopin met the celebrated French woman novelist who called herself George Sand but whose real name was Amandine Aurore Dupin. "What a repellent woman she is," he exclaimed. "Is she really a woman? I'm ready to doubt it." His fastidious nature recoiled at her masculine attitudes and habits. She not only assumed a man's name, but even masculine clothing, and, like a man, she smoked cigars. Her long succession of highly publicized liaisons with the great and near great (as well as her illegitimate birth) was calculated to upset Chopin's inherent prudery. Besides, she was five years older than he and physically most unappealing, and Chopin had always been drawn to young, attractive women.

And yet, though he did not recognize it himself at first, he was drawn to George Sand; and she, in turn, adored him. She was unquestionably one of the most brilliant women of her generation, a woman of letters admired, even venerated, by some of the foremost literary figures of the day. Chopin, ever partial to famous people, could not altogether suppress an interest in her. But beyond this, her powerful and dynamic masculinity seemed to answer some vital need in his own rather effeminate personality; and her older age may well have made her, in his eyes, a substitute for the mother he had always loved.

Before long they were always seen together. In the summer of 1838 she invited him to spend the summer with her at her château in Nohant. Chopin, then ill, felt the need for tenderness and maternal care, and accepted. There was no question in his mind any longer that he was in love with her. They made a strange pair—opposites in temperament, personality, and outlook. And their love affair was as stormy as it was intense.

The illness of George Sand's son sent her to the island of Majorca in the winter of 1838. Chopin decided to follow her there. Their life at Palma, which he had hoped would be idyllic in the setting of a Mediterranean paradise, was an uninterrupted nightmare. The townspeople were openly antagonistic to them because they did not attend church. The weather was continually cold and wet. When Chopin became sick with bronchitis the rumor began spreading throughout the island that he was a victim of tuberculosis. The terrified townspeople demanded that he leave and even threatened his life.

The ménage had to abandon its villa and find a home in Valdemosa, in a bleak, musty, depressing fifteenth-century monastery, the rooms of which were stone cells resembling coffins, as Chopin once said. Nobody would work for them. The food was often inedible. Under such conditions Chopin's health gave way completely. He became a victim of hemorrhages, then of hallucinations and nightmares. One evening George Sand found him "before his piano, his eyes wild, his hair almost standing on end. It was some minutes before he recognized us." As an invalid he was carried aboard a freighter for his return to France. In Barcelona, where he suffered another hemorrhage attack, he lost so much blood that for a time they thought he would die. But eventually they got him back to Nohant—a shadow of his former self. There was only one rewarding result from his otherwise sordid vacation: Chopin sketched there most of his magnificent preludes, Op. 28.

Fortunately, in the happier environment of Paris and Nohant, Chopin recovered from this experience. He was at the height of his fame—and at the height of his powers. Respected and pampered, he produced some of his most ambitious works. For two years he kept up a truly prodigious creative effort, writing the Sonata in B-flat minor (the one with the famous funeral march), two ballades, the monumental Fantaisie in F minor, the F-sharp major Impromptu, etc. This Herculean endeavor sapped his strength and vitality. After 1841 his health disintegrated.

The tensions between George Sand and himself were increasing. Perhaps she had grown weary of him and was seeking a break in their relationship. The final rupture was caused by a comparatively minor episode: Chopin had sided with George Sand's daughter in a family quarrel. There are those who suggest that Sand had skillfully maneuvered Chopin into this quarrel as the pretext for a complete rupture. Chopin and Sand went their separate ways. Sand continued her career and proud station, apparently unaffected emotionally by this separation. Chopin went on to die. For as Liszt wrote: "Chopin felt and often repeated that in breaking this long affection, this powerful bond, he had broken his life."

Despite his poor health he gave a concert in Paris on February 16, 1848—his last public appearance. He was also prevailed upon by his friend and admirer Jane Stirling to visit England and Scotland.

The trip, which took place in 1848, only undermined his health and spirits further. He came back to Paris to become virtually a recluse at his home in Rue de Chaillot. Rich friends kept him in funds—for he could no longer earn anything—and the nobility paid him frequent calls. From Poland came his sister and brother-in-law to attend him. His life was ebbing. He instructed his sister to destroy his unpublished manuscripts (he wanted only the best of his work to survive him) and just before his death, neurotically afraid of being buried alive, he begged that his body be cut open after he had died.

Chopin died on the morning of October 17, 1849, several hours after receiving extreme unction. His funeral took place at the Madeleine Church where, as he had requested, Mozart's Requiem was performed in the presence of the social and musical great of Paris. His body was buried in the cemetery of Père Lachaise, together with the urn of Polish earth he had received from his teacher Elsner when he left Poland for good.

HIS MUSIC

Chopin is the only one of the world's great composers who made a specialty of the piano. The bulk of his music, 169 works in all, is for that solo instrument; the remaining handful use the piano. No other composer made such a bountiful contribution to piano literature, no other composer was so original, no other composer was so influential in developing modern piano technique and style and sound. His harmonic writing was often revolutionary, with its indulgences in discords. He obtained color effects, sonorities, and dynamics which no one before him had realized. He increased both the technical and artistic resources of the piano as an instrument so immensely that it can truthfully be said to have achieved complete emancipation and artistic self-sufficiency. Chopin was one of the first composers to write piano music with only the piano in mind, instead of trying to translate other kinds of music for the piano. Beethoven was frequently orchestral in his piano works, and Schubert was often vocal. Chopin was always *pianistic*.

Chopin stands apart from the other masters in music in several other ways, too. He is perhaps the only great composer upon whom the influence of earlier composers is negligible; who had to create his own world with his own materials; who had to evolve his piano methods and idioms without precedent to guide him.

Chopin is also the only one of the great composers specializing in the smaller forms, whose greatness actually rests securely on them. He knew that the large classical forms restricted the mobility of his music, that he did not know to make these forms the servant of his ideas. He therefore leaned toward more flexible, less inhibiting structures. He recognized his inability to supply long-sustained thought, his weakness in the kind of enlargement, development, and transformation demanded by the concerto, sonata, or symphony. He realized—and probably better than his critics—that his two concertos and three sonatas were essentially made up of smaller pieces, each piece effective by itself, yet together lacking that organization and integration demanded by those large forms. He decided consequently to work in smaller molds—usually in such dance forms as the waltz, the polonaise, and the mazurka—to become "great in small things" even as he was "small in great things," as J. Cuthbert Hadden wrote. As composers at that time were expected to produce concertos, symphonies, operas, and oratorios, his true artistic significance was for a long time not completely appreciated even by his most intimate friends.

Within small spheres Chopin's imagination was so rich, his invention so original, his ideas so inexhaustibly varied, his style so personal and aristocratic, his technique so sure that he cannot be denied a place at the side of the greatest masters of music. Today it is generally accepted that the greatest of Chopin's works are on the highest plane of inspiration and are the ultimate in elegance and sophistication. Less familiar is the equally significant point that with Chopin greatness was the rule. The lifework of few composers maintains such a consistently high standard; or, to put it another way, few composers have such a formidable percentage of their works in the living repertory as Chopin.

One reason for this amazingly high percentage of masterpieces in Chopin's output, and the amazingly small percentage of poor works, is that he was his own severest critic. Just as he insisted in the closing days of his life that all his unpublished pieces be destroyed for fear that something unrepresentative might survive him, so throughout his life he was hypercritical of everything he wrote, fanatically insistent on giving only of the best that was in him.

Ideas apparently came easily. But in working them out he was most painstaking and demanding. He kept on revising and changing, even after a piece had been turned in to its publisher; in more than one work we do have several versions of a single passage. George Sand described his working habits as follows: "He analyzed very much when writing down what was conceived as a whole, and his regret that he could not represent it perfectly made him desperate. For days, he locked himself up in his room, running up and down, breaking pens, repeating, changing one single measure a hundred times, writing, scratching it out, and the next morning starting all over again with painstaking and desperate efforts. He would work six weeks on one single page. . . ."

One more point about Chopin should be emphasized. Long before nationalism swept over the world of music like a tidal wave, he was his country's voice in music. In his mazurkas and polonaises he not only borrowed Polish dance forms, but also filled them with some of the identifiable traits of Polish folk music: its tonalities; its rhythms; its tendency to repeat single phrases or to build entire sequences upon those phrases. Chopin's polonaises and mazurkas, while remaining unmistakably Chopinesque, are also Polish to their very sinew and marrow—thereby placing their composer among the earliest masters to find a bountiful source of inspiration and material in national sources.

ANALYTICAL NOTES

Orchestral Music. The two concertos for piano and orchestra, Chopin's rare attempts at orchestral writing, are early productions. The Concerto No. 2 in F minor, Op. 21, was written first (it is referred to as the Second Concerto because it was published after the First); it came in Chopin's nineteenth year. The Concerto No. 1 in E minor, Op. 11, was completed one year later. In both works the thematic material is invariably of a high order. This, together with the often beautiful writing for the piano, is the reason why both concertos are popular.

The Concerto No. 1 begins with an orchestral prologue in which the two main themes of the movement appear. The first is bold and energetic and appears immediately in the first violins; the second, also in the strings, is tender. Both themes are later worked out by the solo pianist, sometimes with delicate embellishments, sometimes with powerful arpeggios; but it is the second melody that receives the more prominent attention throughout the movement. Chopin called his slow movement a "romanza," and it is poetic and sentimental. After twelve measures of introduction by muted strings the piano presents the main melody, out of which evolves the haunting, nocturnal music of the entire movement. "It is intended," the composer explained in describing this movement, "to convey the impression which one receives when the eye rests on a beloved landscape that calls up in one's soul beautiful memories— for instance, on a fine moonlit spring night." The concluding rondo is spirited throughout; it opens with a vigorous dialogue between strings and winds, after which the piano enters with an infectious dancelike theme. That theme is worked out by the piano before being adopted by the orchestra. A transitional orchestral passage leads to the second vigorous subject of the movement, also played by the solo piano against a delicate accompanying figure in the strings. Virtuoso music for the piano follows, and then vigorous passages for the orchestra. A powerful coda concludes the work.

Chopin himself introduced the Concerto in E minor, at a concert in Warsaw on October 11, 1830, which marked his farewell appearance in Poland. It is amusing to note that in order to make the comparatively long work a bit more palatable to the audience, and possibly to help reduce boredom, a pleasing little aria written by the conductor was sung by soloist and chorus between the first and second movements.

The Concerto No. 2 in F minor was also introduced by Chopin in Warsaw—on March 17, 1830. Here too the attempt was made to break up the monotony of a three-movement concerto, in this case by interpolating a *divertissement* for French horn between the first and second movements.

The writing of the concerto appears to have been stimulated by the composer's frustrated love for Constantia Gladkowska. He confessed that the slow movement was written "while my thoughts were with her."

There are two exposition sections in the first movement. The first is orchestral, with the two main themes presented respectively by the strings and by the oboes. After four introductory measures by the piano, the soloist begins the second exposition, taking up the two themes and then embarking on passage work. In the development section, it is the first theme that is worked out. The larghetto is a song of wistful and nostalgic beauty, one of Chopin's most poetic effusions. Its main theme is heard in the piano after six introductory measures. The evocative tenderness of this music yields to darker pages as the piano brings forth an atmosphere of mystery and foreboding against tremolo strings. Then the first theme returns, greatly embellished, and the movement ends with a restatement of the opening orchestral introduction. The concluding movement is fiery and brilliant, with many pages of virtuoso writing for the solo instrument. The two themes, both originally heard in the piano, have the fiery character and the lusty pace of a mazurka.

Piano Music. Of the three sonatas that Chopin wrote, the first in C minor, Op. 4, belongs to the years of his apprenticeship, having been written when he was only eighteen. The other two—the B-flat minor, Op. 35, and the B minor, Op. 58—came in 1839 and 1844 respectively; they represent his most ambitious projects for solo piano, though not necessarily his most successful. Chopin unfortunately was not at home in the formal sonata. He had neither the power of organization and integration nor the gift for development and transformation so essential to sonata writing. What he did was to string together four pieces of music—often strikingly beautiful pieces, it must be confessed—each of which would have been effective as an individual composition, but which bore no relation to the sonata as a whole. What Schumann once wrote of the Sonata No. 2 in B-flat minor was also true of its successor: "To have called this a sonata must be reckoned a freak, if not a piece of pride. For he has simply linked together four of his maddest children in order to introduce them by fraud under this name into a place which otherwise they would perhaps never have entered."

The Sonata No. 2 in B-flat minor contains the famous funeral march. This solemn threnody, with its tender trio, is the most famous funeral march in all musical literature. Many authorities have found the presence of death in the other three movements: in the breathless terror of the first, with its opening measures, at turns lugubrious and stormy, followed by the agitation of the first theme and the pathos of the second one; the impetuous, headlong progress of the second-movement scherzo, which carries with it so much foreboding; and the immense tragedy and at times the demoniac force of the brief finale.

The Sonata No. 3 also has a third movement that is solemn and funereal in mood, a largo. This is not a formal funeral march, but a poetic expression of unrestrained grief. The most celebrated movement of this sonata, however, is not the third but the fourth, the presto non tanto. It is music in the grand manner: dramatic, heroic, yet of quicksilver motion—among the finest music produced by Chopin, if not by any Romantic composer.

The library of piano music produced by Chopin in forms smaller than the sonata is most remarkable for its amazing variety of moods. The Chopin that most often comes to mind—the sensitive dreamer, the sentimentalist, the yearning Romantic—is, of course, found in many works, notably the nocturnes. But there are other attitudes that are no less characteristic of Chopin. In the waltzes he is the sophisticated child of the Parisian *salons;* in the mazurkas and polonaises he is the fiery, passionate nationalist given often to tempestuous, even savage, declarations; he is a dramatist and poet on a grand scale in the ballades, and an exquisite miniaturist in the preludes and études. Anton Rubinstein recognized this creative versatility: "Tragic, romantic, lyric, heroic, dramatic, fantastic, soulful, sweet, dreamy, brilliant, grand, simple: all possible expressions are found in his compositions, and all are sung by him upon his instrument."

The four ballades (1835–41) are in a form larger than the nocturne, étude, prelude, or waltz. They have an improvisational character in which ideas are presented and then developed freely and elastically. As the name implies, the ballade appears to be telling a story, though no definite program is followed. Of Chopin's ballades, the first, in G minor, Op. 23, is characteristic; Schumann regarded it as "the most spirited and daring" of Chopin's works up to that time (1835). It alternates fiery and tender moods. The first seven bars are an introduction. This is passionate music with tragic undertones, ending in a discord. This composition is grounded in *Konrad Valendrod,* describing the battle of the Christian knights against pagan Lithuanians. Two other ballades have literary sources: the F major, Op. 38, having its source in *Le Lac de Willis,* and the A-flat major, Op. 47, in *Undine.* The fourth ballade—in F minor, Op. 52— is so rich in melodic and harmonic invention that James Gibbons Huneker described its music as "irresistible witchery."

The études are collected in two volumes, each containing twelve pieces (Op. 10 and Op. 25). They were written between 1829–34. Many composers before Chopin had written piano études (exercise pieces to develop piano technique) and had prepared books of études to explore a whole group of technical problems in a unified manner. The études by Karl Czerny (1791–1857) and J. B. Cramer (1771– 1858) are still indispensable on the piano student. Chopin, in writing his études, was also concerned with technical problems, and the studies are of great educational value. Here we find exercises in arpeggios, thirds, sixths, octaves, staccato and legato, and so forth. But Chopin brought to any form he touched a world of enchantment; his études are also of great artistic importance. They are among his most felicitous flights of inspiration. Some of his finest études have acquired identifying names: the *Black Key,* in G-flat major (Op. 10, No. 5), which, as its nickname implies, emphasizes the use of black keys—in the right hand; the tempestuous *Revolutionary,* in C minor (Op. 10, No. 12), inspired by the fall of Warsaw; the programmatic *The Bees,* in F minor (Op. 25, No. 2), a vivid picture of bees in buzzing flight; the delicate *Butterfly,* in G-flat major (Op. 25, No. 9), study in sixths; the pictorial *Winter Wind,* in A minor (Op. 25, No. 11), a study in octaves.

Of the other études, the E-flat minor (Op. 10, No. 6) boasts a poetic, nocturne-like melody; the F major (Op. 10, No. 8) is memorable for its rich sonorities; the A-flat major (Op. 10, No. 10) has a *salon*-like grace and elegance; and the C-sharp minor (Op. 25, No. 7) is distinguished for its tender, elegiac beauty.

In addition to Op. 10 and 25, there exist three études published posthumously: F minor, A-flat major, and D-flat major.

The Fantaisie in F minor, Op. 49 (1841) is not only the greatest of Chopin's four compositions in the fantasy form but also one of his monumental creations. The spacious and malleable form of the fantasia is handled with a sureness and inexorable logic we do not usually find in his large forms. In it he gives voice to ideas that are dramatic, beautiful, tempestuous, and gently reflective. As Niecks wrote: "Chopin's genius had not reached the most perfect stage of its development, and was radiating with all the intensity of which its nature was capable."

The highly popular Fantaisie-Impromptu in C-sharp minor (1834), published posthumously, provided the American popular-song composer Harry Carroll with the melody for a resounding "hit," "I'm Always Chasing Rainbows." The fantaisie is not first-class Chopin. Indeed, the composer himself thought so little of it that he never permitted its publication.

In the mazurkas and polonaises we hear the voice of the nationalist. Without abandoning his personal mannerisms Chopin here assimilated some important traits of Polish folk music: the tonality suggesting medieval church modes, so often found in Polish folk songs; the melodic mannerism of building up an entire paragraph but of a single phrase, either repeated or altered; the rhythm and personality of the two most characteristic folk dances of Poland.

The mazurka, which is in 3/4 time, is slower than the waltz, with the accent on the third, instead of the first, beat. The fifty-five mazurkas are more poetic and sensitive than the polonaises. They have greater freedom of form, more variety of rhythm, and a wider emotional span. Some are sad, such as the E minor, Op. 17, No. 2, and the A-flat, Op. 17, No. 3 (1832–33), while others are spirited and gay, such as the B minor, Op. 33, No. 4 (1837–38). Some have extraordinary rhythmic vitality, such as the B major, Op. 41, No. 3 (1839). Some—like the A minor, Op. 17, No. 4 (1825)— are miniature tone poems. The mazurka was the last form used by Chopin. The last two pieces of music he was destined to write came in 1849, the Mazurkas in A minor and F minor, Op. 68, Nos. 2 and 4.

The polonaise is a stately dance in triple time. Originally the opening dance at court festivities, it soon began to symbolize the old-world chivalry of the Polish in love and war. Most of the eleven polonaises are martial in spirit: for example, the most famous one of them all, the *Military* Polonaise in A major, Op. 40, No. 1 (1838); also the *Heroic* Polonaise in A-flat major, Op. 53 (1824). The *Serbian* Polonaise in E-flat minor, Op. 26, No. 2 (1838), is partly martial and partly reflective. There are other polonaises that are mainly elegiac, such as the three in Op. 71 (1846), in the keys of D minor, B-flat major, and F minor. There is still some virility and heroism in this music, but with them a prevailing melancholy as well.

Chopin's nocturnes are pieces of the starlit night, music of peace, mystery, and romance. Some wear, as James Gibbons Huneker wrote, "an agitated, remorseful countenance; others are seen in profile only; while many are like whisperings at dusk—Verlaine moods." The nocturne for piano did not originate with Chopin. He acquired the form and style from the Irish-born composer John Field (1782–1837), who wrote his first piano nocturne in 1814 and introduced some of them at a Paris concert in 1832 which Chopin attended. Less than a year later Chopin wrote his first three nocturnes (Op. 9)—B-flat minor, E-flat major, and B major—bringing at once a magic of mood and atmosphere and a subtlety of nuance that the Field nocturne had never known. The second nocturne of this first set is among the most popular of the lot, familiar not only in its original form, but also in numerous transcriptions, the best being by Pablo de Sarasate (for violin and piano) and David Popper (for cello and piano). Here we encounter that kind of haunting, poetical melody—amply embellished—which so distinguishes Chopin's nocturne writing.

The following are some of the other frequently heard and widely admired nocturnes: the G minor, Op. 15, No. 3 (1831), inspired by a performance of *Hamlet;* the C-sharp minor, Op. 27, No. 1 (1835), which the composer said describes "a calm night at Venice where, after a murder, the corpse is thrown into the sea"; the D-flat major, Op. 27, No. 2 (1835), with its sublime lyricism; the A-flat major, Op. 32, No. 2 (1837), used so prominently in the familiar ballet whose score is built around Chopin's music, *Les Sylphides;* the C minor, Op. 48, No. 1 (1841), with its tragic implications and its strong dramatic interest; and the exquisite miniature, the F minor, Op. 55, No. 1 (1843).

The preludes collected in Op. 28 (1836–39) are twenty-four in number. But there are two additional preludes less often heard: that in C-sharp major, Op. 45 (1841), and that in A-flat major, discovered in 1918 when it was published posthumously. Before Chopin's time the term "prelude" signified a brief composition serving as a preface to a fugue, or a suite, or an opera or drama.

With Chopin the prelude became a self-sufficient composition—brief and compact. Each of his preludes is a little poem, but each quite different from the others in mood and feeling. In one there is morbid reflection (No. 2, in A minor); in another, an evanescent pensive mood (No. 4, in E minor); in a third, an elfin kind of grace (No. 10, in C-sharp minor). A tortured dream is evoked in the twelfth (G-sharp minor), which is contrasted with a romantic and sensitive tone-picture in the thirteenth (F-sharp major). The twentieth (C minor) has cathedral-like solemnity, and the twenty-second (G minor) is febrile and stormy. The so-called *Raindrop* Prelude (No. 15, in D-flat major) acquired its name from the insistent rhythm in the left hand suggesting the tapping of raindrops on the roof or window.

In the waltzes, Chopin was inspired by the Viennese pieces of the first Johann Strauss (1804–49), father of the Strauss who composed *The Blue Danube,* and himself a composer of famous waltzes. Strauss's music was written primarily for dancing. The waltzes of Chopin are for listening; they are, as Huneker put it so well, "dances for the soul, not for the body." There is another important difference. The waltzes of the first Johann Strauss had an abandon betraying their peasant ancestry; those of Chopin are the offspring of the Parisian *salons* and are refined, elegant, and suave.

Chopin wrote fifteen waltzes. The most celebrated are: the E-flat major, Op. 18 (1829), better known as the *Grande valse brillante;* the D-flat major, Op. 64, No. 1 (1847), familiar as the *Minute* Waltz (*not* a sixty-second waltz, it must be remembered, but a "small" waltz after the French word *minute*); and probably the most famous of all, that in C-sharp minor, Op. 64, No. 2 (1847).*

Among other pieces by Chopin the following are of special interest: the F-sharp minor Barcarolle, Op. 60 (1846), which Huneker interpreted as a threnody for the vanished splendors of old Venice; the Berceuse in D-flat major, Op. 57 (1843), the only such cradle song, or lullaby, in Chopin's literature; the Impromptu in A-flat

---

* In 1967, there was discovered the long-lost manuscripts of two of Chopin's waltzes: the G-flat major, Op. 70, No. 1, and the E-flat major, Op. 18. They were found at the Château de Thoiry in Yvelines, France, in the family residence of Count Paul de la Panouse, and were authenticated by François Lesure, a distinguished Chopin authority. Both compositions reveal less embellishments, and a less sentimental approach, than the familiar versions now in general use, the changes probably made by various anonymous editors.

major, Op. 29 (1837), one of four compositions in this form, and the one that has the character of an improvisation with turbulent passages alternating with serene ones; and the Scherzo in C-sharp minor, Op. 39 (1839)—also one of four scherzos—written during the composer's miserable stay at Majorca.

Aaron Copland

"Here is at last an American that we may place unapologetically beside the great recognized creative figures of any other country."

ARTHUR V. BERGER

BORN: Brooklyn, New York, November 14, 1900.
MAJOR WORKS: *Ballets*—Appalachian Spring; Billy the Kid; Rodeo; Dance Panels. *Chamber Music*—Violin Sonata; Piano Quartet; Nonet, for strings; Duo, for flute and piano. *Choral Music*—In the Beginning; Canticle of Freedom. *Operas*—The Second Hurricane (children's opera); The Tender Land. *Orchestral Music*—3 symphonies; Music for the Theater; Piano Concerto; Symphonic Ode (revised 1955); Short Symphony; El Salón México; An Outdoor Overture; Quiet City; Lincoln Portrait; Concerto for Clarinet and String Orchestra; The Red Pony, suite; Orchestral Variations (adapted from Piano Variations); Connotations; Music for a Great City; Inscape; Three Latin-American Sketches. *Piano Music*—Piano Variations, Sonata; Piano Fantasy. *Vocal Music*—Twelve Poems of Emily Dickinson; Old American Songs, two sets; Dirge in the Woods.

HIS LIFE

There was nothing in Copland's ancestry, background, or environment to suggest that he might become a composer at all, let alone one of the best-known and most highly respected American composers of our generation. His childhood was spent in what he himself described as a "drab" street in Brooklyn. "Music," he wrote, "was the last thing anyone would have connected with it." As for the Copland family, it was only superficially musical. An older brother was an amateur violinist, while a sister played the piano. They used to perform potpourris from the operas, and ragtime; that was about the extent of the family's concern with music. They never talked about music and never went to concerts.

His parents had no intention of giving him a musical training, since they believed (and possibly with justification) that the sums of money already spent on lessons for the other children had been wasted. But Aaron instinctively felt the need for making music, particularly after attending his first concert, a piano recital by Paderewski. One year after this experience, when he was fourteen, Copland began studying the piano, first with his sister, and after that with Leopold Wolfsohn, a local teacher. "The idea of becoming a composer seems gradually to have dawned upon me sometime around 1916." During this period he was attending Boys' High School in Brooklyn. His piano teacher arranged for him to enter Rubin Goldmark's class in harmony after Copland had made a brief but unsuccessful attempt to learn harmony through a correspondence course. Rubin Goldmark was a sound theoretician who could be expected to give his students a good grounding in the fundamentals of harmony, and Copland profited by his instruction. But Goldmark was, unfortunately, uninterested in anything new. He could hardly encourage Copland's interest in the moderns. And he was certainly unsympathetic to his pupil's first attempts to write in their vein. One day Copland brought his teacher one of his piano pieces, *The Cat and the Mouse.* "Goldmark regretfully admitted that he had no criteria by which to judge such music," Copland later recalled. Copland compromised by preparing for Goldmark the kind of exercises the teacher could understand and appreciate, while reserving the writing of modern pieces for the privacy of his own home.

When Copland was graduated from high school in 1918 he decided to concentrate his studies on music. In those days the eyes of every music student were inevitably fixed on Europe, so Copland too decided to go abroad. He had read that a new music school was being founded exclusively for Americans in Fontainebleau, France. He applied and found himself to be the first student to get accepted.

Living and studying near Paris was an exciting experience to a young man from Brooklyn. But Copland soon found the instruction he received from Paul Vidal at the Fontainebleau Conservatory just as academic and stuffy as that he had known in New York. "He was a French version of Rubin Goldmark," is Copland's description, "except that he was harder to understand because of the peculiar French patois that he talked." But one day Copland sat in on a harmony class presided over by a young woman named Nadia Boulanger. "I immediately suspected that I had found my teacher." That fall he became a private pupil of Mademoiselle Boulanger—not without some misgivings, for who had ever heard of anybody studying composition with a *woman*? She was a decisive influence in his development. And so was all the new music that he was to hear in Paris.

He returned to the United States in June 1924. He had been gone three years, had completed his studies, had become intimate with all the progressive tendencies in contemporary music, and had written a few works of his own including a ballet, *Grohg,* and some choral and piano music. He also brought back with him a commission from Nadia Boulanger to write a symphony for orchestra and organ which she, an organist, could perform during a visit to this country. While earning his living that summer as a pianist with a trio at a resort hotel in Milford, Connecticut, he worked on his symphony.

In the fall of 1924 the League of Composers, then in its infancy, accepted two of his piano pieces for a concert in New York in November of that year. These were the first pieces of music by Copland performed in the United States. The event also marked the beginning of his long association with the League of Composers, whose destinies he was eventually to guide as a member of the executive board and later as chairman of the board of directors. Two months later, on January 11, 1925, came the *première* of his symphony, performed by the New York Symphony Society under Walter Damrosch, with Nadia Boulanger at the organ. "If a young man can write a piece like that at the age of twenty-three," remarked Dr. Damrosch after struggling with the discords at a rehearsal, "he will be ready in five years to commit murder." Copland later rescored the symphony, omitting the organ part but leaving the discords intact.

Serge Koussevitzky, who had recently become the musical director of the Boston Symphony Orchestra, apparently was far more impressed by Copland's symphony than Dr. Damrosch had been. He performed it in Boston on February 20, 1925. He demonstrated his interest in young Copland in another way, by inviting him to write a new work for a concert of modern music which Koussevitsky had promised to conduct in New York for the League of Composers. Copland complied with *Music for the Theater,* an orchestral work in a jazz idiom. Koussevitzky introduced it in Boston on November 20, 1925, eight days before he performed it again in New York at a concert of the League of Composers. From this time on Koussevitzky proved indefatigable in his efforts on behalf of Copland, introducing many of his works; he was responsible for many of Copland's early successes.

As a composer Copland was doing far better than he had dared to hope. Hardly twenty-five, he had already had two of America's greatest orchestras perform his works. But a young composer of serious music could not make any money out of his music, and Copland was faced with the pressing problem of making a living. As long as he was a student in Paris the limited budget of his family provided his needs. Now that his student days were over he was expected to support himself. He opened a piano studio, but found few candidates. For a brief period he was supported by a patron who had been convinced of his promise by the brilliant critic Paul Rosenfeld. But in 1925 Copland became the first musician to win the Guggenheim Fellowship. As the fellowship was renewed the following year, he was freed from financial pressure for two years.

Now able to concentrate on composition, he produced a concerto for piano and orchestra (also in the jazz idiom) which he himself introduced with the Boston Symphony Orchestra, Koussevitzky conducting, on January 20, 1927. His *Dance* Symphony followed (adapted from his music for the ballet *Grohg,* which he had written in Paris a few years earlier); it won a $5000 prize in a contest for a symphonic work conducted by the RCA-Victor Company. And his next major work for orchestra, *Symphonic Ode,* was written to commemorate the fiftieth anniversary of the Boston Symphony Orchestra, which of course introduced it in Boston on February 19, 1932; in 1955 Copland revised the *Ode* extensively.

In the early 1930s, Copland began taking stock of himself as a composer. He was displeased with his findings. Except for his brief flirtation with jazz in *Music for the Theater* and the Piano Concerto, he had thus far been producing music that was growing increasingly complex, cerebral, and esoteric. He realized that he had been occupying an ivory tower which had isolated him from all except an intellectual elite. Having lived in France, he was not unfamiliar with the attempts of Erik Satie (1866–1925) and members of the French "Six" to create an "everyday art" (*"musique de tous les jours"*). Nor had he failed to remark the emergence in German music of the 1920s of *"Zeitkunst"* or "contemporary art" and *"Gebrauchsmusik"* or "functional music" in which composers like Kurt Weill and Hindemith were addressing themselves to large, responsive audiences. Copland found enough in this development to merit emulation. He now began feeling with growing conviction that "it was worth the effort to see if I couldn't say what I had to say in the simplest possible terms."

Simplicity, however, was only one of several ways to address oneself to large audiences; another was to use familiar materials—folk or popular music. During a visit to Mexico in the fall of 1932 he visited a popular dance hall in Mexico City where he heard and became fascinated with native dance tunes. This gave him the idea to write a symphonic work reflecting the spirit of these Mexican songs and also the spirit of Mexico as the American tourist knew it. *El Salón México* was the result. Introduced in Mexico City on August 27, 1937, Carlos Chávez conducting—and then heard over the NBC radio network on May 14, 1938, with Adrian Boult conducting the NBC Symphony—*El Salón México* proved an enormous success. It was extensively performed, and it was recorded. Both audiences and critics were most enthusiastic. Copland knew he was on the right track.

The step from Mexican to American folk music is a short step which Copland was not slow in taking. It was in the area of American folk (and at times popular) music that, during the next decade, Copland produced those compositions which placed him with the leading creative figures in twentieth-century music. These works included the scores of two ballets in which cowboy and other Western folk songs were used prominently: *Billy the Kid* in 1938 and *Rodeo* in 1942. The first was introduced in Chicago by the Ballet Caravan on October 16, 1938; the latter in New York by the Ballet Russe de Monte Carlo on October 16, 1942. In a third ballet score, *Appalachian Spring*—written for Martha Graham, who introduced it with her dancers in Washington, D.C., on October 30, 1944—the folk source was the Shaker tunes of the mountain folk in Pennsylvania. Here the quotations appear far more sparingly, with most of the melodic material Copland's own invention. The ballet received the award of the New York Music Critics Circle. A symphonic suite which the composer adapted from this music went on to capture the Pulitzer Prize in music.

Also strongly influenced by American folk music—but once again with infrequent resort to actual quotations—are Copland's Third Symphony and his opera *The Tender Land*. The symphony is one of Copland's masterworks. It was introduced by the Boston Symphony under Koussevitzky on October 18, 1946, following which it received the Music Critics Circle Award and the Boston Symphony Award of Merit. Koussevitzky said of it: "This is the greatest American symphony—it goes from the heart to the heart."

The opera *The Tender Land* had been commissioned by Richard Rodgers and Oscar Hammerstein II to help celebrate the thirtieth anniversary of the League of Composers. Its world *première* took place in New York on April 1, 1954. The opera has since been greatly revised, the new version being heard in New York in 1959 in performances at the Juilliard School of Music.

As part of his aim to communicate through music with a large audience everywhere, Copland also produced a good deal of functional music: for the theater (*Quiet City*); for motion pictures (*Of Mice and Men, Our Town, The Red Pony,* and *The Heiress,* the last of which received the Academy Award); for radio (*Music for Radio*); for television (the signature for the "CBS-TV Theater"); for public schools (*Outdoor* Overture, and the little opera *The Second Hurricane*). Here too—as in his concert works and opera—he was producing music that had tremendous audience appeal without sacrificing his artistic integrity or lowering his standards.

No biography of Copland could be complete without some comment on his activities to promote the interest of contemporary composers. As the founder of the Copland-Sessions concerts and the summer Yaddo Festival at Saratoga Springs in New York; as a dominating figure in the League of Composers; through his affiliations with the Koussevitzky Music Foundation and the International Society for Contemporary Music—in all this he helped to provide composers with an opportunity to get their music performed. Copland organized and directed the American Composers Alliance, which sought to protect and further the financial interests of American composers. As a writer, lecturer, and teacher he had been an indefatigable one-man propaganda agency for comtemporary music in all its varied facets. Between 1940 and 1965 he headed the composition department at the Berkshire Music Center at Tanglewood, during a part of that period (from 1957 to 1965) also filling the shoes of chairman of the faculty.

By the time he celebrated his sixtieth birthday he had become universally accepted as "the dean of American music." He had been made a member of the American Academy of Arts and Letters, and he had received an honorary doctorate from Princeton. He had been invited to Harvard as Charles Eliot Norton lecturer. He had successfully toured South America, the Soviet Union, and Israel in performances of his works. Further significant honors and commissions kept coming after 1960 to add further to the growth of his importance in American music. Among the former was the Presidential Medal of Freedom which President Johnson awarded him in 1964. From the latter came the writing of *Connotations for Orchestra,* for the opening concert of the New York Philharmonic at its new auditorium at the Lincoln Center for the Performing Arts, on September 23, 1962.

For many years Copland made his home in New York City apartments. Then, feeling the need for more serenity, he acquired a house atop a hill in Poughkeepsie, New York, overlooking the Hudson River Valley. This is his home, and here is his workbench. Tall and upright, with craggy features and a large head, he has, in the opinion of Eric Salzman, "a kind of Old Testament grandeur."

Copland's seventieth birthday in 1970 was celebrated internationally with concerts, telecasts, honorary degrees, government decorations, and elaborate tributes in the press. In 1972 he was elected president of the American Academy of Arts and Letters.

HIS MUSIC

Copland's early career represented a search for a creative identity. He experimented with jazz styles and idioms in *Music for the*

Theater and the Piano Concerto. From this he progressed in his Piano Variations, the Piano Sonata, and in *Statements* and *Symphonic Ode,* the last two for orchestra, to the kind of advanced thinking and writing, and complex technique, then so much in vogue with the modernists of the 1920s. His style now became astringent, austere, and esoteric. In the *Vitebsk* Trio, introduced at a concert of the League of Composers on February 16, 1929, he even tried writing music of Hebraic content and interest. All this time he was struggling to find himself as a composer. He found himself in the middle 1930s when he became impelled to subject himself to the discipline of simplicity, economy, clarity, lucidity, and directness, and when he began achieving a thoroughly American language through the stimulation and quotation of American folk songs. He was no longer afraid of using well-shaped melodies and catchy rhythms. His splendid technique, which never failed him, now served his ideas and not vice versa. With ballets like *Billy the Kid, Rodeo,* and *Appalachian Spring* he now became identifiably American just as he became palatable. He was now widely performed and universally esteemed.

From quotation of American folk music Copland graduated into assimilation. His Symphony No. 3 in 1946 had material that was entirely Copland's own, even though the personality and charm of this music were derived from its kinship to the spirit of American folk songs and dances. And this was equally true of his Concerto for Clarinet and Orchestra in 1948, and his opera *The Tender Land* in 1954. Meanwhile, in 1950, with his Piano Quartet, Copland became interested for the first time in the twelve-tone technique, which he used with extraordinary skill and effect in his orchestral compositions *Connotations* in 1962 and *Inscape* in 1967.

ANALYTICAL NOTES

Chamber Music. Copland wrote two important chamber music compositions, and both are in a more intricate and esoteric style than that encountered in his American-oriented ballets and orchestral works that preceded them. Indeed, the Quartet for Piano and Strings (1950) is in the twelve-tone system—Copland's first excursion into dodecaphony. The row is found in the first theme of the opening adagio serioso movement. The second theme in this movement is the twelve-tone row in retrograde. The middle movement is lively and the closing one introspective.

A decade later, in 1960, came the Nonet, for three violins, three violas, and three cellos. (This work can also be played by a string ensemble numbering as many as forty-eight players. When the violas and cellos are doubled in number, the violins are quadrupled; when the violas and cellos are tripled, the violins are sextupled.) This composition, which is in a single movement, goes backward in time to the Baroque era, through the employment of the contrapuntal form of the ricercare and through the way in which the three groups of string instruments are deployed.

Orchestral Music. *El Salón México* is the first of Copland's works to make use of folk materials, in this instance those of Mexican origin. He wrote it in 1936, inspired by a visit four years earlier to a Mexican dance hall, Salón México, in Mexico City. "All that I could hope to do was to reflect the Mexico of the tourists, and that is why I thought of *Salón México*. Because in that 'hot spot' one felt, in a very natural and unaffected way, a close contact with the Mexican people. It wasn't the music I heard, but the spirit I felt there, which attracted me. Something of that spirit is what I hope to have put into my music." He did not get around to sketching the work until he was back in this country in 1933, and he did not complete it until two years after that.

El Salón México may be regarded as an overture of Mexican popular melodies. It is a work that wears its heart on its sleeve; no elaborate analysis is required to uncover for the listener its infectious tunes and rhythms. After a few spirited and catchingly rhythmic introductory measures, in which fragments of two folk tunes are contained ("El Parlo Verde" and "La Jesuíta") there comes the song "El Mosco" in solo trumpet—"the most direct quotation of a complete melody," Copland tells us. Other Mexican tunes follow in rapid succession. One of these has the sensuous quality of a Spanish tango; the rhythm of another has kinesthetic impact. Midway, a jaunty tune for solo clarinet contributes a piquant note of happy irresponsibility.

Two years after *El Salón México*, Copland passed on from Mexican folk tunes to American ones. He did this with his ballet score for *Billy the Kid*. Eugene Loring's choreography and Lincoln Kirstein's scenario traced the career of the notorious Western outlaw from the time he launched his infamous career by avenging his mother's death to the moment he meets his own end at the hands of a posse. But this ballet is not so much interested in presenting a biography of Billy the Kid as it is in painting the pioneer background against which he moved. In his music Copland made extensive use of cowboy tunes, including "Git Along Little Dogie," "The Old Chisholm Trail," "Goodbye, Old Paint," and "O Bury Me Not on the Lone Prairie." The seven-movement orchestral suite which Copland adapted from this score has become extremely popular. These are the movement headings: The Open Prairie; In a Frontier Town; Card Game at Night; Gun Battle; Celebration Dance; Billy's Death; and The Open Prairie Again.

Rodeo, in 1942, was Copland's second ballet score using American folk songs of the West. Here both the scenario and the choreography were the work of Agnes de Mille. Once again we are thrust back into the pioneer times during the building of America's West. The action concerns the adventures of a cowgirl at a rodeo, where a roper and a wrangler fight over her, with the roper proving victorious. In his music Copland uses square-dance tunes ("Bonyparte" and "McLoed's Reel") and two Western folk songs ("Sis Joe" and "If He'd Be a Buckaroo by His Trade"). The four-movement orchestral suite which the composer derived from his ballet score has the following titles: Buckaroo Holiday; Corral Nocturne; Saturday Night Waltz; and Hoedown. The last of these has become a particular favorite not only in its original orchestral version but also in an arrangement for violin and piano.

In *Lincoln Portrait,* for narrator and orchestra, Copland quotes snatches of Stephen Foster's song "De Camptown Races," and from the Appalachian Mountains ballad "Springfield Mountain." Copland wrote *Lincoln Portrait* in 1942 on a commission from André Kostelanetz, who introduced it with the Cincinnati Symphony on May 14 of that year. The composition sets extracts of letters and speeches by Lincoln, concluding with the final part of the Gettysburg Address. There are three sections. The first portrays Lincoln's personality, what the composer called "the mysterious sense of fatality" that surrounded him, together with "something of his gentleness and simplicity of spirit." In the sprightly middle part Lincoln's background is sketched, while the final section serves as a frame for Lincoln's eloquent words.

Appalachian Spring (1944) scored its first major success as a ballet. The title (but nothing else) was taken from a poem by Hart Crane, while the ballet scenario was prepared by Martha Graham, the dancer who had commissioned Copland to write his score and who introduced the ballet. The main action is built around the celebration— by Pennsylvanian pioneers in the Appalachian Mountains—of a newly constructed farmhouse about to become the home of a bride and her farmer-husband. A neighbor provides the couple with the benefit of his advice and experience. A revivalist and his followers tell the couple about the caprices of fate. At last the married pair are left alone to begin their life together, confidently and proudly, in their new home.

The orchestral suite is in eight sections, which are played without interruption. The following analysis, prepared by the composer himself, is definitive:

(1) *Very slowly*—Introduction of the characters, one by one, in a suffused light.

(2) *Fast*—Sudden burst of unison strings in A major arpeggios starts the action.

(3) *Moderate*—Duo for the Bride and Her Intended—Scene of tenderness and passion.

(4) *Quite fast*—The Revivalist and his flock. Folksy feelings—Suggestions of square dances and country fiddlers.

(5) *Still faster*—Solo dance of the Bride—Presentiment of motherhood. Extremes of joy and fear and wonder.

(6) *Very slowly* (as at first)—Transition scene to music reminiscent of the introduction.

(7) *Calm and flowing*—Scenes of daily activity for the Bride and her Farmer-husband. There are five variations on a Shaker theme. The theme— sung by a solo clarinet—was taken from a collection of Shaker melodies compiled by Edward D. Andrews and published under the title *The Gift to Be Simple*. The melody I borrowed and used almost literally is called "Simple Gifts." . . .

(8) *Moderate*—Coda—The Bride takes her place among her neighbors. At the end the couple are left "quiet and strong in their new house." Muted strings intone a hushed prayerlike passage. The close is reminiscent of the opening music.

The Symphony No. 3 (1946), which Copland completed two years after *Appalachian Spring,* does not quote any folk songs or rhythms. But it has about it the character and personality of American folk music. The critic for the Boston *Post* amusingly subtitled it "Shostakovich in the Appalachians." However, as Copland took pains to explain, "any reference to . . . folk material in this work was purely unconscious."

The symphony was commissioned by the Koussevitzky Foundation and was introduced by the Boston Symphony Orchestra under Serge Koussevitzky on October 18, 1946. It subsequently won the Boston Symphony Award of Merit and the Music Critics Circle Award.

The first movement, which the composer describes as "broad and expressive," is built out of three clearly stated themes. The first is heard in the strings at the beginning; the second appears in violas and oboes; and the third, more vigorous than the other two, is heard in trombones and horns. "The general form," the composer explains, "is that of an arch, in which the central portion is more animated, and the final section, an extended coda, presenting a broadened version of the opening material." The second movement is in the form of a scherzo. After a brief introduction by the brass, the main theme is heard three times, first in horns and violas, then in unison strings, and finally in lower brass. The trio follows; solo woodwinds present the main melody before it is assumed by the strings. The main melody of the opening returns somewhat altered in the piano before its restatement by full orchestra. The movement ends with a reminiscence of the trio's lyrical melody, presented canonically and loudly by the entire orchestra.

The slow movement is built out of a series of sections, one blending into the other. The first section is an introduction to the body of the movement. The main melody "that supplies the thematic substance for the sectional metamorphosis that follows" is heard in the solo flute. The final movement proceeds without pause. It opens with a fanfare which Copland had previously used in a short orchestral work entitled *Fanfare for the Common Man.* The main body of this movement consists of the following materials: "a first theme in animated sixteenth-note motion; a second theme—broader and more songlike in character; a full-blown development and a refashioned return to the earlier material of the movement, leading to a peroration." Toward the close of the symphony, the first theme of the first movement returns in the violins and later on in the solo trombone; this is followed by a restatement of the second theme of the first movement in horns and trombones. With a loud and majestic declaration of the opening phrase of the symphony, the work comes to its conclusion.

Connotations (1962) and *Inscape* (1967) are two short compositions for orchestra in a twelve-tone technique. In *Connotations* the row first appears vertically in three four-voice chords. This material becomes the basis of a number of variations. *Inscape*—written on commission to help celebrate the 125th anniversary of the New York Philharmonic Orchestra, which introduced it under Leonard Bernstein's direction at the University of Michigan on September 13, 1967—is a ten-minute work constructed from two twelve-tone rows. A subdued mood is maintained consistently. To the composer, "inscape" (borrowed from Gerard Manley Hopkins) is a kind of "quasi-mystical illumination" applying to the creation of music.

Claude Debussy

"He was the incomparable painter of mystery, silence, and the infinite, of the passing cloud, and the sunlit shimmer of waves—subtleties which none before him had been capable of suggesting."

HENRI PRUNIÈRES

BORN: Saint-Germain-en-Laye, near Paris, August 22, 1862.
DIED: Paris, March 25, 1918.
MAJOR WORKS: *Ballets*—Jeux; La Bôite à joujoux (children's ballet). *Chamber Music*—String Quartet in G minor; Rhapsody for Saxophone and Piano; Rhapsody for Clarinet and Piano; Sonata for Cello and Piano; Sonata for Flute, Viola, and Harp; Sonata for Violin and Piano. *Choral Music*—L'Enfant prodigue; La Demoiselle élue. *Opera*—Pelléas et Mélisande. *Orchestral Music*—Afternoon of a Faun; Nocturnes; Danses sacrée et profane, for harp and strings; La Mer; Le Martyre de Saint-Sébastien, incidental music; Images. *Piano Music*—Pour le piano; Estampes; Masques; L'Ile joyeuse; Suite bergamasque; Images, two series; Children's Corner; La Plus que lente; preludes, two books; études, two books; En blanc et noir, for two pianos; Six Epigraphes antiques, for piano duet. *Vocal Music*—Mandoline; Cinq poèmes de Baudelaire; Ariettes oubliées; Fêtes galantes, two series; Proses lyriques; Chansons de Bilitis; Trois ballades de François Villon; Trois poèmes de Stéphane Mallarmé.

HIS LIFE

One day in 1882 Léo Delibes, professor of composition at the Paris Conservatory, was absent from the classroom. One of the students, Claude Debussy, elected to show his fellow students how harmony should *really* be taught. He went to the piano and produced such overwhelming discords and terrifying progressions that the awful sounds attracted the Conservatory director, who rushed into the room and ejected the culprit.

The desire to make a *new* kind of music—a kind of music that was not taught at the Conservatory and which was not found in the works of the masters—seemed to have been strong in Debussy long before he arrived at a clearly formulated philosophy of musical aesthetics. Again and again in the classroom he startled both his teachers and fellow students with the musical daring of his improvisations and, in his exercises, with his rebellious disregard for the rules of the textbook. "He astonished us all with his bizarre playing," recalled a fellow student, Gabriel Pierné (1863–1937), after he had become famous as composer and conductor. More than once did the harmony professor, Emile Durand, slam down the lid of Debussy's piano when, suddenly and inexplicably, the student would go off on his strange musical adventures. Durand did find ingenuity in Debussy's harmonizations to a given bass. But he would shake his head at some of the strange chords and exclaim, "It's all so utterly unorthodox!" Debussy considered his discordant writing to be a "feast for the ear." He remarked mockingly to those who objected to his discords: "Look at them! Can't they listen to chords without knowing their names?"

After the Conservatory days ended Debussy grew more audacious, more defiant of the traditions of the academicians. In Rome, as the winner of the Prix de Rome, he wrote: "I can only make my *own* music." And he would proceed to write compositions which startled and horrified the graybeards at the Conservatory. In short, he was led to the new and the unorthodox through a compulsion which, in his boyhood and youth, had been instinctive. It was a compulsion too powerful to be resisted.

Debussy's father was the owner of a humble china shop in Saint-

Germain-en-Laye, a suburb of Paris, which went into bankruptcy when the child was three years old. The family moved into Paris where the father engaged in various jobs. The family, which now numbered five children, suffered such poverty that, to relieve some of the economic pressure, four children had to go to live with a comparatively well-to-do aunt. Debussy, however, was brought up by his parents—by a mother who pampered and overprotected him; by a father who had set his heart on his son's becoming a sailor.

One of the boy's greatest pleasures came from listening to the open-air concerts in the Luxembourg and Tuileries gardens. When his aunt made it possible for him to take piano lessons from an Italian named Cerutti, Debussy revealed not only innate musical ability, but also the curiosity to try out new sounds. When his unusual talent became obvious his aunt engaged Madame Mauté de Fleurville, onetime pupil of Chopin, to teach him. She was an admirable teacher, and Debussy a receptive pupil. By the time he was eleven years old he was fully prepared to enter the Paris Conservatory.

Debussy remained at the Conservatory for eleven years. While, as we have already seen, he shocked and irritated such academicians as Marmontel and Durand with his undisguised disapproval of text-book rules, and while they did not understand what he was aiming at, his exceptional gifts were not altogether overlooked. He won several prizes, as well as the respect and encouragement of such sympathetic and progressive teachers as Lavignac and Guiraud, for his first compositions, a number of songs to texts by Théodore de Banville, completed in 1876. Even such a die-hard as Marmontel, upset as he was by the radical thinking of the young man, was finally won over to his ability. When a Russian patroness inquired at the Conservatory for a household pianist for the summer months, Marmontel did not hesitate to recommend Debussy.

The patroness who engaged Debussy was Nadezhda Filaretovna von Meck, the woman who played such a dramatic role in Tchaikovsky's life as his mysterious "beloved friend" and benefactor. She wanted Debussy for her château in the Loire district of France—to play duets with her, teach her daughters the piano, and be a member of a household trio. In the summer of 1880 Debussy traveled with the Von Meck family in France, Italy, and Austria. He was re-engaged for the summers of 1881 and 1882, which he spent with the Von Mecks at their estate in Russia.

A brief infatuation for one of the Von Meck girls was soon supplanted by a much deeper and more profound attachment, the first of Debussy's major love affairs. Madame Vasnier was a singing student whom Debussy occasionally accompanied at the piano. She was older than he and married—two points that did not appear to concern him greatly. Both Madame and Monsieur Vasnier apparently became attached to him and made him welcome at their home. From infatuation Debussy passed to adoration. He haunted the Vasnier household every day in the week, and for a period of almost five years! In the Vasnier home he did his composing and studying; he tried to get a smattering of education by reading their books; occasionally he entertained them either by playing the piano or with amusing drolleries; sometimes he joined them in a game of cards. But always he worshiped Madame Vasnier. For her he wrote and to her he dedicated his first beautiful songs—"En sourdine," "Mandoline," "Claire de lune," and so forth (1880–82). It is not improbable that Madame Vasnier responded to Debussy's ardent love; she would have been a little less than human if she had not by turns been flattered and touched by this unashamed adulation.

Debussy made two attempts at winning the Prix de Rome; both times he failed and was heartbroken. In 1884 he made a third attempt with a cantata, *L'Enfant prodigue,* and on June 27 was proclaimed the winner. Now that he had finally achieved his goal he no longer wanted it. What concerned him most of all was separation from his beloved Madame Vasnier—for as a Prix de Rome winner he would have to live three years at the Villa Medici in Rome. But to turn down a Prix de Rome was unthinkable. Debussy went to Rome on January 27, 1885—and hated it. Everything upset him: the climate, the people, the food, the music, and most of all the many stifling restrictions imposed upon him at the Villa Medici. He sought escape from misery by studying the Wagnerian music dramas, which he now came to admire passionately. When that was not sufficient he fled to Paris, probably with the intention of never returning to Rome. The Vasniers convinced him of his folly and he was back at the Villa Medici, determined to complete his three years' stay and fulfill his obligations.

One of the obligations of a Prix de Rome winner was to send back to the Conservatory, at periodic intervals, new musical works, called *envois,* as evidence of progress. The first *envoi* sent back by Debussy was *Zulëima,* an adaptation of Heine's *Alamanzor.* The academicians in Paris denounced it as "bizarre, incomprehensible, and impossible to execute." The second *envoi, Printemps*—inspired by Botticelli's *Primavera*—was somewhat better liked; but there was still severe criticism of Debussy's frequent heresy in his harmonic thinking.

In the spring of 1887 Debussy decided once and for all to escape from the "Roman jail" and to return to his beloved Paris, even though his three-year period was not yet up. He placated his conscience by submitting the last of his *envois: La Demoiselle élue (The Blessed Damozel),* text based on Dante Gabriel Rossetti. The judges condemned the vagueness of the writing, considering it below the acceptable standards of the Prix de Rome. But it was an original score, and a daring one, and the first in which Debussy's later style can be said to have been hinted at. It took many years for *La Demoiselle élue* to get heard, that performance taking place on April 8, 1893, at a concert of the Société Nationale in Paris. Several notable musicians and critics—including Vincent d'Indy and Julien Tiersot—praised it highly.

For a while Debussy tried to re-establish himself with the Vasniers. But the flame could not be revived. He turned for consolation to Gabrielle Dupont—"Gaby of the green eyes" as he liked to call her— and set up house with her in the Rue de Londres. For the next ten years she managed his household, tended to him, guarded him from interruptions and distractions when he worked—and appeared to make him both comfortable and happy.

In the cafés which he now frequented Debussy came into contact with the progressive tendencies in French poetry and art by meeting and talking to their spokesmen: the Symbolist poet Stéphane Mallarmé, for example, and the Impressionist painters Manet and Renoir. Each Tuesday evening these men and their followers gathered to discuss the aesthetics of the new movements; and before long Debussy was one of them. Influenced by their ideas—and by his conversations with the eccentric and revolutionary French musician Erik Satie (1866–1925), whom he met for the first time in 1891 at the café Auberge de Clou, and whom he then befriended—Debussy crystallized his own thinking about music in general and his own music in particular. He now tried to approximate in music what the Symbolists and the Impressionists were doing in poetry and art without abandoning his own stylistic tendencies. He aspired to become a *French* musician (*"musicien français"* as he began calling himself), a composer of lean, objective, precise music, a music that with its understatement and economy stood in direct opposition to the inflated methods of the German Romantic school.

And he began producing masterworks. On December 29, 1893, the Ysaÿe Quartet introduced in Paris Debussy's Quartet in G minor. Because its language was so new, many critics failed to recognize its greatness. One of them described it as "orgies of modulation"; others objected to its unorthodox part writing. Paul Dukas was definitely in the minority when he wrote: "Debussy is one of the most gifted and original artists of the younger generation of musicians."

But Debussy continued writing in his own way, and he kept growing all the time. One year after the quartet, on December 22, 1894, came his exquisite orchestral prelude, *L'Après-midi d'un faune* (*The Afternoon of a Faun*). Between 1893 and 1899 he completed the three Nocturnes, for orchestra, and the song cycles *Proses lyriques* and *Chansons de Bilitis*. Meanwhile, in 1892, he started working on his most ambitious project of all, an opera based on Maurice Maeterlinck's drama *Pelléas et Mélisande,* the writing of which was to consume ten years and which was to contain the quintessence of his art.

His personal life was changing. "Gaby of the green eyes" was succeeded by Rosalie Texier, a dressmaker of plebeian mind, bourgeois tastes, and no musical intelligence to speak of. But she had chestnut hair, a delicate mouth, an infectious charm—and Debussy fell in love. They were married on October 19, 1899. After a brief celebration at dinner and the circus the Debussys returned to their modest apartment on the Rue Cardinet. For a period, at any rate, Debussy was singularly attached to this woman, whom he lovingly called "Lily-Lilo," and whose interests were so different from his. "This manuscript belongs to my Lily-Lilo. . . . It is proof of the deep and passionate joy I find in being her husband." So he wrote on the title page of his Nocturnes in 1901—just three years before he abandoned her. But that comes later.

In the first three years of his life with "Lily-Lilo" at the Rue Cardinet, Debussy completed his magnum opus, *Pelléas et Mélisande*. It was introduced at the Opéra-Comique on April 30, 1902.

That *première* took place in an atmosphere charged with hostility, scandal, controversy, and misunderstanding. Perhaps no other epoch-making work was ever launched under such storm and stress.

The story of that dramatic *première* begins sometime in 1901, when Debussy went to Passy to play his score for Maurice Maeterlinck, the author of the play. It is doubtful if Maeterlinck knew what he was hearing; it would have required a far more astute musical perceptiveness than Maeterlinck's to recognize the greatness of the score, divested as it now was of orchestral accompaniment and adequate singers. The story goes that Maeterlinck gave visible signs of boredom and before Debussy was through was even half asleep. Only one point interested Maeterlinck about the forthcoming production: His mistress, Georgette Leblanc, had to sing the principal role. Debussy consented; Georgette Leblanc began studying the role, several times coached by Debussy.

But Albert Carré, director of the Opéra-Comique, had other ideas. For the role of Mélisande he selected the glamorous Scottish-American soprano, Mary Garden. The news, when it reached Maeterlinck, had the impact of an atomic blast. Georgette screamed of "betrayal." Maeterlinck was so furious that he jumped out of the window of his ground-floor apartment, cane in hand, with the intention of giving the composer the beating of his life—feeling that Mary Garden would have never been chosen without Debussy's permission. The beating was not administered, and a few days later he spoke of challenging the composer to a duel.

As the evening for the *première* drew near, Maeterlinck did everything in his power to discredit the opera. On April 13, 1902, he published an open letter in *Le Figaro* announcing that the opera was being presented "against my will." He added that *Pelléas et Mélisande* "is a piece which has become almost an enemy alien to me. Barred from all control of my work, I am compelled to wish that its failure should be resounding and prompt."

As if matters were not bad enough for Debussy, there were complications of a different nature. Rehearsals with the orchestra were becoming increasingly disturbed, due largely to the sloppy manuscript prepared by an inexperienced copyist. Robert Jardillier tells the story in his book about *Pelléas*. "He wrote sharps for flats, so that Debussy himself could not make out which was which. Frequently, the change of clef or time signature after a rest was left out. Result: exasperating rehearsals; impossible to proceed; every time a stop. 'Is this a sharp?' . . . A first-desk player declares that the music makes no sense." There was trouble with the scenic designers too.

"To gain time, the scenery is entrusted to two great specialists. . . . Catastrophe! *Pelléas* demands thirteen changes of scenery, but it is impossible to accomplish in the hall. The stage technicians swear a thousand oaths, and, to save the situation, Debussy sits down to compose, between two rehearsals, the necessary interludes; it is a miracle that the stitches do not show." There was even trouble with the censor. In one of the scenes the betrayed husband lifts up his son to spy through the window whether the lovers are near the bed. This was found "inadmissible on the stage of a subsidized theater."

All these production difficulties were eventually solved. But the unwavering antagonism of Maeterlinck was a more serious business. On the day of the dress rehearsal, April 28, a satirical brochure about the opera was distributed outside the Opéra-Comique. Some insisted that it was the work of Maeterlinck himself, who would stop at nothing to reduce the coming performance to the ridiculous. Largely due to this brochure, the dress rehearsal took place in a charged atmosphere. The friends of the dramatist were out in full force. At different times their loud guffaws could be heard ringing in the theater. It was because of these guffaws that the censor demanded the deletion of the window episode. But there was more than laughter, disturbed arguments, shouts of approval and disapproval; there was almost a riot.

But in spite of the disturbances the entire performance took place. And in spite of a repetition of similar episodes and disturbances the *première* was witnessed on the evening of April 30. The conflicting opinions in the press reflected the attitude of the audience. Some were plainly hostile. They described the opera as "decadent," "morbid," "nihilistic," "spineless," a "musical hashish and kaleidoscope of sound," etc. One Paris correspondent to a London journal found the work "amusing in its absurdity," while S. Marchesi reported in the *Monthly Musical Record* that "the opinion of the best musical critics is unanimous in declaring *Pelléas et Mélisande* a work of musical decline."

The admirers were equally articulate and effusive. "The inspiration never weakens for a moment," wrote Gustave Bret. To Vincent d'Indy the score enhanced the design of the play, revealing "hidden images" and intensifying "its expression, while always permitting the word to be discernible through the fluid element of the music."

But in spite of its admirers *Pelléas et Mélisande* appeared doomed.

The opposition was indefatigable in its attacks. To offset its influence Carré filled the balcony with sympathetic students who could be counted upon to serve as a claque. But what actually saved the opera was the public's curiosity about a work that had aroused so much discussion and conflicting opinion. By its seventh performance *Pelléas et Mélisande* was able to sell out the theater. It was seen fourteen times in May and June. And interest in it remained so alive that it returned to the repertory the following season and was given ten presentations.

Debussy now became one of the most famous and provocative composers in France: the center of a cult; worshiped and attacked with equal extravagance. Almost oblivious to all reactions, positive or negative, he kept on writing his music, and kept on producing masterworks for the orchestra, for the piano, and for the voice.

By 1904 Debussy began to see "Lily-Lilo" as she really was. He started looking for tenderness and understanding elsewhere, finding them in the person of Emma Bardac, wife of a wealthy banker. When "Lily-Lilo" tried to commit suicide by shooting herself Debussy became the object of scandal and vituperation. A few of his friends never spoke to him again. "I have seen so many desertions around me!" Debussy wrote to Laloy, one friend who had remained loyal. "Enough to be forever disgusted by anything that bears the name of man. . . . I want to tell you what I've been through. It's ugly, tragic. I have suffered greatly, morally." But nothing could keep Debussy from marrying Emma on October 15, 1905, once the double divorce had been consummated. For the rest of his life he remained tenderly devoted to her. They had a daughter, Claude-Emma, whom Debussy always called by the affectionate nickname of "Chouchou."

The last decade of Debussy's life was filled with physical and mental agony. Suffering from cancer, he had to undergo two painful operations which left him, in his own words, "a walking corpse." To make matters worse, with the outbreak of World War I he was beset by such pressing financial problems that often he did not have the price for fuel or food. And yet he kept on working, frequently in intense pain. He completed two important works for the keyboard, *En blanc et noir,* for two pianos, and the two books of études, for solo piano; also three sonatas, the first for cello and piano, the second for flute, viola, and piano, and the third for violin and piano.

The last time he appeared on the concert platform was for the world *première* of his Violin Sonata, on May 5, 1917, when he shared the performances with the violinist, Gaston Poulet. By now Debussy was revealing the ravages that illness and deprivations had inflicted on him. Here is how André Suares described him at this time: "His complexion was the color of melted wax or of ashes. In his eyes there was no feverish flame, but the dull reflections of silent pools. There was not even bitterness in his gloomy smile. . . . His fat, plump hand, like the hand of a priest, hung from his arm, his arm from his shoulder and his head from his body. . . . As he sat down, his eyes, under their flickering lids, moved slowly round, like those of people who would see without being seen, who steal a glance at something they seem only half to see. . . ."

On March 17, 1918, Debussy applied for a seat recently vacated at the Académie de France. He did not live to receive it, passing away at his home eight days later. The papers hardly noticed his death. France was then too deep in the war to concern itself with much else. The funeral was drab, attended only by a few relatives and friends. As the funeral procession progressed from the Avenue du Bois-de-Boulogne to Père-Lachaise, few, indeed, knew who the dead man was. The closest to identification came from a shopkeeper as the hearse passed by: "It seems," he said, "that it was some musician." It was only after Debussy had been dead for some time —and after his body had been removed from Père-Lachaise to its permanent resting place at Passy—that the world of music suddenly realized that the greatest musician of France was no longer alive.

In the prime of his life Debussy was a familiar and easily recognizable figure in the streets and cafés of Paris. He looked the typical Bohemian of Montparnasse, particularly in his favorite costume of flowing cape and broad-brimmed felt hat. His face had a kind of Levantine swarthiness; it was said he looked like a Syrian. It was dominated by a high forehead and a black beard. His curly hair fell over one eyebrow, drawing attention to his dark and intense eyes.

"Of medium height," writes Oscar Thompson, "he was short-legged and large of trunk. His shoulders were wide. His voice was low but, as Lerolle remembered it, of a marked nasal quality. . . . His figure was flabby and suggested indolence." Nevertheless his movements had feline grace. Indeed, as Oscar Thompson remarked in the very opening line of his biography of Debussy, "something feline in his nature was noted again and again by those who knew him." An interesting point—for if Debussy had any single passion outside of music it was for cats; his household was never without one or without feline images in colored porcelain.

His weakness was to stay up late at night with his artist and writer friends at his favorite cafés—the Chat Noir, Chez Weber, Brasserie Pousset. "He was a moderate eater and an equally moderate drinker," says Thompson, "usually content with a ham sandwich and a mug of Strasbourg beer or fine, pale English ale." Other diversions included the circus (he was fond of the clowns), the card game bezique (at which he was known to cheat occasionally), and collecting books (which he rarely read).

HIS MUSIC

Though Debussy disliked the term "Impressionism," particularly as applied to his music, he was the father of that style in music. Many have been influenced by it; many have imitated it. But nobody surpassed Debussy in the magic and enchantment with which it was used.

The word "Impressionism" is so inextricably associated with Debussy that a review of some essential facts about the movement, however familiar, is illuminating. Two sources are usually given for the word "Impressionism." One is a painting by Claude Monet of a sunrise at sea which he called *"Une impression."* Another is a quotation from a catalogue of Edouard Manet's pictures exhibited in 1867, which explains that the painter's intention was to render "his impression." In any case, a school of French painters arose in the closing decades of the nineteenth century—paralleling a similar movement in poetry known as Symbolism—which sought in art not the expression of a subject or an idea, but rather the feelings and impressions that the subject or idea arouses.

All his life Debussy had been impelled to search for something new in musical expression. He tried out new chords, progressions, cadences, and tone colors because the traditional ones did not satisfy him. Yet he had no clear direction or purpose in these experimental efforts. Listening to the discussions of the Impressionists and Symbolists he suddenly realized—possibly with the excitement of an explorer coming upon a new world—that these people were formalizing what he had long felt instinctively. Their ideas about poetry and painting were applicable to music as well—or, at any rate, to the kind of music he wanted to write.

In 1891 Debussy met Erik Satie. Satie was then earning his living by playing the piano in a Montmartre cabaret. But he was also the composer of strange, exotic pieces for the piano which bore outlandish titles (*Desiccated Embryos, Flabby Preludes for a Dog*) and utilized unorthodox techniques (barless notation, consecutive chords of the ninth). Satie's unusual music was not just the caprice of a quixotic personality, but the fruition of a definite and clearly thought-out philosophy about music. Satie was rebelling against the large forms, the excessive emotions, and the occasional philosophical implications of the music of the German Romantic composers; he wanted to stand at the opposite artistic pole to Wagner, with the latter's super-structures and sensuousness. In short, Satie was striving for a characteristically French art—as opposed to the German—an art that was simple, refined, witty, and above everything else lean and economical.

Satie's ideas made a profound impression on Debussy. For one thing, after two visits to Bayreuth, Debussy had passed from adulation of Wagner to outright revolt. "Don't you see that Wagner with all his formidable power—yes, in spite of his power—has led music astray into sterile and pernicious paths?" he would argue with the Symbolists. Besides, he too felt the need for sensitive, terse, and objective self-expression. Satie's ideas complemented for him the principles set down by the Symbolists and Impressionists, giving him still a clearer musical aesthetic.

In 1892 Debussy's artistic goal became set; he progressed toward it with courage and without wavering. In 1893 he wrote the Quartet in G minor and one year later *L'Après-midi d'un faune*. With these two works, musical Impressionism can be said to have been born.

In developing his style he became one of music's great innovators, introducing a new concept of harmony, tonality, tone color, and form which anticipated and made possible the revolutions of the *enfants terribles* who followed him. He filled his music with chords which moved about freely without dependence on those that preceded or followed them, and without concern for a tonal center—with unresolved ninth and eleventh chords often contributing discord. He was partial to unusual scales and modes, and made the whole-tone scale the basic tool of his Impressionist workshop. In further defiance of accepted procedures, he avoided formal cadences; did not hesitate to allow intervals of fourths, fifths, and octaves to move in parallel motion; and, in his orchestration, compelled individual timbres to stand out with wonderful clarity while creating new tone qualities through his individual way of writing for the woodwinds and the percussion. He changed meters and rhythms frequently, often so subtly concealing the beat and at times so effectively removing the limitations of the bar line that a continuous and uninterrupted pulse was produced.

But he was, of course, much more than just an innovator. The novelty of his sounds no longer startles the ear; but their magic never palls. Not only was he the first of the great painters in music; up to now he is still the greatest of them all. He was, as Oscar Thompson put it so well,* "the poet of mists and fountains, clouds and rain; of dusk and of glints of sunlight through the leaves; he was moonstruck and seastruck and a lost soul under a sky bespent with stars."

ANALYTICAL NOTES

Chamber Music. Debussy's chamber music came at both ends of his career. Strangely enough, his masterwork came at its dawn and represents the first flowering of the composer's genius. All the rest—three sonatas—marked the dusk of his career and the decline of his powers.

The masterwork was the Quartet in G minor, completed in 1893. The form is throughout traditional, one of the last instances in which Debussy did not use a structural scheme of his own. The first movement is in the accepted sonata form; the second is a scherzo; the third is in the three-part song form; and the last is the kind of finale often found in other and earlier quartets. But here the subservience to the past ends. Throughout the quartet the writing is so daring that it took almost a decade for the work to be fully appreciated. Tone color is given greater importance than form; subtle innuendos are given preference to outright statements. Exquisite effects are sought after, and achieved through vagueness of tonality. The nebulous harmonic texture and delicate timbres, the spectrum of colors—all this was decidedly new in quartet writing in 1893.

* *Debussy: Man and Artist*, by Oscar Thompson. New York: Dodd, Mead & Co., 1937.

The first movement is made up of two themes. The first is sharply accented and becomes the motto for the entire quartet. This is later contrasted with a poignant melody dominated by solo passages in the violin and viola. The second movement is concerned mostly with the motto theme, but altered in rhythm, tempo, and intervallic structure; it appears first in the viola, with a pizzicato background, and after that in the violin. The slow movement that follows is the finest page of the quartet. Muted strings present a sensuous song. After the middle section, in which violin and cello are prominent in a second sustained flight of melody, the opening material returns. The powerful finale pays particular attention to the motto theme. It is heard, inverted in the violin, after a one-measure introduction by the cello; and after that the theme becomes the core of a fugato section.

Opera. *Pelléas et Mélisande,* completed in 1902, is Debussy's only opera. It is one of the most successful attempts to create a single artistic entity out of music and drama; and it opened new vistas for opera. Maurice Maeterlinck's poetic play, set in a misty dreamworld in which the characters move like shadows, is filled with imagery and symbolism. Debussy sensed at once that this was a text most ideally suited for his style.

Maeterlinck's drama was a variation of the Tristan and Isolde story. Golaud comes upon Mélisande at a fountain, falls in love with her, and brings her back to the castle of his father, King Arkel. After they are married his brother Pelléas is so struck by her beauty that he falls in love with her. They become lovers. Golaud, inflamed by his jealousy, kills Pelléas. Mélisande, who has given birth to a child, dies soon after this; a repentant Golaud is at her side begging her for forgiveness.

In the vagueness of its musical writing and the unity of its mood, Debussy's score caught magically the essence of the poetical drama. Music is made subservient to the play. Without the text, the score loses an inextricable part of its meaning and poignancy.

The style and structure of the opera are unorthodox. In place of set arias and ensemble numbers there are declamations which closely imitate the patterns of speech. "The characters of the drama," Debussy wrote in explanation, "endeavor to sing like real persons, and not in an arbitrary language or antiquated traditions." In place of big scenes or dramatic conflicts, so long an element of the theater, there are only the most delicate suggestions and nuances, evanescent moods, misty atmospheres. All is understatement. Strings are frequently muted. The rest of the orchestra also whispers. Only in the entr'actes is the full orchestra used, while throughout the score there are just four fortissimos. Even when the story rises toward a dramatic peak—as when Pelléas and Mélisande first reveal to each other how much they are in love with one another, or in the closing scene when a grief-stricken Golaud tries to win forgiveness from a dead Mélisande—the music does little more than faintly suggest the emotional upheaval involved.

The score also boasts harmonic daring: iconoclastic harmonies of the seventh and ninth moving in organum-like parallel motion. In other ways, too, the opera is unusual, and most particularly in the free and fluid way in which declamation courses throughout the opera, its motion frequently unimpeded by bar lines—an expressive, eloquent declamation that is half song and half speech and which replaces the arias, duets, and ensemble numbers traditional with opera. "I have tried," as Debussy explained, "to trace a path that others may follow, broadening it with individual discoveries which will, perhaps, free dramatic music from the heavy yoke under which it existed for so long a time."

Pelléas et Mélisande created a revolution in opera. Oscar Thompson gives three reasons why this is so: "because of (1) the word setting, which enables the sung text to move with almost the naturalness of speech; (2) the suggestive background of the orchestra, which supplies for the drama what may be termed a tonal envelope, without constituting itself either an accompaniment for the singers or a series of symphonic expansions in competition with them; (3) the mood expressiveness of the score which, in its reticence and lack of emotional stress, takes on the mystery of the other-worldly, and ends in being profoundly human in its sympathy and pathos."

Because of the oneness of its style, mood, and texture, *Pelléas et Mélisande* does not have individual arias or ensemble numbers that have become popular independent of the opera. Every part of the opera relies for its artistic interest on its place in the whole; divorced from that place, it loses something vital and indispensable.

Orchestral Music. *L'Après-midi d'un faune,* or *The Afternoon of a Faun,* (1892–94) is one of Debussy's perfect creations, sustaining a delicate, nebulous atmosphere from the first bar to the last while evoking an impressionist picture with exquisite sensibility. Its inspiration was Stéphane Mallarmé's poem of the same name. The reason why Debussy called this composition a prelude was because he had originally planned a triptych based on the Mallarmé poem—comprising a prelude, an interlude, and a finale. He finally decided to abandon this project in favor of a single movement which he had intended to be the opening prelude.

The poem itself is in the vague style of the Symbolists. It is a languorous description of a faun in a delicious state between waking and dreaming, imagining he has seen a nymph. He is now awake, trying to understand the sensations he has just felt and to analyze the visions he has just seen. His feelings become intense and turbulent. Then he succumbs once more to sleep, to return to his vanished dream.

This half-real world of the faun is created in the opening bars with a lonely chant for solo flute, the principal theme. With a chord in the woodwinds, the call of horns, and after that arpeggios in the harp, the sylvan setting of the faun is brought to us in all its shimmering beauty. The song of the flute returns, more extended than before. Soon there is another sensual melody, this time in the oboe. The music grows more passionate. A brief subject for the woodwinds and horns leads directly to a climax. But the spell so suddenly broken is restored with a monologue for solo violin and with the return of the principal melody in the flutes. This melody now passes to flute and solo cello and appears in a disfigured form in muted horns and violins. After a gentle chord in the flutes, the music dissolves. The hazy world of the nymph vanishes; the spell is gone.

The Nocturnes for Orchestra were completed in 1899, five years after the orchestral prelude. In writing orchestral nocturnes the composer intended his title "to have a more general and, above all, a more decorative meaning," as he explained. "We are not concerned with the form of the Nocturne, but with everything that this word includes in the way of diversified impressions and special lights."

Debussy provided a program for each of the three Nocturnes. The first, *"Nuages"* ("Clouds"), portrays the "unchangeable appearance of the sky, with the slow and solemn march of clouds dissolving in a gray agony tinted with white." The movement of the clouds is suggested with subdued chords for clarinets and bassoons soon supplemented by oboes. The nebulous chords move to different parts of the orchestra as the English horn plays a poignant theme. After that the solo viola is heard in a song against a background of two oboes. Still another subject is found first in the flute and harp, and after that in the solo strings. Earlier material is recalled to end the piece.

The second Nocturne, *"Fêtes"* ("Festivals"), is, as Debussy explained, "rich with movement, rhythm, dancing. . . . There is also the episode of a procession . . . passing through the festival and blended with it. But the main idea remains the festival and its blended music." The rhythm of a dance is presented by the violins. A gay tune for English horn and clarinets moves against this rhythm. After a fanfare for brass and glissandos on the harp, the original theme reappears in flutes and oboes, though in a slightly altered version. A new subject is found in the woodwinds after calls in the trumpet and oboe; this subject is developed intensely until a climax erupts from the orchestra. The procession is now described with a march rhythm clearly articulated by harps, drums, and plucked strings. The march theme is then sounded by the trumpets, repeated by the woodwinds, and taken up by the brass. The mood changes suddenly. There is a song for the oboe. The revelry dies down, echoing in the distance and ebbing away.

These two Nocturnes are the most famous of the set. The third, *"Sirènes"* ("Sirens"), is heard less frequently. Debussy's description follows: "The sea and its innumerable rhythms; then amid the billows silvered by the moon the mysterious song of the Sirens is heard; they laugh, and the song passes on." The song of the Sirens is a wordless chant for eight mezzo-soprano voices.

La Mer (*The Sea*), completed in 1905, is structurally the composer's most ambitious work for orchestra. In many respects it is one of the most elusive of his works to analyze. As Oscar Thompson noted, the work "lacks those fixed points which can be recognized in the description of a symphony and to which can be related details of departure from, as well as conformity with, the familiar patterns. It is not feasible to refer to tonalities, since there is a kind of incessant modulation. To attempt to particularize thematic material is also futile, because of equally incessant transformations." Nor did Debussy leave a detailed and specific program to guide us. The listener is compelled to respond intuitively to Debussy's many-sided portrait of the sea—

even as Debussy himself responded intuitively to the beauty and majesty of the sea he portrayed.

The work is in three movements, or "sketches," as Debussy preferred to call them. There is a subtle bond unifying the three parts, which are integrated into a single over-all concept so wonderfully that no single movement can stand by itself successfully (in the way that individual movements of the Nocturnes or the orchestral *Images* can). As a matter of fact the final movement is dependent on the first, since thematic material is repeated.

The first "sketch" is called *"De l'aube à midi sur la mer"* ("From Dawn to Noon at Sea"). It begins with rising and falling figures suggesting the undulations of waves. A passage for muted horn and trumpet brings up the peaceful scene. The music swells, changes colors, even as does the sea at different times of the day. The movement ends with a noble chorale for the brass, "the chorale of the depths," as it has been described. The second part begins without pause: *"Jeux de vagues"* ("Play of the Waves"). Here snatches of themes are altered so frequently that it is difficult to follow the various transformations. The ever changing rhythms and tone colors bring up a picture of the sport of waves. But the playful caprice of the sea becomes wild and elemental in the final "sketch," *"Dialogue du vent et de la mer"* ("Dialogue of the Wind and the Sea"). There are rushing figures in the whole-tone scale, as the immensity of the sea is before us. Two of the main ideas of the first movement (the subject for muted horns and trumpet, and the chorale theme) return; the latter is built up into a powerful climax. The music ends with soft undulating harmonies, as the waves of the sea become more passive.

Ibéria is the second, and the most famous, of the three works for orchestra collectively entitled *Images* (not to be confused with the two sets of *Images* for the piano). It was completed in 1910. One year before he had completed *Gigues* and *Rondes de printemps,* which became the first and third parts of *Images.* The music of *Gigues* was derived from English folk music, specifically the English jig. Its principal melody is given by a solo oboe d'amore after a twenty-measure introduction. French folk song was the musical source of *Rondes de printemps,* just as springtime was its inspiration. The published score quotes the following line as a clue to the music's meaning: "Long live the month of May! Welcome to May with its savage banner!"

Ibéria is often played independently of the other parts of *Images*. Debussy did not here intend a portrait of Spain, but a description of the feelings and impressions aroused in him by that country. Truth to tell, his knowledge of Spain was meager. The sum total of his personal experience with it was a one-hour visit to the town of San Sebastián, where he attended a bullfight. What he knew about Spanish backgrounds, folk songs, and dances was acquired by reading books, looking at pictures, and hearing flamenco songs and the music of the Spanish guitarists at the Paris Exposition of 1889–90. Yet despite this superficial information he succeeded in catching the essence of Spain in his music. One who was no less than the foremost contemporary composer of Spain, Manuel de Falla, regarded *Ibéria* as more authentic than similar works by many Spanish composers. Here is what Falla wrote: "The echoes from the villages, a kind of *sevillana*—the generic theme of the work—which seems to float in a clear atmosphere of scintillating light; the intoxicating spell of Andalusian nights; the festive gaiety of a people dancing to the joyous strains of a *banda* of guitars and *bandurrias* . . . all this whirls in the air, approaches and recedes, and our imagination is continually kept awake and dazzled by the power of an intensely expressive and richly varied music."

Ibéria is in three movements. The first, *"Par les rues et par les chemins"* ("In the Streets and Byways"), opens with a riot of rhythm and color; for the streets of Spain are vivid with sights and sounds. A saucy tune is played by two clarinets, accompanied by harmonies in the oboes and bassoons and a persistent rhythm in the tambourine. The theme is repeated by different instruments of the orchestra before a new subject is heard in the viola and oboe. A change of tempo brings on a marchlike theme for four horns in unison. After persistent repetitions of this theme, the principal subject returns in the oboes.

The second movement, *"Les Parfums de la nuit"* ("The Perfumes of the Night"), evokes the romance of a night in Spain. A languorous subject is given by muted divided violins and violas. Glissandos and chromatic runs set the stage for a haunting melody for oboe against harmonies in divided violas and strings. After muted strings recall one of the main themes of the first movement, a stirring climax develops. Earlier subjects are briefly recalled, after which the movement ends with the tolling of bells.

The third part, *"Le Matin d'un jour de fête"* ("The Morning of a Festive Day"), enters without interruption. A march rhythm is forcefully enunciated. Different instruments of the orchestra enter gradually. There is some recollection of moods and themes from the preceding two movements, sometimes with a suggestion of parody. The tempo quickens; the sonority expands. The festivities now become abandoned as merrymakers lose all restraint and surrender to gaiety.

Piano Music. The preludes of Debussy form one of the landmarks in piano music. No one since Chopin had so changed the character and technique of piano writing as did Debussy. The essence of that change is found in the preludes. The new colors, nuances, effects, atmospheres created by Debussy—largely through his harmonic writing and a new approach to resonance—brought an expressiveness to the keyboard it did not know even with Chopin and Liszt.

Debussy wrote two sets of preludes, twelve in each set, between 1910 and 1913. Each prelude is free in form and has the character of an improvisation. They are far different in style from a Chopin prelude, which is the medium for expressing stormy, passionate, poetic moods. With Debussy a prelude is a fleeting mood or impression, reserved and objective, and not necessarily carrying out the programmatic implications of its title. In this connection it is significant to point out that Debussy placed the title of each prelude at the *end* of the composition. One reason was that on several occasions the title came to him after the piece had been written; another was his wish to have each piece heard as objective music.

Not all the preludes are of equal quality, but the best of them are among the finest miniatures in piano music. In the first set, five may be regarded as representative. *"Les Sons et les parfums tournent dans l'air du soir"* ("Sounds and Odors Blend in the Evening Air")—title from Baudelaire—is voluptuous music. *"Les Collines d'Anacapri"* ("The Hills of Anacapri") combines the rhythm of a tarantella with a melody that sounds like a Neapolitan folk song. *"Des pas sur la neige"* ("Steps on the Snow") is a melancholy portrait of an icebound landscape. *"La Fille aux cheveux de lin"* ("The Girl with the Flaxen Hair"), one of Debussy's most exquisite melodies, was inspired by Leconte de Lisle's *Chanson écos-saise*. *"La Cathédrale engloutie"* ("The Engulfed Cathedral") is an interpretation of the same Breton legend that Edouard Lalo (1823–92) used for his opera *Le Roi d'Ys*. In the clear light of morning, so the legend says, it is possible to see the cathedral of Ys rising out of the waves. Bells toll; the priests chant their prayers. Slowly the cathedral returns into the depths of the water. The principal melodic ideas represent, respectively, the chant of the priests, the quiet sea, the gentle surge of the waves, the tolling bells, and the chant of the priests.

On the whole, the second set of preludes is less consistently in-spired than the first. There is a great deal of dross here, since when this was written (1913) Debussy's creative strength was on the decline. But there is some gold too. The following preludes are in Debussy's best vein: *"La Puerta del Vino,"* a vivid picture of the gate of the Alhambra, stylistically marked by the use of the habanera rhythm in conjunction with an ornamented Andalusian melody; *"Les Terrasses des audiences au clair de lune"* ("Reception in the Moonlight"), a dreamy picture of the night which quotes the popular French tune "Au clair de la lune"; and *"Ondine,"* the por-trait of a playful nymph.

The *Estampes*—"prints" or "etchings"—date from 1903 and com-prise three descriptive pieces. The first, *"Pagodes,"* re-creates a Chinese atmosphere through the use of the oriental pentatonic scale and the simulation of tolling bells. This is followed by an etching of Spain called *"Soirée dans Grenade"* ("Evening in Granada") about which Manuel de Falla said it "conjures up the effect of images mirrored by the moonlight upon the limpid waters of the large *albercas* ad-joining the Alhambra." A Spanish serenade is here accompanied by chords suggesting the strummings of a mandolin. In the concluding movement, *"Jardins sous la pluie,"* ("Gardens in the Rain"), the spatter of rain is described in delicate arpeggios; the return of the sun, dissipating the storm, is suggested through a subtle modulation. Melodically this piece is characterized by its quotation of two French songs: "Nous n'irons plus au bois" and the lullaby, "Do, do, l'enfant do."

In the *Suite bergamasque* (the allusion here is to Verlaine's al-literative phrase *"masques et bergamasques"*), Debussy tried to re-create the refined style of the French harpsichord composers of the sixteenth and seventeenth centuries. The suite begins with a prelude and includes two old dance forms found in the old French suites, a minuet and a passepied. But the suite has remained famous largely due to the third movement (which comes between the minuet and the passepied), which is probably one of the most popular pieces written by Debussy. It is that evocative, pure, impressionistic picture of night called *"Clair de lune."*

Debussy had originally intended *L'Ile joyeuse* (*Happy Island*) for *Suite bergamasque,* but he finally decided to publish it as an independent number, which he did in 1904. This sensual music is intended to portray through tones Watteau's *Embarquement pour Cythère;* it is particularly fascinating for its rhythmic ingenuity and for the way the piano sonorities simulate orchestral sound.

There are two series of *Images* for the piano, the first appearing in 1905, and the second two years after that; each series comprises three numbers. The essence of Debussy's impressionism is found in the opening piece of the first series: *"Reflets dans l'eau"* ("Reflections in the Water"). Picturesque chords and shimmering arpeggios create images reflected on the surface of still water. Debussy himself regarded the writing of this piece to embody "the newest discoveries in harmonic writing"; many of the chords, made up from the whole-tone and pentatonic scales, are used in revolutionary sequences. The remaining two numbers in this first series are *"Hommage à Rameau"* and *"Mouvement."*

In the second series of *Images,* the gem is *"Poissons d'or"* ("Goldfish"), the concluding number. Debussy's inspiration was said to be a precious oriental lacquer on which a water faun was depicted. The music, then, is not intended to describe goldfish, as its title implies, but to re-create the sensations of the composer in the presence of a beautiful piece of art work.

With the *Children's Corner,* Debussy enters the world of the child and describes what he sees. He wrote this suite between 1906 and 1908 for his little daughter, "Chouchou." English titles were used both for the entire work and for its respective movements to suggest games played with a French child by an English governess. There are six sections. In the first, "Doctor Gradus ad Parnassum," a child struggles with his piano exercises. This is followed by "Jimbo's Lullaby," Jimbo being a toy elephant. The three sections that follow are little tone pictures, the title of each providing the clue to the program: "Serenade of the Doll," "The Snow Is Dancing," and "The Little Shepherd." In the concluding piece, "Golliwogg's Cakewalk," Debussy uses the strutting rhythm of that American popular dance the cakewalk. The discerning ear will also detect in this piece a brief satirical quotation from Wagner's *Tristan and Isolde*.

Among Debussy's last works for the piano are a composition for four hands (*Six Epigraphes antigues,* in 1914) and another for two pianos (*En blanc et noir,* in 1915). Two volumes of études, in 1915, were the composer's last works for the solo piano. While intended to present and solve various technical problems for the student, these études actually sum up the composer's own lifelong experiments with his methods, idioms, techniques, and approaches in writing for the keyboard.

Vocal Music. Debussy was not only one of the greatest of all French composers of the art song, but also one of the most French of all song composers. In songs he fully realized his mission to be *"un musicien français."* His hypersensitive response to French poetry; his extraordinary capacity to mold his lyric line along the contours of the inflections and cadences of the French language; and his consummate success in adapting the means and the materials of Impressionism to the requirements of his texts, enabling him to find the exact musical equivalent for every shade and nuance of the poem he was setting—all this gave him an eminent place among French song composers. Whether he was writing music for the verses of Verlaine or Baudelaire, Mallarmé or Pierre Louÿs, Villon or Charles d'Orléans, Debussy (as James Husst Hall noted) "intensified the mood and clarified the meaning of the poem." For Debussy, as Hall stated further, "the words were after all only the husks or outer coating of the images which were half concealed; the sensitive musician divined the hidden secrets and revealed them in movement and tone."

The first piece of music Debussy produced was a song: "Nuit d'étoiles," written in 1876 when he was only fourteen. For the next forty years Debussy continued writing songs, ending his career in this area with "Noël des enfants qui n'ont plus des maisons" in 1915. In his maiden efforts he was under the spell of Massenet. But it was not long before he began arriving at his own identity. Indeed, his first song gems appeared long before he had crystallized his

impressionist art and produced his first masterworks. Thirteen years
before the G minor String Quartet and fourteen years before *Afternoon of a Faun* he wrote the graceful serenade "Mandoline" (poem
by Verlaine), in which he anticipated his later remarkable powers
in translating Symbolist poetry into Impressionist music. Also before
the string quartet and the orchestral prelude came such significant
song cycles as the *Cinq poèmes de Baudelaire* (1887–88) and the
Ariettes oubliées (1888) and the first set of *Fêtes galantes* (1892),
the latter two to poems by Verlaine. Edward Lockspeiser has remarked how in the *Cinq poèmes de Baudelaire* Debussy was "more
articulately sensuous" than he had been up to this time, and how
these settings of Baudelaire's verses were "remarkable for the impassioned and declamatory style of vocal writing, the ornate accompaniment creating the illusion of an orchestra and the recurrence of melodic phrases marking the repetition of lines at the
opening and close of each verse."

Debussy reached the heights of his powers as composer of songs
with the second set of *Fétes galantes* (1904), the *Trois ballades de
François Villon* (1910), and the *Trois poèmes de Stéphane Mallarmé*
(1913). "The poets of Debussy's inspiration," says Lockspeiser, "are
each endowed with the musician's novel and arresting vision which,
however, is capable of the most bold transformations according to
the demands of his fantasy. The empurpled style of the erotic
Baudelaire songs, or the subdued pastel shades of the settings of
Verlaine, the noble medieval severity of the Villon ballads . . . almost
all the definable aspects of the rich and varied nature of the great
artist are consecutively presented in this enchanting gallery."

Frederick Delius

"To all that he touched he gave a new meaning, a new color, a new outline, a new loveliness, and a new poignancy."

BERNARD VAN DIEREN

BORN: Bradford, England, January 29, 1862.
DIED: Grez-sur-Loing, France, June 10, 1934.
MAJOR WORKS: *Chamber Music*—3 violin sonatas; 2 string quartets; Sonata for Cello and Piano. *Choral Music*—Appalachia; Sea Drift; A Mass of Life; Songs of Sunset; A Song of High Hills; Requiem; A Poem of Life and Love; Songs of Farewell. *Operas*—Koanga; A Village Romeo and Juliet; Fennimore and Gerda. *Orchestral Music*—Over the Hills and Far Away; Paris: The Song of a Great City; Brigg Fair; In a Summer Garden; A Dance Rhapsody, Nos. 1 and 2; Summer Night on the River; On Hearing the First Cuckoo in Spring; Concerto for Violin and Orchestra; Eventyr; A Song Before Sunrise; Concerto for Cello and Orchestra; A Song of Summer.

HIS LIFE

For one half of his life, Delius sought out the world. He traveled extensively, at times lived recklessly. For the next half of his life he withdrew from the world, isolating himself in a small French town.

The boy Delius was gifted in music. He early learned to play the violin and piano. While attending Bradford Grammar School, where he was for the most part an inept student, he was always making music. His father, a prosperous wool merchant of German extraction, had little sympathy for these musical inclinations. He wanted the boy to follow him in his business and saw to it that he received a sound business training. Between 1877 and 1880 Delius was a student at a business college at Spring Grove at Isleworth (International College). Music was not neglected: Delius took lessons on the violin, participated enthusiastically in local musical performances, and attended concerts during frequent trips to London. In 1881, he entered his father's business, first in the capacity of bookkeeper, and then as salesman. Determined to give his son the best possible business training, the father soon dispatched the young man to Chemnitz, in Saxony, Germany, to serve an apprenticeship in a thriving German wool establishment. Delius applied himself to the wool business with only half a heart. His enthusiasm as well as his industry belonged to music. He made pilgrimages to major German cities to hear important performances of operatic and symphonic music. During one of these visits he heard a performance of Wagner's *Die Meistersinger* which convinced him more than ever that music was his first love.

Nevertheless, back in England, Delius continued to work for his father, with whom he stayed until 1884. Restricted to a desk and to an occupation that bored him, Delius continually dreamed of escape to far-off places. Several trips to Sweden, Norway, and France failed to satisfy his wanderlust. One day he read about Florida; its languorous climate, peaceful surroundings, and primitive communities excited his imagination. He begged his father to let him go there. As the old man had by now come to the unhappy conclusion that his son was not cut out to be a wool merchant and would never be successful as one, he gave his consent. He did even more than this. He made arrangements for the purchase of an orange plantation in Solano, Florida, which Delius could supervise as a means of earning a living.

Solano was remote and virgin territory on the Saint Johns River, accessible only by water. Delius went there in 1884 and was immediately taken with its wild, primitive beauty. The languor of its life enchanted him. He succumbed to its spell. He allowed the oranges to rot. Instead of tending to them he devoted himself to reading, contemplation, canoeing with his Negro friends, listening to Negro songs and watching their dances. Sometimes there were hardier pastimes, such as a night alligator hunt. In his complete detachment from the world outside—a detachment emphasized by the fact that he was a white man in a community of Negroes—he found happiness.

He started to make music on the violin he had brought with him. Then the need for a piano sent him on a three-day journey to Jacksonville. While trying out various instruments there he was accosted by a stranger who introduced himself: Thomas F. Ward, organist from Brooklyn, New York, who had come south for his health. Ward had been attracted to the strange and often beautiful chords Delius had been playing on the various pianos. They began talking about music and continued their talk at dinner. Delius prevailed on Ward to return with him to Solano. Ward remained six months, paying his way by teaching Delius harmony and counterpoint. Apparently he was a remarkable teacher. Delius confessed that his later study in the Leipzig Conservatory brought him nothing that Ward had not already given him. "Ward's counterpoint lessons were the only lessons from which I derived any benefit," Delius recalled much later in life. "Towards the end of my course with him . . . he showed wonderful insight in helping me to find out just how much in the way of traditional technique would be useful to me."

During the six-month period of study with Ward, Delius realized that he had at long last found the only career that appealed to him, that of composer. Recognizing the fact that he could not develop creatively in the isolation of Solano, he decided to return to the world he had so long rejected. In August 1885 he sailed up the Saint Johns River and settled in Jacksonville. There he sang for a while in the choir of a Jewish synagogue. With glowing letters of recommendation from the chief rabbi he went on to Danville, Virginia, where he became a teacher of music at the Old Roanoke Female School. Mrs. Belle McGhee Phifer recalled Delius' visit to Danville in an interview in 1942, shortly before her death: "He charmed all of us, this modest young Englishman with such nice manners. My husband was quickly convinced of his virtuosity at the piano, especially the chromatic quality of his extemporizations which seemed to violate the known rules of harmony. I remember my husband used to sit entranced as the young man played and often remarked 'that man has music in his mind, but when he sets it down it is almost impossible to play it.'"

Delius' playing of the Mendelssohn Concerto so enchanted his audience that he became something of a local celebrity. The wealthy planters sent him their daughters for music lessons. In about a year's time Delius had earned enough and saved enough to realize an ambition which Ward had aroused in him: to attend the Leipzig Conservatory. He went there in the summer of 1886, studied with Sitt, Jadassohn, and Reinecke at the Conservatory, and haunted the concert auditoriums. Vacation time was spent in walking trips to Norway, a country he had come to love.

In the winter of 1887 Edvard Grieg visited Leipzig. Delius was introduced to him and made a favorable impression. Hearing one of Delius' orchestral works (the suite *Florida,* inspired by dance melodies Delius had heard Negroes perform) further increased Grieg's high opinion of the young man. Thus when Father Delius began showing signs of impatience with his son's musical activities, Grieg did not hesitate to use the influence of his reputation to win the old man over. Father Delius consented to provide his son with a small but regular stipend to allow him to follow his ambition. That stipend was supplemented with a subsidy from Delius' uncle, who left him a legacy in 1894.

Now able to pursue his ambition to become a composer, Delius settled in the Latin Quarter of Paris where he lived for the next eight years. He published his first work in 1892: a *Legend,* for violin and orchestra. Between 1890 and 1897 he completed three operas: *Irmelin, The Magic Fountain,* and *Koanga.* He also wrote several songs, some chamber music works, and a fantasy-overture for orchestra, *Over the Hills and Far Away.* By 1899 he had completed a piano concerto and two significant compositions for orchestra, the tone poem *Life's Dance* and the nocturne *Paris: The Song of a Great City.* A concert devoted entirely to his works took place in London on May 30, 1899. "England ought to know something about one of the few composers of genius she has had the good fortune to possess," wrote one unidentified critic. But this critic was a voice in the wilderness. Most of the others regarded Delius' music as the "bizarre affectations of a clever young man" or as "discordant, harsh, and uninviting." No other Delius work was heard in London for the next eight years.

Meanwhile in 1897, he married Jelka Rosen, an event that must be regarded as the major turning point in his life. She was cultured (what had attracted them to each other was their mutual admiration for Nietzsche), gifted (she was a fine painter whose work had been exhibited from her seventeenth year), and well-to-do. She brought

Delius security, emotional as well as financial—that, and the kind of sympathetic encouragement he needed.

Before long they bought a quiet house and garden in the small French town of Grez-sur-Loing. This was Delius' renunciation of the outside world, of which up to now he had been too much a part. He became a recluse, giving himself to music and to little else.

This withdrawal became almost psychopathic. He saw less and less of people. He had nothing whatsoever to do with his neighbors, refusing even to give them a nod of recognition or a "good day" when he passed them in the street. When a visitor came to call, Delius usually enveloped himself in one of his profound silences. Even the arrival of famous musicians, coming to play his works for him, often could not break down his aloofness. A guest at the Delius dinner table might find himself suddenly dismissed when Delius could stand him no longer; or, Delius might dismiss himself, by having his man suddenly read to him.

In solitude and in contemplation he seemed to find new creative strength. Up to then he had been a promising composer. After 1900—soon after he made his escape to Grez-sur-Loing—he became a great one. In 1901 he completed the opera *A Village Romeo and Juliet*. Between 1903–7 he created three important choral works: *Sea Drift, A Mass of Life,* and *Songs of Sunset*. And beginning with 1907, with *Brigg Fair,* he began writing those sensitive pieces for orchestra with which his name is identified, including *In a Summer Garden, On Hearing the First Cuckoo in Spring,* and *Summer Night on the River*.

Recognition came—but it came slowly. His absence from the musical market place may have had something to do with its tardiness. The refinement and delicacy of his music may have been another reason; it is not the kind of music that sweeps an audience off its feet. In any case, although Delius was writing one masterwork after another he remained a more or less unknown composer. There were a few successful performances in Germany, including the world *première* of his opera *A Village Romeo and Juliet* in Berlin on February 21, 1907, but not enough to lift him out of obscurity.

In England a few devoted admirers set themselves the task of selling him to English audiences. Henry J. Wood introduced the Piano Concerto at a Promenade Concert in 1907 and followed it with *Sea Drift* at the Sheffield Festival. Beginning with 1909 the most devoted of all Delius admirers began to propagandize for his music—the brilliant conductor Sir Thomas Beecham. Thenceforth Beecham was indefatigable in performing Delius' works. After introducing *A Mass of Life* in 1909, he gave the first performance in England of *A Village Romeo and Juliet* in 1910, and then presented an all-Delius concert in 1911. Familiarity with Delius' music made the English public more receptive to it; his important position in English music became established.

During World War I, with the thunder of German cannon shattering the tranquillity of Grez-sur-Loing, Delius and his wife escaped to London. They took with them only one possession: a painting by Gauguin. During this period Delius wrote only one major work, his Requiem, to honor the young artists of England who died in the war.

The war over, he returned to his beloved haven. Soon after the turn of the second decade he began suffering inertia and excessive fatigue. These were the first signs of the physical disintegration that was soon to take place in 1922. Partial paralysis was followed in 1925 by total blindness. His withdrawal from the world was now complete.

He accepted the terrible tragedy with strength and serenity. Each afternoon he would sit in his garden, listen to his wife read to him, talk to one or two intimate friends, or plan new works. He had to find pleasure in little things: the feel of the sun on his face; the delights of the table, which he was fortunately still able to enjoy; the joy of hearing his own works on phonograph records. "Not being able to see does not bother me," he once said stoically. "I have my imagination. Besides, I have seen the best of earth and done everything that is worth doing. I am content. I have had a wonderful life."

Most important of all, he could still create. He acquired the services of a young Yorkshire musician, Eric Fenby, who came to live with him. Fenby became Delius' eyes and hands. Painstakingly, and with a fantastic concentration on every detail, Delius dictated his last works to Fenby, note by note. It was a difficult process, taxing him greatly, but a job Delius would not shirk. "He could not keep still," Fenby has recorded, "but would wriggle about in his armchair, gesticulating wildly with his hands to a degree that would have been impossible in a more collected mood until, bathed in perspiration, he could go on no longer. Then he would be carried away." Thus he completed the *Songs of Farewell, A Song of Summer,* the Sonata No. 3 for Violin and Piano.

In October 1929 Sir Thomas Beecham arranged a monumental festival of Delius' music in London. Six concerts were performed between October 12 and November 1. Beecham successfully prevailed upon the composer to come to England for the event. "He was carried in his invalid chair, propped up with cushions, down the gangway to a waiting ambulance," wrote Delius' sister. "All that the pressman . . . could see was a figure with silvered hair, wearing a gray felt hat, a heavy overcoat, with his sightless eyes shielded by tortoise-shell glasses, and a pale, wrinkled, ascetic face."

In his armchair Delius was witness to the greatest triumph of his life. There were ovations after each concert, and a moving, unforgettable demonstration after the concluding performance. Arthur Hutchings recalled in his biography of Delius,*

Those who were present can testify that never has music cast so uncanny a spell over an audience as it did on the last night of the festival. . . . A tense silence followed the last audible sounds; Beecham and the players did not move. Then began the applause and cheering, such as is not heard even in the football-match atmosphere of the last night of a promenade season. . . . The first cheers and noise, after the silence was broken, lasted a full ten minutes, and all eyes turned to the balcony where Delius lay on his litter surrounded by flowers. For the first time, and the last, his compatriots heard his voice in public. Slowly but clearly he uttered a few sentences of thanks for his reception and for the performance, adding: "This festival has been the time of my life."

Other impressive honors came his way that week. The king made him Companion of Honor, while the city of Bradford gave him the Freedom of the City. There were elaborate tributes in the papers. A society was launched to record his works. Oxford extended him an honorary degree.

This was his last public appearance. His health continued to disintegrate. By early 1934 he was victim of excruciating pains and violent spasms demanding an almost continual use of morphine. On the all-too-rare occasions when he had a respite from pain he was cheered with the progress made by the Delius Society in recording his works or lulled by having a favorite novel read to him by Fenby.

* *Delius* by Arthur Hutchings. London: Macmillan & Co., Ltd., 1948.

He died on June 10 and was buried in the cemetery at Grez without any religious ceremony. He had, however, expressed a wish to be buried near a church "where the winds are warm and the sun friendly." One year after his death his friends fulfilled this wish. Delius' body was transported from France to southern England. In the churchyard of the small town of Limpsfield a second funeral service took place. In the church itself Sir Thomas Beecham conducted a concert of Delius' most famous works: *On Hearing the First Cuckoo in Spring* and *Summer Night on the River*. To the elegiac strains of the music Delius was buried in the churchyard under a tree, his grave lighted by two hurricane lamps and lined with laurel leaves.

HIS MUSIC

Delius' music could have come only from a man who had divorced himself from the outside world. It is serene; it is contemplative; it is emotionally restrained; it is touched with mysticism. When it becomes melancholy it has resignation. Emotional turmoil, excitement, dramatic climaxes rarely disturb its placidity.

He was an Impressionist, with the Impressionist's concern with color, nuance, shade, and refinement. When he sustains a mood the spell is seldom allowed to break. However, Delius was no imitator, not even of Debussy, whose influence was great. He had a warmth not found in Debussy, and a gentle, tender vein all his own. Others could be more sensuous than he, more heroic, more grandiose, and more profound. But none could realize beauty so poignantly. An English critic, reviewing his last violin sonata, remarked: "It is wonderful that he gets so far, using the same means." True—his means were limited. But his inspiration was ever high. He was the poet of dawn and sunsets, of hills, the countryside, and the sea. Circumscribed as his sphere may be, in it he was at least unique.

ANALYTICAL NOTES

Orchestral Music. *On Hearing the First Cuckoo in Spring* (1912) is one of the finest examples of Delius' sensitive, Impressionist art. It may be a miniature, but it is a fully realized work of art. It begins with a slow three-bar introduction. We then hear a sequence of phrases that simulate the distant calls of a cuckoo. They appear in the oboe and then in divided strings. This cuckoo call is the first of two principal themes. Out of the simple phrase is built a gentle, nostalgic, tender page of music, with strings and oboe often exchanging phrases. Next comes the second theme, a melody derived from the Norwegian folk song "In Osa Valley." It is presented by the first violins. After the second theme is heard and enlarged, cuckoo calls return in the clarinet. The work ends peacefully.

Summer Night on the River was completed in the same year as *On Hearing the First Cuckoo in Spring* (1912) and may be regarded as a companion piece. They are similar in mood. Both works were, as a matter of fact, introduced at the same concert, in Leipzig on October 2, 1913. *Summer Night on the River* is more literally programmatic than its companion. Diaphanous chords in the wind instruments bring up the image of a river surrounded by the darkness of night; one can sense the mist in the nebulous music. Swirling figures in the wind instruments suggest the rocking of small boats. Suddenly we hear in the cellos a wonderful song (different members of the orchestra take turns in weaving little arabesque figures around it); it speaks of the beauty and mystery of night. The song is assumed by strings, and other material in a similar vein is heard in strings and woodwinds; the mystery of the night is maintained in the nebulous harmonies. Then the song returns in the cello, and the enchantment of night and the river remains unbroken.

Brigg Fair (1907) was described by Delius as a rhapsody, but it is actually in the theme-and-variations form. The theme is a folk song found in the English countryside by Percy Grainger (1882–1961), who made a setting of it in 1906. One year later Delius wrote his "rhapsody" around it and dedicated the work to Grainger. The theme appears in the oboe after a short slow introduction. The variations present the melody in several different moods. One of the most effective variations is a solemn passage for trumpet and trombones in octaves, with bells, and with off-beat chords in divided strings. Another fine variation is, by way of contrast, a gay section scored for brass alone.

In a Summer Garden, a fantasy, written in 1908, is an impressionistic portrait evoking the sensations aroused by a garden in full bloom—obviously Delius' own garden in Grez-sur-Loing. Two quotations, published in the score, provide the key to its emotional (but not programmatic) content. The first is a couplet by Dante Gabriel Rossetti:

All are my blooms; and all sweet blooms of love
To thee I give while Spring and Summer sang.

The second, of unknown authorship, is as follows: "Roses, lilies, and a thousand scented flowers. Bright butterflies flitting from petal to petal, and gold-brown bees humming in the warm, quivering summer air. Beneath the shade of ancient trees, a quiet river with water lilies. In a boat, almost hidden, two people. A thrush is singing in the distance."

The work is built out of a consecutive series of melodic ideas. The opening theme, heard in the woodwinds and repeated in the strings, makes Arthur Hutchings think of "our sadness in the presence of beauty and our reflection that it must fade as the flowers." The English horn then presents a brief figure which is worked up into a dreamy section. The music becomes livelier. The principal theme is a broad melody for violas accompanied by figures in the woodwinds and chords in the lower strings. This is worked out with intensity. The atmosphere now becomes subdued, but only briefly. A new febrile idea appears in the violins and is taken over by the woodwinds. But tranquillity returns. Earlier material is repeated, and the tone poem ends in mystery as the music ebbs away.

Eventyr, or *Once upon a Time* (1917), owes its origin to Norwegian folklore: to a collection of Norwegian fairy tales published in 1841. Delius here tried to re-create the world of imagination and fantasy that had so enchanted him in this anthology. The tone poem has five sections played without interruption. A slow twenty-measure introduction offers a theme shared by lower strings and woodwinds. This is followed by a melody for strings, and another one for the bassoons. The second part introduces a new thought in the strings which is transformed, developed, and carried to a climax in the third and fourth parts. The final section represents a summation of earlier material.

One other orchestral composition has become familiar, but this one comes from an opera—*A Village Romeo and Juliet* (1901). It is *The Walk to the Paradise Garden,* an orchestral intermezzo. The opera (text by the composer adapted from a tale by Gottfried Keller) tells the love story of a girl and a young man from families who are feuding. They decide to elope, and after various adventures come to a tragic end. To Philip Heseltine, Delius' biographer, the orchestral intermezzo offers a tonal résumé of the whole opera. In the introduction a waltzlike theme is heard in the cellos and bassoons. In the main part, two haunting melodies are prominent. The first comes in horns and bassoons, and the other in oboes with a countersubject in the basses.

Gaetano Donizetti

"When he chose to take trouble, he was capable of attaining remarkable heights."

CECIL GRAY

Born: Bergamo, Italy, November 29, 1797.
Died: Bergamo, April 8, 1848.
Major Works: *Choral Music*—Cantatas, Masses, motets, psalms; Vespers; Ave Maria; Requiem. *Operas*—Anna Bolena; L'Elisir d'amore; Lucrezia Borgia; Lucia di Lammermoor; Il Campanello di notte; La Fille du régiment; La Favorita; Linda di Chamounix; Don Pasquale.

HIS LIFE

Donizetti's father, originally a weaver and then a pawnbroker, apprenticed the boy to an architect. A listless apprentice, Donizetti was neglectful of his trade, giving himself up either to daydreaming or to scribbling verses and melodies. Architecture was soon abandoned. Donizetti was then directed by his father to law. But the boy remained apathetic. His only interest was in art: music, drawing, poetry.

At last his father gave his reluctant consent for Donizetti to enter the Bergamo School of Music. There the greatest single influence was not a teacher, but the music of his contemporary Rossini, which Donizetti came to know through published scores. He had to study these operas in the strictest privacy, for the school did not permit its students to devote themselves to anything that was not in the regular curriculum. Fortunately, Donizetti had managed to gain the friendship of the school librarian, who smuggled the Rossini scores, one by one, into Donizetti's room. Rossini's operas gave the young student direction and a goal. He too would become an opera composer, and he would write the way Rossini did.

When Donizetti was seventeen his father sent him to the Liceo Filarmonico in Bologna. The father had not completely reconciled himself to his son's becoming a composer instead of a respectable tradesman. But he was willing to accept such a fate if Donizetti concentrated on church music. The Liceo was a good place to get such a training. One of Donizetti's teachers there was Padre Mattei, who had also taught Rossini. Studying with him further stimulated Donizetti's ambition to follow in the footsteps of his favorite composer.

The determination on the part of Donizetti to write for the theater instead of the church made his father intransigent. He would never allow his son to follow music as a profession, but insisted that the young man must now consider teaching. Unable to bend this decision, Donizetti suddenly entered the Austrian Army. While in uniform he devoted all his leisure time to writing music. He completed three operas before one got performed—*Enrico di Borgogna,* introduced in Venice on November 14, 1818, where it was favorably received.

Donizetti wrote four more operas before arriving at his first great success. This took place in Rome on January 28, 1822, with *Zoraïde di Granata.* After the *première* he was carried aloft on the shoulders of the opera lovers to the city Capitol, where they crowned him "king of the opera." The Government recognized his success. It released him from further military duty so that he could spend all his time writing operas.

He proceeded to write operas with amazing, even breath-taking, rapidity: four in 1822; four in 1823; two in 1824; three in 1826; four in 1827; four in 1828. In all these, as in the earlier operas, the hand was Donizetti's, but the voice was Rossini's. Meanwhile in 1824 he married a sixteen-year-old girl, Virginia Vasselli. They had three children, two of whom were stillborn while a third died two weeks after birth. Tragedies notwithstanding, the marriage was an idyllic one, until Virginia died of cholera in 1838.

Rossini wrote his last opera in 1829. It is a curious fact that not until Rossini stopped writing operas was Donizetti able to free himself from a slavish imitation of the master. Donizetti could not have known that Rossini would write no more—for the master was only thirty-seven in 1829, in good health apparently, with a long, productive life still ahead of him. Yet it was almost as if Donizetti sensed that, beginning in 1829, he was Rossini's rightful successor, a position that carried the artistic responsibility that he imitate no more, but set off in his own direction. In any case, in 1830 Donizetti entered upon the second phase of his career by writing for the distinguished Italian opera stars, Rubini and Pasta, the first opera in which his own abilities were not completely overshadowed by the style of Rossini. *Anna Bolena,* introduced in Milan on December 26, 1830, was a triumph. It was soon performed throughout all of Europe (the great bass Luigi Lablache scored his first major success in England with it), and made Donizetti a composer of international fame. For many years thereafter *Anna Bolena* was regarded by Donizetti's contemporaries as his magnum opus.

In this second creative phase Donizetti finally arrived at his own full identity with two operas that belong with his finest creations. One was a comic opera, *L'Elisir d'amore,* heard first in Milan on May 12, 1832. The other was a tragedy, *Lucia di Lammermoor,* whose *première* took place in Naples on September 26, 1835.

He was now a celebrity, and he traveled extensively throughout Europe, assisting at performances of his operas. In 1837 he was appointed director of the Collegio di Musica in Naples (where since 1834 he had been professor of counterpoint and composition). He did not hold this position long. In 1839 he became embroiled in a bitter controversy with the censors, who objected to the performance of his opera *Poliuto,* based on Corneille's *Polyeucte.* He became so incensed that he decided to leave Italy. He came to Paris to assist at the production of some of his earlier works. He also stepped into a new phase of his creative development by writing several new operas—French operas. The most important were *La Fille du régiment* and *La Favorita,* both introduced in 1840, the first at the Opéra-Comique on February 11, and the other at the Opéra on December 2.

His star never shone more brightly than at this time. In Vienna, which he visited in 1842 after a brief return to Italy, he was given a hero's acclaim. The *première* there of his new opera, *Linda di*

Chamounix, on May 19, 1842, was a musical event of the first magnitude, and its success brought him the honorary titles of Court Composer and Master of the Imperial Chapel, conferred by the Emperor himself.

He was back in Paris in 1842 to write two new works for the French lyric theater, one of them being his masterpiece, *Don Pasquale,* performed at the Théâtre des Italiens on January 3, 1843, with an extraordinary cast including Lablache, Tamburini, Norina, and Mario. One year later, on January 12, 1844, there took place in Naples the *première* of *Catarina Cornaro*—his last opera.

For some time now he had been subject to violent headaches, intense depressions, and then hallucinations. One morning in 1845 he was found stretched out on the floor of his bedroom, paralyzed. His mental condition deteriorated. He spent all of 1846 and half of 1847 in an insane asylum at Ivry. For periods at a time he would sit in his room in complete silence, which he would suddenly and inexplicably break by exclaiming: "Dom Sebastino . . . Dom Sebastino."

He was released from the asylum in October 1847 and put in the care of his brother at Bergamo. Thus he was brought back to die in the city of his birth. Donizetti's valet recorded:

More than four thousand persons were present at the funeral. The procession was composed of the numerous clergy of Bergamo, the most illustrious members of the community and its environs and of the civic guard of the town and suburbs. The discharge of musketry, mingled with the light of three or four thousand torches, presented a fine effect; the whole was enhanced by the presence of three military bands. The young gentlemen of Bergamo insisted on bearing the remains of their illustrious fellow townsman, although the cemetery was a league and a half from the town. Never hitherto had such great honors been bestowed on any member of that city.

HIS MUSIC

Together with Vincenzo Bellini (1801–35), composer of *Norma,* Gaetano Donizetti represents the transition in Italian opera from Rossini to Verdi. In that period much of the tradition of Italian opera style and format was established; Donizetti and Bellini went a long way in helping to establish it. Bellini was the lyrical genius with a gift for song so varied and expressive and aristocratic that it could fulfill all the aesthetic needs of his dramas. Donizetti combined a gift for lyricism with other qualities.

His greatest characteristic as a composer—and his greatest weakness —was his facility. He wrote with incredible speed. He could complete an entire opera, text as well as music, in less than two weeks. It is said that he sketched and wrote most of the last act of *La Favorita* in a few hours. Such facility inevitably brought with it much that was trite, conventional, and formalized. It is for this reason that most of the sixty-seven operas of Donizetti have long been forgotten.

But, as Cecil Gray noted, on the rare occasions when he took pains with his composition he was able to touch greatness. He was at his best in the field of the *opera buffa,* or comic opera, where he wrote with verve, ebullience, freshness, tongue-in-cheek sentimentality, and malice that remind us of Rossini at his best. But in his best tragic operas, which so often go in for sententious scenes and melodrama, there are pages of irresistible power and beauty. He had, first and foremost, a wonderful lyric gift, all the more remarkable for its variety and expressiveness when we recall that most of his arias were tailored to exploit the virtuosity of specific voices. He was also a master of ensemble writing, writing not only with polyphonic skill, but often without losing sight of the identity of individual characters. He also, on occasion, introduced in his scores little subtleties of melody or rhythm or tempo changes which heightened an artistic effect or forcefully pointed up a situation or character trait.

ANALYTICAL NOTES

Operas. In the second phase of his creative development, in which once and for all Donizetti had stopped imitating Rossini to become himself, he produced a masterwork in each of the two genres of opera in which he proved himself a consummate master: *opera buffa* and *opera seria.* The comic opera was *L'Elisir d'amore,* or *The Elixir of Love.* The tragic opera was *Lucia di Lammermoor.*

L'Elisir d'amore (1832) is the earliest Donizetti opera to have retained its popularity up to the present time; and one of its arias, *"Una furtiva lagrima"* is probably the most famous one he ever wrote. The gay text—the work of Felice Romani based on a libretto by

Eugène Scribe—spins merrily on the pivot of a magic elixir capable of inspiring love. This is a commodity marketed by Dr. Dulcamara. He finds a ready and willing customer in Nemorino, since Nemorino is in love with Adina and he has a serious rival in the army sergeant, Belcore. Even though the magic potion is nothing more than cheap wine, Nemorino is so convinced of its powers that he is confident Adina will select him as husband even though she has already announced her intention to marry the sergeant. To get money to buy the elixir, Nemorino joins the Army, recruits being given a cash bonus for signing up. However, it is not the magic potion that causes a change of heart in Adina, nor even the news that Nemorino has come into an inheritance, but the fact she has loved him all the while and had coquettishly been teasing him. To Adina's dismay she now finds that all the village girls are pursuing Nemorino, but is reassured by him that it is she alone whom he loves. Adina procures Nemorino's release from the Army and, to be sure, he wins his girl. He is now thoroughly convinced that it is Dr. Dulcamara's elixir that has worked the trick for him.

"Una furtiva lagrima"—the most celebrated aria in the opera—is the romance Nemorino sings about his love for Adina. Several other numbers, while less famous, reveal Donizetti's remarkable gifts at *bel canto*. The best are those also sung by Nemorino: *"Quanto è bella," "Adina credimi,"* and his hymn to the powers of the elixir, *"Dell' elisir mirabile."*

Lucia di Lammermoor (1835), which came three years after *L'Elisir d'amore,* offers us a far different Donizetti from the one encountered in the *opera buffa.* Here Donizetti is the tragedian—in the grand manner.

The text, based on Sir Walter Scott's *The Bride of Lammermoor,* is filled with violent emotions: love, hate, and jealousy of the most intense kind. Lucy and Edgar Ravenswood are in love. But Lucy's brother, Henry Ashton—trying to rehabilitate the fortunes of his family—has pledged her to Lord Arthur Bucklaw. When Edgar Ravenswood goes off on a mission in France, Henry Ashton intercepts his letters to Lucy and forges others to prove her lover's infidelity. He finally succeeds in winning Lucy's consent to marrying Lord Arthur Bucklaw. No sooner is the marriage contract signed than Edgar Ravenswood suddenly makes his appearance. Overwhelmed on learning that Lucy has apparently jilted him to marry someone else, he curses the house of Lammermoor. On her wedding night Lucy loses her mind. She kills her husband and commits suicide. Ravenswood, too, commits suicide when he learns the truth.

Suicide, murder, forgery, and insanity—the librettist appears to have neglected nothing that could serve the purposes of stark melodrama. Later composers would have used the fullest resources of harmony, orchestration, and rhythm to convey such violent incidents. But Donizetti relied primarily on his lyricism. That lyricism is so varied and fresh that, even apart from the opera, the best arias and ensemble numbers never fail to produce a powerful effect. The sextet in Act II, Scene 2 (*"Chi mi frena"*) is deservedly one of the finest and most famous ensemble numbers in all opera; Cecil Gray considers it one of the finest existing examples of concerted vocal music. The "Mad Scene" in Act III, Scene 1 (*"Spargi d'amaro pianto"*) is one of the most exacting and effective coloratura arias in operatic literature. Edgar's aria in the closing scene, his farewell to the world (*"Tu che a Dio"*), is Italian lyricism at its most poignant.

These great lyrical moments are so expressive, and they arise so logically out of the texture of the play, that their emotional force increases when they are heard within the opera. Thus, the sextet is the logical climax of the opera. Ravenswood, on his sudden return from France, discovers that his beloved has signed a marriage contract with somebody else. The music that follows is not only a skillful piece of vocal writing, but a vibrant expression of vengeance and hate, as each character voices his or her own reaction to what has taken place. The Mad Scene is filled with Lucy's grief, expressed in a simple and touching melody; but the wanderings of her lost mind are caught in the florid passages. And the "Tomb Scene," with Edgar's last, moving aria, highlights the immense tragedy that has struck the houses of Ravenswood and Lammermoor.

Among the operas Donizetti wrote for Paris, three maintain their interest today in varying degrees. One is an *opera buffa, Don Pasquale;* the second, an *opéra comique, La Fille du régiment,* or *The Daughter of the Regiment;* the third is an *opera seria, La Favorita.*

The most celebrated of these is, to be sure, *Don Pasquale.* Indeed, this is the composer's magnum opus, his one opera which is all of a piece, consistently inspired and completely integrated. It is an *opera buffa* in the style of Rossini's *The Barber of Seville.* But Donizetti is not an imitator here; he is a creator in his own right. The text, by Salvatore Gammerano, follows the *opera buffa* tradition of using everyday characters inextricably enmeshed in amatory complications. Don Pasquale is a wealthy bachelor who opposes the marriage of his nephew Ernesto to the beautiful widow Norina, whom he has never actually met. Pasquale is duped into a mock marriage with the ravishingly beautiful "sister" of his physician, who (of course) is Norina. After the mock ceremony Norina proceeds at once to become an extravagant, unfaithful shrew whose volatile moods and explosive temper send Pasquale to despair. He bewails the fact that he has entered upon so disastrous a marriage! Then the hoax is revealed to him. His relief at this good news makes him more amenable to Ernesto's marriage.

The opera is introduced by one of those brisk and tuneful little overtures with which the world of *opera buffa* abounds. It is built out of two main arias. The first is Ernesto's serenade in Act III, which, after a short introduction, appears in the clarinet and after that in horn and flute. The second is a part of Norina's cavatina in Act I. These two ideas are worked out with sprightliness, creating the proper mood for the merry play to come.

The opera is filled with many wonderful lyrical sequences. In the first act there is Ernesto's farewell to love when he realizes that Pasquale will stand in the way of his marriage, "*Sogno soave e casto de' miei prim'anni.*" Within the context, and flanked by gaiety and satire, this tender little apostrophe provides a refreshing change of pace. In the second scene of the same act Norina sings lightheartedly of the ways of love, in which, she says, she is well versed: "*So anchio la virtù magica.*" Ernesto's determination to escape to foreign lands in order to forget his unrequited love in Act II ("*Chercherò lontana terra*") has a whimsical sentimentality which is just right for comic opera—it is sentimental, yet it does not take its sorrow too completely to heart. Ernesto's serenade in Act III ("*Com' è gentil la notte*") is in the best traditions of Italian *bel canto*.

But beyond its varied lyricism *Don Pasquale* has laughter and mockery. A turn of melody, a change of tempo, a saucy rhythmic phrase reflect the subtlest change of mood and feeling in the characters. Quicksilver figures in the orchestra provide an amusing commentary on Norina's sudden splurge of extravagance after her mock marriage to Pasquale, or Ernesto's incredulity on hearing from Pasquale that the latter is about to get married. There are numbers which are farcical and which have mock seriousness. There are enchanting ensembles, such as the quartet in the second act in which each of the characters provides his own commentary on Norina's ruthless marital behavior. There is the spicy flavor of sardonic wit in the closing page of the opera which points out the moral that a man of Pasquale's age should never marry.

A good deal of the interest in *La Fille du régiment* (1840) lies in its martial tunes and patriotic airs. Two of the heroine's most stirring arias are in this class: her ringing tribute to the regiment (*"Chacun le sait"*) and her hymn to France with which the opera ends (*"Salut à la France"*). In addition there is the song of the French troops in praise of war and victory, *"Rataplan, rataplan."* For France, therefore, *La Fille du régiment* has special significance and interest, the reason why this opera has remained so popular in that country. Outside France, the opera has lent itself to timely (though not always relevant) interpolations during times of stress. During World War I, for example, Frieda Hempel included a rendition of the popular English war ballad "Keep the Home Fires Burning" during her appearance in this work at the Metropolitan Opera; also at the Metropolitan Opera—after the Nazi occupation of Paris in World War II— Lily Pons improvised a patriotic scene by draping a French flag around her body and singing the "Marseillaise."

The heroine in the opera, Marie, is a canteen manager of the 21st French Regiment during the French invasion of the Tyrol in or about 1815. The troops are devoted to her. Consequently, they are concerned when the man with whom she is in love—Tonio, a peasant—is falsely accused of being a spy. Another obstacle to the romance is the fact that Marie must leave the troops to live with her aunt, the Countess of Berkenfeld, who plans for her a marriage of convenience with a duke. The French troops invade the palace of the Countess and are responsible for bringing about a happy resolution to Marie's love affair.

When *La Favorita* (1840) is occasionally revived, it is mainly for some of its wonderful arias, such as *"O Mio Fernando"* (the most celebrated in the opera), *"Spirto gentil,"* and *"Una vergine."* Beyond these memorable pages the opera is attractive for its eye-filling ceremonials, processions, and other big scenes. The plot involves Fernando, a novice monk, in a love affair with Leonora de Guzman. He abandons his religious order to marry her. Only then does he learn that she had been the king's mistress. This shattering revelation sends him back to the monastery where Leonora seeks him out and dies in his arms.

Antonín Dvořák

"The vernacular and folk poetry invariably touched the depths of his musician's heart. The roots of his creation are the melody and rhythm of folk song and folk dance."

PAUL STEFAN

BORN: Nelahozeves, Bohemia, September 8, 1841.
DIED: Prague, May 1, 1904.
MAJOR WORKS: *Chamber Music*—13 string quartets; 4 piano trios; 3 string quintets; 2 piano quintets; String Sextet in A major; Violin Sonata in F major. *Choral Music*—Stabat Mater; The Spectre's Bride; Mass in D major; Requiem; Te Deum. *Operas*—The Pigheaded Peasants; Vanda; The Cunning Peasant; Dimitrij; The Jacobin; The Devil and Kate; Rusalka; Armida. *Orchestral Music*—9 symphonies; 4 tone poems based on ballads by Erben (The Water Sprite, The Midday Witch, The Golden Spinning Wheel, The Wood Dove); 3 concert overtures (In Nature's Realm, Carnival, Othello); 3 Slavonic Rhapsodies; Slavonic Dances, two sets; Legends; Scherzo capriccioso; Piano Concerto in G minor; Violin Concerto in A minor; Cello Concerto in B minor. *Piano Music*—From the Bohemian Forest, for piano duet; Poetic Pictures; Suite in A major, "American"; Dumky Trio, Humoresques, mazurkas, waltzes. *Vocal Music*—Evening Songs; Gypsy Songs (including "Songs My Mother Taught Me"); 10 Biblical Songs; various individual songs for voice and piano.

HIS LIFE

It is said that in Bohemia when a child was born his parents would place a silver spoon near one hand of the infant and a violin near the other. Whichever object was reached for by the child would suggest his future, either as a wealthy tradesman or an indigent musician.

We do not know if this proverbial test was made when Dvořák was born. But the legendary silver spoon and violin were important symbols in his early life. His father, a humble innkeeper and butcher, wanted his son to reach for the silver spoon, while the boy appeared to want only the violin.

Fortunately the Bohemian people were essentially musical. They might frown on a musical career as impractical, but they regarded music as a fundamental part of life. "Every child must learn music," Dvořák later explained about the Bohemian people, "and if possible sing in the church. After church the people revel in music and dancing, sometimes until early morning."

Father Dvořák played the violin and zither, sang agreeably, and played in the village band. He most certainly would not prevent his son from making music too. As a boy Dvořák learned to play the violin and soon entertained his father's clientele with merry dance tunes and sad village melodies. He also performed at village fairs and sang in the church choir. When he was not playing music, he was listening to it. He would sit fascinated at concerts of visiting gypsy bands; he never tired of hearing the older folk sing their songs. While he managed to receive a bit of formal instruction from the local schoolmaster, Joseph Spitz, his early musical training consisted in hearing and learning the songs of his people.

This preoccupation with music was well and good, but there was the problem of learning a trade. Father Dvořák was hopeful of making his son an innkeeper too. When Dvořák was fourteen he was sent to live with his uncle in the nearby town of Zlonice for the purpose of learning German; a good innkeeper had to know that language. In Zlonice he found a sympathetic music teacher in Antonín Liehmann, who was probably the first to recognize his unusual talent. Liehmann taught Dvořák the viola, piano, and organ, and under his instruction the boy made swift strides. (Later on Dvořák was to give repeated evidence of his high esteem for the teacher of his boyhood. In 1880, one year after Liehmann's death, he conducted a concert in Zlonice to raise funds for a gravestone. And after that he wrote an opera, *The Jacobin,* in which a major character is a village schoolmaster modeled after Liehmann.)

Antonín Liehmann was too astute, and too humble, not to realize that there was only so much he was equipped to teach the boy, that Dvořák needed the expert instruction only a metropolis such as Prague could provide. He became indefatigable in his efforts to get Dvořák to go to Prague. He went to the father and begged him for the consent and the monetary support for this undertaking. But the father was firm. Things had been going badly for him at the inn. He had been forced to close down the inn he had in Nelahozeves and to open another in Zlonice. He needed badly the help of his son and expected it. Besides, even if this had not been the case, he would never allow a son of his to become a professional musician; music, he insisted, was a pastime and not an occupation.

In order to separate his son from the unhealthy influences at Zlonice that would make him a professional musician, Father Dvořák sent him to Böhmisch-Kamnitz. There, as in Zlonice, Dvořák found sympathetic musicians to encourage and direct him. The spark that Liehmann had ignited within him to become a musician was kept alive.

After a year Dvořák was back in Zlonice, working for his father at the inn. But music remained the primary interest of his life. He played the violin and piano continually, and before long started composing little pieces for the town orchestra. And he kept on studying with Antonín Liehmann. The teacher, more convinced than ever of the boy's ability, had not relaxed his efforts to send him to Prague. At last he won the support of Dvořák's uncle, who stood ready to provide the funds even against the father's violent opposition.

Dovřák, sixteen years old, entered the reputable Organ School in Prague, where he remained for about a decade. His teachers regarded him as an industrious student, more proficient in the performance of music than in the theoretical studies. But the boy worked with passion. He studied the organ, played in the orchestra, memorized the scores with which a friend provided him, and did some composing.

The funds that had been coming from Zlonice were suddenly

stopped. Dvořák could go back and work in his father's inn, or he could stay in Prague and make his way as best he could. He chose the latter course. He tried to earn a living by playing in a small band that went from café to café giving concerts and by accepting other little orchestral jobs. What he earned was hardly enough to feed and clothe him. He often went cold and hungry. But he was able to continue his studies at the Organ School; and if he had had the price of admission to concerts and operas, he would have been idyllically happy.

After finishing his studies at the school Dvořák worked in the orchestra of the National Opera, which was opened in 1862, a position he held for eleven years. His poverty was still great; for a long time he could not even afford to rent a piano. Those were years, as he put it, of "hard study, occasional composing, much revision, a great deal of thinking, and very little eating." As for his teachers at this time: "I studied with God, with the birds, and the trees—and myself." The major influence at this time was the Bohemian composer Bedřich Smetana, who was a conductor at the National Opera. Dvořák's personal contact with Smetana, and his participation in the *première* of Smetana's folk opera *The Bartered Bride,* directed his thinking toward the writing of Bohemian national music.

In 1873 Dvořák gave up his orchestral post to become organist of the St. Adalbert Church, and soon after that he married his pupil Anna Cermáková. For a while, as he put it, "I ate less and gave more lessons." But he also worked on composition as never before, and with a new creative richness and strength. For a long time, and largely as a result of his friendship with Smetana, he had been growing increasingly dissatisfied with the works of his early manhood—chamber music, several symphonies, the opera *Alfred*—much of which he destroyed. Instead of trying to arrive at his own identity he had been imitating the German composers: Wagner in his opera; Beethoven, Mozart, and Liszt in his concert works. Now he abandoned his German models, freed himself once and for all of his Wagner obsession, and set off on his own by writing Bohemian music. Just before his marriage, he had written a patriotic hymn called "The Heirs of the White Mountain," which was a resounding success when introduced on March 9, 1873. This success, Dvořák's first, inspired in him an unprecedented burst of creative activity. His Symphony in E-flat major was heard in Prague in 1874 and received the Austrian

State Prize one year later. He wrote a comic opera in a folk vein, *The King and the Collier,* which the National Opera had commissioned and which it introduced on November 24, 1874. It was a failure, and Dvořák set about rewriting it immediately. In the new version it was better received, but Dvořák was still dissatisfied. He rewrote it several more times, and then wrote an entirely new score to the same libretto. He also produced many new orchestral and chamber music works, songs, and even operas. The best of these were derived from Bohemian folk sources.

One of these Bohemian works, *Airs from Moravia,* he submitted to the Austrian Commission, which had given him a prize for his symphony. This new work made such a deep impression on the committee that it awarded the composer a pension amounting to $250 a year. Even more important than this pension was the fact that the *Airs from Moravia* won for Dvořák the devoted friendship and the unsparing help of Johannes Brahms. Brahms, a member of the committee that made the award, was now one of the most powerful and celebrated musicians in Vienna. He used his position and his fame to further the career of the still unknown Dvořák. He persuaded the publisher Simrock to issue the young composer's music; he influenced performers and conductors to introduce Dvořák's works in Vienna; he provided Dvořák with funds; he even corrected the proofs of Dvořák's music when the composer was unable to do so. "I can hardly tell you, esteemed Master, all that is in my heart," Dvořák once wrote appreciatively to Brahms. "I can only say that I shall all my life owe you the deepest gratitude for your good and noble intentions towards me, which are worthy of a truly great artist and man."

It was due to Brahms's persuasion that Simrock commissioned Dvořák to write a set of Slavonic dances in the style of Brahms's Hungarian Dances, which had been so successful. The Slavonic Dances of Dvořák were outstandingly successful. While they brought the composer very little revenue—he had sold them outright for a flat fee—they did succeed in making Dvořák famous throughout Europe. This fame was further enhanced by the efforts on his behalf by such powerful musicians as Hans von Bülow, Joseph Joachim, Hans Richter, and Franz Liszt, who performed his major works in Europe's leading capitals. Major works left his pen in profusion. His three Slavonic Rhapsodies for orchestra came in 1878; the Violin Concerto in A minor, the Symphony in D major, and the Gypsy Songs followed in

1880; the ten *Legends* (originally for piano duet, but later orchestrated) were written in 1881. On October 8, 1882, a folk opera, *Dimitrij,* was produced at the National Theater. He was now besieged with offers to conduct his works in Germany and Austria, and was overwhelmed with commissions for new works.

Now that he was a celebrity Dvořák was invited to London in 1884 to direct three concerts of his works. He was the man of the hour. "As soon as I appeared, I received a tempestuous welcome from the audience of 12,000." This success was also financially rewarding. Besides being paid handsomely for his appearances, Dvořák received a fee of 2000 pounds from the publishers Novello for a new choral work (*The Spectre's Bride,* introduced at the Birmingham Festival in 1885).

He was in a position to bring to realization a lifelong dream. He bought a spacious summer villa in the forests of Vysoka, thenceforth to be his beloved retreat for several months each year. The peasant returns to the soil where he belongs. For, notwithstanding his fame, Dvořák did not outgrow his humble peasant origin. To the end of his days he remained shy, uncomfortable in the presence of those he regarded as his social superiors, and frequently remiss in his social behavior. He was never completely at ease in large cities, with the demands they made on him. Actually he had a pathological fear of city streets and would never cross a busy thoroughfare if a friend was not with him. He was happiest when he was close to the soil, raising pigeons, taking long, solitary walks in the hills and forests of the Bohemia he loved so deeply. Yet he was by no means a recluse. In the company of his intimate friends, particularly after a few beers, he was voluble, gregarious, expansive, and good-humored.

For all his travels he never lost the naïveté of boyhood. Like a boy, he was passionately fond of locomotives and boats. He often traveled distances to watch, for a few moments, a train pass by. And he never missed an opportunity to visit an ocean liner and inspect it from bow to stern. He also had a boyish delight in games. When he played cards he was a poor loser, sometimes furiously flinging his cards across the room after an unsuccessful hand.

On one occasion, when an acquaintance complained bitterly that outside of music Dvořák was incapable of discussing anything, he was told, "Did you try talking to him about pigs?" Dvořák's entire intellectual world was music; away from it he was lost. And in that world he had one god: Beethoven. "Why don't all of you kneel?" he once exclaimed to his students in Prague when they were dissecting one of Beethoven's masterworks. Figuratively he was always kneeling before the master. On one occasion his townspeople brought him a gift of a laurel wreath bearing this inscription: "To the greatest composer in the world." They later found the wreath in Dvořák's study, but the inscription had been placed around a bust of Beethoven.

Dvořák's great fame soon spanned the Atlantic Ocean. Jeanette Thurber, who had helped establish the National Conservatory of Music in New York in 1885, called on him to become director of that institution. The salary—$15,000 a year, or more than twenty times as much as Dvořák earned in Prague—was a powerful selling point.

Dvořák set sail with his wife and two of their children aboard the *Saale,* which left Bremen, Germany, on September 17. The crossing was quiet except for one particularly stormy day. Everybody was seasick then—everybody except Dvořák, who was the only passenger in the dining room that evening. The ship came to New York Harbor on September 26. Due to an epidemic of cholera in Europe, all passengers were placed in quarantine for a full day. When they were finally allowed to disembark, the Dvořáks were transported to the Hotel Clarendon on Eighteenth Street. A few days later they moved to their permanent New York home: an apartment at 327 East Seventeenth Street, a stone's throw from the Conservatory.

When the New York press first interviewed Dvořák they expected a "wild man"—perhaps because he was a Bohemian; perhaps because his famous Slavonic Rhapsodies and Dances suggested that their creator might have a combustible temperament. The press was rather surprised to discover that Dvořák was a mild, meek, agreeable little man with a soft voice and a parson's gentle manner.

He was also gentle as a teacher—but only to talented students, who were given a free hand to develop in their own way. With less gifted pupils, however, he was a martinet. He insisted on having them learn and obey the textbook rules. His irony had a sharp edge, but he did not use it indiscriminately. And those on whom it was applied surgically would eventually agree they deserved it.

Dvořák liked the New World, and he soon became one of the earliest and most staunch advocates of its folk music. The eminent critic James Gibbons Huneker and one of Dvořák's pupils, H. T.

Burleigh (a Negro), had introduced Dvořák to the Negro spiritual, and Dvořák was instantly enchanted. He also became acquainted with and interested in another facet of American music—the music of the American Indian. He built several of his most ambitious works around the idioms of Negro and American Indian songs and dances.

But he was homesick. He was partially able to assuage this pain by spending his summers in a little town in Iowa, Spillville, populated by Bohemians. Here he could speak in his native tongue, play Bohemian melodies on the church organ for people who could respond to this music instinctively, feel at ease with simple folk whose early background had been his as well, and move in a setting whose scenery reminded him of his Bohemian homeland. When his villagers celebrated his fifty-second birthday with a feast in the best Bohemian tradition, he almost felt he was home again.

He was therefore happy in Spillville and able to do there some of his best work. He orchestrated a new symphony, which he subtitled *From the New World* and which was inspired by Negro songs. It was introduced by the New York Philharmonic Orchestra under Anton Seidl on December 15, 1893, and was a success. After the second movement there was a scene described as one "of wild enthusiasm" as the composer was forced to take bow after bow from his seat in an upper-tier box. "The success of the symphony was magnificent," Dvořák himself reported. "The newspapers say that never has a composer had such a triumph. . . . The public applauded so much that I felt like a king in my box." Such acclaim demanded that the symphony be repeated. The New York Philharmonic played it twice more the same season. The Boston Symphony introduced it in Boston two weeks after the *première* in New York and had to repeat it at least once each season between 1895 and 1897 inclusive.

But, for all the honor and glory that were his in this country, Dvořák was growing restive. He wanted to go home. "Whether or not they extend my contract," he confided to a friend, "I simply must see Bohemia again." The National Conservatory did extend his contract, but Dvořák would remain no more. In 1895 he left the United States for Prague.

Soon after his return to Prague he wrote a piece for the piano which is undoubtedly his most popular work, the Humoresque. During his stay in America he had been gathering in his notebooks material for gay, witty, and whimsical pieces for the piano. Back in

Prague he wrote eight of these pieces within a period of seventeen days, entitled them collectively *Humoresques,* and published them as Op. 101. It is the seventh number of this piano cycle that is *the* famous Humoresque: a staple in the violinist's repertory (in Fritz Kreisler's transcription); a perennial favorite of *salon* orchestras; the inspiration for the famous short story of Fannie Hurst which, in turn, was the source for two motion pictures.

In 1901 Dvořák became director of the Prague Conservatory, holding this post until the end of his life. The celebration of his sixtieth birthday throughout Bohemia brought him an appointment as member of the Austrian House of Lords.

But his last years were somber. He was suffering from Bright's disease. But physical pain was not the only thing that tormented him. In 1904 the National Theater presented his opera *Armida.* It was such a disastrous failure that the composer thought his heart would break. He died soon after this—suddenly at a dinner table. The cause of his death was not a broken heart, but an apoplectic stroke. His funeral, on May 5, 1904, caused a national day of mourning.

HIS MUSIC

As the man is, so the music. The composer was unsophisticated almost to the point of naïveté, without culture, artifice, subtlety, or guile. He wrote as his heart dictated. Like Schubert he wrote abundantly, easily, spontaneously, and was completely incapable of a creative method requiring fastidious workmanship in details or a painstaking working out of germinal ideas. The ideas came from him copiously, as the did from Schubert, and he allowed them to pour out munificently in his works.

At his best he wrote with a most ingratiating charm, sensitivity of feeling, lyrical freshness, and a wealth of tenderness and beauty. And his music is at its best when it carries recollections of the Bohemian landscape, its songs and dances, backgrounds, feast days, and ceremonies: the Slavonic Dances and Rhapsodies; the concert overtures, *Carnival, My Home,* and *In Nature's Realm;* the *Dumky* Trio; the Symphony No. 1; the piano duets *From the Bohemian Forest.* Here his melodies have the immediate and inescapable appeal of folk songs; his rhythms are infectious in their freedom and variety; his colors are vivid; his feelings, warm and direct.

He was at his weakest when he tried to become grandiose or heroic or profound. "He was not a man to translate pictures, statues, poems, a system of metaphysics, a gospel of pessimism in music," as Philip Hale once wrote.

Some of his best and most famous works were inspired not by Bohemian but by American folk idioms. The songs of the Negro had made a deep impression on him. Some have described how the tears came to his eyes as he listened to them. "These beautiful and varied themes are the products of the soil," he later said. "They are American. They are the folk songs of America, and your composers must turn to them. In the Negro melodies of America I discovered all that is needed for a great and noble school of music." He proceeded to prove his point by imitating these melodies in his *Symphony from the New World* and parts of his Concerto for Cello and Orchestra.

He was also strongly affected by the music of the American Indian, with which he came into contact in Spillville, Iowa, in the summer of 1893, when three Iroquois Indians visited him and performed for him authentic Indian music. Stimulated by this experience Dvořák wrote the *American* Quartet and the Quintet in E-flat major. But Dvořák did not actually employ Indian themes. He explained that "I have simply written original themes embodying the peculiarities of Indian music, and, using these themes as subjects, have developed them with all the resources of modern rhythm, harmony, counterpoint, and orchestral color."

ANALYTICAL NOTES

Chamber Music. Though Dvořák's two most famous chamber music works owe their inspiration and material to native American sources, the Piano Quintet in A major, Op. 81 (1887) is thoroughly Bohemian. The second movement is a dumka—a *dumka* meaning "passing thought" in Russian, but used by Dvořák to designate elegiac music. On the other hand, the third movement is a furiant, a native Bohemian dance form. But even in the first and final movements we encounter the sharp contrasts of mood prevalent in Bohemian folk music, together with melodies and rhythms of unmistakable Bohemian personality.

Bohemian, too, is the popular *Dumky* Trio, Op. 90 (1891), for piano, violin, and cello. As the title suggests, this trio is made up of a number of elegiac movements. There are six in all in various keys: the first and sixth movements in E minor, the second in C-sharp minor, the third in A major, the fourth in D minor, and the fifth in E-flat major. Paul Stefan made an interesting observation when he pointed out that the six movements can actually be regarded as a traditional four-movement work. The first three dumky, in his opinion, form the introductory movement in a kind of rondo form; the fourth is the slow movement; the fifth is the scherzo; and the sixth, the finale.

Though there are occasional outbursts of passion, the music is for the most part plaintive. Otakar Sourek notes that this alternation between agitation and a subdued melancholy provided Dvořák with an opportunity to express his own "complex and fiery temperament, which plunged at times into revery and showed itself at other moments in outbursts of gladness."

The two chamber music masterworks that are of American inspiration and origin are companion pieces. They are the Quartet in F major, *American,* Op. 96, and the String Quintet in E-flat major, Op. 97. They were written in the same period, the summer of 1893. They are similar in style and spirit, deriving their personality from the folk music of the American Indian.

The Indian element is pronounced in the first two movements of the *American* Quartet. The first is made up of three Indian themes. The initial theme is introduced by the viola and after that taken up by the first violin. The second appears as a duet for the two violins. The third is heard in the first violin against chords in the rest of the strings. The second movement presents an exotic Indian song, played by the first violin in the opening measures; in the end the melody is recalled by the cello to a pizzicato accompaniment. The two concluding movements are in Dvořák's Bohemian vein, rather than in the Indian style, and include a whimsical scherzo and a finale that is vital with Bohemian dance rhythms.

The use of Indian rhythm is prominent in the quintet. Indian drumlike rhythms are used with compelling effect as a background to the first theme of the first movement and in the scherzo. The slow movement features an expressive melody in the viola and five variations. The main idea of the concluding rondo is a strongly accented theme; two subsidiary thoughts have once again an American Indian personality.

Choral Music. Both of Dvořák's major works for chorus are funereal. The earlier one is the Stabat Mater, Op. 58. He began sketching it in 1876, but did not get around to writing it until the tragic death of his child in September of 1877. The music is permeated with Dvořák's grief at the loss of his loved one. The first part is dramatic, abounding with realistic writing. The second part combines spiritual exaltation with surpassing tenderness.

Thirteen years later came the Requiem, Op. 89 (1890). Here too we find two clearly demarcated sections. The first, which concludes just before the Offertory, suggests the horror of death. The second part brings hope for salvation and finds peace through faith in God. An integrating feature in this composition is a two-measure *leitmotiv* (poco lento), which makes its first appearance in the cellos in the opening of the first section. A curious blood relationship between the Stabat Mater and the Requiem is established by having the main subject of the *Recordare* in the latter work an inversion of the theme in the *Quis est homo* from the Stabat Mater.

Orchestral Music. In recent years a significant renumbering of Dvořák's symphonies has taken place. For a long time, only five of Dvořák's symphonies were officially numbered, even though it had been known that Dvořák had written several earlier symphonies. Thus the D major Symphony, Op. 60, was long accepted as Dvořák's Symphony No. 1, just as the *Symphony from the New World* was accepted as Symphony No. 5. Since 1960, and the promotion of four early Dvořák symphonies through recordings and performances, Dvořák's symphonies have acquired new numbers to take into account the earlier compositions. What had once been Symphony No. 1 is now Symphony No. 5, and so on.

The four early symphonies are still novelties. The first, in C minor, is named *The Bells of Zlonice.* Dvořák wrote it in 1865 for a competition, and it is the only one of these four early works that he did not later revise. Symphony No. 2 in B-flat was also written in 1865, and revised in the late 1880s. Symphony No. 3 in E-flat and Symphony No. 4 in D minor were completed between 1873 and 1874, and revised in the late 1880s. Discussing these early symphonic works for *High Fidelity* magazine, David Hamilton has said: "None of these . . . symphonies of Dvořák is a fully realized work, but in sum they are full of characteristic touches—the (occasionally distracting) fertility of thematic invention, the rhythmic vitality, the contrapuntal skill are all present, if not yet under control."

Dvořák first achieves maturity within the symphonic form in what was formerly known as Symphony No. 1 but is now identified as Symphony No. 5—the Symphony in D major, Op. 60 (1880). This is music that brims over with youthful verve and enthusiasm, that is consistently engaging for its buoyant lyricism and its vital rhythmic pulse. Of especial interest is the folklike song of the second movement, and the spirited Bohemian dance music of the third-movement furiant.

The Symphony No. 6 in D minor, Op. 70 (1885)—once known as Symphony No. 2—has far greater sobriety. It opens solemnly with a subject in the lower strings, and later on in the same movement presents a tender melody for woodwinds accompanied by the strings. There are overtones of tragedy and conflict. But in the second movement, dominated by a chorale for the woodwinds, and in the sprightly scherzo, a lighter mood is introduced. The finale, however, is once again at turns solemn and agitated.

Symphony No. 7 in F major, Op. 24 (formerly Symphony No. 3), is an early work and is rarely heard. It was written in 1875 and revised in 1887. But Symphony No. 8 in G major, Op. 88 (formerly Symphony No. 4), is the most popular of all the Dvořák symphonies except for the *New World* which followed it. Some have identified the Eighth Symphony as *English,* because it was published in England. The London *Times,* in 1890, called it *Pastoral* because it suggests "rural sights and sounds." Most, however, refer to it as the *Bohemian* due to its national identity. In none of his symphonies is Dvořák more engagingly lyrical, more spontaneous, more lovable. The work opens with a tender minor-key subject for woodwinds and cellos. After a change of key we hear the principal idea, a happy thought first given by the flutes. A similarly lighthearted mood is then projected by flutes and clarinets as the second theme. The main melody of the second movement has pastoral serenity. Though new, intriguing ideas are later introduced, the bucolic atmosphere of the opening is maintained. A graceful scherzo, with a lively waltzlike tune in its trio, is followed by a summons from the trumpet, with which the finale begins. A vigorous Bohemian tune in the cellos is then followed by another vividly national idea in violins and violas—the principal subjects.

Dvořák's most celebrated symphony—indeed, his most famous work of all—is the Symphony No. 9 (formerly Symphony No. 5) in E minor, Op. 95 (1893), better known as the *Symphony from the New World*. It has been the subject of a violent controversy. Is it an American work by a Bohemian? Or is it a Bohemian work with superficial American traits? The German critic Kretzschmar belonged to the school that insisted it was American to the core, and he even went so far as to say it included American melodies not of Dvořák's invention (which, of course, is not the case). Others pointed to stylistic traits in the melodic and rhythmic writing that are in Dvořák's identifiable Bohemian vein. Dvořák himself entered the controversy when he wrote: "Omit the nonsense about my having made use of . . . 'American' motives. It is a lie. I tried to write only in the spirit of these national melodies." Whether American or Bohemian—the problem no longer seems important or even interesting—the work remains one of the best-loved in the symphonic repertory.

It opens with a slow introduction in which the main theme of the first movement is suggested in horns and lower strings. This theme, which is syncopated, is presented by the horns and carried over by the woodwinds. A transitional subject in flutes and oboes then leads to the second main theme, which is introduced by the flute and after that assumed by the violins. This second theme has more than a passing resemblance to the Negro spiritual "Swing Low, Sweet Chariot."

The second movement is one of the most celebrated in all symphonic music. It is built around an elegiac melody for the English horn over harmonies in the strings. This melody has the unmistakable personality of a spiritual, so much so that Dvořák is sometimes falsely assumed to have expropriated it. (One of Dvořák's pupils, William Arms Fisher, later wrote words to it. The song that resulted, "Goin' Home," is now almost as famous as the original.) Two subsidiary ideas are introduced after this melody, the first in the flute and oboe and the second in the oboe. After this the main melody returns and the movement ends as it began, with a few quiet chords.

The lively first theme of the scherzo, which sounds like an Indian ritual dance, is heard in flute and oboe and answered by the clarinet. A gentle second idea is presented by the flute and oboe. There are two spirited trios, in two different keys (E major and C major). In the coda, which appears after a repetition of the opening section, the principal theme of the first movement is heard in the horns, develops in volume, and then dies out.

After a brief introduction the jubilant main theme of the finale is proclaimed by horns and trumpets against sharp chords in the rest of the orchestra. A transitional section follows. We then hear the second theme, in triplets, presented by the clarinet against a tremolo background in the strings. In the development these two themes are worked out. But the composer also recalls in the development the main theme of the slow movement, a fragment of the scherzo, and the principal subject of the first movement. The recapitulation presents again the new material of this finale, but in the coda (which is built up with tremendous force) the materials of the preceding movement are reviewed for the last time.

The Concerto in A minor for Violin and Orchestra, Op. 53, was written for the eminent Hungarian violinist Joseph Joachim between 1879 and 1880. The exacting Hungarian musician suggested so many changes that Dvořák had to rewrite most of the violin part; and it is undoubtedly due to Joachim's painstaking criticism and advice that it turned out to be so grateful a work for the violin.

The concerto is broad and rhapsodical; the writing for the violin frequently assumes the character of an improvisation. There are three basic themes in the first movement. The first, somewhat stark and dramatic, is shared by the orchestra and the solo violin. After the orchestra enlarges on this theme, the violins present the second melody in octaves against a countermelody in the woodwinds. After the working out of this material, a third melody appears in the solo violin.

The second movement, a romanza, is built out of melodies that are of Bohemian nationality. Against a woodwind setting the soloist plays the first melody. It is assumed by the woodwinds, before the solo violin enters with a second theme. After some passage work by the violin, the strings in the orchestra appear with the third melody. There follows a long and rhapsodic section for the solo violin. After a reappearance of the three themes, either in the solo instrument or in the orchestra or in both, two horns present the opening theme to embellishments by the soloist.

The concluding rondo is built out of three lively themes, all first introduced by the solo instrument and all having the personality of Bohemian folk dances.

The Concerto in B minor for Cello and Orchestra, Op. 104, came fifteen years after the Violin Concerto. It was completed in Prague in 1895, but most of it was written during Dvořák's stay in the United States, and it includes melodic material that stems from American folk sources.

A long orchestral prelude presents the two main themes of the first movement. The first theme, which appears in varied forms and colors throughout the entire work, is heard in the clarinets. The second, betraying the influence the Negro spiritual had on Dvořák at this time, is presented by solo horn against a string background. The orchestral introduction over, the main body of the movement begins with the entrance of the solo cello. It discusses the two themes, then embarks on formidable virtuoso passages in which the two themes are embellished and developed.

The beautiful slow movement passes from tender to somber feelings. It is one of the most strongly felt and emotional of Dvořák's slow movements. It is built out of two poignant melodies, the first appearing in clarinet with accompaniment by oboe and bassoon. After the solo instrument echoes this theme, the strings appear with the second theme to an accompanying subject by clarinet.

There is so much joyous feeling in the concluding movement that Paul Stefan, Dvořák's biographer, is convinced that it expresses Dvořák's exhilaration on returning to his native land after his long stay in America. A powerfully rhythmic figure in the winds opens the movement. Solo cello, and after it the orchestra, presents the first theme, which is something like a peasant dance. The second theme, also vivacious, appears in the clarinet with intriguing decorative trimmings by the cello. The two melodies are worked out vigorously, with a great variety of moods and often with a high degree of virtuosity on the part of the soloist. The movement ends, in Dvořák's own description, "like a breath, with reminiscences of the first and second movements; the solo dies away to a pianissimo, then there is a crescendo, and the last measures are taken up by the orchestra, ending stormily."

The Slavonic Dances originated as four-hand pieces for the piano. Dvořák wrote them on a commission from the publisher Simrock, producing a set of eight dances, Op. 46 (1878), based on rhythms and melodies of Bohemian folk songs and dances. When these Slavonic Dances became extraordinarily popular (to the point of spreading Dvořák's name not only throughout Europe but also in the United States) Simrock commissioned Dvořák to orchestrate them. In 1886, Dvořák produced a second set of dances, Op. 72, once again for piano duet, and then for orchestra. This time he based his melodies on Yugoslav and Little Russian rhythms and melodies.

Their contagious rhythms and infectious moods, both sad and gay, reflective and abandoned, make for success. It is no wonder, then, that the Slavonic Dances proved as popular as they did. They carry the very essence of Slavic personality. These are the most celebrated ones: C major, Op. 46, No. 1; E minor, Op. 46, No. 2; D major, Op. 46, No. 3; A-flat major, Op. 46, No. 6; G minor, Op. 46, No. 8; E minor, Op. 72, No. 2; and C major, Op. 72, No. 7. Fritz Kreisler transcribed for violin and piano Nos. 1 and 2 in the Op. 46 group and No. 2 in the Op. 72 set—all extremely popular in the violin repertory.

The three Slavonic Rhapsodies, Op. 45 (1878), bring up the old Bohemian world of knights, fair ladies, and tournaments. The first (D major) depicts a tournament of knights, the second (G minor) a lover's tryst, and the third (A-flat major) a hunt. The last is the most famous. It opens solemnly with a solo harp. When the theme is taken up by the orchestra it becomes a vital folk dance. This melody is enlarged and varied, ever changing in mood and atmosphere. The somber mood of the opening returns to end the work.

The Scherzo capriccioso in D-flat major, Op. 66 (1883), is also one of its composer's popular works in a short orchestral form. The first part is brilliant and festive but then becomes lyrical and emotional with a stately melody for full orchestra and a light waltz subject for the violins. The second section is a trio which opens with a theme for English horn, as preface to a significant thought for strings and wind. The broad melody of the first part returns to receive extended treatment before the significant thought of the trio is remembered. The concluding coda pays attention to the festive subject with which the composition opened.

Carnival Overture, Op. 92, is one of three concert overtures written in 1891, the other two being *In Nature's Realm,* Op. 91, and *Othello,* Op. 93. Originally, Dvořák wanted this set to be a trilogy describing the "great creative forces of the Universe—Nature, Life and Love." But in time he lost interest in this idea and instead completed three compositions that could be played independently of one another. *Carnival* is the most popular. Here is the composer's own program for this music: "A lonely contemplative wanderer reaches the city at nightfall where a carnival of pleasure reigns supreme. On every side is heard the clangor of instruments, mingled with shouts of joy and unrestrained hilarity of the people, giving vent to their feelings in song and dances."

The opening, in its bright orchestral colors and dynamic urge, brings up the picture of a carnival. An important melody is then presented by oboes and clarinets, soon to receive important amplification. A recall of the brilliant opening helps to set the stage for a haunting, passionate episode for flutes and violins, accompanied by English horn, intended to suggest a tender exchange between lovers. The overture ends as vigorously and as brilliantly as it began.

Vocal Music. The nourishment Dvořák received from Bohemian folk music strengthened him in the writing of his songs. In these works we continually encounter either the languorous, sensuous moods of the Bohemian folk song or the vital, cogent rhythms of the Bohemian dance tune.

The most famous song Dvořák wrote was "Songs My Mother Taught Me." This is the fourth of seven songs in a cycle entitled *Gypsy Songs,* Op. 55 (1880)—typical of the composer's talent for spinning a long, simple melodic line and dressing it with the most sensitive emotion. "Songs My Mother Taught Me" has become popular in various transcriptions. Another familiar number in this cycle is the first one, "I Chant My Lay," particularly noteworthy for the way in which voice and piano accompaniment blend together inextricably.

Another significant song cycle by Dvořák is the *Biblical Songs,* Op. 99 (1894)—a setting of parts of a seventeenth-century Bohemian translation of the Bible. There are ten songs in this group. The mood throughout is lugubrious (reflecting the composer's deep sorrow upon learning of Tchaikovsky's death); but the deep melancholy is at times combined with spirituality, as in "By the Waters of Babylon," which has been likened to a Negro spiritual, and "Turn Thee to Me."

Sir Edward Elgar

"Edward Elgar was the first composer to bring England to the front rank in the field of orchestral music."

BASIL MAINE

BORN: Broadheath, near Worcester, England, June 2, 1857.
DIED: Worcester, February 23, 1934.
MAJOR WORKS: *Chamber Music*—Violin Sonata; String Quartet; Piano Quintet. *Choral Music*—The Light of Life; The Dream of Gerontius; The Apostles; The Kingdom. *Orchestral Music*—2 symphonies; Enigma Variations; Pomp and Circumstance, five marches; Cockaigne; Introduction and Allegro for String Quartet and String Orchestra; In the South; Violin Concerto; Falstaff; Cello Concerto.

HIS LIFE

The death of Henry Purcell in 1695 brought a flourishing period in English music to an end. It had produced the madrigals, the keyboard music of the Elizabethan virginalists, as well as Purcell's opera *Dido and Aeneas* and his instrumental works. One would imagine that such a tradition would be the soil for a great and flourishing art. And yet this was not the case. For two hundred years England produced composers who were respectable craftsmen rather than inspired or original creators, most of whose works have since been forgotten.

Not until the closing year of the nineteenth century did there arise in England a figure who could be compared in ability to the great composers of other lands. He was Edward Elgar, whose *Enigma* Variations and *The Dream of Gerontius* might be said to have inaugurated a renaissance in English music.

Elgar's father, proprietor of a music store, was an excellent musician. He was the organist at the St. George's Cathedral in Worcester and he played the violin in local orchestras. Elgar acquired from him his early fascination and talent for music. But the boy showed a keen interest and gift for other art forms as well.

It was music that finally claimed him. He spent hours at the feet of his father listening to his performances of Bach's organ works. Finding scores of symphonies and operas in the house, Elgar studied them until he knew many of them from memory. He also began studying counterpoint, harmony, and thorough bass by himself— with only textbooks to guide him. His first formal instruction in the violin, as well as the piano, was given him at a local "ladies' school." He also managed to acquire by himself enough of a facility at the organ to be able to substitute for his father occasionally at church. And he tried his hand at composition. While attending Littleton House, where he was getting his early schooling, he wrote in 1869 the score for a children's play, *The Wand of Youth.* Two suites assembled from this music were finally introduced in London between 1907 and 1908.

But his father wanted him to be a lawyer. Upon leaving school Elgar worked as clerk in the office of a solicitor. Then, one year later, he came to London to begin a three-year course of study in law. But homesickness and his real interest in music soon sent him home. Law was now abandoned for good as Elgar applied himself passionately to his beloved music. He played the violin in the local orchestra; he joined a wind quintet; he gave local violin recitals; he took on jobs as orchestrator; he was the bandmaster at the County Lunatic Asylum; and he played the organ at church.

He was drifting about aimlessly in music until 1889 when he married Caroline Alice Roberts, daughter of a major general. She was a remarkable woman of great perception, integrity, and vision. She believed that her husband was capable of important musical achievements, though thus far he had been little more than a dilettante. She made him give up his various jobs. She arranged for both of them to leave Worcester and live in London where the rich and varied musical life might stimulate him. And she encouraged him, even urged him, to turn to the writing of music that was serious in intent and ambitious in scope.

Though not a trained musician, she had such taste and judgment that throughout her life she was Elgar's most discriminating critic. He came to lean on her, to rely on her opinions, to follow her tactful advice. Later in life he acknowledged his debt to her.

I play phrases and tunes to her because she always likes to see what progress I have been making. . . . A few nights before . . . I played some of the music I had written that day, and she nodded her head appreciatively, except over one passage, at which she sat up, rather grimly I thought. However, I went to bed leaving it as it was; but I got up as soon as it was light and went down to look over what I had written. I found it as I had left it, except that there was a little piece of paper, pinned over the offending bars, on which was written, "All of it is beautiful and just right, except this ending. Don't you think, dear Edward, that this end is just a little . . . ?" Well, I scrapped the end. Not a word was ever said about it; but I rewrote it; and as I heard no more I knew that it was approved.

Soon after his marriage Elgar wrote *Froissart*, a concert overture which had a successful hearing on September 9, 1890. Meanwhile the Elgars felt that the life of a great city was too distracting for sustained creative effort. They moved to the smaller community of Malvern where they remained for the next thirteen years and where Elgar wrote some ambitious choral works. *The Black Knight*, based on a poem by Uhland translated by Longfellow, was heard at the Worcester Festival on April 18, 1893. *The Light of Life*, adapted from the Scriptures, was given at the same festival on September 10, 1896. *Caractacus* received its world *première* at the Leeds Festival on October 5, 1898.

Success came between 1899 and 1900 with two contrasting works which up to the present time are regarded as among Elgar's best. One of them was the Variations on an Original Theme (more familiarly known as the *Enigma* Variations). It was discovered by the eminent conductor Hans Richter. Searching for some new English works to introduce at his concerts, Richter came upon Elgar's Variations, which an agent had submitted to him. Its melodic freshness and its uninhibited emotional content impressed Richter. He conducted the work for the first time in London on June 19, 1899.

Subsequently the composer revised it and himself directed the *première* of the new version at the Worcester Festival. It has since that time become one of the most popular works in the repertory of English orchestral music, as well as the first piece of orchestral music by an Englishman to acquire a permanent place in the repertory.

The success of the Variations was pronounced. But an even greater triumph was eventually to be won by the second of Elgar's works completed in 1900, the oratorio *The Dream of Gerontius,* based on the poem of Cardinal Newman. Actually *The Dream of Gerontius* was not initially successful. Introduced at the Birmingham Festival on October 3, 1900, it was appreciated by only a few discerning musicians (one of them was Bernard Shaw). But at the Lower Rhine Festival, the following year, the work was acclaimed. And when heard again in England it was accepted as a masterwork. Since that time English music audiences have come to regard *The Dream of Gerontius* in the class of Handel's *Messiah* and Mendelssohn's *Elijah.*

Beginning with the turn of the twentieth century Elgar assumed a position of first importance in England which, with passing years, he continued to solidify. He was commissioned by the Government to write the music for the coronation of Edward VII. In 1904 there took place a three-day Elgar festival in London, and soon after that he was knighted. In 1905 a chair of music was created for him at the University of Birmingham (which he occupied for only one year). He received the Order of Merit in 1911. Other honors came to him at a later day: an appointment as Master of the King's Music in 1924, and baronetcy in 1931.

Elgar paid his only visits to the United States in 1905 and 1907, the first time to receive an honorary doctorate from Yale, and the second time to direct his oratorio *The Apostles* (1903) in New York. During World War I, he served his country in whatever capacity he could. At first he was a special constable in the Hampstead Division, then a member of the Hampstead Volunteer Reserve. He also wrote martial music.

By 1920 he had produced his finest works, including two symphonies, two concertos (one for the violin and the other for the cello), several concert overtures, several oratorios, and some highly personal and intimate chamber music works. He was at the height of his critical and popular acclaim when suddenly he would write no more. The death of his beloved wife, in 1920, had destroyed his will to create. He deserted the homes in which he and his wife had been living for many years—Severn House in Hampstead and a country place in Sussex—to rent a modest apartment at St. James's Place in London. This was his home until 1929. After that, up to the end of his life, he resided at Marl Bank, in Rainbow Hill in Worcester.

This self-imposed silence lasted over a decade. It was finally broken in 1929 when he wrote a hymn of prayer for the recovery of George V, then seriously ill. He now confided to his friends that he would work again. He spoke of undertaking the writing of a third symphony and even began making sketches. He did not live to complete it. Suffering from sciatica, he had to undergo an operation from which he never recovered. Three weeks before his death, which took place on February 23, 1934, at his home at Marl Bank, he assisted from his bedside in recording one of his works, the march from *Caractacus*. He was buried beside his beloved wife in the cemetery at Malvern.

Tall, stately, erect—bearing himself with dignity—Elgar was the very model of a model Englishman. But his personality revealed facets and sides far different from that suggested by his imposing appearance. In an article for a London journal, which Robert J. Buckley had written early in Elgar's career, he made a jocular comment that Elgar's personality changed chameleon-like with the costume he favored at any given time. The man who dressed in rough tweeds and leggings, and in an informal outdoor jacket, was the one who enjoyed taking long walks in the country or setting off on bicycle trips. The one who put on a silk waistcoat was the one who enjoyed musing in front of his fireplace smoking a pipe, or engaging his friends in conversation. The gentleman in top hat and evening dress was the elegant man about town, while the one who was partial to solemn dark-colored suits and unostentatious shirts and ties was the businessman who talked, behaved, and thought like an astute banker or broker.

He was, in short, many men in one: a brilliant, penetrating conversationalist who at turns enchanted and amazed his listeners with the wide range of his interests and the depth of his information on many varied subjects. He also had a boy's inordinate delight in games, and the plebeian's passion for doping out and betting on the horses. His other enthusiasms ranged from cryptograms to flowers, from throwing boomerangs to fishing, from experimenting with test tubes and Bunsen burners in a laboratory to engaging village folk in small talk.

HIS MUSIC

Elgar was not an original composer. There is no work of his which does not echo or re-echo the styles and mannerisms of other composers—sometimes Wagner, sometimes Brahms, sometimes Schumann. He recognized this fact and acknowledged it. On one occasion he took pains to point out to a critic how, in one of his pieces, he had been influenced by Léo Delibes (1836–91). And his music, so strongly and unmistakably influenced, had almost no effect on that of his own and succeeding generations; it was too derivative to be able to shape and form the speech of any other composer.

He was, for better or for worse, essentially the voice of an era now dead, the so-called Edwardian age; and his music has the nostalgic quality of belonging to the past. "In a broad sense," wrote Basil Maine, "the First Symphony can be regarded as a salute to national heritage and attainment, the Second Symphony as a last exulting in the glories of an epoch which has already closed, and the Violoncello Concerto as a lament for irrevocable years. They are respectively a paean, an epic, and an elegy."

At his best Elgar was a composer of inescapable charm. His music has taste and breeding. It has feeling, dignity, beauty—and, at times, a genuine nobility.

ANALYTICAL NOTES

Choral Music. *The Dream of Gerontius,* Op. 38 (1900), is probably the most significant oratorio by an English composer. The text comes from the celebrated poem by Cardinal Newman portraying the doctrine of purgatory as expounded by the Catholic Church. Elgar's music, like Newman's poem, passes swiftly from dramatic to lyrical pages, from feverish agitation to spirituality.

The oratorio has two sections. An orchestral prelude offers some of the thematic ideas encountered throughout the score: the awesome

Judgment theme; the motives of Gerontius' fear and religious conviction; the prayer subject. The oratorio then begins with Gerontius' solo, "Jesus, Maria, I am near to death" in which we feel the utter desolation and despair that have seized him. He grows increasingly agitated, but is calmed by the chorus of "assistants" chanting *Kyrie eleison*. When their voices die out, Gerontius expresses his faith in God, in the Church and its teachings (*"Sanctus fortus, Sanctus Deus"*) while the assistants plead for his salvation.

Falling back feverish and exhausted, Gerontius—tortured and dismayed—begs Jesus for help and Mary to pray for him. The assistants continue to intercede for him with a noble litany. Somewhat calmed, Gerontius now commends his soul to God. As the priests intone a solemn prayer, the soul of Gerontius begins its journey.

The second part begins with what Ernest Newman has called "music of felicity." It is music of incomparable serenity. The soul of Gerontius explains that it is refreshed, filled with an inexpressible lightness and a sense of freedom. A dialogue ensues between Gerontius' soul and the Angel, during which (in music of awesome spirituality) the Angel describes the stigmata of St. Francis of Assisi. This is followed by the chorus of the Angels, "Praise to the Holiest," culminating in a mighty hymn of praise. Now the Judgment of Gerontius is at hand. His friends and the priest recite the *Subvenite* and the Angel of Agony pleads for him before the Throne of God. On earth people cry out for mercy. Then the Guardian Angel cries out *Alleluia* with joy and rapture. Gerontius, having experienced the beauty of God, exclaims: "Take me away, and in the lowest deep there let me be." Then, in what is probably the noblest page in the entire score, the Guardian Angel tenderly bids Gerontius farewell: "Softly and gently, dearly-ransomed soul, in my most loving arms, I now enfold thee." The Angels sing the praises of the "Holiest in the heights" and the oratorio comes to an exultant end with a rousing *Amen*.

Orchestral Music. The *Enigma* Variations, Op. 36 (1899)—or, more officially, the Variations on an Original Theme—established Elgar's reputation. It is still Elgar's best-known and best-liked work for orchestra. Elgar intended it as a tonal portrait of fourteen close friends, appending initials or nicknames to each of the variations to identify the person being discussed.

Elgar is believed to have introduced a "hidden" theme which, though never actually played, is suggested, sometimes intended as a kind of "silent accompaniment" to each of the variations. What this hidden theme is has never been revealed, and it is for this reason that the work is known as *Enigma*. Some have said that it is "Auld Lang Syne," though Elgar denied this vehemently. Henry E. Krehbiel suggested that it was a motive from Wagner's *Parsifal*.

The principal theme is a beautiful and somewhat sad melody played by the strings in the opening measures. The fourteen variations that follow can be described as follows:

1. "C.A.E." (Elgar's wife, Alice). The theme, slightly altered, is now tender and expressive, as the composer limns the personality of the woman who was his lifelong companion and inspiration.

2. "H.D.S-P." (H. D. Stuart-Powell, a pianist). The theme becomes more vigorous as Stuart's personal idiosyncrasy of exercising his fingers before playing the piano is amusingly described in the opening bars.

3. "R.T.B." (Richard Baxter Townshend, an amateur actor). The theme is briefly quoted in pizzicato strings and oboe. The woodwinds now introduce a mocking subject describing the actor's ability to change his resonant voice to a piping falsetto whenever he impersonated old men.

4. "W.M.B." (William M. Baker). A strenuous movement, in which kettledrums and trumpets participate, suggests the vigor and headstrong personality of this friend.

5. "R.P.A." (Richard P. Arnold, son of the famous English poet Matthew Arnold). The theme becomes moody. Violins introduce a countermelody that is livelier in character. This combination of introspection and vivacity depicts the dual personality of the young man.

6. "Ysobel" (Isabel Fitton, an amateur violist). This is a romantic movement as the viola sings a melody of melancholy beauty.

7. "Troyte" (Arthur Troyte Griffith). Griffith was one of Elgar's more explosive friends. His excitable nature is reflected in this boisterous section.

8. "W.N." (Winifred Norbury). A gracious and sedate version of the theme is given by the clarinets, describing a splendid lady whom Elgar admired greatly and who lived with dignity in her eighteenth-century house.

9. "Nimrod" (August Jaeger). Elgar himself said of this deeply

moving variation: "It is a record of a long summer evening walk when my friend Jaeger grew nobly eloquent—as only he could—on the grandeur of Beethoven, and especially of his slow movements."

10. "Dorabella" (Miss Penny). In capricious music the composer simulates the hesitancy of speech which was a physical trait of this lady.

11. "G.R.S." (George Roberts Sinclair, organist of the Hereford Cathedral). Sir Ivor Atkins believes that this variation is not so much a portrait of Sinclair as of Sinclair's bulldog, Dan. Sir Ivor points to the rapid descending passage for strings as a picture of the dog hurling himself down a riverbank, and to the succeeding bars, with their undulating rhythm, as a description of the dog's swim in the water.

12. "B.G.N." (Basil G. Nevinson, a cellist). Once again Elgar becomes poetic as he creates a poignant solo for the cello.

13. "***" (Lady Mary Lugon). Elgar said about this section, which he subtitled a "romanza": "The soft tremor of the drums suggests the distant throb of the engines of a liner, over which the clarinet quotes a phrase from Mendelssohn's overture, *Calm Sea and Prosperous Voyage,* while the quiet undulations of the violas suggest the peaceful motion of the waters."

14. "E.D.U." (This is believed to be a self-portrait. E.D.U. stands for "Edoo," the affectionate nickname by which Elgar's wife called him). The composer here speaks of his illusions and frustrations, dreams and ideals. The principal theme is given exultantly. The organ enters with majestic peals as if to reaffirm Elgar's faith in life and art. The work ends with a delightful presto.

Elgar completed his Symphony No. 1 in A-flat major, Op. 55, in 1908. At that time the composer explained that this music was "written out of a full life-experience and is meant to include the innumerable phases of joy and sorrow, struggle and conquest, and especially between the ideal and the actual life." This work is in three movements. The first generates power, while the second is somber and deeply emotional. The finale has three parts, an adagio, a lento, and an allegro. Themes heard first in the introduction of the opening movement are recalled to give the symphony an over-all unity.

The Symphony No. 2 in E-flat, Op. 63, followed the first symphony by three years. The two symphonies are quite different. The second is almost consistently joyous and buoyant where the first had been, for the most part, dark and brooding.

In the published score of the Second Symphony, Elgar quoted the following opening lines from Shelley's *Invocation:*

> Rarely, rarely comes thou
> Spirit of Delight!

But since these opening lines are despondent, and the general mood of the symphony is optimistic, Ernest Newman insists that they do not indicate the programmatic intent of the music. He feels that the closing lines of *Invocation* are more indicative of the composer's meaning:

> Spirit, I love thee—
> Thou art love and life! O come!
> Make once more thy heart my own.

Elgar dedicated this symphony "to the memory of His Late Majesty King Edward VII"; thus F. H. Shera may be justified in regarding it as an "epic of the Edwardian age. . . . This symphony certainly stands as the epitome of an age marked by a brilliance and splendor which dissolved in a moment on August 4, 1914."

In any case, since the music was partly written before the death of Edward VII, it has good humor as well as deep feeling and strength. In the first movement the main subject—heard in the full orchestra without preliminaries—is energetic. The second theme, appearing in the cellos, has a somber character. As it is the first idea, rather than the second, that is given prominence in the development, the entire movement generates joyous feelings. The entire second movement is reflective, the principal melody coming pianissimo in the flutes after a few quiet chords for the strings. But the third movement is ebullient throughout; as Ernest Newman said, its themes are filled with "quips and surprises" and the "pure joy of motion." The finale is majestic. It opens with a proud dissertation in low wind instruments and cellos, and continues with two other ideas, both dignified. The material is worked out vigorously. After a climax there is a quiet restatement of the opening theme of the first movement.

As in the symphony, so in the concerto: Elgar produced only two works, and each holds a place of prime importance among his creations. The first was the Concerto for Violin and Orchestra in B minor, Op. 61 (1910), whose world *première* was given in London by Fritz Kreisler in the year of its composition. This work has several original approaches. A telling effect is achieved in the opening of the first movement by having the solo instrument enter, not after the close of the orchestral introduction, but with its concluding bars. In the third movement, the traditional cadenza becomes untraditional by acquiring a gentle orchestral accompaniment and by concerning itself with the materials of the first two movements rather than with those of the third.

But the concerto is most noteworthy not for its originality, but for its romanticism, poetry, and flights of eloquence. That it is a personal document is proved by the words appearing on the flyleaf of the published score: "Here is enshrined the soul of . . ." It is also a spacious work, containing rhapsodical pages (such as the opening orchestral introduction, and the molto maestoso section of the third movement) contrasted with themes of great beauty which are like integrated songs (the second theme of the first movement, the main melody of the second, and the second theme of the third).

The Concerto for Cello and Orchestra in E minor, Op. 85 (1919), is also characterized by deeply personal utterances—such as the recitative for solo cello with which the work opens, and the sixty-measure reflective song shared by cello and orchestra in the second movement. The emphasis on affecting lyricism continues in the more vigorous finale, which is in rondo form, particularly in the eloquent second subject heard in the solo cello, which is followed by an extended passage with the kind of meditative repose previously encountered in the slow movement. A sudden return of the recitative of the concerto's opening measures breaks the spell and helps carry the work to a spirited conclusion.

Elgar's orchestral works include several highly successful and familiar shorter compositions. Unquestionably, the most celebrated is the *Pomp and Circumstance March* No. 1 in D major (1901). Its main broad melody for strings (for which Laurence Housman wrote the lyric "Land of Hope and Glory") is almost as intimately associated with the British Empire as "God Save the King." (In the United States, many, indeed, have marched to its strains to receive a diploma at graduating exercises!) This melody is preceded and followed by a contrasting brisk and energetic subject for strings.

This march is one of a set of five collectively entitled *Pomp and Circumstance,* Op. 39 (1901–30). The phrase "pomp and circumstance" originated in *Othello:* "pomp and circumstance of glorious war." Elgar wrote these marches to prove that a serious composer could produce distinctive music within this form. Two were written in 1901, one in 1905, one in 1907, and the last in 1930. The most familiar of the other four marches is the fourth, in G major, called *The Song of Liberty.* Here, too, the opening and closing are brisk and spirited, enframing a stately melody for full orchestra.

Among Elgar's concert overtures two have retained their place in the repertory. *Cockaigne,* Op. 40 (1901), is a vivid and realistic picture of the city of London. This is a programmatic work describing a stroll through "London Town" by two lovers. The hubbub of the streets, the sounds of a passing brass band, and organ music coming from a nearby church are all picturesquely caught in the music. Its heart is an expressive melody for strings: Our lovers have stopped off to rest and give voice to their romantic feelings.

In the South, or *Alassio,* Op. 50 (1903), was inspired by the composer's visit to the Ligurian resort. The following quotation appears in the published score: "A land which *was* the mightiest in its old command, and *is* the loveliest; wherein were cast the men of Rome. Thou art the garden of the world." This concert overture is a tonal study of Nature, opening with a lively tune for clarinets and progressing toward a pastoral section for woodwinds and muted strings descriptive of a shepherd and his flock.

Among Elgar's less orthodox orchestral compositions is the Introduction and Allegro for Solo String Quartet and Strings, Op. 47 (1905). It is somewhat in the style of the Baroque concerto grosso, with the solo quartet serving as the concertante and the string orchestra as the tutti. The principal subject is a Welsh melody in the minor mode (heard in the introduction in solo viola). This is characterized by the cadence of a falling third characteristic of Welsh folk songs. In the ensuing allegro, this melody returns in the major. New material is introduced by the solo quartet and as the germ of a fugato passage. The composition ends with a loud recall of the Welsh melody by solo quartet and strings.

Manuel de Falla

"The story of Manuel de Falla's art is that of an unceasing quest for the musical soul of Spain."

GILBERT CHASE

BORN: Cádiz, Spain, November 23, 1876.
DIED: Alta Gracia, Argentina, November 14, 1946.
MAJOR WORKS: *Ballets*—El Amor brujo; The Three-Cornered Hat. *Chamber Music*—Concerto for Harpsichord, Flute, Oboe, Clarinet, Violin, and Cello. *Choral Music*—Atlántida (completed by Ernesto Halffter). *Orchestral Music*—Nights in the Gardens of Spain. *Piano Music*—Pièces espagnoles. *Vocal Music*—Siete canciones populares españolas.

HIS LIFE

There are some composers who, while they themselves have failed to produce great music, have nevertheless succeeded in inspiring others to do so. These composers are remembered only in the history book and by the research scholar. One such composer was a Spanish scholar who devoted his life to research in the field of Spanish folk music: Felipe Pedrell (1841–1922). Of the extensive library of operatic, orchestral, choral, and church music Pedrell created, not a single page has remained in the repertory. For Pedrell's most important works were not compositions—but *composers*. It was due to him that Isaac Albéniz (1860–1909) was transformed from a composer of inconsequential pieces to the first of the great Spanish nationalists. And it was due to Pedrell that Manuel de Falla did not become a mere concert pianist but the greatest of all Spanish composers.

Two childhood experiences were responsible for later making Falla receptive to Pedrell's influence. One took place when Falla was ten years old. On a visit to Seville he witnessed a religious pageant (much like the one his compatriot Albéniz set to music in *Fête-Dieu à Seville*). Its pomp and majesty—which then moved him to tears and ever after remained a glowing memory—first aroused in him a feeling of pride in country. The second experience was musical. Sometime after his visit to Seville, Falla heard his first orchestral concert. This took place in Cádiz; the program included a Beethoven symphony. Falla later said that his life as a musician began with the hearing of this symphony.

He had been receiving musical instruction from childhood on, for the Falla household was one of the most cultured in Cádiz and the mother was an excellent pianist. She gave him his first lessons, then passed him on for further piano study to Elois Galluzo, and for lessons in harmony and theory to Alejandro Odero and Enrique Broca. In 1888 he performed with his mother a four-hand arrangement of Haydn's *Seven Last Words of Christ* at the San Francesco Church in Cádiz. (Haydn had written this work for another of Cádiz' churches.) Later on he played his first attempts at composition (subsequently destroyed) at the home of Don Salvador Viniegra, a gentleman of great musical ability, where regular chamber music concerts took place.

Falla's musical talent was unmistakable. As he later told Gilbert Chase, he supplemented formal study by "analyzing with avid curiosity every piece of music that held a real interest for me because of its affinity with certain secret aspirations whose realization, nevertheless, seemed to me scarcely possible." Feeling the need of supplementing the formal instruction he was getting at Cádiz, he began making regular trips to Madrid for special piano lessons. There, when he was fourteen, he received first prize in a competition for pianists. During this period he also wrote a good deal of music, but none of it has survived.

When he was twenty, Falla became a regularly enrolled student at the Madrid Conservatory. There his piano teacher, José Tragó, was so impressed with his ability that he urged Falla to concentrate on his piano studies in preparation for a virtuoso career. When Falla won two prizes in piano playing at the Conservatory the ambition of his teacher appeared to be realized. But Falla was next to feel the impact of a much more powerful, and much more decisive, influence. His teacher in composition was Pedrell. Pedrell was then sixty years old. He was still to complete his most valuable research in the fields of Spanish church and folk music. But already Pedrell had interested himself in Spanish national music, and he wanted to see all Spanish composers using the Spanish folk song and dance as a basis of their works.

Recognizing unmistakable talent in Falla, Pedrell directed him toward composition and aroused his national consciousness. Pedrell's influence was far-reaching. As Falla later confessed, "It is to the lessons of Pedrell and to the powerful stimulation exercised on me by his works that I owe my artistic life." It was because of Pedrell that Falla once and for all rejected the career of virtuoso for that of composer. And it was because of Pedrell that from this time on Falla dedicated himself to the writing of *Spanish* music. Nor was the winning of the important Ortis y Cussó prize in piano playing, in 1905, to deflect him from his purpose.

As his aim was to be a composer, and as he wanted to learn everything he could about writing music, his immediate goal was Paris, where so much exciting new music was written and performed. He set about earning the money for such an expedition, and, as is so often the case, the shortest route he chose proved to be a dead end: He wrote music for popular operettas, zarzuelas, one of which was a complete failure and another not even produced. He had to earn money the hard way, by playing the piano with chamber music groups and at concerts, and by teaching. At the same time he continued composing—serious music this time. He wrote a Spanish opera, *La Vida breve,* to a Spanish text by his friend Carlos Fernandez Shaw. For the first time he tried to produce authentic Spanish music. He entered it in a competition for a national opera conducted by the Academy of Fine Arts in Madrid in 1905 and won first prize; but it was some time before it was performed.

By this time he had saved enough money to undertake a seven-day trip to Paris. He left Spain in 1907. He remained not seven days, but seven years. To a young composer Paris of 1907 was just about the most exciting city in the world. It was the city in which only recently opera had charted a new course with Charpentier's *Louise* in 1900 and Debussy's *Pelléas et Mélisande* in 1902. Debussy was the musician of the hour, a provocative figure who was admired as extravagantly by the *avant-garde* as he was attacked by the reactionaries. He was the apostle of the new music. Gabriel Fauré, director of the Paris Conservatory, was at the height of his success. Paul Dukas (1865–1935), composer of the charming orchestral scherzo *L'Apprenti sorcier,* had just had performed his Impressionist opera, *Ariane et Barbe-bleue.* The up-and-coming composers who were creating a stir included the thirty-seven-year-old Florent Schmitt (1870–1958) and the thirty-eight-year-old Albert Roussel (1869–1937), and, most important of all, the thirty-two-year-old Maurice Ravel, himself an object of violent controversy. To be able to move among such composers, to be able to attend concerts of new music all the time, to be in contact with the latest ideas not only in music but in all art—all this would have been a tremendous experience for any young musician.

During his seven years in Paris, Falla wrote comparatively little: *Pièces espagnoles,* four pieces for the piano, in 1908; *Trois mélodies,* on poems by Théophile Gautier, in 1909; and some parts of *Noches en los jardines de España* (*Nights in the Gardens of Spain*). He was too busy assimilating musical experiences to write music, too eager to absorb what others around him were doing (and doing so brilliantly) to venture on his own.

It was a stimulating period for young Falla. But it was also a trying one, for his poverty was intense and frequently he had to forgo regular meals. His friends did what they could to help him. One day the pianist Ricardo Viñes brought him the name and address of a wealthy young piano student who sought a teacher. The fee was handsome, and he set off without delay to her home. As the prospective student lived near his laundress, he took along a bundle of his soiled clothing. Unfortunately the laundress was out for lunch when he arrived; Falla had to make his visit to the prospective student with the bundle under his arm. When the servant opened the door for him and saw the bundle she mistook him for a tradesman and gave him a bitter tongue-lashing for coming by the front door. Timidly, Falla went to the back entrance, to confront there the mistress of the house, who also rebuked him for having dared to come the front way. Falla was so humiliated and embarrassed that he found it impossible to make the necessary explanations. He fled, preferring to lose a profitable music lesson than to reveal his identity.

Slowly—much more slowly than was the case with most other outstanding contemporary composers—his music was getting heard. The four Spanish pieces for piano were introduced by Ricardo Viñes at a concert of the Société Nationale de Musique in Paris in 1908. Three years after that Falla himself played these pieces in London. In 1910 his *Trois mélodies* was introduced at a concert of the Société Indépendante, and was published. In October of the same year, Falla presented these three songs together with his four piano pieces in an all-Falla concert in Paris at which he was making his French debut as pianist. On April 1, 1913, his opera *La Vida breve* was finally introduced—at the Casino in Nice. It was so successful there that about a year and a half later the Opéra-Comique in Paris presented it.

A few months before the outbreak of World War I, Falla decided to return home, where *La Vida breve* was to receive its Spanish *première*. He must have felt the need of returning to Spain to draw from it the strength and inspiration he now required. Though his home was in Madrid, he traveled about Spain a good deal, to come in closer contact with its geography, local customs, and folk songs and dances. The return to Spain appears to have revitalized him, for he now produced his first two masterworks. In 1915 he completed the orchestral nocturnes for piano and orchestra, *Nights in the Gardens of Spain,* which he had begun as far back as 1911, and the ballet *El Amor brujo* (*Love, the Magician*). The *première* of the ballet took place at the Teatro Lara in Madrid on April 5, 1915, while that of *Nights in the Gardens of Spain* followed in Madrid on April 9, 1916. These two works placed him in the vanguard of living Spanish composers. During the next few years he solidified that position with a handful of other major works: the ballet *El Sombrero de tres picos* (*The Three-Cornered Hat*), which he wrote in 1919 on a commission from Serge Diaghilev and which the Ballets Russes introduced in London (with scenery and costumes by Pablo Picasso) on July 22, 1919; a little marionette opera *El Retablo de Maese Pedro* (*Master Peter's Puppet Show*) based on scenes from *Don Quixote,* completed in 1922 and first performed in the Paris *salon* of the Princesse de Polignac a year later; and the Concerto for Harpsichord, Flute, Oboe, Clarinet, Violin, and Cello, written for the harpsichordist

Wanda Landowska in 1925 and first performed by her in Barcelona on November 5, 1926.

In 1922 Falla moved to Granada. For the next seventeen years he was to live in the same small house in the shadow of the Alhambra.

He looked like a monk, with his spare, even frail build, sunken cheeks, thin and firm mouth, stark eyes, and hair closely cropped like a tonsure. And he lived like one. A simple man, he had an aversion to honors, property, crowds, ceremonials. His home was bare of everything except basic essentials. There he led such a quiet and withdrawn existence that he became virtually a recluse. His day was routinized. He rose early, took a short walk, then attended Mass at the nearby San Cecilio Church. After that came several hours of composition. He was such a slow and painstaking workman that a single composition might take him a year or more to produce; a lifetime of productivity yielded only a handful of works, each the product of a most fastidious and discriminating creator. After a noonday meal and a siesta he would be host to a few intimate friends. In the evening he returned to work, after which he retired at an early hour. Once a year he took what he described as a "solitude cure." He would go off by himself to a remote, sparsely populated Andalusian village to spend there two weeks or more in total silence. He said this period refreshed and renewed him for creativity.

He was devoid of all vanity. He did not like to talk about himself and his work, and rarely did. Particularly after 1922, he seemed oblivious to success or failure as far as his work went. He even reduced to a bare minimum his presence at concerts offering his works. Material benefits of success interested him as little as the kudos and praise of public and critics. He was totally disinterested in how much money he was earning since his needs were so few that whatever income came his way was more than enough to pay his bills. He never made a bid for commissions, prizes, or significant performances.

In the last decades of his life he was a sick man; but even before that he suffered from hypochondria. He had a horror of drafts, insisted that the equinoctial seasons were bad for his health, and believed implicitly that the full moon was harmful. During the full moon, and in March and September, he would refuse to see visitors.

Being a profoundly religious man, he sided with the Franco forces during the Spanish Civil War; he was convinced that the

Nationalists would serve as a check to the anti-religious sentiment that had been sweeping the country since the overthrow of the monarchy. In return for his support, Franco appointed him President of the Institute of Spain in 1938. Disenchantment with the Franco regime, however, was not slow in taking place. In 1939 Falla decided to leave Spain for good; he was too well aware of his physical condition not to realize that it was hardly likely that he would ever again return to his native land. He conducted a few concerts in South America, then settled at the Villa del Lago in Alta Gracia, about twenty-five miles from Córdoba, in Argentina. There, patiently and solicitously attended by his sister, he spent the last years of his life. Such was his poverty that for a long time he could not afford to get a piano. In addition he was tormented by his rapidly declining physical strength and by omnipresent fears he could not explain or dissipate. Nevertheless, he was able to labor on a giant project that had engaged his efforts and interests for many years now, a "scenic cantata," *Atlántida,* whose text was based on a nineteenth-century poem by Jacinto Verdaguer. Scored for solo voices, chorus, and orchestra, this was an epical creation describing the loss of the continent of Atlantis, the saving of Spain by Hercules, and the discovery of the New World. Falla did not live to complete the cantata. (This was done for him by his pupil, Ernesto Halffter.) And he did not live to witness its *première,* which took place in a concert version in Barcelona on November 24, 1961, followed by a staged presentation at La Scala in Milan, on June 18, 1962. "There emerges," said Enrique Franco of this monumental work, "a sacred polyphony, both vocal and instrumental, more beautiful than anything we have had since Victoria. . . . As the music unfolds, from the grandiose to the detailed and finely wrought, *Atlántida* takes its sure place as the only Spanish work of such great magnitude, duration, quality, and depth of conception."

When, in the early morning of November 14, 1946, Falla's servant came to his bedroom to deliver his breakfast, she found him dead, the victim of a heart attack. Following services at the Cathedral in Córdoba, the body was transferred to Cádiz, where impressive funeral ceremonies took place on January 9, 1947. The Capella Classica of Cádiz sang a Bach chorale during the procession, and a Requiem by Tomás Luis de Victoria (1548–1611) when the body was being lowered in the crypt at the Santa María de las Cuevas Church. The inscription over his grave is one which Falla himself had written: "Honor and glory belong only to God." A monument, the work of José Menéndez Pidal, was unveiled at Falla's tomb on September 8, 1960.

HIS MUSIC

The influence of Pedrell on Falla has already been pointed out. It was Pedrell who encouraged Falla to become a composer of national music. And it was Pedrell who introduced him to Spanish folk and church music. From that source, Falla derived his basic stylistic elements: the sinuous, throbbing oriental melody of the flamenco song (*canto hondo,* or "deep song"); the ever changing vital rhythms of the Spanish dance, often imitating the clicking of castanets or the strumming of a guitar; the modal writing of Spanish ecclesiastical chants.

But there was a second influence as well, almost as far-reaching as that of Pedrell: his friendship with and the music of Debussy. Debussy's advanced harmonic thinking, hypersensitive lyricism, delicate instrumental colorations also helped to mold Falla's style. And there was another way in which Debussy affected Falla, in the example he set for the younger man with his own Spanish music. Strange!—Debussy, who had never lived in Spain and who knew the country and its folklore only superficially, was able to write pieces of music to serve as a prototype for Falla's national art. *Ibéria,* one of the orchestral *Images,* and such piano preludes as "*Soirée dans Grenade*" and "*La Puerta del Vino*" gave Falla an altogether new perspective on Spanish national music. Up to the time he came into contact with these works, Falla had tried to imitate Andalusian music down to details of melody, harmony, and rhythm. Debussy had demonstrated that not the letter of Spanish music was important, but the spirit—the *evocación,* as the Spanish called it. And it was the spirit of Spain, rather than the literal details of its folk music, that Falla tried to convey in his music.

He became the mystic, evoking the very soul of Spain and the Spanish people rather than the superficial externals of Spanish life. He once told a French interviewer, "The essentials are in the people. I do not like taking actual folk material; but you must go to natural, living sources, study the sounds, the rhythms, use their essence, not just their externals. You must go really deep, so as not to make any sort of caricature. In Spain every region has its own essential music. The gypsies have theirs in some Hindu roots."

ANALYTICAL NOTES

Chamber Music. Falla wrote his remarkable Concerto for Harpsichord, Flute, Oboe, Clarinet, Violin, and Cello between 1923 and 1926 at the request of Wanda Landowska, the distinguished harpsichordist. Their mutual aim was to demonstrate that this Baroque instrument still had artistic validity in contemporary music. But in creating his work, Falla did not give undue prominence to the harpsichord, but made it the equal partner to the other instruments in projecting his musical thoughts. Stylistically, and at times idiomatically, Falla reached back to the harpsichord sonatas of Domenico Scarlatti (1685–1757). But here, as in other Falla masterworks, the influence of Spanish folk and church music is unmistakable.

In the first movement, the guitar playing of Spanish gypsies is subtly suggested. The second movement has been said to describe a religious procession, while the third movement abounds with the vital, dynamic rhythms of Spanish folk dances.

Orchestral Music. *El Almor brujo* (1915) originated as a ballet; but it is best known as a suite for orchestra. It emphasizes the gypsy element in Spanish folk art, its melodies simulating the *canto hondo* of the gypsy and its scenario being derived by Gregorio Martínez Sierra from an old Andalusian gypsy tale. Falla wrote the ballet for the distinguished Spanish dancer Pastora Impervio, who wanted a vehicle for her voice as well as her terpsichore. And it was Pastora's mother who related to Sierra the Andalusian tale which he adapted into a ballet scenario. The story centers around the love of Candelas— of course a volatile, sensuous, and beautiful gypsy—and Carmelo. But Candelas is haunted by the memory of another gypsy lover, now dead, and she is ever tormented with the fear that he may return, in spirit if not in flesh, to harass her. The shadow of her dead lover darkens her love affair with Carmelo. Before long the ghost of the dead lover does appear, seeking his lost love. Despair gives birth to inspiration: Carmelo conceives an idea to deflect the ghost from Candelas. He induces the coquettish and seductive gypsy Lucia to flirt with the specter, who, even in death, is as susceptible to the wiles of a beautiful girl as he had been when alive. Thus Candelas and Carmelo are free to pursue their own love, without supernatural disturbances.

Pastora Impervio appeared in the *première* of *El Amor brujo* in Madrid on April 15, 1915. Soon after this Falla adapted the ballet score into an orchestral suite, which has since become one of his most celebrated scores.

It is in twelve uninterrupted, and sometimes episodic, sections. In the first, "Introduction and Scene," a trumpet call rises against a background of vigorous rhythms. This motive is a motto theme that appears throughout the suite. "The Gypsies: Evening" follows. An air of mystery is evoked in a thirty-three-measure prelude; the oboe then begins an oriental-like improvisation. The first of the gypsy songs for mezzo-soprano is heard in the "Song of the Sorrows of Love," to a poetic text beginning "Ay, do I not know what I feel, nor what passes over me." A briskly accented subject in muted trumpet opens "The Apparition." Woodwinds, strings, and piano then present a demoniac passage consisting of glissandos and running scales. We next hear a wild and abandoned dance called "Dance of Terror," introduced by oboe and muted trumpet. The striking of a clock is simulated in the brief "The Magic Circle." The seventh section is undoubtedly the most celebrated of the entire work, often heard independently not only in its original orchestral version but also in transcriptions for solo piano and two pianos. It is the popular "Ritual Fire Dance." Diabolical trills bring on the first theme in the oboe; a vigorous second theme appears loudly in unison horns and is quietly echoed by muted trumpets. "The Scene" begins with an improvisation for solo oboe. After the motto theme is recalled by the strings, the section concludes with solos for flute and for oboe. "The Song of the Will-o-the-Wisp" is the second gypsy song, the opening line of which is "Oh, this love's a Jack-o-lantern." One of the most beautiful pages in the score, a dreamy and nostalgic nocturne, is heard in "Pantomime." The full orchestra is heard in the motto theme, which is repeated elegiacally by the strings. Then, against an accompaniment of flutes, strings, and piano, the solo cello presents a brooding melody, soon taken up tenderly by first violins and violas. The song ends, and an oboe brings up a variation of the motto theme. But the solo violin returns with the tender song. Before this section

ends the trumpet quickly recalls the motto theme. The suite concludes with two more gypsy songs. The first, "Dance of the Game of
Love," is set to a text beginning "You are the wicked gypsy that a
gypsy loved." The second is introduced by a peal of tolling bells. The
complete text follows:

> And now the day is dawning.
> Ring out, O bells, ring out!
> For the glory of my love returns!

Nights in the Gardens of Spain (1915), symphonic impressions for
piano and orchestra, contains the essence of Falla's *evocación*. Though
the material is derived from the rhythms, cadences, modes, and melodic turns of Andalusian popular music, and though the instrumentation often simulates effects peculiar to popular Spanish instruments,
the music never gives the impression of being derivative. It is a
highly personal and individual art.

The work is in three sections. The first, "At Generalife," was inspired by the beautiful gardens near the Alhambra, "with its fountains and ancient cypresses contemplating the city below," according
to the description of W. R. Anderson, who writes: "In the influence
of the night, the fountains, dreamy patios, melancholy thickets and
flowering pomegranates in the summer palace of the Moorish sultan,
we can feel a sense of mystery and ghosts of the past." The principal
theme of the movement is sensuous and exotic; it appears in the
solo viola in unison with the harp. After the entrance of the piano,
a second theme is suggested by the orchestra. The piano develops
this theme, then embarks on a short cadenza. The first theme returns
provocatively again and again, assuming significance in the concluding
coda as the horn presents it pianissimo against a string background.

"A Far-Off Dance" follows. The flute and English horn present
the basic dance theme. After a brief transition in the piano, a second
dance melody is heard in flute and strings. After this melody has
been repeated by the English horn, clarinet, and first violins, a strong
and persistent rhythm is maintained to the end of the section.

The third part, "In the Gardens of the Sierra at Córdoba," proceeds without interruption, the transition being, in Falla's own words,
"a tremolo on the violins in the highest register," over which "are
sprinkled like distant echoes, the notes which begin the fundamental

theme of the 'Distant Dance.' The bridge ends with an ascending passage for the piano in octaves, which is resolved in a *tutti* with which the third and last nocturne begins." Wild, passionate music—music rooted in the East—is now heard. We are in the world of the gypsy, with his uninhibited dances and languorous, sensuous songs. There is an ominous feeling of anticipation as the movement opens. The shimmering voice of the strings in upper register, punctuated by phrases in the woodwinds, is foreboding. The piano enters softly with an insistent rhythm; this rhythm grows louder and louder. Then the full orchestra erupts in a demoniac outburst. Ideas follow one another in rapid succession. Interspersed among the more virile passages are haunting strains of gypsy song—the *canto hondo*. The section ends on a note of peace and mystery.

The Three-Cornered Hat (1919) is a ballet (or "pantomime") based on a novel of Alarcón adapted by Martínez Sierra. Serge Diaghilev, the impresario of the Ballets Russes, heard parts of Falla's score when he visited the composer. For a long time he had been planning a ballet which would synthesize the Spanish arts. In listening to Falla's music, and following Sierra's text, he recognized here the basis for such a project. He suggested some changes, then had Pablo Picasso design the costumes and scenery. The ballet was introduced by the Ballets Russes in London on July 22, 1919. It was one of the company's major triumphs and was largely responsible for bringing international recognition to the composer.

The text is a saucy, spicy tale which had previously been used by Hugo Wolf for his opera *Der Corregidor*. A miller, his wife, and a governor (whose badge of office is a three-cornered hat) are involved in a love triangle. The governor literally pursues his love, is eluded by the coquettish wife, and falls into a nearby stream. He has to remove his wet clothes and warm up in the miller's bed while waiting for them to dry. The miller returns suddenly to find the governor in this compromising situation. But he is by no means upset by this discovery. In a note to the governor he points out that the latter's wife is also highly desirable and that he is now free to pursue her without interference.

The three dances from *The Three-Cornered Hat* are deservedly popular and are often heard at symphony concerts. In the first, "The Neighbors," the main theme is heard immediately in the first violins; an interesting effect is produced in transitional passages by having the orchestra simulate a strumming guitar. The second, "The Miller's Dance," has two ideas. The first is rhythmic: a sharply accented theme for strings suggesting the vigorous stamping of feet in a Spanish dance. The second is melodic: a haunting melody in the oboe. The main dance melody of the "Final Dance" is a rousing jota for full orchestra.

There are also two effective Spanish dances in Falla's early opera *La Vida breve* (1905), whose principal action involves an Andalusian lad, Paco, and the gypsy girl he has forsaken, Salud. While Paco is getting married to Carmela, Salud invades the ceremonies to denounce him, and falls dead at his feet. The Spanish Dance No. 1 is especially famous. Here the rhythm of clicking castanets is imitated, against which surges a warm-blooded melody. Fritz Kreisler has made a fine arrangement of this for violin and piano.

Gabriel Fauré

"It is the spirit of Hellenism, as well as its forms, which is reborn in him. . . . He, too, thrusts himself beyond the spheres in order to bring back pure beauty."

JULIEN TIERSOT

BORN: Pamiers, Ariège, France, May 12, 1845.
DIED: Paris, November 4, 1924.
MAJOR WORKS: *Chamber Music*—2 piano quintets; 2 piano quartets; 2 violin sonatas; 2 cello sonatas; String Quartet in E minor. *Choral Music*—Messe de Requiem; Ave verum; offertories. *Operas*—Prométhée; Pénélope. *Orchestral Music*—Symphony; Pelléas and Mélisande, suite; Ballade for Piano and Orchestra; Fantaisie for Piano and Orchestra; Masques et bergamasques. *Piano Music*—Barcarolles, impromptus, nocturnes, preludes, valse-caprices; Dolly, for four hands; Theme and Variations; Mazurka. *Vocal Music*—La Bonne Chanson; La Chanson d'Eve; Le Jardin clos; Mirages; L'Horizon chimérique; numerous individual songs for voice and piano.

HIS LIFE

Fauré became interested in music at an early age. In his childhood he was one day shown the town organ. Then and there he made up his mind he would learn to play it; and he did so after a long and painstaking period of trial and error. His obvious aptitude for music impressed a local music lover, who convinced Fauré's father to send him to Paris for intensive study. Fauré arrived there in his ninth year and played for Abraham Louis Niedermeyer, director of the famous Ecole Niedermeyer. The director, convinced of the boy's talent, accepted him for his school without fee. There, as Fauré later recalled in a magazine article, "we were impregnated with music, we lived in it as in a bath, and it entered our system by every pore." The Ecole placed particular emphasis on the singing of *a cappella* religious music of the fifteenth and sixteenth centuries, a training responsible for Fauré's later interest in liturgical music and Gregorian chants. One of Fauré's teachers (piano) was Camille Saint-Saëns, a major influence in Fauré's early development, and in later years a devoted friend. While he was attending the Ecole, Fauré's first published piece of music made its appearance, *Trois Romances sans paroles,* for the piano.

In 1865, Fauré's studies at the Ecole Niedermeyer ended with prizes in piano, harmony, organ, and composition. He was now ready to begin his professional career. His first post was as organist at a church in Rennes, Brittany, where he stayed four years. He was dismissed because late one evening, after a party, he came to church to fulfill his function as organist dressed in evening dress. Actually, his congregation had long been displeased with the kind of music he insisted upon performing at services. From Rennes, Fauré went to Paris in 1870 to occupy the organ bench at the Notre-Dame-de-Clignancourt. He held this post only a short time when the Franco-Prussian War broke out, sending him into uniform in the infantry. The war ended, Fauré returned to Paris where he now became organist of the Saint-Honoré-d'Eylau Church.

Saint-Saëns introduced him to the musical *salon* of Pauline Viardot, the celebrated prima donna, in 1873. It was a rendezvous for many brilliant figures in the cultural life of Paris, and here Fauré met writers such as Turgenev and Flaubert, and musicians such as Gounod. Here he was introduced to the poetry of Verlaine and Baudelaire, some of whose poems he now set to music. The songs were performed and well received.

He also fell in love with Mme. Viardot's daughter, Marianne. The romance lasted four years, culminated in an engagement, and then was broken off permanently. In all probability, the practical young lady came to the decision that a struggling young musician was not the best possible candidate for matrimony.

Through Saint-Saëns two events took place in 1877. The first was a meeting with Franz Liszt in Weimar. Saint-Saëns invited Fauré to accompany him to Weimar to attend the world *première* of his opera *Samson et Dalila*. This visit offered Fauré an opportunity to show the master one of his more ambitious works. Unfortunately, Liszt was not impressed. His only comment was: "It's too difficult." The second event was more gratifying. At Saint-Saëns' recommendation, Fauré was appointed assistant organist of the Madeleine Church; eventually, in 1896, he became first organist.

Fauré's career as a church organist was long and distinguished. But no less productive were his achievements as a teacher. After conducting composition classes at the Ecole Niedermeyer, Fauré took over a similar class at the Paris Conservatory in 1895, in succession to Jules Massenet, the famous composer of *Manon*. In 1905 Fauré became director of the Conservatory; he held this position for the next fifteen years.

An entire generation of young French composers studied under him. Many of them have expressed their indebtedness to him for their development; they include Ravel, Schmitt, Roger-Ducasse, and Aubert. Charles Koechlin wrote:

As our teacher he was perceived as a purist who detested errors or awkwardness. But most important was the spirit of emulation which he and his inestimable art incited in us. His pupils could not but submit the best that was in them, fearing to come before so perfect a musician with anything so unworthy as concession or platitude. When such a thing did happen, Fauré would remain silent. He would appear distant, preoccupied; and, the audition over, he would turn away with pretended casualness and say quietly, with a detached air, "Is there anything else?" We understood—all, of course, but the incorrigible offenders.

Meanwhile he kept working on his compositions, and he kept growing. He first revealed individual gifts with songs in the 1860s, notably with "Lydia" and "Après un rêve." In the 1870s his creative powers expanded into the writing of such chamber music works as his first violin sonata and the Piano Quartet in C minor. In 1881 came his most significant work for solo instrument and orchestra, the Ballade in F-sharp minor, and in 1883, his most celebrated work for chorus, the Messe de Requiem, the latter given its first performance at the Madeleine Church in 1888.

A marriage of convenience had also taken place—in 1883 with Marie Fremiet, daughter of a sculptor. Despite the lack of romance in their relationship, this was a good marriage. Marie was a devoted, sympathetic housewife who provided her husband with domestic tranquillity and comfort.

By the early 1900s Fauré was generally recognized as one of the great men in French music, and he was the recipient of many honors. In 1909 he was elected to the Académie des Beaux-Arts; one year later he was made Commander of the Legion of Honor. In 1922 he was honored with the *grand cordon* of the Legion of Honor (the highest class) at a time when he was given a testimonial at the Sorbonne by national decree, in which some of France's greatest musical and political figures officiated.

His creative force showed no signs of diminishing. Two of his finest song cycles came in 1910 and 1922 respectively, *La Chanson d'Eve* and *L'Horizon chimérique*. His most significant work for the stage, the lyric drama *Pénélope*, was successfully introduced in Monte Carlo on March 4, 1913. His last composition was the String Quartet in E minor, upon which he was at work at Annecy during a summer rest cure. Sensing he had not much longer to live, Fauré returned to Paris where he spent his last months. Among the last words he uttered was the question "what of my music; will it live?" followed by his own answer, "But, then, that is of little importance."

During the last twenty years of his life Fauré grew increasingly deaf. He tried pathetically to keep it a carefully guarded secret during all those years for fear of jeopardizing his cherished position as director of the Conservatory. Intimate friends guessed the truth, and they helped him to keep up the pretense by ignoring telltale symptoms. In 1920 Fauré, deciding that he could no longer fulfill his duties, resigned his directorial post. But he insisted on maintaining the secret of his deafness until the end of his life, which came four years later. It was only several years after Fauré's death that the musicologist Paul Landormy revealed the truth of Fauré's condition; many who had known Fauré well were shocked at this revelation.

HIS MUSIC

In Fauré's music we have the art of understatement. The pure and classic beauty which pervades his greatest works is derived from simplicity, restraint, delicate sensibility, refinement, and repose. It is the kind of beauty that lends itself best to smaller forms and the more intimate mediums of musical expression. Consequently, Fauré was at his best in writing songs, chamber music, and piano pieces. (This remains true even though he produced an eloquent Requiem, an excellent lyric drama, *Pénélope,* and a symphony.) He was a classicist by nature, but—as Paul Landormy pointed out—a classicist "of the French type, more closely related to Couperin and Rameau than to Mozart or Beethoven. . . . His language, always moderate, is like well-bred discourse. He never raises his voice too high. He works in quiet colors. He is most discreet. He leaves much to be inferred. And his reserve is something quite as eloquent as louder outbursts."

The works by Fauré which we hear most often were written comparatively early in his career. They are aristocratic in workmanship over which hovers the spirit of Hellenism; their principal concern is the projection of beauty. The process of continual refinement to which he subjected his writing continued throughout his life, making his later works more subtle in expression, more nebulous and elusive in content, and therefore less likely to win popular favor. To his last works, written in deafness (the Second Piano Quintet, completed in 1921; the song cycle *L'Horizon chimérique,* 1922; the Trio in D minor, 1923, and the String Quartet in E minor, 1924) he brought a spiritual radiance not found in earlier creations.

ANALYTICAL NOTES

Chamber Music. While it is true that Fauré's later works in the chamber music field have greater subtlety of expression and more originality of thought and structure than the earlier ones, it is the works of his youth and early manhood that are heard most frequently.

The Sonata No. 1 in A major for Violin and Piano, Op. 13, was written in 1876, Fauré's thirty-second year. Today it appears as romantic music, pleasing melodically and harmonically. But in its time it was daring in harmonic construction and original in thematic evolution. Tendencies of French romantic music crystallized in Franck's Sonata for Violin and Piano are so strongly suggested in this sonata by Fauré (which preceded Franck's by a decade) that Charles

Koechlin remarked it was necessary "to render unto Gabriel, and not unto César, that which is Gabriel's."

There are two main themes in the first movement. The first, introduced by the piano before being taken up by the violin, is energetic; the second has sobriety. Both themes are worked out with polyphonic skill. The second movement is a song as gentle as a benediction; it is unfolded in its entirety by the violin. This is followed by a scherzo of quicksilver movement, capricious in mood; a tender middle section for the violin is a contrast. The finale opens with an expressive subject for the violin. The mood is agitated until midway there comes a delicate melody described by Florent Schmitt as "Schumannesque." But the movement continues in the more dramatic character of the opening and ends with a brief scherzo-like passage for the violin.

Forty years later Fauré wrote a second violin sonata, in E minor, Op. 108 (1917). The romanticism of the earlier works gives way to such an ultrasophistication in structure and expression that the exquisite and sensitive beauty of this music is elusive at first hearing. An interesting technical feature is the way in which the composer uses some stylistic element or idiom to unify each of his three movements. In the first, it is an appoggiatura rhythm, first encountered in the first theme, then recurring as the bass to the second theme. In the second movement, the melody progresses in octave ascents before and after it proceeds in single degrees of the scale. Quaver and semiquaver figures characterize the main themes of the finale where further unification takes place through the quotation of material from the first movement.

The Quartet in G minor for Piano and Strings, Op. 45, was the second such work by Fauré. The first, the Quartet in C minor, Op. 15, had been completed in 1879. Its successor came seven years later. It opens with an intense melody for unison strings about which Florent Schmitt said that "it alone would have assured immortality to its composer." The second theme is serene. The second movement, a scherzo without a trio, is built out of a perpetual-motion theme. The introduction to the slow movement that follows sounds like the tolling of bells. The viola then appears with a sensitive theme that sounds like a barcarolle. Later on in the movement the strings take over the "bell" theme while the piano presents the barcarolle melody. The quartet ends with a stormy finale, emotionally disturbed and not in Fauré's usual vein; the second theme was described by Schmitt as "a long phrase . . . which implores and shrieks like a chorus of lost souls."

Fauré produced two piano quintets. The first, in D minor, Op. 89, was written in 1906. Fifteen years later came the Quintet No. 2 in C minor, Op. 115, the more distinguished of these two works. It opens with a measure for the piano as preface to a suggestion of the first theme by the viola. As strings enter one after another, this first theme becomes fully projected. The second subject is a vigorous statement comprising forceful chords. The second movement is a light-handed, vivacious scherzo. As a sharp contrast, this is followed by music of great melancholy. First the strings are heard in a grief-stricken four-measure theme. Then comes an emotional exchange between piano and strings. Finally the piano presents a third poignant idea. In the fourth movement sorrow is replaced by vigor, with music that is at turns agitated and spirited.

Choral Music. The Messe de Requiem, Op. 48 (1887) is not only Fauré's most famous work for chorus but also one of the most distinguished in French choral literature. Fauré was impelled to write it in memory of his father, who had died in 1885. Since it took three years to get performed, its *première* became a memorial service for his mother as well.

Fauré's grief did not express itself in emotional or dramatic outbursts—not even in the *Dies irae* section where turbulence and agitation might be expected. Throughout, Fauré sustains a quiet, intimate tone, almost an otherworldly kind of serenity together with contemplation, as he prefers to devote himself to the tranquillity that death brings rather than to its torment. The composition (scored for soprano and baritone solos, as well as for the chorus, organ, and orchestra) has seven sections, beginning with an Introit and *Kyrie,* a prayer for eternal rest, and concluding with *In paradisum* where the soul is welcomed into paradise by angels and martyrs.

Orchestral Music. The earliest orchestral work by Fauré to remain in the permanent repertory is the Pavane, Op. 50 (1887), a resuscitation of the stately Baroque dance. The principal melody is a serene subject first heard in flute, then taken over by the woodwinds and after that shared by woodwinds and violins over a plucked string accompaniment.

Fauré's most successful work for orchestra is the *Pelléas and Mélisande* Suite, Op. 80 (1898). It originated as incidental music for a production of Maurice Maeterlinck's drama given in London on June 21, 1898. Thus Fauré's music preceded Debussy's more famous and more epoch-making adaptation of the Maeterlinck drama by four years. Soon after the production of the play Fauré adapted his score into an orchestral suite.

The suite consists of four sections. The first, "Prelude," is the prelude to the play. It is a movement of subdued beauty, consisting of two gentle themes, the first in the strings and the second in solo cello, flutes, and bassoons; an atmosphere of melancholy and mystery sets the mood for the play to come. The second section, "The Spinner," describes Mélisande at the spinning wheel. The spinning is imitated in the strings, accompanying several melodies in various woodwind instruments. The third section (sometimes omitted) is "Siciliana," a slow and undulating piece of music which Fauré had originally written as a piece for cello and piano (Op. 78) and which he later orchestrated and interpolated into his incidental music. The suite ends with "The Death of Mélisande," an elegy which begins quietly in the winds and continues in the strings, but grows in emotional intensity as the dynamics increase.

Fauré never wrote a piano concerto, but he did produce two extended compositions for piano and orchestra: the Ballade in F-sharp minor, Op. 19 (1881), and the Fantaisie, Op. 111 (1919). The earlier work is the more popular. Though the structure and tradition of the ballade calls for a richly romantic approach, Fauré's attitude is one of classic reserve. Repose, contemplation, and a sensitive poetry characterize the composition not only in the presentation and enlargement of its haunting basic melodic subject but also in the delicacy and refinement of the orchestration.

Vocal Music. Fauré's place among the finest creators of French song is secure. His refined and sensitive lyricism—with its partiality to long, sinuous phrases—was ideally suited for vocal writing. His uncommon talent in writing for the piano made it possible for him to produce accompaniments remarkably rich in harmonic texture and subtlety of mood and nuance. He paid unusual attention to his harmonic writing, often using a harmonic scheme as his point of departure, and only then devising the melody best suited for that harmony.

He possessed an exceptional gift for capturing elusive moods, volatile emotions, and the subtlest feelings of all his texts: poems by Baudelaire, Verlaine, Hugo, Gautier, and so forth. His sensitive melodies, subtle modulations, exotic moods, and unusual chords kept pace with every changing thought and feeling of the poems. His songs sometimes consist of mere declamation, but the effect remains lyric rather than dramatic. Frequently there is very little variation of tempo or dynamics—yet the songs never become monotonous. Something else is deserving of mention: the way in which the melodic line now simulates and now follows the inflections and rhythms of the French language.

He wrote his first songs in 1865, when he was twenty, and his last songs in 1922, two years before his death. The writing of songs, therefore, engaged him virtually throughout his career. Among his earliest songs we find two that have never lost their appeal: "Lydia," Op. 4, No. 2, and "Après un rêve," Op. 7, No. 1. Their sustained popularity notwithstanding, these two songs find Fauré still in the formative stage. He arrived at complete maturity of style in 1880. He now began the production of some of the most exquisite songs in French music, including "Rencontre," Op. 21, No. 1 (1881); "Chanson d'amour," Op. 27, No. 1 (1883); "Les Roses d'Ispahan," Op. 39, No. 4 (1884); "Au Cimetière," Op. 51, No. 2 (1889); "En Prière," (no opus number, 1890); and "Soir," Op. 83, No. 2 (1900). A landmark was reached in 1887, for it was then that he set to music for the first time a poem by Paul Verlaine, "Clair de lune," Op. 46, No. 2. In 1892 he produced some of his most important songs up to that time, the cycle *La Bonne Chanson,* Op. 61, a setting of nine out of twenty-one Verlaine love lyrics. His vocal style was further developed and perfected in later songs. Two song cycles have particular interest. *La Chanson d'Eve,* Op. 95 (1910), is a setting of ten pantheistic poems by Charles van Lerberghe. *L'Horizon chimérique,* Op. 118 (1922), was Fauré's last composition for voice and piano. This cycle consists of four poems by Jean de la Ville de Mirmont in which the sea becomes a symbol of the undiscovered. Now in his old age, Fauré looked upon de Mirmont's sea as a symbol of the Great Beyond. This is the reason why the prevailing feeling of these songs is a profound sadness.

César Franck

"He stands out from among his contemporaries like a man of some other age. They are self-advertising, he worked in silence. They seek glory, he was content to await it. They aim at easily acquired reputation . . . he built enduring monuments amid the calm of a retired life."

GUY DE ROPARTZ

BORN: Liège, Belgium, December 10, 1822.
DIED: Paris, November 8, 1890.
MAJOR WORKS: *Chamber Music*—Piano Quintet; Violin Sonata; String Quartet. *Choral Music*—Rédemption; Les Béatitudes. *Operas*—Le Valet de ferme; Hulda; Ghisèle (unfinished). *Orchestral Music*—Les Eolides; Le Chasseur maudit; Les Djinns, for piano and orchestra; symphonic variations for Piano and Orchestra; Symphony; Psyché (with chorus). *Organ Music*—Six pièces pour grand orgue; 44 Petites pièces (also for harmonium); L'Organiste, 55 pieces for harmonium; Trois chorales. *Piano Music*—Prelude, Chorale, and Fugue; Prelude, Aria, and Finale. *Vocal Music*—Various songs for voice and piano including "Ave Maria" and "Panis angelicus."

HIS LIFE

In August of 1885 César Franck was awarded the ribbon of the Chevalier of the Legion of Honor. His services as professor of the organ were thus being recognized. It is both ironical and characteristic that when some measure of recognition came to the sixty-two-year-old musician it should have been for the wrong thing. By this time Franck had produced the Piano Quintet, the oratorio *Les Béatitudes,* the symphonic poem *Les Eolides,* and some fine organ pieces. Yet it was not for this that he was decorated, but because he was a teacher.

Few great composers of any period suffered so at the hands of their contemporaries as Franck did. His first major public success as a composer did not come until he was sixty-eight years old (the last year of his life) when the *première* of his String Quartet received an ovation. Before then he was continually confronted by the apathy of the Paris public and, worse still, by the antagonism of his powerful colleagues. The typical attitude was that of the conductor Colonne, who rehearsed the symphonic poem *Les Djinns* in the early 1880s. Midway in his rehearsal he stopped the orchestra and turned to the composer to ask, "Does it please you?" Franck replied that he was very pleased indeed. Colonne then turned back to the orchestra men and added, "It's all frightful music, gentlemen, but we'll go on anyway." Typical, too, was the private performance of *Les Béatitudes,* which, after ten years of devoted labor, Franck was ready to reveal to Parisian musicians. In 1879 he invited the most important musical figures of the time to his home to hear the work. But one after another the guests sent in polite apologies, many of them at the last minute, giving specious reasons why they were unable to come. Only two people were present to hear Franck play his oratorio.

Most of those who knew him regarded him as a quaint man who always wore an overcoat too large for him, over trousers that were invariably too short; who was always rushing from one place to another—to the Conservatory, where he taught the organ; to the Sainte-Clotilde Church, where he played; to the houses of his various pupils, where he taught piano and theory—making grimaces as he hurried along the streets; who was notoriously absent-minded; whose specialty was the organ, but who insisted on writing a great deal of music nobody was interested in.

A simple man, Franck served music and God with reverence and humility. He was happy in that service; he asked no more from life but that he be allowed to continue it. He had the serenity of a man who was at peace not only with the world around him but with himself.

He allowed several hours each day for silent meditation and reflection, as indispensable to his well-being as the time he spent composing. His sweetness of spirit was untouched by the bitterness of frustration or the turmoil of struggle. He was, as Claude Debussy wrote of him, a man without guile. "The discovery of a beautiful harmony was sufficient to make him as happy as the day was long. . . . This man who was unfortunate, unrecognized, possessed the soul of a child, and one so good that neither contradictory circumstances nor the wickedness of others could ever make him feel bitter."

When confronted with his only major success—the ovation given to his String Quartet in 1890—his first instinctive reaction was that of pleasure that the performers should be thus acclaimed. It never occurred to him that the applause might be for him! But when it dawned on him finally that he had been cheered, he remarked to Vincent d'Indy, "There, you see—the public is at last beginning to understand me." That they had not understood him up to then—his sixty-ninth year—was not even a fleeting shadow over his joy.

His father, a music-loving banker of German extraction, wanted his son to become a musician; he dreamed of a brilliant and triumphant career for the boy as a virtuoso of the piano. Consequently, César Franck was early taught the piano at the Liège Conservatory, and his progress was so rapid that when he was eleven he made a concert tour of Belgium and at thirteen won first prize for piano playing at the Conservatory. The greater advantages of music study in Paris were now required. The Franck family came to the French capital in the fall of 1835. After a period of study with Anton Reicha, who had been a friend of Beethoven, the boy was enrolled in the Paris Conservatory. He was a brilliant pupil and probably would have run off with most of the prizes if a perverse streak had not occasionally tempted him to shock his teachers. At his first-year examinations he was required to read at sight a concerto by Hummel; some caprice led him to transpose it from its original key of A minor to F-sharp major. Cherubini was so flustered by this impudence that he withheld the first prize, giving Franck the second prize instead. For his fourth-year examination he was set two themes, one to be improvised into a fugue and the other into a sonata. Once again Franck preferred to be different, using both themes within the sonata form, containing a fugue; and once again he was given second prize instead of first. Nevertheless, he won first prize for counterpoint and piano and organ playing, and in 1842 made plans to compete for the Prix de Rome.

Father Franck was not pleased with his son's development. All signs at the Conservatory pointed to Franck's becoming either an organist or a composer. The boy seemed particularly interested in composition. In his fifteenth year he completed a piano concerto which he himself introduced in Paris; one year later he wrote three trios, which became his Op. 1, and one of which was later performed. But Father Franck was insistent that his son seek the rewards and personal glory of the concert stage. He withdrew the boy from the Conservatory in 1842, returned to Belgium, and arranged for several recitals, one of them for the king. But these concerts did little to advance César Franck's virtuoso career. By 1844 the Francks were back in Paris, where César made his French debut as pianist and composer on March 17, 1843, with a program devoted entirely to his own works. The Francks also set up something of a musical *salon* in the Rue La Bruyère so that young César might exhibit his virtuoso gifts for specially invited guests. For these performances the young musician wrote various *pièces d'occasion*. These were his first and last attempts at the writing of functional music. Before long his serious musicianship and his deeply religious nature led him into more ambitious creative spheres. He began writing large religious works. The first of these was a biblical eclogue, *Ruth,* performed at the Conservatory on January 4, 1846, before a distinguished musical audience that included Liszt and Meyerbeer; some members of the audience liked the work.

In 1848 Franck married an actress, Mademoiselle Desmousseaux. Revolution had just broken out in Paris. To reach the church the couple had to surmount barricades. This marriage was instrumental in bringing about the final break in the increasingly strained relations of father and son. It had for some time been evident to the father that his dream for his son was not destined for realization, that the young man was determined to follow the obscure career of a composer and church organist rather than the dazzling one of a concert pianist. Now that his son was to share his humble life with—of all people!—an actress, Father Franck decided that he would no longer have anything to do with him.

César Franck now devoted himself humbly to his many activities as a musician. He held various organ posts: first as assistant at the Notre-Dame-de-Lorette, then in 1851 as principal organist at Saint-Jean-Saint-François au Marais, finally in 1858 in a similar capacity at Sainte-Clotilde, an office he held until his death. "There he spent the better part of his life," wrote his pupil Vincent d'Indy. "There for thirty years, every Sunday, every festival day, toward the last, every Friday morning he came to stir up the fire of his genius on admirable improvisations frequently far loftier than hosts of pieces cleverly worked out." Many of his pupils would sit near him in the organ loft listening to those improvisations, never failing to marvel at their imagination and beauty. Franz Liszt once attended, on April 3, 1866, and left the church mumbling that Bach had just been brought back to life.

He also gave private lessons in piano and solfeggio. After 1872 he served as professor of the organ at the Paris Conservatory. More often than not he would forget the lesson at hand and impatiently push aside the text and try to impart to the student his own enthusiasm for Bach or Gluck, spending the time in minutely analyzing a passacaglia or toccata or in going through an act from *Iphigénie en Aulide*. Most of his students considered him a bit odd. But a handful recognized his genius and loved him as a man. They gave him their adulation and unwavering devotion—men like Debussy, Vincent d'Indy (1851–1931), Ernest Chausson (1855–99), and Henri Duparc (1848–1933)—and they were inspired by him.

It was a busy life. A friend, the organist Tournemire, wrote: "The first years of his marriage were 'close.' One must live! From half past five in the morning until half past seven, Franck composed. At eight he left the house to 'comb' Paris. He dispensed solfeggio and piano for the convenience of pupils in the Jesuit school of Vaugirard (lessons 1 franc 80 centimes a half hour, from eleven until two!). He had only a bite of fruit or cheese to sustain him. . . . He would go to Auteuil, to a fashionable institution for young ladies of society who often constrained him to teach them impossible novelties of the hour."

Always uppermost in his mind, and often even when he was teaching, was his own music. His mind was cluttered with ideas he would use in new works. "It frequently happened," wrote Vincent d'Indy, "that during his lessons he would suddenly get up and retire into a corner of the room to jot down a few measures which he was anxious not to forget and then come back almost immediately to take up once more the demonstration or examination. Important works were composed in this manner, in bits, casually indicated, and their connection never failed to be logical and consecutive."

He produced one ambitious work after another; and he was fated to suffer one major disappointment after another. An opera, *Le Valet de ferme,* on which he had expended so much energy and time that he was brought to the brink of a nervous breakdown, was never performed. Franck himself had to concede sadly that it was not even worth publishing. The oratorio *Rédemption* was so miserably performed at a Concert Spirituel on April 10, 1873, that its true spiritual beauty and eloquence were altogether obfuscated. *Les Béatitudes,* the fruit of ten years of labor, had (as we have seen) an audience of two when Franck tried to introduce it to Paris' foremost musicians. It was never again heard in its entirety during Franck's lifetime. An all-Franck concert on May 1, 1885—arranged by his pupils and friends in an effort to bring him, at last, deserved recognition—was shabbily performed.

On February 17, 1889, the *première* of his now celebrated Symphony in D minor was a major fiasco. Most of the members of the Paris Conservatory Orchestra were opposed to playing it. Only the firm insistence of its conductor, Jules Garcin, prevented cancellation of the performance. The audience, which included many famous musicians and authorities, appeared puzzled by the music. One of the Conservatory professors commented: *"That* a symphony? Who ever heard of writing for the English horn in a symphony?" Charles Gounod, leaving the auditorium, told a group of admiring girls that the work was "the affirmation of incompetence pushed to dogmatic lengths." Léo Delibes, who had had the temerity to applaud the work at one point, was taken to task for compromising himself in such a fashion. The attitude of musical Paris was perhaps best reflected in an acid comment made by one music lover to a Franck pupil: "Why play this symphony here? Who is Professor Franck? An organ professor—I believe."

But the impact of this disaster did not seem to touch the composer. His pupil de Bréville wrote: "Going out we trembled to find Father Franck saddened by the coldness of the public. He was radiant. He had heard his music played . . . he planned new compositions, he promised himself to write for the brass otherwise than he had done in the finale."

When Franck came home his wife besieged him with questions about the performance. Did the public like the symphony? Had it been well played? Franck smiled. Not a word about the violent opposition to his music, not a word betraying disappointment or resentment. All he said was: "It sounded well, just as I thought it would."

There was one brief taste of success—and that was all. On April 19, 1890, the *première* of his String Quartet was acclaimed at a concert of the Société Nationale de Musique. Its success was so great that a repeat performance was arranged for the following month. Meanwhile, on his way to a pupil—hurrying in the streets as always, concentrating on some piece of music—he was struck by an *autobus*. He managed to get to his pupil's apartment, where he fainted. After recovering he insisted on proceeding with his lesson. He discounted the seriousness of the accident and kept on living and working as if it had never happened. But his physical condition was deteriorating. In the fall he was confined to bed with pleurisy. Even though his condition was serious he left his bed one day to visit his beloved organ loft and play for the last time the last of his works, the Three Chorales for Organ. Its score rested on his bed when the Last Sacraments were administered.

HIS MUSIC

Up to the last work Franck's music represents unfaltering growth and continued enrichment. His evolution was slow. The apprentice works reveal no premonition of his later greatness. His first important work, *Rédemption,* was completed when he was fifty-two. Now in his maturity, he produced within the next five years his Piano Quintet and *Les Béatitudes,* unmistakable evidence of greatness. And he kept growing all the time. His greatest works are the fruits of his old age, produced in the last four years of his life: the Symphony in D minor, the Sonata for Violin and Piano, the String Quartet, the Three Chorales for Organ, and the Prelude, Aria, and Finale for Piano.

His aim was to write romantic music within classical structures. (His enemies—failing to see the forest for the trees—used to say that he betrayed the ideals of French music for German academism.) From his training at the organ he brought to his writing an inclination for improvisation and a love for contrasting timbres. Other little idiosyncrasies of his style include the frequent use of shifting harmonies and quick modulations, a tendency to dissect melodies into fragments, and a preference for inorganic structures. But his individuality is not found in such stylistic mannerisms. It is found in the general feeling, mood, and poetry of his speech. He filled his music with serenity and deep religious feeling. It is music without conflict, the music of a man at peace with himself. It is music for a cathedral and it has a kind of purifying effect on responsive listeners.

His one innovation was structural: the use of the "cyclical form." This method consisted in building up fully developed themes out of melodic germs (these germs have been described as "generative phrases"), and in repeating in later movements of a work thematic material used earlier, to arrive at unity.

In his own quiet and unobtrusive way he exerted a profound influence on those near him. Several fine examples of French Romantic music—the works of Chausson and d'Indy, for example—owe their character to Franck's music. The purity, mysticism, and serenity in these works are the unmistakable fingerprints of the *"maître des maîtres,"* as they always lovingly referred to their teacher.

ANALYTICAL NOTES

Chamber Music. The Quintet in F minor for Piano and Strings (1879) marked Franck's return to chamber music after more than thirty-five years. He had written some trios when he was twenty years old. They were the derivative works of a comparative novice. The quintet, completed in 1878, was the work of a master. Its personal language was spiritual and mystic; the work is filled with themes of otherworldly beauty, themes that are worked out with consummate mastery.

It is in three movements instead of the traditional four (the third-movement scherzo is omitted). Structurally it is characterized by the use of the sonata form—exposition, development, and recapitulation—in all three movements; the first and third movements have an introduction and coda. Another structural characteristic is the cyclic use of a single theme which appears and reappears throughout the work in various forms and welds the entire work into a unity. It is found in the second theme of the first movement, in the middle of the second movement—where it arrives as a kind of climax—and in the extended coda of the third movement.

The Quartet in D major (1889), one of Franck's last works, brought him belated success. Harvey Grace believes that no other of his works contains so much the essence of Franck as this one. It has a serene, remote beauty which often makes us think of the last quartets of Beethoven. The first movement is built out of a slow, reflective song which, later in the movement, is given a fugal treatment that is mystic. A change of pace in the second movement brings us an engaging scherzo, in which the song of the first movement is briefly quoted. The slow movement that follows is among the noblest music Franck ever wrote, sustained in its eloquence and intensity of feeling. In the finale an introductory section recalls the themes of preceding movements, after which the movement proper begins with a transformation of the song theme of the first movement. The second theme of this movement is built out of the traditional motive of the first movement, while in the coda the themes of all the previous movements are again quoted, sometimes polyphonically; the affecting melody of the slow movement helps to end the quartet on a sublime note.

The Sonata in A major for Violin and Piano is one of the finest in the repertory, well deserving a place at the side of the violin sonatas of Beethoven and Brahms. Franck wrote it in 1886 for the Belgian violinist Eugène Ysaÿe, who introduced it, but not with any degree of success. The first movement is in a condensed sonata form, as it has no development section; the recapitulation follows immediately after the exposition. The first theme, heard in the violins after a few introductory notes in the piano, combines yearning with reverie. This mood is continued with the second theme, heard in the piano. The yearning grows restless, as the two melodies return with figurations or with changing tone colors. But in the closing measures there are peace and resignation. The second movement is agitated—one of the few examples in Franck of turbulent feelings. A stormy first theme appears in the piano. In a transitional passage we hear echoed a melodic idea from the first movement. The second theme now arrives in the violin. These ideas are worked out with vehemence, completely dispelling the mystic mood of the first movement. The movement that follows is called a "recitative-fantasia." After a brief dialogue between piano and violin—in which several ideas are projected, including a recollection of the main theme of the first movement—there takes place an extended rhapsody on these themes, free in form, and in Franck's improvisational manner. There is some of the unrest of the preceding movement; but there is also a somber forlornness. In the finale we return to the calm and spiritual beauty of the first movement. A graceful theme is presented canonically by piano and violin. A climax is reached, after which the somber theme of the third movement is quoted by piano with figurations by the violin. The canonic melody returns; as it is being worked out, further quotations from the second and third movement are interpolated. Now the somber theme of the third movement becomes a fiery utterance in the violin. But once again the canonic melody returns, more exultant than before.

Orchestral Music. The Symphony in D minor, written in 1888, is Franck's only symphony. (An apprentice symphony, *The Sermon on the Mount,* written in or about 1846, was never published.)

A majestic lento introduction opens the first movement. A questioning phrase, heard in the cellos and basses—the germ of one of the principal themes of the movement—is powerfully built up. An air of mystery is injected with tremolos in violas and cellos. At last the allegro non troppo section erupts with the vigorous first theme in the strings. There are two other principal themes. One is yearning, treated canonically in the strings. The second, which follows in full orchestra without delay, is like a proud affirmation of faith and hope. This third theme is plaintively echoed in solo horn and in the woodwinds to aid in the development. Quick modulations and changes of orchestral color provide rapidly contrasting moods as these three themes are varied and developed. The conclusion of the development —the final coda of the movement—is made up of a vigorous canonic treatment of the opening questioning phrase.

Plucked strings and harp provide the harmonic and rhythmic background for the first principal melody of the second movement. It is a song of stately beauty, begun by the English horn (then carried on by the clarinet and after that by unison horns) against a poignant countermelody in violas and cellos. The second melody—no less tender and poetic than the first—appears in the first violins and is treated in some detail. The English horn and the other winds bring up a fragment of the opening melody as a transition to an extended scherzo section, which begins with muted triplets in the strings. There now comes a third melody—one of those incomparably serene songs which are so often found in Franck's music. It is given by the clarinet, against triplet rhythm, and taken over by the strings. The scherzo theme returns; it is now combined with the opening melody. The third theme then is treated in great length and with great feeling. A single arpeggio in the harp, and the movement ends as gently as it began.

The third and concluding movement is a summation of what has been heard before; but not without the presentation of new material. It opens in a joyful vein as a spirited melody is presented by the cellos and taken over by full orchestra. A second new theme is a stouthearted subject for brass. But now the first melody of the second movement returns—again in the English horn. The mood becomes agitated, reaching a climax with a restatement of the joyful new theme. But we return to earlier material again. The beautiful first melody of the second movement resounds jubilantly in the brass against the tremolo of the strings. Now the third theme of the first movement is brought back to be worked in with the lento phrase that opened the symphony. But it is the new joyful subject, rather than one of the earlier themes, that brings the movement and the symphony to an exultant finish.

The *Symphonic* Variations (*Variations symphoniques*) for Piano and Orchestra is the nearest that Franck came to writing a piano concerto after an adolescent experiment in the form. He completed the Variations in 1885. The form is unorthodox. Unlike so many other works in the variation form, it does not present its main theme at the outset of the work and then transform it in a series of formal variations. The work consists of an introduction, a middle section, and a finale. It is the middle section that utilizes the variation technique. In the introduction and the finale the variation-theme is only vaguely suggested.

The introduction consists of a dialogue: a dramatic recitative for strings alternating with a gentle answering phrase of the piano. When the tempo changes, the strings present the first two phrases of what will later be the variation theme. The piano then engages in a long solo discourse, and when the orchestra returns, the initial dialogue is recalled. A powerful climax is reached, bringing the introduction to an end. It is now that the variation theme appears, a singularly beautiful melody in the piano. Six variations are heard. Donald Francis Tovey has given the following analysis of the variations:

The first . . . is in dialogue (figure by figure) between piano and orchestra. In the second variation, the cellos have the theme. The third is in flowing movement for the piano accompanied by pizzicato chords for strings, the wind gradually joining in melodically. The fourth variation takes the theme fortissimo, passing through various keys. It expands dramatically and leads to a softer but not less lively accompaniment. The fifth variation . . . dies away into the original key . . . before it is complete; and the sixth variation sails in slowly. . . . A beautiful meandering counterpoint ripples throughout the piano part while the theme, in the cellos, forms the bass for the first eight bars. The rest is given by the wind instruments. Then the mode changes to minor and slowly, below the flowing arpeggios of the piano, the cellos spell out a wonderful dream on the theme of the piano's original entry. There is no more thought now of variation; the rest of the work is concerned with building up a brilliant finale on this other theme.

The finale is gay throughout, with contrast provided by a meditative cadenzalike passage for piano, in the middle of which the flute repeats the principal theme of the movement.

Les Eolides (1876) and *Le Chasseur maudit* (1882) are among Franck's most familiar shorter works for orchestra. Both are tone poems. *Les Eolides* has for its literary source a poem by Leconte de Lisle that reads: "O floating breezes of the skies, sweet breaths of fair spring, that caress the hills and plains with freakish kisses. Virgins, daughters of Aeolus, lovers of peace, eternal nature awakens to your songs; and the dryad seated amid the thick foliage sheds the tears of the scarlet dawn upon the mosses."

The tone poem opens gently, an important figure in clarinet appearing in the seventeenth measure. It is then repeated by the oboe. A molto espressivo section has for its basic subject a plaintive melody. The clarinet plays it first, and then the violins present it. As this material is being worked out, the mood becomes turbulent, but the tone poem ends as serenely as it had begun, with a final reminder of the opening clarinet figure.

Le Chausseur maudit, or *The Accursed Huntsman,* has for its program a ballad by Gottfried August Bürger based on an old legend. This is how the ballad is summarized in the published score:

It is Sunday morning. In the distance are heard the joyous pealing of bells and the sacred chanting of the worshipers. What desecration! The wild Count of the Rhine sounds his hunting horn. The chase goes on over grain fields, moors, and prairies. "Hold on, Count, I pray thee; listen to the pious chants!" "No!" and the rider rushes on like a whirlwind. Suddenly, the count is alone. His horse cannot move, nor his horn any longer give forth a sound. A grim, pitiless voice curses him: "Desecrator!" it says, "be thou forever pursued by the Evil One!" The flames blaze up on all sides. The Count, mad with terror and pursued by a pack of demons, flees ever faster and faster—across the abysses by day and through the sky by night.

The tone poem has four sections. A hunting theme for horns is heard first, setting the stage for the chase. The cellos present a somber melody in the second part representing the warning that the huntsman ignores. The third part offers a description of the huntsman—unable to sound his horn, incapable of getting his horse to move—in a theme for bass tuba, which the brass choir takes over. The demons, in pursuit of the huntsman, are realistically depicted in the final part.

Piano Music. Franck's two most significant works for solo piano came toward the end of his life: the Prelude, Chorale, and Fugue (1884), and the Prelude, Aria, and Finale (1887).

The first of these compositions represents a return to the polyphonic practices of Johann Sebastian Bach without abandoning Franck's own brand of romanticism and mysticism. There are two main subjects in the prelude—the first, solemn; the second, vigorous. A religious chorale precedes the fugue, whose subject is a descending chromatic figure. The Prelude, Aria, and Finale begins with a slow chorale. The aria that follows is an exalted melody that maintains the spiritual character of the preceding prelude. In the finale there takes place a summation of earlier thematic material.

George Gershwin

"He is the present, with all its audacity, impertinence, its feverish delight in motion, its lapses into rhythmically exotic melancholy."

SAMUEL CHOTZINOFF

BORN: Brooklyn, New York, September 26, 1898.
DIED: Hollywood, California, July 11, 1937.
MAJOR WORKS: *Opera*—Porgy and Bess. *Orchestral Music*—Rhapsody in Blue; Concerto for Piano and Orchestra; An American in Paris; Second Rhapsody; Cuban Overture; Variations on "I Got Rhythm" for Piano and Orchestra. *Piano Music*—Three Preludes.

HIS LIFE

When he died in 1937, Gershwin was looked upon more as one of Tin Pan Alley's great success stories than as one of the great creative figures in American music. He was the man who outgrew a song plugger's cubicle to become box-office magic on Broadway and in Hollywood. He was the composer whose annual income went into six figures, who had lived in a swank duplex apartment in New York and on an estate in Beverly Hills in California. The general consensus of editorial and feature writers and music critics in 1937 was that Gershwin would survive in his popular songs, but that his serious efforts—from the *Rhapsody in Blue* through *Porgy and Bess*—would be consigned to permanent oblivion.

The popular songs *have* survived. Indeed, the best of them have as wide a circulation today as they had when first written, and are now sung not only by leading popular performers but also by major stars of the concert hall and opera house. These songs were the saving grace of the Gershwin screen biography, *Rhapsody in Blue,* released in 1945; they helped still another motion picture musical to win an Academy Award, *An American in Paris,* in 1951.

But the serious Gershwin has not fallen by the wayside, as most people said would happen. On the contrary! The growth in importance of Gershwin's concert music and opera throughout the civilized world is something of a phenomenon. Perhaps nothing points up this posthumous growth in importance of the serious Gershwin than Toscanini's attitude toward him. It was no secret that when Gershwin was alive the maestro held neither the composer nor his music in very high esteem. But five years after Gershwin's death, Toscanini conducted the *Rhapsody in Blue* with the NBC Symphony; and in the next two years he also led performances of the Concerto in F and *An American in Paris.* He now told Samuel Chotzinoff, general music director of NBC, that "Gershwin's music is the only *real* American music."

The proliferation of all-Gershwin concerts in the capitals of the world is one of many barometers of Gershwin's mounting posthumous fame. All-Gershwin concerts, of course, had already become something of an established institution when he was alive. But the principal attraction there—even more than the music itself—was Gershwin, appearing as either pianist or conductor. It hardly seemed likely that with Gershwin dead the vogue for all-Gershwin concerts could continue. But with each passing year more and more of these all-Gershwin concerts increased in popularity—so much so that in 1953 the Gershwin Concert Orchestra was formed to tour the United States in Gershwin programs, a tour that was expanded in 1954. (This is undoubtedly the first time in musical history that an orchestra was founded just to perform the compositions of a single composer.) Since then, all-Gershwin concerts have become invitations to sold-out houses and to ovations wherever they are given. And they are given everywhere, from Paris to Tel Aviv, from London to places behind the Iron Curtain, from New York to the Orient and even Tanganyika. In May of 1968 there even took place a three-night Gershwin festival in Venice. What is extraordinary about this is that no American composer—possibly no composer in the twentieth century—can boast of having entire programs of his works given annually so often and in so many places. More noteworthy still is the fact that, since the repertory of Gershwin concert music is meager, the permutations and combinations of Gershwin compositions to make up a program are highly limited. Yet in spite of such limitations, every repetition of the self-same work inspires excitement as if the audience were hearing this music for the first time.

More remarkable still is what has happened to Gershwin's folk opera, *Porgy and Bess,* since his death. In 1937 it seemed certain that it had been consigned to that permanent limbo which seems to be the fate of all American operas. Then slowly things began happening to *Porgy and Bess.* First it received the David Bispham medal "for distinguished contribution to native American opera." Then, in 1938, it was successfully revived in California. Brought back to New York in 1942 for the first time since its none-too-successful *première,* it had an eight-month run, the longest of any musical revival in Broadway history. In addition, the New York Music Critics Circle singled it out for special attention. Most of the leading music critics in New York (many of whom had condemned the opera when they had first heard it) now reversed themselves to call it a master-work and to hail it as the most significant opera by an American.

After that, *Porgy and Bess* was produced by resident companies in Denmark and Sweden, as well as in Moscow and Zurich. Between 1952 and 1956, *Porgy and Bess* was performed by a traveling American all-Negro company throughout Europe, the Middle East, the Soviet Union, Latin America, and the Far East. It was the first opera by an American-born composer given at the historic La Scala in Milan. In Austria it scored the greatest success of any new foreign opera since *Cavalleria Rusticana* a half century earlier. In Yugoslavia, London, Paris, Israel, Germany, and the Soviet Union the success was just as spectacular. Then, in 1965, *Porgy and Bess* entered the permanent repertory of the famous Volksoper in Vienna. In 1967 it was performed by the Oslo Opera in Norway, in 1967–68 by several opera companies in France, and in 1968 a production was mounted in Ankara, Turkey, with a part Negro, part Turkish cast. Meanwhile, in 1959, it had been made into a handsome and lavish motion picture—a Samuel Goldwyn production that also circled the globe.

More and more posthumous honors were heaped upon Gershwin

himself, beginning with the honorary membership to the St. Cecilia Academy in Rome, the highest honor Italy could give a foreign composer. Gershwin's name was given to two competitions for American composers, to a collection of manuscripts at Fisk University in Nashville, to a theater workshop in Boston, to a Liberty ship during World War II, to a theater at Brooklyn College in New York, to a junior high school also in Brooklyn, and even to a street in Hull, England (the last being the first instance in which an American musician had a European street named after him). There is a George Gershwin collection at the Library of Congress in Washington, D.C., and another one at the Museum of the City of New York.

All this adds up to an impressive sum: Gershwin now belongs to those great creators of the past who have helped shape an American culture. He speaks for America to the rest of the world, and he speaks about Americans, in the way that Mark Twain, Stephen Foster, Jack London, Edith Wharton, Carl Sandburg, Robert Frost, Eugene O'Neill, or Ernest Hemingway have spoken in song, poetry, and story. Today Gershwin's serious efforts as composer are universally accepted as classics, and their composer has become something of a legend.

This posthumous recognition of his greatness would have pleased Gershwin no end—far more than his material success did. A friend once visited him with a volume of Schubert songs under his arm. He took the book, ruffled the pages until his eye caught the "Ave Maria." "You know," he said softly, "I'd gladly trade in everything I've got for a bit of the genius it took to write that song."

The truth is that Gershwin, who wrote popular music, was driven by artistic impulses and by an idealism no less powerful than that of composers of symphonies or oratorios. When in his teens Gershwin continually tried proving to his teacher that the American popular song had value as music. Gershwin studied Debussy and Chopin assiduously and made good progress in harmony and in piano playing. But when he played an Irving Berlin ragtime number he knew with an unshakable conviction that this was the kind of music he would like to write if he ever turned to composition. "The boy is a genius," Hambitzer, Gershwin's first important piano teacher, wrote to his sister at the time. "He's just crazy about music and can't wait until it is time to take his lessons. He wants to go in for this modern stuff, jazz and what-not. But I'm not going to let him for a while."

Later, when he was famous, Gershwin wrote articles emphasizing his belief in the artistic importance of jazz as a serious musical idiom. To prove this importance to the world was a mission from which he was never deflected. The significant point is that though in his youth he was less articulate, he was no less certain of his own direction and the direction of jazz. When he was a piano demonstrator for Remick's he often spent his free moments in his cubicle—practicing Bach's preludes and fugues. A fellow demonstrator asked him, "Are you practicing to become a conert pianist?" Gershwin answered soberly, "No. I'm practicing to become a popular-song composer." He sometimes put it into words to Hambitzer and to his mother. His ambition was to become a great composer—but in the medium of American popular music.

He was, however, no prodigy. The setting in which he was born and in which he functioned as a child was not calculated to produce a genius. No Gershwin had ever shown particular aptitude for music.

The early years of George's life were devoted to the normal activities of city streets: roller skating, punchball, "cat," street hockey, gang rivalries. He was a rooter for the New York Giants, and together with his cronies he considered any boy that went in for music a "Maggie."

When he was nine he heard Rubinstein's Melody in F. "The peculiar jumps in the music held me rooted," he later revealed. "To this day I can't hear the tune without picturing myself outside the arcade on 125th Street, standing there barefoot and in overalls, drinking it all in avidly." At about this time, too, he fell in love with a girl only because she sang sweetly. But the full awakening to music came in or about his tenth year. He was playing ball outside Public School No. 25, on the Lower East Side of Manhattan, when he heard Dvořák's Humoresque played on a violin. A local prodigy by the name of Maxie Rosenzweig (later to become the concert violinist Max Rosen) was giving a concert in the school auditorium. "It was," Gershwin said many years later, "a revelation." A few days later he sought out Maxie and became his friend. Through Maxie he began discovering the world of music. He secretly tried writing music of his own on Maxie's piano; significantly enough, it was not a piece of music such as Maxie might play, but a popular song. Proudly he exhibited it to Maxie. The latter, probably expecting distillations of

Mendelssohn and Chopin, was taken aback by the ragtime rhythms and harmonies. "I'm sorry," he said at last, "but you haven't got the talent to be a composer."

The Gershwins had by then acquired a piano, so that George's older brother, Ira, might take lessons. George soon appropriated it for himself. His first teacher was a Miss Green, who charged fifty cents a lesson. George soon realized that she was not for him. She was succeeded by a Professor Goldfarb (he was given the honorary title of "professor" by the neighborhood because he charged $1.50 a lesson!), who fed him simple arrangements of opera potpourris; Professor Goldfarb did not believe in scales or exercises. At about this time George was introduced to Charles Hambitzer, a composer of operettas who was an extraordinary musician. George played for him the *William Tell* Overture, which the professor had taught him. "Listen," Hambitzer said when Gershwin finished, "you and I will now go out and hunt up the teacher who taught you to play that way. We'll shoot him—and without an apple on his head, either."

Gershwin now became a pupil of Hambitzer, his first good teacher. Hambitzer gave him a sound training at the piano, initiated him into the great literature of music, and, later on, insisted that he take theory lessons with Edward Kilenyi. George was, as he himself put it, "crazy" about Hambitzer, even though the latter was not receptive to his ambition to write popular music. "Don't you see," Hambitzer would argue with him, "that these songs you like so much are just hack stuff, with no imagination whatsoever?" And Gershwin would provide a hot rebuttal. He seemed to realize even then that despite their naïveté and gaucheries these popular idioms could become something important, and something *American,* in the hands of a good musician.

Gershwin soon decided to get a job in the only conservatory where he could possibly learn about popular music: Tin Pan Alley. When he was sixteen he became a piano demonstrator for the publishing house of Remick. It was not long before he began writing songs in an uninterrupted stream. One of his songs was published in 1916, "When You Want 'Em You Can't Get 'Em." Soon after this another song, "Making of a Girl," was interpolated into a Broadway musical, *The Passing Show of 1916.*

There were those who already were recognizing something vital and original in Gershwin's still-primitive song attempts. Irving Berlin thought so highly of Gershwin that he offered him a job as his musical secretary, at a salary several times larger than what Gershwin was earning at that time. "But I hope you don't take the job," Berlin added reflectively. "As my secretary you'll probably start imitating me. And you're meant for much bigger things than that." Gershwin did not take the job and learned the wisdom of Berlin's advice. But there was another encouraging offer he could and did take. Max Dreyfus, head of the powerful publishing house of Harms, gave him $35 a week to write songs and to show them to him; there were no other set duties. Largely through Dreyfus' influence, Gershwin got his first commission to write the music for a Broadway revue, *Half-Past Eight,* and soon after that for a Broadway musical comedy, *La, La, Lucille.* At about this time too—the year was 1919—Al Jolson sang Gershwin's song "Swanee" in *Sinbad* and made it a million-copy sheet-music hit and a resounding best seller on records.

Gershwin did not stop studying; he would continue studying for the rest of his life, now with one teacher, and now with another. Under Kilenyi's guidance he began to take lessons in instrumentation in 1919 by engaging various performers to teach him the basic elements of playing their instruments. Occasionally he would bring to Kilenyi the orchestrations that others made of his music to dissect them. "He had an extraordinary faculty or genius," Kilenyi said, "to absorb everything, and to apply what he learned to his own music."

A few years later Gershwin entered the harmony class of Rubin Goldmark. Goldmark did not think much of his pupil, principally because the young man would bring into his class exercises that had the bounce and swing of jazz and ragtime. One day, as a peace offering, Gershwin brought his teacher a Lullaby for String Quartet which he had actually written in 1919, a few years before becoming Goldmark's pupil. "That's much better," the venerable teacher said. "I can see that you are finally beginning to make some progress." (The manuscript of Lullaby lay hidden in the Gershwin archives of the Library of Congress for many years before it was discovered by the Juilliard String Quartet. The much belated *première* of this quartet— Gershwin's first attempt to use American popular idioms with serious intent, since the basic melody of the Lullaby was a blues—took place in Washington, D.C., on October 19, 1967.)

Beginning in 1920 Gershwin began writing the music for George White's annual lavish revue, *Scandals.* Musical comedies starring Ed Wynn and Irene Bordoni also used his songs. There was even a commission from London for a musical-comedy score. Hardly past his twenty-third birthday, Gershwin was one of the most successful composers in Tin Pan Alley. And one of the best, too. Such songs as "I'll Build a Stairway to Paradise," "Do It Again," and "Somebody Loves Me" were setting a new standard for melodic freshness and rhythmic ingenuity.

As early as 1922 a serious musician (the concert pianist Beryl Rubinstein, later the head of a great conservatory) was able to describe Gershwin to an interviewer as a "great composer." When the interviewer was startled by this, Rubinstein added, "I am absolutely in earnest. This young fellow has the spark of musical genius which is definite in his serious moods." And he went on to say with remarkably prophetic insight, "With Gershwin's style and seriousness he is not definitely of the popular-music school, but is one of the really outstanding figures in this country's serious musical efforts."

Rubinstein was not the only serious artist aware of Gershwin's potentialities. Another was the celebrated singer Eva Gauthier. On November 1, 1923, she gave a recital at Aeolian Hall, the program of which included songs by such great composers of the past and present as Byrd, Purcell, Bellini, Bartók, Schoenberg, Mihaud, and Hindemith. The last group was devoted to American popular songs, three of them by Gershwin. "I consider this one of the very important events in musical history," wrote Carl van Vechten, the novelist, to a friend. "Mind you, I prophesy that the Philharmonic will be doing it in two years!" (Exactly two years later the *première* of Gershwin's jazz Piano Concerto took place at a concert of the New York Symphony Society.)

He was, in short, making a vital and self-respecting art out of the popular song, by bringing to it the harmonic, rhythmic, and melodic resources of serious music. But he was not satisfied. He wanted to bring the styles and techniques of Tin Pan Alley into serious musical forms. Gershwin's first effort in this direction since the 1919 Lullaby for String Quartet was a one-act opera originally called *Blue Monday,* later renamed *135th Street,* written in 1923 for the *Scandals. Blue Monday* stayed in the *Scandals* only for a single evening; it was considered too gloomy. But it made a deep impression on the conductor of the *Scandals* orchestra, Paul Whiteman.

In 1924 Whiteman planned an all-American music concert in Aeolian Hall designed to prove that jazz was a serious affair. To give point to his contention, and to provide a fitting climax for his concert, he commissioned Gershwin to write a new concert work in the jazz idiom. That work was the *Rhapsody in Blue*. Fittingly enough, it was introduced on Lincoln's birthday—February 12, 1924—for it proved to be the emancipation proclamation of American popular music. Walter Damrosch put it another way: "Gershwin made a lady out of jazz." In any event Gershwin had produced a composition which more than any work that had preceded it proved that there was artistic importance to the popular style, if treated with dignity and with conviction. It set into motion a trend that swept the world of music, the writing of large works in the jazz style; it stimulated such composers as Constant Lambert, Kurt Weill, Ernst Křenek, Maurice Ravel, Aaron Copland, Morton Gould, Ferde Grofé, and many others. And it made Gershwin world-famous.

From this time on, and up to his untimately death in Hollywood, Gershwin was to devote himself both to Tin Pan Alley and Carnegie Hall. He produced a long succession of successful scores for the Broadway theater and the Hollywood screen, climaxed by *Of Thee I Sing,* which, in 1932, became the first musical comedy ever to win the Pulitzer Prize. He wrote a piano concerto, the tone poem *An American in Paris,* the Second Rhapsody and the *Cuban* Overture, which were performed by most of the great American orchestras. His last work proved to be his greatest—the folk opera, *Porgy and Bess,* presented by the Theatre Guild in Boston on September 30, 1935, and in New York on October 10.

With *Porgy and Bess* out of the way, Gershwin went to Hollywood in 1936 to write music for the movies. By early 1937 it was obvious something was seriously wrong with his health. For many years he had been suffering from a chronic ailment he called his "composer's stomach" which led him to follow a strict diet and give up smoking cigars. But while the stomach condition had not improved (in spite of the efforts of medical specialists through the years and the subsequent sessions with a New York psychiatrist) this was not what was now harassing him. At an all-Gershwin concert in Los Angeles, on February 11, 1937, he suddenly had a lapse of memory during the playing of his piano concerto; he also experienced the strange sensation of smelling burned rubber. A few months later, in April, he once again suffered a brief blackout and the smell of burned rubber.

Then excruciating headaches began plaguing him, followed by a crushing depression, and then by a loss of muscular co-ordination.

His doctors were so convinced he was suffering from a neurosis or imminent nervous breakdown that they placed him again in the hands of a psychiatrist. But what Gershwin was suffering from was a cystic degeneration of a tumor on that part of the brain that could not be touched. And this was the cause of his death, at the Cedars of Lebanon Hospital in Hollywood on the morning of July 11, 1937. Death had proved merciful. Had Gershwin lived he would have been afflicted by paralysis or blindness or both.

His body was brought back to New York where funeral services were held at Temple Emanu-El on Fifth Avenue. Thousands of admirers who could not gain admission into the temple stood outside in a downpour during the services. The funeral then proceeded to Hastings-on-Hudson where Gershwin was buried in Mount Hope Cemetery.

Despite the chronic stomach trouble that had bothered him for most of his adult life, there was nothing physically effete about Gershwin. He was athletic in build, with the muscular resiliency of one who enjoyed participating in sports. He exercised daily at a small gymnasium which he set up in one of the rooms of each of his lavish apartments: first the seventeenth-floor penthouse at 33 Riverside Drive, which he occupied between 1928 and 1933; then in the fourteen-room duplex at 132 East Seventy-second Street. Nor did his physical discomfort contain his extraordinary energy or dampen his irrepressible enthusiasms. He was a human dynamo, whether at work or play. At play, his diversions were many and varied. He liked games—preferably those that taxed his muscles; when he became interested in one he pursued it with the most extraordinary intensity until he became extremely adept at it. Then he would drop it for another hobby. At one time or another in his life he was a rabid golfer, fisherman, horseman, croquet player, ping-pong player, photographer. Except for roulette, in which he became fascinated late in life, he had no interest whatsoever in games of chance. Also toward the end of his life he became absorbed with painting, in which he revealed such remarkable talent that several distinguished critics were convinced he would have become a great painter had he lived.

But music, especially his own music, was his passion. Everything else assumed comparative insignificance in his scheme of things, even love. Many times in his life he was deeply in love, and on several occasions he came close to the altar. But he never married, partly because he was too busy with his music to get around to it, partly because the women he loved were incapable of penetrating the protective wall with which he surrounded himself whenever he became absorbed with creative problems. One woman to whom he was particularly attached decided she would wait for Gershwin no longer and proceeded to marry someone else. Gershwin reported the news to his brother, Ira, who wrote the lyrics for his songs. "I'd be terribly heartbroken, if I weren't so awfully busy."

He liked best writing his music late at night. Seated at his piano half-undressed, he would sometimes work right through the night without fatigue, even though he had just gone through a busy day. When in the mood he could even work in a crowded and noisy room. Ideas came easily, but working them out cost him sweat and tears. One night (when he was still living with his family in the five-story house on 103rd Street) his father was sitting on the stairs outside the room in which George was at work, listening raptly as George composed. Whenever the piano suddenly fell silent his father went through mental torture, knowing that George was struggling with his ideas. Once, when the piano was mute for an intolerably long period, he could contain himself no longer. Opening the door, he shyly thrust his round face inside, hurriedly whistled a snatch of melody, and asked, "Does *that* help you, George?"

Next to working on his music, he liked best playing it and talking about it. He never missed an opportunity to do so. A party with Gershwin present soon turned out to be a Gershwin party. He never drank. His only dissipation was to sit at the piano and play his music, sometimes for hours on end. During the grueling rehearsals for *Porgy and Bess,* Gershwin suddenly decided to run away from it all for a weekend; he invited the conductor, Alexander Smallens, and the director, Rouben Mamoulian, to his place on Long Island. "You must come out," Gershwin told them, "and relax and forget all about *Porgy and Bess* for a few days." They went, only to spend all Saturday and Sunday listening to him play the opera score on the piano. His mother once scolded him for continually playing his own music at parties. "But, Ma," he said candidly, "if I don't play my music at these parties, I get bored stiff!" It was at one of these *soirées,* after Gershwin had monopolized the evening, that Oscar Levant asked him acidly, "If you had to do it all over again, George, would you still fall in love with yourself?"

Yet he was no egocentric by any means. The reason why he continued studying music throughout his life (with Henry Cowell and Joseph Schillinger in later years) was because he was aware of his technical shortcomings. He was always poring over modern scores, particularly those by Hindemith, Schoenberg, and Berg; and whenever he was in the company of great musicians, he was continually "picking their brains" for answers to creative or performing problems to which he was seeking solutions. But if he was ever seeking help for himself, he was also the soul of generosity in helping others. A good deal of the history of American popular music can be written with the careers of brilliant composers to whom Gershwin gave a helping hand through advice and criticism, through recommendations to publishers and producers, through performances on his regular radio program, and through financial assistance when needed.

HIS MUSIC

Gershwin's inspiration is finer than his technique. His training was inadequate. Consequently he often had to call upon trial and error—and intuition—rather than rules and examples in solving his problems. It was a laborious process. There is no point in brushing aside the frequent structural clumsiness in his larger works, the sometimes self-conscious modulations, the frequent lack of clarity in instrumentation, the occasional inability to enlarge his ideas without resorting to dull repetition. There are flaws in all his large works.

But these flaws become insignificant when placed beside the many strong points; the amazing melodic inventiveness; the never failing freshness of ideas; the basic feeling for rhythm; the extraordinary instincts which dictated the proper effect and the precise means; the unfailing inspiration in getting the idea required by the big moment. His talent, in short, was a conservatory in itself, guiding him (even if at times falteringly) to his inevitable destination.

He created a handful of works which are among the finest achievements of any American composer. And he also began a trend. He was not the first composer to impose the styles of American popular music on large, serious musical forms. Before him had been Satie,

Debussy, Stravinsky, and Milhaud. But the influence of their music in the popular American idioms was negligible, while that of Gershwin has had a permanent effect.

ANALYTICAL NOTES

Opera. *Porgy and Bess* (1935) was Gershwin's last major work. He ended his career as a serious composer as he had begun it, with operatic music. His first experiment had been a one-act "opera" called *Blue Monday* (later titled *135th Street*), completed in 1923. It was little more than a patchwork quilt of several "blues" and jazz melodies for a silly little text devoid of any understanding of the requirements of good theater. *Porgy and Bess* came twelve years later —and what growth had taken place! It boasted a fine Negro play by DuBose Heyward (originally produced by the Theatre Guild), which he adapted into a pliable libretto in collaboration with Ira Gershwin. And Gershwin's music brought to the play dramatic power, humor, tragedy, rich atmospheric colors, and finely drawn characterizations.

Before writing his score Gershwin lived in South Carolina to get a firsthand feeling for his background. In Charleston he heard the declamatory street cries of the vendors. Then he stayed on James Island, some miles from Charleston, to come into contact for the first time with the primitive religious "shouts" and the wailing spirituals of the Gullah Negroes. DuBose Heyward has left us a vivid account of Gershwin's reaction to this Negro music:

I shall never forget the night when, at a Negro meeting on a remote sea island, George started shouting with them—and eventually to their huge delight stole the show from their champion "shouter." I think that he is probably the only white man in America who could have done it. Another night as we were about to enter a dilapidated cabin that had been taken as a meeting house by a group of Negro Holy Rollers, George caught my arm and held me. The sound that had arrested him was one to which, through long familiarity, I attached no special importance. But now, listening to it with him, and noticing his excitement, I began to catch its extraordinary quality. It consisted of perhaps a dozen voices raised in loud rhythmic prayer. The odd thing about it was that while each had started at a different time, upon a different theme, they formed a clearly defined rhythmic pattern, and that this, with the actual words lost, and the inevitable pounding of the rhythm, produced an effect almost terrifying in its primitive intensity. Inspired by the extraordinary effect, George wrote six simultaneous prayers producing a terrifying primitive invocation to God in the face of hurricane.

It is not difficult to trace the effect these musical experiences had on Gershwin in the writing of his score. Without quoting a single melody, he created street cries that seem to belong to the Charleston streets, powerful religious "shouts" and spirituals and work songs that seem to be torn from the very heart of the Negro race. Without borrowing a single bar, Gershwin produced folk music. Thus *Porgy and Bess* is not only good opera, but good folk opera—perhaps the first genuine folk opera to have been written in America.

As the curtain rises on the first act, after a brief orchestral prelude, we are in Catfish Row, in Charleston, South Carolina. Clara is singing her baby to sleep with the tender lullaby "Summertime." But this opening mood is not maintained. For in Catfish Row we have a generous slice of Negro life in the Charleston of that period. There is a crap game, the players being further stimulated by alcohol and dope. Emotions are aroused. Anger and hate instigate a brawl in which Crown kills the husband of Serena. Crown escapes before the police arrive. His girl, Bess, finds a welcome refuge in the home of the cripple Porgy.

The scene changes to Serena's room, where the neighbors have gathered for the wake. Gershwin's writing here achieves dramatic intensity in spirituals and shouts like "Overflow, overflow," "He's a-gone, gone, gone," and "Oh, the train is at the station." Here, too, Serena sings her lament, "My Man's Gone Now."

We return to Catfish Row in the second act. Porgy, now in love with Bess, expresses his exhilaration in "I Got Plenty of Nuttin'." For the time being, at any rate, Bess is true to him; for the time being she can withstand the temptations offered her by Sportin' Life to run away with him to New York. She has even begun to respond to Porgy's tenderness with warmth and gratitude, and is able to join him in an exchange of love sentiments in the duet "Bess, You Is My Woman Now."

In the next scene the residents of Catfish Row have come to Kittiwah Island for a lodge picnic. Sportin' Life entertains them with his cynical commentary on religion, "It Ain't Necessarily So." The island is also the hiding place for the fugitive Crown, who, finding Bess alone, convinces her that she should stay with him in his refuge for a few days. She is sick and delirious when she returns to Porgy, but is tenderly nursed back to health by the crippled beggar.

In the concluding act Porgy, fearing Crown may take Bess away from him, kills him. Porgy is jailed, but only for a week; and when he returns, eager and impatient to be with Bess again, he learns to his horror that, her will shattered by dope, she has gone off to New York with Sportin' Life. Heartbroken, Porgy follows her in his goat cart. "O Lawd," he sings to his neighbors as he sets forth on his journey, "I'm on my way, I'm on my way to Heavenly Lan.'"

There are several other important vocal numbers beyond those singled out in the above summary of the plot. These include Jake's cynical commentary on women as he rocks his baby to sleep in the opening scene, "A Woman Is a Sometime Thing"; the work song of the fishermen as they repair their nets at the beginning of the second act, "It Take a Long Pull to Get There"; Porgy's "Buzzard Song" in the same act, in which he senses imminent disaster for himself as he watches the flight of an overhead buzzard; and, in the third act, Crown's irreverent and mocking tune, "A Red-Headed Woman Makes a Choochoo Jump Its Track," and Sportin' Life's attempts to lure Bess to New York, "There's a Boat That's Leavin' Soon for New York."

All-Gershwin programs frequently offer a symphonic adaptation of the opera's principal melodies which Robert Russell Bennett prepared and called *A Symphonic Picture.* He made it at the request of the conductor Fritz Reiner, who introduced it with the Pittsburgh Symphony on February 5, 1942. This composition (actually a tone poem) is made up of the following episodes: scene of Catfish Row with the peddler's calls; opening of Act II; "Summertime" and opening of Act I; "I Got Plenty of Nuttin'"; storm music; "Bess, You Is My Woman Now"; "It Ain't Necessarily So"; and the finale.

Porgy and Bess, as Gershwin wrote it, was first heard without any deletions at the Blossom Music Center in Cleveland on August 16, 1975, in a concert presentation by the Cleveland Orchestra, Lorin Maazel conducting. The complete opera was first staged by the Houston Grand Opera in Texas in the Spring of 1976, a production successfully brought to New York City on September 15, 1976.

Orchestral Music. The *Rhapsody in Blue,* written in 1924, was Gershwin's first successful attempt to produce serious music in a popular style. It has remained his best orchestral work and the most popular; one can even go further and say it is the best-loved and most frequently heard serious American work in the entire literature for orchestra.

It is in three sections, the first and third being fast, and the middle slow. It opens with a low trill in the solo clarinet, the base of an ascending scale which, when the uppermost note has been reached, erupts into the first theme of the work. It is a headstrong, irresponsible tune; perhaps nowhere has a decade notorious for its abandon and license found a more fitting expression. A transitional figure by the wind section leads to a repetition of this theme by muted trumpet, then by full orchestra. But this transitional figure becomes the second theme in the piano. The opening clarinet theme returns to be worked out with considerable detail by piano, orchestra, and piano and orchestra, until it is stated forcefully by full orchestra and piano. A second transitional passage—a bawdy subject for winds against a piano embellishment—leads to a shrill return of the first theme in the clarinet. The orchestra then appears with the second theme. Three incisive chords invoke a long and detailed oration by the piano, built mostly around the second theme, with a later casual suggestion of the second transitional idea in the bass. A few ascending chords in the piano bring on the slow movement. It is the wonderful song for strings which is the heart of the entire work and one of the most famous passages in American music. The full orchestra repeats this melody exultantly, and it is briefly commented upon by the piano. A change of tempo, and the final section arrives. The opening phrase of the melody, but in quickened tempo, is hastily quoted by the orchestra. Repetitions of this phrase bring on an acceleration of pace and a growth of sonority until a dissonant chord is reached. The music now rushes to its climax: a thundering statement of the opening clarinet theme by the entire orchestra. A few bars of the second theme in the piano lead to the closing chord.

In its original version, as introduced by Paul Whiteman, the *Rhapsody* was orchestrated by Ferde Grofé, Whiteman's arranger. Subsequently, Gershwin provided his own orchestration, which is the version now played.

The Concerto in F for Piano and Orchestra came one year after the *Rhapsody*. It was commissioned by Walter Damrosch for the New York Symphony Society. Gershwin completed it in a few months, orchestrating it himself, and its world *première* took place in New York on December 3, 1925.

The eight-measure introduction to the first movement is a dynamic Charleston motive shared by percussion and woodwinds. The bassoon announces the first theme. After a recall of the Charleston idea, this theme is repeated by the rest of the orchestra. There is a roll from the percussion, and the piano enters with a short glissando, progressing immediately to the second theme of the movement—a plaintive melody. Further on in the movement there is still a third major lyrical subject, a broad, slow waltz melody for strings, the piano providing trimmings. It is immediately taken up passionately by the orchestra.

In the second movement a muted trumpet plays a poignant song against a misty harmonic background of three clarinets. An oboe enters with a piercing wail; the lament continues, before the trumpet solo's return. When the orchestral introduction has concluded, the piano enters with a jaunty tune against a brisk rhythm in the strings. This tune is elaborated upon until the solo violin provides a transitional passage bringing back the opening song in a slightly varied form. After a brief cadenza for piano, the strings engage in a romantic, rhapsodic passage, a characteristic Gershwin effusion. Earlier material is then repeated, but the main melody returns first in the piano and then in the entire orchestra. There is a sudden pause. The opening phrases of the movement are repeated; in this misty atmosphere the movement ends.

The finale explodes in a riot of rhythm and instrumental color. Main melodies from the preceding two movements are woven skillfully into the texture of the music, without abandoning the spirit of gaiety that prevails throughout. The concerto ends with a passionate restatement by the strings of the plaintive second theme of the first movement.

An American in Paris—completed in 1928 and introduced in New York on December 13, 1928, by the New York Philharmonic Orchestra conducted by Walter Damrosch—is the only orchestral work by Gershwin with a detailed program. It was inspired by, and written during, a visit to Europe and is probably autobiographical in its description of the American tourist's nostalgia for home.

An American is walking along the boulevard. A sprightly theme, which opens the work, describes his brisk walk. We now hear the angry noise of Paris taxi horns, for the American appears to be oblivious to the traffic. The snatch of a popular melody in the trombone tells us that a music hall is nearby. But the American passes it quickly; a second walking theme, also rhythmic and vigorous, appears in the clarinet. The walk continues. A lady accosts him; she is represented by a solo violin. She detains him momentarily; the music becomes tender. But eventually he continues his walk. Suddenly he is seized by homesickness. A wailing "blues" melody betrays the fact that he is thinking of his own country. But the homesickness is soon dispelled. Two trumpets bring on a rousing Charleston theme. It seems that the American has met a compatriot, and they can enjoy Paris together. The "blues" theme, when it returns, is no longer a lament, but full of exhilaration. Home is wonderful, but Paris is wonderful too; the surging strings suggest how intoxicating Paris really is. In a riot of sound, which brings the work to its end, the American enjoys the city to the full.

Seven years separate Gershwin's two orchestral rhapsodies. Gershwin originally planned calling his Second Rhapsody the *Rhapsody of the Rivets*. This was because the work was an enlargement of background music he had then recently prepared for a motion picture depicting city noises, including the sounds of riveting. Since that motion picture (*Delicious*) used only a minute of this material Gershwin decided to adapt the rest of it into a new rhapsody. Only after he had finished this chore did he decide to select a non-descriptive title. As the Second Rhapsody it was introduced by the Boston Symphony under Serge Koussevitzky on January 29, 1932. The suggestion of riveting is found in the rhythmic subject for piano with which the rhapsody opens. The main melody (like that in *An American in Paris*) is a blues, heard first in strings, then in brass, and after that embellished upon by solo piano and orchestra.

The *Cuban* Overture (1932) was the result of a holiday in Havana where Gershwin became fascinated with Cuban instruments and rhythms. In writing his overture, he made extensive use of such native instruments as the maraca, the bondo, the gourd, and the Cuban stick. The overture is in three parts. In the first, the strings present two Cuban tunes, the second of which is then juxtaposed contrapuntally against fragments of the first one. A clarinet cadenza leads into the middle section, in which a two-voice canon is developed, unusual in that it is given a harmonic background. After a climax, comes the finale, in which earlier themes are reviewed. The composition ends with an exciting rumba in which the native instruments are prominent.

The *Cuban* Overture received its *première* at an all-Gershwin concert at Lewisohn Stadium in New York on August 16, 1932, Albert Coates conducting. The Variations on "I Got Rhythm" for Piano and Orchestra (1934) was heard first in Boston on January 14, 1934, in a performance by the Leo Reisman Orchestra with the composer at the piano.

"I Got Rhythm" was one of the hit songs that first made Ethel Merman a star of the first magnitude—in her Broadway debut in the Gershwin musical *Girl Crazy* (1930). The Variations opens with a four-note ascending phrase (the initial two measures of the chorus of the song) played by the clarinet. This phrase is taken over by solo piano, then by full orchestra, before the piano is heard in the complete melody of the song's chorus. In the variations that follow, the melody changes its moods chameleonlike from gaiety and exuberance and pyrotechnical brilliance to melancholia.

Piano Music. Gershwin wrote a set of five piano preludes for a concert he was sharing with the singer Marguerite d'Alvarez in New York on December 4, 1926. Two of these preludes are no longer heard. Three have become popular, have been extensively performed and recorded by leading piano virtuosos, and have been transcribed for orchestra.

The first, in B-flat major, is an excursion into abandoned rhythm, with suggestions of the tango and the Charleston. The middle one, in C-sharp minor, is a plangent, throbbing three-part blues. The third, in E-flat major, like the first, gives vent to uninhibited feeling through exciting rhythms and changing meters.

Christoph Willibald Gluck

"He thrust the doors open and allowed the daylight of human naturalness to fall upon the opera world of the time."

PAUL BEKKER

BORN: Erasbach, Upper Palatinate, July 2, 1714.
DIED: Vienna, November 15, 1787.
MAJOR WORKS: *Ballets*—Don Juan; Semiramide. *Chamber Music*—6 sonates for two violins and continuo. *Choral Music*—Frühlingsfeier; De Profundis. *Operas*—Il re pastore; L'Ivrogne corrigé; Le Cadi dupé; Orfeo ed Euridice; Alceste; Paride ed Elena; Iphigénie en Aulide; Armide; Iphigénie en Tauride; Echo et Narcisse.

HIS LIFE

In 1736 Christoph Willibald Gluck came to Vienna for the first time. He was twenty-two years old, a large-boned, ruddy-complexioned peasant who had come to the city of the Hapsburgs to make a career for himself in music. He was conscious of his talent. The son of a forester employed on the summer estate of Prince Lobkowitz, he had begun his musical education in the Catholic schools in Kamnitz and Albersdorf. He also received some private instruction in singing, the violin, and organ. In his eighteenth year he came to Prague. He then traveled throughout the Upper Palatinate, earning a few coins here, a few coins there, by singing in church choirs or playing the violin at village fairs. Inevitably his eyes turned toward distant Vienna. He knew that in that metropolis he would have opportunities for self-advancement. It had a magnificent court orchestra and a nobility lavish in its spending for music and musicians.

He was not disappointed. Prince Lobkowitz (son of his father's employer) engaged him for his household orchestra. Later on, Gluck attracted the interest and admiration of Prince Melzi, who not only took him along on a tour of Italy, but also financed his music study there. Gluck's teacher was a highly respected composer of Italian opera, Giovanni Battista Sammartini (1701–75), who directed the student to the writing of Italian operas, the first of which, *Artaserse,* was produced in Milan on December 26, 1741. Eight more operas followed, all in the accepted Italian manner, all produced in Italy between 1742–45, and all adding to Gluck's growing stature.

He returned to Vienna by a circuitous route that brought him to several other European countries. In England, at the King's Theatre in the Haymarket, he had produced two operas in 1746, both failures. He also met the great Handel, who appeared with him at one of his public concerts and who regarded Gluck's music as "detestable." ("He knows no more counterpoint than my cook," Handel is reputed to have said.) In Hamburg, Leipzig, and Dresden he conducted a traveling opera company. A brief visit to his native land to be at the bedside of his dying father—and he was back again in Vienna. The year was 1748; Gluck had been gone twelve years.

He was no longer the petitioner after favors, but a musician who had established his reputation and who would now be sought after. He was so highly regarded that he was commissioned to write an opera for the birthday of Empress Maria Theresa. That opera, *Semiramide riconosciuta,* helped to reopen the court opera, the Burgtheater, on May 14, 1748. Its text was by the celebrated poet and favorite of the Vienna court Pietro Metastasio, whose flowery dramas in the grand manner provided most of the great Italian opera composers of the day with their librettos. The opera, in the accepted Italian style Vienna liked so well, was a great success; the Empress, who attended, expressed unqualified enthusiasm.

For two years Gluck traveled about in various important European music centers where new operas by him, all to texts by Metastasio, were produced. Back in Vienna by 1750, he married that year Marianne Pergin, daughter of a wealthy merchant; he was to live with her until his death thirty-seven years later. He proceeded to solidify his position in Vienna, to become a favorite in the palaces—and a particular favorite of the Empress, who appointed him court composer in 1754.

All this while, Gluck was becoming increasingly dissatisfied with the kind of operas he was writing. He objected to Metastasio's texts, which were based on stilted and ornately treated biblical or historical subjects. He also objected to the kind of artificial music that was required for such texts, music calling for pompousness and the meretricious lyricism that could exploit the technical powers of singers. He felt a compelling need for simplicity and naturalness. Fortunately, there were two powerful figures in Vienna who thought as he did. One was Count Giacomo Durazzo, director of the court theaters. Durazzo was an admirer of French culture. As French drama and music were at an opposite aesthetic pole to the Italian, Durazzo encouraged Gluck in revolting against the long-held traditions of opera writing. The second ally was Ranieri de' Calzabigi, chamber councilor to the exchequer, and a poet who was also a believer in French art.

The three decided to pool their influence and talent in effecting a French reform in the Viennese theater. Their first collaborative effort was a ballet, *Don Juan,* introduced on October 17, 1761. Calzabigi wrote the scenario, which was based on a play of Molière's; Gluck wrote the music; Durazzo saw to it that it was produced. It was the kind of ballet that could be seen in the Parisian theaters, and thus was responsible for the infiltration of French ideas into Vienna.

The three collaborators now embarked on an even more ambitious project, an opera which would once and for all overthrow the influence of Metastasio and the established Italian tradition. And they created *Orfeo ed Euridice,* presented on October 5, 1762. Because *Orfeo* was new, it was not at first appreciated—it was not to be successful for another two years. But its authors were not discouraged. They were determined to be even bolder in their approach to the opera. *Alceste,* presented on December 26, 1767, was even more daring in carrying out the new principles of simplicity, economy, and directness set forth in *Orfeo.* It, too, was a failure; and so was the opera that succeeded it, *Paride ed Elena,* introduced on November 3, 1770.

Gluck was discouraged. "I flattered myself," he wrote at this time, 'that the others would be eager to follow the road I had broken for them, in order to destroy the evil practices which have crept into Italian opera and have dishonored it. I am not convinced that my hopes were in vain. The half-learned, the judges and legislators of art—a class of persons unfortunately too numerous, and at the same time of greater disadvantage to art than ignoramuses—rage against a method which, if established, would obviously endanger their criteria." But he would not desert his mission. "No obstacles will deter me from making new attempts to achieve my purposes. *Sufficit mihi unus Plato per cuncto populo;* I would rather have one Plato on my side than all the populace."

He decided on a change of scene. Marie Antoinette had repeatedly urged him to come to Paris; and in Paris, he felt, he might find a more sympathetic audience for his ideas. In 1773, therefore, Gluck left Vienna. But he had not escaped from struggles, misunderstanding, intrigues, and the fierce opposition of enemies. He wrote a new opera for Paris, still along the new lines, *Iphigénie en Aulide.* Its course was not smooth. Everywhere Gluck encountered opposition. There were those who resented the fact that he was a foreigner. There were others who were true to the Italian principles of opera. Continually, obstacles were placed in his way, and if it had not been for the intervention of Marie Antoinette herself, the opera would probably never have reached performance.

Iphigénie en Aulide, presented on April 19, 1774, produced a sensation. "At last a triumph!" wrote Marie Antoinette. "I was carried away by it. We can find nothing else to talk about. You can scarcely imagine what excitement reigns in all minds in regard to this event. It is incredible." The opera was the prevailing topic of conversation in the *salons.* Women began wearing their hair *à l'Iphigénie.* Receipts at the box office soared to unprecedented heights. In spite of all this, many of the French critics were not impressed. Some of them complained that Gluck lacked the gift of song, while others insisted that Gluck too often set to music episodes and incidents that simply did not lend themselves to music.

A presentation in Paris of *Orfeo ed Euridice* on August 2, 1775, was even more successful with the public than *Iphigénie en Aulide.* It now appeared that the victory of Gluck's ideas was established. But there were enemies in Paris no less powerful than those in Vienna;

and they were indefatigable in undermining Gluck's influence and prestige. When Gluck was engaged to write the score for a new opera, *Roland,* these enemies—taking advantage of Gluck's temporary return to Vienna—arranged to have one of Italy's most popular opera composers, Niccolò Piccinni (1728–1800), commissioned to do an opera on the same text. This maneuver so infuriated Gluck that he rushed back to Paris where he published a vehement letter of protest in *L'Année littéraire.* That letter was instrumental in splitting musical Paris into two warring camps. The faction on the side of Gluck was headed by the philosopher Jean Jacques Rousseau, who had formerly been a staunch advocate of the Italian tradition, but who had finally been won over to Gluck's style. "Gluck alone," Rousseau now wrote, "appears to set himself the aim of giving to each of the personages the style that is proper to him." The Italian camp found a spokesman in Marmontel, who condemned Gluck's music for being full of "harsh and rugged harmony, incoherent modulations and incongruities, mutilations, and so forth." When a presentation at the Paris Opéra of Gluck's *Alceste* on April 23, 1776, was a dismal failure, it appeared that Gluck's enemies had the winning hand. But then the Gluck forces countered with a successful presentation of a new Gluck opera, *Armide,* on September 23, 1777.

The battle reached fever pitch. "Women and men alike entered the fray," is a contemporary report from Baroness Oberkirch. "Such passion and fury were roused that people had to be separated. Many friends and even lovers quarreled on this account." Mme. Riccoboni wrote to David Garrick: "They are tearing each other's eyes out, for or against Gluck."

The director of the Opéra, recognizing the full publicity value of this intense rivalry, decided to capitalize on it. To settle once and for all the issue as to which style of operatic writing was superior—that of Gluck or that of the Italians—he commissioned both Gluck and Piccinni to write music to the same text, *Iphigénie en Tauride,* the two operas to be presented in swift succession.

Gluck's opera was seen on May 18, 1779. It was a triumph of major proportions. "I know not," wrote Melchoir Grimm after the first performance, "whether what we have heard is melody. Perhaps it is something even better. I forget the opera, and find myself in a Greek tragedy." The extent of Gluck's success impelled Piccinni to try withdrawing his opera from production, but he was held to his contract. His work was a fiasco. There could no longer be any question of the complete and unqualified victory of Gluck's ideas. "The works of Gluck," reported the *Mercure de France* in June 1781, "are about the only fortune of operatic music."

One more new opera by Gluck was produced in Paris: *Echo et Narcisse* on September 24, 1779. Gluck then returned to Vienna, to live there for the rest of his life, a composer whose greatness was recognized throughout the world. To his house in Perchtoldsdorf, on the outskirts of Vienna, the great of the earth came to pay him homage, among them Grand Duke Peter of Russia. Gluck was not only world-famous, but a man of substantial fortune. He died of an apoplectic stroke on November 15, 1787, and was buried in the cemetery of Matzleinsdof. The inscription of his tombstone reads: "Here lies an upright German man. A zealous Christian. A faithful spouse. Christoph Willibald Gluck. Of the Noble Art of Music a Great Master." The fact that the mention of his art was left to the last line did not disturb Romain Rolland, always a great admirer of Gluck's music. To Rolland it seemed to show "that his greatness was more in the soul than in his art. And that is as it should be, for one of the secrets of the irresistible fascination of that art was that it came from a breath of moral nobility, of loyalty, of honesty, and of virtue. It is this word 'virtue' which seems to me to sum up the music of *Alceste* or *Orfeo* or the chaste *Iphigénie*. By 'virtue' this composer endears himself to other men; in that he was, like Beethoven, something finer than a great musician—he was a great man with a clean heart."

Roland's personal portrait of Gluck is penetrating. It is well worth quoting in detail, for it provides a singularly illuminating insight into the composer.

He was tall, broad-shouldered, strong, moderately stout, and of compact and muscular frame. His head was round, and he had a large red face strongly pitted with the marks of smallpox. His eyes were gray, small, and deep-set but very bright; and his expression was intelligent but hard. He had raised eyebrows, a large nose, full cheeks and chin, and a thick neck. . . . He had little singing voice, and what there was sounded hoarse though expressive. . . .

In society he wore a stiff and solemn air, but he was quickly roused to anger. . . . Gluck lacked self-control, was irritable, and could not get used to the customs of society. He was plain-spoken to the verge of coarseness. . . . He was insensible to flattery but was enthusiastic about his own works. That did not prevent him, however, from judging them fairly. He liked few people—his wife, his niece, and some friends; but was undemonstrative and without any of the sentimentality of the period; he also held all exaggeration in horror and never made much of his own people. He was a jolly fellow, nevertheless, especially after drinking—for he drank and ate heartily. . . . There was no idealism about him, and he had no illusions about either men or things. He loved money and did not conceal that fact. He was also very selfish. . . . On the whole he was a rough sort and in no way a man of the world. . . . He had unusual intelligence in matters outside his art and would have made a writer of no small ability. . . . Truly he had so much revolutionary and republican spirit in him that there was no one to equal him in that direction. . . . Gluck allowed the courtiers to pay him attentions. At rehearsals he appeared in a nightcap and without his wig and would get the noble lords present to help him with his toilet, so that it became an honor to be able to hand him his coat or his wig. He held the Duchess of Kingston in esteem because she once said that "genius generally signified a sturdy spirit and a love of liberty." In all these traits one sees the Encyclopedists' man—the mistrustful artist jealous for his freedom, the plebeian genius, and Rousseau's revolutionary.

HIS MUSIC

Gluck was one of the most important pioneers in the evolution of opera. Through his theories, and through his application of those theories in dramatic works, he brought to an end one epoch and ushered in another. The epoch that passed was that of the Italian grand opera as stylized by the librettos of Metastasio. The plots were so intricate as to be often indecipherable; the poetry was euphuistic; elaborate ballets and pageantry were emphasized to the detriment of the drama; the characters were made of cardboard. And the music written for these plays was just as stilted. Meretricious arias dominated the score, their sole purpose being the glorification of the vocal flexibility and range of the *castrati* (eunuch singers); the accompaniments were formal; the music made no apparent attempt to interpret the text.

Against all this Gluck rebelled violently; for the intellectual revolution sweeping over Europe—transforming its literature, art, and society

—found in him an articulate spokesman. He wrote: "When one wishes to keep to the truth, one's style must be adapted to the subjected that is being treated. The greatest beauties of melody and harmony became imperfections when they are out of place in the whole." And again: "I do not by any means believe that you would gain pleasure in hearing a beautiful piece of music. I assure you, on the contrary, that you would have lost by it. For a beauty in the wrong place has not only the disadvantage of losing a great part of its effect but also of injuring the whole by leading the spectator astray, who then does not so easily find himself in a fitting position to follow with interest the course of the music drama." And finally: "Before I work, I try above everything else to forget that I am a musician. I forget myself in order to see only my characters."

In the preface to his opera *Alceste,* Gluck clearly and forcefully stated his position.

I endeavored to restrict music to its proper function, that of seconding the poetry by enforcing the expression of the sentiment and the interest of the situation without interrupting the action or weakening it by superfluous ornament. . . . I have been careful never to interrupt a singer in the heat of the dialogue in order to introduce a tedious ritornello, nor to stop him in the middle of a word for the purpose of displaying the flexibility of his voice on some favorable vowel. . . . I have also thought that my chief endeavor should be to attain a grand simplicity, and consequently I have avoided making a parade of difficulties at the cost of clearness; I have set no value on novelty as such, unless it was naturally suggested by the situation and suited to the expression.

He sought and he achieved an integrated unity between text and music. The play was simple and direct, unencumbered by lavish scenes, complex plot, elaborate ballets, or abundance of characters, with stress placed on human and emotional values. The music was just as lean and economical, always serving the drama, underscoring the emotions, emphasizing them, and interpreting them. Singers, chorus, dancers were assigned that role in the artistic whole that enhanced the play rather than impeded it. Decorative writing for the singer was eliminated; for the song and not the singer was now of first importance. Harmonic colors, rhythms, and modulations were called upon to increase the expressiveness of the spoken word.

By accomplishing these things Gluck ushered in a new era. It was that of the music drama, as distinguished from grand opera. No wonder, then, that many years later Richard Wagner spoke with such admiration and humility of *Alceste*. For *Alceste*—and the other great Gluck operas—made possible the emergence of *Tristan and Isolde*.

ANALYTICAL NOTES

Opera. *Orfeo ed Euridice* (1762) is the oldest opera to have remained in the permanent repertory. This is one of its distinctions, but not the only one. It may be regarded as the first music drama, the first successful conscious attempt to create an inextricable unity of music and text. But most important of all, it is an opera that achieves great emotional and expressive power through the simplest possible means. There are only three characters. The plot and action are the final words in economy. There are no big scenes, no magnificent climaxes, no majestic processions, no elaborate ballets; everything is reduced in scale; everything is unadorned, clear, and direct. And yet with the most elementary tools and materials Gluck built a monument. For *Orfeo ed Euridice* is not only a milestone in the evolution of opera. It is one of the most moving works of art in the operatic form. "There is no other opera in the world's long list," wrote the English critic Henry Chorley, "which, with merely three female voices and a chorus, can return to the stage in days like ours to make the heart throb and the eyes water."

The legendary tale of Orfeo and Euridice had been a favorite of opera composers long before Gluck. The man generally regarded as the first of all opera composers, Jacopo Peri (1561–1633) wrote *Euridice,* presented on February 9, 1600. His immediate successor Giulio Caccini (1546–1618) also wrote a *Euridice* in 1600. And the first of the operatic masters, Claudio Monteverdi (1567–1643) produced his most celebrated opera, *Orfeo,* on the same theme, seen in Mantua on February 24, 1607.

The text prepared by Ranieri de' Calzabigi for Gluck followed the traditional Greek legend with one major alteration: A happy ending was interpolated. Grief-stricken by the death of his wife, Euridice, Orfeo is permitted by Amor to descend to the other world to regain her. Only one condition stands between him and his beloved wife: He must not look at her until he has brought her back to earth. In the cave of the Furies, Orfeo appeases the evil spirits with his wondrous song. He passes on to the Happy Valley, where he finds his wife. He conducts her back to earth. But Euridice is convinced that her husband loves her no more because he will not look at her. She is so unhappy that Orfeo, forgetting the set conditions, looks at his wife and brings about her death again. But Amor pities him. Admiring the great love of husband and wife, Amor revives Euridice and permits the two to return safely to earth.

The male character of Orfeo is most frequently sung today by a woman because Gluck wrote it for a *castrato,* the renowned Gaetano Guadagni. A *castrato,* of course, was a singing eunuch so popular in those days because his voice had feminine range and quality, and he was capable of remarkable breath control.

One of the remarkable features of the opera—considering the year in which it was written—is its realistic tone painting, which heightens and intensifies the dramatic and emotional elements of the play. Gluck uses discords to describe the horror of Hades and the Corybantic of the Furies; and he enlists the pure silver voice of the flute, in an angelic melody, to portray the Blessed Spirits of Elysium.

The most famous aria in the opera is Orfeo's lament, *"Che farò senza Euridice?",* when he loses his wife for the second time. There are three other noteworthy vocal pages sung by Orfeo in the opera: his grief at the death of his wife when the opera opens, *"Chiamo il mio ben così";* his poignant plea to the Furies to pity him, *"Deh placatevi con me!";* and his song of wonder at the beatific beauty of Elysium, *"Che puro ciel,"* introduced by an eloquent oboe solo. The most familiar orchestral passage is the otherworldly music describing the Elysian Fields, "The Dance of the Blessed Spirits."

Gluck carried on his ideal to create a musical drama in the French tradition in *Alceste* (1767). Here Calzabigi adapted a drama by Euripides. Alcestis, wife of King Admetus of Thessaly, mourns the imminent death of her husband. In *"Grands dieux du destin"* she prays to Apollo to save the king's life. Stately music now brings to the scene the high priest and his retinue. He reveals that the king's life can be spared if somebody stands ready to take his place in death. In *"Divinités du Styx"* (the noblest aria in the opera), Alcestis announces her readiness to die in her husband's place. The king recovers, and his people rejoice. His own joy, however, is soon dissipated when he discovers that Alcestis must leave him to descend into the lower world in order to fulfill her bargain. He follows her, catches up with her at the gates of Hades, and tries to make her change her mind. But Alcestis cannot be swayed. Such devotion of husband and wife moves Apollo's heart, who permits the royal couple to return to earth.

Alceste begins on a note of sublimity without preliminaries: with an intrada, or introduction, of rare grandeur, intended by the composer to set the proper mood for his opera. It opens with descending chords in the orchestra, like the implacable voice of a relentless fate. An expressive slow passage for strings follows, occasionally growing in intensity of feeling. The music now quickens and surges on restlessly. The ominous opening chords return, and all earlier material is repeated.

The orchestral introduction (or overture) to *Alceste* is a symphonic staple. So is that to *Iphigénie en Aulide* (1774). This opera has a text by du Rollet based on Racine's version of the tragedy by Euripides. In a deeply moving address, *"Diane impitoyable,"* Agamemnon informs his people he must sacrifice his daughter, Iphigenia, to the gods, if the Greeks, temporarily halted in Aulis, can proceed to Troy. In an attempt to save his daughter, he tries to get her to leave Aulis by telling her that her beloved Achilles has been unfaithful. Achilles, however, assures her that this is not the case. They are about to get married, and Agamemnon, torn between love and duty, wavers between murdering his daughter and saving her. Parental love conquers. He commands his wife, Clytemnestra, to take Iphigenia off to Mycenae. But the Greek people insist that Iphigenia must be sacrificed to placate the gods, and Achilles is determined that his bride must stay in Aulis. Iphigenia, however, remains determined to sacrifice herself. She bids her people farewell in the most moving aria in the opera, *"Adieu, conservez dans votre âme."* Achilles and his followers come to do battle with the Greeks in an effort to save Iphigenia. Then Calchas, the priest, announces that the gods have been appeased, that no sacrifice is necessary. The people rejoice as Iphigenia and Achilles are reunited.

The famous introduction, or overture, has for its beginning a broad, funereal passage for strings which Wagner interpreted as an invocation for deliverance from affliction. The main theme is Agamemnon's air, *"Diane impitoyable."* This is followed by a heroic idea for full orchestra (explained by Wagner as an assertion of imperious will), and a sympathetic melody for violins, representing to Wagner the "maidenly tenderness" of Iphigenia. A fourth idea—stated by flutes and oboes alternating with strings—suggested "painful, tormenting pity" to Wagner. These subjects are elaborated upon as the music passes from dramatic force to tenderness.

Originally this introduction had no formal concert ending. To make the music available for concert purpose, endings have been devised by various composers. The one most frequently heard is that of Wagner: It is an adaptation of the opening funereal passage against the background of an ascending figure of four notes which is the opening phrase of the strong, decisive subject. At last only the ascending figure is heard, bringing the overture to its conclusion.

Orchestral Music. Gluck's two most famous works for orchestra—the introductions, or overtures, to *Alceste* and *Iphigénie en Aulide*—are discussed in the opera section above.

Another work representing Gluck on symphony programs is the so-called Ballet Suite, which is actually a free adaptation of some of the ballet music from various Gluck works made by the German conductor Felix Mottl. It begins with the courtly music that opens the *Don Juan* ballet. The gentle ballet music from the first act of *Iphigénie en Aulide* is used by Mottl as a contrasting middle section, after which the more vigorous page from *Don Juan* returns. The second section consists of the serene music of the Blessed Spirits from *Orfeo ed Euridice*. This is followed by the third section: a slow pastoral dance in three-part form, known as the musette; it is from *Armide*. The concluding movement begins with a festive dance from the first act of *Iphigénie en Aulide*. Once again, as in the first part, Mottl takes a contrasting dance as a middle section: the sedate sicilienne from *Armide*. A repetition of the festive music from *Iphigénie en Aulide* brings the suite to a brilliant close.

There exists a second Ballet Suite using Gluck's music. This one is an adaptation by François Auguste Gevaert, Belgian composer and musicologist. Gevaert took his material from just two Gluck operas, *Iphigénie en Aulide* and *Armide*. From the former come "Air," "Danse," "Tambourin," and "Chaconne"; from the latter, "Musette."

Charles Gounod

"Gounod created a musical language of his own, one of extraordinary sweetness, of wondrous fascination."

ARTHUR HERVEY

BORN: Paris, June 17, 1818.
DIED: Paris, October 18, 1893.
MAJOR WORKS: *Chamber Music*—String Quartet. *Choral Music*—Rédemption; Mors et Vita; Masses, Psalms, Requiems. *Operas*—Sapho; Le Médecin malgré lui; Faust; La Reine de Saba; Mireille; Roméo et Juliette. *Orchestral Music*—2 symphonies; Funeral March of a Marionette; Marche religieuse. *Vocal Music*—About 200 songs for voice and piano including "Ave Maria" (accompaniment, Bach's Prelude in C major), "Jésus de Nazareth," "Où voulez-vous aller?" and "Serenade."

HIS LIFE

When Gounod was very young he knew with finality that he wanted to become a musician. His father, a lithographer and a highly gifted painter, died when Charles was five years old. The child was raised by his mother, a pianist, who gave him his first music lessons. She placed him in the Lycée St. Louis, a boarding school, where the music classes were the ones that held the greatest interest for him. In his thirteenth year, he was taken to the opera for the first time by his mother. "I felt as if I were in some temple," he later recalled, "as if a heavenly vision might shortly rise upon my sight. . . . Oh that night! What rapture! What Elysium!"

He went to his mother and quietly announced he wanted to become a musician; that he wanted to abandon all academic studies. She could be sympathetic to such ambitions, being a talented musician in her own right. But she was the kind of levelheaded woman who could run both her household and her late husband's lithography business successfully. Her practical nature insisted on a good academic background even for a potential musician. Charles would have to finish his schooling before devoting himself to music. To implement this decision she went to the principal of the Lycée to enlist his co-operation. The principal called the boy into his office for a brief interview. Why did the boy think he wanted to become a musician? "Because I love music," the boy answered firmly. Did not the boy realize that the life of a musician was a hard one? "That makes no difference," the boy replied. "Then," said the principal, "you ought to give me some proof of your talent." He gave the boy a poem to set to music then and there. The melody was produced in short order. Then the boy sat down to the piano, improvised an accompaniment, and sang it. The principal commented quietly, "You are right. You will be a musician."

Gounod completed his academic schooling as his mother had insisted. Then, in his eighteenth year, he entered the Paris Conservatory, where for three years he studied counterpoint and fugue with Halévy and composition with Lesueur. He was a good student, and in 1839 (after three attempts) he won the much coveted Prix de Rome with the cantata *Fernand*.

The three years spent in Rome as the Prix de Rome winner brought Gounod into contact with Italian church music. As he was profoundly religious, this kind of music struck a particularly responsive chord within him. He attended the choral services at the Sistine Chapel. He made an intensive study of the music of Giovanni Pierluigi de Palestrina (1525–94), foremost of Italian polyphonic composers. Such absorption led Gounod to the writing of his own church music. He completed two Masses, one of which was performed in Rome in 1841, the other in Vienna—which he visited at this time—a year later.

After his return to Paris, Gounod became organist at a little church on the Rue du Bac, *Les Missions Etrangères.* His deeply religious nature and his intimate association with the church made him begin to think seriously of becoming a priest. He even began theological studies at Saint-Sulpice, started wearing clerical garb, and even designated himself as "Abbé." But he discovered soon enough that he was unable to desert music. The ambition to become a priest was discarded; as a substitute he once again directed his musical activity into religious channels by producing another Mass.

He would probably have concentrated on church music, with a random excursion into the symphonic field, but for a chance meeting in Rome in 1850 with the famous prima donna Pauline Viardot. The encounter seemed to have made a great impression on the singer, who did not forget it. She asked Gounod to write an opera expressly for her. Madame Viardot was not only a celebrated singer, but an influential figure in Parisian music; her request was not to be taken lightly, particularly by an unknown composer. Though he had never before tried writing for the stage, Gounod wrote his first opera, *Sapho.* Madame Viardot's influence was instrumental in having it produced by the Paris Opéra on April 16, 1851, with herself in the title role. It was not very successful, closing after six performances. But one critic—none other than Hector Berlioz, the famous composer of the *Symphonie fantastique*—referred to Gounod as "a young man richly endowed with noble aspirations; one to whom every encouragement should be given at a time when musical taste is so vitiated."

Between 1852 and 1860 Gounod conducted the Orphéon Society, a distinguished choral group. He continued writing music for the theater. The incidental music he wrote for a tragedy by Ponsard, *Ulysse,* presented in 1852, was a failure. So was the five-act opera *La Nonne sanglante,* produced in 1854, which passed into oblivion after eleven performances. His next opera, seen on January 18, 1858, was mildly successful: *Le Médecin malgré lui,* based on the play of Molière. But in 1859 came his greatest work, the opera *Faust.*

Faust was a child of misfortune. It was originally accepted by Carvalho, director of the Théâtre Lyrique in Paris. Unfortunately, a play on the Faust theme was being presented with spectacular fireworks and lavish scenery at the nearby Théâtre de la Porte Saint-Martin. Carvalho feared the rivalry of this successful Faust play and decided to delay his own production. While the opera awaited its *première*

Carvalho continually harassed the authors with suggestions for deletions and alterations. At least one of these suggestions proved fruitful. A song of Valentine was omitted to allow for the interpolation of a new choral number. Gounod reached into his trunk and withdrew a chorus from one of his other operas, *Ivan the Terrible*. This became the high point of *Faust,* for it emerged as the "Soldiers' Chorus."

At last the opera was put into rehearsal. But misfortune dogged its steps. The principal tenor, a fine artist by the name of Guardi, became sick and had to withdraw. As it was seriously doubted that anyone could learn the part in time for the first performance, Gounod offered to sing the role himself. But at the last moment a tenor named Barbot was found who could learn the part quickly; he proved to be a sorry substitute.

Then there was the problem of censorship. The censor feared that the cathedral scene might offend the Catholic Church and insisted on its deletion. Carvalho invited the Apostolic Nuncio at Paris to attend the final rehearsals, then brought the censor to him. Did the Monseigneur think that the cathedral scene would offend Rome? The Nuncio was emphatic that it did not; indeed, he would like many other theatrical spectacles to have scenes like that. That ended the trouble with the censor, who never learned that the Nuncio was blind.

Faust, in its *première* performance on March 19, 1859, was not an overwhelming success. Some did not like the way the libretto treated the Goethe play; some said that the opera was an experiment that did not quite come off. No publisher would issue it until a friend of Gounod prevailed upon a newcomer in the field, Choudens, to take a chance. The publication of *Faust* established the success of Choudens. The story is told that many years after the publication of *Faust,* Gounod met Choudens, who was wearing a handsome fur coat and a shabby hat. Gounod touched the coat and asked: *"Faust?"* A moment later he pointed to Choudens' hat and asked: *"Roméo et Juliette?"*

Although it had no major success in its first season, *Faust* did manage to receive fifty-seven performances. On March 3, 1869, *Faust* was revived by the Paris Opéra. Spoken dialogue was now replaced by recitatives; ballet episodes were interpolated. These changes helped no end. This time the opera was a triumph. It stayed in the repertory. In little more than half a century, *Faust* received more than two thousand performances in Paris alone. In London in the 1870s it was regarded as the most popular opera of all; just before her death Queen Victoria had parts of it sung for her. In the United States it was the opera selected to open the newly founded Metropolitan Opera Company in New York on October 22, 1883.

Germany was the only country in which *Faust* was, for a long time, regarded with dismay. The Germans considered it a shocking travesty of Goethe's great epic. To this day there are many Germans who look upon Gounod's opera condescendingly; and for this reason, whenever the opera is performed in Germany (which is not often) it is announced as *Margaretha* to distinguish it sharply from the Goethe poem.

After *Faust,* Gounod wrote eight operas. Six were failures. The two successful ones were *Mireille,* based on the Provençal poem of Mistral, produced at the Théâtre Lyrique on March 19, 1864, and *Roméo et Juliette,* at the same opera house on April 27, 1867. One has remained in the repertory—*Roméo et Juliette.* But he never achieved a second *Faust.*

As choral conductor, Gounod was inevitably brought back to his first love, religious music. He produced several Masses and many religious songs. But out of the great volume of music for the church created in a productive lifetime, one small gem has retained its primordial glitter: the melody "Méditation," or, as it is better known, "Ave Maria," which he wrote in or about 1854 to the accompaniment of the first prelude, in C major, of Bach's *Well-Tempered Clavier.*

Because of the outbreak of the Franco-Prussian War, Gounod left Paris in 1870 and for four years settled in London. He was greatly honored there, making personal appearances as conductor of his own works and helping to found the Albert Hall Choral Society.

He returned to Paris in 1875. Though he completed four more operas, from this time on he became more and more absorbed with religious mysticism in his music. His last opera was *Le Tribut de Zamora,* completed in 1880, and introduced on April 1, 1881. From then on he devoted himself exclusively to religious music, addressing himself to this task with such piety that at one time he spoke of creating one of his works on bended knee. His most ambitious compositions were the oratorios *La Rédemption* (1881) and *Mors et Vita* (1884), both of them receiving their world *premières* at Birmingham in England. The last work that engaged him was a Requiem. But, as had happened with Mozart before him, he wrote this Requiem for himself, for he was at work on it when a congestion of the brain attacked him. He fell unconscious on his piano. Three days later, on October 18, 1893, he was dead.

Here is how Howard Paul described Gounod's daily life in *The Musician* after paying him a visit a few years before the composer's death:

Gounod was a late riser. . . . He dressed with scrupulous care, and at home wore a black velvet cap and very finely made patent leather shoes. When his toilet was over, he repaired to his sanctum, drank a glass of milk, and sat down to a table to work in an immense room with a vaulted ceiling suggesting a church, and principally furnished with an organ, two grand pianos, and a fine musical library. He sometimes smoked as he wrote, then he received visitors, and at twelve o'clock he breakfasted with his wife. His afternoons, four days a week, were devoted to work, and he was not a persistent diner out, though he received numerous invitations. He was fond of passing his evenings at the opera, occasionally the Boulevard theaters, and now and again, by way of what he termed a naughty spree, he went to the broad farces at the Palais Royal. . . . He was exceedingly fond of walking in the Bois, and most Saturdays he attended the meeting of the Académie des Beaux-Arts.

HIS MUSIC

In the evolution of French opera of the nineteenth century from the artificiality and grandiosity of Meyerbeer to human appeal and economy, Gounod was a significant force. Others who worked in this direction (notably Bizet) had greater dramatic power and finer theatrical instincts than he: Gounod's weakness in the dramatic element was one reason why he produced so many failures, and so few successes, in the operatic form. But none of his colleagues surpassed him in sweetness of lyricism, expressiveness of harmonies, and refinement of style. These positive qualities more than compensated for dramatic weaknesses. When the spirit was upon him, as it was in *Faust,* these qualities were sufficient to enable him to create an enduring monument.

ANALYTICAL NOTES

Opera. *Faust* (1859) is one of the most popular operas in most places where opera is performed. It is not difficult to understand why. It has all those things which audiences look for and delight in in the lyric theater. It is filled with wonderful arias for the different voices, ranging in emotion from the tender and the nostalgic to the sardonic. It has rousing choruses and colorful ballets. Its music mirrors the play in its continual change of pace, from the dramatic to the sentimental and the tender, from the passionate and sensual to the spiritual, from the spectacular to the intimate. Whatever else one may say of *Faust* one can never complain that it invites tedium.

The legend of Faust has been a favorite subject for composers. Liszt wrote a *Faust* Symphony and the *Mephisto* Waltz; Boïto wrote *Mefistofele;* Berlioz wrote the dramatic legend *The Damnation of Faust;* Schumann produced *Scenes from Goethe's Faust;* Wagner conceived a *Faust* Overture. It is sometimes said—though with questionable authenticity—that Wagner intended writing an opera about Faust but was dissuaded only because Gounod had done it so well.

Although the musical versions of Faust are many and varied, there is one that comes to mind whenever the subject is broached—Gounod's lovable opera. The adaptation, prepared by Jules Barbier and Michel Carré, was derived from the epic drama of Goethe. But the opera text does not concern itself with Goethe's metaphysical ideas; it centers entirely around the love affair of Faust and Marguerite and the tragedy it brought them.

The story is well-known: Faust, the aged philosopher and alchemist, trades his soul for his lost youth with Mephistopheles. He returns to make love to Marguerite, betrays her, and deserts her. Her brother, Valentine, seeking revenge, challenges both Faust and Mephistopheles, and is killed. Marguerite meanwhile has killed the child that was born to her and must suffer execution. Faust comes to save her. It is too late. She withstands Faust's urging, swoons, and is carried aloft by the angels.

The opera literally overflows with famous arias, choruses, and instrumental numbers. In the second act, which is laid in the public square on the day of a village fair, there are three outstanding excerpts.

Valentine, Marguerite's brother, is about to leave for the army. He sings an invocation (*"Avant de quitter ces lieux"*) in which he expresses concern over leaving his orphan sister alone. This is followed by Mephistopheles' hymn to Mammon and Greed (*"Le Veau d'or"*). Valentine succeeds in sending Mephistopheles away. As the crowd is again seized with merriment and festive gaiety there takes place the celebrated waltz (*"Ainsi que la brise"*—"The Kermesse Waltz"), one of the most infectious instrumental numbers of the entire opera.

In the third act, which takes place in the garden in front of Marguerite's house, we have Faust's beautiful apostrophe to Marguerite and her home (*"Salut! demeure chaste et pure"*). Marguerite meanwhile is sitting at her spinning wheel. As she thinks of Faust, whom she has just come to love, she sings a tender ballad (*"Il était un roi de Thulé"*). She finds a casket of jewels that Mephistopheles has placed near at hand, puts them on deliriously, and inspects herself in the mirror, singing the famous "Jewel Song."

In the third scene of Act IV, which takes place on a square in front of the church, comes one of the best-loved of all opera choral numbers: the "Soldiers' Chorus," marking the return of Valentine. Meanwhile Mephistopheles and Faust come back, the former singing a mocking serenade under Marguerite's window (*"Vous qui faites l'endormie"*). In the closing scene of the opera, the trio *"Alerte, alerte"* is one of the opera's most poignant ensemble numbers. The trio includes *"Anges purs, anges radieux!"* in which Marguerite prays to the hosts of angels to carry her soul to heaven.

Roméo et Juliette (1867) is once again (as had been the case with *Faust*) a most successful attempt to make an opera out of its literary source. It is no *Faust* by any means, lacking as it does the sustained dramatic and emotional impact of the earlier opera. But Gounod, ever the sensitive and poetic melodist, has time and again soared to heights of eloquence in *Roméo et Juliette:* Juliet's justly celebrated first-act waltz, *"Je veux vivre dans ce rêve"*; Romeo's cavatina to Juliet in the second act, *"Ah, leve-toi, soleil"*; and the duets of Romeo and Juliet, *"Ange adorable"* and *"O Nuit divine."*

Mireille (1864) is remembered for its melodious overture and such soaringly beautiful arias as Mireille's waltz. *"Légère hirondelle"* and the farandole shared by Mireille and Vincent, *"Mon coeur ne peut changer."* This opera is based on *Mirèio,* a Provençal poem by Frédéric Mistral adapted into a libretto by Michel Carré. The

story takes place in the province of Millaine in legendary times.
Mireille and the basket-weaver Vincent are in love; but her father
wants her to marry Ourrias, the drover. The rivalry of the two men
for Mireille leads them to a consultation with a sorceress, during
which they come to blows and Vincent gets hurt. Thinking Vincent
dead, Ourrias escapes on a barge down the river Rhone. It capsizes
and sends him to his death. Also in the belief that Vincent is dead,
Mireille, sick at heart and spirit, seeks solace in church where she
collapses and dies in Vincent's arms.

Edvard Grieg

"The Chopin of the North."

HANS VON BULOW

BORN: Bergen, Norway, June 15, 1843.
DIED: Bergen, September 4, 1907.
MAJOR WORKS: *Chamber Music*—3 violin sonatas; Cello Sonata; String Quartet. *Orchestral Music*—Piano Concerto; in Autumn; Two Elegiac Melodies; Holberg Suite; Norwegian Dances; Peer Gynt, two suites; Sigurd Jorsalfar, suite; Symphonic Dances; Lyric Suite. *Piano Music*—Sonata; Lyric Pieces, ten volumes; Moods; Norwegian Mountain Tunes; Norwegian Peasant Dances; Albumblätter, ballades, Humoresques. *Vocal Music*—German Songs; Danish Songs; Children's Songs; individual songs for voice and piano including "A Bird Song," "A Dream," "Eros," "I Love You," "Spring," "A Swan," "While I Wait," "With a Primrose," "With a Water Lily," and "The Wounded Heart."

HIS LIFE

Grieg is a national hero in Norway, not only because he was its greatest composer, but more especially because he was the musical embodiment of the land and its people.

There are nationalist composers of other lands who turned, as Grieg did, to native songs and dances for stimulation and musical materials. But with few composers anywhere was the land and the music so inextricably one as it was with Grieg. Listening to Grieg's music we are suddenly brought into the world of Norwegian geography, sagas, customs, and people. We have in Grieg's works rustic dances and peasant songs, bridal processions and carnivals, pictures of folk life and village scenes, the sounds of church bells and mountain streams.

When Grieg was a boy, the great Norwegian violinist and composer Ole Bull (1810–80) said to him, "Do you see the fjords over there— the lakes and streams, the valleys and forests, and the blue sky over all? They have made my music—not I. Frequently when I am playing, it seems to me as if I merely made mechanical motions and were only a silent listener while the Soul of Norway sings in my soul." So too might Grieg have spoken many years later. It is Norway that made Grieg's music; Grieg was only an instrument. He too was the silent listener while "the Soul of Norway" sang in his soul.

When he was young Grieg did not think he would become a musician. And when he became a musician he did not know for a long time that he would identify himself completely with his native land. As a child he was dreamy and indolent. Inexplicable yearnings and soaring flights of imagination led him to unorthodox ambitions. At one time he felt he would like to become a parson; then, allowing free rein to his fancy, he decided he would be more than a parson, a biblical prophet. On another occasion he expressed the wish to become a poet, like the bards of old.

He preferred the dream world to the real one. At the Bergen school he was regarded as both lazy and stupid. He devised all kinds of ingenious methods for being sent home from school, or for coming to school late. He hated his studies and resented being a continual object of ridicule for his teachers. "At that time," Grieg later recalled in an autobiographical sketch, "the school seemed to me nothing but an unmitigated nuisance. I could not understand in what respect all the torment connected with it was to a child's advantage. Even today I have not the least doubt that the school developed only what was bad in me and left the good untouched."

In music, things went somewhat better. When he was six years old his mother playfully placed him on a high stool in front of the piano keyboard. He put his fingers on the keys and to his amazement produced musical sound. His first discovery that the striking of several keys could produce a concord of sound was a thrill he never forgot. One year after being introduced to the piano he begged his mother for lessons, only to experience disillusion when he realized that learning music meant long and intensive practice. His indolence rebelled against such application, and he avoided practice periods scrupulously. Fortunately his instincts and a natural aptitude for music made it possible for him to overcome some of the technical problems with a minimum of effort. By the time he was twelve he could play the piano acceptably; he also wrote his first composition, Variations on a German Theme. Proudly he brought his first brain child to school, with the hope of receiving that homage that he felt was his due. The children responded as Grieg had hoped they would. But this taste of glory vanished when he heard the teacher's reaction. "Next time," he said sternly, "bring to school your German homework, and leave this stupid stuff at home."

But Grieg was not without encouragement. Both of his parents were musical; his mother was a particularly fine pianist. They not only loved music, but were ready and eager to encourage their son. Ole Bull heard Grieg's first piece of music and forthwith pronounced it to be a work of genuine talent. He prevailed upon Grieg's parents to send him for further music study to the Conservatory at Leipzig.

He was fifteen years old when he arrived in Leipzig, found a room in a boarding house, and enrolled at the Conservatory. The Conservatory student was not much better than the Bergen school pupil. He was still lazy, shiftless, given to dreaming instead of study-ing. He resented practicing the exercises of Czerny and Clementi, avoided whenever possible the routines imposed on Conservatory students, and refused to accept as dogma the rules of the textbook. When Ignaz Moscheles, the famous piano teacher, ridiculed in class the music of Chopin, Grieg grew furious, for he had already come to admire Chopin as his favorite composer. However, Moscheles—and also Wenzel and Reinecke—were among the better teachers of the Conservatory, and to them Grieg was for the most part highly sympathetic. The pedants—men like the piano teacher Louis Plaidy and the harmony teacher E. F. Richter—he disliked violently.

His friendship with a few of the more industrious students of the Conservatory, among whom was the young Englishman Arthur Sulli-van (1842–1900)—later one half of the famous comic-opera partner-ship of Gilbert and Sullivan—aroused his industry and his ambition to do well in his studies. He went to an opposite extreme, working so hard at his studies by day and night that he undermined his health.

He developed pleurisy and for a while he was seriously ill; his left lung was permanently damaged, leaving him for the rest of his life in poor health and impaired energy.

After recuperating in Bergen, he returned to Leipzig, remaining at the Conservatory until his graduation in 1862. He finally achieved high honors as a student, and made an excellent impression both as pianist and as composer when he played some of his piano pieces at a public concert in the Gewandhaus. However, he did not like anything he had written thus far. His works were distillations of the German Romantic composers, and he knew it; he knew also that he would have to arrive at a more personal style if he was to achieve recognition as a composer. But he was at a loss to know what that style should be.

Back in Bergen he gave a concert of his works in the spring of 1863. It was highly successful and financially profitable, but it did little to give Grieg confidence in his music. Still in search of something—he knew not precisely what—he left Bergen to live for a while in Copenhagen, then the most active musical center in Scandinavia. He met and was encouraged by Niels Gade (1817–90), the dean of Scandinavian composers, who gave him valuable advice and criticism; Grieg later said he profited more from Gade than from his years at the Leipzig Conservatory. Gade urged Grieg to write a symphony, which he did. But the result, though it inspired Gade to lavish praise, pleased Grieg no more than his earlier works had done. He was still imitating the style of others.

Then, early in 1864, still in Copenhagen, Grieg became a friend of a young Norwegian musician named Rikard Nordraak (1842–66), composer of the Norwegian national anthem and a cousin of the celebrated dramatist Björnson. Nordraak introduced Grieg to a library of Norwegian folk songs and dances which he possessed; more than that, he inflamed Grieg with his own burning ideal to create a Norwegian music touched with the spirit of the Norse race. The two friends solemnly vowed to dedicate their lives toward freeing Norwegian music from its subservience to Germany and toward the creation of authentic Norwegian music based on folk sources. "It was as if the scales fell from my eyes," Grieg wrote. "From Nordraak I learned for the first time what the Norwegian folk song was, and learned to know my own nature."

Back in Bergen, Grieg started working to bring his new ideals to fruition. With Nordraak he helped found a Nordic music society, "Euterpe," which was concerned with performing the music of Norwegian composers, and which its founders hoped to make a forum for the dissemination of their ideas about national Norwegian music. Grieg also started writing music in a new vein—Norwegian music. His first effort in this direction was the *Humoresques,* for piano, Op. 6 (1865), dedicated to Nordraak.

At about this time, Greig became engaged to his own cousin, Nina Hagerup, a talented singer. Her parents objected to the marriage. "He is nothing. He has nothing. And he makes music no one wants to hear." Thus did her mother evaluate the young composer. Marriage, then, would have to wait. Meanwhile he would sublimate his love in music, by writing for Nina, in 1864, his most celebrated song, on a poem of Hans Christian Andersen, "I Love You."

In the winter of 1865 he visited Italy, where he met for the first time his distinguished compatriot, the dramatist Henrik Ibsen. He now completed his first work for orchestra, the overture *In Autumn.* Later on, when he showed his manuscript to Gade, the older man said abruptly, "This is trash, Grieg. Go home and write something better." However, when Grieg submitted the overture in a four-hand piano arrangement to the Stockholm Academy of Music it received first prize. One of the judges who voted for it was Gade himself, who had apparently forgotten his previous severe criticism!

While in Rome, Grieg heard the crushing news that his dear friend Nordraak had just died in Paris. The immediate result was to overwhelm Grieg both emotionally and physically. He collapsed; for a period his condition was serious. When he recovered, his determination to create a national Nordic musical art was strengthened; he would work toward that goal singlehandedly, as a memorial to his friend. Back in Scandinavia (in Christiania this time, because his beloved was there) he arranged a concert of Norwegian music on October 15, 1866, the first such to be held. Two of his own works were on the program: a piano sonata and the Sonata in F major, for Violin and Piano. There were also songs by other Norwegian composers, including Nordraak. The concert, because it was a novelty, was an outstanding success. It did much to further Grieg's career at the time. He was invited to be the conductor of the Philharmonic Society, which he led in several fine choral and orchestral concerts; he founded the Norwegian Academy of Music;

he was besieged with pupils; he had an audience to hear his piano recitals. Now able to support a wife, he married his sweetheart on June 11, 1867, despite her mother's continued opposition.

The cause for Norwegian music was not yet won. When the novelty wore off, Grieg's indefatigable attempts to win recognition for the music and the composers of his native land were met first by indifference, then by outright opposition. Two farsighted and idealistic men became his allies. But, unfortunately, one of them (Halfdan Kjerulf, teacher of Jenny Lind and himself a national composer) died; the other (the poet Björnson) was usually away traveling. Grieg, then, was mostly alone in the struggle, which grew increasingly severe. This difficulty in overcoming the phlegmatic reactions of Scandinavian music lovers to his self-appointed mission brought on depression and at moments a stifling feeling of futility. Nor were things made any easier for Grieg when his first and only child, a thirteen-month-old girl, died in 1869. But he would not give up, either as a missionary or as a composer.

This period of despair was suddenly and unexpectedly brought to an end. In 1869 he received a letter from Rome which brought him the warmth of encouragement and appreciation. It was from Franz Liszt himself. He had come upon Grieg's Sonata in F major for Violin and Piano, and was profoundly impressed by it. "It evidences a powerful, logically creative, ingenious, and excellent constructive talent for composition, which needs only to follow its natural development to attain high rank. I could hope that you are finding in your own country the success and encouragement you deserve; you will not fail of them elsewhere." Liszt finally urged Grieg to visit him.

A small Government endowment (had Liszt been an instrument?) enabled Grieg to make the trip to Italy to visit the master. Grieg played one of his works. Then Liszt impulsively took the music and played it at sight. "I laughed like an idiot," Grieg wrote to his mother in explaining his reaction to Liszt's phenomenal exhibition. Liszt's response was: "Well, what do you expect? An old hand like me ought to manage a bit of sight reading, don't you think?"

Giovanni Sgambati (Liszt's pupil) and Ettore Pinelli played Grieg's Violin Sonata at a public concert. Liszt, who was in the audience, helped create a warm demonstration for the work. A few days later

Grieg brought him a new work, his most ambitious up to that time. It was the Concerto in A minor for Piano and Orchestra. Liszt went through it with painstaking thoroughness, once again playing at sight, and was enthusiastic about its Scandinavian personality. The concerto received a triumphant *première* at the hands of Eduard Neupart in Copenhagen on April 3, 1869.

Up to 1874 Grieg divided his time between Christiania and Copenhagen (doing some conducting, some teaching, and a great deal of composing). He was slowly gaining recognition, both in and out of Scandinavia. The powerful efforts made on his behalf by Liszt and Grieg's German publisher, Peters, were instrumental in popularizing Grieg's music throughout Europe. Before long Grieg's piano music became something of a household fixture in musical living rooms everywhere. The prophet was also being appreciated in his own country. A Government subsidy of approximately $500 a year enabled him to give up all activities except composing, assuring him of a certain measure of financial security for the rest of his life.

In a few years Grieg's rapidly growing fame was further enhanced with the writing of his most popular work, the incidental music to Henrik Ibsen's *Peer Gynt,* which the dramatist had asked Grieg to compose. The music was heard in Christiania on February 24, 1876, in a performance of Ibsen's play, and was acclaimed. It was soon heard throughout Europe. Eduard Hanslick, the trenchant Viennese critic, went so far as to prophesy that Ibsen's drama would survive only because of Grieg's music, and to a certain measure he was right. To a great many people throughout the world *Peer Gynt,* today, means Grieg and not Ibsen.

At last, in 1885, Grieg had the financial means to realize a lifelong ambition. He had the villa Trollhaugen ("Hill of Mountain Men"), built for him six miles out of Bergen. It was a secluded setting of woodlands and mountains, overlooking the Hardanger Fjord, that was typically Norwegian, a setting in which Grieg could be at peace. On a rock overlooking the fjord he had a special hut for his piano and music, and there he composed. He lived at Trollhaugen for the rest of his life. It was not long before the villa became a mecca for the music lovers of the world. The stream of admirers was so steady that Grieg had to post a sign: "Edvard Grieg does not desire to receive callers earlier than four in the afternoon."

Not only admirers, but honors, too, now came his way: an appointment to the Swedish Academy in 1872 and to the Leyden Academy one year later; election to the French Academy of Arts in 1890; an honorary doctorate from Cambridge University in 1893 and another from Oxford in 1906. His sixtieth birthday, in 1903, was celebrated almost like a national holiday, with Björnson delivering two orations. Commemorative concerts were also given throughout the world. It was on this occasion that Grieg received the only tribute which touched him profoundly and which he valued: His bust was placed in the entrance of the Gewandhaus in Leipzig.

Most other honors he had dismissed casually, tossing the orders and decorations into a drawer as soon as he received them and forgetting them a moment later. He was a simple man, embarrassed by public marks of attention and homage. By temperament he was a hermit, preferring the monastic seclusion of his little hut overlooking the fjords and mountains of his beloved Norway to the activity of city life. Yet when he met the great of the earth, which occurred frequently in his later years, he displayed the poise of a cosmopolitan. He always met them on equal terms, for he was a passionate democrat. During the Dreyfus scandal in France he allied himself volubly and courageously with the persecuted Jewish officer. In 1899, when Grieg was invited by Colonne to appear with his orchestra in Paris, Grieg refused, explaining in an open letter that he could not perform in a country where justice was flouted so flagrantly. For taking this position he was later hissed in one of the Paris concert halls and he was the recipient of slanderous letters.

One of Grieg's friends, Gerhard Schjelderup, has left us the following description of the composer:

Grieg was of small stature, delicate but impressive. . . . His light blue eyes under the bushy eyebrows sparkled like those of a child when listening to a fairy tale. They mostly had a joyful though gentle and dreamy expression, but when roused to sudden anger or indignation, they could flash like lightning. For with his short, stumpy nose, the fine flowing hair, the firm expressive mouth under the strong moustache, the resolute chin, he had dynamic energy and an impatient and passionate temperament. As in Wagner's features there was in his a marked contrast between the upper and lower parts of the face. The forehead reveals the dreamer, the mouth and chin a strong determination to live a life of untiring activity. Grieg's astounding energy gave to his frail body an elastic and impressive gaity and more than once in his life he performed true feats of endurance.

He conducted two concerts of his works in London in May 1906. The demonstration of the English public was so effusive that he promised to return the following year to participate in the Leeds Festival. On his way to England for that event he suffered a heart attack in Bergen and was taken to the hospital. "This is the end," he said quietly to his wife. He asked that his funeral be modest and that he be cremated, with his remains interred in a grotto near Trollhaugen overlooking the fjord. A few days later he died in his sleep.

His request for a simple ceremony was ignored. He was given a state funeral. His body lay in state in the Museum of Art and Industry, as thousands upon thousands passed his bier to see him for the last time. An orchestra played some of his elegiac pieces, as fifty-seven representatives of foreign Governments and musical organizations placed wreaths near his body. More than four hundred thousand Norwegians lined the streets of Bergen when his ashes were taken back to the setting where he had been happiest.

HIS MUSIC

Grieg's music is deeply rooted in the soil of his native land. He molded his style and technique on the idioms of Norwegian folk music. Nordic polyphony gives his work its archaistic flavor; the tonal language of Norwegian folk songs and dances provides some of its primitivism. He rarely quoted folk song material directly in his music. So completely did he assimilate the idiom of Norwegian folk music that his own works inevitably acquired the physiognomy and spirit of his country's folk expressions. He was, of course, a profound student of folklore; he edited and published several volumes of authentic folk songs and dances. But in his creative work he was not the scientist, analyzing and dissecting his country's folk art. He was the romanticist, inspired by his background, his people, his country's music, inspired to create an art which expressed these things and yet remained his own voice.

Percy Grainger, who knew Grieg intimately, made an astute observation about him: a middle-class townsman, the composer was ineluctably drawn to the peasant even though he could not mix with him gracefully. Grainger wrote:

Grieg was much chagrined by his inability to identify himself with the Norwegian peasants and to feel at home with them in their daily life. Grieg was by birth and association a middle-class man. The genius in Grieg urged him to rise out of his middle-class beginnings into becoming an all-round Norwegian. So, as a part of this all-roundness, he tried to mix with the peasants—to take part in their festivities. On such occasions the communal beer-bowl is passed around the table and every feaster is expected to drink with it. But here Grieg's middle-class squeamishness found him out. "When I saw the great bowl approach me, its rim dark with tobacco juice, my heart sank within me," he told me. This urge "to feel at one with the peasants" is a more vital necessity for a Norwegian artist than a non-Norwegian might be able to guess.

This paragraph throws a new light on Grieg the artist. The townsman, or cosmopolitan, who would mingle with the peasant is seen in Grieg's music. The cosmopolitan was the composer of the sonatas, the Piano Concerto, the *Peer Gynt* Suites (even though here, too, we can occasionally detect echoes of peasant voices). The peasant is discovered in his native costume: the songs, the Norwegian Dances, the Ballade in G minor, many morsels in the Lyric Pieces for piano, the *Holberg* Suite, the *Scenes from Peasant Life*.

And Grieg was able to achieve in art what he failed to reach in actual life. In his nationalist music we have no feeling of the townsman's discomfort in the company of peasants; in his nationalist music Grieg identifies himself completely and gracefully with the masses. Their merrymaking becomes his; their mannerisms and idiosyncrasies are his too. His nationalist music is inspired, as one unnamed writer said of all Norwegian peasant music, "by the spirit voices of the fjords, the mountains, the waterfalls, the forests. . . . There is a bewitching fascination about these tunes; of a thrill of the deepest poetic sentiment, often a wail of profound melancholy. . . . It is the untrammeled outpouring of the inner lives of the Norwegian people; an expression of their character, their indomitable will, the dauntless energy, the deep feeling that are the natural characteristics of the Norseman."

But what is important today is not that Grieg was a successful nationalist composer, but that he was able to fashion the national idiom into enduring works of art. Hans von Bülow's famous description of Grieg as "the Chopin of the North" puts a finger squarely on the principal traits of Grieg's music. Like Chopin, Grieg was a miniaturist; like Chopin, he filled his music with poetic sentiments; like Chopin, he was singularly successful in writing for the piano. But he was no imitator, not even of Chopin. "Grieg," Lawrence Gilman wrote, "has individuality—individuality that is seizing and indubitable. That, one feels, is his distinguishing possession. His accent is unmistakable. His speech may sway one, or it may not; but always the voice is the voice of Grieg. . . . Grieg is thrice-admirable in this: he wears no man's mantle; he borrows no man's speech.

ANALYTICAL NOTES

Chamber Music. Grieg wrote only one string quartet, the String Quartet in G minor, Op. 27 (1878). The introduction to the first movement presents a motto theme that recurs throughout the work: It comes out of one of Grieg's songs from the *Minstrels* group, Op. 25 (1876). In the first movement the motto theme is found in the first measure of the opening theme. In the romantic second movement, dominated by a melody of folk song character, it provides material for the second theme. A brief intermezzo separates this slow movement from the fiery finale, which has the rhythm and personality of a saltarello and in which the motto theme is used in imitation.

Grieg produced three violin sonatas. The second, in G major, Op. 13 (1867), is a romantic effusion, full of ardent emotion—and with good reason. Written one month after Grieg's marriage to his beloved Nina, it speaks his ebullient feelings at the time. His best sonata is the third, in C minor, Op. 45 (1887). This is music of far greater sobriety, introspection, and poetic thought than its predecessor. It begins at once with its vigorous first theme (in the violin), for which the mellow second theme provides emotional contrast. The slow movement that follows is a haunting folk song with a contrasting rapid section. The rhythms of Norwegian dances dramatize the finale, whose two main themes, both lively, are first stated by the violin.

Orchestral Music. The Concerto in A minor for Piano and Orchestra, Op. 16 (1868), is Grieg's most ambitious work. And it is perhaps the only work in which he was artistically as successful in a large and spacious form as he was in the smaller forms.

The main theme of the first movement appears quietly in the woodwinds after an introductory drum roll and an important subject of descending chords in the piano. The piano takes up the theme. A skipping passage for piano and for orchestra then brings on the second melody, a poetic dialogue for the cellos and woodwinds which is repeated with greater feeling by the piano. The development section works out both themes, sometimes in a reflective vein, sometimes dramatically. A loud recall of the main theme introduces the cadenza, which elaborates on the main theme in an improvisatory manner. The coda, too, is built out of the main theme and its variation.

Muted strings present the melancholy song of the second movement. When the song is finished the piano engages in an improvisational monologue, answered by a soft commentary by the strings. This dialogue continues; soon the woodwinds join in. Then the opening song returns loudly in piano and orchestra. The mood grows calmer and the music ebbs away.

The third movement, which enters without interruption, is rich with the color, movement, and spirit of the Norwegian folk dance. Two dance melodies are heard in the first section. After a vigorous introductory passage, the first dance melody is presented by the piano and is taken over by the orchestra. The second dance follows, also in the piano. The second section begins with a theme whose identity with the Norwegian folk song is inescapable. It is heard first in the flute, then in the piano, and subsequently is worked out by both the piano and the orchestra. The coda, introduced by scale passages in the piano, builds up the first dance theme with rhythmic verve, both in the piano and in the orchestra. The folk song melody now returns in trumpet, woodwinds, cellos, and violas against robust arpeggios in the piano. The piano repeats this theme forcefully, then it is quoted for the last time by brass and violins. The concerto ends with forceful chords.

The incidental music to *Peer Gynt,* Op. 23 (1875), which Grieg subsequently adapted into two orchestral suites, was undertaken with reluctance. Ibsen came to him in 1874 for the music, but Grieg could not summon up enthusiasm for the project. For one thing, he knew that his talent was more lyrical than dramatic; for another, he did not respond sympathetically to Ibsen's poetic, allegorical drama; for a third, he did not believe that the play lent itself to musical treatment. Nevertheless he accepted. The writing cost him more effort and soul-searching doubts than any other work of his. In the end, almost as if in compensation, this music, begun so grudgingly and written so painfully, was to be his greatest success of all.

Grieg himself provided a summary of Ibsen's play in the preface to his Suite No. 2:

Peer Gynt . . . is . . . a character of morbidly developed fancy and a prey to megalomania. In his youth he has many wild adventures—comes, for instance, to a peasants' wedding where he carries off the bride up to the mountain peaks. Here he leaves her to roam about with wild cowherd girls. He then enters the kingdom of the mountain king, whose daughter falls in love with him and dances to him. But he laughs at the dance and the droll music, whereupon the enraged mountain folk wish to kill him. But he succeeds in escaping and wanders to foreign countries, among others to Morocco, where he appears as a prophet and is greeted by Arab girls. After many wonderful guidings of Fate he at last returns as an old man, after suffering shipwreck on his way to his home, as poor as when he left it. Here the sweetheart of his youth, Solvejg, who has stayed true to him all these years, meets him, and his weary head at last finds rest in her lap.

From the twenty-two numbers Grieg wrote for the play, eight were selected by the composer to form two orchestral suites.

The Suite No. 1, Op. 46, is particularly celebrated. It opens with "Morning," which, in the style of a barcarolle, gives a musical portrait of a sunlit morning, the air echoing with a mountain yodel and the tinkling of cowbells. This is followed by "Åse's Death"—Åse being Peer Gynt's mother—a threnody for muted strings. The third section is "Anitra's Dance," an oriental melody in the tempo of a mazurka. The suite ends with "In the Hall of the Mountain King," a march in a grotesque vein.

Only one movement of the Suite No. 2, Op. 55, is as famous as the four sections of the first one. This is the concluding number, "Solvejg's Song," a song for muted strings in Grieg's finest lyrical style. The three sections that precede this beautiful melody are: "Ingrid's Lament," "Arabian Dance," and "Peer Gynt's Homecoming." (There was originally a fifth part, "Dance of the Daughter of the Mountain King," but Grieg preferred that it be omitted.)

The *Two Elegiac Melodies,* Op. 34 (1880), is an adaptation for string orchestra of two Grieg songs to lyrics by A. O. Vinje: "Wounded Heart" and "The Last Spring." Both are lugubrious melodies touched with tenderness.

Two Northern Melodies, for string orchestra, Op. 63 (1895) makes highly effective use of folk song material with the utmost simplicity. In the first the cellos are heard in a slow folk tune after several introductory measures. In the second, the folk song "The Cowherd's Tune" is presented by the strings, and is followed by a peasant dance.

Piano Music. The Ballade in G minor, Op. 24 (1875), is one of Grieg's finest works for the piano. Walter Niemann, the German critic, has described it as "the most perfect embodiment of Norway and the Norwegian people, of its agonized longing for light and sun, and at the same time the most perfect embodiment in music of Grieg the man." It is not in the free rhapsodic form of Chopin's ballades, but is a series of variations. The theme is a plaintive Norwegian folk melody, presented at the beginning of the ballade. The variations that follow alter the melody into many different rhythmic and melodic designs, often—as in the cases of the first and ninth variations—music of compelling power and originality.

The *Lyric Pieces* (1867–1901) consist of sixty-six pieces collected in ten volumes—Op. 12, 38, 43, 47, 54, 57, 62, 65, 68, and 71. In no other of his works are there such a wide variety of feeling—from the light, the fanciful, and the capricious to the melancholy and the elegiac. These pieces are all miniatures; the shortest ones are usually the best. Many of them portray different facets of Norwegian life and backgrounds. Others are exquisite nature pictures. Still others are sentimental or romantic reflections. Among the best-known are: "Butterfly," Op. 43, No. 1; "To the Spring," Op. 43, No. 6; "Shepherd Boy," Op. 54, No. 1; "Norwegian Peasant March," Op. 54, No. 2; "March of the Dwarfs," Op. 54, No. 5; "Nocturne," Op. 54, No. 3; "Wedding Day at Trollhaugen," Op. 65, No. 6; and "At the Cradle," Op. 68, No. 5.

Four of these pieces were orchestrated by Grieg and assembled into the *Lyric* Suite, Op. 54: "Shepherd Boy," romantic music scored entirely for strings; "Norwegian Peasant March," for full orchestra, vigorous music whose main subject is a ponderous, rhythmic idea first heard in clarinets; "Nocturne," whose principal theme is given first by the first violins; and "March of the Dwarfs," in which a fantastic march tune (first given by the violins) alternates with an expressive melody (introduced by solo violin).

The *Holberg* Suite, Op. 40 (1884)—which originated as a work for the piano and was subsequently transcribed by the composer for string orchestra—was Grieg's tribute to Ludvig Holberg, founder of Danish literature, the bicentenary of whose birth was celebrated in 1884. In honoring the great Scandinavian of the past, Grieg decided to use musical forms contemporary with Holberg: a seventeenth-century type suite comprising classical dances. The prelude presents a vigorous melody against a restless rhythm. Three quick and graceful classical dances follow: the sarabande, gavotte, and musette. An affecting and emotional "Air" succeeds these dances; while of classical design, it has nevertheless an unmistakable Norse character. The rigaudon that concludes the suite is in the gay and light-footed early style of this Provençal dance, rather than the dignified dance of a later evolution. Although the forms were of the past, the musical writing is in Grieg's romantic vein. Thus this graceful fusion of the old and the new may be regarded as a kind of forerunner to the neoclassic movement of our own day.

The ever popular Norwegian Dance No. 2 also started out as music for the keyboard, though this time for piano duet. It is found in Four Norwegian Dances, Op. 35 (1881), which Grieg subsequently orchestrated. The second dance, in the key of A minor, has three sections, the first and last being a rustic dance tune, with the middle part fast and vigorous contrasting music. The other three Norwegian dances are in the keys of D minor, G major, and D major.

Vocal Music. Grieg wrote almost 150 songs which place him with the most important song writers to come out of Scandinavia. His earliest songs have a German identity, beginning with his Op. 2 (1862), in which he sets to music poems by Heine and Chamisso. A Norwegian identity begins to enter his song writing with "The Fair-haired Maiden" (no opus number) in 1867. Thereafter, Grieg wrote music for many Norwegian and Danish texts; and it is here we confront his song masterpieces.

His most famous song (though by no means his best one) is the one he wrote as a testimonial of his love for Nina Hagerup:

"I Love You," or "Ich liebe dich," poem by Hans Christian Andersen. This is the third number in a group entitled *Heart Melodies,* Op. 5 (1864).

Some of his subsequent song gems are to poems by Henrik Ibsen. These include "A Swan," "With a Water Lily," and "A Bird Song," found in Op. 25 (1876). Others are to poems by Aasmund Vinje, including those in Op. 33 (1873–80), two of which—"The Wounded Heart" and "Spring"—Grieg orchestrated and renamed *Two Elegiac Melodies.* But whether using Norwegian or Danish texts, his economy of means and mastery of technique are always combined with a lyricism whose simplicity, poignancy, and personality all spring from the soil of the Norwegian folk song.

George Frideric Handel

"To him I bend the knee. For Handel is the greatest, ablest composer that ever lived."

BEETHOVEN

BORN: Halle, Saxony, February 23, 1685.
DIED: London, April 14, 1759.
MAJOR WORKS: *Chamber Music*—Various sonatas for solo instruments and continuo; trio sonatas. *Choral Music*—Esther; Alexander's Feast; Saul; Ode for St. Cecilia's Day; Israel in Egypt; L'Allegro; Messiah; Samson; Dettingen Te Deum; Semele; Hercules; Belshazzar; Judas Maccabaeus; Joshusa; Susanna; Solomon; Theodora; Jephtha. *Harpsichord Music*—Capriccios, fantasias, fugues, suites. *Operas*—Rinaldo; Acis and Galatea; Giulio Cesare; Rodelinda; Alcina; Atalanta; Berenice; Serse. *Orchestral Music*—18 concerti grossi; various concertos for solo instruments and orchestra; overtures. *Vocal Music*—72 Italian cantatas for voice and continuo; various other cantatas for solo voice and instruments; 22 Italian Duets with continuo; English Songs; French Songs; German Songs.

HIS LIFE

Not once, but several times in his life, Handel was fated to see his seemingly impregnable position in music completely undermined; and each time he was able to rebuild that position more strongly than before. Twice he was swept from success to ruin. For example, in 1715, he was the most famous composer alive, but fifteen years later his popularity was dead and his onetime fame had dissipated to such a degree that he was faced with debt, disgrace, and possible imprisonment. He emerged from that overwhelming trial as he was to emerge from all disasters—proud and victorious.

During his fifties he came face to face with the realization that he was through in the sphere in which for so many years he had been uniquely productive and successful: opera. He faced this realization and found another sphere in which to achieve even greater triumphs than had been his before, that of the oratorio. Then came the greatest blow of all—blindness. He could compose no more. But this was no defeat. He continued his musical career as the incomparable organist he had always been and as a conductor of his great oratorios.

His ever changing fortunes—the cataclysmic or the benevolent—never stemmed the tide of his prodigious production. He completed forty-six operas, thirty-two oratorios, more than a hundred large vocal works, numerous dramatic pieces, and many, many solo instrumental and orchestral compositions. Perhaps more than any other composer he was able to prevent the realities of everyday life from encroaching on and interfering with his spiritual existence. When his mother died, and to nobody was he more attached, he could write a lighthearted opera, *Poro*. When, in or about 1737, he knew only despair, he could produce some of the most jovial music of his career, the comic parts of *Serse* and the spirited *Alexander's Feast*. Even more, when he was most viciously, ruthlessly, and unfairly attacked by envious and prejudiced cliques—and when these cliques seemed successful in their efforts to destroy him—he was most fertile, sometimes creating three operas a year as well as many other works.

It takes a tranquillity of spirit to divorce oneself from the turmoil of a hectic life and create uninterruptedly and with sustained inspiration. Handel had that tranquillity when he sat at his working table. It took tremendous courage and will to create when apparently one's entire world had just crumbled. Handel had that will. And it took moral strength to fight disaster again and again and over a period of several decades. Handel had that strength. Time and again, for some forty years, it appeared that his enemies had finally triumphed over him. Time and again he returned—now with a new opera, now with new singers—to reclaim his position.

It took courage for him to become a musician in the first place. His father—a barber who later became a surgeon—not only opposed a musical career for his son (he wanted him to become a lawyer) but also hated music, considering indulgence in it a sign of weakness. In spite of the restrictions imposed on Handel, he managed to learn to play the organ and the spinet. One story has it that a spinet was smuggled up to his attic by his sympathetic mother. Handel smothered the strings with strips of cloth and thereby was able to practice each night without being discovered by his father.

When Handel was seven his father took him to Saxe-Weissenfels, at whose ducal court his stepbrother was employed as valet. Somehow, at one of the Sunday services, Handel managed to play the organ for the duke, who was so greatly impressed that he filled the boy's pockets with gold and urged the father to allow him to study. Father gave his consent grudgingly. The boy was entrusted to F. W. Zachau, organist of the Lutheran Church at Halle, who was not slow to recognize that a genius had come into his hands. He gave Handel a thorough training in every phase of music and opened up to the student his fine library of musical scores. Handel studied with Zachau for three years. Under his teacher's painstaking guidance he became a splendid instrumentalist. Then, in 1696, Zachau confessed that there was nothing more he could teach the boy.

In his eleventh year, Handel appears to have paid a visit to Berlin, though why he went, or why he was allowed to go alone, has never been clarified. He electrified the court with his performances at the clavichord and the organ. The Elector of Brandenburg stood ready to provide him with funds for continuing his study in Italy. But Father Handel ordered his son back home. This musical nonsense had been allowed to go far enough. Handel reached his father's house just in time to be with him when he died.

Handel was now free to pursue music without interference. He assumed the office of assistant organist at the Halle Cathedral, and he wrote music for church services. But a strong sense of duty, or sentimentality, made him in 1702 continue his academic studies, as his father had wanted him to do. While he was attending the University of Halle, beginning a preliminary study of law, the post of organist at the Cathedral of Moritzburg was vacated. It speaks volumes for Handel's ability and reputation that he should have been offered the job. For Handel was only eighteen years old. Besides, he was a Lutheran and the church was Calvinist. He fulfilled his function as organist for a year with brilliance; already there were some who spoke of him as "the famous Handel."

He had become convinced of his destiny. Once and for all he abandoned law. Conscious of his powers, he felt the need for greater horizons than those found in Halle and its vicinity. In 1703 he resigned his organ post and proceeded to Hamburg.

At that time Hamburg was the seat of German opera, over which presided Reinhard Keiser (1674–1739), prolific and famous composer of German operas. Handel found employment as second violinist in the opera house orchestra. But it soon became obvious that a seat in the orchestra would not contain him. One day he substituted for an absent harpsichordist, giving unmistakable proof of extraordinary musicianship. He wrote a major religious work, the *Passion According to St. John,* which did not fail to attract favorable attention when performed.

On one occasion the venerable Keiser found he could not fulfill an assignment to complete an opera, *Almira.* (Keiser's dissolute extramusical activities were too demanding on his time and energies.) He turned the libretto over to Handel. Handel's *Almira,* seen on January 8, 1705, was such a huge success that Keiser, recognizing the presence of a formidable rival, became Handel's most bitter antagonist. When Handel wrote a second opera, *Nero,* Keiser immediately went to work and wrote a *Nero* of his own, to demonstrate that he was still the master. Actually he proved nothing at all, for his *Nero* and that of Handel were both failures. But Keiser, aroused, was indefatigable in discrediting his rival and in trying to destroy him. And he was successful. After *Nero,* Handel wrote no more for the Hamburg Opera, devoting himself to teaching and to writing music for his pupils. And before long Handel left Hamburg altogether.

Handel had aroused the envy of still another influential musician in Hamburg, and with consequences that might have proved fatal. Soon after Handel arrived there he developed a warm friendship for Johann Mattheson, a fine musician employed at the Opera as both singer and harpsichordist. As long as Handel was the obscure second violinist, Mattheson was fond of him and tried to be helpful. When rumor had it that a successor was sought in Lübeck for Buxtehude's post at the Marienkirche, Mattheson prevailed on Handel to join him in trying to get the post. The two young musicians discovered in Lübeck that Buxtehude's successor would have to marry the master's daughter before he could get the post; they withdrew politely. (A few years earlier, Johann Sebastian Bach had declined the same post for the same reason.) Back in Hamburg, Handel's rising star transformed Mattheson's unselfish friendship into undisguised jealousy. Their relationship became increasingly strained. In 1704 Handel directed a performance of Mattheson's opera *Cleopatra,* in which the composer sang the part of Antony. When Antony died, early in the opera, Mattheson insisted upon going down into the orchestra pit and taking over the direction of the opera from Handel. Handel refused. An ugly brawl developed in which Mattheson challenged Handel to a duel. Mattheson's sword split in two when it struck one of Handel's buttons; had it struck a more vulnerable spot, Handel's career would have ended before it began.

Handel had had enough of Hamburg, of its corrupt life, its envies and cabals, its petty jealousies, its rapidly disintegrating musical activity. In 1706 he left the city for Italy. His first Italian opera, *Rodrigo,* was performed in Florence in 1707 without causing much of a stir. In Rome, where a papal ban forbade opera performances, Handel turned in 1708 to religious music, writing an oratorio, *La Resurrezione,* which was introduced on April 8, 1708. (Arcangelo Corelli, then one of Italy's most celebrated composers and violinists, was the conductor.) It was a triumph. *"Il Sassone"* ("the Saxon"), as he was now called by the Italians, was one of the most talked-about musicians in Rome. In Venice, Handel scored an even greater triumph with the opera *Agrippina,* which at its *première* on December 26, 1709, had the Venetians shouting at the top of their lungs: *"Viva il caro Sassone!"* ("Long live the dear Saxon!"). He also aroused considerable wonder at his accomplishment as a virtuoso. Legend would have it that one evening he attended a masquerade party where, disguised by mask and costume, he sat down at the harpsichord to play for the guests. One of them was Domenico Scarlatti, himself a virtuoso of the first rank as well as an acclaimed composer. In this apocryphal story Scarlatti is quoted to have remarked after the performance: "He is either the devil—or *that* Saxon."

One of the many famous musicians Handel met in Italy was Agostino Steffani, Kapellmeister to the Elector of Hanover. Steffani was planning to resign, and he urged Handel to succeed him. Handel consented, assuming that position in 1710. Hardly was he installed when he asked for a leave of absence, to visit London. (One of the conditions of his accepting the post was that he be allowed periodic leaves of absence.) He arrived in London late in 1710, bringing with him a new opera—*Rinaldo*—introduced on February 24, 1711. *Rinaldo* set a new standard for Italian opera in England; and it established Handel's reputation there. Fifteen performances were given to sold-out houses. Its publisher made such a huge profit that Handel remarked wryly, "Next time I will have *him* write an opera and I will publish it." Indicative of its great success was the fact that Handel made both all-powerful allies and friends *and* enemies. In the vanguard of the latter group were the brilliant essayists Addison and Steele, who bitterly attacked Handel in the *Spectator*—Addison because he had himself previously written a libretto for an opera that had been a dud; Steele because he had invested in the theater where this ill-fated opera was performed.

But the allies were more potent than the enemies. Handel was feted, adulated, quoted, and sought after. He would have liked to stay in London permanently, but he had already overextended his stay and by mid-June of 1711 had to be back in Hanover. There he diligently fulfilled his duties as director of a small orchestra, teacher, and composer. But one who has tasted glory in London is hardly likely to be satisfied with Hanover. It was not long before Handel once again appealed to his Elector for a leave of absence. It was granted on the condition that Handel return "in a reasonable period." In the fall of 1712 Handel was back in London. This time he overstayed his leave by forty-seven years; he remained in England for the rest of his life, becoming a citizen of that country in 1727.

No musician of his generation soared so high. He was in London only a few months when he completed and saw produced two new operas. Although neither one remained long on the boards, his popularity was unimpaired. He was called upon to write the music celebrating Queen Anne's birthday and the signing of the Peace of

Utrecht (his first works using English texts), which gave him the status of a court composer, a status made more or less official when he received from the queen a life pension of two hundred pounds a year.

In 1714 Queen Anne died; she was succeeded by Handel's employer, the Elector of Hanover. Legend would have us believe that for a long time the new king, bitter at Handel's prolonged absence from Hanover, would have no traffic with him. The legend would further have us believe that reconciliation was effected through the magic of Handel's *Water Music*. For—so goes the familiar story—two of Handel's royal friends arranged a water party on the Thames and had the royal barge followed by musicians performing Handel's music. When the king discovered that this wonderful music was by his delinquent Kapellmeister, he forgave and forgot, restoring Handel to his good graces. Unfortunately, history is more prosaic. The *Water Music* was written in 1717, and not 1714 or 1715, and on the express request of the king. The king provided eloquent testimony of the high esteem with which he regarded Handel by engaging him as music master to the royal family, doubling his pension, and even taking him on a short trip to Hanover.

In 1717 opera in England was temporarily in a moribund state. Handel decided to accept an appointment as music master to the Duke of Chandos, who had some years earlier built himself a sumptuous estate at Canons, near London. This magnificent setting was the scene for fine music-making under the direction of Johann Christoph Pepusch (1667–1752), later to achieve renown with his music for *The Beggar's Opera*. Handel became Pepusch's successor. During the three years he worked for the duke, he produced anthems, masques, and other works for the stage, including the delightful secular cantata *Acis and Galatea*. At the same time, in his position as royal music master to the daughters of the Prince of Wales, he wrote harpsichord suites. One of them included the most famous piece of instrumental music he ever wrote, known under the nickname of *The Harmonious Blacksmith*.

A revival of London's interest in opera brought Handel back to that city and lifted him to the summit of his fame. A powerful group of opera lovers founded in 1719 the Royal Academy of Music in London for the purpose of presenting Italian opera. Handel was made its artistic director. Handel combed all of Germany for the finest singers,

and he wrote new operas. The *première* of the first of these—
Radamisto, on April 27, 1720—was an event of national interest. Seats
were at a premium; the king and his entourage attended. The great
success of *Radamisto* augured well for the future of the new opera
house.

But with Handel in an apparently unassailable position, admired
alike by royalty and the masses, opposition forces were gathering
their strength to overthrow him. The sad truth was that he, who had
the capacity of holding friends and winning the lifelong gratitude
and love of the underprivileged, could also make enemies. Those
who disliked him—whether because he was a foreigner; or because
he was so successful; or because he was favored by the wrong pro-
tectors; or because those working under him were abused by his
tyrannical demands—easily found in him material for either ridicule
or contempt. His very appearance had a suggestion of the ludicrous.
He was huge in size (they used to call him the "great bear"),
swamped in fat, bowlegged, and with a face sometimes described as
"horselike," at other times as "bovine." As he strode, none too gracefully, through the streets of London, he could clearly be heard mut-
tering to himself, giving expression to violent oaths in his absurd
and comical accent. In personal contacts he was known to be imperious, arbitrary, gruff, blunt, and given to violent tempers. He was not
polished in manner; a glutton, his eating habits were even said to be
repulsive.

The opposition forces gathered around the personality of the Earl of
Burlington, who wanted a return to the purer operatic principles of
the Italians. These forces brought to the Academy an exponent of
those principles, one of Italy's most popular and prolific opera composers, Giovanni Battista Bononcini (1670–1747). A spirited and not
always good-natured rivalry developed between Bononcini and Handel, each vociferously backed by his own coterie of faithfuls. For a
while it seemed that the Italian had the upper hand. His first opera
at the Academy, *Astarto,* was an immense success. Handel countered
with *Floridante,* which was only mildly received, whereupon Bononcini replied with not one but three operas, all acclaimed. But one
season later it was Handel who was on top. His *Ottone,* with the
extraordinary singer Francesca Cuzzoni, swept London off its feet
on January 12, 1723. Thereafter, Bononcini faded from the picture.
About all that has survived from this historic competition is a phrase:

"tweedledum and tweedledee." The Bononcini-Handel affair inspired the following bit of verse by John Byrom in which the phrase was coined:

> Some say, compared to Bononcini
> That Mynheer Handel's but a ninny.
> Others aver that he to Handel
> Is scarcely fit to hold a candle.
> Strange all this difference should be
> 'Twixt tweedledum and tweedledee.

If Handel was victorious it was, alas, to be a Pyrrhic victory. The Academy was about to enter on evil days. Its directors had depleted the treasury with their extravagance. Huge salaries, paid out to famous singers, imposed a staggering financial burden. Besides, the English public had grown weary of Italian opera. It had found a new fancy, the delightful satire *The Beggar's Opera,* whose topical text and popular tunes made it a travesty on grand opera in general and Handelian opera in particular. In 1728 the Academy went into bankruptcy.

The "great bear" would not accept defeat. In partnership with Heidegger he rented the King's Theatre, formed his own company, and set out to continue where the Academy had left off. With his customary formidable energy he wrote one new opera after another for his theater: *Lotario* (1729), *Partenope* (1730), *Poro* (1731), *Ezio* (1732), *Sosarme* (1732), *Orlando* (1733), *Arianna* (1734). But Italian opera had lost its audience. This fact alone would have spelled ruin for Handel. Besides this, a rival company had been set up under the sponsorship of the Prince of Wales to draw away from Handel not only his best singers but the little patronage he possessed. Handel closed shop, but only temporarily. Before long he was trying to win back his audiences, first in one opera house, then in a second. But it was hopeless. He faced bankruptcy, even debtors' prison. Worse still, financial disaster was accompanied by a collapse in health. First Handel was afflicted by rheumatism, then by an agonizing paralytic stroke; he even showed signs of losing his mind. Ironically, in Vauxhall Gardens they erected his statue, perhaps in memory of things past—almost as if that proud figure in stone (whose music was heard almost every night in the Gardens) was someone completely different from the Handel who was now broken in health, spirit, and financial resources.

But a rest cure in Aix-la-Chapelle worked wonders in rehabilitating his health and spirits. He returned to London with renewed energy and renewed determination. One or two new operas and one or two revivals of old ones, however, failed to win back his lost glory. He had to face it. He had come to the end of his career as an opera composer—and not only because he had lost his audience, but also because (he could no longer evade the truth) he had nothing more to say within that form. He had to find a new medium for his prodigious creative energy. His last opera was *Deidamia,* produced on January 10, 1741. From then on he was to concentrate on oratorios in English.

He had written his first oratorio, *La Resurrezione,* as far back as 1708. But not until 1732 was he to suspect that that medium held for him promises of great success in England. In that year there was revived a work he had written for the Duke of Chandos, *Esther,* Handel's first English oratorio. It was presented by a cast of children, with costumes and scenery. So enthusiastic was the audience that Handel decided to present *Esther* again, this time with professional singers. But the church forbade public stage representations of religious subjects. Handel therefore gave *Esther* in concert version, without scenery or costumes. The overwhelming response to this work led him to venture a similar kind of performance for another oratorio, *Deborah,* in 1733. With *Saul* and *Israel in Egypt,* both in 1738, oratorio found a secure place in English musical life for the first time. After 1741 Handel knew that he had found a new medium for his genius, and for him the greatest medium of all.

In 1741 Handel was invited to Dublin by the Duke of Devonshire, the Lord Lieutenant of Dublin, and the governors of three charitable organizations to direct a performance of one of his works for charity. For that occasion Handel produced a new oratorio, *Messiah,* which he had written in twenty-five feverish days. He found Dublin ready to cooperate with him to its fullest resources in the presentation of his new work. An excellent orchestra had been assembled, placed under the leadership of one of Ireland's outstanding orchestral musicians, Dubourg. Two choruses from leading cathedrals were enlisted, both painstakingly trained for the occasion. The solo singers included

Mesdames Avolio and Cibber, two of the most highly respected artists of the time.

Handel's fame had never waned in Ireland. He was overwhelmed by visitors who sought to pay him homage: Curiosity seekers crowded outside his house to peek through the windows and catch a glimpse of the great man. The *première* of *Messiah* was looked forward to with great expectancy. Long before the first performance every available space in the hall was taken. The Dublin papers begged the women coming to the concert not to wear hoops and the gentlemen to leave their swords at home, so that there might be a bit more space in which to move about.

Seven hundred music lovers crowded the Music Hall in Fishamble Street on the evening of April 13, 1742. (Technically this was not the first performance; one week earlier, on April 8, the last general rehearsal was open to holders of tickets for the regular concert.) Several hundred more swarmed outside hoping to catch a few strains of the new music. And the audience was profoundly moved by what it heard. "Words are wanting to express the exquisite delight it afforded the admiring, crowded audience," reported the *Faulkner Journal*. One of the Dublin music critics wrote as follows about the music: "The sublime, the grand, and the tender, adapted to the most elevated, majestic and moving words, conspired to transport the ravished heart and ear." After Madame Cibber had sung the air "He was despised" with particular eloquence, a Dr. Delany (mindful of the singer's notorious reputation for immorality) exclaimed, "Woman, for this, thy sins be forgiven thee!" The concert brought in about $1800, which was distributed equally among three charities.

On March 23, 1743, *Messiah* was introduced in London. On that occasion George II was present; he was so awed by the "Hallelujah Chorus" that involuntarily he rose in his seat and stood during the entire section. The audience, seeing the king rise, had to rise too and remain standing as long as their monarch did. What began as a spontaneous gesture became a tradition: Since then it has been habitual for audiences to rise during the singing of the "Hallelujah."

That first London performance provided no hint of how formidable a place *Messiah* would soon occupy in that city's musical life. (An expert in such matters recently computed that if a royalty fee were paid for every London performance of *Messiah,* even at the lowest possible rate, the sum would exceed $10,000,000!) It was not successful. Some resented having a work about the Omnipotent presented in a public theater, regarding *Messiah* as sacrilegious. Others disliked the use of prose, instead of a poetic text. Still others failed completely to penetrate through the originality of the music to find its beauty and grandeur.

In 1749 Handel presented to the Foundling Hospital in London a new organ, which he dedicated on May 1, 1750, with a performance of *Messiah*. Thereafter, for nine consecutive years, Handel directed annual benefit performances of *Messiah* at the Foundling Hospital. These performances helped to establish the overwhelming success of that work in London.

Messiah proved decisively that once again he was the "great Handel." And once again the tide of his production had the surge of an ocean. *Samson* came in 1741, *Semele* in 1744, *Belshazzar* and *Hercules* in 1745, *Judas Maccabaeus* in 1746, *Joshua* in 1747, *Solomon* in 1748, *Theodora* in 1749, *Choice of Hercules* in 1750, *Jephtha* in 1751. This outpouring of genius—which Arnold Schering considers the greatest period of all in oratorio history—found Handel at the peak of his creative powers. In this period he also wrote other works, such as the Dettingen Te Deum, written in 1743 to celebrate the victory of the English over the French at Dettingen, and the *Fireworks Music* for orchestra, completed in 1749 to celebrate the signing of peace between the English and the French at Aix-la-Chapelle. When the *Fireworks Music* was played for the first time, twelve thousand people crowded every corner of Vauxhall Gardens to hear it; so many tried to gain admission that traffic to the Gardens was held up for several hours.

Once again the giant was laid low by a blow that was not dealt by mortals. He was working on his last oratorio, *Jephtha,* when midway his sight gave way. On January 27, 1753, the *Theatrical Record* reported dutifully: "Mr. Handel has at length, unhappily, quite lost his sight." He was operated on several times, once by the surgeon who had tried to save Bach's eyesight, and with no greater success than in Bach's case.

Blind, Handel refused to concede that his life had come to an end. He gave concerts at the organ and conducted performances of his oratorios almost to his last days. He was directing a performance of *Messiah* in London on April 6, 1759, when, during "The trumpet shall sound," he felt somewhat faint. Neither he nor the musicians near him took this indisposition seriously. He even seemed fully recovered when, after the final Amen, he turned to receive a thunderous acclaim. But a few moments after the ovation subsided he fainted and had to be helped home. He was put to bed, from which he was never again to rise. "I should like to die on Good Friday," he said simply. He died only a few hours after that, early on the morning of Good Saturday. His last wish expressed in his will, was faithfully carried out: He was buried in Westminster Abbey.

Over his grave there stands a statue by Roubiliac which portrays Handel in front of his working table. On the table are his quills and the score of *Messiah* open at the passage: "I know that my Redeemer liveth."

HIS MUSIC

Few of the giant figures in the history of music were as productive as Handel. In the case of all other composers, the majority of their works are part of the living repertory. This is not true of Handel's works. What do we hear by Handel today? Of his more than forty operas only *Giulio Cesare* has become familiar in the United States, and this mainly since its revival in 1967 by the New York City Opera and the subsequent recording of that performance. Of his some twenty oratorios there is the *Messiah* to be sure, and to a much lesser degree *Israel in Egypt*. Most of the others remain *terra incognita* to most music lovers, except for random vocal excerpts. Several of his concerti grossi, the *Water Music,* sometimes the *Fireworks Music,* much less frequently a concerto for solo instrument and orchestra represent him on present-day orchestral programs. From his works for harpsichord, only a scattered handful are played—most frequently, *The Harmonious Blacksmith;* while from the mass of his vocal works, masques, and other entertainments little is remembered.

In short, though there is no hesitancy in calling him one of music's greatest masters, the present-day music world is not generous in keeping his music alive. This can mean one of two things: Either Handel has been too long overestimated or his music has been too long neglected. The grandeur and majesty of his best music can only point to the latter conclusion. Handel is more neglected than overestimated. What was true of Johann Sebastian Bach a century ago is probably true of Handel today. There are still immeasurable riches to be uncovered in the long list of his works.

For the first half century of his life Handel was primarily a composer of Italian operas. These operas are victims of a tradition that was already beginning to decay in Handel's day. Because he made no effort to change that tradition, Handel's operas have died with it.

The oratorios are a different story. There is much more in Handel than *Messiah* or even *Israel in Egypt.* On the rare occasions when we are privileged to hear revived such oratorios as *Judas Maccabaeus* or *Solomon* or *Samson* or *Saul* we are aware of the same titanic creative forces that move in *Messiah.*

When Handel stepped from opera to oratorio he was not moving far afield. The Handel oratorios are really Handel operas without scenery or costume, and in the English language. They are not essentially church music, even though they often abound with the deepest religious feeling. They are monumental choral dramas, built out of recitatives and arias of the greatest lyrical variety, as Handel was no longer constricted by the necessity of writing for specific voices. But there is this basic difference between the opera and the oratorio (indeed, between the Handel oratorio and that of his predecessors): The drama was also projected in mighty choruses, cathedral-like in their majesty. In writing the choruses Handel brought not only the fullest resources of the polyphonic art—used with such lucidity that its complexity often eludes the ear—but also a wealth of humanity and compassion.

Handel carried the oratorio form to such an advanced stage of structural and aesthetic development that to follow him in that field was to emulate him. He also created the English oratorio, thenceforth to become a basic part of English musical life. Before the revival of *Esther* in 1732, the oratorio form was virtually unused in England. The success of *Esther,* and the rapidly increasing popularity of Handel's subsequent works in that form, established the oratorio as an English institution. According to Paul Henry Lang* the Handelian oratorio glorified "the rise of the free people of England." Lang explains: "The people of Israel became the prototype of the English nation, the chosen people of God reincarnated in Christendom, and

* *Music in Western Civilization,* by Paul Henry Lang. New York: W. W. Norton & Company, Inc., 1941.

magnificent Psalms of thanksgiving and marches of victory in imperial baroque splendor proclaimed the grandiose consciousness of England's world-conquering power. The Handelian oratorios were entirely the product of English social and spiritual environment." To the English people the oratorio became a fitting substitute for a national opera. "The public which spurned his operas turned avidly to his edifying, colorful and massive oratorios, seeing in their monumental Biblical choruses its own triumphal progress and recognizing in them its own religion."

Oratorios were being written outside of England, too, and by composers other than Handel. There was, for example, the overworked cantor of Leipzig, Johann Sebastian Bach. These two giants dominated the music of the first half of the eighteenth century. They were born in the same year (Handel was four weeks older); they came from the same region in central Germany; yet they never met. Bach was the provincial who all his life functioned in a circumscribed area. Handel was the cosmopolitan who had traveled extensively. Bach was regarded condescendingly and was little appreciated by those around him. Handel, at least when fortune was favorable, was the monarch of all he surveyed. Musically, too, they were poles apart. Handel was the apotheosis of Italian musical culture; Bach represented and glorified the German. One was the genius of dramatic and lyrical expression, the other of religious thought. Handel was the realist, the human dramatist. Bach divorced his music from the realities of the world outside. Handel interpreted human experience, whereas Bach idealized it. Handel was satisfied with existing conventions and formulas and yielded to them. Bach rose above them when they constrained him, shattering all barriers that would stop the flight of his imagination. Handel wrote for an audience and was always sure of one; Bach wrote only for his conscience. Bach was the genius in every musical form he adopted. Handel—for all his flashes of greatness in the operas and orchestral works—was the supreme master only in the oratorio.

ANALYTICAL NOTES

Choral Music. *Messiah* (1742) is the greatest oratorio ever written. Huge in scale (it comprises fifty sections and requires two and a half hours for performance), sublime in concept, unfaltering in its eloquence, it remains one of man's most grandiose conceptions. Only an inspired man could have produced it at all, let alone in the incredibly short period of twenty-five days.

Detailed accounts of its writing reveal that Handel was such an inspired man. From the moment he started working on *Messiah* he was under an uninterrupted spell, in a kind of trance. He did not leave his house; he allowed no visitors to disturb him. The food that was brought to him was usually left untouched, and when he did eat something he would munch on a piece of bread without stopping his work. He did without sleep, too. When his domestics tried to get him to rest or eat he would answer them with ill-tempered and sometimes even incoherent retorts—his eyes blazing with a wild fury—so that they sometimes thought he was losing his mind. "Day and night he kept hard at his task, living wholly in the realm where rhythm and tone reigned supreme. As the work neared an end, he was increasingly inspired, increasingly tortured by the fury of inspiration. He had become a captive of himself, a prisoner within the four walls of his study; he strummed on the harpsichord; he sang; then, sitting at his work table he worked and worked until his fingers gave out. Never had he experienced such a frenzy of creation, never before had he so lived and fought with music."*

Never a religious man in the same sense as Bach, Handel became the God-intoxicated man while writing *Messiah*. When he completed the "Hallelujah Chorus" he exclaimed to his servant, "I did think I did see all Heaven before me, and the great God himself." Again and again his servants found him in tears as he put to paper an awesome phrase or a devout passage. And then, after the last monumental Amen had been written, he confided simply to a physician, "I think God has visited me." The exaltation with which *Messiah* was created is found on every page of the score.

Messiah is in three parts. The first contains the prophecy of the coming of the Messiah. This is followed by the sufferings and death of Christ. The concluding section deals with the Resurrection. To the text provided by his friend Charles Jennens, adapted from the Scriptures (there are some inclined to believe that Jennens' secretary, Pooley, actually wrote it), Handel wrote fifty musical numbers. Recitatives, arias, and chorales concerned themselves with the emotion rather than the dramatic implications of the words, providing such a

---

* *Tides of Fortune*, by Stefan Zweig. New York: The Viking Press, Inc., 1936.

variety of feeling—from compassion and pathos to serenity, spirituality, and ecstatic joy—that there is never a faltering of pace or lack of contrast.

The overture is in the French style, by which we mean it is in two distinct sections. The first part is slow and stately, played by strings, trombones, bassoons, and the organ. To August Kretzschmar this music depicts the world as yet untouched by the presence of the Messiah. The stately music yields to a quick fugal passage, played by strings alone, the vigorous theme being stated first by first violins before passing on, in turn, to second violins, violas, and cellos.

A recitative for tenor, "Comfort ye," is followed by a florid aria warm with the fresh breath of the vernal season, "Every valley shall be exalted." The chorus proceeds with a rousing paean, "And the glory of the Lord." Thus the opening sections of *Messiah* are already touched with radiance. Only a composer drunk with inspiration could proceed from this point to ever higher levels of greatness. In this first section we have other unforgettable moments: the compassionate bass aria "But who shall abide?"; the joyous melody for contralto "O thou that tellest good tidings to Zion"; the gloom of the bass air "The people that walked in darkness." After the exultant chorus "For unto us a child is born" there comes the "Pastoral Symphony," in which the Nativity is portrayed by muted strings in a gentle melody which Handel had heard thirty years earlier in Calabria and never forgotten. This is followed by such beautiful sections as the brilliant soprano aria "Rejoice greatly, O daughter of Zion," the overwhelmingly tender aria for soprano "He shall feed His flock," and the lighthearted concluding chorus "His yoke is easy."

The second part begins with a chorus touched with mysticism, "Behold the Lamb of God." In this part we have some of the most sublime pages in the score, beginning with the terrible sorrow of "He was despised," an aria for alto, passing on to the unutterable pathos of "Surely He hath borne our grief," for chorus, and to one of Handel's most wonderful lyric creations, the soprano aria "How beautiful are the feet." The music sweeps onward until the magnificent final chorus is reached—that incomparable song of joy which is also one of the miracles of polyphonic writing, the "Hallelujah Chorus."

It is incredible that the concluding part of *Messiah* should not seem anticlimactic after all the immensity that precedes it. We have only to hear the opening soprano aria, "I know that my Redeemer liveth"

—with its ineffable serenity—to realize that Handel is still capable of further elevation. A moving choral passage, "Since by man came death," and a recitative and aria for bass (remarkable for variety of color) lead to the monumental closing chorus, "Worthy is the Lamb." This concluding chorus is in three parts. The first alternates a slow and a fast passage. After this, to the words "Blessing and honor, glory and power," there comes a joyous fugal section. At last the chorus—and *Messiah*—concludes with a spacious, exultant "Amen." "These two abrupt and short syllables," wrote Stefan Zweig, "were to be built into a monument which would reach to the skies. One voice tossed it to another; the syllables became long and protracted, to be reknit again, and then rent apart, more glowing. Like God's breath, Handel's inspiration resounded in the concluding word of the sublime prayer, which thus became as wide and as manifold as the universe."

Israel in Egypt (1739), which preceded *Messiah* by three years, is an oratorio of somewhat different form and character. If it does not have the spiritual radiance and exaltation of *Messiah,* it has an overpowering dramatic impact. In its own way it is no less a work of genius than *Messiah;* Romain Rolland goes so far as to say that it is "the most gigantic effort ever made in the oratorio."

Musically it differs from *Messiah* on two major points. For one thing, it utilizes a Narrator, whose recitatives are used to explain what is about to take place. For another, it places so much emphasis on the chorus (in *Messiah,* Handel divided his most felicitous ideas between solo voices and the chorus) that the chorus is regarded as the principal protagonist of the work. In few oratorios is the chorus treated so prominently or, for that matter, with such variety and grandeur.

The Narrator is heard at once—there is no overture—"Now there arose a new king in Egypt which knew not Joseph." This is followed by a double chorus of epic design setting forth the lamentation of the Israelites over their bondage in Egypt. The Narrator returns to explain: "Then sent he Moses." The next six sections describe the plagues inflicted on the Egyptians. With amazing realism Handel finds the musical equivalent—either through rhythm, or harmony, or sonority, or orchestration—for the hopping of frogs, buzzing of flies, patter of hailstones, and so on. Program writing had never before been realized with such literalness and on such a scale. This first part of the oratorio concludes with five consecutive choruses describing the passing through the Red Sea and the jubilation of the Israelites at "that great work that the Lord did upon the Egyptians."

The second and concluding section of *Israel in Egypt* is subtitled "Song of Moses." One of the finest pages here is a duet for two basses, music martial in character, "The Lord is a man of war." But the chorus does not yield its dominating role. There is the proud and exultant double chorus "I will sing unto the Lord," heard early in this half of the oratorio; there are the highly descriptive choruses "Thou sendest forth Thy wrath" and "And with the blast of Thy nostrils"; and that page of music whose incomparable power and magnificence is such that Donald Francis Tovey has called it the greatest of all Handel choruses, "The people shall hear and be afraid."

Parts of other Handel oratorios are far more famous than the whole. As these contain some of the noblest melodies conceived by that master they are heard in our concert halls and have enjoyed numerous recordings. Among the finest excerpts—orchestral as well as vocal—from these lesser-known oratorios are: the four-part overture and the "Death Music" from *Saul* (1738); "Let the bright seraphim" from *Samson* (1743); "Wher'er you walk" and "O sleep, why dost thou leave me?" from *Semele* (1744); "Sound an alarm" and "See the conquering hero comes" from *Judas Maccabaeus* (1746); "Oh had I Jubal's lyre" from *Joshua* (1748); "The Arrival of the Queen of Sheba" from *Solomon* (1749); "Ask if yon damask rose be fair" from *Susanna* (1749); "Angels ever bright and fair" from *Theodora* (1749); and "Waft her, angels" from *Jephtha* (1750).

Handel, of course, produced a rich literature of choral music outside of the field of the oratorio. *Acis and Galatea* (1720) is a masque, text by John Gay with additional parts by Dryden and Pope. The story of the shepherd Acis, who, crushed by the monster Polypheme, is transformed into a fountain by his beloved Galatea, comes out of the seventh fable in the thirteenth book of Ovid's *Metamorphoses*. The masque consists of thirty numbers, beginning with the chorus "Oh, the pleasures of the plains" and ending with "Galatea, dry thy tears," also a choral number. Other notable choral pages include the one that closes the first section, "Happy we," and another that opens the second part, "Wretched lovers." Distinguished airs include that of Acis, "Love sounds the alarm," and that of Polypheme, "O ruddier than the cherry."

Handel made two musical settings of Dryden's famous poem in praise of St. Cecilia, patron saint of music, *Alexander's Feast.* Both are notable. One is the ode *Alexander's Feast* (1736), and the other, *Ode for St. Cecilia's Day* (1739). Though the choral writing is of a high order in *Alexander's Feast,* two of its airs—one for the tenor, and the other for the bass—are the most familiar pieces of music from this score: "War is toil ad trouble" and "Revenge, Timotheus cries."

The *Ode for St. Cecilia's Day* is the finer of the two works. There are twelve sections, beginning with an overture and concluding with a fugue. Natural phenomena are described realistically in the first vocal number, the tenor recitative "From harmony, from heavenly harmony." A choral episode precedes two effective arias, "What passion cannot music raise," for soprano, and "The trumpet's loud clangors," for tenor. Four more arias follow a march for orchestra. After the soprano recitative "But bright Cecilia" there comes an air for soprano and chorus, "As from the power of sacred lays," and the monumental closing fugue.

The Dettingen Te Deum (1743) was intended to celebrate the victory of the English over the French at Dettingen in the War of the Austrian Succession. The text comes from the Hymn of St. Ambrose of Milan in the Book of Common Prayer. Music which for the most part is full of pomp and ceremony, the Te Deum is made up of eighteen sections, beginning with the rousing chorus "We praise Thee, O God." Affecting pages for solo voices (such as "All the earth does worship Thee," or (for baritone) "When Thou tookest upon Thee to deliver man," are combined with stirring choruses, of which "To Thee all angels cry aloud," "To Thee cherubim and seraphim continually do cry," and "Thou art the King of Glory" are distinguished examples. The work ends with an exalted air for alto and chorus, "O Lord, in Thee have I trusted."

Operas. What has previously been said about Handel's oratorios outside of the *Messiah* and *Israel in Egypt* holds true for his operas: The parts are better (and more famous) than the whole. The genius who could scale the heights of nobility and eloquence in his oratorios still speaks to us in page after page of operas which otherwise, with one or two exceptions, are little better than museum pieces— faded relics of a dead tradition.

Unfortunately, Handel was content to work within the formal, stilted patterns of the Italian opera of his time. The absurd euphuistic texts (always on remote historical or legendary subjects), the lifeless characters, the absence of action were as much a part of the existing Italian conventions as were the dull and inflexible succession of recitative and aria, the florid melodies tailored for specific voices, and the superfluous pageants and ballets. Rameau in France and Gluck in Vienna administered the death blow to these conventions. As soon as the conventions crumbled, Handel's operas lost both their artistic validity and their popular appeal.

Bernard Shaw was fully justified in referring to Handel's operas as merely "stage concerts." They have no dramatic verity whatsoever. They are formal procedures by which Handel's ever wonderful airs could be heard. These opera arias, however, are among the noblest pages in vocal music, of a grandeur, a majesty, and a beauty which (for lack of a better descriptive term) we have since come to describe as "Handelian." There is *"Lascia ch'io piango"* and *"Cara sposa"* from *Rinaldo* (1711); *"Sommi dei"* from *Radamisto* (1720); *"Alma mia"* and *"Caro amore"* from *Floridante* (1721); *"Care selve"* from *Atalanta* (1735); *"Verdi prati"* from *Alcina* (1735); *"Ombra mai fu"* (the celebrated Largo) from *Serse* (1738); and so forth. Undoubtedly, these melodies, and many others like them, justify occasional revivals of Handel's operas.

The most frequently and successfully revived of Handel's operas is *Giulio Cesare in Egitto,* or *Julius Caesar in Egypt* (1724). It was revived in the ruins of Pompeii in July of 1952 with a cast headed by Renata Tebaldi and Cesare Siepi; at La Scala in Milan in 1956–57 with Giulietta Simionato and Nicola Rossi-Lemeni; at the bicentenary commemoration of Handel's death in Halle, Germany, in 1959; and by the New York City Opera in 1967.

Niccolò Francesco Haym prepared the text, which opens with Caesar's arrival in Egypt. Welcomed as a hero, he is given the gift of Pompey's head—Pompey having been murdered by Ptolemy, brother of Cleopatra. Shocked, Caesar denounces both the gift and its bearer, then pays tribute to Pompey by visiting his tomb. Cleopatra, in an attempt to win Caesar's love, arranges a sumptuous feast in his honor, and woos him with her seductive singing. When an avenging mob comes to demand Caesar's head he escapes. But in time he comes back to Egypt to crown her queen and to accept her love.

Donald Jay Grout points out that "in every case the realization not only of mood but also of personality comes from the music. . . . Only through Handel's music does his character [Caesar] receive those qualities which make him a truly dramatic figure." Once again, as had been the case with other Handel operas, affecting arias are the central points of interest: three delivered by Cleopatra (*"Se pietà di me non senti," "Voi, che mie fide ancelle,"* and *"V'adoro, pupille"*), and two by Caesar (*"Alma den gran Pompeo"* and *"Dall' ondoso periglio"*). Pages such as these, as Mr. Grout has said further, are "the direct emanation of Handel's own spirit, expressed in music with an immediacy that had no parallel outside Beethoven. It is the incarnation of a great soul."

Orchestral Music. The twelve concerti grossi collected in Op. 6 (1739) rank with Bach's Brandenburg Concertos as a summit in concerto grosso writing. Nineteen years earlier, in or about 1720, Handel had produced a set of six concerti grossi, Op. 3, after having met Arcangelo Corelli, father of the concerto grosso, and having become acquainted with Corelli's music. The Handel concerto grosso became, like that of Corelli, a several-movement work for string orchestra in which a small group (called the concertino, and usually consisting of two violins and a cello) was used in conjunction with the larger body of strings (known as the ripieno); sometimes the two groups were used in unison, more often in contrast to each other. A harpsichord provided an accompanying harmonic background.

When one listens to a Handel concerto grosso it is not difficult to recognize the Corelli parentage. But how the child has outgrown his father! In place of the all-too-formal treatment of light and shade in sonority, the more or less stilted alternation of slow and fast tempos, and the rather limited resources of melodic development and harmony, there is a wonderful expansion of design, materials, and musical line. As Paul Henry Lang remarked:* "The features are larger, the melodic arches wider, and the form and logic of construction more monumental in their straightforwardness. Once an allegro movement is started, it rolls along with the impetuousness of a

* *Music in Western Civilization,* by Paul Henry Lang. New York: W. W. Norton & Company, Inc., 1941.

mountain stream, while the broad pathos of the slow movements spins garlands around quietly ambling melodies."

While the Op. 3 set was stimulated by Corelli's concerti grossi, it represents a step forward for this structure: in the amplitude of the symphonic writing; in the independence of the passages for solo instruments; in the freedom of structure and even thought in some of the fantasia passages. The first concerto grosso has three movements; the second, third, and fifth have five movements; the fourth has four movements; and the sixth has two. A distinguishing feature in all these concerti grossi is the prominence accorded to the oboe.

Handel's most significant concerti grossi, however, are found in the Op. 6, of which the sixth in G minor and the twelfth in B minor are representative. Both are in five movements. The sixth begins with a spacious slow movement for string orchestra touched with melancholy, yet not without nobility; phrases interpolated by the concertino are an inextricable part of the design. A four-part fugue based on a chromatic chord follows; the chromatic theme appears in the first violins before passing on to the second violins, then to violas and cello. There next comes one of Handel's most famous pieces of orchestral music, a musette. A wondrous melody rises above a sustained drone in the basses, described by Romain Rolland as a dream of pastoral happiness. Two vigorous allegros provide the concluding movements.

Like the sixth concerto grosso, the twelfth opens with a solemn movement, a largo. In the vigorous allegro that follows, the solo instruments receive attention in themes with wide-spaced intervals. The third movement presents a two-part aria and variations. A lyrical slow section precedes the closing movement, which opens with a six-measure slow introduction for harpsichord and a four-part fugue.

The *Water Music* (1717) is a suite of dances, airs, fanfares, and so forth, written for a royal water pageant on the Thames. The event was described in the London *Daily Courant* of July 19, 1717:

On Wednesday evening about 8, the King took water at Whitehall in an open barge . . . and went up the river toward Chelsea. Many other barges with persons of quality attended, and so great was the number of boats, that the whole river in a manner was covered. A city company's barge was employed for the music, where were fifty instruments of all sorts, who played all the way from Lambeth . . . the finest symphonies, composed expressly for this occasion by Mr. Handel: which His Majesty liked so well that he caused it to be played over three times in going and returning.

The legend that both the water pageant and Handel's music were arranged to effect a reconciliation between the composer and George I has already been discussed, and disposed of, in the biographical section.

The *Water Music* as Handel wrote it—comprising about twenty pieces—is almost never heard any longer. As performed in our present-day concert auditorium it appears in an orchestral transcription by Sir Hamilton Harty which contains only six of the items. The first is an overture in the French style: A slow section, comprising fanfares and emphasizing the horns, is followed by a brisk fugal section. A poignant air is then heard, in the character of an old English folk song. Next comes a bourrée: a fast dance, two beats to a measure, which originated in the Auvergne region of France. A lively English dance follows, the hornpipe. Another song, gentle and mannered, precedes the concluding movement. The last is music of royal pomp in which horns and trumpets are effectively employed; a diaphanous and graceful middle section provides contrast.

The *Royal Fireworks Music* (1749) is also best-known to us through an arrangement by Sir Hamilton Harty made up of five movements. Handel wrote his *Fireworks Music* to celebrate the peace treaty of Aix-la-Chapelle, concluding hostilities between France and England in 1748. This celebration was to take place at Green Park, in London, on April 27, 1749. A fire, caused by the fireworks, destroyed the main building and dispersed the crowds almost in a panic. However, this did not happen until Handel's music had been played by a huge band comprising twenty-four oboes, twelve bassoons, nine trumpets, nine horns, one contrabassoon, three pairs of tympani, and a "serpent" (a now obsolete member of the cornet family).

Sir Hamilton Harty's transcribed five sections for symphony orchestra begins with an overture. The second movement, called *"Le Paix,"* or *"The Peace,"* is in celebration of the happy occasion, while the third movement—*"Le Réjouissance"* or *"Rejoicing"*—is intended to reflect the happy mood of the people with the coming of peace.

After that comes a bourrée, with a final movement comprising two minuets.

Though concertos for harpsichord and orchestra or harp and orchestra by Handel are sometimes performed or recorded, they are actually alternate versions of concertos which the master originally wrote for organ and orchestra. Handel himself had suggested that his first set of organ concertos, Op. 4 (c.1735), could be performed by harpsichord and orchestra, and that the second set (no opus number, 1749) might be given by harp and orchestra. However, he provided no alternate instrument for his third set of organ concertos, Op. 7 (1740–51).

The Concerto in D minor, the tenth work in the third set, is a familiar item on symphony programs. Slow and stately adagio music alternates with brisk, vigorous allegros in the four movements, beginning with an adagio.

However, perhaps the most popular of all Handel's concertos for organ and orchestra are not to be found in these three sets. One of them is the Organ Concerto in D major, which Sir Hamilton Harty adapted from an organ concerto he found in the Handel Gesellschaft Edition (Vol. 47). This work is in three movements: an adagio, an allegro moderato, and an allegro con brio. The other is known as *The Cuckoo and the Nightingale* because the voices of these birds are simulated in the second movement. In the key of F major, this concerto was published independently. In this work Handel uses material from his own Concerto Grosso No. 9, Op. 6, and from his Trio Sonatas Nos. 5 and 6. It has five movements, beginning with a larghetto and continuing with an allegro, adagio, larghetto, and allegro.

Piano (Harpsichord) Music. *The Harmonious Blacksmith,* Handel's best-known work for the harpsichord, now most often performed on the piano, is not an independent work. It is the fourth movement (an air and variations) from the Suite No. 5 in E major for Harpsichord. The air of *The Harmonious Blacksmith* is a pleasing little eight-bar tune in two parts; the five variations provide rhythmic and melodic alterations in the formal and routined manner of the seventeenth and early eighteenth centuries.

A legend has survived to the effect that during a thunderstorm Handel sought refuge in a blacksmith's shop. The even beating of the blacksmith's hammer suggested to the composer the air of *The Harmonious Blacksmith*—hence the origin of the title. The facts, however, are these: the nickname *Harmonious Blacksmith* was concocted not by Handel but by an enterprising publisher in Bath in or about 1822. And the publisher arrived at this piquant title by virtue of the circumstance that a blacksmith in Bath, fond of Handel's tune, always sang it at the top of his voice and came to be known in his neighborhood as the "harmonious blacksmith."

Howard Hanson

> "Hanson is not a chauvinist; he is not an advocate of a 'nationalist' school. To him, American music means music written by Americans."
>
> JOHN TASKER HOWARD

BORN: Wahoo, Nebraska, October 28, 1896.

DIED: Rochester, New York, February 26, 1981.

MAJOR WORKS: *Chamber Music*—Piano Quintet; String Quartet; Concerto da Camera for Piano and Strings. *Choral Music*— The Lament for Beowulf; Heroic Elegy; Hymn for the Pioneers; How Excellent Thy Name; Song of Democracy; The Song of Human Rights; Two Psalms; Streams in the Desert; The Mystic Trumpeter; New Land, New Covenant. *Opera*— Merry Mount. *Orchestral Music*—6 symphonies; Lux Aeterna; Pan and the Priest; Fantasy for String Orchestra; Piano Concerto; Pastoral for Oboe and Strings; Fantasy-Variations on a Theme of Youth; Elegy; Mosaics; Summer Seascape; Bold Island Suite; Dies Natalis. *Piano Music*—Sonata; Scandinavian Suite; Three Etudes; Two Yuletide Pieces. *Vocal Music*— Three Songs from Walt Whitman; Two Songs from the Rubaiyat; Three Swedish Folk Songs; Three Swedish Songs.

HIS LIFE

At the approach to the town of Wahoo, Nebraska, there is displayed prominently a sign reading: "Wahoo, Birthplace of Howard Hanson." Many of those who drive through Wahoo and are attracted by this sign might be startled to discover that Howard Hanson, thus being honored by his birthplace, is not a war hero, an ex-congressman, or some founding father; that he is a composer, a composer of serious music, and (most incredible of all) a *living* composer.

Wahoo is a Midwestern city which, in the days gone by, was settled by Swedish pioneers. Hanson's parents were also Swedish. The ancestral blood that flows in Hanson's veins was responsible for his writing such works as the *Nordic* Symphony (a tribute to the motherland of Hanson's parents), the Symphony No. 3 (homage to the spiritual contributions made to America by the Swedish people), the early tone poem *North and West,* and the choral *Hymn for the Pioneers.* For Hanson keenly feels the influence of his heredity and early environment; despite his world travel he has never shaken loose from them.

Both the study of music with his mother and attempts at composition began early, the former when he was six, the latter a year after that. His musical appetite whetted, he organized a string quartet when he was nine, playing the cello because none of his other friends could play that instrument. While attending Wahoo's high school, he enrolled at the School of Music at Luther College for the study of the piano and cello, and harmony and counterpoint. His extracurricular activities included the conducting of the school orchestra. When he completed his courses at Luther College he was given special permission to graduate, since he was not yet seventeen; nevertheless, he was graduated with highest honors.

For about six months he traveled about Nebraska playing the cello and saving his money so that he might have the funds to continue his music study at the Institute of Musical Art in New York. For a year he studied the piano there with James Friskin and composition with Percy Goetschius. Then, having gathered some more funds by spending the summer months playing the cello again, he came to Northwestern University in Evanston, Illinois, where he received a Bachelor of Arts degree.

He was only twenty when he was appointed professor of theory and composition at the College of the Pacific in San Jose, California. As if this were not sufficient evidence of precocity, he became dean of the Conservatory of Fine Arts when he was twenty-one, becoming the youngest man in the country to serve as the dean of a school of music. He had also begun to write music seriously, completing the *Symphonic Prelude* in 1916, the *Symphonic Legend* in 1917, and the *Symphonic Rhapsody* in 1919; the *Legend* was heard in San Francisco in 1917, and the *Rhapsody* in Los Angeles in 1919. He also completed in 1920 music for the *California Forest Play,* which he conducted at the open-air festival under the giant redwood trees.

In 1920 a jury of the American Academy of Rome had been formed for the purpose of giving gifted young American composers the benefit of Italian study and background. Having read an announcement about this, Hanson submitted both his tone poem and his score for the *California Forest Play.* He was accepted, becoming the first Fellow.

He spent three years in Rome, where his most vital musical experiences were derived from the Italian church music of the past, of which he made an intensive study. In Italy he wrote a tone poem, *Lux Aeterna,* which he introduced at an Augusteo concert in Rome. He also wrote his Symphony No. 1, the *Nordic,* and directed its *première* performance in Rome on May 20, 1923. Back in the United States in 1924, he directed the American *première* of his *Nordic* Symphony in Rochester, New York, on March 19, 1924. The work made a good impression. It was instrumental in bringing him to the attention of George Eastman, head of the powerful Eastman-Kodak Company located in Rochester, and the patron who had generously provided several million dollars for the establishment of the Eastman School of Music in the same city. Eastman was so impressed by both Hanson's music and his personality that despite the musician's comparative youth—he was only twenty-eight—he appointed him director of the school.

Eastman's faith in Hanson was fully justified. Under Hanson's direction the Eastman School of Music became one of the leading and most progressive musical institutions of learning in the country. From its halls emerged many promising young men of music, such as David Diamond, Gardner Read, William Bergsma, and Bernard Rogers. But this was not the full extent of Hanson's achievements. On May 1, 1925, he inaugurated the American Composer's Concerts (a daring adventure at a time when contemporary American music was being comparatively ignored)—a festival devoted entirely to American composers. This became an annual event. By the time Hanson retired from the Eastman School of Music, this festival had given a hearing to some fifteen hundred compositions by seven hundred composers, many of them *premières.*

Between November 1961 and February 1962, Hanson took the Eastman School Orchestra on a tour of Europe, the Middle East, and the Soviet Union, under the auspices of the State Department. Hanson was also financed by the Oberlaender Trust of the Carl Schurz Memorial Foundation to appear as a guest conductor of leading German orchestras in all-American programs. Meanwhile, through the years, he was also a tireless advocate of the American composer during his many appearances as guest conductor of most of the major American symphony orchestras.

Just as his conducting activity was not confined to his work with the Eastman School Orchestra, so his contributions to pedagogy were not reserved exclusively for the Eastman School during his forty years as its director. He also served as president of the National Music Council, as chairman of the Commission on Graduate Study of the National Association of the Schools of Music, as member of the National Guild for Community Schools, and as director of the Institute of American Music.

Hanson's activities as a musical administrator, teacher, and conductor notwithstanding, he was indefatigable in the writing of ambitious musical works. The first major work he completed following his return to the United States in 1924 was *The Lament for Beowulf*, for chorus and orchestra, a setting of *Beowulf* as translated by William Morris and A. J. Wyatt. "My intention," the composer explained, "has been to realize in the music the austerity and stoicism and the heroic atmosphere of the poem. This is true Anglo-Saxon poetry and may well serve as the basis for music composed by an American." *The Lament for Beowulf* was heard at the Ann Arbor Festival in 1926.

His choral and orchestral music after that was performed by most of the major musical organizations of the United States, bringing him to the front rank of living American composers. In 1933 came his only opera, *Merry Mount*, text by Richard L. Stokes based on Nathaniel Hawthorne's story *The Maypole of Merry Mount*. Set in New England in 1625, the opera tells the story of the passionate love of Pastor Bradford, a Puritan clergyman, for Lady Marigold Sandys, a Cavalier woman. Both meet death within the flames of a church when Indians attack and set fire to the settlement. The opera's staged *première*—at the Metropolitan Opera House on February 10, 1934—was an event attracting nationwide attention. (It had previously been heard in a concert version at Ann Arbor, Michigan, on May 20, 1933.) Headlines in the New York newspapers reported that it was given a "stirring ovation—reception most enthusiastic of ten years at the Metropolitan," that "fifty curtain calls cap opening." The critics found Hanson's rich and varied lyricism especially to their liking, a lyricism that spilled over from the solo vocal pages into the choruses and the dances.

Ten years later Hanson's Symphony No. 4 became the first such work to win the Pulitzer Prize. Among the other awards and honors that Hanson accumulated through the years are about twenty honorary degrees, the first such being a doctorate in music from Northwestern University in 1924, and one of the latest a similar degree from the University of Michigan in 1960. He was also elected member of the National Institute of Arts and Letters (1935); appointed Fellow of the Royal Academy of Music in Sweden (1938); presented the Ditson Award for "unfailing service to American music" (1945), together with a Peabody Award (1946) and a citation from the National Federation of Music Clubs (1957); and awarded the Medal of Honor from the National Arts Club for "notable and inspired contribution to music" (1962).

On July 24, 1946, Hanson married Margaret Elizabeth Nelson— his first marriage. They maintained their permanent home in Rochester, New York, even after 1964 when Hanson retired as director of the Eastman School of Music. (Upon his retirement, he was made director of the then newly founded Institute of American Music of the University of Rochester, which joined forces with the Eastman School to sponsor the annual American Music Festival, which Hanson continued to direct and whose programs he continued to select.)

Summers were spent by the Hansons (and their dogs, Peter Bolshoi and Tamara) on Bold Island, off the coast of Maine. Here Hanson could indulge in his favorite sports, swimming and boating. His height of over six feet, his dignified demeanor, and the short, pointed beard he wore since he was twenty-four all combined to give the false impression that this was a cold, austere, and forbidding man, which was most certainly not the case. Hanson had great warmth and affection, was highly gregarious, and made friends easily and kept them permanently. Outside music and his outdoor sports, his main interests embraced literature (non-fiction for the most part), mathematics, and an occasional game of cards (poker or hearts). He died in Rochester, New York, on February 26, 1981.

HIS MUSIC

The titles Hanson gave to his first two symphonies can serve to point up two essential traits of his musical style. The Symphony No. 2 is the *Romantic*. And there is little question but that, in all his works, he was essentially a romanticist concerned primarily with divulging his emotional responses in music that has melodic and harmonic warmth and graciousness. His Symphony No. 1 is called *Nordic,* and this describes a secondary quality of his music, the restraint in instrumental color and the somewhat exotic character of so many of his modal melodies.

He said: "My music springs from the soil of the American Midwest. It is music of the plains rather than of the city and reflects, I believe, something of the broad prairies of my native Nebraska." It was this faith in the essential American identity of his music—a faith which, it can be added, was completely justified—that made him dismiss impatiently any attempt to label him an "American Sibelius." "It may be of interest," he wrote, "that my *Nordic* Symphony, which first gained for me the title, was written *before* I was familiar with the music of Sibelius!"

ANALYTICAL NOTES

Orchestral Music. While it is a comparatively early work, the Symphony No. 2, *Romantic,* Op. 30 (1930), represents its composer in his full maturity. He wrote it in 1930 on a commission from the Boston Symphony Orchestra to celebrate its fiftieth anniversary, and that orchestra under Serge Koussevitzky presented the world *première* on November 28, 1930. Since then the work has been directed by most of the celebrated conductors in the United States.

A slow introduction precedes the appearance of the first principal theme of the first movement. This theme is presented by four horns in unison. After several transitional ideas (the most important being a quiet theme for oboe) the secondary theme of the movement is heard in the strings with a countersubject in the solo horn. The development that follows pays considerable attention to the transitional subject as well as to the two main themes. Ideas from the first movement are recalled in the second. But before this happens there comes in the second movement a new lyrical subject for woodwinds against strings. A part of the slow introduction in the brass and the horn solo theme, both from the first movement, come after this lyrical subject. Some florid passages in the woodwinds bring on the principal theme of the second movement, with which this movement ends.

The finale consists of two sections. The first section has two basic ideas: The first idea, stalwart and resonant, is introduced by four horns and repeated by the basses; the second, less virile, is announced by the cellos and taken up by the English horn. After the second idea has been developed, the second section of the movement arrives, opening with a horn call that is supported by pizzicatos in the strings. The call yields to a fanfare, first in the trumpets, then in the horn and woodwinds, and after that in the trumpets and woodwinds. At a climax of this fanfare, the main theme of the first movement is brought back in the trumpets (set against the fanfare theme in the woodwinds). The second theme of the first movement is also brought back loudly. A coda develops all this material briefly, after which the symphony ends with a final announcement of the fanfare theme.

In the Symphony No. 3, Op. 33, written between 1936 and 1937, Hanson reverts to the Nordic style and temperament of his Symphony No. 1. He explains that he wrote this third symphony to pay tribute to the "epic qualities" of the pioneers who founded the first Swedish settlement on the Delaware in 1638 and later forged a road to the West. The heroism and the conflicts of these pioneers are found in the virile and sometimes turbulent music of the first movement. This is followed by a peaceful and brooding slow movement. The third part, in the tempo of a fast scherzo, is markedly rhythmic. The fourth movement begins in the character of the first, but eventually the mood becomes one of uninhibited joy. The main part of this finale is an extended chorale in antiphonal style. After the chorale has arrived at a climax, the main melody of the second movement emerges. The symphony ends, as the composer explains, "in a note of exultation and rejoicing."

The Symphony No. 4, Op. 34, completed in 1944, is on the other

hand a Requiem inspired by the death of the composer's father. The
four movements bear the Latin titles from a Requiem Mass: *Kyrie,
Requiescat, Dies irae,* and *Lux aeterna.* The first movement is strongly
felt music. The main theme (the *Kyrie* melody) is presented by four
horns and later repeated by full orchestra. Through changes of tempo
and mood this *Kyrie* theme appears and reappears, worked in with
subsidiary ideas. In the second movement, *Requiescat,* a plaintive,
scalelike melody is heard in the bassoon. It is repeated by different
choirs of the orchestra, sometimes with slight variations. The *Dies
irae* is a scherzo, described by one anonymous commentator as "furious and bitter"; the *Kyrie* theme returns in this section. The closing
Lux aeterna begins with a pastoral theme whose serenity is sometimes disturbed by exclamations in the brass. Some of the thematic
ideas of the first movement are quoted briefly, including the *Kyrie*
theme.

The Symphony No. 5, Op. 43, came eleven years after the fourth,
in 1954. Hanson called it the *Sinfonia sacra* because it is a musical
treatment (emotional, atmospheric, and mystical rather than programmatic and realistic) of the Easter story as told in the Gospel According to St. John. The work has three sections, but is played without
interruption. The first part is made up of three introductions. In the
second part, three major themes are discussed: the first, "Pesante,"
the second, "Gregorian," and the third, "Pastorale." The last of
these is carried to a climax which then brings on the concluding section, in which the first and second themes are brought back (the
latter in the form of a chorale), separated by an agitato section.

Roy Harris

"In producing a composer such as this . . . America has placed herself in the front rank amongst those nations who are concerned with building a music for the future."

ALFREDO CASELLA

BORN: Lincoln County, Oklahoma, February 12, 1898.
MAJOR WORKS: *Ballets*—From This Earth; What So Proudly We Hail. *Chamber Music*—3 string quartets; Concerto for Piano, Clarinet, and String Quartet; String Sextet; Piano Trio; Piano Quintet; String Quintet; Violin Sonata; String Quartet in One Movement. *Choral Music*—Symphony for Voices; American Creed; Alleluia; Easter Motet; Israel; Mass; Cindy; Festival Folk Fantasy, for folk singer, chorus, and amplified piano. *Orchestral Music*—14 symphonies; When Johnny Comes Marching Home; Violin Concerto; Two-Piano Concerto; Kentucky Spring; Cumberland Concerto; Piano Concerto; Abraham Lincoln Walks at Midnight, for soprano, piano, and orchestra; Fantasy for Piano and Orchestra; Canticle to the Sun, for coloratura soprano and chamber orchestra; Ode to Consonance; Horn of Plenty; Rhythms and Spaces (an expansion of String Quartet No. 3) *Piano Music*—Sonata; American Ballads; Toccata.

HIS LIFE

There is the blood of the American pioneer in the veins of Roy Harris. His grandfather had driven a pony express between Chicago and points west. Later on he and his son (Roy Harris' father) participated in the Cimarron rush to Oklahoma, traveling by oxcart with only an ax, a gun, and a few basic provisions. They staked a claim, felled the trees, and built a log cabin. In the uniquely American setting of a log cabin, situated on the plains of the frontier, one of the most American of our composers was born. And with equal appropriateness he was born on Lincoln's birthday—in Lincoln County.

The Harris family stayed in Oklahoma for the first six years of Roy's life. A malaria epidemic which claimed two of Roy's brothers as victims sent the family farther west, to the Gabriel Valley in California. They bought a parcel of land in Covina and began to farm it. It was still pioneer country. But as Roy Harris grew up he saw the country around him also grow; before his eyes the frontier became a part of modern industrial America.

He attended a public school in Covina, took some piano lessons, first from his mother and after that from a local teacher. The organ and the clarinet he learned to play by himself. He was obviously musical. But, then, the whole Harris household was musical. It was the only home in the neighborhood with a piano. "Mother played quite well by ear," Harris later recalled,* "and used to accompany a cousin of mine, who played the violin. . . . My father bought us a phonograph—an Edison with cylindrical records. Each new record was an event in our family. We played them nearly every evening— even in the late summer evenings after a long day's work."

Though he made some public appearances as pianist, there was no thought or suspicion of his becoming a musician. Music was only one of several important elements in his life then. Another was books: He read everything he could put his hands on, from mail-order catalogues to Shakespeare. A third element was philosophy. "And so, as I finished high school, my world was dividing into two parts. Music, philosophy, poetry, and the wonder of clouds, mountains, bird-songs,

---

* This and subsequent autobiographical quotations are from an article by Roy Harris, "Perspective at Forty," in *The Magazine of Art*, November 1939.

and sunsets—all belonged to the beckoning unknown world. The farming and the bank account belonged to a very sure, well-known world which laughed at the other."

In his eighteenth year Harris acquired his own farm, which he cultivated for the next two years. At the same time he kept on reading, making music, and studying Greek philosophy. The need for study made him finally rent out his farm and go back for further schooling. When World War I erupted Harris enlisted in the Army as a private in the artillery.

The war represented a definite and permanent cleavage with his farming past. When he got out of uniform he enrolled in the Southern branch of the University of California as a special student in philosophy and economics. While there he also attended a class in harmony, his initiation into the world of musical theory. To support himself he drove a dairy truck every day, distributing eggs and butter to the outlying communities in California. In the evenings he concentrated on his studies. Those years of study, Harris has said, must be regarded as uneventful. "But," he adds, "they were years crowded with enthusiasms. Each new harmony, each new melody, each new composer discovered was a milestone."

The need for additional music study became pressing. From Charles Demarest he took lessons in the organ, and from Fannie Charles Dillon in the piano. Then, determined to make some headway as a composer, he contacted the well-known composer and teacher Arthur Farwell (1872–1952) asking to become, and being accepted as, a pupil in composition.

Harris studied with Farwell for two years. "I was convinced," Farwell later wrote, "that he would one day challenge the world." Stimulated and inspired by his teacher, Harris wrote *Impressions of a Rainy Day,* for string quartet. Its *première* in Los Angeles on March 15, 1926, became his first piece of music to receive a public performance. He also completed writing an orchestral piece, the Andante, which made such an impression on Howard Hanson that he conducted its world *première* in Rochester, New York, on April 23, 1926. The Andante was soon heard at Lewisohn Stadium in New York City and at the Hollywood Bowl in Los Angeles—and with such success that funds were raised to send Harris to Paris for further music study.

He went to Paris in 1926 to study with Nadia Boulanger. When Mademoiselle Boulanger gave him an assignment to produce 20 melodies in different styles he returned with 107! But his studies with that great teacher were, as he put it, a disappointment. He was impatient to begin writing music and to tackle the more ambitious forms; he had come to Mademoiselle Boulanger expecting direction in his creative activity. "I was like an Army rookie who came to France to win the war." Mademoiselle Boulanger subjected Harris to the severe and none-too-inspiring discipline of counterpoint, solfeggio, and harmony. Harris had to work out his destiny in his own way. What he would not accept from formal instruction he received from the music of the past. First he came upon the last quartets of Beethoven; then it was the music of Bach; after that the works of the Netherland school of contrapuntal music. "Boulanger co-operated with grace, and from this point on my life unfolded swiftly and with exciting logic." All his life he has remained true to Bach, and the music of the old contrapuntal schools has remained one of the greatest influences in the development of his personal style.

After six months Harris completed his first mature work, the Concerto for String Quartet, Piano, and Clarinet. It was performed in Paris on May 8, 1927, by the Roth String Quartet, supplemented by Mademoiselle Boulanger at the piano and Monsieur Cahuzac, clarinetist. It was enthusiastically received. One French critic wrote: "It has warmth, life, a rhythm, an accent which denotes a nature of the first order." This concerto was introduced in the United States on February 12, 1928, was broadcast over a national radio hookup on June 14, 1933, and after that was both published and recorded.

The success of the concerto brought him a Guggenheim Fellowship in 1927, which was renewed for a second year in 1928. After the end of the fellowship's second year Harris was struck by misfortune. He fell down a flight of stairs in his cottage near Paris, breaking his spine. For five months he was in a plaster cast. Then he was brought back to the United States, on a stretcher, for an extremely difficult and painful operation. It was successful beyond expectation, and Harris recovered completely. But first he had to suffer a long period of hospitalization. Confined to his bed for months, Harris tried to escape boredom by writing music. He finished a string quartet.

That accident was almost as important to his evolution as a composer as his apprenticeship in Paris. Up to the time he was hospitalized Harris had done all his composing at the piano; his music was written in terms of the piano. In a hospital bed the piano had to be dispensed with. He was now able—and for the first time—to think exclusively in terms of the instrument for which he was writing. More than that, he could give his ideas greater freedom of movement and could now submit to his natural bent for counterpoint.

After the accident Harris started producing the first works in which his pronounced individuality revealed itself. He completed the String Sextet in 1932 and the Symphony: 1933. (The latter had been commissioned by Serge Koussevitzky, who introduced it with the Boston Symphony on January 26, 1934.) While writing these works he was relieved from financial pressure by a two-year creative fellowship from the Pasadena Music and Arts Association. In 1933 he assumed his first teaching post when he was appointed teacher of composition at the Westminster Choir School in Princeton, New Jersey, holding this position for four years.

His spectacular rise to fame in the 1930s has few precedents. Up to about 1933 he was known and admired by a small and comparatively esoteric group. In about a year's time he became one of the best-known, most widely heard, and most frequently praised of American composers. Major orchestras sought to present his new works: On February 28, 1936, for example, almost within the same hour, two of America's greatest orchestras (the Boston Symphony and the Philadelphia Orchestra) presented world *premières* of two different Harris works. His *Symphony: 1933* became the first American symphony to be recorded commercially. In 1935 a nationwide poll among its radio listeners by the New York Philharmonic Orchestra placed Harris in the first place among American composers; among the composers of the world he received only a few votes less than César Franck. Once again, in a phonograph-record poll conducted by *Scribner's Magazine* in 1937, he received more votes than any American composer. Commissions for new works came to him from many different sources, including the first ever given a composer by a record company.

The word "genius" was now being used to describe Harris. It redounded to Harris' credit that he survived this period of excessive attention and praise; that he did not allow it to influence the kind of music he was writing; that he proceeded to produce works of increasing importance. In 1937 he completed two chamber music compositions which the critics hailed as among the best by any American: the String Quartet No. 3 and the Piano Quintet. The former was the only contemporary American composition played by the Roth Quartet at the International Congress of Musicologists in New York in 1939. The Symphony No. 3, completed in 1938, became almost immediately one of the most highly respected and most frequently played symphonic works by an American. When Koussevitzky introduced it with the Boston Symphony Orchestra on February 24, 1939, he referred to it as "the greatest orchestral work yet written in America." It was soon presented by virtually every major conductor in the United States (including Toscanini, who was now performing an American symphony for the first time in his long career!). During the London blitz, in the early years of World War II, when it appeared that the day of doom was at hand for civilization, a Britisher recommended that recordings of one hundred great works of music be preserved as our heritage to some future civilization; and the only American work on his list was this Harris symphony.

In his next symphony, Harris identified himself more closely than heretofore with American music by reaching for his material into the reservoir of American folk music. That symphony, his fourth, was called *Folk Song,* and it made skillful and elaborate use of several American folk and popular songs within the large framework of a seven-movement symphony scored for chorus and orchestra. This symphony, completed in 1939, was first heard only in parts in Rochester, New York, on April 25, 1940, with its first complete performance taking place the following December in Cleveland, when the National Federation of Music Clubs presented it with a prize of $500 as the year's most important symphonic composition. Harris then revised the symphony by changing the arrangement of the movements, the version now regarded as definitive; its *première* was given by the New York Philharmonic under Dimitri Mitropoulos in 1942. Meanwhile, in 1941, Harris completed the writing of a violin sonata, which was awarded the Elizabeth Sprague Coolidge medal.

During World War II Harris was appointed head of the music section of the overseas branch of the Office of War Information. To fill this post he received a leave of absence from his position as composer-in-residence at Cornell University, a position which he had assumed in 1938. After the war, Harris affiliated himself with various American institutions of higher learning, from 1957 to 1960 at Indiana University, in 1960 as director of the International Institute of Music, of the Inter-American University in Puerto Rico, and for a decade after 1961 at the University of California in Los Angeles.

He thrives on the adulation of his students. This atmosphere is maintained at home by his talented wife, Johana Harris (whom he married in 1936 and who has often been the performer in those of his works that require a pianist). It is a crowded household, for besides their five children, it often includes the presence of a friend or two who comes for a brief visit but remains for several days or weeks.

Harris has an irresistible creative drive which makes it necessary for him to write music all the time. "It is natural for me to write music, and lots of it, and quickly," he once wrote to Nicolas Slonimsky. "In other words, I am not a phony who has to go through strange experiences in his living, and tortuous effort in his writing, to produce music."

That drive, however, is only one explanation for his fecundity. Another is his unfaltering conviction that he is a great composer. There is nothing vulgar or brash about him; his overpowering belief in himself and his music is not offensive. He has always had it. As far back as 1933, when he was still an unknown composer, he could write to Slonimsky: "I hope to become a really great composer." Since his great success, and his general acceptance by the world of music as a master, he has come to accept his powers as normally and as unquestioningly as he does the facts that he eats, breathes, and sleeps. And he expects his personal friends to accept and acknowledge his genius just as implicitly.

About each of his new works he generates such spontaneous excitement and enthusiasm that Slonimsky once applied to this state of mind the medical term of "euphoria." "I have just finished two movements of my Fifth Symphony," he wrote Slonimsky. "And it is wonderful beyond my wildest hopes. I am sure you will be happy about it." A fellow composer, Henry Cowell, once remarked, "Harris often convinces his friends and listeners of the extreme value of his works by his own indefatigable enthusiasm for them."

This self-confidence—call it cocksureness if you must—is an American trait that made possible the opening up of the West and the fashioning of the American dream. Another American trait in Harris is his irrepressible energy. He must always be doing something. When he isn't working or teaching he is gardening, or reading, or playing tennis or chess, or taking long walks, or just pacing the room nervously. There is also his passion for speed. Whatever he does he must do quickly. There is nothing he enjoys more than to race his car on open highways at a speed of ninety miles an hour. Automobiles, in fact, are such a passion that he is always changing cars for a newer and flashier model. Baseball is another passion; in fact, the whole Harris family are stalwart baseball fans.

When Harris celebrated his fiftieth birthday in 1948, the Governor of Colorado gave him a citation for distinguished citizenship. His sixtieth birthday was the occasion for performances of major works by some of America's leading musical organizations. In 1965, Sweden conferred on him the Military Order of Saint Saviour and of Saint Bridget. Harris also became the first American composer to conduct his own music in the Soviet Union. This happened on October 15, 1958, when he led a performance of his Fifth Symphony over the Moscow Radio.

HIS MUSIC

The qualities which place the stamp of nationalism on the works of so many other composers are not found in Roy Harris. The quotation of folk songs or rhythms is not a general practice with him. It is found in one or two of his works, but this resource is an exception rather than a rule. Nor has he ever modeled his own melodic, rhythmic, or harmonic patterns after those of the American folk song and dance. His style is entirely his own, evolved in his own way; it has no identity with any other American music. His traits are easily recognizable: the long, flowing melodic line; the asymmetrical rhythms; the angular structure; the partiality to techniques of other musical eras, particularly the polyphony of the sixteenth century and Greek modality.

And yet (though the process by which he arrived at it is not easy to identify) he has produced authentic American music, music that simply could not have arisen in any other country; and he has created vibrantly modern music, for all its dependence on old styles. His music has the expanse of the Western plains; it has wind-swept freshness; it has the energy and strength of a young country looking into the future rather than living in past glories. It has American optimism, enthusiasm, and zest; there is nothing decadent or effete about it. Someone somewhere once referred to Harris as the Carl Sandburg of music; for Harris speaks about America, for Americans, and in accents unmistakably American.

ANALYTICAL NOTES

Chamber Music. The two chamber music works that Harris completed in 1937 are still among his best works in this genre. The Piano Quintet consists of a passacaglia, cadenza, and fugue. The main theme of the passacaglia, in a modal structure, is in Harris' spacious vein. It is a great sweep of melody which gives the movement a heroic cast. To Lazare Saminsky, who was not often given to such sweeping phrases, this passacaglia "is a world in itself, and its achievement is a summit of American artistry . . . a work of genius and the best piece of music that has been written during the three hundred years of its [America's] history." The cadenza that follows is of a virtuoso character, with an introspective recitative for string quartet and a powerful and imaginative cadenza for the piano. The concluding movement is one of Harris' most astute and imaginative exercises in polyphonic writing.

In the String Quartet No. 3 Harris indulges in his predilection for modal writing. It is in four movements, each of which is a prelude and fugue; and each of the preludes and fugues is in one of the Greek modes.

The Sonata for Violin and Piano (1941) one of the few compositions by Harris to resort to quotation. This takes place in the second movement, a pastorale, in which is heard an adaptation of the American-English folk song "I'll Be True to My Love, If My Love Will Be True to Me." The first movement is a fantasia illustrating the freedom of melodic qualities on the four strings of the violin. The third movement, an andante religioso, emphasizes the violin's singing quality, while the finale is a toccata full of motor energy for both the violin and the piano.

Orchestral Music. The Symphony No. 3, which Harris wrote in 1938, is one of the few symphonies by a living American whose survival seems assured. Despite the complexity of its construction and the occasional elusiveness of its style, it won immediate success; for even on first hearing audiences sensed its inherent powers and originality.

It is in a single compact movement made up of five parts. The first was described by the composer as "Tragic—low string sonorities." Here the main theme appears in the violins in the sixtieth bar: one of those broad, expansive flights of song so characteristic of Harris. After this melody is worked out, the second section, "Lyric—strings, horns, woodwinds," is brought in by a brief flute solo. Nine bars later there comes the main subject, another elastic melody for violins. In the section that follows, "Pastoral—emphasizing the woodwind," there are several ideas presented successively by the English horn, oboe, and bassoon and bass clarinet against arpeggiated chords in divided strings. The fourth section is a "Fugue—dramatic," the theme of which appears in the strings. An important rhythmic figure brings on the concluding part, "Dramatic—Tragic," in which strings and woodwinds present again the first beautiful melody of the symphony in canonic form. After this, brass and percussion work out the rhythmic figure that opened this section. In the coda the main melodies of the first and second sections are developed.

The *Folk Song* Symphony, for orchestra and chorus, Harris' fourth, is simple and forthright music whose appeal is immediate. Harris wrote it in 1939 for use by high school or community musical groups. There are five choral sections and two instrumental interludes built out of Negro, cowboy, minstrel-show, Civil War, and mountain songs— many of them very familiar and easily recognizable in Harris' version. In the first part we hear "The Gal I Left Behind." The second part is made up of cowboy melodies, two of which are the very popular "Streets of Laredo" and "Oh Bury Me Not on the Lone Prairie." An instrumental interlude consists of dance tunes for strings and percussion. This is followed by a mountaineer love song, "I'm Goin' Away For to Stay a Little While." A second interlude of dance tunes now appears in full orchestra. The fourth choral section is made up entirely of a single Negro song, "De Trumpet Sound in My Soul," while in the concluding movement we hear the song made popular during the Spanish-American War, "When Johnny Comes Marching Home." This melody was also the basis of an orchestral overture written by Harris a few years earlier.

The Symphony No. 5, completed in 1942—and dedicated to "the heroic and freedom-loving people of our great ally, the Union of Soviet Socialist Republics"—reflects the war period in which it was written, as well as Harris' faith in his country and his people. "I hoped to express the qualities of our people," he said. "We . . . have qualities of heroic strength, determination, will to struggle, faith in our destiny.

We are possessed of a fierce, driving power—optimistic, young, rough, and ready."

It is in three movements, the first being a prelude, the second a chorale, and the third a fugue. Its martial character is immediately established with a theme for horn that resembles a bugle call. It has a vigorous rhythm, which generates the energetic drive of this entire section. In the second movement we have an interesting contrast of major and minor triads—major for the brass and minor for the strings. The first theme, which is melancholy, is given by the English horn and bassoon. After it is developed, there comes the middle section of the movement, a majestic Harrisian sweep of melody which evolves for 118 bars before catching its breath. This section ends with a chorale. The concluding fugue is built out of two themes (it is a double fugue), one energetic and highly accented, the other broad and expressive. Harris explained its form as follows: "It is a large A-B-A form in which 'B' is in itself a double fugue with two twelve-tone subjects, both of which are derived from the major-minor third and sixth relationships of the opening motive. The return to subject 'A' is a working out in more dramatic terms of all three subjects."

The Symphony No. 6, written in 1944, was also inspired by the crisis of World War II. Harris explained that in attempting to write a symphony expressive of the critical period in which our country found itself in 1944, he "turned to one of the great moments in the history of our nation for guidance." And the great moment he had in mind was the Gettysburg Address of Lincoln. The four movements of the symphony give a musical interpretation to four different parts of that speech. The opening movement, "Awakening," was stimulated by the opening lines, beginning "Fourscore and seven years ago." In the second movement, "Conflict," the music reflects the following lines about the Civil War: "Now we are engaged in a great civil war, testing whether that nation—or any nation, so conceived and so dedicated —can long endure." The third movement, "Dedication," is a chorale inspired by the part beginning with "We are met on a great battlefield of war" and ending with "The world will little note nor long remember what we say here; but it can never forget what they did here." The finale, "Affirmation," which is in the form of a fugue, speaks for the concluding lines of the address, beginning with: "It is for us the living, rather, to be dedicated here to the unfinished work which they who fought here thus far so nobly advanced."

Harris' Seventh Symphony, perhaps his most significant work in that form, was originally completed in 1951, but was radically revised a few years later, in which form it was introduced in 1955 in Copenhagen, Eugene Ormandy conducting. Described by its composer as a dance symphony, this work is in a single movement. The first half is made up of a passacaglia and five variations; the second half has three subdivisions, "contrapuntal variations in assymetrical rhythms," "in symmetrical rhythms," and in "symmetrical meters," as the composer explained. The symphony ends with a coda which is a final variation of these rhythmic materials.

Harris' Symphony No. 8 (1961) bears the title of *San Francisco* because it was written on a commission from the San Francisco Symphony for its fiftieth anniversary. The work was intended as music about the life of St. Francis of Assisi, since St. Francis is the patron saint of San Francisco. In a single movement, it expresses the moods of five dominant periods in the life of that saint: childhood and youth; renunciation of worldly living for the mantle of spiritual aspiration; the building of the chapel with his own hands; the joy of pantheistic beauty as a gift of God; a final period of ecstasy after his premonition of death.

Commissioned by Eugene Ormandy and the Philadelphia Orchestra to write a symphony, Harris produced his Symphony No. 9—1963 dedicating it to Philadelphia as "the cradle of American democracy." The Preamble to the Constitution provided Harris with the form and substance of his symphony. The work opens with a prelude inspired by the Preamble's opening words, "We the people." Harris wanted this music to provide "a swift-moving panorama of all kinds of people in their basic drives and emotions—a kind of quick Dance of Life, of rhythms, melodies, dynamics and instrumental colors." The second movement is a chorale, whose point of departure is the words "to form a more perfect Union," while the words "to promote the general welfare" stimulated the writing of the closing movement, which bears the title "Contrapuntal Structures." Three mottoes taken from Walt Whitman are quoted for each of the three principal thematic subjects in this finale: "Of Life Immense in Passion, Pulse and Power," "Cheerful for Freest Action Formed," and "The Modern Man I Sing."

In his Symphony No. 10 (1965), Harris returned to the man whom he had previously glorified in his Symphony No. 6—Abraham Lincoln. The composer explains that this symphony was strongly influenced by Carl Sandburg's biography of Lincoln. "I have chosen" Harris explains, "two moods from the youth of Lincoln, and three moods expressing his profound concern for the destiny of our democratic institutions." This is a five-movement work which bears the following programmatic titles: "Lonesome Boy in the Wilderness," "The Young Wrestler," "Abraham Lincoln's Convictions," "Civil War, Brother Against Brother," and "Praise and Thanksgiving for Peace." The scoring is unusual, calling for three choruses (women's, men's, and mixed) and a brass choir, two amplified pianos, and percussion. For his text, Harris used material from Lincoln's writings and speeches in the third and fourth movements (including the Gettysburg Address, which he had previously set in the Symphony No. 6). In the first, second, and fifth movements, the composer wrote his own textual material.

Harris' Symphony No. 11 (1967) had been commissioned by the New York Philharmonic to help celebrate its 125th anniversary. Actually, its world *première* on February 8, 1968—with the composer conducting the Philharmonic—also helped celebrate (though a few days prematurely) Harris' seventieth birthday. The symphony is a twenty-minute work which the composer described as "highly dramatic and almost operatic. It begins in a mood of nervous agitation, dips downwards, and ends in an expansive affirmation and optimism."

His next symphony, the twelfth (1967), also came about through a commission—this time from the Father Marquette Tercentenary Commission. Entitled the *Père Marquette Symphony,* it was introduced by the Milwaukee Symphony on February 24, 1968, under the composer's direction. As its title suggests, the symphony was intended as a tribute to Father Marquette, whose voyages made him the first white man to see the confluence of the Mississippi and Wisconsin rivers.

The Symphony No. 14, which was introduced by the National Symphony Orchestra in Washington D.C., in February of 1976, was written to commemorate America's bicentenary. Based on the anthem "America," it is a five-section work calling for a narrator and chorus as well as orchestra.

Joseph Haydn

"He alone has the secret of making me smile and touching me to the bottom of my soul."

MOZART

BORN: Rohrau, Lower Austria, March 31, 1732.
DIED: Vienna, May 31, 1809.
MAJOR WORKS: *Chamber Music*—125 trios for various combinations; 82 string quartets; 35 piano trios; 18 string trios; Cassations, divertimenti, nocturnes, quintets, sextets, sonatas. *Choral Music*—14 Masses; The Creation; The Seasons. *Operas*— L'Infedeltà delusa; Il Mondo della luna; L'Isola disabitata; Armida; Orfeo ed Euridice. *Orchestral Music*—104 symphonies; 15 piano concertos; 3 violin concertos; 3 cello concertos; 2 horn concertos; other concertos for solo instruments and orchestra; The Seven Last Words of Christ; Divertimentos, German Dances, marches, minuets, nocturnes, overtures. *Piano Music*— 52 sonatas; Fantasia in C major; Capriccio in G major; Variations in F minor; 10 German Dances. *Vocal Music*—Various songs for voice and piano including "Das Leben Ist ein Traum," "My Mother Bids Me Bind My Hair," "Piercing Eyes," "The Sailor's Song," "She Never Told Her Love," "The Spirit Song"; Canons, cantatas, rounds, vocal duets, vocal trios, vocal quartets.

HIS LIFE

The life of Haydn is seen most clearly within the framework of his times and setting. Most of his life was spent in or near Vienna, where he arrived in 1740. At that time music belonged almost exclusively to the aristocracy, and depended for its existence and development upon the patronage of the nobility. There were no public orchestras or concerts. The first concert orchestra did not emerge until 1772, with the Tonkünstlersocietat, while garden concerts (later so popular) came into being with Mozart in 1782. Before that time musical activity took place almost exclusively within the glittering halls of palaces. The people heard some music in the church and in the streets, where serenades were played and sung by roving minstrels. But those who could not gain access to the homes of the great were not likely to hear much good music or to become acquainted with the works of leading composers of the age.

And yet Vienna was a musical city, for there was hardly an important household that did not have its own orchestra or employ a Kapellmeister to direct and write the music. The wealthier establishments even had their own opera companies. Many of the aristocrats were exceedingly musical, some were even fine performers. The love of great music was as sincere in Vienna as it was stylish. Rarely was there an important dinner or social function at which a specially planned musical entertainment did not take place.

Naturally, much of the new music written in Vienna was dictated by the preferences of the patrons, the prevailing vogues, and the size and quality of the musical forces the composer had at his disposal. Music was generally written to order for specific occasions. The composer wrote with the perfunctory dispatch of a cook preparing meals; the many occasions for which new works had to be tailored did not allow their creator to wait for inspiration.

In such a society the composer was regarded more as a menial employee than as an artist. He lived with the other servants in the house of his employer, for whom he worked exclusively, often made to suffer petty indignities which he expected and accepted as part of his job. He was given explicit orders on how to dress and behave. The contract that Haydn signed when he became the Kapellmeister for the Esterházys was characteristic: "The said Haydn . . . must be temperate, not showing himself overbearing toward his musicians, but mild and lenient, straightforward and composed. . . . The said Joseph Haydn shall take care that he . . . appear in white stockings and white linen, powdered, and with either a pigtail or a tiewig. . . . He should conduct himself in an exemplary manner, abstaining from undue familiarity, and from vulgarity in eating, drinking, and conversation." And when Haydn accepted such terms he was already one of Austria's most celebrated musicians!

The patronage system had obvious humiliations and limitations. But it also had benefits. A good composer was assured of a livelihood, a home, an audience, and performances for his works. A great composer such as Haydn had at his beck and call instrumental and vocal forces with which he could experiment in a way denied to later composers. Writing for specific occasions gave these composers an incentive for continued production; the praise of superiors and their material gifts provided badly needed stimulation. It is true that the age produced a great deal of routine, methodical, factory-made music, written for special occasions, functions, and purposes. But it is also true that it helped rather than killed outstanding talent, as the development and evolution of Haydn can serve to demonstrate.

Before he came to Vienna, Haydn had shown unmistakably the direction his life would take. The humble wagoner and cook who were his father and mother respectively were sympathetic to some of the better things of life. Their home, in the little village of Rohrau, was the scene for continual music-making, in which members of the family and neighbors collaborated. Haydn responded to this music even as an infant; soon he was singing the tunes he had heard. While still a child he participated in these family concerts by picking up two sticks and pretending that they were a violin and bow. His father (who as a sideline was the sexton of the local church) wanted him to become a priest, but he did not try to stifle the child's musical development. First the village schoolmaster was recruited to teach Haydn his first lessons. Then a relative, Johann Matthias Frankh, a professional musician, was called upon for guidance. Frankh readily recognized Haydn's exceptional ability. He received the boy into his own household in nearby Hainburg (Haydn was then about five) in order to give him personally a comprehensive training.

Haydn spent three years in Frankh's house, and they were years of undiluted misery. Frankh was a merciless disciplinarian who did not spare the rod. At his hands the boy suffered mental and physical abuse as he was put through the rigorous paces of harmony, composition, violin playing, harpsichord playing, and solfeggio. Frankh's wife was no more sympathetic to Haydn. She resented the fact that she had one more mouth to feed, neglected completely his everyday needs, and mistreated him sorely. To make matters even worse, he had no friends. A scrawny boy, ungainly, self-conscious, awkward, given to rapidly changing moods, he easily became the object of taunts and teasing; out of self-protection he avoided the company of other children altogether.

This miserable existence had compensations which the mature Haydn was better able to appreciate and be grateful for than the sadly maltreated child. For Frankh, who was an excellent teacher, gave his ward an exhaustive musical training. Thus when the Kapellmeister of St. Stephen's Church in Vienna came to Hainburg in 1740 to find fresh voices for his celebrated choir, he did not have to put Haydn through an extensive test to realize that here was not only a born musician but a carefully trained one.

As a choirboy of St. Stephen's in Vienna, Haydn was fed, clothed, and taught music. To the eight-year-old boy, departure from the Frankh household could be only for the good; but life was made neither easier nor more gracious in Vienna. The activities of a choirboy were many and varied. He had to learn the harpsichord, violin, singing, psalm reading, Latin; he had to participate in cathedral services, sacred processions, funerals, and occasionally in performances at the royal palace. So far so good—for neither intensive study of music nor its continual practice could disturb a boy with Haydn's avid desire to learn and make music. But everyday life was hard. The pittance provided by the Government for the choir school made it impossible to provide the boys with adequate food and lodging. Their rooms were cold; their meals were so frugal that the boys were always hungry. Haydn often sang in the streets to earn a few kreuzer with which to buy some bread or soup, or he would try to get some menial job at a nobleman's palace so that he might be fed in the kitchen.

All this would have been tolerable to Haydn if the musical activities had been satisfying. But the Kapellmeister, Karl Georg Reutter, disliked the boys, treating them with both suspicion and contempt. Whenever possible he managed to sidestep his responsibilities as a teacher. He was particularly impatient with Haydn, who, for one thing, perpetually plied him with eager questions, and, for another, annoyed him with an uncontrolled bent for mischief. He neglected Haydn's education even more than that of the other boys. Left for the most part to his own resources, Haydn had to acquire musical learning by memorizing treatises, practicing endlessly on the harpsichord, and trying to write church music. When he submitted a twelve-part Salve Regina to Reutter, the teacher tossed the manuscript aside impatiently and growled, "You could put your time to better use by studying your solfeggio, young man!"

Haydn was always getting into trouble. The story goes that he and his companions had climbed the perilous heights of a scaffold which then surrounded the palace of Schönbrunn. The empress caught sight of him from her window and ordered Kapellmeister Reutter to administer a sound thrashing to the culprits. On another occasion, in the classroom, he snipped off the pigtail of the fellow chorister in front of him with a pair of scissors.

When Haydn's voice broke, in his seventeenth year, Reutter was only too glad to be rid of him. He was turned out of St. Stephen's to shift for himself as best he could. Alone, without money, and without friends, Haydn would undoubtedly have experienced a period of great suffering if another ex-chorister by the name of Spangler had not taken pity on him and, poor though Spangler was, offered him food and lodging in his own wretched rooms. Before long Haydn was able to get a few pupils and some engagements as a violinist, earning enough to keep alive.

In the spring of 1750, aided by a loan from a tradesman, Haydn was able to set up house in a garret of Michaelerhaus on the Kohlmarkt. It was cramped, cold, and badly lighted; during heavy rains water would drip steadily through the ceiling. Yet it was his own and he was happy. "When I sat down to my old worm-eaten harpsichord, I envied no king his good fortune." He earned his living by teaching, performing, and doing hack work. At the same time he was studying with a passion greater than ever and writing his own music. One of his serenades appealed so greatly to a well-known Viennese actor that he commissioned Haydn to write the music for one of his own farces. The "opera"—*Der neue krumme Teufel*—was performed at the Burgtheater in 1752 and was well liked. Unfortunately an important Viennese nobleman regarded the work as a satire on him and used his influence to have it withdrawn after two performances. But in later years the opera was successfully presented in Berlin, Prague, Saxony, and Breisgau.

In the Michaelerhaus, on the third floor, there lived the imperial court poet, Pietro Metastasio, whose poetic dramas provided most of the great Italian opera composers of the period with their librettos. Metastasio came to know Haydn, to like him, and to admire his industry. Metastasio, if he wished, could be a powerful ally; and he wanted to help Haydn. He soon acquired for the young composer his first permanent job, as accompanist to the well-known singing teacher and opera composer Niccolò Porpora (1686–1768). In return Porpora gave Haydn singing lessons and taught him the art of writing vocal music. It was a fair exchange, even though it was one of Haydn's duties to serve as personal valet and house servant to the master. From Porpora, Haydn learned a great deal about the art of Italian vocalization. And through Porpora he was able to meet some of Vienna's leading musicians (including Gluck) and some of its princely patrons. Among the latter was Baron Karl Joseph von Fürnberg, a wealthy music lover. The baron engaged Haydn to direct musical performances and to write new works for the splendid entertainments held regularly at his palace in Weinzierl. For Fürnberg, Haydn wrote, in short order, eighteen orchestral pieces —and he wrote his first string quartet in 1755.

At Weinzierl, Haydn came to know Count Ferdinand Maximilian von Morzin, who needed a Kapellmeister at his palace in Pilsen. He lured Haydn away from Baron von Fürnberg. For two years Haydn worked for the count, for whom in 1759 he wrote his first symphony.

On November 26, 1760, Haydn was married to Anna Maria Keller, daughter of a wigmaker. He had actually been in love with Anna's younger sister, but accepted Anna as a substitute when the other suddenly entered a convent. He was not in love with Anna when he married her, and their marriage was not a happy one. Anna was a shrew, incapable of understanding or appreciating her husband. They fought frequently, particularly when she insisted on using Haydn's manuscripts as curling papers. After a few unhappy years they separated and lived apart for the rest of their lives. But with his customary generosity, Haydn, after the separation, not only provided for her handsomely for the remainder of her life, but also was never heard to express an un-kind thought about her.

Financial difficulties compelled Count von Morzin to disband his orchestra in 1761. As he was by then a celebrated musician, Haydn did not have to search for another post; it was waiting for him. One of Vienna's greatest music patrons, Prince Paul Anton Esterházy, had often expressed the wish to have Haydn work for him. Once he was free Haydn was welcomed with open arms by Prince Esterházy, who engaged him as second Kapellmeister at his palace in Eisenstadt.

For the next three decades, the best part of his remaining years, Haydn worked for Esterházy. After a new, magnificent palace had been built near Odenburg in 1766, Haydn became first Kapellmeister. Work was plentiful; there was always a great deal of music-making at Esterház. Haydn was in charge of rehearsals and concerts; he directed the orchestra and wrote music for the regular concerts and special occasions. Events such as a wedding or the visit of a royal personage required performances on a grand scale and new, ambitious works. And besides all this, Haydn had to supervise the life, conduct, and ap-pearance of all musicians working under him.

It was a busy, well-ordered, productive, and uneventful life. Re-moved from the distractions of a great city, Haydn could write abundantly: symphonies, quartets, trios, divertimentos, serenades, concertos, sonatas, operas, Masses. He could also become more original and independent in his use of form and in his style. For, as he ex-plained, "Cut off as I was from the world, there was no one to con-fuse me and torment me and I was forced to become original." And so the years passed—quietly, peacefully—years in which a gifted and talented composer became a master, the most famous and gifted musician of his time.

His fame spread throughout Austria, then to other parts of Europe. As early as 1764 he had some of his symphonies published in Paris, and one year later a few of his works appeared in Amsterdam. By 1765 the *Wiener Diarium* was referring to him as "the darling of our nation." In a city as far distant as Madrid they wrote a poem in his honor, "The Art of Music." Commissions came to him from many different places: from Paris for two sets of symphonies; from Cádiz, in Spain, for an orchestral work entitled *The Seven Last Words of Christ*. In Esterház the great of Austria paid him homage, among them none other than the empress herself, Maria Theresa.

His position and his increasing creative powers could not change the man. He remained simple, direct, honest, and incorruptible. There was no artifice in him, no pretentiousness. He never forgot that he had risen from humble origins, and he was proud to have made something of himself "out of nothing." "I have associated with kings and many great ones," he said late in life, "and have received from their lips much flattery. But I have never wished to live on a level of intimacy with them, for I had rather hold to the people of my own station."

His favorite adage was the key to his personality: "Be good and industrious and serve God continually." He *was* a good man, ethically as well as morally. His kindliness, his gentleness, and his warmth were some of his most endearing qualities. He was generous to a fault, his purse always open to anyone in need. In his will, for example, he remembered charitable acts done more than fifty years earlier and rewarded them handsomely. The loan which a tradesman had made to him so that he could set up his own home—a loan which had been repaid!—brought a hundred florins to his benefactor's daughter; the daughter of Frankh (Frankh who had treated him so shabbily) he remembered with another hundred florins. He was as incapable of harboring malice as he was of ingratitude. It is a rare person who has so few enemies and so many who love him.

He was industrious. His working day spanned sixteen hours. Requiring little sleep, he awoke early and followed a rigid program from which he was rarely deflected. He was ever faithful to his many duties, and at the same time he found both the time and the energy to write a prodigious amount of music. He often worked on several compositions at one time, never neglecting to bring to each his most conscientious effort and his most painstaking thoroughness.

Above all, he served God continually, with humility and piety. He never forgot to thank Him for his talent and the favors he enjoyed. Each of his works began with the words "In the name of the Lord" and ended with "In praise of the Lord." He often said that he was able to write fine works only because God was good to him and helped him. "I rise early, and as soon as I am dressed, I fall on my knees and pray to God and the Holy Virgin that I may succeed again today."

Haydn's good friend, the painter Albert Christoph Dies, described the master as follows:

Haydn was something under middle height. The lower half of his figure was too short for the upper . . . very noticeable because he kept to the antiquated style of trousers reaching only to the hips. . . . His features were rather regular, his glance fiery yet temperate, kindly and inviting. When he was in a serious mood his features, along with his glance, expressed dignity. . . . Haydn had a moderately strong build; his muscles were spare. His hawk nose (he suffered much from a nasal polyp which doubtless actually enlarged this organ) as well as the rest of his face was deeply marked with smallpox. The nose itself was pockmarked, so that the nostrils each had a different shape. Haydn considered himself ugly and mentioned to me a prince and his wife who could not stand his appearance "because," he said, "I was too ugly for them." But this supposed ugliness lay not at all in the cut of his features but solely in his skin, eaten away with pockmarks and of a brown tint.

He was not a happy man. There were some of his contemporaries who never heard him laugh and who remarked that, for all his wit, there was always an indefinable sadness in his eyes. He was terribly lonely. What he missed most of all was the love and tenderness of a wife (though for a while he did get solace from his love affair with Luigia Polzelli). And there were many times when he keenly felt his separation from the world outside of Esterház. "Here I sit in my desert," he once wrote, "forsaken, a poor orphan, almost without human companionship. . . . Where are those beautiful evenings which one can merely remember, but not describe?"

To one friend above all others was he attached: Mozart. When they met for the first time in 1781, Haydn was forty-nine years old and Mozart twenty-five. They were drawn to each other immediately, not only by respect and admiration for each other's genius, but also by genuine tenderness for each other. Haydn spoke to Mozart as a teacher who perceived the greater genius of his pupil. And Mozart, openhearted, passionately in search of understanding, turned to the older man, learned from him freely, and always acknowledged himself the debtor. But, strange as it may sound, Haydn learned much from his young friend. Mozart's originality and daring and flaming genius made Haydn take notice. Although Haydn was already acknowledged to be the greatest composer alive, he began to emulate Mozart and, by emulating him, to bring to his writing greater enrichment and profundity.

On his infrequent visits to Vienna, Haydn would visit Mozart at his home in Schulerstrasse. There, one day in 1785, Mozart and his colleagues performed a new set of quartets which he had written in honor of his friend Haydn. Mozart's father was also present. After the performance Hadyn went up to the old man and said, "I tell you before God and as an honest man—your son is the greatest composer I know, either personally or by name."

Haydn's post at Esterház was terminated in 1790. Haydn's employer died that year, and his successor, little interested in music, radically reduced his musical forces. Haydn was not sorry to leave. He could now return and live in Vienna, enjoy the society of friends and colleagues who meant much to him. But he did not have much of a chance to get settled. Late in 1790 an English impresario, Johann Peter Salomon, came to Vienna expressly to engage Haydn to conduct orchestral concerts in, and write a set of new symphonies for, London. The fee was munificent: twelve hundred pounds.

Tearfully Mozart bade Haydn farewell. "We shall never meet again," he said firmly, as if he knew that one year later he would be dead. Then, on December 15, 1790, Haydn set forth on the journey. En route he stopped off at Bonn, where he heard a Mass by a young composer named Beethoven. "He is a man of talent," Haydn exclaimed. Then he crossed the Channel over a stormy sea, arriving in London on the first day of 1791.

London feted and honored Haydn in a manner that few other visiting musicians had enjoyed. To his modest lodgings in Golden Square came some of England's most honored citizens to pay their respects. And they opened wide their homes to him. Haydn was forced to dine away from home on six out of seven days. He had to devote his late evenings to social functions planned for him, or even to royal festivities to which he was invited. In spite of this whirligig, which taxed him severely, he had to find the time to rehearse his orchestra and to complete the new symphonies commissioned for the concerts. "My mind is very weak, and it is only the help of God that will supply what is wanting in my power. I daily pray to Him. Without His assistance I am but a poor creature."

His first concert, at the Hanover Square Rooms on March 11, attracted a brilliant audience and was outstandingly successful. And the new symphony Haydn had written for this concert—the so-called *Surprise* Symphony—received an ovation; the slow movement had to be repeated. The second concert was attended by the Prince of Wales, who was as enthusiastic as his subjects. Thereafter, all of Haydn's concerts were oversubscribed.

Between performances he was a guest at balls, picnics, and river excursions. The Lord Mayor of London gave a banquet in his honor, attended by more than a thousand people. Oxford University conferred an honorary degree on him. In the midst of all this frenetic activity there came to him the crushing news that Mozart had died on December 5, 1791.

Haydn made his second visit to London in 1794. (Meanwhile in Vienna he gave lessons to young Beethoven, fresh from Bonn, whom he could not understand or get along with.) Once again he came to conduct concerts; once again he wrote a set of symphonies; and once again he became enmeshed in the endless rounds of social calls, invitations, and ceremonies.

After the second London visit Haydn spent his declining years in the Gumpendorf suburb of Vienna—a rich man, a man of world renown. But there was no decline in his creative powers, for he was now to produce two of his greatest works: the oratorios *The Creation* and *The Seasons*. He was also to write the Austrian national anthem at the request of the Minister of the Interior; it was officially introduced on the emperor's birthday, February 12, 1797, in all the theaters of the empire. "You have expressed what is in every loyal Austrian heart," the emperor told Haydn, "and through your melody Austria will always be honored."

On December 26, 1803, Haydn directed a performance of *The Seven Last Words of Christ* in Vienna. Thereafter he divorced himself from the world. He was deteriorating physically. He could no longer hear very well; his mind became fogged; his tongue was slow and heavy. Callers—who came in an uninterrupted stream to pay him tribute—wearied him to distraction. At last he printed cards which his servant handed out to visitors; they read "Fled forever is my strength; old and weak am I" and included a musical quotation from his vocal quartet *Der Greis* (*The Hoary Old Man*). Most of the time he suffered from severe headaches, even forgetfulness. When his mind was clear he liked to finger the many gifts he had received.

On March 2, 1808, his seventy-sixth birthday was celebrated in Vienna four days prematurely with a performance of *The Creation*. Prince Esterházy sent his personal carriage, and Haydn—old and sick though he was—was able to make his last public appearance. The demonstration of love and reverence given him by his fellow Viennese brought tears to his eyes. When they carried him in a chair out of the hall, the audience rose to its feet and stood in homage.

The occupation of Vienna by the invading French Army intensified the depression of his last months. He had his servant carry him to his piano, where he played his national anthem several times. One day a French officer came calling—not as a conqueror, but as a humble admirer. At first Haydn would not see him. The visitor walked over to the piano and played and sang "In native worth" from *The Creation*. Haydn received the officer and embraced him. "God bless you, my son, you have made me very happy today."

He knew he did not have much longer to live. On May 26 he drew up his will, forgetting no one and commending his soul "to my all-merciful Creator." He gathered his household around him, bade them a gentle farewell, then played for them his national anthem for the last time. He died on the last day of the month, mourned in the principal churches of Vienna not only by his countrymen but also by the French. Napoleon ordered a special guard of honor placed at his house and had important officers conduct his body to the churchyard of Hundsthurm where it was buried. Two weeks later, on June 15, Mozart's Requiem was sung in Haydn's honor at the Scots Church. It was the final tribute, and the one which he would probably have appreciated the most.

In 1820, Haydn's body was disinterred and reburied in its final resting place in Eisenstadt.

HIS MUSIC

The creative activity of Haydn spanned half a century. His first period began in 1750, with the writing of some instrumental serenades; his last period ended with *The Seasons*, completed in 1801. During this span of years the art of music underwent a radical transformation. In 1750 Johann Sebastian Bach died, and with him an epoch had passed. In 1800 the *première* of Beethoven's First Symphony announced a brave new world for music. Between these two historic events—the death of the culminating figure in contrapuntal music and the birth of the first symphony by the greatest of all symphonists—musical style changed completely. Homophony (the single melody with harmonic background) became the basis of musical expression, in place of counterpoint, or polyphony (the simultaneous interweaving of equally important melodies). New forms replaced the old: The symphony, the sonata, the string quartet, and the instrumental concerto occupied the composer's attention instead of the Mass, the oratorio, the part song, the suite, the fugue, the concerto grosso, and so forth. The focal point of musical activity was transferred from the church to the palace of the nobility and after that to the concert platform; with this transfer came a profound change of musical values. Poetic expressiveness, individuality, independent thinking, and unorthodox techniques slowly began to supersede formality of structure, rigidity of style, and subservience to tradition.

Haydn was the first major force in bringing about this evolution. History refers to him as the "father" of the symphony, sonata, and string quartet. Strictly speaking, this is not so. Before Haydn's time symphonies were being written in the city of Mannheim, where a composer such as Johann Wenzel Stamitz (1717–57) produced three-movement works for orchestra, already called symphonies, which arrived at unity, balance, and contrast. The piano sonatas of Karl Philipp Emanuel Bach (1714–88) were the starting point of Haydn's writing of sonatas; Haydn himself conceded the overwhelming influence that Karl Philipp Emanuel Bach had had upon him. An Italian by the name of Gregorio Allegri (1582–1652) had written a string quartet a century or so before Haydn.

But while Haydn did not create these forms—and thus, strictly speaking, was not their "father"—he did succeed in developing them. Haydn enlarged the outlines of the symphony, the sonata, and the string quartet, bringing to them altogether new structural dimensions and crystallizing the basic form they were thenceforth to assume. By his ceaseless experiments with orchestration and by his introduction of new instruments into the orchestral ensemble, he helped to establish once and for all the foundation of the modern symphony group. Through the extraordinary variety of his lyricism and through the increasing wealth of his harmonic structures, he brought to instrumental music an expressive content and a wide gamut of feelings it had not known up to then. He introduced the concept of thematic development, demonstrated the artistic potentialities of the variation form within the symphonic mold, and with remarkable audacity injected effects, whimsical moods, and nuances which immediately extended the horizons of musical thought. When his work was done music had been brought to the threshold of modernity, through which Beethoven was then to pass.

Haydn developed slowly. If he had died as young as Schubert or Mozart (at the ages of thirty-one and thirty-five respectively), he would today be remembered only by the musicologist and he would be heard only when some adventurous conductor or performer went searching into the past for a pleasing novelty. Not until his fortieth year did Haydn begin writing works which are likely to be heard today, such as the *Farewell* Symphony or the Op. 20 string quartets. But if he developed late, he kept on growing to the end of his life. Always he continued studying, experimenting, and changing; always he continued to smash down what he described as "mechanical regulations." To each succeeding series of works he brought a new enrichment of speech, a greater emotional intensity, a greater technical daring. Always was he dissatisfied with what he had accomplished and tried always to uncover new ways of expressing himself in his music. Just before his death he told a friend, "I have only just learned in my old age how to use the wind instruments, and now that I do understand them, I must leave the world."

Wit, gaiety, kindliness, laughter, sunny humor, mischief—these are the qualities frequently associated with Haydn's style. For these qualities he acquired the nickname of "Papa." But there is also a deeper and profounder vein in Haydn's music. In many of the slow movements of his string quartets and symphonies he gives voice to a tragedy or achieves a kind of poetic revelation which we associate with Beethoven. There are fugal episodes in his later quartets which have Beethovian mysticism, just as there is Handelian sublimity in pages of *The Creation,* and the nobility and majesty of a Bach in his greatest Masses.

ANALYTICAL NOTES

Chamber Music. The eighty or so string quarters of Haydn are the foundation on which were to rest all later quartet structures, from Mozart to Bartók. Haydn did not originate the idea of writing music for four stringed instruments: two violins, viola, and cello. In this he was anticipated by Thommaso Antonio Vitali (c. 1665–?), Alessandro Scarlatti (1660–1725), Giuseppe Tartini (1692–1770), and Giovanni Battista Sammartini (1701–75). But Haydn was the first to recognize fully its artistic potentialities, to fulfill these potentialities at least partially, and once and for all to establish the form, style, and personality of the string quartet. His later quartets are the first in music history in which we can clearly and unmistakably recognize the form and medium as we know them today. He went a long way toward realizing the individuality of each of the four instruments. He arrived at a definite chamber music style (lucid, transparent, and sensitive) as opposed to the orchestral style; more remarkable still, he achieved a *string quartet* style as opposed to that of other chamber music combinations. No wonder, then, that Mozart conceded he had learned to write string quartets from Haydn!

Into his quartets Haydn put more of himself than in any other musical medium. To them he confided his most personal thoughts and feelings; they reflect his personality completely. Otto Jahn, Haydn's biographer, noted: "It is not often that a composer hits so exactly upon the form suited to his conceptions. The quartet was Haydn's natural mode of expressing his feelings. The poet and the peasant, the lonely man and the man of mirth and wit, the devout Christian and the lover of earthy joys reveal themselves in some of the most poignant, or radiant, or ingratiating, or rowdy, or tragic music that he was to write."

His first quartets, Op. 1 and 2 (c. 1755), like his first symphonies, followed the old suite form, combining four or five movements (two of them usually minuets), each brief and episodic. This music is conventional and superficial, reminding us that it was written to entertain the nobility; it taxes neither the intellect nor the emotions. Throughout there is little concept of the individuality of the four instruments, instead of which Haydn approximates chamber-orchestral writing reduced to a skeleton.

Six quartets gathered in Op. 3 (1763) represent a transition from this manner of writing in a chamber-orchestral style to one that is distinctly string quartet. A movement from the Fifth Quartet in F major has become popular apart from the rest of the work. It is the second movement, a serenade with the tempo marking of andante cantabile, in which a courtly melody in the first violin is accompanied by plucked strings. This nocturne has become familiar in transcriptions for orchestra.

Haydn was to write about forty string quartets before the form became crystallized. Full crystallization takes place with six works completed in 1772, grouped in Op. 20. They acquired the name *Sun* Quartets because to some they represented "a sunrise over the domain of the sonata style as well as of quartets in particular"; also because the publisher's trademark on an early Berlin edition depicted the sun. The sonata form is here adapted into quartet literature once and for all. Each of the four instruments finally achieves emancipation, but without the sacrifice of balance and unity. There is here much more, too. Such a wealth of beauty and emotion was released in these quartets that what had been a stylized and artificial form suddenly became a great art.

The Quartet in D major (Op. 20, No. 4) reveals Haydn's adventurousness: in the abrupt changes of themes and rhythms in the first movement, where the composer appears unable to contain his ebullience; in the unprecedented importance accorded to the cello in the second variation of the second movement; in the displaced accents in the minuet; and in the changing rhythms and harmonic innovations of the fourth movement.

The Quartet in F minor (Op. 20, No. 5) is remarkable for its profound feelings, particularly in the tragic accents of the third movement, one of the most moving pages of music in this set of quartets. The finale is a fugue in two subjects, of such dramatic and tragic content that W. W. Cobbett regards this movement as a "hint of the emotional and dramatic impulse which became so volcanic in Beethoven's fugues."

Nine years elapsed between the completion of the Op. 20 quartets and the writing of a second set of six works (Op. 33). During this period Haydn had come into contact with the quartets of Mozart; their emotional depth and daring inventiveness had made a profound impression upon him. As Haydn himself said, he was now writing quartets "in an entirely new manner." The leader became the follower; Mozart's influence widened the sphere of Haydn's quartet writing. The Op. 33 quartets are known as the *Russian* Quartets because they are dedicated to Grand Duke Paul of Russia; they are also known as the *Gli scherzi* Quartets, due to the fact that Haydn replaced the traditional minuet movement with a scherzo, though it must be confessed that the change is in name only and not in the character of the music itself.

The Quartet in E-flat major (Op. 33, No. 2), popularly called *The Joke,* reflects Haydn's bent for mischievous fun. In the finale, a rondo, he tried to prove that women are always involved in gossip while listening to music. To catch them he put in a short adagio at the close of the movement, after which he repeated the principal theme, inserting a two-bar rest after each phrase; then he included a four-bar rest before repeating the opening phrase of the theme. These pauses were intended to betray the gossiping women.

In the Quartet in C major (Op. 33, No. 3) the main theme of the first movement is trimmed with grace notes (each of the four instruments take up these notes in the development section) which bear such a resemblance to chirping birds that the quartet is called *The Bird.* There is also a suggestion of bird chirping in the duet between first and second violins in the trio part of the scherzo. But it is in the slow movement that Haydn writes his greatest page of the work. No longer is he the genial and whimsical "Papa," but a poet who feels deeply and who translates his feelings into eloquence.

It is in the quartets written after 1784 that Haydn arrives at the height of his creative powers. More and more he is influenced by Mozart, particularly by those six remarkable quartets which Mozart dedicated to him and which were introduced in 1785. Ever profounder and subtler grows Haydn's expression, ever braver and freer his use of his materials. His slow movements often glow with a beatific radiance as he reaches unfalteringly for the spiritual and the sublime.

In 1787 came the six *Prussian* Quartets, Op. 50, called so because they were dedicated to the King of Prussia. Here we occasionally encounter a new structural method for Haydn, a monothematic process in which the second subject within the sonata-allegro form (or the second group of subjects) is derived from or is a variation of the first subject (or group of subjects). Haydn's increasing independence of method and thought (an unmistakable Mozart influence) can be discerned further in the opening of the Third Quartet in E-flat major where both of the principal subjects are stated at once, the second derived from the first. Of particular interest in the Fourth Quartet in F-sharp minor is the fugue in the finale, in which a mighty tragedy seems to unfold. The Sixth Quartet in D major is popularly known as *The Frog* due to the repetition of the same notes, performed by alternate instruments, in the finale, which seems to sound like the croakings of a frog.

The *Prussian* Quartets were followed in 1789–90 by the *Tost* Quartets, Op. 54, 55, 64, twelve quartets dedicated to a certain Johann Tost, about whom we know very little. One of the most distinguished compositions in this group is the Quartet in D major, Op. 64, No. 5, referred to as *The Lark*. This is because the main melody of the first movement seems to soar heavenward like a lark's song. Few pages in Haydn achieve such sublimity.

But there is sublimity as well as tragedy and nobility and grandeur in the set of six quartets, Op. 76, dedicated to Count Erdödy. These works, completed in 1799, are the apex of Haydn's quartet writing.

The Quartet in D minor (Op. 76, No. 2) is perhaps the best-integrated and most consistently inspired of the group. All four movements, which significantly are in the same key, have a subtle relationship with each other. The basic theme of the first movement, heard immediately, has melodic skips in fifths, which is the reason why the work is known as the *Quinten* Quartet. The entire movement is evolved from this subject, as Haydn does not make use here of a second major theme. In the slow movement that follows, Haydn soars once again; no more poignant piece of music has come from him.

The Quartet in C major (Op. 76, No. 3), the *Emperor,* is the work into which he incorporated his Austrian national anthem as a second movement. It serves for a series of variations, so elementary in treatment that they often consist of nothing more than the transfer of the melody from one instrument to another. The first movement has greater originality. The first five notes of the opening theme are the fundamental materials out of which Haydn builds a movement of spacious proportions, another proof of his constructional genius.

In the Quartet in D major (Op. 76, No. 5) such an exalted plane of eloquence is achieved in the largo movement—only in the slow movements of Beethoven's quartets do we enter such rarefied spheres! —that the entire work is designated as the *Largo* Quartet.

Choral Music. *The Creation* (*Die Schöpfung*), written in 1798 when he was sixty-six years old, was Haydn's first attempt at an oratorio. He had come belatedly to this medium, after having produced works in virtually every other known form of music, because of his high esteem for Handel and his feeling of insufficiency to compete with him.

The intrusion of Handel's name is perhaps inescapable in the discussion of any oratorio, but particularly so in the case of *The Creation*. The text, combining parts of Genesis and Milton's *Paradise Lost*, had originally been prepared by Liddell for Handel. Only because Handel had turned it down was it eventually brought to the attention of Haydn, probably by the impresario Salomon. Haydn seized upon it, for he had always nursed the ambition to write an oratorio in the Handel manner, and the text provided him with the necessary stimulus.

The writing of *The Creation* (like that of Handel's *Messiah*) was as much an act of piety as of musical composition. It was Haydn's service to God. He confessed that he had never been so pious as when he wrote this music. "Daily I fell on my knees and begged God to vouchsafe me strength for the fortunate outcome of my work." And again: "I felt myself so penetrated with religious feeling that before I sat down to the pianoforte I prayed to God with earnestness that He would enable me to praise Him worthily." Like Handel before him, Haydn sometimes felt that the music came to him from a Higher Being. About one of the passages he said simply, "It came from on high," even as Handel had said of the "Hallelujah Chorus," "I do think I did see all Heaven before me and the great God himself." The feeling of reverence pervades *The Creation* and almost puts it in the class of *Messiah* as a medium of religious worship.

The Creation is a work of great strength and many weaknesses, of sublimity and of naïveté, of true inspiration and stilted formality. Haydn put his best foot forward in the orchestral introduction, "Description of Chaos," one of the most remarkable examples of atmospheric tone painting in the orchestral music of the eighteenth century. Through the most advanced use of dynamics, instrumental color, and harmony for that period, Haydn portrays the resolution of chaos into order. The hushed tones of the orchestra melt into the opening phrase of Raphael's recitative "In the beginning." The ensuing chorus, "And the Spirit of God," contains a blinding flash of musical genius: the blazing chords which accompany the word "light" in the phrase "Let there be light." But Haydn can descend quickly from the heights. In the chorus "Now furious storms" he yields to musical realism of disarming ingenuousness—describing thunder, lightning, rainfall, and snowstorms with naïve representation. The next two sections, on the other hand, are among his finest arias: The first, for basso, is a song of simple eloquence, "Rolling in foaming billows," followed by the gentle and pastoral "In verdure clad," for soprano. A monumental chorus, the celebrated "The heavens are telling," brings the first part of the oratorio to an exultant conclusion.

In the second part, following Gabriel's soaring melody depicting the eagle's flight, Haydn's realism becomes penetrating. With overpowering effect, and through subtle suggestion rather than literal painting, he creates the awe and mystery of things bursting to life in the soil: Raphael's recitative "Be fruitful, all." Later on in this part we hear the beautiful tenor aria "In native worth."

The third part begins with another fine atmospheric tone picture: fresh and verdant morning. The duet of Adam and Eve that follows, together with the interpolated choruses, is one of the longest and most original parts of the score. We are now in the presence of the miracle of the Creation; the glory of the Creator is hymned by the chorus in resplendent music. The love duet of Adam and Eve follows, music of the flesh rather than the spirit. *The Creation* ends with a magnificent paean to God for chorus and vocal quartet, "Sing to the Lord."

Haydn's second and last oratorio was *The Seasons* (*Die Jahreszeiten*), which followed *The Creation* by three years, in 1801. The two works are contrasts. Where *The Creation* is dramatic and at times sublime, *The Seasons* is atmospheric, pastoral, and effervescent. For in *The Seasons* Haydn is speaking of his love of nature, just as his deeply religious nature finds voice in *The Creation*.

The Seasons has four sections, each a self-sufficient unit, each devoted to one of the seasons of the year, beginning with spring. An orchestral prelude precedes each part, so descriptive of the season it is discussing that it is virtually a tone poem, at times highly vivid in its pictorialism, and generally original in its harmonic and instrumental writing.

The music of *The Seasons* is for the most part buoyant and ebullient in spirit. It begins with a lusty chorus of the peasants, "Come gentle spring," followed by a lively song, "Happily the farmer goes to the field," in which Haydn quotes a theme from his own *Surprise* Symphony. Breezy choruses, lyrical vocal solos, and vivid orchestral tone painting then carry on the message which the composer finds in each of the seasons. Since Haydn looked upon winter as the symbol of old age, a quiet sadness momentarily enters into his writing toward the end of the oratorio. But his good spirit finally prevails again in "Let us never tire of doing good," a hymn in praise of the wonders of nature, and in the concluding "Amen" which follows.

Haydn's library of choral literature includes many Masses. The greatest of these came toward the end of his life, between 1796 and 1802. How remarkable this music is, and how significantly it looms among Haydn's compositions, became apparent only in recent years when it became familiar through recordings.

The *Missa in tempore belli* (*Mass in Time of War*), completed in 1796, makes such effective and extensive use of the tympani in the *Agnus Dei* that the entire work has come to be known as the *Paukenmesse* (*Tympani* Mass). A martial feeling is also injected into the opening *Kyrie* with the presence of the tympani and with trumpet calls. The *Heiligmesse* (*Holy* Mass), also a product of the year of 1796, gets its title from the quotation of the hymn *"Heilig, heilig"* in the *Sanctus*. In the *Nelsonmissa* (*Nelson* Mass), in 1798, Nelson's victory at the Battle of the Nile is believed to have been the inspiration for the stirring trumpet music in the *Benedictus*. The *Theresienmesse,* in 1799, was probably written for and named after Maria Theresa. The *Schöpfungsmesse* (*Creation* Mass)—also known as the *Missa Solennis*—lifts the melody of "The dewy morning" from *The Creation* in the *Qui tollis* and *Miserere*. This work came in 1801. Haydn's last Mass was the *Harmoniemesse* in 1802, to which the master brings supreme command not only of choral music and the polyphonic technique we find in the other Masses but also of symphonic writing. This is why this work has been described as a "choral symphony."

Orchestral Music. In comparison to the symphonies Haydn wrote for London late in his life, a similar work by one of his distinguished predecessors is a primitive creation. The orchestra for which Stamitz usually wrote was mostly a quartet of strings, with only occasionally the intrusion of a horn, an oboe, a flute, or a bassoon. The "London" Symphonies of Haydn are scored for strings, two oboes, bassoons, horns, trumpets, a single flute, and tympani; and in the Symphony in E-flat major (No. 99) there are also two clarinets. The dynamics of a Stamitz symphony were regarded revolutionary because they introduced crescendos and diminuendos. The Haydn symphony explores a world of color, effects, and nuances. The Stamitz symphony consisted of no more than a presentation of pleasing little melodies within formal rhythms. In Haydn we get themes, greatly varied in emotional color, which move with freedom and are altered and elaborated with great imagination. The Stamitz symphony is enslaved by the basso continuo—figured bass—in which the orchestra is tied together by formal chords in the harpsichord or cembalo. By abandoning the basso continuo Haydn brought a greater elasticity not only to the harmonic writing, but also to tempo and rhythm.

But before he produced the twelve London Symphonies, the crown of his orchestral output, Haydn went through a long period of development. The first symphonies he wrote were not symphonies at all, but instrumental serenades, divertimentos, and cassations—eighteenth-century developments of the classical suites, comprising many small movements for limited ensembles. The first symphony which Haydn wrote for the Esterházy orchestra, that in C major (1761), was in style and instrumentation more like a concerto grosso, while its five brief movements still suggest the divertimento. This symphony is known as *Le Midi* (*The Afternoon*), and is one of a set of three works, the other two of which are called *Le Matin* (*The Morning*) and *Le Soir* (*The Evening*).

But by 1770 Haydn began producing works in the recognizable structure of the Haydn symphonies. These works are in four movements: The first, a fast movement, is built around two basic themes; the second is a slow movement full of feeling (*Empfindsamkeit*); the third is a cheerful minuet; the finale is a fast movement, lively in mood. And the Haydn charm, vivacity, and originality became recognizable for the first time, too.

The Symphony in F-sharp minor (No. 45), known as the *Farewell* Symphony and written in 1772, is one of the earliest Haydn symphonies still performed. The straightforward character of the musical ideas and the simple outlines of the form suggest a Stamitz symphony. But there are essential differences. One is Haydn's greater variety of orchestral color and richer instrumental texture; another is the charm and sparkle of his melodic ideas; still another is the human quality of the slow movement and its profound feelings; a fourth difference is the use of a minuet movement as the third part of the symphony. The symphony's most original feature is the scoring of the finale, which is the reason the work acquired its name of *Farewell.* The story (highly dubious), goes that Haydn's musicians needed a vacation, a fact that Haydn attempted to impart to his employer tactfully through his music. In the closing pages of the finale, the various instruments of the orchestra are allowed to withdraw from the stage, one by one, until only the two first violins remain to end the symphony. It is said that the employer took the hint and gave the band its leave.

The Symphony in G major (No. 88) is one of Haydn's masterpieces. It belongs to a group of symphonies written in 1786–87 on a commission from Paris. Here, too, we have an innovation found first in Haydn: the slow and majestic introduction that precedes the fast opening of the first movement. In this case the slow introduction consists of strong chords alternating with softer phrases. A gay theme in the violins comes as the first theme; it is repeated more loudly and elaborated upon by the entire orchestra. The second theme, also in the strings, maintains the lively character of the movement. The slow movement is a beautiful song, the first part found in cellos and oboe, the second in the strings. Change of instrumentation, and picturesque contrapuntal trimmings in the violins, add to the interest of the melody. Midway the serenity is interrupted briefly by loud, surging chords in the orchestra, but it returns with a second poignant theme first in woodwinds, then in the strings, before the main song is repeated. The minuet that follows has greater vigor than we usually associate with this courtly dance. The middle trio section actually becomes a kind of peasant dance, defying the harmony textbook by utilizing consecutive fifths in the bass, possibly to simulate the droning of a hurdy-gurdy. The finale is in rondo form; the interpolation of a rondo in the symphony is still another Haydn "first." Its character, like that of the preceding movement, is suggestive of peasant dance music, gay and vigorous as only Haydn could be in his more vivacious moods.

The Symphony in G major (No. 92) has acquired the name *Oxford* because it was performed on the occasion of Haydn's receiving an honorary degree of Doctor of Music from that university in July of 1791. However, this is not the symphony that Haydn wrote as his doctoral "thesis." There was not enough time to rehearse the new work, which musicians found difficult, and Haydn had to substitute this earlier symphony, which he had written for Paris in 1788.

The *Oxford* Symphony begins with a tender twenty-measure introduction, mostly for strings alone. The strings set into motion the ensuing allegro spiritoso with a theme which begins somewhat haltingly but which, once momentum is gained, proceeds at a breathless pace. After a vigorous development the second theme, also in the strings, brings a more gentle mood. This theme is soon repeated with decorative filigree work in the flute. The second movement is a three-part song, one of Haydn's most moving lyrical pages. The melody begins in strings alone, but is soon doubled by the flute; the contrasting section of this melody is heard entirely in the strings, and when the first part returns it is the oboe instead of the flute that reinforces the orchestral texture. Loud chords and four descending notes in bassoon introduce the middle section of the movement, which is in a rebellious temper; then the original song is brought back. The minuet is in the formal Haydn pattern; the minuet theme is heard vigorously in full orchestra, while the principal theme of the trio is in bassoons and horns against an accompaniment of plucked strings. As so often happens in Haydn's symphonies, the dance element is maintained in the finale. A graceful elfin dance is heard in the strings. A second theme, in the delicate spirit of the first, appears in the strings. The first theme, stated loudly in a minor key, brings on the development, to which it contributes the subject of a fugato. After a restatement of the second theme, a transitional figure leads to the recapitulation section, in which all the earlier material is repeated.

The London Symphonies comprise twelve works in two sets of six, each set written for one of Haydn's two visits to London, in 1791 and 1794 respectively. They are his greatest works in the symphonic form, and with Mozart's best symphonies they represent the highest summit of symphonic writing before Beethoven. Each of the twelve symphonies is a work of major importance whose place in the symphonic repertory is permanent. But we shall confine ourselves to discussing only those which are heard most often.

In the first of these London Symphonies, that in D major (No. 93), what is of particular significance is the largo movement, in which Haydn's expressiveness, or *Empfindsamkeit,* achieves the kind of intensity and spirituality which are a precursor of the expressiveness of Beethoven's slow movements.

The Symphony in G major (No. 94) is better known as the *Surprise (Paukenschlag)* Symphony. The "surprise" comes in the second movement where, after a quiet and gentle theme for strings, a loud chord for full orchestra erupts suddenly and unexpectedly. Legend would have us believe that this chord was interpolated by Haydn to wake up those in the audience who habitually become drowsy in slow movements. Otherwise the procedures are not much different from what they were in the preceding London symphony. A slow introduction leads to the main body of the first movement, the two main themes of which are buoyant and vivacious and both presented by the strings. The second movement, which has been commented upon, is a theme and variations; after the presentation of the lovable melody there ensue four simple variations. A fifth variation is begun, but before it is realized the movement comes to a quiet end. The minuet that follows requires no comment, following as it does the traditional form. The finale is in an abandoned mood. The form is a rondo, and it consists of two delightful themes.

The Symphony in D major (No. 96) has been named *Miracle*. The reason for this is supposed to be as follows: Just before this symphony was introduced at Hanover Rooms in London on March 11, 1791, a huge chandelier fell from the ceiling upon empty seats, whose occupants had only a moment before rushed to the front of the stage for a better view of Haydn. Upon realizing that nobody was hurt, the audience shouted the word "miracle," which then became the popular sobriquet for the symphony that was performed as soon as the pandemonium died down. However, historic truth compels the admission that the "miracle" took place just before the performance of the Symphony in B-flat major (No. 102); the one in D major, was played *after* the accident. If any symphony should be called *Miracle,* it is the former, and not the latter.

A second popular symphony in the key of G major is found in the London group; it is No. 100. Because it utilizes the bass drums, cymbals, and a triangle (instruments which the eighteeenth century usually employed for military music), as well as bugle calls, it has been baptized the *Military* Symphony. These instruments are found in the second movement, which begins with a charming little tune for first violins and flute (Haydn had used the same melody in several other works). After this theme has been repeated and developed there comes a loud section in the minor key in which the so-called "military" instruments are sounded. Toward the end of the movement bugle calls are sounded. Except for these superficial traits there is nothing particularly martial about the symphony as a whole; it is Haydnesque in its ingratiating charm.

The Symphony in D major (No. 101) has its central point of interest in the second movement. Here a slow, steady rhythm, like the beating of a clock, is set forth by staccato notes in the bassoons and plucked notes in some of the strings; against this background there soars a beautiful melody in the first violins. Because of this persistent rhythm in the second movement, the work as a whole has come to be known as the *Clock* Symphony.

The Symphony in E-flat major (No. 103) derives the name of *Drum Roll* (*Mit dem Paukenwirbel*) Symphony from the first movement, where a roll of the tympani appears in the first bar. The drum roll is heard again unexpectedly in the middle of the movement with comic effect.

The Symphony in D major (No. 104) bears the name *London,* just as does the whole set of twelve symphonies—though why this should be so has never been explained. In the first movement Haydn does not present two contrasting subjects as might be expected. Instead of a second subject, he repeats the first theme in the dominant. The slow movement gives prominence to a haunting melody, while the scherzo combines whimsey with vigor. The finale opens with a dance melody over a pedal point in cellos and horns and subsequently presents a second lively idea, both of which are given interesting harmonic and contrapuntal treatment.

For a long time Haydn was believed to have been the composer of the so-called *Toy* Symphony, in C major. This is a curiosity that has become popular at children's concerts. Only three formal orchestral instruments are used (two violins and a bass), supplemented by a whole array of toy instruments (penny trumpet, quail call, rattle, cuckoo, screech-owl whistle, a little drum in G, and a little triangle). It is now conceded that this charming trifle was the work of either Mozart's father, Leopold, or Haydn's brother, Michael.

There has also been a good deal of controversy for many years as to who wrote the celebrated Concerto in D major for Cello and Orchestra, Op. 101. A nineteenth-century encyclopedist maintained that the concerto was actually the work of a cellist in the Esterház orchestra, Anton Kraft (1752–1820), and not of Haydn; the testimony was that of Kraft's son. The disappearance of Haydn's original manuscript made refutation difficult. That manuscript, however, was finally discovered in the 1950s to provide incontrovertible proof that the concerto was the work of Haydn, and that he wrote it in 1783.

As heard today, the concerto is not in the version originally put down on paper by Haydn. Haydn's work was of smaller dimensions, calling for a chamber orchestra. The late nineteenth-century Belgian conductor and musicologist François Auguste Gevaert edited it extensively, extending the orchestration, amplifying the solo parts, and contributing candenzas. Gevaert's edition is the one utilized in the present-day concert hall.

The concerto begins in a gracious manner with a delightful melody for strings, soon joined by flutes, which some have described as Mozartean because it resembles Leporello's "Catalogue Aria" in *Don Giovanni*. This melody is repeated more loudly and in variation, it is enlarged, and it ends in forte. Oboes and clarinets now present the second pleasing theme of the movement. These two principal subjects are taken over by the solo cellist, who elaborates on them and then engages the orchestra in working them out in great detail.

The second movement, music of luminous beauty, is made up of three melodies. The first is a stately dance appearing in the solo instrument. After it has been repeated by the orchestra with great vigor, the soloist enters with a second radiant melody. After a brief recapitulation of the opening subject, still a third song appears in the solo cello.

The ebullient closing movement, a rondo, has the earthy quality of folk music, to remind us that there was peasant blood in Haydn. The principal subject is a healthy dance tune for the solo instrument, repeated vigorously by full orchestra. An infectious mood is maintained until the end of the concerto.

The Concerto in D major for Harpsichord and Orchestra (identified as Op. 21 to distinguish it from another harpsichord concerto in the same key) is the last and the finest of Haydn's concertos for that instrument. Like the Cello Concerto in D major, it was written in 1783. The music abounds with such grace and refinement that to mate it to the piano instead of the harpsichord, as is sometimes done at concerts, is only to destroy its identity.

The principal material of the first movement is found in the extended orchestral introduction: first a tender tune in the strings, which is then taken up by the entire orchestra and amplified; then a second delicate theme, also in the strings, supplemented by the woodwinds.

The harpsichord then takes over the two ideas, embellishes them, changes them now rhythmically and now tonally, but never breaks a kind of spell. The spell grows more poetic and more rarefied in the second movement with an eloquent song heard in the violins before it is taken up and transformed by the harpsichord. Later the harpsichord enlarges on this melodic idea in a prolonged and exalted discourse. A rondo in the Hungarian style follows. The fiery spirit of the music, flashing and scintillating in its rhythms, does not destroy the essentially fragile character of the work as a whole.

Piano Music. Haydn's earliest piano sonatas were influenced by his study of and admiration for the sonatas of Karl Philipp Emanuel Bach (1714–88). As Haydn himself said: "Whoever knows me well will see how much I owe to Karl Philipp Emanuel Bach, and how I have understood and thoroughly studied him." From Bach, Haydn inherited not only the sonata structure but also the gift to endow homophonic writing with expressiveness (*Empfindsamkeit*).

Haydn produced some fifty sonatas for the piano. Though his inspiration in this medium is not of the exalted order we so often confront in his best string quartets, symphonies, and choral music, nevertheless there can be no doubt that under his hand the piano sonata experienced considerable growth both structurally and in expressiveness. In Haydn we find a greater expansiveness of form, an increasing richness of thematic growth, and a greater variety of style than can be found in the Bach sonatas—so much so, in fact, that the Haydn piano sonatas, even more than those of Mozart, can be regarded as a direct link between Karl Philipp Emanuel Bach and Beethoven.

Rococo grace and charm are omnipresent, and so is elegance of structure and a wealth of the most lovely thematic material—as in the ever popular Sonata in C major, No. 35 (1780), or the extraordinary Sonata in E-flat major, No. 49 (1790). But with these qualities we also get a deepening of emotion and a soul-searching beauty that is almost Beethovian—the slow movement of the Sonata in A-flat major, No. 43 (1785), for example. And in works like the Sonata in D major, No. 51 (1792), there exists an iconoclastic attitude towards the *status quo* in thematic and rhythmic procedures which suggest a brave new world for the sonata.

Haydn's literature for the solo piano also includes some shorter pieces. The most famous are the Fantasia in C, Op. 58 (1789), and the Variations in F minor, Op. 83 (1793). The former is a remarkable exercise in improvisation, with continually effective changes of mood and emotion, and unusual modulations and distribution of voices between the two hands. The latter is made up of two themes, a trio, two variations, and an extended coda.

Paul Hindemith

"There is nothing at all academic about Hindemith. He is simply a musician who produces music as a tree bears fruit, without further philosophic purpose."

ALFRED EINSTEIN

BORN: Hanau, Germany, November 16, 1895.
DIED: Frankfurt, Germany, December 29, 1963.
MAJOR WORKS: *Ballet*—St. Francis, or Nobilissima Visione. *Chamber Music*—Kammermusik, Nos. 2 and 3, for various solo and accompanying instruments; string quartets; 3 violin sonatas; 2 sonatas for unaccompanied violin; 2 string trios; various sonatas for solo instruments and piano; Kleine Kammermusik, for wind quintet; Septet; Octet. *Choral Music*—Das Unaufhörliche; When Lilacs Last in the Dooryard Bloom'd; Apparebit repentina dies; Six Madrigals; Mass. *Operas*—Cardillac; Neues vom Tage; Mathis der Maler; Die Harmonie der Welt; The Long Christmas Dinner. *Orchestral Music*—2 piano concertos; 2 cello concertos; Concerto for Orchestra; Konzertmusik for Strings and Brass; Philharmonic Concerto; Mathis der Maler, symphony; Der Schwanendreher, for viola and strings; Symphonic Dances; Nobilissima Visione; Violin Concerto; Symphony in E-flat; Symphonic Metamorphosis of Themes by Karl Maria von Weber; Theme and Variations According to the Four Temperaments; Herodiade, for chamber orchestra; Symphonia Serena; Clarinet Concerto; Concerto for Trumpet, Bassoon, and String Orchestra; Sinfonietta; Horn Concerto; Die Harmonie der Welt, symphony; Pittsburgh Sym-

phony; Organ Concerto. *Piano Music*—4 sonatas; Sonata for
Two Pianos; Ludus Tonalis. *Vocal Music*—Die junge Magd;
Die Serenaden; Das Marienleben; Nine English Songs.

HIS LIFE

When the Nazis came to power in Germany, branding the swastika not
only upon its political and social life but also on its culture, Paul
Hindemith (like so many other great men of free spirit) had to
adopt a new homeland. For many years after that he was assimilated
into American culture. Having found a setting in which he could
continue functioning as his artistic conscience dictated (rather than
according to laws, principles, and even whims of the Nazi Chamber
of Culture), Hindemith's growth as one of the most original and
productive musical figures of our generation had not been stunted.

When Hindemith left Germany in 1935 he was already one of its
great men of music. In the late 1920s the Hugo Riemann *Lexikon* referred to him as "the most full-blooded talent" in German music. And
this was before Hindemith had produced such exciting works as the
operas *Neues vom Tage* and *Mathis der Maler,* the oratorio *Das
Unaufhörliche,* and the *Konzertmusik,* Op. 50! And his activity as a
composer had been only a single facet of a musical life. As professor of
composition at the Berlin Hochschule, he was one of Germany's
greatest teachers; as a violist, he was a virtuoso of the first rank as well
as a member of a great string quartet up to 1929. It was in recognition
of his many services to German music, as well as of his position as a
composer, that he was elected a member of the august German
Academy.

But in the upheaval that took place in 1933 with the assumption of
power by the Nazis, an upheaval which overturned all existing values
of the civilized world, Hindemith suddenly became *persona non grata.*
The new rules regarded him as a degenerate influence. "When a man
like Hindemith," wrote Alfred Rosenberg, chief of the Nazi Foreign
Affairs Bureau, in *Die Musik* (January 1935), "commits the foulest
perversions of German music we have the right to reject him. The
accomplishments of such an artist . . . and the laurels received by
him in that now-overthrown Republic, are by right of no value to our
movement."

Hindemith was rejected because he was married to a half-Jewess, had made recordings with Jews, and had refused to break his associations with famous Jewish musicians. The Nazis also found Hindemith's music unacceptable. The progressive tendencies in all art were undesirable. But there were also specific objections to Hindemith's works. A provocative jazz opera like *Neues vom Tage* was found to be symptomatic of Hindemith's "degeneracy." "Technical mastery is not an excuse but an obligation," pompously exclaimed Dr. Goebbels. "To misuse it for meaningless musical trifles is to besmirch true genius. Opportunity creates not only thieves but also atonal musicians who in order to make a sensation exhibit on the stage nude women in the most disgusting and obscene situations, and further befoul the scenes with the most atrocious dissonance of musical impotence." The Nazis were even more disturbed by Hindemith's later opera *Mathis der Maler,* whose theme—the defeat of German liberalism during the Peasants' War—had, for 1934, dangerous implications.

Hindemith could stay in Germany no longer. In an atmosphere charged with malice and hate, the first phase of his great career came to a close. It had been a richly productive phase.

His father, a successful painter and decorator, had been opposed to his making music a career. But the boy could not be denied. When he was eleven he ran away from home to find not adventure, but music. He studied the violin and the viola by himself, then earned his living by playing the former instrument in café and theater orchestras. At the same time he attended the Frankfurt Conservatory, where his teachers included Arnold Mendelssohn and Bernhard Sekles. The winning of the Mendelssohn Prize for his First String Quartet, Op. 2, drew attention to his creative talent.

When Hindemith's studies ended he spent a year in the German Army. In 1915 he joined the orchestra of the Frankfurt Opera, and served as its concertmaster for an eight-year period. During this time he distinguished himself in other ways, too. In 1921 he helped found the Donaueschingen Festival at Baden-Baden where new music could get a hearing. He also helped organize the Amar Quartet, which made a specialty of performing the works of modern composers, propagandizing this music throughout Germany. He remained its violist and guiding spirit until 1929; and for it he wrote some of his early important chamber music works.

The performance of two insignificant one-act operas, *Das Nusch-*

Nuschi and *Murder, Hope of Women,* in Stuttgart on June 4, 1921,
was his first important emergence in public as composer. These little
operas did not make much of an impression. Richard Strauss told
him: "You don't have to write this way because *you* have talent."
One of these operas was so unhappy a marriage of text and music
that the wits had Hindemith saying: "Never again will I compose
music for a libretto I haven't read!" But performances of other,
more serious, Hindemith works were more successful. On August 1,
1922, his Second String Quartet, Op. 22, written for the Amar Quartet, was introduced by that organization at the Donaueschingen Festival; the work was so well received that it was repeated the following
year at the same festival. His music continued to be performed with
mounting success: The Kammermusik No. 1, Op. 24, which quoted
a German fox trot, and the song cycle *Die junge Magd* were heard
at the Donaueschingen Festival in 1922; the magnificent song cycle
Das Marienleben, at the same festival in 1923; the Quintet for
Clarinet and Strings, Op. 30, and the String Trio, Op. 34, at Salzburg
in 1923 and 1924 respectively; the Kammermusik No. 2, Op. 36, No. 1,
in Venice in 1925. With his first full-length opera, *Cardillac,* at the
Dresden Opera on November 9, 1926, he became the most important
composer to emerge in Germany after World War I.

In these works he was becoming increasingly objective in his style
and approach, increasingly interested in polyphonic procedures but
in an atonal idiom. These elements of Hindemith's maturing style
were particularly evident in *Cardillac,* which Gerhart von Westerman
has called "a perfect example of the ideal anti-romantic opera as
envisaged by musicians of the 1920s." The text, based on a romantic
tale by E. T. A. Hoffmann, had for its principal character a jeweler in
the seventeenth century who would rather murder his clients than
part with the art works he has fashioned for them on commission.
Utilizing the fullest resources of his polyphonic art, within the framework of such instrumental forms as fugue, canon, and passacaglia,
Hindemith here produced an opera with greater intellectual interest
than dramatic. Eventually Hindemith came to realize how guilty he
had been here of sacrificing emotional and dramatic values for intrin-
sically musical ones. A quarter of a century later he revised the opera
extensively, rewriting the libretto and introducing into his score a
breath of romanticism and touches of dramatic interest which the

earlier version had lacked. The new version was successfully received when it was introduced in Zurich on June 20, 1952.

Hindemith married Gertrud Rottenburg, the daughter of the conductor of the Frankfurt Opera, in 1924. Three years later, Hindemith left Frankfurt for Berlin where he was appointed professor of composition at the Berlin High School for Music and made a member of the German Academy. This was the time and the place when he became conscious of his responsibility to society and of his necessity to speak in terms that could be understood and appreciated by large audiences. "What is to be generally regretted today," he wrote in 1927, "is the loose relation maintained by music between producer and consumer. A composer these days should never write unless he is acquainted with the demand for his work." To meet a wider and more popular demand Hindemith did not abandon the writing of his complex and individual works. He supplemented them with other kinds of musical works intended for mass consumption and for different media: the radio, pianola, brass bands, theater, motion pictures. He wrote educational music for various instrumental ensembles and music to accompany children's plays. He produced choral numbers in which the audience could participate. For these works the term *Gebrauchsmusik* —"functional music"—was coined.

In addition to producing *Gebrauchsmusik* during this period Hindemith was also a spokesman for an aesthetic cult then popular in Germany—*Zeitkunst*, "Contemporary Art." *Zeitkunst* was partial to contemporary subject matter treated in a racy, popular manner. This was the movement that produced Ernst Křenek's jazz opera *Jonny spielt auf!* (1927) and Kurt Weill's provocative, social-conscious production *The Three-Penny Opera,* text by Bertolt Brecht (1928). Infected with the spirit of the times, Hindemith contributed to *Zeitkunst* one of his most controversial scores, the opera *Neues vom Tage* (*News of the Day*), introduced in Berlin on June 8, 1929. The text described a divorce proceedings that makes front-page news. Hindemith's score, much of it in a popular or jazz style, included such sensational items as an aria to hot water sung in a bathtub, a chorus of stenographers accompanied by the clicking of typewriters, and a "hate duet," instead of the more usual love duet.

But the writing of *Gebrauchsmusik* and *Zeitkunst* represented for Hindemith a passing phase. The creation of serious works in his personal, complicated contrapuntal style continued without any concession to public needs, tastes, or fashions. And it was his serious works, far more than his functional or topical ones, that made Hindemith one of the most celebrated figures in the music of pre-Hitler Germany, second in fame only to the venerable master Richard Strauss. These serious works included the Konzertmusik for Strings and Brass, Op. 50 (1930); the *Philharmonic* Concerto, completed in 1932 to help celebrate the fiftieth birthday of the Berlin Philharmonic Orchestra; and, most significantly, *Mathis der Maler* (1934), which appeared in two versions, as an opera and as a symphony.

It was because of *Mathis der Maler* that Hindemith became the center of a violent political storm during the early years of the Nazi regime. On March 12, 1934, Wilhelm Furtwängler conducted the world *première* of the symphony *Mathis der Maler* at a concert of the Berlin Philharmonic. This was such an immense success that Furtwängler now made plans to stage the opera. The Nazi bigwigs, however, vetoed the plan, first because they objected to Hindemith's affiliations with Jews, then because they regarded Hindemith's music as "decadent," and finally because they objected on the grounds of political expediency to an opera whose central theme concerned the uprising of peasants against autocracy. This led Furtwängler to publish a fiery letter of protest in the *Deutsche Allgemeine Zeitung* on November 25, 1934, which brought down on him the wrath of Hitler himself. Furtwängler was relieved of his musical posts and denied permission to leave the country; it was many months before he was able to reinstate himself into the good graces of the ruling powers. For Hindemith, the scandal meant he had to leave Germany once and for all.

He went to Turkey where he had been invited by the Government to assist in the rehabilitation of its musical life. This assignment took him more than a year and was completed with consummate skill and success. Then, on an invitation from Elizabeth Sprague Coolidge, he paid his first visit to the United States, making his American debut at a concert in Washington, D.C., on April 10, 1937, following which he made numerous appearances throughout the United States as violist and conductor. In 1938–39 Hindemith returned to the United States for a second visit when his ballet *St. Francis* was given its American *première* by the Ballet Russe de Monte Carlo; at this time he led a master class in composition at the Berkshire Music Center at Tanglewood.

With war breaking out in Europe in September of 1939, Hindemith decided to establish his home permanently in the United States; in 1936 he became an American citizen.

Soon after Hindemith arrived in the United States for permanent residence, the distinguished German critic H. H. Stuckenschmidt presented the following intimate sketch of the composer in *Modern Music:*

A friendly boyish head, its blond hair tinged of late years with gray, surmounts a lithe, youthful figure. Small in stature, Paul Hindemith likes to make himself smaller still by sitting on a low hassock. He prefers to remain close to the earth. From this vantage point, he leads the conversation unobtrusively, a clever, learned, inexorably logical participant, a little malicious, but friendly even in his malice. His knowledge embraces not only the music of every age, but also the oldest and newest arts of poetry and painting. His talk is not abstract but concrete, his point of view realistic. . . .

His fundamental characteristic is a sustained and bantering cheerfulness. Hindemith loves to laugh, but his laughter does not glance off the surface of things. . . .

To learn and to teach are his passions. Even after he was a composer of world fame he took special lessons in branches of musical science that with his manifold activities he would not have been able to master alone. His pupils bear him an affection which is not the expression of a fanatic cult. He is never the distant *"Meister,"* but the co-worker, an older, more experienced colleague of his pupils. There is really no other musician who has attracted such a large following of young men.

Strongly attached to his South German fatherland, Hindemith suffered greatly in the struggle waged against him. But he retained his poise of spirit and lives a calm life, aloof from politics, occupied with his work, a representative figure in his conduct and his character.

The second phase of Hindemith's career took place during his many years of residence in the United States. He enriched American musical life immeasurably with his unceasing activities not only as a composer but also as a teacher (as professor of music at Yale and as visiting lecturer at Harvard), as theorist (a significant volume of his outlook and methods was published in 1954, *A Composer's World: Horizons and Limitations*), and as conductor and violist. Major works came from his industrious pen in profusion, in every possible medium, all of them on the highest possible plane of integrity and artistic purpose: the *Theme and Variations According to the Four Temperaments* (1940), the Symphony in E-flat (1940), the *Symphonic Metamorphosis of Themes by Karl Maria von Weber* (1943), the *Symphonia Serena* (1946), the Sinfonietta in E (1950), and the symphony *Die Harmonie der Welt* (1950), all for orchestra; the opera *Die Harmonie der Welt* (1950); the *Ludus Tonalis,* for piano (1943); *When Lilacs Last in the Dooryard Bloom'd,* for chorus (1945); and the Piano Concerto (1945). No recess from activity here; no diminution of creative power!

In 1949, Hindemith paid a brief visit to Germany, his first return home since the war. He was now acclaimed by the press and honored by having a street named after him. The leading German musicians urged him to make his return permanent, but Hindemith refused. In 1953, when he finally decided to re-establish himself in Europe, he went to live in Zurich, where he joined the music faculty of the University of Zurich. Nevertheless, he continued to pay return visits to the United States in the ensuing decades. During one of these, in 1963, he participated in a four-day Hindemith festival in New York when his last opera was introduced to America, *The Long Christmas Dinner,* libretto by Thornton Wilder; its world *première* had previously taken place in Mannheim on December 17, 1961.

In 1955, Hindemith was the recipient of the Sibelius Award of $35,000 presented each year to an outstanding musician. In 1960 he was given the New York Music Critics Circle Award for his Six Madrigals, and in 1962, the Italian Balzan Prize of $52,000.

Despite his hyperintellectual interests and pursuits, Hindemith for many years was not above indulging in such boyish hobbies as playing with an elaborate system of toy trains on his living room floor. Later in his life he took an interest in cartooning, for which he demonstrated a marked gift; he would habitually send his own drawings as Christmas greetings to friends and acquaintances. On occasion, he also enjoyed carpentry.

On November 12, 1963, Hindemith conducted in Berlin an *a cappella* Mass. As it turned out, this was his last composition, and this appearance was his last in public. A few weeks later he suffered a stroke in Frankfurt, and died in a hospital in that city on December 29, 1963.

HIS MUSIC

Like so many other twentieth-century composers Hindemith went through various stages of development. First he embraced German Romanticism. Then he began to lean toward expressionism. Finally, he came to linear counterpoint and evolved his own idiom by combining polyphony with the most modern tonal devices and resources.

He arrived at his individual style in his second and third string quartets, Op. 22 and 32 (1922, 1924), in the first version of his song cycle *Das Marienleben,* Op. 27 (1923), and in the series of works called Kammermusik (Chamber Music), beginning with the second, Op. 36, No. 1 (1924). Stylistically many of these works looked backward and forward at the same time—backward to the contrapuntal music of Bach, forward to the complete freedom of tonality of the twentieth century. One German critic described some of his Kammermusik compositions as "Brandenburg Concertos—upside down." This linear technique was also evident in his first full-length opera, *Cardillac,* the first version of which was completed in 1926.

This, then, was a composer who, without rejecting the past, was a spokesman for his own times. While writing contrapuntally Hindemith felt that all tone combinations are possible as a new conception of "key" is realized. He wanted melody to be freed from its dependence on harmony, to achieve for the different voices of polyphony a complete freedom of movement.

The same trenchant intelligence that made Hindemith one of the finest teachers and theoreticians of our day is present in his music. His works abound with subtle processes of thought which cannot unfold themselves completely to the hearer at first acquaintance. While it is possible to enjoy a Hindemith work at first hearing, because it always *sounds* well, it is not at first possible to understand its logic fully. A Hindemith composition has heart, but that heart is not worn upon its sleeve. The listener must penetrate to the very core of the music to understand it intimately. Hindemith's thinking, however, is by no means abstruse, though it is usually penetrating; and his technique is never esoteric, though generally it is intricate.

Hindemith was one of the most prolific composers of our day. This is just one more way, beyond his partiality for polyphony, in which he reminded us of the Baroque composer. His production was voluminous and embraced every possible area. No year passed without several Hindemith works, large and small, being added to this formidable list. In spite of his fertility, Hindemith maintained a remarkably high standard of artistic achievement. His works never betray haste. He was one of the most skillful technicians of his time; his compositions are always models of astute craftsmanship; they never suffer from glibness. Complex in texture, involved in thought, original in structural outlines, his music is ever a rewarding experience for those prepared to give it the concentration it requires.

ANALYTICAL NOTES

Chamber Music. Three of the compositions Hindemith identified as Kammermusik, or Chamber Music, belong within the chamber music category, but only three; the others are orchestral works.

Kleine Kammermusik, Op. 24, No. 2 (1922), is for flute, oboe, clarinet, horn, and bassoon. It reveals Hindemith's early interest in satire, parody, and humor, and his then occasional tendency to use a popular idiom. Kammermusik Nos. 2 and 3, Op. 36, Nos. 1 and 2 (1924–25), though concertos, are still within the boundaries of chamber music. The first is for piano and twelve solo instruments, while the latter is for cello and ten solo instruments. It is here that Hindemith's austere and objective attitudes become fixed for the first time, as he begins to develop his linear technique.

Hindemith wrote seven string quartets. His free use of tonality and his growing contrapuntal skill both become evident in his third and fourth quartets, Op. 16 and 22 (1922). In the third quartet, the first movement includes an atonal fugato, while in the fourth, the voices of the first-movement fugue and double fugue move with independence. In the latter composition, Hindemith's already impressive compositional skill is revealed in the closing movement's passacaglia, twenty-seven variations of a theme ending with a powerful fugato.

The fifth string quartet, Op. 32 (1924), and the sixth (1944) both designate a key for the entire work, in each instance the signature being E-flat major. But the tonality remains highly flexible throughout, even to the extent of including in the fifth quartet polytonal sequences. Hindemith's last string quartet, in 1945, however, once again abandons an identifying key. "Having earlier shown the way to the logical expansion of polyphonic concepts which led to the dissonant style of linear counterpoint," says Homer Ulrich of Hindemith's later quartets, "he has now developed an equally vigorous but more restrained manner which again allows subjective emotional expression to emerge. . . . Great energy has always been characteristic of Hindemith's music; here the energy of earlier works has been transformed into vitality and driving power."

Choral Music. The death of President Franklin D. Roosevelt in 1945 (and a commission from the Collegiate Chorale and its conductor, Robert Shaw) led to the writing of one of Hindemith's most poignant, most personal compositions: *When Lilacs Last in the Dooryard Bloom'd*. Walt Whitman's poem, inspired by the death of President Lincoln, provided Hindemith with an appropriate text.

Scored for soprano, baritone, chorus, and orchestra, the work is in four sections. It opens with a solemn orchestral prelude as the preface to the opening lines, "When lilacs last in the dooryard bloom'd," sung by baritone and chorus. This is followed by an affecting arioso for soprano and an extended march for chorus with which Lincoln's coffin is carried from Washington to its burial place in Springfield, Illinois. The second part is confined to baritone and chorus, and soprano and chorus, and ends up with a dramatic fugue. The third part comprises a baritone recitative, a hymn for baritone and orchestra, a duet for soprano and baritone, and a concluding carol for chorus to the words "Come, lovely and soothing Death." In the finale, a stirring recitative for the baritone leads to the deeply moving closing chorus, "And carried hither and yon through the smoke, and torn and bloody."

Operas. The turbulent early history of Hindemith's most famous opera, *Mathis der Maler*—the frustrated attempts to have it performed in Berlin during the early years of the Nazi regime—has been described in his biography. The opera was not staged until May 28, 1938, and then, of course, not in Nazi Germany, but in Zurich, where it enjoyed an overwhelming success. Not until 1959 did *Mathis der Maler* finally come home to the Berlin State Opera.

The central character of Hindemith's opera is the German religious painter Matthias Grünewald. Explaining his libretto, Hindemith wrote:

This man, who wants to delve into the most obscure motives for creative work, sinks into a fit of unfruitful brooding, despairs of his mission and becomes absorbed in problems, the solution of which now seems to him more important for the well-being of his oppressed fellow man than the creation of works of art. He goes to war and fights on the side of the rebellious peasants against the nobles and the church and thus against his own master, Cardinal Albrecht of Mayence. There is a gross contradiction between the imaginary ideal of a fair combat and just victory and the ugly reality of the Peasants' War.

Mathis soon sees the wide gulf separating him from his companions in arms, and when the peasants suffer a decisive defeat, he is so completely engulfed in despair that not even death by his own hand or a stranger's has mercy upon him. In an allegorical scene he experiences the temptation of St. Anthony; all the promptings of conscience within his tortured soul rise to assail and plague him and call him to account for his actions. . . . St. Paul, under whose allegorical disguise Cardinal Albrecht is to be recognized, enlightens Mathis, in the likeness of Anthony, about his mistakes and instructs him to the right road which he is to follow in the future. The conversion to conscious, supreme artistic endeavor is successful. Mathis devotes the remainder of his days to his art, which is henceforth rooted in the talent bestowed upon him by God and in his attachment to his native soil.

Hindemith assembled three extended orchestral episodes from the opera into a symphony which has become one of his most frequently performed orchestral compositions. Actually, the work is no symphony in the accepted sense of the term; it is more of a suite. Each section is a tonal representation of one of the panels on the Isenheim altar, which Grünewald painted and which is often regarded as his masterwork. In the opera each of these paintings is used to symbolize the dramatic action.

The first movement, entitled "Concert of Angels," is the opera's overture. Its principal theme is heard in the trombones in the eighth bar. This melody, *"Es sungen drei Engel,"* makes a frequent appearance throughout the opera. The entire section is serene and tender. The second movement, "The Entombment," appears in the sixth scene. There are two themes here: The first appears in muted strings and woodwinds, and the second is presented first by the oboe, then by the flute, against a pizzicato background. "The Temptation of St. Anthony"—which in the opera occurs in the final scene—begins with a brief introduction in the A-B-A structure. The main section, which is in a rapid, jiglike manner, culminates in a fugato. The movement ends with a majestic chorale for the woodwinds (with a countermelody in the horn and more counterpoint in the violins) followed by another chorale in the brass.

Hindemith had written his own text for *Mathis der Maler,* and he did this once again for his opera *Die Harmonie der Welt* (*Harmony of the World*), which he completed in 1950, and whose world *première* took place in Munich on August 11, 1957. The opera is built around the spiritual and physical life of Johannes Kepler, the astronomer and mathematician, and its background is the Thirty Years' War. In presenting a pageant of Kepler's life and times, Hindemith includes the three women who played vital roles in his career: his mother, Katharina, a woman with mystical tendencies who is accused of being a witch but who is rescued from death by her son; his little daughter by a first marriage, Susanna; and his second wife, also called Susanna, his inspiring partner in his development as a scientist.

Once again, as he had done with *Mathis der Maler,* Hindemith extracted three orchestral episodes for a "symphony." The first, "Musica Instrumentalis," touches on Kepler's unhappy childhood. Here the main musical materials are a stately theme for brass, a march tune, and a fugal episode. The second part, "Musica Humana," speaking of Kepler's spiritual development, is in two sections. The first is dominated by themes built from the interval of the fourth; and the second is introduced by an oboe solo and is brought to a climax for full orchestra. The finale, "Musica Mundana," or Kepler's mundane existence, consists of a passacaglia with twenty-one variations ending in a fugue.

Orchestral Music. Hindemith's most famous work for orchestra is the *Mathis der Maler* Symphony, which is discussed in the opera section. Another symphony adapted from opera, *Die Harmonie der Welt,* is also commented upon there.

The Symphony in E-flat, written in 1940, follows a more traditional symphonic pattern. It is in the four movements of the classical form.

In the first movement the main theme, which is loud and rhythmic, is announced by the brass section. After it has been discussed and after other subsidiary ideas derived from this basic one have been stated briefly, there comes the second principal subject, a lyrical passage for the woodwinds against pizzicato strings. This idea is also worked out; and it plays a prominent part in the coda that brings the movement to a close. In the second movement there is an insistent rhythm in the tympani which appears intermittently. Against this background the first main theme is immediately projected in the English horn, clarinet, and trumpet. The oboe brings on the second subject against chords in the violins. When the entire orchestra takes over the second subject, the rhythm becomes more and more assertive. The first theme is now worked out canonically in first violins and violas. This is followed by the coda, which emphasizes the rhythmic pattern.

The third movement is in the nature of a scherzo, with the scherzo-music tendency to indulge in good humor. There are three distinct sections. In the first the two principal themes are presented by the violins and the woodwinds respectively. The middle section, a trio, is also made up of two melodies, one for the oboe, the other for English horn and oboe. The opening material is then restored, though with alterations. The finale proceeds without a pause. A melody appears in the violins, is repeated and developed, and yields to a second theme in the brass. The middle part of this movement is in the nature of an intermezzo for flute and piccolo and subsequently for oboe. The earlier material of the movement is repeated. As the tempo slackens, the first theme is played by the trombones and repeated by the trumpets, and the movement comes to a loud and passionate close.

The *Symphonia Serena* was completed on the last day of 1946 for the Dallas Symphony Orchestra, which had commissioned it. It is a departure from Hindemith's other symphonies in its orchestration, with the first and last movements scored for full orchestra, the second exclusively for the winds, and the third for the strings alone. Another interesting feature of the symphony is its dependence, in the second movement, on two little-known marches for military band which Beethoven wrote in 1809.

When the Dallas Symphony Orchestra introduced the work on February 2, 1947, its conductor, Antal Dorati, provided what has since become its definitive analysis. "The first movement is in sonata form, a rather typical example of first movements of classical symphonies. . . . Its opening theme, with its descending fifths and ascending fourths, is one of the strongest I have heard in modern symphony writing. . . . The second theme is marked 'grazioso.' The third theme has the character of a coda. The themes are developed in the usual symphonic fashion. The exposition is brought back in the customary reprise, and the movement ends in a strong climax." The second movement, which utilizes the march melodies of Beethoven, assumes the role of a scherzo.

Under a fluent and steady current of woodwind passages, which provides a continuous thematic background, the Beethoven theme is stated in little bits at a time first and gradually becomes stronger, more and more coherent, and develops into a fast march, with which the scherzo closes brilliantly.

The third movement is written for string orchestra divided into two groups. The first puts forth a serious and tender slow theme. The second group plays a faster scherzando section, pizzicato. These two sections are connected by a recitative-like passage for two solo violins, one of them playing backstage. After the pizzicato section, again a recitative-like passage is played, this time by two solo violas in the same fashion as before, the second answering the first from behind the scene; and following that section, the movement ends with the first and second string groups playing their respective themes simultaneously.

The finale . . . opens with a very short, fanfare-like introduction; then, by way of a symphonic exposition, introduces no less than five themes, each of which is already developed right when introduced. Following this section comes one which is nearest to a sonata development section, in which themes Nos. 3 and 4 from the exposition are developed, and, at the same time, the main theme of the first movement of the symphony is brought back rather grandiosely. An abbreviated reprise follows, which reintroduces the themes of the exposition, minus those which were developed in the second section of the movement. A short coda, which gives new, thematic importance to an accompanying figure used throughout the movement, closes with a repetition of the fanfare-like passage with which the movement has begun, and closes brilliantly.

The Konzertmusik for Strings and Brass (Op. 50) is one of Hindemith's finest shorter works for orchestra. He wrote it in 1930 on a commission from the Boston Symphony Orchestra to commemorate its fiftieth anniversary. It is in two movements. The first begins with a powerful subject for trumpets and trombones in unison against a rhythmic accompaniment by the strings. This is followed by a second theme for brass alone. We now have a section for strings alone in which the accompaniment to the first theme is elaborated. The second theme comes in for some treatment by the full orchestra, after which the accompanying material of the strings is repeated. The movement ends with the first theme loudly proclaimed by the strings. The second movement is a three-voice fugue. The theme of the fugue appears first in the violins, then in the violas, and finally in the cellos and basses. Material of contrasting nature interrupts the fugue, which returns to conclude the work.

Nobilissima Visione is an orchestral suite adapted from the score for the ballet *St. Francis,* written in 1937 for the Ballet Russe de Monte Carlo. The composer has provided his own description of the suite's three movements and their connection with the ballet:

The introduction consists of that part of the original music during which the hero of the action is sunk in deep meditation. The Rondo corresponds to the music in the stage score for the mystic union of the Saint to Mistress Poverty, the scene having been inspired by an old Tuscan legend. The music reflects the blessed peace and unworldly cheer with which the guests at the wedding participate in the wedding feast—dry bread and water only. The second movement pictures the march of a troop of medieval soldiers. First heard but distantly, their gradual approach is observed. The middle portion of the movement suggests the brutality with which these mercenaries set upon a traveling burgher and rob him. The third and closing movement, Passacaglia, corresponds to that portion in the ballet score representing the dance, Hymn to the Sun. Here all the symbolic personifications of heavenly and earthly existence mingle in the course of the different Variations through which the six-measure theme of the Passacaglia is transformed.

Theme and Variations According to the Four Temperaments (1940) had originally been intended for a ballet, which never materialized. Hindemith adapted his score as a concert work for piano and strings. (This music has since been used for ballet.) The composition consists of a series of three themes stated at the beginning, followed by four variations, each of which represents a different mood: "Melancholic," "Sanguinic," "Phlegmatic," and "Choleric."

In *Symphonic Metamorphosis on Themes by Karl Maria von*

Weber (1943), Hindemith lifts four themes from some less familiar compositions by Weber. In the first, third, and last movements the material comes out of *All'Ongarese,* Op. 60, for piano four hands, while the second movement quotes a theme from Weber's overture to *Turandot.* The four movements are an allegro, a moderato, an andantino, and a march.

The Sinfonietta in E is a four-movement composition which Hindemith wrote for the Louisville Orchestra in Kentucky in 1950. The first movement has the surge and sweep of an opening movement in a Baroque concerto grosso. The second movement begins with a reflective adagio section and passes on to a vigorous fugato. In the third movement the subject is an ostinato figure that passes from one group of instruments to another. The sinfonietta ends with a light, vivacious finale.

In the series of compositions that Hindemith identified as Kammermusik will be found four concertos for solo instruments and chamber orchestra: No. 4—Op. 36, No. 3 (1925)—is for the violin; No. 5—Op. 36, No. 4 (1927)—is for viola; No. 6—Op. 46, No. 1 (1930)—is for viola d'amore; and No. 7—Op. 46, No. 2 (1928)—is for the organ.

But Hindemith's most important concertos for solo instruments and orchestra are not found in this group. One of them, for viola and orchestra, is called *Der Schwanendreher* (*The Organ Grinder*). It was written in 1935. All of its thematic material is derived from German folk tunes of the fifteenth and sixteenth centuries; and the name of the work is derived from the folk melody "Seid ihr nicht der Schwanendreher" ("Are You Not the Organ Grinder"), which appears in the third movement. In the first movement we hear the tune "Zwischen Berg und tiefem Tal," ("Between Hill and Dale") presented by the horns after a brief viola solo. The second movement is in two parts, each based on a folk song. The first, "Nun laube, Lindlein, laube" ("Linden, Now Is the Time to Leaf"), emerges as a duet for solo viola and harp. A ten-bar solo passage for viola leads to the second melody, "Der Gutzgauch auf dem Zaune sass" ("The Cuckoo Sat on the Fence"), presented as a fugato. The finale is a set of five variations on the melody "Seid ihr nicht der Schwanendreher."

The Concerto for Violin and Orchestra, which came in 1939, is made up of expansive melodies. Two of them appear in the first movement, presented by the solo instrument; the first is an ecstatic song for the high register, while the second is in a more tranquil vein. Another extended melody makes up the second movement. It is introduced by the solo violin, after an introductory passage for the woodwinds, and is taken up later by a clarinet solo to embellishments by the violin soloist. The third movement, a rondo, is made up of dance melodies.

The Concerto for Piano and Orchestra followed the Violin Concerto by six years. The most interesting movement of this work is the third, an elaboration of a fourteenth-century dance tune called "Tre Fontane" ("Three Fountains"). The first two movements are highly lyrical. In the first movement, the two principal themes are presented, respectively, by the clarinet (and then taken up by the piano) and by two clarinets and bass clarinet (also repeated immediately by the piano). The second movement is in a three-part-song form. In the first part there are two dominant themes: The first is for the cellos and bass clarinet in unison, the second is for the piano. After a middle section—made up of a single idea for the piano repeated by the horn—the material of the initial section appears with slight variation.

In 1949 Hindemith wrote the Concerto for Woodwinds, Harp, and Orchestra as a birthday gift for his wife. With this occasion in mind he interpolated into the closing rondo movement a brief quotation from the "Wedding March" in Mendelssohn's *A Midsummer Night's Dream* Suite. This kind of levity prevails throughout the entire concerto, which is so predominantly light of heart that one annotator described the work as a "fun piece." In the second movement, Hindemith dispenses in his orchestration with trumpets and trombones, and in one episode uses the horns to double the lower strings. Here the main idea is a sustained lyrical thought in the woodwinds, accompanied by the strings.

Piano Music. Hindemith's reverence for Johann Sebastian Bach and his partiality for polyphony led him to emulate the master in a major work for the keyboard. At the dusk of his career, Bach wrote *The Art of the Fugue* to demonstrate the technical resources of contrapuntal writing and at the same time probably to demonstrate his ówn powers with this technique. Hindemith might very well have had the same goals in mind when in 1943 he wrote *Ludus Tonalis*

(*Tonal Play*), a giant work for solo piano that takes forty-five minutes to perform. Hindemith subtitled his work "Studies in Counterpoint, Tonal Organization, and Piano Playing." It comprises twelve fugues in three voices, each in a different key of the chromatic scale. Interludes, providing contrast through lightness of mood and lyricism, separate each of the fugues. The work as a whole opens with a praeludium and concludes with a postludium which is the praeludium inverted and in retrograde.

Vocal Music. Though written comparatively early in Hindemith's career, in 1923, the song cycle *Das Marienleben* (*The Life of Mary*) is one of his masterworks. Hindemith himself fully recognized the importance of this music, and revealed his sustained interest in it when eighteen years after writing it he revised it extensively to have it comply more faithfully to his now mature style and to take into greater consideration the limitations as well as the potentials of the singing voice.

The cycle is a setting of thirteen poems by Rilke, which narrate the life of the Virgin Mary. The composer divides these poems into four groups. In the first he concentrates on Mary's personal experiences and here the musical treatment is either lyric or epic. The second group has greater dramatic interest, though several numbers are of an idyllic nature. "In these songs," the composer has explained, "a considerable number of persons, actions, scenes and circumstances are shown, and only in the last of them does our central figure again actively appear." The third group describes Mary's suffering in music that is at times highly intense and at times sublime. The fourth group reaches, the composer says, "the highest point of abstraction, in which purely musical ideas and forms prevail. This is an epilogue in which persons and actions no longer play any role."

Arthur Honegger

"He has a large vision, and goes his own way unconcerned about passing infatuations and fashions."

HENRI PRUNIÈRES

BORN: Le Havre, France, March 10, 1892.
DIED: Paris, France, November 27, 1955.
MAJOR WORKS: *Ballets*—Skating Rink; Le Cantique des cantiques; L'Appel de la montagne; De la musique. *Chamber Music*—3 string quartets; 2 violin sonatas; Viola Sonata; Cello Sonata; Sonata for Solo Violin. *Choral Music*—Le Roi David; Jeanne d'Arc au bûcher; La Danse des morts; Nicolas de Flue; Cantata de Noël. *Operas*—Judith; Antigone; Amphion. *Orchestral Music*—5 symphonies; Pastorale d'été; Horace victorieux; Chant de joie; Pacific 231; Piano Concertino; Rugby; Cello Concerto; Mouvement symphonique No. 3; Concerto da camera for Flute, English Horn, and Strings; Suite archaïque; Monopartita. *Piano Music*—Prelude, Arioso, et Fughetta sur le nom de Bach; Partita for Two Pianos. *Vocal Music*—Quatre poèmes; Poésies de Jean Cocteau; Trois psaumes.

HIS LIFE

Although Honegger was born in France and maintained his permanent home in Paris, he regarded himself as a Swiss composer. He never gave up his Swiss citizenship, which he acquired by virtue of his parents being Swiss. They had come from Zurich to the French seaport of Le Havre to set up business importing café-house fixtures. At the harbor the boy Honegger spent fascinated hours watching boats and trains, for which he never outgrew his passion. His first major musical impression came from hearing a Bach cantata performed in Le Havre under André Caplet's direction. Honegger had acquired a love for music from hearing his mother play the piano and had undertaken the study of the violin with a local teacher named Sautreuil. But the Bach work opened up new musical horizons, awakening in him for the first time the desire to become a composer. He did not wait too long to bring this ambition to realization. Hearing his mother play a potpourri of melodies from Mozart's *The Magic Flute*—and having heard *Faust* and *Les Huguenots* at the opera house—he decided that he would write an opera, text as well as music. He wrote not one opera but two (entirely in the treble clef because he was at the time acquainted with no other), as well as some sonatas; it must be confessed, though, that any resemblance to the actual forms of opera and sonata was purely coincidental.

From the town organist Honegger acquired an elementary training in harmony and composition. The idea of becoming a professional musician was still remote. In his sixteenth year he entered his father's business. But his heart was elsewhere, as his father recognized before very long. The father decided to send him to the Zurich Conservatory for additional music study. Friedrich Hegar, director of the Conservatory, soon convinced the father that his son had unusual talent and won him over to the idea of sending the boy to the Paris Conservatory. Honegger went to Paris in 1912. At the Conservatory he studied under Gédalge, Widor, Capet, and Vincent d'Indy in classes that included Darius Milhaud (later to be coupled with Honegger in a new so-called school of young French composers) and Andrée Vaurabourg (subsequently Mrs. Honegger).

In 1914 Honegger was called back to Switzerland to complete the year of military service required of all Swiss citizens. He spent his leisure time writing music, mostly songs. But in 1915 he was back at the Conservatory and on July 13, 1916, he made his debut as a composer when a few of his songs were heard in a small Paris hall. Later the same year, on December 15, Andrée Vaurabourg introduced his Toccata and Variations for Piano at a concert of the Cercle Musical et Dramatique in Paris. He also wrote a great deal of chamber music, as well as his first work for orchestra, an overture to Maeterlinck's play *Aglavaine et Sélysette,* whose world *première* took place at the Paris Conservatory on April 3, 1917, the composer conducting.

He was to come to prominence in conjunction with a group of other young French composers self-styled *"les nouveaux jeunes,"* which gave its first concert at the Vieux Colombier on January 15, 1918. This group, which included Roland-Manuel, Georges Auric, Germaine Tailleferre, and Francis Poulenc, besides Honegger, did not at first attract much attention. Nor was any greater attention paid to performances of Honegger's works which took place the same year: a concert of his chamber music in a Paris studio on January 19 and a performance of his incidental music to Paul Méral's play *Le Dit des jeux du monde* at the Vieux Colombier on December 3.

But in 1920 the group came into sudden recognition, and not entirely by its own efforts. On January 16, Henri Collet reviewed in *Comoedia* an album of piano pieces by Honegger, Auric, Milhaud, Poulenc, Tailleferre, and Louis Durey. In this article Collet referred to these composers as "The French Six," drawing a parallel between them and the Russian nationalist school known as "The Five." "The six Frenchmen," he wrote, "have by a magnificent and voluntary return to simplicity brought about a renaissance of French music." There is magic in a catch phrase! The six composers, banded together by Collet into a single new school of French music, were different in temperament and artistic approach. They were friends and were interested in each other's work. But they had no intention of traveling together under any single artistic banner—Honegger least of all. (Though on one occasion five of them—Durey was the exception—collaborated on a score for a Jean Cocteau ballet, *Les Mariés de la tour Eiffel,* presented by the Ballets Suédois in Paris on June 19, 1921.) But the name "The French Six" caught on. It became a powerful instrument for presenting the names of these new composers to the music public and for inviting important performances of their works.

In his own way Honegger proved that there was no unifying element in the works of these six composers; for there was no unifying element in his own endeavors. In 1921 he created an oratorio in the Handelian manner, *King David* (*Le Roi David*). It was given a stage presentation in Switzerland on June 11 of the same year. Later on Honegger adapted the work for concert purposes;

performed in Paris, Zurich, Rome, and New York from 1924–26 it was a tremendous success. But no sooner was Honegger identified as an archconservative than he proceeded to write music in the advanced polytonal and dissonant manner of the times: *Horace victorieux* and the notorious *Pacific 231*. The former was heard in Lausanne on October 30, 1921, and the latter at a Koussevitzky concert in Paris on May 8, 1924.

Between the two world wars Honegger crystallized his style and produced the works which elevated him to a dominating position in French music—operas, chamber music, orchestral music, vocal music, and choral music.

Honegger married Andrée Vaurabourg on May 10, 1926. They made their home in Paris where they raised a daughter. In 1929, Honegger paid his first visit to the United States where he made many appearances with major orchestras in the presentation of his compositions.

During the 1930s, Honegger wrote some of his greatest works for orchestra, notably the oratorios *Jeanne d'Arc au bûcher* and *La Danse des morts*. Both received their world *premières* in Basel, the former on May 10, 1938, and the latter on March 2, 1940.

During World War II, with the Nazi occupation of Paris, Honegger remained a virtual recluse in his apartment, writing music and serving as an important link in the chain of the French Resistance forces. Time and again he was invited by the Nazis to conduct both in Germany and over the German-controlled radio in France, and each time he turned them down contemptuously. The Nazis did not interfere with him, however, and he was able to complete several important works deeply affected by the mood and spirit of the times. One of these was the Symphony for Strings, his finest work for orchestra up to then; it was introduced in Basel on May 18, 1942. Another was a large work for baritone, chorus, and orchestra, prophetically entitled *Chant de Libération,* which was finally performed in Paris on October 22, 1944, two months after Paris had been liberated.

In 1947, Honegger was invited by Serge Koussevitzky to visit the United States and teach composition during the summer at the Berkshire Music Center in Lenox, Massachusetts. A heart attack made it impossible for him to complete this assignment. Despite the deterioration of his health, Honegger continued to produce major works after his return to Paris, including his fifth and last symphony, whose first performance took place in Boston on March 9, 1951, and the *Monopartita,* for orchestra, its *première* following that of the symphony by three months, in Zurich on June 12. Honegger's death in Paris on November 27, 1955, was brought about by a second heart attack.

HIS MUSIC

The early Honegger vacillated in almost successive works from one style to another: from the conservatism of *King David* (1921) to the polytonal thinking of *Horace victorieux* (1921) and the discords of *Pacific 231* (1923); from the playful wit of the Piano Concertino (1924) to the powerful dramatic surges of the biblical drama *Judith* (1926) and the musical tragedy *Antigone* (1927). He was groping for the style best suited to his nature. When he arrived at it the style was far different from that generally associated with "The French Six": neoclassic economy, restraint, and lucidity on the one hand; Gallic wit and satire on the other. Honegger's style was virile, even passionate; emphasis was placed on musical architecture, vigorous rhythms, dissonant harmonies, sometimes linear counterpoint, and vague tonalities; expressive lyricism, however, was not sacrificed. This style reached maturity with the Concerto for Cello and Orchestra (1929), the First Symphony (1930), and the Mouvement symphonique No. 3 (1932). In later works, religious feeling—even mysticism and spirituality—enter Honegger's writing to endow it with exalted qualities his music rarely possessed before this; in this category belong the oratorios of the 1930s and the symphonies of the 1940s and 1950s.

ANALYTICAL NOTES

Choral Music. Honegger's two most significant oratorios came fourteen years apart. The first, *Le Roi David* (*King David*), represented his first success, at a time when his style had not yet achieved an identifying profile. In the other, *Jeanne d'Arc au bûcher* (*Joan of Arc at the Stake*), his style had not only become fully personalized but also had begun to assimilate spiritual values.

Le Roi David (1921) is an oratorio in the Handelian format, and with continual suggestions of a Handelian style in the choral pages, particularly in the use of polyphonic resources. Utilizing a text by René Morat, *Le Roi David* is made up of twenty-eight sections divided among three large segments. The first segment traces David's life from the time he was a shepherd through his battle with Goliath and his confrontation with King Saul. A psalm for unison chorus, the march of the Philistines, and the Jewish song of mourning are some of the notable episodes in this section. The second segment opens with the song and dance celebrating the crowning of King David and concludes with an exultant Alleluia. The third and concluding segment brings the David story to its end with his death. Here the memorable parts include the march of the Israelites and two songs of penitence. The Alleluia that had closed the second segment is brought back to end the oratorio where it is placed contrapuntally against a chorale.

Jeanne d'Arc au bûcher (1935)—text by Paul Claudel—is much less conventional than *Le Roi David* both as to structure and style. Though designated as an oratorio (and often performed today as such) it was originally intended by its composer as a mimodrama—in other words, as a stage production with scenery and costumes. Honegger wrote it for the dancer Ida Rubinstein, who appeared as Joan when this oratorio received its world *première,* in Basel in 1938. The role of Joan is a speaking one exclusively (as is also the case with the part of Frère Dominique). She stands on one level of the stage throughout the performance, fastened to the stake. On another level stands Frère Dominique, a narrator who recalls episodes from Joan's life. The chorus, placed on different levels, represents the people and makes comments not only on phases of Joan's life and martyrdom, but also on the Church and society of Joan's time. Since Paul Claudel's drama is more of a morality play than an oratorio text, it is filled with symbolic figures suggesting pride, ignorance, or avarice; animals perform human judicial functions or reflect the less noble attributes of the French people; a game of cards serves to illustrate the game of war and the gamelike functions of state.

The oratorio consists of a prologue and eleven scenes. The prologue has the chorus describing the low state of morality, ideals, and human conscience to which France had fallen. The French people cry out to be saved. Highlights of Joan's life are then told in flashbacks, commentaries, and dramatic episodes. The oratorio closes eloquently, first with Joan's recollection of her girlhood in Lorraine with a simple folk tune, and then with a mighty choral episode entitled "The Burning of Joan" where the chorus comments bitterly that the "holy Joan" has been condemned as a sorcerer as Joan herself passes from disbelief through fear to triumph. A final comment is contributed by the chorus of saints and children's voices: "Greater love hath no man than this—to give his life for those he loves."

Honegger himself designated his work as a "dramatic oratorio," and it is the dramatic element that is most pronounced throughout his musical writing, though religious and spiritual overtones are not absent. His score is a skillful blend of music and spoken dialogue, of accompanied recitatives and dialogue, of stirring choruses and equally effective orchestral interludes, of soaring lyricism and dramatic *Sprechstimme*.

These are the titles which Claudel gave to the eleven scenes: The Voices of Heaven; The Book; The Voices of Earth; Joan Delivered to the Beasts; Joan at the Stake; The Kings, or the Invention of the Card Game; Catherine and Marguerite; The King Who Goes to Rheims; Joan's Swords; "Trimazo"—Rehearsal of the Merry Month of May; and Joan of Arc in Flames.

Orchestral Music. *Pacific 231,* more than any other early work of Honegger, gave him the reputation of being music's *enfant terrible.* In 1923, when it was written, it appeared to be the last word in daring discords and rapidly changing meters and rhythms. Our ears have since become accustomed to much sterner stuff. The shock is there no more. Instead we hear an interesting musical study of movement, the realistic picture of a train in motion. The appeal of this music is largely kinesthetic, through the impact of its rhythms, cacophony, and motor energy. Nervous rhythms and abrupt chords in the opening of the piece suggest the chugging of the train as it is set into motion. The rhythms grow increasingly complex; the speed gains momentum. Then discords are piled one on top of another as the train travels at lightning speed. At the end of the work, heavy chords and halting rhythms bring the train to a lumbering halt.

Another short and early orchestral piece by Honegger has a

much different character. It is *Pastorale d'été* (1921), a delicate tone portrait of nature constructed from two bucolic themes, the first for the horn and the other for clarinet. Some conductors have performed this pastoral music on the same program as *Pacific 231* as a study in contrasts.

The delightful Concertino for Piano and Orchestra which followed *Pastorale d'été* by three years and *Pacific 231* by one is the kind of slight and witty music the French (particularly the students of Nadia Boulanger) write so well: with epigrammatic themes (often touched with whimsey), high-spirited moods, and even jazz rhythms. In the first movement there is a sprightly little dialogue between piano and orchestra. There follows a fugal passage, after which the dialogue returns. A wistful little melody appears in the piano against accompanying strings in the second movement. This melody is elaborated upon by the orchestra. In the finale the violins establish a strong rhythm by striking the backs of the bows on the strings. The piano then enters with a jazzy, highly syncopated subject. Another tune appears in the violas and bassoons. A climax is reached through a crescendo, and the movement ends with healthy animal spirits.

The Symphony No. 2, for string orchestra, was one of Honegger's greatest and most deeply emotional works up to that time. It was written in 1941, a year of crisis. The Nazis were occupying Paris. Some have found this music expressive of those terrible times and Honegger's reaction to them. André George wrote that the symphony "embodies much of the mood of occupied Paris, to which the composer remained faithful under all conditions." And Olin Downes saw in the music a picture of France of that day—now desperate, now defiant. Honegger, however, has disavowed all programmatic interpretations for the work.

The symphony opens with a slow introduction made up, for the most part, of a figure first heard in the solo viola. In the allegro that follows, this figure becomes converted into a vigorously rhythmic theme for low strings. There is a second theme of more lyric character, played by the first violins. The two themes are worked out with brutal strength, as dissonances and dynamic rhythms sound the shrill note of defiance; but there are also passages of great gloom. After the development, the material of the introduction is brought back for elaboration and repetition. In the coda, the rhythmic first theme, this time presented very quietly, is prominent.

The second movement is in the form of a passacaglia. The passacaglia ground bass subject appears in the first eight measures in the cellos. Eight variations follow. Up through the fourth variation there is an increase in sonority and in intensity of feeling. The entire movement passes from subdued pain to uncontrolled grief. But in the last movement (which has the character of a rondo) there is optimism, even gaiety, as one theme succeeds another in rapid succession. In the closing pages there is an exultant chorale hymn in the first violins supplemented by a single trumpet.

The Symphony No. 2 was Honegger's second work in that form. (The first was written in 1930 to commemorate the fiftieth anniversary of the Boston Symphony Orchestra.) The Symphony No. 3, *Liturgique*, came in 1946. The only clues to the programmatic implications of each of its three movements are found in the Latin liturgical phrases heading each: the first is *Dies irae;* the second, *De profundis clamavis;* and the third, *Dona nobis pacem*. But the dramatic expressiveness and the emotional turbulence of the music lend themselves to extramusical interpretation. To Charles Munch, to whom the symphony is dedicated, it represents the revolt of man against a higher will, followed by man's voluntary submission to it. To Arthur Hoerée the symphony is the expression "of a spirit in search of serenity amid all the unrest which is our present state." If there is unrest, it is found in the first and third movements, in the turbulent rhythms, vigorous syncopation, abrupt accents; if there is serenity, it can be heard in the fervent song of the second movement, particularly in the gentle and idyllic solo for flute with which the movement ends.

The Symphony No. 4, written in 1946, was subtitled *Deliciae Basilienses* (*Basel Delights*) because old popular songs of Basel are incorporated. In the second movement, the song "Z'Basel an mi'm Rhi" is heard in its entirety, and in its original form, in the horn. The tune "Basler Morgenstreich" is woven into the polyphonic texture of the third movement.

The Symphony No. 5 was completed in 1950 on a commission from the Koussevitzky Music Foundation. This work is subtitled *Di tre re* (*Of three D's*) because a unifying element is the note "D" tapped quietly on the drum at the end of each of the three movements. A majestic theme for full orchestra launches the first movement; the second theme of the movement is, by contrast, a gently flowing figure in clarinets and English horn. In the second movement, the traditional slow and scherzo movements of the symphony are telescoped into one. It opens lightly with a delicate duet between clarinet and first violins. An adagio section appears after a climax, and is followed by the return of the opening quick part. The finale features an incisive staccato rhythmic motto in the brass.

Aram Khatchaturian

"Khatchaturian's works weave the traditional musical art of his people on a modern frame."

BORIS ASAFIEV

BORN: Tiflis, Russia, June 6, 1903.
MAJOR WORKS: *Ballets*—Gayane; Spartacus. *Chamber Music*—String Quartet; Trio for Clarinet, Violin, and Piano; Violin Sonata. *Orchestral Music*—3 symphonies; Violin Concerto; Piano Concerto; Concerto for Violin, Cello, and Orchestra; Cello Concerto; Masquerade, suite; Russian Fantasy; Concerto-Rhapsody for Violin and Orchestra; Concerto-Rhapsody for Piano and Orchestra; Concerto-Rhapsody for Cello and Orchestra; Flute Concerto.

HIS LIFE

Russian composers, particularly the nationalists, have always been partial to the musical idiom of the Russian Orient. But at last there has arisen a composer who was actually born in one of the Caucasian countries and who uses the folk materials of his own people.

He is Aram Khatchaturian, Soviet composer of Armenian birth. Unfortunately, his father, a bookbinder, was too poor to allow his son to indulge his apparent musical gifts. Up to the time he was nineteen, Aram knew nothing about theory and was unacquainted with even the basic works in the musical repertory. The only music he knew—and that music he knew well—was the songs and dances which he heard all around him from childhood.

But he had an insatiable curiosity and a burning desire to learn, which remained unsatisfied until after the Khatchaturian family had moved to Moscow in 1920. In 1923, Aram was enrolled in the Gnesin School of Music where his advance was so rapid that in two years' time he was able to write a piece of music good enough to get published. That piece, a dance for violin and piano (1926), was derived from the folk music of the Transcaucasian peoples, as was his second published composition, a poem for piano, in 1927.

In 1929 he went on from the Gnesin School to the Moscow Conservatory, where his teachers included Miaskovsky and Vassilenko. He continued to study and learn; he also kept on writing new works: in 1932 a trio (for clarinet, violin, and piano), in which he used not only Armenian melodies and rhythms but also those of other Caucasian republics; in 1933 his first work for orchestra, a dance suite. For his graduation he produced his most ambitious work up to that time, the three-movement Symphony No. 1, written to honor the fifteenth anniversary of the Sovietization of Armenia. When introduced by the Moscow Philharmonic under Eugene Szenkar, in 1934, it was received enthusiastically. "This fine composition," wrote Khubov, "may without exaggeration be described as an important peak . . . in the general development of Soviet symphonism."

From then on Khatchaturian's rise as one of the most widely acclaimed and most highly honored of Soviet composers were meteoric. One year after the symphony, he produced his Concerto for Piano and Orchestra, which was a phenomenal success when introduced on July 5, 1937. Critics regarded it as an "event in Soviet music" which succeeded (as they put it) in rehabilitating the importance of the piano concerto in Soviet music. It has remained one of Khatchaturian's most popular works; it is even more familiar outside of the Soviet Union than in it.

The then much coveted Stalin Prize came to him for the first time in 1941 with the Concerto for Violin and Orchestra, which he had written in 1938, and which had received its world *première* in Moscow on November 16, 1940. The successes enjoyed by his ballet *Gayane,* when produced in Molotov on December 9, 1942, and his Second Symphony, first heard in Moscow on December 30, 1943, also led to Stalin Prizes. Meanwhile other honors came his way. In 1939 he received the Order of Lenin for his services in developing music of Armenia. In 1943 his name was inscribed on a marble tablet in the hall of the Moscow Conservatory as one of its celebrated graduates.

Despite his importance in Soviet music and his ever expanding successes Khatchaturian did not escape official criticism when, on February 10, 1948, the Central Committee of the Communist Party hurled accusation of "decadent formalism" at the leading composers of the Soviet Union and subjected them to the severest censure. The full story of that incident, which rocked the world of music, is told in a later chapter (*see* Prokofiev). What is particularly interesting in Khatchaturian's case—and particularly paradoxical—is that he had been writing the kind of music the Soviet officialdom now set up as the desirable standard: music avoiding all extremes of style and technique, pleasing in melodic and harmonic content, deriving its material from folk sources.

At the time, Khatchaturian freely confessed the error of his ways, accompanying his breast-beating with a promise he would write music hewing more closely to the lines drawn by the Central Committee. But a half year after Stalin's death in 1953, Khatchaturian published in *Soviet Music* an attack on the policies so long adopted by the Government for Soviet composers. At the same time he sent out a call to these composers to liberate themselves by giving freer rein to creative innovation. That this article was published at all represented a thaw in the cold war between the Government and the leading composers of the Soviet Union. That letter represented the beginnings of a new Soviet policy which was finally enunciated in 1958, in which Soviet composers were given greater latitude for self-expression and experiment and in which the onetime condemnation of composers like Khatchaturian, Shostakovich, and Prokofiev was considered ill-advised.

If there was any doubt that Khatchaturian had been completely exonerated, that doubt was certainly dispelled only a half year after the article appeared. In 1954, he was given the Lenin Prize for his ballet *Spartacus.* (A revival of *Spartacus,* with new choreography by Yuri Grigorovich, became in 1968 the greatest success of any new production by the Bolshoi Ballet in Moscow in twenty years.) His sixtieth birthday, in 1963, became an event for national celebration, and soon thereafter Khatchaturian was given one of the highest distinctions his Government could give him when he received the honorary title of People's Artist of the U.S.S.R.

For many years Khatchaturian has pursued a successful career as professor of composition at both of his alma maters—the Gnesin School and the Moscow Conservatory. He and his wife, Nina Markova (whom he had met and fallen in love with when both attended the Moscow Conservatory, and who has become one of the most celebrated women composers in the Soviet Union), maintain an apartment in Moscow, in the same house where reside both Shostakovich and the distinguished cellist Mstislav Rostropovich. The Khatchaturians maintain a country home where they spend most of their time and do most of their composing. They own two automobiles and employ a chauffeur.

Khatchaturian has made many appearances in Europe conducting his music. He paid his first visit to the United States in 1960, but his American debut as conductor did not take place until January 23, 1968, when he appeared with the National Symphony Orchestra in Washington, D.C. On that occasion he presented the American *première* of his Concerto-Rhapsody for Cello and Orchestra, with Rostropovich as soloist. This is one work of a triptych, having been preceded by the Concerto-Rhapsody for Violin and Orchestra, and followed by the Concerto-Rhapsody for Piano and Orchestra.

HIS MUSIC

"Folk music for me," Khatchaturian once wrote, "is not an end in itself, but a means to an end."

Early in his career Khatchaturian tried writing music in the dissonant style of the modern Europeans. But he immediately discovered that he had no sympathy whatsoever for such an idiom, that it did not come naturally to him, and that as a consequence the result was artificial and stilted. When he wrote music which he felt deeply within him, he found himself imitating the melodies and rhythms he had known and loved since childhood—the music of his people. He therefore accepted the folk style as his own, not for the express purpose of creating a national art, but because it served his artistic purpose. His music abounds with the Caucasian rhythms, oriental colors, striking contrasts of mood, and long, rambling, improvisational melodies that are found so plentifully in the folk songs of the *ashugs* (bards) and in Armenian folk dances. Many of his harmonies derive their complex physiognomy from his studied attempt to imitate the effects peculiar to native Armenian instruments.

ANALYTICAL NOTES

Orchestral Music. The compositions that first brought Khatchaturian his enormous popularity in the world's concert auditoriums—the large works produced between 1935 and 1946—are still those representing him most often on programs today.

The first of these is the Concerto for Piano and Orchestra (1935), whose pronounced orientalism encouraged Soviet critics to describe it as "Borodinesque." It is fresh in its exotic melodies, which are made up of small intervals and built out of eight-note and nine-note scales; it is exciting in rhythmic force; it is striking in its contrasts of orchestral color. The forceful, even barbaric, first main theme of the first movement is heard at once in the piano, immediately after a brief and savage orchestral outburst. The movement is for the most part percussive, given to virtuoso passages for the piano. But the glowing second theme, introduced by the oboe and elaborated upon by the piano, brings an emotional respite with its oriental languor.

In the second movement we hear an exotic Eastern melody of rare beauty unfolding in the piano as the low notes of the flute provide a piquant background. It is such melodies as this which made some writers remark that Khatchaturian's lyricism has caught the improvisational character of the songs of Armenian bards (the *ashugs*). Later the strings take over the melody and the piano provides delicate filigree work. There is soon a second poignant theme, given by the flute and taken over by the piano.

If the second movement is poetic and rhapsodic, the third is barbaric and uninhibited. The piano thunders out a few chords, after which a trumpet solo is heard in a racy theme which the piano continues. The music achieves a frenzy of color and sound; the piano is involved in the savage proceedings. Toward the close of the movement the trumpet theme is heard once again, leading to a recall of the main theme of the first movement magnificently orated by the brass. The concerto ends with a coda in which the main themes of both the first and third movements are sounded simultaneously.

The Concerto for Violin and Orchestra came three years after the Piano Concerto, and was given the Stalin Prize in 1941. Like the Piano Concerto, it opens in a forceful vein. The first theme, heard in the solo instrument after a brief orchestral exhortation, has primitive force and rhythmic interest; the momentum is intensified when the theme is shared between the solo violin and the orchestra. A languorous second theme, given by the solo violin, brings temporary repose. The second movement is an extended song for the violin with the character of a Slavic lament; it appears in the solo instrument after a dramatic orchestral preface. The finale is vertiginous music which abounds with passionate gypsy melodies and rhythms.

Gayane (or *Gayaneh*) is a patriotic folk ballet which was introduced by the Kirov Theater for Opera and Ballet (a subsidiary of the Leningrad State Academy) in Molotov on December 19, 1942, and subsequently won for its composer the Stalin Prize. But it is known and admired by concert audiences outside of the Soviet Union through the two suites of twelve dances—eight in the first, four in the second—which the composer derived from the ballet score. At least one of these pieces—the "Saber Dance"—assumed in the United States the status of a popular hit by getting heard not only in its original version for large orchestra but also in all kinds of transcriptions, including some for jazz ensembles.

The action takes place on a collective farm. The lovely Gayane is married to the cruel Giko, traitor to the regime. Giko joins a band of smugglers, then sets fire to the farm. But it is saved by Kazakov, the Red commander of a border patrol. As Kazakov is in love with Gayane, he marries her after Giko has been eliminated.

The ballet's great strength rests in its many and varied folk dances (some of them found in the final scene celebrating the engagement of Gayane and Kazakov). There are shepherd, folk, peasant, and exotic dances—Armenian, Kurdish, Georgian, Ukrainian, and so forth. Their emotional range is wide. Many of them are wild and primitive: "Dance of the Young Kurds," "Hopak," "Dance of the Kurds," "Lezghinka," "Armen's Variations," "Fire," and (most famous of all) the breath-taking "Saber Dance." But there are gentler moods, too. The "Dance of the Rose Maidens" is by turns graceful and gay, brilliant in its contrast of tone colors. "Lullaby" has pastoral refinement; "The Dance of Ayshe" is elegiac; and the "Russian Dance" has a simple folkish character. Two of the dances, with the nondescript titles of "Andante: Introduction" and "Gayane's Adagio," are introspective, intended as tonal portraits of Gayane; the latter is a particularly beautiful song for the strings.

Khatchaturian's Symphony No. 2 was written in 1942 during World War II when the Nazis invaded the Soviet Union. The war left its fingerprints on this music. The third movement, for example, is basically a funeral march speaking for the suffering of the Soviet people during this harrowing period; the fourth movement, which opens with vivid fanfares, speaks loud and clear for the people's heroism, particularly in a ringing page for the brass which has been described as a "chorus of glory." A unifying element in this work is a bell motive with which the symphony opens. The third movement ends with this bell motive built up with climactic power, and the fourth movement also reaches a dramatic climax with a statement of the motive, used here to proclaim the inevitable triumph of the Soviet Union over Nazism.

The orchestral suite *Masquerade* is one of Khatchaturian's lighter efforts, and ranks second only to *Gayane* in popularity among his works. This a delightful, easy-to-listen-to, five-movement work derived from incidental music Khatchaturian had written in 1939 for a play by Mikhail Lermontov. The suite was prepared in 1944. The movements are: Waltz, Nocturne, Romance, Mazurka, and Galop.

Zoltán Kodály

"With a modern equipment he has managed to blend peculiarly Hungarian folk forms with Western musical culture."

GUIDO PANNAIN

BORN: Keczkemét, Hungary, December 16, 1882.
DIED: Budapest, March 6, 1967.
MAJOR WORKS: *Chamber Music*—2 string quartets; Cello Sonata; Sonata for Unaccompanied Cello; Duo for Violin and Piano; Serenade for Two Violins and Viola. *Choral Music*—Psalmus Hungaricus; Te Deum; Missa Brevis. *Operas*—Háry János; The Spinning Room; Czinka Panna. *Orchestral Music*—Summer Evening; Dances of Marosszék (also for piano); Dances of Galánta; Peacock Variations; Concerto for Orchestra; Symphony.

HIS LIFE

Soon after Béla Bartók's death there took place in Pecs, Hungary, a memorial concert in his honor. At this concert Zoltán Kodály delivered a touching eulogy—his farewell not only to a colleague but also to his closest friend.

He must have felt that with Bartók a part of himself had also passed away. For the lives and careers of Bartók and Kodály, Hungary's two greatest composers of the twentieth century, were curiously intertwined. They first met in 1900, when Kodály joined the class of Hans Koessler at the Budapest Conservatory. Bartók was also in that class, and a friendship was immediately initiated between the two young men.

Five years later Kodály (won over to his friend's enthusiasm for and interest in Hungarian folk music) joined Bartók in the first of several expeditions through Hungary to uncover indigenous examples of folk song and dance. It was, as one of Kodály's pupils, Adjoran Atvos, explained, a task of heroic proportions, "far more taxing than that of other explorers of folk music. For it should be understood that no people on earth are as unmusical as the Magyars. Meeting in a convivial spirit they do not sing; they whoop it up. No one in Hungary has ever heard peasants sing quietly, much less in harmony. Each voice improvises its own variations. Every air is differently interpreted by different people. It requires a rare knack, indeed, and courageous labor to trace one's way through this muddle of melody." But both Bartók and Kodály most assuredly did trace their way. Their collaborative endeavor resulted in the rediscovery of several thousand folk melodies, at that time completely unknown not only outside of Hungary but even outside of the regions where they had arisen. They edited, arranged, and published these melodies. Kodály made his own individual contributions, too.

Like Bartók, Kodály allowed his studies in Hungarian folk music to affect his entire creative outlook. Thus the careers of both men, begun simultaneously, progressed along similar lines. It is surely fitting and proper that, when Bartók died, Zoltán Kodály would have been at once universally accepted as Bartók's successor, as the greatest living Hungarian composer.

Kodály believed it necessary for every composer to retain his connections with his ancestral sources. His own connections were always particularly close. In an autobiographical sketch he recalled his musical experiences as a child in a provincial Hungarian town:

My father was a stationmaster in our tiny townlet. . . . He adored music. When the last fast train thundered down the valley . . . he would hasten home, seize his violin and, with friends equally enamored, begin to play quartets. Those distant evenings of childhood! I have only to close my eyes and they return in all their vividness: the dark, rapt faces above the music racks, the sweep of the bow, the twang of the pizzicati, and myself standing big-eyed in the corner completely enthralled. Thus I learned the quartets of Haydn. . . . Apart from my father's music, and that of his friends, I listened to the gypsy orchestra, the only "professional" music one could hear in a little Magyar town. These then were my first teachers: my father's violin, the gypsies, and the rhythmic rumble of the great trains which passed or stopped a minute before our little station.

He combined these musical contacts with learning to play the violin, mostly by himself, and with singing in the cathedral choir at Nagyszombat. Although he knew nothing about theory he also tried writing music, at first a few religious works, including a Mass. He was fifteen when his orchestral overture was played by a student orchestra of the Nagyszombat High School and seventeen when he completed a trio that was tried out at a family concert.

He went to Budapest in 1900 to concentrate on the study of science. But at the same time he enrolled in the Royal Academy of Music. His teacher there, Hans Koessler—and his young friend Bartók—made him decide to specialize in music instead of science. He wrote little during this period, though he did manage to get something of his published, an Adagio for Violin and Piano, in 1901. He was too busy acquiring a basic technique for the first time and in freeing himself from the influence that Brahms was having on his writing.

Kodály was graduated from the Royal Academy in 1905, and in 1906 he received a doctorate from the University of Budapest, where he had been attending classes in French culture and Latin humanism. Meanwhile in 1905 he began the first of a few trips with Bartók to uncover the native music of different racial elements of Transylvania. His doctoral thesis, in 1906, was *The Strophic Construction in Hungarian Folk Song,* a fruit of this first expedition. Another fruit was *Summer Evening,* in 1906, an orchestral tone poem whose principal subject matter had assimilated the physiognomy of the Hungarian folk song. In 1908 he completed several songs on Hungarian texts, Op. 1. These were followed by some chamber music works including his First String Quartet, Op. 2, and a Sonata for Cello and Piano, Op. 4. Some of his music was now receiving important performances not only in Hungary but also in Paris and at the Zurich Festival, and his First String Quartet received a hearing in the United States in 1915 at the hands of the Kneisel Quartet. Meanwhile, in 1906, he had been appointed professor at the Royal Academy where, in 1919, he became assistant director. He had also embarked on marriage in 1910 with Emma Gruber, a woman twenty years older than he.

Kodály suffered a period of creative sterility between 1919 and 1923, from which he emerged to become a nationalist composer of first importance. The work that first established him as such was the *Psalmus Hungaricus,* an extraordinary success (the greatest Kodály had known up to that time) when introduced in Budapest on November 19, 1923. Another great triumph was soon at hand. On October 16, 1926, there took place at the Budapest Royal Opera the *première* of Kodály's folk opera *Háry János. Háry János* and the works that followed it soon thereafter—the *Dances of Marosszék* in 1930, the *Dances of Galánta* in 1934, the Te Deum in 1936, and in 1939 the Concerto for Orchestra and the *Peacock* Variations for Orchestra—brought Kodály to a leading position not only in Hungarian music (second only to that of Bartók) but in all contemporary music. The Hungarian Government conferred on him the Order of Merit in 1930, and four years after that Kodály became a member of the National Hungarian Arts Council. Programs devoted entirely to his works were heard throughout Hungary when his fiftieth birthday was celebrated in 1932.

His great fame in his native country and the great respect paid him by his countrymen were instrumental in saving his life during World War II. After the Nazis occupied Hungary, Kodály was ordered to divorce his Jewish wife. He stoutly refused to do so. What is more, he further defied the Nazis by engaging in the underground activity of finding a refuge for fleeing Jews. Eventually the Gestapo caught on to Kodály's work and questioned him. Within the shadow of the concentration camp—and threatened with physical torture—Kodály refused to disclose the identity of his collaborators, nor would he reveal the methods by which Jewish refugees were brought to safety. Only his immense reputation saved Kodály. Rather than set off repercussions throughout Hungary, the Nazis decided to leave him alone.

The war left Kodály destitute. As he confided in a letter to an American friend, all he had left were "two suits and a half-wrecked apartment in Budapest." But with the restoration of normalcy Kodály's fortunes were rehabilitated. He now played a giant role in helping rebuild the musical life of his country. He became president of the National Arts Council, a member of the National Assembly, and director of the Academy of Music. He also devised and developed a monumental program for the teaching of music to children, inventing a system by which children from earliest years could be taught singing by means of hand symbols.

In the winter of 1946 Kodály served as a delegate to the Congress of the International Confederation of Authors' Societies held in Washington, D.C. This was his first visit to the United States, and on this occasion he made numerous appearances in performances of his works; on November 22, 1946, he led the American *première* of his *Peacock* Variations at a concert of the Philadelphia Orchestra. He revisited the United States during the summer of 1965 when he was composer-in-residence at Dartmouth College in Hanover, New Hampshire. At the Congregation of the Arts at the college, four concerts of his music were given in his honor.

Kodály's wife died in 1958 at the age of ninety-five. When he remarried on December 18, 1959, it was to Sarolta Péczeli, a nineteen-year-old girl who had been his pupil at the Academy of Music. This period of readjustment in his personal life saw the writing of his last masterwork, and his most ambitious work for orchestra— a symphony (the first time he had attempted to write one). Interrupted by his first wife's death and by his own serious illness, the symphony was several years in the writing. It was finally completed in May of 1961 and introduced in Lucerne, Switzerland, on August 16 of that year.

In old age, Kodály interested himself more in researches into Hungarian folk music and in developing the music-education system in the schools than in composition. Old age robbed him neither of his enthusiasms nor of his physical vigor. He continued to the end of his life his practice of swimming daily in an open-air pool regardless of the season, and to take long hikes or brisk sprints in the woods. He liked to drop in on schools to conduct children in their singing performances and to study at first hand the progress they were making in his methods. When the American composer Norman Dello Joio attended the International Society for Music Education in Budapest in 1964 he did not fail to notice and admire

Kodály's "punctual attendance at every session and concert." Kodály's "grueling day," said Dello Joio, always started early in the morning and continued without time off for rest or relaxation until after the concert performance late in the evening.

Kodály's eightieth birthday sparked monumental celebrations in every part of Hungary—in villages as well as cities. Gala performances were given of practically everything he had ever written. The event that stirred Kodály most deeply, however, was a concert sponsored by the Ministry of Culture and the Hungarian Association of Musicians in Budapest at which one thousand children joined in a choral performance. Another tribute was a composition using a theme from Kodály's First String Quartet to which each of twenty-three of Kodály's pupils contributed a variation; this work was broadcast over the Hungarian Radio. Five years after this celebration, Zoltán Kodály died in Budapest—on March 6, 1967.

HIS MUSIC

Kodály's musical language, like that of Bartók, was shaped by the highly individual stylistic traits of the Hungarian folk song and dance. Before 1905 Kodály imitated Brahms and other German post-Romanticists. After his contact with the Hungarian folk song idiom his music changed character completely; it became a music that could have been written by none but a contemporary Hungarian. Without resorting to the advanced musical techniques of the twentieth century, and working within the long-accepted principles of tonality, Kodály nevertheless succeeded in producing a new and individual kind of music, strong, astringent, and personal. The modality of the Hungarian folk song often gave Kodály's work an exotic character. The frequent repetition of a melodic or rhythmic phrase—together with the brusqueness of accent and complexity and variety of rhythm—gave it force.

These observations might also be made of Bartók's music. But the music of Kodály is essentially different from that of his colleague and friend. For one thing, unlike Bartók, Kodály frequently quotes Hungarian folk songs even in important major works, such as his operas and orchestral compositions. In addition, Kodály is more lyrical; his music has greater clarity and lucidity; it has a greater inclination toward gentle and contemplative moods; and it is much more easily assimilable.

ANALYTICAL NOTES

Choral Music. It was with *Psalmus Hungaricus* that Kodály's significance as a nationalist Hungarian composer first attracted world attention. Kodály completed this work in 1923 on a commission from his Government to commemorate the fiftieth anniversary of the union of Buda and Pest. For his text he went to a sixteenth-century poem by Michael Veg based on the Fifty-fifth Psalm, but including Veg's own lines in which he bewailed the plight of Hungary under Turkish oppression. His poem, consequently, was more patriotic and national than religious. Kodály's music followed suit by using old Hungarian modes and various idioms of Hungarian folk songs and thereby creating a Hungarian musical epic. The work is scored for tenor solo, mixed chorus, a children's chorus, and orchestra. After a sixteen-measure orchestral introduction, altos and basses are heard in a unison passage that later becomes a recurring refrain: "Sad was the king, dismal and downcast." This is followed by a prayer for the tenor in which he pleads to God not to turn from the misery of the Hungarian people. An eloquent slow section for orchestra precedes another deeply moving solo for tenor ("Now does the French courage enter my soul") and the closing chorus that praises God, whose justice and mercy will surely bring doom to Hungary's enemies.

More religious than national is Kodály's most famous work for chorus and orchestra, the Te Deum, for solo voices, chorus, and orchestra (1936). But the folk element, of course, is not absent. The Te Deum was written to honor the 250th anniversary of the delivery of Budapest from the hands of the Turks. Two unifying elements are important here: the trumpet call that opens the composition, and an expansive melodic thought to the words *Pleni sunt* that gets fugal treatment. Hungarian folk elements beautifully coalesce with religious ones to create music that passes from power to spirituality. The composition ends with a poignant air for soprano and chorus, *Tu Patris Sempiternus*, whose Hungarian identity is readily recognized.

Orchestral Music. Kodály's best-known work for orchestra is his suite from the folk opera *Háry János,* in which he gathered some of the opera's most tuneful and infectious musical episodes. The opera was completed in 1925, and the suite was prepared two years later. Háry János is a character familiar in Hungarian folklore. To Hungarians he is a kind of symbol of Magyar bravado and conceit. He is a fabulous liar. In Kodály's opera Háry spins an incredible yarn in which Marie Louise, wife of Napoleon, falls in love with him. There ensues a war between France and Austria. Singlehanded, Háry lays the enemy low. Returning to Vienna in great triumph, Háry rejects Marie Louise for his boyhood sweetheart, Orzse.

The suite is in six movements. Prefacing the first movement, "The Tale Begins," is an orchestral simulation of a sneeze; for legend has it that if someone sneezes while a tale is being told, then this tale must be true. A pause, and Háry's fantastic story begins. The main melodic idea in this section is an expressive melody heard first in the cellos and basses and later developed into a climax by the strings. The melody speaks for the sentimentality and the undisciplined imagination of the hero. He is now ready to begin his tall stories.

In the ensuing five sections we have various episodes in Háry Janós' imagined exploits. In "The Viennese Musical Clock," Háry has come to Vienna and is impressed by the musical clock on the imperial palace. The musical clock is depicted by a saucy tune given by woodwinds, horns, piano, and chimes; the military atmosphere is projected in a little march theme for trumpets and percussion. The "Song"—a simple but intense folk melody presented by viola solo—describes Háry's tenderness for his boyhood sweetheart, Orzse. In this movement Kodály interpolated passages for the cembalon, an instrument peculiar to Central Europe; but in most orchestral performances the piano is substituted. There follows the strident martial music of "The Battle and Defeat of Napoleon." Soon we hear a brief dirge quoting a few notes from the "Marseillaise"; if we have had any doubts, we are now informed that Napoleon is defeated. A glissando in the bass tuba and bass trombone portrays Háry's vulgar and impudent gesture of contempt toward the defeated emperor. Strings and woodwinds give forth a passionate Hungarian czardas in the "Intermezzo." A rhythmic fanfare for percussion introduces the concluding portion of the suite, "Entrance of the Emperor and His Court." There is then sounded a march full of ceremony, climaxed by clashing of cymbals; Háry Janós is brought before the Emperor of Austria.

Dances of Marosszék originated in 1927 as a composition for the piano. At Toscanini's suggestion, Kodály orchestrated it in 1930, the version in which it is more familiar to concertgoers. Marosszék is a town in the Hungarian province of Székely. Within a rondo structure, Kodály places six dance tunes from that region, the most significant of which is the one that violas, cellos, and clarinets present at the beginning.

Dances of Galánta is a unified suite of five dances (played without pause) prefaced by an introduction and concluded with a coda. Kodály wrote this orchestral piece in 1934 for the eightieth anniversary of the Budapest Philharmonic. Galánta is a little market town near the Austro-Hungarian border. There, as a child, Kodály heard a great deal of gypsy music performed by gypsy orchestras. The *Dances of Galánta* is gypsy music—now wild and fiery, now melancholy, now nostalgic.

The main material of the introduction is a theme given by the cellos and subsequently repeated by horns and other instrumental combinations. The first dance is a theme in solo clarinet. The second, much more rhythmic, appears in solo flute. A brief recollection of the first dance brings on the third: an expansive melody appearing first in solo oboe, then in the rest of the woodwinds, and finally in full orchestra. Once again the first dance theme is brought back, in a slight variation. A delicate folk dance, made up of two sections, is the fourth. The fifth and final dance is a gypsy tune in strings and solo flute. After the fourth dance has been quickly recalled there come the coda, built out of the first dance theme, and a cadenza for solo clarinet. The suite ends with the final return of the gypsy dance.

The Variations on a Hungarian Folk Song, more popularly known as the *Peacock* Variations, came in 1939 for the fiftieth anniversary of the Concertgebouw Orchestra in Amsterdam. The work is built around a folk melody from Somogy on the western end of Lake Balaton, "Fly, Peacock, Fly." This melody is presented in the second section, "Theme," following a brief "Introduction." It is given by muted oboe to string accompaniment. Sixteen variations of the melody are given in the third part, after which the finale opens with a variant of theme that receives a dramatic build-up and rises toward a resounding coda.

In the Concerto for Orchestra (1939), Kodály attempted a revival of the Baroque structure of the concerto grosso. Like the old concerto, this one alternates fast and slow movements, being in five parts (played without interruption) and beginning and ending in a fast tempo. The energetic Hungarian melody in unison strings which opens the first movement recurs extensively in the third, where it eventually receives fugal treatment, and in the finale; an important motive for cello in the second movement recurs in the fourth. Kodály wrote his concerto on a commission from the Chicago Symphony for its fiftieth anniversary.

Kodály's only symphony, the Symphony in C major, was a child of his old age. He began sketching some ideas for it in the early 1930s, but not until the 1950s did he begin to work seriously. It still took a long time to get written, being completed in 1961 when Kodály was seventy-nine. It is in three movements, the second and third played without interruption. The first opens with an atmospheric introduction before the main body is projected; its first theme is heard in cellos and basses, and its second, in clarinets, the latter of Hungarian folk song origin. The folk element once again becomes pronounced in the second movement with its main thought, heard in muted violins. Horns present the virile first subject of the finale, which is then commented upon in detail. A structural feature of this finale is the repetition of the interval of the fourth. It appears in the opening preface, recurs throughout the movement, and then is used with dramatic impact in the coda.

Franz Liszt

"The most important germinative force in modern music."

CECIL GRAY

BORN: Raiding, Hungary, October 22, 1811.
DIED: Bayreuth, Bavaria, July 31, 1886.
MAJOR WORKS: *Choral Music*—Requiem; Die Legende von der heiligen Elisabeth; Christus; Hungaria; Die heilige Cäcilia. *Orchestral Music*—13 tone poems including Mazeppa, Tasso, Les Préludes, and Orpheus; 2 piano concertos; A Faust Symphony; A Symphony to Dante's Divine Comedy; Two Episodes from Lenau's Faust; Second Mephisto Waltz; Hungarian Fantasy for Piano and Orchestra; Totentanz, for piano and orchestra. *Piano Music*—19 Hungarian Rhapsodies; 2 Concert Studies; Two Legends; Etudes d'exécution transcendante; Album d'un voyageur; Années de pèlerinage; Harmonies poétiques et religieuses; Sonata in B minor; Albumblätter, ballades, caprices, Consolations, Ländler, Liebesträume, mazurkas, rhapsodies. *Vocal Music*—Songs for voice and piano including "Du bist wie eine Blume," "Es muss ein Wunderbares sein," "Kling leise, mein Lied," "O Lieb', so lang du lieben kannst," "O quand je dors."

HIS LIFE

Franz Liszt was many people in one. He was spiritual and he was earthy, idealistic and insincere, egocentric and humble. He was a musician who could function on the highest levels of his art. Few served music with such generosity, self-effacement, tolerance, and courage as Liszt did in Weimar as Kapellmeister. Yet placed in front of the piano he became a flamboyant showman, given to dramatics and theatricalism, frequently calling on shoddy music to advertise his phenomenal technique. He, who could demand the most scrupulous integrity from other composers, did not hesitate to write potboilers himself.

The man was as contradictory as the musician. He was given to religious contemplation and the life of the recluse, but at the very same time he filled the role of darling of the aristocratic *salon* with undisguised joy. He fawned before a nobleman, yet he could give a tongue-lashing even to royalty when their bad manners interfered with his music-making. He could wear the modest cassock of an *abbé,* but on other occasions strut in the outlandish costume of a Magyar prince or the equally preposterous dress of a fop. He followed the Church and he pursued sensual pleasures. In Rome, when he turned to religion, he spent his days in the cloister of the Santa Maria Church in prayer and contemplation; but in the evening, and without apparent qualms of conscience, he sought less spiritual diversion in other places. He might on occasions be the man of spirit, but he was never to deny the flesh. When not a recluse he lived in an atmosphere of luxury. He loved extravagantly. One German biographer (with characteristic Teutonic thoroughness) uncovered twenty-six major love affairs, some of which yielded illegitimate offspring. Even in his old age he was enmeshed in ugly scandals with peasant girls and noble ladies.

He was the poseur, the mountebank, but—make no mistake about it!—he was also one of the greatest musicians of his generation. Which was the *real* Liszt? In vain do we comb the details of his biography to uncover the true man. The biographical facts provide evidence for whatever conception one wishes to entertain about him, while also offering disconcerting testimony to the contrary.

He was raised as a child prodigy, taught to cater to the public, to bid continually for its smiling favor; this early conditioning did much to shape the man. His father, Adam Liszt, was capable of recognizing his talent. Although Adam was a humble servant on the Esterházy estate in Raiding, he was a splendid amateur musician. Franz, then, was early taught the piano, beginning when he was just six. Three years later he was able to appear publicly in various towns in Hungary playing ambitious compositions, including a concerto by Hummel, and extemporizing on given themes. Proudly, Adam exhibited his son to his employer, who was so impressed that he arranged for Franz to give a concert at his palace for his friends. They contributed to a fund to pay for the boy's musical education for the next six years.

The Liszts settled in Vienna in 1821, where Franz made a successful debut as pianist on December 1, 1822. He studied with Karl Czerny (who soon refused to accept any payment for such a privilege) and composition with Salieri. At one of his concerts, in 1823, Beethoven was in the audience. He lifted the child in his arms and kissed him. The boy also made his appearance as composer; he was one of several composers invited to contribute a variation to an air by Diabelli, the set being published in 1823 under the title of *Vaterländische Künstlerverein*.

Twelve years old, and admirably trained, Liszt left Vienna for Paris with the intention of entering the Conservatory. He soon learned that the Conservatory excluded foreigners; its director, Cherubini, was not the kind of man to waive rules even for a phenomenon. The boy consequently was placed with private teachers, to study composition with Reicha and Paër. As for the piano, he now shifted for himself without the benefit of formal instruction. While studying, he performed publicly, the first of his concerts taking place at the Opéra on March 8, 1824. The story is that he played a concerto so excellently that the men of the orchestra stopped their playing to listen enraptured. After the concert the boy was conducted from one box to the next, to be coddled by the great ladies of the city. Inevitably, the fashionable *salons* welcomed him. He came, he played, and he conquered; he became at once the much admired, the greatly spoiled pet of Paris society.

The same summer he won London as decisively as he had Paris. His debut at the Argyll Rooms was sensational, and he was commanded to perform for George IV. Already we find one of the London papers assigning to him "a place among the principal pianists of Europe; nay, some have gone so far as to say he yields the palm to Hummel alone."

Back in Paris he not only continued his concerts, but also completed an opera, *Don Sanche,* introduced by the Opéra on October 17, 1825. It attracted attention primarily because it was the work of a fourteen-year-old boy. But this curiosity could not make the opera a success. It was seen four more times, then shelved for good. Some fifty years later the score was consumed by a fire that destroyed the Opéra library—or so it was believed at the time. It is doubtful if Liszt himself lamented the loss. In any case, he never again tried writing an opera. Although the score was rediscovered in 1903, complete and safe, *Don Sanche* was never again performed.

There was no question about his continued popularity as a virtuoso. For the next two years Liszt played in France and England, meeting adulation and acclaim everywhere.

On his deathbed, in 1827, old Adam Liszt surveyed the world he was leaving and found it good. His son was famous throughout Europe; he was financially self-sufficient; he was tremendously gifted. Nothing would stand in the way of his continued success—nothing, that is, except Woman. Adam Liszt had already remarked, and with no little misgiving, the way his gifted and strikingly handsome son had attracted women and how he was attracted to them.

The death of his father brought on some pious resolutions. He would give up once and for all the good life for asceticism. He would turn over his fortune to his mother, as it was she who had made it possible. He would renounce the vacuous life of a pampered concert virtuoso for more meaningful activity. "I would rather be anything in the world than a musician in the pay of great folk, patronized and paid for by them, like a conjurer or a clever dog," he exclaimed at the time. His appearances, for the next few years at any rate, were few and far between. Finally, he would avoid women. The last resolution was the one to be broken first.

For he was already embarking on his first great love affair. She was one of his pupils, Caroline de Saint-Cricq—young (sixteen), attractive, and highborn. They spoke of marriage, but Caroline's father intervened and smashed the budding affair. Liszt took his disappointment with the gravity of an adolescent and the exaggerated turmoil of a Romantic. For a while he appeared to be on the verge of nervous collapse. Then he sought refuge in religion. He wanted to embrace the Church, but, failing that, he read religious books avidly. "I hoped it might be granted me to live the life of the saints and perhaps die the death of martyrs." But religion alone did not satisfy him. He suddenly became interested in politics: During the crisis of 1830 he wanted to be a revolutionist and fight on the barricades, but was finally dissuaded by his mother. Instead he devoured books of poetry, philosophy, belles-lettres. "Teach me *all* French literature," he begged a literary friend passionately. The friend's comment was: "Within the head of this young man only confusion reigns."

Soon after 1830 Liszt met three musicians who brought him from his political, literary, and religious digressions back to music. Chopin and Berlioz—both still young and unknown, the one sensitive and poetic, the other vital and experimental—introduced Liszt to a new kind of music. Each in his own way was the spirit of Romanticism, to which Liszt could respond—and did. The third musician was the fabulous virtuoso of the violin, Paganini. "What a man, what a violin, what an artist!" Liszt wrote to a friend. "Heavens! what sufferings, what misery, what tortures in those four strings!" Chopin and Berlioz fired him with the ambition to write a bold, fresh, and adventurous kind of music—but that would come later. A more immediate objective was to return to the concert stage and become the "Paganini of the piano," the greatest virtuoso of his time.

During the next two years Liszt hurled himself into the study of the piano and the mastery of his technique; he worked with a savage determination and with a passion that defied fatigue. When he left the piano, it was to read voraciously. Thus he divided himself between music and literature. "Here is a whole fortnight that my mind and fingers have been working like two lost spirits—Homer, the Bible, Plato, Locke, Byron, Hugo, Lamartine, Chateaubriand, Beethoven, Bach, Hummel, Mozart, Weber are all around me," he wrote at this time. "I study them, meditate on them, devour them with fury. Besides this, I practice four to five hours of exercises (thirds, sixths, eighths, tremolos, repetitions of the notes, cadenzas, etc.). Ah! provided I don't go mad you will find an artist in me! Yes, an artist such as you desire, such as is required nowadays."

By 1833 two important things had happened to Liszt. He had returned to the concert stage and his public, who welcomed him as a conquering hero. And he had become involved in a *grande passion*. The Countess d'Agoult possessed most of the qualities that Liszt sought in a woman: station, intelligence, beauty, romantic ardor, and the capacity to adore him. She also had a husband and three children, but these Liszt could ignore. The love affair finally burst its bounds. The countess deserted her family and went with Liszt to Geneva, where a child was born to them. Two other children came from this idyll, one of whom was Cosima, destined to play a major role in the life of Richard Wagner.

This interlude kept Liszt from the Paris concert scene for two years. When he returned he discovered to his chagrin that another pianist had usurped the limelight: Sigismond Thalberg. His vanity piqued, Liszt set out to prove to Paris that he was still the first pianist of the world. Whenever Thalberg gave a concert Liszt gave one too—calling on his immense technique and his showy transcriptions to dazzle his audience into submission. Each of the two pianists had his own coterie of devoted admirers; for a while the question as to which was the greater pianist remained unresolved. Princess Cristina Belgojoso decided to settle the issue by having both appear at her *salon* in a musical "duel." Thalberg played his meretricious fantasy on Rossini's *Moses*. Liszt followed with a still more dazzling transcription of melodies from a now forgotten opera by a forgotten composer. The consensus favored Liszt.

For the next decade or so Liszt played throughout Europe. Not a rival could now threaten his fame. Perhaps no concert performer was attended with the kind of hero worship that met Liszt wherever he played. He had an incomparable sense of style when he chose to play something more substantial than pyrotechnical fantasias. "Such marvels of executive skill and power, I could never have imagined"—so wrote Charles Hallé (later a famous conductor) after hearing him. But he was also the born showman. Dramatics, even hysterics, heightened the effect of his playing. With the consummate skill of the born actor he used facial contortions, a toss of his majestic mane, and eloquent sweeps of his hands across the keyboard to intensify the drama.

"Constantly tossing back his long hair, with lips quivering, he swept the auditorium with the glance of a smiling master." So wrote the dramatist Legouvé. No means were too extravagant for him to dramatize himself and his playing. He sometimes even went into a swooning act. An unidentified witness has reported: "As the closing strains began I saw Liszt's countenance assume that agony of expression, mingled with radiant smiles of joy, which I never saw in any other human face except in the paintings of our Saviour by some early masters. . . . He fainted in the arms of a friend who was turning over the pages for him, and we bore him out in a strong fit of hysterics. The effect of the scene was really dreadful. The whole room sat breathless with fear, till Hiller came forward and announced that Liszt was already restored to consciousness and was comparatively well again."

The modern piano virtuoso was born with him. He was the originator of the piano recital—the first who dared to give an entire concert without the embellishments of an orchestra or assisting artists. This happened in Rome in 1839 when he was the exclusive attraction at a concert which he labeled a "musical soliloquy." The term "recital" was used for the first time at another of Liszt's performances, this time in London, on May 1, 1840. He was also the first to establish the tradition of playing the piano in public in a profile position. The concert pianist had previously faced the audience or had his back to it. Conscious of his handsome profile, and its effect on his female admirers, Liszt insisted on performing in the position most favorable to his appearance.

As Liszt's triumphs mounted, the liaison with Countess d'Agoult disintegrated. His prolonged absences enabled her to view him with perspective. She did not like what she saw: a man of colossal vanity, continually bragging of the honors heaped upon him and the great men he met; a musician who would stop at nothing to make an impression; a lover who was not beyond indulging in passing liaisons. By 1840 they knew that the affair was at an end. They went their separate ways, she with her children, he on his paths of glory. By 1844 they had agreed to make the separation permanent.

Liszt found someone else to fill the vacancy. In Kiev, in 1847, his personality and playing were, as usual, irresistible, particularly to Princess Carolyne von Sayn-Wittgenstein. She invited him to visit her at her vast estate; he came and stayed. Extremely intelligent, and the victim of an unhappy marriage, the princess soon found much more to attract her to Liszt than his genius and Byronic appearance. They read great literature together; he was inspired by a reading of Dante to plan a symphony. She discovered to her delight that her own inclination toward religion and mysticism struck a responsive chord in Liszt. They spoke continually of finding peace in the spiritual life —even while the princess vigorously puffed on her black cigar or was his ardent lover. Smoking cigars was only one of several eccentricities. She had a morbid fear of fresh air. She sealed her rooms so that the atmosphere was always fetid; and she would have all visitors wait in an anteroom for ten or fifteen minutes so that they might come to her "deventilated." She made it a practice to work most of the night—for she had dedicated herself to the writing of a twenty-four-volume magnum opus, *The Inner Causes of the Outer Weakness of the Church*—wearing fantastically colored and designed dresses all the time.

In 1848 Liszt was appointed Kapellmeister to the Grand Duke of Weimar, for whom he was required to direct performances of symphonic and operatic music. He rented a villa where, with his mistress, he was to live for the next ten years. During that decade Liszt's devoted efforts to bring recognition to unknown composers and neglected works presents a startling contrast to his preceding shenanigans as a virtuoso. Personal penchants or prejudices never dictated the kind of music he presented, nor did expediency. He played works of many different styles and idioms. He courageously fought the battle even for neglected composers he personally disliked or who had abused him. Through him, Weimar became one of Germany's greatest music centers. Where else in Germany—where else in all Europe—could one hear so many provocative *premières?* What other center was the refuge for so many neglected works, those by Berlioz, for example? Who else would have dared to revive *Tannhäuser* and then give the world *première* of *Lohengrin* when their composer was a political revolutionary sought by the Dresden police?

The paths of Wagner and Liszt had already crossed. Liszt first met Wagner in Paris in 1840, but became conscious of the younger man's potentialities with a hearing of *Rienzi* four years later. As a fugitive, Wagner came to Weimar and lived with Liszt for a brief period in 1849. Thereafter, Liszt was to be among the most passionate of all Wagnerites, tireless in bringing performances and recognition to the mighty Wagnerian music dramas. After directing *Tannhäuser* and *The Flying Dutchman* and introducing *Lohengrin,* Liszt fought bitterly with the Duke of Weimar for the funds with which to present the entire *Ring* cycle, or at least *Tristan and Isolde.* Failure to get these funds was one of several forces which drove Liszt away from the Kapellmeister post.

Another was the increasing resentment of Weimar music lovers toward the new music he was continually presenting. They hissed his presentation of Peter Cornelius' *The Barber of Bagdad* (also a *première*). He would stay in Weimar no longer, at least not as its Kapellmeister.

While he resigned from his musical duties in 1859, he remained in Weimar until 1861. After 1861 he found himself drawn back to religion. He longed for the priesthood, but his past life and his continuing amatory entanglements made that impossible. He could get only the minor orders. In 1865 he submitted to the tonsure, assumed the cassock of an *abbé,* and entered the Third Order of St. Francis of Assisi.

He now divided his year between religious interests in Rome and activities as a teacher of the piano in Pest and Weimar. Piano students came from all parts of the world to study with him—Moriz Rosenthal, Hans von Bülow, Karl Tausig, Giovanni Sgambati, and Emil Sauer, among many others. With almost unparalleled generosity he gave of himself and his time to anyone who asked for them; he never asked a fee. When Moriz Rosenthal wrote "Liszt was more wonderful than anybody I have ever known" he was echoing the sentiments of an entire legion of famous Liszt pupils.

Another of his pupils, Amy Fay, an American, left the following description of Liszt.

He is tall and slight, with deep-set eyes, shaggy eyebrows, and long iron-gray hair which he wears parted in the middle. His mouth turns up in the corners which gives him a most crafty and Mephistophelean expression when he smiles, and his whole appearance and manner have a sort of Jesuitical elegance and ease. His hands are very narrow, with long and slender fingers that look as if they had twice as many joints as other people's! . . . But the most extraordinary thing about Liszt is his wonderful variety of expression and play of feature. One moment his face will look dreamy, shadowy, tragic. The next he will be insinuating, amiable, ironic, sardonic; but always the same captivating grace of manner.

When Wagner broke up the marriage of Liszt's daughter Cosima, and started living illicitly with her, Liszt could not forgive. Thenceforth he would have no further personal contact with Wagner, though he was too sincere a musician to allow this to influence his continued efforts on behalf of Wagner's music. Not until 1872 did reconciliation take place, enabling Liszt to participate in laying the cornerstone of the festival theater in Bayreuth. Later, Liszt was a frequent visitor to the Bayreuth Festivals. The death of Wagner, on February 13, 1883, was a terrible blow. Liszt's daughter Cosima did not help matters either. Unable to forget her father's onetime severe denunciation of her love affair with Wagner, she now insisted that he stay away from her husband's funeral and for the next three years stoutly refused to see Liszt.

But some consolation came to him with a last personal triumph. This took place in 1886, when he visited England despite his rapidly failing strength. He played the piano again as only he could (including a private concert for Queen Victoria at Windsor Castle) and attended a public performance of his oratorio *St. Elizabeth*. The tremendous homage given him stirred him profoundly. He stayed in England one week longer than he had intended, then left for Bavaria to attend again the Bayreuth Festival. He fell ill in Bayreuth. Defying the orders of his doctor, he went to hear *Parsifal* and after that *Tristan and Isolde*. But he was so sick during *Tristan* that he had to leave before the performance was over. Pneumonia set in and after that congestion of the lungs. One of his last requests was a drink of brandy, which his physician denied him; and the last word he uttered was "Tristan."

HIS MUSIC

The composer was not different from the virtuoso. Both wooed the public, but on other occasions humbly served art. It is the less ambitious and more meretricious items of Liszt that, unfortunately, continue to be heard, particularly the lesser works for the piano. He wrote these pieces to win a public and the public has never outgrown its enthusiasm for them. In this category belong the ubiquitous Hungarian Rhapsodies and the perhaps too frequently heard *Liebestraum,* the Concerto No. 1 for Piano and Orchestra, and the tone poem *Les Préludes.* Much less often heard are the far more important and ambitious works he produced for the piano, such as the *Années de pèlerinage,* various études, the *Funérailles,* the Sonata in B minor. His other works—the oratorios and the vast *Dante* and *Faust* symphonies with which he placated his conscience and hoped to scale the heights—are also rarely performed, and when performed even more rarely meet the approval of the general music public.

His failings as a human being were also his artistic shortcomings. He lacked integration. His music passes recklessly from moments of real eloquence to sham dramatics, from an intense, original, and powerful creative logic to diffuseness and triviality. He is stirring, or overpowering, or beguiling, and at times even poetic. But it is rare that his music is more than surface gloss.

He was not a great composer; but he was an important one. The tone poem, or symphonic poem—transmutation into musical terms (and within an elastic musical form) of a poem, or a prose text, or a story, or a painting, or an idea—was his creation. He established the form of the rhapsody. For this alone more than one great composer was to be indebted to him. But he also gave an increasing articulateness to program music; he made the use of a recurrent theme (the *idée fixe,* as Berlioz called it) an integral technique of orchestral writing; he brought a new sense of freedom to musical form; he was a striking innovator in harmonic writing and instrumentation.

ANALYTICAL NOTES

Orchestral Music. Though they do not get as frequent a representation on programs as they deserve, the two monumental symphonies which Liszt completed between 1856 and 1857 are his most significant works for orchestra. The first was *A Symphony to Dante's Divine Comedy* (1856) and the other *A Faust Symphony* (1857).

The *Dante Symphony*—for solo voice, chorus, and orchestra—comprises two sections, each of which may be regarded as a tone poem. The first is entitled "Inferno" and the other "Purgatorio." The first opens with a recitative to the words of the famous inscription over hell's door in Dante's *Divine Comedy.* Trombones and horns soon contribute to the portentous atmosphere thus far evoked. Hell's torments are then described in a section dramatized by discords, chromatic sequences, and brilliant sonorities. A quiet part for bass clarinet and English horn tells the story of Paolo and Francesca da Rimini. But the idyllic mood is soon shattered by the return of the music suggestive of hell.

The second part projects a religious mood with a chorale-like melody, a temporary emotional respite between the torments of hell and the turbulence of purgatory. After an extended fugal section, we get an exultant Magnificat for solo voice, chorus, and orchestra with which the symphony ends.

A Faust Symphony—for tenor solo, male chorus, and orchestra—is a setting of Goethe's epic drama. There are three movements, each devoted to one of the main characters—Faust, Marguerite, and Mephistopheles. The portrait of Faust reveals the philosopher with all his unfulfilled yearnings, bitter frustrations, inner torment, and passionate longings for Marguerite. The second movement presents Marguerite's ardent song of love in oboe accompanied by viola arpeggios. This is followed by another tender episode, this time for the flute. After this the music gains in sensuality as Marguerite becomes aware of her physical desires. In the end her innocence conquers over her sensual yearnings. The symphony's finale is a scherzo with ironic, at times sardonic, overtones. Material from the first two movements is recalled (including Marguerite's beautiful long song) before the music gives way to frenzy. The peals of an organ bring on the *chorus mysticus* for tenor solo and male chorus in the closing lines by Goethe in praise of Woman and Love.

It is in the tone poems that Liszt is certainly most familiar as an orchestra composer—three tone poems in particular. The most celebrated, of course, is *Les Préludes* (1854), the third of those thirteen orchestral compositions to which Liszt applied the happy generic term of symphonic poem, or tone poem. The program is taken from Lamartine's *Méditations poétiques:*

What is our life but a series of Preludes to that unknown song of which death strikes the first solemn note? Love is the enchanted dawn of every life; but where is the destiny in which the first pleasures of happiness are not interrupted by some storm, whose deadly breath dissipates its fair illusions, whose fatal thunderbolt consumes its altar? And where is the soul which, cruelly wounded, does not seek, at the coming of one of these storms, to calm its memories in the tranquil life of the country? Man, however, cannot long resign himself to the kindly tedium which has at first charmed him in the companionship of nature, and when "the trumpet has sounded the signal of alarms," he hastens to the post of peril, whatever may be the strife which calls him to his ranks, in order to regain in combat the full consciousness of himself and the complete command of his powers.

There are two plucked notes in the strings before a broad and solemn theme is pronounced by the double basses. This is the heart of the entire tone poem. After this theme has been enlarged it reappears in a slight variation, exultantly in brass and basses. Twelve measures later a more introspective version of the theme is heard in the cellos. There is some development before a new melody is heard, expressive of "happiness in love," unfolded by four horns, strings, and harp. It passes on to the woodwinds. This is worked up into a climax which is quickly dissolved. A new variant of the main theme calls in the "storm" music, full of lashing chromaticism and turbulent diminished sevenths. The storm spends itself. A pastoral mood arrives with an extension of the main theme in the oboe. The suggestion of a country dance is heard in the horn. The "love" melody comes back. The music grows more agitated and a martial mood is established. More and more turbulent does the music grow, until in the coda it realizes a dramatic apotheosis. A majestic restatement of the main theme in one of its variants provides a stirring ending.

Tasso and *Mazeppa* are the only other Liszt tone poems which enjoy performances nowadays. *Tasso* had originated in 1840 as a piece for the piano. In 1843, Liszt orchestrated it so that it might serve as a prelude to a performance of Goethe's drama *Tasso* in Weimar. This orchestral prelude was then revised as a tone poem.

The "lament and triumph" of Tasso inspired both Goethe and Byron, but Liszt was affected more strongly by the epic poem of the Englishman than by the poetic drama of the German. Liszt provided his own program: "Tasso loved and suffered at Ferrara. He was avenged at Rome. His glory still lives in the folk songs of Venice. These three elements are inseparable from his immortal memory. To represent them in music, we first called up his august spirit as he still haunts the waters of Venice. Then we beheld his proud and melancholy figure as he passed through the festivals of Ferrara, where he had produced his masterpieces. Finally we followed him to Rome, the Eternal City, which offered him the crown and glorified in him the martyr and the poet."

A strong theme for cellos and double basses brings up the "august spirit" of Tasso. It is the principal motive of the work. A melancholy folk melody for bass clarinet, accompanied by strings and harps, projects Tasso's suffering. The concluding section describes Tasso's ultimate triumph, as the opening Tasso melody is transformed into proud and heroic music.

Mazeppa (1851) is a musical description of Victor Hugo's famous poem. The central figure is the chieftain, who is tied to an untamed steed and forced to ride for three days across the plains of the Ukraine before the horse collapses with fatigue. "The horse devours space," explained Camille Saint-Saëns, who regarded *Mazeppa* as one of

Liszt's finest works, "but all the interest is concentrated on the man, who thinks and suffers. Toward the middle of the composition one is impressed by immensity; horse and rider fly over the boundless steppe, and the man feels conquered by a thousand details of the expanse, and the more because he does not see them."

The tone poem begins with agitated music. A brief ascending phrase for the winds precedes the main theme: a virile subject for trombones, cellos, and double basses, which portrays Mazeppa. This theme is worked out in great detail before the ride is re-created with electrifying realism. The tone poem ends with a return of the Mazeppa theme and a recollection of the opening fiery material.

Mephisto Waltz (1861), while not a tone poem, is another of Liszt's better known short works for orchestra. It is an unbridled, demoniac orchestral setting of an episode in Nikolaus Lenau's poem based on the Faust legend: a wedding at a village inn. Here is the program as it appears in the published score: "There is a wedding feast in progress in the village inn, with music, dancing, carousing. Mephistopheles and Faust pass by, and Mephistopheles induces Faust to enter and take part in the festivites. Mephistopheles snatches the instrument from the hands of the lethargic fiddler, and draws from it indescribably seductive and intoxicating strains. The amorous Faust whirls about with a full-blooded village beauty in a wild dance; they waltz in mad abandon, out of the room, into the open, away to the wood. The sound of the fiddler grows softer and softer, and the nightingale warbles his love-laden song."

Liszt uses two central melodic ideas. The first is strongly accented and appears in the cellos, bringing up the gay dancing of the wedding feast. The other is gentler, but still an impassioned song for strings— Mephistopheles' "seductive strains." James Gibbons Huneker regarded this second subject as "one of the most voluptuous episodes outside of the *Tristan* score."

The precise year when Liszt completed the writing of his Concerto No. 1 in E-flat major for Piano and Orchestra is not known, but it was not after 1849. For many years this concerto was regarded by Viennese pianists as a sure bid for failure, from the time that the distinguished critic Eduard Hanslick derisively dubbed it a "triangle concerto" when it was performed in Vienna in 1857. (The triangle makes a discreet and inoffensive appearance in the scherzo movement.) But in 1869 Lina Ramann defied the prevailing prejudice and revived the work in Vienna with considerable success. Since then it has been a favored tour de force for concert pianists everywhere.

The concerto is played without interruption. The first important theme is heard at once. It is a vigorous statement for strings, with supplementary chords in the winds. The piano enters in the fifth measure and engages the first theme. Muted basses, followed by the violins, introduce the second subject, which is a lyrical and plaintive adagio. Once again the piano discourses on the idea. After the material is developed, an altogether new theme appears in the solo flute against a sustained trill in the piano. A phrase for the clarinet is the transition to a scherzo section in which the triangle, which so offended Hanslick, appears rather timidly. The main theme of this scherzo section is a sprightly subject, first foreshadowed in plucked strings and then appearing in the piano. This movement concludes with a return of the flute melody of the preceding section against the piano trill. The sonorities grow and the pace quickens. After a brief restatement of the principal theme, the finale enters vigorously. Liszt himself explained that this finale

is merely an urgent recapitulation of the earlier subject matter with quickened, livelier rhythm, and contains no new motive. . . . The method of binding together and rounding off a whole piece at its close is somewhat my own, but it is quite maintained and justified from the standpoint of musical form. The trombones and basses take up the second part of the motive of the Adagio [the lyrical and plaintive second theme]. The piano figure which follows is no other than the reproduction of the motive which was given in the Adagio by flute and clarinet, just as the concluding passage is a variant and working up in the major of the motive of the Scherzo, until finally the first motive . . . with a trill accompaniment, comes in and concludes the whole.

The Concerto No. 2 in A major is less popular than the First Piano Concerto because it is more sentimental and given more often to the commonplace. Liszt obviously was not satisfied with it since he revised and rewrote it many times after having produced his first draft between 1840 and 1845. Liszt described this work as a "concerto symphonique" to point up its symphonic character. It has only one movement, in which the dominant thought is immediately heard in the woodwinds. The first part of the concerto is slow and solemn, but stormy music erupts after a change of tempo. A tender and lyrical thought reminiscent of the first theme is later given by the solo cello, while the first theme itself returns in march rhythm before the closing coda.

Liszt wrote two more important works for piano and orchestra. *Totentanz*, or *Danse Macabre* (1849), is a fantasy which makes significant use of the famous melody of the *Dies irae*, which receives its first hearing from the woodwinds, brass, and strings. This melody is transformed several times after that, while a diabolic mood is being projected.

The Hungarian Fantasy for Piano and Orchestra is an orchestral adaptation of the Hungarian Rhapsody No. 14 for piano solo. Liszt completed it in 1860, eight yers after writing the rhapsody (*see* Hungarian Rhapsodies below).

Piano Music. The Hungarian Rhapsodies, written between 1846 and 1885, are undoubtedly the works with which the name of Liszt is most often associated. In view of the fact that some of the rhapsodies are often heard in orchestral transcriptions (either by Liszt himself or by Franz Doppler) it should be borne in mind that they were originally written for piano solo. These works are as much the outgrowth of Liszt's researches in the field of Hungarian folk music as were the ten volumes of *Hungarian Folk Melodies* which he edited and published between 1839 and 1847. The rhapsodies are filled with actual gypsy melodies and Hungarian rhythms and dances, adapted, organized, and developed by Liszt with tremendous effect. Dramatic use is made of variety of rhythms, the gradual quickening of the tempo until the music becomes vertiginous, the sudden intrusion of sentimental and gaily ornamented gypsy melodies, powerfully impelled climaxes. The rhapsodies make no pretense at subtlety; every effect is on the surface. Their impact on an audience is inescapable.

All Liszt rhapsodies have one thing in common: They are studies in quick contrasts. Slow, languorous music (called *lassan*) continually alternates with frivolous, abandoned passages (*friskan*) with telling and often exciting theatrical effect.

The most popular of these works—the most popular of all Liszt's works—is undoubtedly the Hungarian Rhapsody No. 2. Neither this nor the other better-known rhapsodies require analytical comment. This is not only highly familiar music, but also music which does not call for a schooled ear to be appreciated at first hearing. The other popular rhapsodies include the Ninth (*Carnaval de Pesth*), Twelfth, Thirteenth, Fourteenth (also adapted by Liszt into a work for piano and orchestra and renamed Hungarian Fantasy), and the Fifteenth (*Rakoczy March,* not to be confused with a composition of the same name by Berlioz).

The universal appeal of *Liebestraum* (*Love's Dream*) is rivaled only by that of the Second Hungarian Rhapsody. Liszt wrote not one but three *Liebesträume,* all of them in 1850. But when we speak of *Liebestraum* we mean only one piece of music, the Third in A-flat, a sentimental idyll that has melted more hearts than any other piece of piano music. Liszt wrote his three *Liebesträume* as songs before adapting them for the piano; the third is based on "O Lieb', so lang du lieben kannst." It is for this reason that the expansive melodic line has such a vocal quality.

The Sonata in B minor (1853), like everything else Liszt created on a large scale, combines the very good with the inferior. It has grandeur, eloquent poetic content, and a magnetizing power. But it also indulges in shallow dramatics, prolixity, and sprawling disorganization. It is a long work even though it is in a single movement. Its greatest fault is that, despite its magnificent pages, it always *sounds* long.

It opens in an epic vein, with a stirring theme in octaves leaping out of an effective harmonic texture. A mocking section follows, and after that a chorale. The epic theme returns to lead into the finale section: a dazzling prestissimo which James Gibbons Huneker considers one of the most brilliant pages in all piano literature.

The extensive library of Liszt's piano music includes many other compositions, large and small, which belong in the pianist's repertory: ballades; Consolations; études which include adaptations of six Paganini caprices (1838), the third of which, in A-flat minor, is *La Campanella;* the programmatic legends *St. François d'Assise prédication aux oiseaux* and *St. François de Paule marchant sur les flots* (1866). There are also three sets of tone pictures collectively entitled *Années de pèlerinage.* The first (1835–36) was inspired by Switzerland and includes Liszt's delicate impression of a spring of water, *Au bord d'une source.* The second set (1838–39) was stimulated by a visit to Italy. Here we have the famous descriptive piece *Sonetto 104 del Petrarca,* which as its name indicates is a musical interpretation of Petrarch's 104th Sonnet. The third set (1877) is less distinguished than the other two and consists of a varied assortment of travel portraits. The most interesting is *Les Jeux d'eaux à la Villa d'Este,* which prophetically suggests Impressionistic writing.

One other original Liszt work for the piano should be considered: *"Funérailles,"* the seventh in a collection of ten pieces called *Harmonies poétiques et religieuses* (1849). This is one of the noblest threnodies for the piano, believed to be in memory of Frédéric Chopin, who died one month before it was written. An introductory section is a mighty expression of grief. A heroic funeral march follows. A change of mood comes with a tender, even wistful, trio. A stormy martial section is now built up to a magnificent climax. Earlier material is then recalled, and the work ends on a note of profound poignancy.

There exists still another library of Liszt piano pieces made up of transcriptions of works by other composers. Once again we are confronted by very bad Liszt and very good Liszt. The worst of these transcriptions were calculated to exhibit Liszt's technique and are exclusively display pieces. These are usually elaborate fantasies on melodies from famous operas. More important by far are those transcriptions in which Liszt remained true to the spirit of the original and served as a humble translator. In this category are his excellent adaptations for the piano of many lieder by Schubert and Schumann and of organ works by Bach.

Gustav Mahler

"No one will gainsay me when I say, 'Truly he was a great man!'"

ARNOLD SCHOENBERG

BORN: Kalischt, Bohemia, July 7, 1860.

DIED: Vienna, May 18, 1911.

MAJOR WORKS: *Orchestral Music*—9 symphonies (a tenth symphony reconstructed and completed by Deryck Cooke); Das klagende Lied, for solo voices, chorus, and orchestra; Lieder eines fahrenden Gesellen, for voice and orchestra; Lieder aus Des Knaben Wunderhorn, for voice and orchestra; Kindertotenlieder, for voice and orchestra; Das Lied von der Erde, for solo voices and orchestra. *Vocal Music*—Lieder und Gesänge aus der Jugendzeit; Five Songs to Poems by Rückert; individual songs for voice and piano.

HIS LIFE

Mahler used to enjoy telling two anecdotes. One was about his grandmother, the other about his mother. Since her eighteenth year his grandmother had earned a living by going from house to house selling goods. When she was eighty she violated some new law governing peddlers and received a fine which she considered both undeserved and excessive. She was not the one to accept such injustice with docility. Despite her old age she went to Vienna, insisted upon and received an audience with Emperor Franz Joseph, and pleaded her case. After she had received a complete pardon she returned home and quietly carried on her business.

The story about his mother concerned Mahler when he was a student at the Vienna Conservatory. One day he proudly informed his mother that he had won first prize in composition. "How did Hans Rott do?" his mother asked. Hans Rott was then one of the most brilliant of all the Conservatory students, a fact which Mahler had always conceded. Rott, however, had not even received an honorable mention. His mother cried softly. "Rott's work was better than yours. He deserved the prize," she said.

The proud defiance of his grandmother against anything that stood in her way and the fierce honesty of his mother were two salient traits of Mahler's make-up. Always he had pride, integrity, an uncompromising spirit, and a will of iron that would not bend to expediency. He was a fighter. For these qualities he was both hated and adored. There were those who detested him because he had been born a Jew. They found him vulnerable to their attacks, since he was arrogant, intractable, and bitter of tongue. He was oversensitive, easily irritated, with an easily wounded vanity. With disagreeable people, or with people with whom he could not establish a bond of understanding, he was, as Guido Adler once wrote of him, "mistrustful and reserved . . . and he was capable of striking out with the harshest home truths, so that now and then he hurt." In addition to all this he was egocentric—a composer of huge symphonies trying to express world philsophies, a composer with a passion for greatness and a sublime faith in his power. Those who worked for him may have recognized that he was one of the world's greatest conductors, but some of them nevertheless resented the physical and spiritual ordeals to which he continually subjected them in his unsparing efforts to attain ideal performances. They ridiculed him, plotted against him, and—in the end—succeeded in destroying him.

There was another side to Mahler, a side which made those who knew him well love him. Guido Adler tells us that, in spite of Mahler's inflexible will, "his temper was mild, his heart soft. He was generous; like a child he felt with his fellow men, with great and small, with grownups and with the young. He was touching in his friendship, in his attachment; he was open, reserved to the point of self-abnegation. He could enjoy everything. . . . He was communicative and confiding toward friends whom he won and recognized as such. . . . He could bear the most acute pain without complaint."

There were also those who saw in him an uncompromising artist with the highest ideals—as composer as well as conductor. Men such as the conductor Bruno Walter (who for many years worked as his assistant) and the composer Arnold Schoenberg (who was inspired by him) described him as a "saint." The singer Theodor Reichmann, of the Vienna Opera, started out by naming him derisively "the Jewish monkey," but ended by referring to him as "the god Mahler." There was, indeed, something religious about his sense of dedication from the very first, about his lifelong denial of the physical for the spiritual.

He was born in the small Bohemian town of Kalischt. Suffering, an emotion well known to him throughout his life, began in childhood. Tragedy stalked the Mahler household. Five of Mahler's brothers and sisters died in childhood of diphtheria. Another brother, to whom the composer was particularly attached, suffered a long illness before dying of hydrocardia at the age of twelve. In the last months of the boy's life Mahler was continually at his side, suffering with him. His oldest sister died of a brain tumor after a brief, unhappy marriage. Another sister succumbed to fantasies that she was dying; again and again she would light candles around her bed and lie down motionless, feigning death. A brother was a simpleton in his youth and a forger in his adult life. Still another brother, a humble musician, committed suicide rather than accept the mediocrity assigned him by fate. Against this background of misery was the unhappy marriage of Mahler's father and mother. The lifelong resentment that Mahler bore his father was due principally to the abuses suffered by his mother, which as a boy he witnessed frequently.

When Mahler was six years old he found an old piano in the attic of his grandmother's house. From then on a new world opened up for him. With supreme patience he sat at the piano day by day solving the mystery of the black and white keys.

His father wanted Mahler to become a respectable shopkeeper; but if his son had talent, he would not stand in his way. One day he brought the boy to Vienna to see Professor Julius Epstein of the Vienna Conservatory. Epstein's judgment would decide whether Gustav was to study music. Gustav played some of the piano pieces he had written. Epstein said, "He is a born musician." His fate was decided. At the age of fifteen Gustav Mahler was enrolled in the Vienna Conservatory. For the next three years he was an earnest and hard-working pupil, winning awards for composition and piano playing. At the same time, between 1877 and 1879, he attended the University of Vienna for courses in history and philosophy.

At the advice of Epstein, Mahler accepted a post as conductor of light opera in a cheap Vienna music hall where he received $12.50 a month. The work was humiliating to a young man of Mahler's ideals and sensibilities. He left it for other jobs not much more gratifying.

Several patrons interested themselves in him and arranged for him to conduct Mendelssohn's *St. Paul* at a Leipzig music festival in 1885. For the first time Mahler was asked to direct a masterwork with adequate musical resources at hand. His performance had such incandescence and technical finish that the audience was stirred profoundly. One of those who heard him was the impresario Angelo Neumann, who offered Mahler a conducting post with the German Opera in Prague.

Mahler's rise as a conductor was now rapid. From Prague he went to Pest, where his performances received the glowing praise of distinguished musicians, including Brahms. Then to Budapest and Hamburg where, during the next five years, he was responsible for completely reorganizing and revitalizing those companies. Praise and honor were now his, but he also met opposition and obstruction. In the provincial opera companies, where mediocrity ruled, he had contended with mockery, slovenliness, and lack of discipline, and he had had to crush them. In the opera houses of the larger cities his demand for perfection—already as much a part of him as breathing—appeared strange to musicians who did not always understand what he was trying to do.

In 1897, on the recommendation of such musicians as Brahms and the musicologist Guido Adler, Mahler became the musical director of the Vienna Royal Opera. It was there that Mahler's achievements as a conductor received world-wide recognition. When he arrived the Vienna Opera was in the process of artistic disintegration. During the ten years he remained with the Opera he made it into the first of the world's musical institutions. He spared no one, least of all himself, in his maniacal devotion to his task, in his pursuit of the ideal performance. He completely renovated the opera company, dismissing old and tired singers and replacing them with fresh personalities. The repertory was rehabilitated: many novelties never before heard in Vienna were introduced, and many new works of promise were heard for the first time. He restored discipline. He laid down the law that no one in the audience was to come late to a performance, refusing to seat anyone during the first act. He banished the claque. He made drastic reforms in stage direction and brought about a complete renovation of scenery and costumes. He insisted on presenting the Wagnerian music dramas without deletions. He subjected the old familiar operas to a most painstaking restudy by all the branches of his company. They used to say in Vienna that the works that emerged from his hand were fresh and new—*"Herrlich wie am ersten Tag"* ("Glorious as on the first day").

But he was hated, hated because he was a Jew, because he was a martinet, and because he was a genius. Directors of the Royal Opera objected to the expenses which his restudied versions of opera performances incurred. Those who sang and played under him were victims of his merciless tongue, his unbridled anger, his imperious will, and even his contempt. Petty intrigues were hatched all around him. He swept them aside and kept on working.

All the while that he was expending such energy in breathing new life into the music of others, he was also producing works of his own. They were ambitious works which tried to bring new dimensions to the symphonic form and give it a new articulateness. Here, too, he met opposition and malice. The Symphony No. 1, first heard in Budapest on November 22, 1889, under Mahler's own direction, was a fiasco. The musicians, who disliked the work as well as its composer, did their best to sabotage the performance. The audience was unmistakably hostile. The review of one of the two critics who attended was mixed with vitriol. The Symphony No. 2, of which three movements were presented by Richard Strauss in Berlin on March 4, 1895, and the entire work by Mahler himself in December of the same year, seemed to find the audiences more appreciative or at any rate less antagonistic. But the critics were devastating. One of them described it as "the cynical impudence of this brutal . . . music maker." And so it continued, as Mahler produced one new symphony after another, each vaster than the preceding one. Always there was misunderstanding and vituperation.

Personal abuse and misunderstanding of his life's work were not the only crosses Mahler had to bear. There was personal tragedy too.

In 1906 his little daughter died of scarlet fever. (Mahler had married Alma Maria Schindler, daughter of a Viennese painter, on March 9, 1902, and their daughter was born in 1903.) Mahler almost went mad with grief. After that he always carried deep within him the guilty feeling that he was partially responsible for his little one's premature death. He felt that he had tempted fate by writing, in 1903, a set of poignant elegies for dead children, on poems of Rückert, entitled *Kindertotenlieder*.

Something else was troubling Mahler. Soon after his daughter's death he submitted to what he thought would be a perfunctory physical examination. It turned out that he was suffering from a serious heart condition. Thenceforth he would have to live with moderation, if he was to survive. Moderation in eating, drinking, and smoking did not mean much to him, for he had never been a slave to physical needs. But moderation in his work—that was impossible! The demon drive within him would not allow him to submit to his physical condition. Indeed, if that were possible, he worked harder than ever before, conscious that time was running out and that he still had so much to accomplish.

On October 15, 1907, Mahler gave his last performance at the Vienna Opera—a beautiful reading of Beethoven's *Fidelio*. He could work no longer in an atmosphere so charged with envy, malice, and hypocrisy, where obstructions were continually put in his way. He did not have to go; no one had asked for his resignation. Even many of those who hated him were ready to concede that he had achieved miracles at the Opera. But Mahler would stay no longer. "I must keep on the heights. I cannot let anything irritate me or drag me down. It is hard enough as it is to keep up on that level all the time." To his colleagues at the Royal Opera he addressed a touching letter of farewell: "Instead of the complete accomplishments of my dreams, I can only leave behind me fragments, as man is ever fated to do. . . . I may venture to say of myself that my intentions were ever honest and my aim lofty. . . . I have always put my whole soul into the work, subordinated my person to the cause, my inclinations to duty. I have not spared myself, and could, therefore, require of others their utmost exertions. In the press of the struggle, in the heat of the moment, neither you nor I have escaped wounds and misunderstandings. But when a work was successful, a problem solved, we forgot the difficulties and the troubles, and all felt richly rewarded."

He felt that what he needed most of all was a change of scene. He came to the United States late in 1907 to conduct at the Metropolitan Opera House, making his American debut on January 1, 1908, in *Tristan and Isolde* (an event made further memorable by the first appearance as Isolde of the brilliant Wagnerian soprano Olive Fremstad). The following autumn he combined his demanding and physically exacting tasks at the Metropolitan Opera with newly assumed duties as conductor of the New York Philharmonic Orchestra. In America, as in Vienna, he worked with zeal and devotion, refusing to make a single concession to his faltering heart. On September 12, 1910, he returned to Munich to conduct the *première* of his monumental Eighth Symphony (after harrowing rehearsals), and witness one of his few triumphs as a composer. The following winter he was back in America, completing a rigorous schedule of sixty-five concerts.

He broke down under the strain of hard work and the continual pressure to popularize his programs, attend social engagements, and make fewer demands on his musicians. He collapsed in New York on February 21, 1911. A streptococcus infection set in. Brought to Paris for serum treatments, he showed no signs of improving. He asked to be taken to Vienna, where he was confined to a nursing home. But it was the end: uremia had set in. Dying, he kept moving a finger as if it were a baton and as if he were directing invisible musicians in inaudible music. The last word he spoke was the name "Mozart." He died an hour before midnight of May 18, 1911, during a terrible storm.

Mahler's widow was subsequently married to two other world-famous cultural figures, the architect Walter Adolf Gropius and the author Franz Werfel.

HIS MUSIC

Except for songs and song cycles, Mahler concentrated his creative energies on the symphony. His output contains no operas or oratorios, no chamber music, no music for solo instruments, no smaller choral works, and no music for chamber orchestra. As he could compose primarily in the summer, when he was released from his pressing duties as conductor, he had to devote himself exclusively to "great works," as he put it, "if I am to achieve an immortal role for posterity."

"Great works" to him meant symphonies (a song cycle such as *Das Lied von der Erde* is actually a symphony too)—but symphonies of great dimensions. Only the First and Fourth Symphonies are of traditional length, requiring three quarters of an hour each for performance and engaging the more or less normal complement of the present-day full-size symphony orchestra. All the others are over-sized. Most of these sprawl out into five or six movements, take from an hour to ninety minutes to be performed, and call for Gargantuan musical forces (including many instruments not usually found in the orchestra) including human voices. His Symphony No. 8, the so-called *Symphony of a Thousand,* requires two mixed choruses, a boys' chorus, eight solo voices, and a mammoth orchestra.

But "great works" meant something more to him than immense size. It must be recalled that he was one of the last great German Romantics, in life and thought as well as in deed. The turmoil of the nineteenth century was in his blood. Deep-rooted pessimism, Dostoyevskyan moral laceration, intense spiritual conflict, Faustian struggle after knowledge—all this was in Mahler and all this is in his music. He wanted to produce works embodying a mystical sense of some transcendent truth. "All my works are anticipations of a future life." Although he hated programs for music—he grew violent whenever he was asked to give one for a symphony of his— he tried to fill the symphonic form with intellectual content. To probe in music the epic problems of the universe, of life and death, was his ultimate goal. "When I conceive a large musical work I always arrive at a point where I am compelled to draw upon the 'word' as the bearer of my musical ideas." He had to make the "word," the idea, a part of his symphonies; he aspired to make the voice, conveyer of the "word," an integral part of the orchestra.

His works were violently attacked in his own day because of their overpretentious aims, musical as well as philosophic. And they had difficulty making headway after their composer's death for these and other reasons. Mahler's severest critics pointed to his shortcomings: his tendency to be prolix, diffuse, bombastic, and even hysterical;

his bathos; his weakness for naïve Austrian folk tunes and march melodies; his sentimentality.

But since Mahler's death there have appeared some who believed implicity in his greatness and expressed supreme faith that his day would surely come. These admirers and disciples worked passionately and indefatigably to bring recognition to his music—conductors like Willem Mengelberg, Bruno Walter, Otto Klemperer, and Richard Strauss. Their efforts have not been in vain. Their victory is further ensured through the further dedicated propagandizing of a new generation of Mahler conductors: Leonard Bernstein, Sir Georg Solti, Bernard Haitink, James Levine, Rafael Kubelik, Eric Leinsdorf, and Pierre Bouliz. When, between September 26 and October 25, 1976, the New York Philharmonic became the first American orchestra ever to present a Mahler festival covering all his symphonies, Irving Kolodin could say: "The rise from obscurity to prominence . . . of Mahler is the most remarkable phenomenon of public musical life in America in the mid decades of the twentieth century."

ANALYTICAL NOTES

Orchestral Music. Mahler's nine symphonies were divided into three groups by his biographer, Paul Stefan. The first four symphonies are subjective, representing a personal struggle against cosmic forces. The next four are the probings of a musician-philosopher seeking the answer to the riddle of the universe; the personal element is now gone. In Symphony No. 9 the struggle with himself and the eternal verities is over. Mahler divorces himself from the problems of the world. Resigned, he now seeks inner peace.

The Symphony No. 1 in D major, the *Titan* (1888), was described by the composer as "the sound of Nature." Others have found more in it. To Bruno Walter it was Mahler's *Werther,* his escape from personal suffering; Gabriel Engel provided still another interpretation, finding in the music the search of a hero for some faith.

When the symphony was performed in Weimar in 1894 (five years after the *première*) Mahler permitted titles, subtitles, and explanatory lines to be appended to the respective movements. The first three movements came under the general heading of "From the Days of Youth." The first movement carried the following legend:

"Spring and no end. The Introduction portrays the awakening of Nature in the early morning." In this long introduction we hear faint woodwind calls simulating the voices of birds. An ascending passage in the basses separates the introduction from the principal section, the main theme of which is given quietly by cellos and double basses; a subsidiary subject in the horns, also subdued, is soon taken up by the cellos. The second movement, heard at the *première* and in Weimar in 1894, has since been deleted. Instead we proceed to a scherzo-like movement described as "Under Full Sail," in which a vigorous peasant dance theme is given by the woodwinds.

The next two movements are captioned: *"Commedia umanae"* ("Human Comedy"). The first is an extended funeral march with ironic overtones. The main theme, which sounds like the familiar canon "Frère Jacques," appears grimly in muted double basses and is treated canonically. A second melody follows in the first violins, a passionate, oriental-like song; the funeral canon is then brought back. The tempestuous finale is "the abrupt outburst of doubt from a deeply wounded heart" according to the Weimar program. Thematic materials from the first movement are recalled and are developed passionately. Toward the close of the movement, a resplendent theme is sounded by seven horns; to Bruno Walter this theme represents the "triumphant victory over life."

The Symphony No. 2 in C minor, the *Resurrection* (1894), was considered by Mahler a sequel to the First, which it followed by five years. He wrote to a German critic: "I have called the first movement 'Celebration of the Dead.' If you wish to know, it is the Hero of my first symphony whom I bear to the grave. Immediately arise the great questions: Why have you lived? Why have you suffered? Has it all been only a huge, frightful joke? We must all somehow answer these questions, if we are to continue living, yes, even if we are only to continue dying. Whoever hears this call must give a reply. And this reply I give in my last movement."

The symphony calls for immense forces. The large orchestra includes a pipe organ, church bells, four off-stage horns, four off-stage trumpets, a large variety of percussion instruments including such unorthodox ones as tam-tams (a variety of gongs) and *Ruthe* (a bundle of sticks), and another percussion group "heard in the distance." The symphony also calls on the human voice—a soprano, a contralto, and a chorus; for the first time Mahler enlists the "word" to supplement his music.

This dramatic music has often been subjected to programmatic interpretation. The aptest one is that which would regard it as an allegory on the life of man. In this interpretation the first movement speaks of death, the second of youthful optimism, the third of life's vulgarities, the fourth of the spiritual life, and the fifth of Judgment Day.

The symphony opens with an angry rumble in the basses; the "why" of human existence is being questioned. The questioning continues in the woodwinds, then loudly in the entire orchestra, until it becomes a frenzied outcry. There comes a quiet melody in the horns and strings, as if in reassurance, but the discontent of the opening returns, and before long we are hurled into the midst of a passionate struggle. The ensuing section is less disturbed. Then the basses present the rhythm of a funeral march; the battle of doubt is soon fought. A chorale begins in a funereal vein, on which brighter colors are gradually superimposed; the mood changes from defeat to victory. Earlier material, particularly the opening questioning, is repeated in varied guises and is worked out dramatically. There is an elegiac song in the strings, carried on by the horns. Basses bring on another variation of the opening material, but the mood for the most part is now restrained until the end of the movement; the struggle is over.

After the turmoil of the first movement, the second (a graceful Austrian folk dance) comes with the ingratiating warmth of sunshine after a summer storm. The theme is heard in the strings. A contrasting fast section follows, after which the dance melody is brought back. The fast section is now developed at some length, often with agitation. A variation of the dance tune restores calm and brings the movement to an end.

Strokes of the tympani invoke the third movement. It is a scherzo both in form and substance. The music has levity (the hero has confronted the vulgarities of life); vivacious themes follow one another and the rhythms become capricious. The middle section is brought in by a brief fugato; the initial material is then repeated. The fourth movement, entitled *"Urlicht"* ("Primal Light"), enters without a break. It is here that Mahler uses the voice for the first time—a contralto. His text was derived from the anthology of German folk poetry entitled *Des Knaben Wunderhorn* (which was also the source of one of Mahler's song cycles). The text begins with the following lines:

Oh, red, red rose!
Man lies in bitter need
Man lies in greatest pain!
Rather would I be in heaven.

Once again there is no interruption between movements. Once again, in the fifth movement, the voice is called upon, this time a soprano and a chorus as well as the contralto. The text here is "The Resurrection" by Klopstock with additional verses by Mahler himself. The orchestra enters with a wild outburst. Judgment Day is heralded by distant horns. The chorale of the first movement is quoted quietly. A phrase from the Resurrection melody to come is provocatively suggested by the winds. The music now is, by turns, full of splendor and anguish. Suddenly we hear a mighty funeral march, as if the dead have arisen from their graves and are filing past in a grim procession. The macabre music is succeeded by spiritual radiance. Then the horns of the Apocalypse sound their call; the voice of the nightingale flutters in a rarefied atmosphere; the shimmering sound of the chorus enters with the song of the Resurrection. More and more exultant does the "word" become; more and more orgiastic are the orchestral colors; more and more heaven-storming are the sonorities. A climax of shattering power is arrived at by the entire orchestra. The symphony ends with the joyous tolling of bells and the majestic voice of the organ.

The Symphony No. 3 in D minor (1895) is the voice of Mahler's pantheism. It starts off with a paean to nature and ends up with a hymn to love. Scored for solo contralto, women's chorus, boys' chorus, and orchestra, this symphony is divided into two parts, with one section in the first part, and five more in the second. The composer himself explained his programmatic intent in this music by appending a title to each of the sections as follows: in the first part, "Introduction: Pan Awakes; Summer Marches In"; in the second, "What the Wild Flowers Tell Me," "What the Animals Tell Me," "What Man Tells Me," "What the Morning Bells Tell Me," and "What Love Tells Me." In the second of these sections

Mahler quotes one of his songs which he had derived from a folk tune; in the third part he uses a text from Nietzsche's *Also sprach Zarathustra*. In commenting on the last part, the composer said that he might have called it "What God Tells Me," explaining that "in such a sense God is only to be understood as love."

The Symphony No. 4 in G major (1900) is one of the shortest and most joyous of the Mahler works. Droll, even gay, moods predominate. But the third movement, the andante, has ecclesiastical majesty. In the fourth movement the "word" is used, as a soprano sings the text of an old Bavarian folk song and a lyric found in *Des Knaben Wunderhorn;* in this movement, as Bruno Walter remarked, the "humorous character" of the symphony is "changed into one of exalted solemnity."

The Symphony No. 5 in C-sharp minor (1902) has acquired the name of the *Giant* due to its size; but it is by no means the largest of the Mahler symphonies. It is arranged in an unorthodox pattern. The five movements are divided into three parts. The first part opens with a funeral march and concludes with a movement filled with stormy music. The second consists entirely of a virile scherzo. The finale begins with a graceful adagietto (the work's most famous movement), whose serenity is touched with sadness, and ends with a rondo, the core of which is a triple fugue.

Mahler himself designated the Symphony No. 6 in A minor as *Tragic* (1904), but it could also be dubbed *Fate*. Fate makes its presence felt in the dramatic "hammer strokes" (to which Mahler was always so partial), a fate motive consisting of a six-note rhythm in the tympani appearing in the first movement (after the first theme has been stated and developed) and recurring three times in the finale. As for tragedy, this emotion permeates the finale, a giant movement taking some thirty minutes to perform in which a lamentation lapses into utter despair.

The Symphony No. 7 in D major (1905) is made up of five movements, two of which are *Nachtmusik,* or "serenades." In the first of these (the second movement) the horn is prominent, first with the opening calls, then with a slow melody. This pastoral atmosphere is intensified later with flutes simulating the voices of birds and cowbells. The second serenade (fourth movement) once again assigns its principal theme to the horn. Mahler's bent for

unusual instrumentation reveals itself in the opening, scored for mandolin and guitar.

The first movement has a solemn beginning, but the main section
is muscular music, its principal subject found in cellos and horns,
and its secondary thought in second violins accompanied by cello
arpeggios. The third movement is a scherzo with four contrasting
trio sections. The finale, introduced by a tympani solo and a horn
fanfare, is dramatized with a march melody and a dynamic episode
for strings and woodwinds. The main subject of the first movement
is brought back, first in the horns and then in the trombones, to
bring the symphony to an exultant end.

In size and structure, in the giant forces it enlists, and in its
Weltanschauung, the Symphony No. 8 in E-flat major (also known
as the *Symphony of a Thousand*) is Mahler's most ambitious composition (1907). It is scored for eight solo voices, two mixed choruses, a boys' choir, and a huge orchestra. It occupies an entire
program, one of the longest symphonies ever written. And its message
is hardly less Gargantuan. "Imagine to yourself the entire universe
suddenly beginning to sound and sing!" said Mahler of this music.
"There are no longer human voices, but revolving suns and planets."

The symphony has two parts. The first, called *"Veni, Creator
Spiritus,"* uses a ninth-century Latin text by the Archbishop of
Mayence subsequently incorporated into the Roman Catholic liturgy
for Pentecost. God and the Holy Ghost are represented in this
music, but also the divine spark that is found in every true creative
spirit. In the traditional sonata-allegro structure, this section is made
up of three principal subjects: the outcry of the chorus, *"Veni,
Creator Spiritus";* a beautiful and plaintive melody for soprano solo,
"Imple superna"; and an expressive thought for the choruses and
orchestra, *"Infirma nostri."* These ideas are developed along monumental lines and end up in a giant double fugue.

The second half of the symphony is a setting of the closing scene
of the Second Part of Goethe's *Faust.* Structurally, it consists of
an andante, a scherzo, and a finale with coda. The music here is
consistently dramatic, after an impressive introduction whose pedal
point (in the key of E-flat) extends for one hundred and sixty-four
measures. In this movement, even more than in the preceding one,
Mahler gives a strongly affirmative answer to life, as Bruno Walter

has noted. "It peals from the *Faust* words and from the torrent of music in which Mahler's own emotion is released."

The Symphony No. 9 in D major (1909) is Mahler's last complete work. Together with the song cycle *Das Lied von der Erde* (written one year earlier) it represents the composer's farewell to the world. It opens and closes with a slow movement; but the music of the first movement is filled with anguish, while that of the last speaks of eternal peace. In between we have a charming Austrian peasant dance (as if commenting on the evanescent pleasures of life) and a bitter rondo, full of mockery and scorn.

Mahler began writing a tenth symphony but did not live to complete it. Two movements were in an advanced stage of completion when he died; the other three movements consisted merely of random sketches. An English musicologist, Deryck Cooke, developed all this material in a full-length five-movement symphony, adhering as closely as he could to Mahler's own intention—an adaptation finally introduced in London in 1960. Obviously this work is hybrid Mahler, but parts, particularly in the last movement, have the kind of rapture and exaltation of which only Mahler seemed capable.

Perhaps more deserving of being considered as Mahler's tenth symphony, though it is not a symphony at all, is his magnificent song cycle for tenor, contralto, and orchestra *Das Lied von der Erde,* or *The Song of the Earth,* which he completed in 1908 after his Eighth Symphony. This work consists of six songs, alternately rendered by a tenor and an alto (or baritone), the texts of which are Chinese poems by Li-Tai-Po and Tchang-Tsi, which Hans Bethge had adapted into his volume *Die Chineische Flöte.* Like the slow movements of the Ninth Symphony, *Das Lied von der Erde* represents the composer's withdrawal from the world of struggle. It is the most somber of Mahler's works, regarding the world as full of strife and woe and renouncing that world with bitterness.

The first is a drinking song of "earthly woe" in which the deep note of pessimism, which sounds throughout the work, is immediately heard in tones of the darkest despondency. "When sorrow approaches, the soul's gardens lie desolate," runs one of the stanzas. "Joy and song wither and die. Dark is life, and dark is death." This is followed by an autumnal picture; the world has grown desolate. The third and fourth songs speak of youth and love and, consequently, provide a brief respite from the prevailing gloom. But in the tenor solo "The Drunken One in Springtime"—like the first, a drinking song—we again have the voice of the pessimist. "What matters Spring to me?" the concluding lines inquire. "Only drunk I want to be." The last section, "Farewell," combines two poems. In a drunken sleep the poet renounces happiness and calls to his friend to bid him farewell. "I am wandering toward my native place, my home," he says sadly. "I seek rest for my lonely heart."

Jules Massenet

"His object was to seduce, and from the time when he found that his music proved effective and became popular, he carefully avoided changing his manner."

M. D. CALVOCORESSI

BORN: Montaud, France, May 12, 1842.
DIED: Paris, August 13, 1912.
MAJOR WORKS: *Ballets*—La Cigale; Espada. *Choral Music*—Marie-Magdeleine; Eve; La Terre promise; Narcisse; La Vierge. *Operas*—Hérodiade; Manon; Le Cid; Werther; Thaïs; La Navarraise; Sapho; Cendrillon; Grisélidis; Le Jongleur de Notre Dame; Don Quichotte. *Orchestral Music*—7 suites (including Scènes pittoresques, Scènes napolitaines, Scènes alsaciennes); 3 overtures (including Phèdre); Marche solennelle; Fantaisie for Cello and Orchestra; Piano Concerto; incidental music to various plays including Les Erinnyes. *Vocal Music*—songs for voice and piano including "Elégie," "Noël païen," "Ouvre tes yeux bleus," and "Sérénade du passant."

HIS LIFE

Massenet's father was an officer in the First Empire who resigned when the Bourbons were restored. He started and managed an ironworks in Montaud, near Saint-Etienne. It was there that Jules, youngest of twenty-one children, was born. The date on which his mother gave him his first piano lesson was never erased from his mind, for on that very day—February 24, 1848—revolution broke out. The firing of shots in the street not only interrupted the lesson but also closed the ironworks. The Massenet family moved on to Paris in 1851, where it lived in poverty. Most of the support came from piano lessons given by the mother to neighborhood children. Her own son Jules was one of her pupils.

When he was ten years old Jules entered the Paris Conservatory. While still attending the Conservatory he supported himself by playing the tympani in various theater orchestras. "During the dialogue I would trace my intervals on the skin of the kettledrum and sketch my fugues for class." He was at first an inattentive and lazy student; his teacher, Bazin, once ordered him to stay out of the classroom for good. But Massenet soon found the kind of sympathetic understanding that his temperament required. Ambroise Thomas particularly inspired him to work hard. Before long Massenet was winning prizes in piano playing and fugue, and in 1863 he received the Prix de Rome for the cantata *David Rizzio*.

"I began to live," Massenet said of his three-year stay in Italy as winner of the Prix de Rome. "During my happy walks with my comrades, painters, sculptors, and in our talks under the oaks of the Villa Borghese, or under the pines of Villa Pamphili, I felt my first stirrings and admiration for Nature and for art." He met several outstanding musicians then living in Italy, including Franz Liszt, who were impressed by his talent. One day Liszt sent Massenet a young girl who wanted piano lessons, Mademoiselle Sainte-Marie. Massenet fell in love with his pupil and married her on October 8, 1866.

Back in Paris, Massenet began writing music in many different forms and with the facility that was to mark his entire career. He did not have to wait long for a performance. His former teacher, Thomas, arranged for his one-act opera *La Grand'tante* to be performed at the Opéra-Comique in 1867. In the same year his First Suite for Orchestra, was introduced by the Pasdeloup Orchestra. Neither work was particularly successful.

During the Franco-Prussian War, Massenet served in the National Guard. After the war he continued his career, this time with rapidly mounting success. His second opera, *Don César de Bazan,* enjoyed a minor success when introduced in 1872. Then came his first claim to fame, with the incidental music he wrote in 1873 for a drama by Leconte de Lisle, *Les Erynnyes.* It was received most enthusiastically when it was introduced at the Odéon on January 6, 1873. One part of that score has remained to this day one of Massenet's most popular pieces of music. It is the "Invocation," which Massenet arranged for cello and piano and retitled *Elégie*. It was also subsequently arranged for violin and piano, and adapted into a song with superimposed lyrics by E. Gallet.

With two successful oratorios—*Marie-Magdeleine* in 1873 and *Eve* in 1875—and with the opera *Le Roi de Lahore* produced at the Opéra in 1877, Massenet became famous throughout France. He was made a member of the Legion of Honor in 1876, and in 1878 became the youngest member ever elected to the Académie des Beaux-Arts. But he was yet to produce the operas that were to immortalize him, which came between 1880 and 1900. On December 19, 1881, the Théâtre de la Monnaie in Brussels introduced *Hérodiade*. Massenet's masterwork, *Manon,* followed on January 19, 1894, at the Paris Opéra-Comique. With *Le Cid* in 1885, *Werther* in 1892, *Thaïs* at the Paris Opéra on March 16, 1894, and *Sapho* in 1897, Massenet arrived at a commanding position in the French lyric theater and became one of the most favored composers of his time in France.

His great success did not bring on indolence. Up to the last years of his life Massenet maintained his industry as a composer. But it did bring on the desire, even the passion, to maintain that success at all costs, to retain his comfortable life, his high station, and what Debussy once described as "the butterfly play of fascinating lady admirers" by whatever means he could. Although he wrote a good deal after 1900, including eleven operas as well as ballets and music for orchestra, he produced nothing that could compare to either *Manon* or *Thaïs*. Two of his later operas, however, deserve mention and are still occasionally revived: *Le Jongleur de Notre Dame* and *Don Quichotte,* each of which was introduced in Monte Carlo, the former in 1902, and the latter in 1910.

His success made him negligent in other musical activities. From 1878 to 1896 he taught advanced composition at the Conservatory, a teacher capable of providing stimulation as well as knowledge to his pupils; they included Gustave Charpentier (1860–1956), Gabriel Pierné (1863–1937), Henri Rabaud (1873–1949), and Florent Schmitt (1870–1958). But after he had arrived at success Massenet grew lax in his duties as a teacher, neglecting his classes and allowing his assistant, André Gedalge, to substitute for him. On one occasion, when Massenet returned to his class after a prolonged absence, Ambroise Thomas, director of the Conservatory, said to him, "It is a pleasure to see you again. But don't you sometimes fear that your pupils—or more accurately the pupils of Gedalge—will forget you altogether?"

He has often been described as an opportunist, and he would sometimes go to absurd lengths to create an impression on those whom he met even casually. The eminent French pianist and teacher Isidor Philipp recalls one such incident that was characteristic of many. Massenet was present when young Philipp, then unknown, came to the publisher Heugel to submit a piano piece, a barcarolle. Massenet listened to it, then convinced Heugel to publish it. Thirty years after this episode Philipp came to Massenet to discuss transcribing some of Massenet's orchestral works for the piano. "Whatever became of your delightful little barcarolle?" Massenet asked suddenly. Philipp was startled to find that Massenet still remembered so trivial an item. "It was a lovely thing," the master added, and then sat down at the piano and played it. This feat of memory dumfounded Philipp, who did not fail to describe it the following day to Heugel. Heugel smiled indulgently and explained, "Massenet came in last week and got a copy of your barcarolle."

Massenet had come to Paris from his home in Egreville to consult physicians when he died suddenly, in 1912. Twenty-two years after his death a bust of Massenet was unveiled at the Opéra-Comique, on which occasion his opera *Don Quichotte* was revived, with Feodor Chaliapin in the title role.

HIS MUSIC

The descriptive word "Massenetique" has found a useful place in the vocabulary of French music critics. It has come to have a specific meaning: a melodic beauty which, though frequently skin-deep, is nevertheless seductive; a vein of tenderness, even sentimentality, that is more beguiling than cloying; a poetic feeling, delicate and sensitive, gently touched with melancholy. These qualities, by which Massenet's finest operas are ever recognizable, are also the identifying traits of the French lyric theater at its very best.

Massenet was the French Romantic, child of the nineteenth century. The new styles that emerged after 1900 were not for him—not the naturalism of Gustave Charpentier nor the Impressionism of Debussy. He clung tenaciously to the fervent Romantic ideal for which he was so extravagantly acclaimed in the 1880s. His refusal to change his style, combined with an overwhelming desire to please, made him imitate himself. But the old spell, the old irresistible charm, were gone; there remained only tiresome mannerisms.

In a fantasy entitled "Posthumous Thoughts," which Massenet published in a magazine just before his death, he imagined himself present at his own funeral services, where a colleague remarked, "Now that he is dead I think he will be played much less frequently." Massenet knew, probably better than his severest critics, how much commonplace music he had produced, particularly in his last dozen years. But he need not have concerned himself about his masterworks. *Manon* and *Thaïs*—Massenet at his best—represent the quintessence of French Romantic opera. They will continue to be heard with delight as long as that literature and that tradition survive.

ANALYTICAL NOTES

Operas. When *Manon* (1884) was introduced at the Opéra-Comique, some critics accused Massenet of succumbing to Wagnerian influences; one derisively nicknamed him "Mademoiselle Wagner." From present-day perspective that is about the most curious criticism that could be leveled against the opera. There was a measure of indebtedness to the Wagnerian music drama, particularly in Massenet's use of the leading motive. But to call *Manon* Wagnerian is to fail completely to recognize its personality. It is as essentially French as is the boulevard or the cancan or onion soup. It is opposed to almost everything for which not only German but also Italian opera stands. Instead of large scenes and arias inflated out of their contextual importance, instead of grandiose climaxes and elaborate techniques we have understatement and refinement. The force of *Manon* lies in its tenderness and sympathy, its gentle French melody, its Gallic economy of dramatic and musical means, its poignant recreation of eighteenth-century French backgrounds through dances *à la Lully*.* And yet dramatic tensions are never sacrificed; *Manon* is always excellent theater. It is perhaps at its dramatic best in a Massenet innovation:

---

* Jean Baptiste Lully (1632–87), who, though of Italian birth, was the founder of French opera.

spoken dialogue (instead of recitative) set against an expressive orchestral background.

The story is based upon the famous novel of Abbé Prévost, *L'Histoire de Manon Lescaut*, adapted for Massenet by Henri Meilhac and Philippe Gille. Chevalier des Grieux falls in love with the beautiful Manon Lescaut and prevails upon her to run away with him. They set up house in Paris. More infatuated with her than ever, Des Grieux is determined to marry Manon, as he writes to his father. To prevent this marriage the father contrives to have his son abducted. Unable to forget his beloved, Des Grieux decides to renounce the world and find peace in priesthood. The arrival of Manon alters this decision; once again he runs away with her. At a gambling house Des Grieux is falsely accused of cheating and is saved from the police only by his father's intervention; but Manon is arrested as a disreputable character. She is sent into exile. On the road to Le Havre, Des Grieux awaits her coach in an attempt to save her. But it is too late: sick and emaciated, Manon dies in his arms.

The brief prelude to Act I is for the most part made up of two important melodic ideas from the opera. The first is the festive music that begins Act III; the other, the ardent love song of Des Grieux to Manon in Act IV. The curtain rises on the courtyard of an inn in Amiens. Manon is due by coach. She arrives, providing a piquant self-portrait in *"Je suis toute étourdie."* Another fine melodic page in this act is the ardent duet of Manon and Des Grieux *"Nous irons à Paris."*

There are two major arias in the second act, which is set in Des Grieux' Paris apartment. In *"Adieu, notre petite table"* we have Manon's poignant recollection of the happiness she has known with Des Grieux, happiness which, she is told, her lover's father is soon to destroy. This is followed by Des Grieux' passionate reassurance. In *"Le Rêve"* he tells her of a dream he has had in which they are sharing their home and happiness.

Imitations of two old French dances evoke the eighteenth century in the third act, which portrays a festival day in Paris at the Cours la Reine. The act is introduced by a tinkling little minuet in the orchestra. Later on Manon participates in the gay proceedings with a gavotte, *"Obéissons quand leur voix appelle."* In the second scene of this act—at the seminary of Saint-Sulpice—we hear the most famous tenor aria of the opera, Des Grieux' renunciation of the outside world for the peace of priesthood, *"Ah, fuyez, douce image."*

The dominant melody in the fourth act, which takes place in a fashionable gambling house in Paris, is Des Grieux' passionate protestation of love to Manon, *"Manon, sphinx étonnant."* In the closing act, on the road to Le Havre, thematic ideas from previous acts are recalled.

Thaïs (1894) is based on the novel of Anatole France, adapted into a prose libretto (one of the few librettos which is not in verse) by Louis Gallet. France's novel represents the conflict of flesh and spirit, the flesh emerging triumphant in one of the characters, while in another it is the spirit that is victorious. In his score Massenet gives greater emphasis to the spiritual aspect of the story than to the physical. With a sweetness of melody, a delicacy of harmony, and a refinement of orchestration Massenet brings to his music an all-pervading radiance. There is a great deal of romantic fervor, even passion, in many pages of *Thaïs*. But the passages that linger most in the memory are those which are filled with religious exaltation and spiritual overtones.

Thaïs, courtesan of old Alexandria, is to be saved by the monk Athanael. Thaïs, who is cynical, tries to arouse the monk with her great beauty. Then, as she grows weary of her dissolute life and luxury, she becomes more and more responsive to the monk's preaching. She follows him through the wilderness into a convent where she finds peace at last. But now Athanael is a victim of physical torment. He is in love with Thaïs; he desires her. Ardently he begs her to abandon the convent and live with him in Alexandria. But Thaïs is now of the spirit and not of the flesh. She dies, stretching out her arms to heaven's gate, which opens before her. Athanael, who is at her side, is overwhelmed by his terrible grief and frustration.

Thaïs does not contain as many individual arias and individual parts as *Manon*. But the following vocal episodes are memorable: Athanael's lament over the corruption of Alexandria, *"Voilà donc la terrible cité"*; Thaïs' plea to Venus to reassure her that she is beautiful, *"Dis moi, que je suis belle"*; Athanael's torment at his love and desire for Thaïs, *"En vain j'ai flagellé ma chair"*; and Thaïs' death song, *"Te souvient-il du lumineux voyage."*

But the most celebrated single excerpt from this opera is not vocal but instrumental; indeed, with the *Elégie*, it represents the most frequently played of all Massenet's compositions. This is the *Médita-tion,* which is presented in the orchestra with violin obbligato at the end of Act II, Scene 1, to express Thaïs' rejection of physical pleasures for the spiritual life. It is again used prominently in Thaïs' death song.

Felix Mendelssohn

"Light, aerial, fairy music is a specialty of Mendelssohn's in which he has never been surpassed."

HUGO LEICHTENTRITT

BORN: Hamburg, February 3, 1809.

DIED: Leipzig, November 4, 1847.

MAJOR WORKS: *Chamber Music*—6 string quartets; 3 piano quartets; 2 string quintets; 2 piano trios; 2 cello sonatas; String Octet; Piano Sextet; Violin Sonata. *Choral Music*—St. Paul; Lobgesang; Die erste Walpurgisnacht; Elijah; Te Deum; Anthems, hymns, motets, Psalms. *Orchestral Music*—5 symphonies (not including his early symphonies); 2 piano concertos; Violin Concerto; A Midsummer Night's Dream Suite; Fingal's Cave (or Hebrides) Overture; Calm Sea and Prosperous Voyage Overture; Ruy Blas; Capriccio brillant, for piano and orchestra; Rondo brillant, for piano and orchestra. *Organ Music*—6 sonatas; preludes and fugues. *Piano Music*—3 sonatas; Seven Characteristic Pieces; Rondo capriccioso; Songs Without Words, eight books; Variations sérieuses; Caprices, études, fugues, preludes, scherzos. *Vocal Music*—Songs for voice and piano including "Auf Flügeln des Gesanges" ("On Wings of Song"), "Gruss," "Ich wollt', meine Liebe, ergösse sich," "Morgengruss," "Sonntagsmorgen," "Wasserfahrt."

HIS LIFE

The name was appropriate: *"Felix,"* Latin for "happy man." The frustrations, maladjustments, and conflicts of most other great composers make the life story of Felix Mendelssohn as refreshing as sunshine. He was born to wealth and position. He was encouraged to follow the direction in which his talents lay and given every opportunity to develop those talents. Success came early and without struggle; it remained with him till the end. He had two large visions: One was to restore the neglected music of Johann Sebastian Bach to the world; the other, to found a great conservatory. He was able to realize both of them. The one woman he loved returned his love. If he died at the premature age of thirty-eight, he died at any rate before the serenity of his life could be seriously disturbed.

Besides wealth and station, the Mendelssohn family had a tradition of culture. Felix's grandfather, Moses Mendelssohn, was a hunchbacked peddler who became one of the great intellectual figures in eighteenth-century Germany. His dialogue on the immortality of the soul, translated into a dozen languages, won him the sobriquet of "the modern Plato." He also did valuable research in the fields of metaphysics and aesthetics. Kant, Herder, and Mirabeau were among the many to admire him. Lessing was believed to have written his play *Nathan the Wise* around him.

Felix's mother, Leah, was a woman of keen intelligence. She was an excellent linguist, read classic Greek literature in the original, was a fine pianist, and had a gift for drawing. The talents of her husband, Abraham, rested elsewhere. Abraham had directed his energies toward building up a comfortable dowry into a powerful Hamburg banking institution. Aware of his own intellectual limitations, he was satisfied to make a great deal of money and allow the cultural prestige of his family to rest, first in his father, then in his wife, and after that in his son, Felix. He himself would often say: "First I was the son of my father. Now I am the father of my son." Or he would put it another way. "I am but a dash uniting Moses and Felix Mendelssohn."

But in the Hamburg household of Abraham and Leah Mendelssohn, culture was never relegated to a secondary role. The children (a girl, Fanny, came first, and after her, Felix) were so early directed toward books and the arts, the pleasures of the mind, that these things became as basic to their everyday lives as food.

When the invading French Army occupied Hamburg, the Mendelssohn family went on to Berlin, where they lived in the spacious house of the children's grandmother on the fashionable Neue Promenade. At that time Felix was three years old. Before long his mother began teaching him and his sister the piano, devoting to this task several five-minute sessions each day. It soon became apparent that both children were exceptionally talented. When the family had to visit Paris for one of Abraham's business trips, the mother engaged a special piano tutor for both children. And when they were back in Berlin the children's musical and academic education was undertaken in earnest. Felix now studied the piano with Ludwig Berger and theory with Karl Friedrich Zelter, as well as the violin, languages, and drawing. The Mendelssohns did not pamper their children. Felix had to get up at dawn and put in a full day at his studies. But the Mendelssohns also had balance: They saw to it that work was relieved by child's play.

At that, music for Felix was more play than work. His sensitive ear, his fantastic memory, and his musical intuition made him assimilate effortlessly what was taught to him. "When Zelter became Mendelssohn's teacher," it was said, "he merely put fish to water and let him swim away as he liked." And so, when Felix was nine he played the piano well enough to appear publicly. A year after that he joined the Singakademie, then directed by his teacher, Zelter. As a member of this famous choral body he was initiated into great choral music. By this time he was also composing—not by fits and starts, but with the complete dedication and concentration of a professional musician. By the time he was twelve he had written out and neatly collated numerous works in many different forms; the production of a single year—that of 1821—included several symphonies, fugues for string quartet, two operas, and a library of smaller works.

Because of his son's ability and the certainty that music would be the boy's lifework Abraham stood ready to take a step he had long regarded with repugnance: conversion to Christianity. His wife's relatives had for a long time urged him to make such a move, and for a long time their arguments had fallen on deaf ears. The realization that many avenues were closed to a musician who was a Jew made Abraham more sympathetic to the idea. But it was a single incident that finally made up his mind. One day Felix came home from the Singakademie in tears. He had been singing with the chorus a passage from Bach's *Passion According to St. Matthew* when a fellow chorister remarked derisively, "The Jew-boy raises his voice to Christ!" Even old Zelter could not suppress a chuckle. It was a little incident, to be sure, but it put an end to Abraham's doubts and hesitations. The next day he took Felix and Fanny to the Protestant Church for conversion, and after that he and his wife followed suit. He later appended the name of "Bartholdy" to "Mendelssohn" to distinguish his family from the other Mendelssohns, who were still of the Jewish faith.

There was always good music at the Mendelssohns'. The Sunday afternoon musicales were particularly celebrated. Professional musicians would join the children in the formal presentation of chamber music and works for small orchestra. The music was of such high caliber that distinguished people from all walks of life, and particularly well-known musicians, gravitated naturally to the Mendelssohn household. For example, when Karl Maria von Weber visited Berlin in 1821 to supervise the *première* of *Der Freischütz,* he was soon seen at the Mendelssohns'. At these concerts Felix often played the piano, had his early works performed, and even led the small orchestra. There was not much doubt in the minds of those who heard him that here was "another Mozart."

Even the great Goethe thought so; and Goethe had heard the child Mozart. In 1821 Felix was brought to Weimar by Zelter and introduced to the great poet. The boy improvised, played Beethoven manuscripts at sight, and performed several Bach fugues. On one occasion his memory failed in the middle of a fugue. Rather than arrest the flow of the music, he improvised the rest of the piece. Goethe was enchanted. "Every morning I get a kiss from the author of *Faust* and *Werther,*" the boy wrote to his parents. The two, becoming warm friends, succeeded in spanning the gap between a seventy-two-year-old genius and a twelve-year-old prodigy. Up to the time of Goethe's death, in 1832, he remained attached to Mendelssohn, who was his guest on several occasions. "I am Saul and you are David," Goethe once wrote to the composer. "Come to me when I am sad and discouraged and quiet my soul with your sweet harmonies."

A vivid impression of the child Mendelssohn comes to us from a distinguished English musician, Julius Benedict (1804–85):

Walking in the streets of Berlin with my master and friend, Karl Maria von Weber, he directed my attention to a boy, apparently about eleven or twelve years old, who, on perceiving the author of the *Freischütz,* ran towards him, giving him a most hearty and friendly greeting. "This is Felix Mendelssohn," said Weber, introducing me at once to the prodigious child, of whose marvelous talent and execution I had heard so much at Dresden. I shall never forget the impression of that day on beholding that beautiful youth, with his auburn hair clustering in ringlets around his shoulders, the ingenuous expression of his clear eyes, and the smile of innocence and candor on his lips. He would have it that we should go with him at once to his father's house; but as Weber had to attend a rehearsal, he took me by the hand and made me run a race until we reached his home. Up he went briskly to the drawing room where, finding his mother, he exclaimed: "Here is a pupil of Weber's who knows a great deal of his music and of the new opera. Pray, ma, ask him to play for us." And so, with an irresistible impetuosity, he pushed me to the piano and made me remain there until I had exhausted the store of my recollections. When I then begged him to let me hear some of his own compositions, he refused, but played from memory such Bach fugues or Cramer exercises as I could name.

He continued to astound all those with whom he came into contact. In 1822 the family went on an extended trip. In Cassel, Felix played improvisations for that celebrated violinist, conductor, and composer Ludwig Spohr (1784–1859). Spohr listened and shook his head with incredulity. In Frankfort, as a guest of the Caecilia Verein, the boy's improvisations on themes from several Bach motets (just performed by that group) was regarded as a miraculous feat. Johann Schelble, the director, said, "This boy . . . is one of God's own." Three years later, in Paris, it was the turn of the venerable Luigi Cherubini (1760–1842), director of the Paris Conservatory and celebrated composer of operas, to be overwhelmed. Felix had set for him a *Kyrie* for voice and orchestra spontaneously and without any apparent effort or difficulty.

He outdistanced his teachers as quickly as he outgrew his clothes. When Mendelssohn's comic opera *The Two Nephews* was presented at his home on the occasion of the boy's fifteenth birthday, Zelter told him, "My dear boy. You are no longer an apprentice but an independent member of the brotherhood of musicians. I proclaim you an independent in the name of Mozart, Haydn, and the older Bach." Old Berger, who had been teaching him the piano conscientiously, could serve him no longer. Ignaz Moscheles, already one of the great pianists of the time, was called to continue these lessons. Moscheles said simply, "He stands in no need of lessons." However, he did offer to give the boy, as he put it, "a hint . . . as to anything new to him." In recording the first of these "lessons" in his diary Moscheles added, "He is a mature artist."

In 1825 the Mendelssohn family moved to a seven-acre estate on the Leipzigerstrasse. An adjoining garden house was converted into a theater for the weekly Mendelssohn concerts. On its grounds Felix could bowl, ride horseback, and swim. Within the beautifully appointed house he indulged in his favorite indoor pastimes: dancing, billiards, and chess. Whatever he did, he did well—some things, such as dancing, he did elegantly; others, such as painting and drawing, with professional skill. This, and the fact that he was extraordinarily handsome, even-tempered, and well poised (besides being a genius in music), inevitably made him the center of all social activity. He was adulated; but there is no evidence that it turned his head. We can be sure that it in no way affected the quality of the music he was writing. For, with his seventeenth birthday at hand, he was already creating his first masterpiece: the overture to *A Midsummer Night's Dream*. The original version, for two pianos, was introduced by Felix and his sister at a Mendelssohn *soirée* in the garden house in the fall of 1826. About six months later Mendelssohn directed the overture, in its orchestral form, in Stettin. Still in his adolescence, Mendelssohn had produced one of his finest and most characteristic works.

But things did not always go smoothly for the young composer, of whom Goethe had said that he "was born on a lucky day." The year that he wrote his overture also saw the completion of an opera, *Die Hochzeit des Camacho,* based upon an episode in *Don Quixote*. Mendelssohn submitted it to Spontini, director of the Berlin Opera, who apparently accepted it but kept it from production for more than a year. He finally mounted it in one of his smaller theaters. The long wait for its production had been trying enough. But the realization that came to Mendelssohn, when he finally heard his opera, that he had written a third-rate work was certainly more vexing. The audience was enthusiastic, as it was made up mostly of Felix's friends and relatives. But it was not a good opera, and Felix knew it. It was given only a single performance, a fact which even its composer did not regret.

In 1829 Mendelssohn realized the first major ambition of his life: to rescue the music of Johann Sebastian Bach from the oblivion into which it had plunged with the general music public after that composer's death. Mendelssohn had been nursed on Bach's music since childhood. Despite the fact that few non-professional musicians knew about Bach at the time—and even fewer were able to evaluate his importance correctly—Mendelssohn's mother had managed to get a copy of Bach's preludes and fugues for the piano and to admire them. They became the bread and butter of Felix's musical diet. Mendelssohn's teacher, Zelter, also had a healthy respect for the music of the Leipzig cantor. He possessed many Bach manuscripts (some of them had been given him by Abraham Mendelssohn); among these treasures was the only existing copy of the *Passion According to St. Matthew.* From time to time Zelter took down a musty copy of some Bach music and pointed out to Felix Mendelssohn a passage, a melody, or a chorus. Occasionally, too, Zelter took some passages from the *Passion* and had members of the Singakademie sing them. Mendelssohn's own enthusiasm for this masterwork was a reflection of his teacher's. One of the boy's prized possessions was a duplicate of the *Passion,* made from Zelter's copy, which his grandmother gave him on Christmas. From then on Mendelssohn came to know the work intimately; and from then on he entertained the ambition of presenting it to the world of music.

His first gesture toward realizing this aim was the formation of a group of sixteen singers, whom he rehearsed in some of the chorales from the *Passion.* One of these choristers was Eduard Devrient, a well-known opera singer. After each rehearsal Devrient and Mendelssohn discussed the seemingly inexhaustible genius of a work so long forgotten. More and more Mendelssohn became fired with the ambition of having the work performed publicly, and Devrient kept that ambition alive. One day they went to Zelter to convince him to have the Singakademie perform it under Mendelssohn's direction. Zelter's reluctance was due entirely to his belief that the world was not yet ready to accept so epical a work. But the contagious enthusiasm of the two young men won him over, and he gave his consent.

That performance took place in Berlin on March 11, 1829, one of the great days in musical history. "Carried along by the performance as a whole," recalled Eduard Devrient in his Memoirs, "I could thus sing with my whole soul, and I felt that the thrill of devotion that ran through me at the most impressive passages was also felt by the hearers who listened in deadly silence. Never have I felt a holier solemnity vested in a congregation than in the performers and audience that evening." Mendelssohn's sister Fanny wrote in a letter: "Everyone was filled with the most solemn devotion. One heard only an occasional involuntary ejaculation that sprang from deep emotion." So successful was this concert that the *Passion* had to be given a second time. There is no doubt but that these concerts started the Bach revival which was finally to carry the composer to the position in the music world that he deserved.

Not long after this performance Felix Mendelssohn undertook an extended period of travel in foreign lands. He went to England, the first of ten visits he was to make to that country. From the very beginning he endeared himself to the English music public as no foreign composer had done since Handel. "London, that smoky nest, is fated to be now and ever my favorite residence," he reported to a friend. "My heart swells when I even think of it." London responded to him with equal enthusiasm. He was feted as a celebrity; the Philharmonic Society elected him an honorary member. He also made his English debut by directing the *première* of his Symphony in C minor. Thenceforth, in each of his visits to England, he was to be welcomed with ever mounting affection and appreciation.

His next stop was Scotland, a visit that stimulated him in sketching the *Fingal's Cave* Overture and was later responsible for the *Scotch* Symphony. After that came a tour of Italy, during which impressions of Italian art and music were absorbed and the writing of the *Italian* Symphony was begun. In Paris he came into contact with Chopin, Liszt, and Meyerbeer. Back in London he conducted the *première* of the *Fingal's Cave* Overture on May 14, 1832, and performed the piano part of his Concerto in G minor on May 22. He also completed the writing of the *Capriccio brillant,* for piano and orchestra, and had the first volume of his *Songs Without Words* published.

In 1833 Mendelssohn was appointed musical director of Düsseldorf, in charge of opera, church music, and two choral bodies. It was the first time he had been called upon to fill a professional musical post, and he was not happy at it. His aims were too high. His exacting demands on performers and his insistence on maintaining the repertory on the highest possible level met with resentment and opposition. After six months he had had enough. But within a year or so (after he had been elected a member of the Berlin Academy of Fine Arts, his first official honor) an even more ambitious post called to him: that of musical director of the celebrated Gewandhaus Orchestra in Leipzig. He assumed this office in 1835, and for the next five years filled it with vitality, imagination, and scholarship. His devotion to new music, his concentration and painstaking attention to the details of interpretation and his concern over orchestral performance raised the Gewandhaus to a leading position among the orchestras of the world. It also marked a definite epoch in the evolution of the art of the orchestral conductor.

The death of his father in 1835 was a blow, but one from which he could recoil resiliently. "The only thing that remains to be done, is one's duty," he said philosophically. His first duty, of course, was to the Gewandhaus Orchestra concerts. His second was to complete his oratorio *St. Paul,* which was a huge success when introduced at the Lower Rhine Festival on May 22, 1836.

Back from the festival, Mendelssohn stopped off briefly at Frankfort. There he became acquainted with a family by the name of Jeanrenaud. His increasingly frequent visits to this home set the tongues to wagging. They began saying that the suave and elegant musician from Leipzig was growing attached to the handsome young widow. Actually, Mendelssohn was paying attention not to the widow, but to her seventeen-year-old daughter, Cecile. A self-imposed absence from Cecile finally convinced him that he was irrevocably in love for the first time in his life. He rushed back to Frankfort, proposed, and was accepted. On March 28, 1837, Cecile and Felix were married. The love affair which had progressed so serenely (like almost everything else in which Mendelssohn had ever been involved) was the prelude to an idyllic marriage that brought them five children.

He had never been happier. He was at the height of his world fame. His activities as conductor of the Gewandhaus excited him. His numerous associations in Leipzig—Ferdinand David, Clara Wieck, Robert Schumann—provided continual exhilaration. And his happy marriage added a luminous glow to it all.

In 1840 Mendelssohn was appointed head of the music department of a projected Academy of Arts in Berlin by the King of Prussia. He was not willing to leave Leipzig, but it was not wise to refuse the offer of a king. Reluctantly, Mendelssohn assumed his new post in 1841. He found himself enmeshed in court intrigues as the Academy of Arts struggled to outgrow the blueprint stage.

The world *première* of his *Scotch* Symphony in Leipzig gave him an excuse to leave Berlin temporarily. After that performance, which took place on March 3, 1842, Mendelssohn went on to England to give two command performances at Buckingham Palace for Queen Victoria. When he returned to Berlin he discovered that the Academy project had been abandoned. He offered his resignation with relief. But he was prevailed upon to assume the honorary post of Kapellmeister to the king, a post which required him to write music for special functions but did not demand his presence in Berlin. In this Kapellmeister post Mendelssohn wrote incidental music for several plays as well as *A Midsummer Night's Dream* Suite, the overture for which he had completed in his adolescence.

He could now return to his beloved Leipzig, continue conducting the Gewandhaus Orchestra in occasional concerts and—most important of all—bring to life a new dream. He had long aspired to see a conservatory of first rank arise in Leipzig and had made overtures to the King of Saxony for such a project. In 1843 the king gave the decree necessary to permit the founding of a conservatory. Mendelssohn had Robert Schumann share with him classes in piano and composition. Ferdinand David took over the violin department. The organization and curriculum carefully worked out, the Leipzig Conservatory opened officially under Mendelssohn's direction on April 3, 1843.

He was now working at a feverish pace: teaching and supervising at the Conservatory; conducting the Gewandhaus Orchestra at intermittent periods; writing such major works as the oratorio *Elijah* and the Concerto for Violin and Orchestra; making numerous guest appearances throughout Europe. Taxing his health severely, he began to feel pains in the head and to experience periods of excessive fatigue. In spite of this he went to England to direct the world *première* of *Elijah* in Birmingham on August 26, 1846. He received one of the greatest ovations of his career. The work was received with such thunderous acclaim that four choruses and four arias had to be encored. "No work of mine ever went so admirably . . . or was received with such enthusiasm," he wrote.

Back in Leipzig after this exciting experience he felt more weary than ever. But he kept on working with his customary drive. In the spring of 1847 he paid still another visit to England to direct several performances of *Elijah,* to play for Queen Victoria at the palace, and to fill many other musical and social engagements.

The news that his beloved sister and lifelong companion, Fanny, had died suddenly in Berlin on May 14, 1847, was a crushing blow. He fell unconscious, rupturing a blood vessel in his head. He recovered, but was never again the same man. Suddenly he had aged, had lost all spirit and energy. He began to suffer violent depressions. Several times he was seized by agonizing pain. His strength was completely dissipated. He was unconscious for a full day before death came, on November 4, 1847.

"In the afternoon the immense throng of the funeral procession began to gather in front of the house," wrote Eduard Devrient. "The coffin was covered with a rich funeral pall of velvet embroidered in silver. . . . Streets and open places were filled with people; all the windows were crowded on the long and circuitous route that the procession was to pass, through the town and by the Gewandhaus, the scene of Mendelssohn's labors. The musicians led the way, playing a hastily instrumented *Song Without Words* (the one in E minor, Book 5). Six clergymen in full robes followed the bier."

Memorial services were also held in London, Manchester, Birmingham, Paris, and most of the principal cities of Germany as the most celebrated and most honored musician of his age was put to final rest in his family vault in Berlin.

HIS MUSIC

Mendelssohn was among the first of the great Romantic composers. But, despite the period in which he worked, he may also be considered the last of the classicists. One of the things Robert Schumann admired about Mendelssohn's music was its harmonious fusion of the classical and Romantic spirits. The classical forms—the sonata, the concerto, the symphony, even the fugue—were bottles into which Mendelssohn could pour the new wine of his Romantic feelings. He had the Romanticist's tenderness, even sentimentality; but he also had the classicist's respect for structural design and the traditional concepts of harmony and counterpoint.

This is at once Mendelssohn's strength and his weakness. Few equaled him and none surpassed him in elegance and beautiful proportions of form and in clarity of writing. He had the gift of expressing himself effortlessly, so much so that his best music has the ingratiating quality of spontaneity. The music, like the personality of its author, has breeding, culture, exquisite taste, and poise. What it lacks most is profundity of either thought or emotion.

The circumstances surrounding Mendelssohn from the cradle were credits toward a full and happy life, but debits toward the complete fulfillment of his native creative powers. He had the equipment to scale the heights. He scaled those heights only in certain pages of *Elijah*. To his other masterworks—and they are masterworks!—he brought a wonderful and incomparable lyricism, exquisite poetic moods, and aristocratic workmanship; they never fail to enchant and seduce. But they do not have the power to inspire or transfix or overwhelm us in the way the *Eroica* Symphony does, or the B minor Mass, or the most spiritual pages of *Parsifal*.

Had Mendelssohn experienced some of the terrible isolation of a Beethoven, the religious ecstasy of a Bach, or the Gargantuan struggles of a Wagner, he too might have been in their company. But as Eduard Devrient once remarked of him: "He wanted to do only what was congenial to his nature, and nothing beyond." He succeeded in being a great composer and in writing great music, because he was a genius. But he never quite succeeded in joining the elect.

ANALYTICAL NOTES

Chamber Music. Two of Mendelssohn's earliest chamber music compositions are among his best. The Octet in E-flat major, for strings, Op. 20 (1825)—one of the earliest works in music history for eight instruments—was written when the composer was sixteen, just before he completed the overture to *A Midsummer Night's Dream*. One of its movements (the third) has the same kind of fleet mobility, diaphanous texture, and grace that distinguish the overture. This is the octet's most celebrated movement. The composer must also have been partial to it since he orchestrated it. Pure Mendelssohnian lyricism, another of the composer's strong suits, is also present in this work, most notably in the slow movement (the second) which has the rhythm of a siciliana, and which contrasts an initial sad melody with a later gay one.

Of Mendelssohn's six string quartets, the first is the best-known— the String Quartet in E-flat major, Op. 12 (1829). The finest movements—as was the case with the octet—are the second and third. The second is a canzonetta, with plucked strings and staccato passages contributing Mendelssohnian delicacy and charm. This is followed by a slow movement which an unidentified critic has described as "a noble song of thanksgiving."

The Piano Trio No. 1 in D minor, Op. 49, is a later work, composed in 1839. The first movement places both principal subjects in the cello. An unusual structural feature here is found in the recapitulation section where these two subjects receive an altogether new development. The slow movement is a two-part song, each part introduced by the piano and repeated by the violin. There is only a single theme in the third-movement scherzo, and no trio. The finale is made up of three important ideas, the first being a gypsy-like tune.

Choral Music. It has sometimes been said that the oratorio *Elijah*, Op. 70 (1846), is as dramatic as an opera. We learn from Mendelssohn himself how much importance he placed on the dramatic interest. To the author of the text, Pastor Julius Schubring, he explained: "I am particularly anxious to do justice to the dramatic element, and . . . no epic narrative must be introduced. If I might make one observation it is that I would fain see the dramatic more prominent as well as more vividly and sharply defined." And on a second occasion he wrote again: "In such a character as that of Elijah . . . it seems to me that the dramatic should predominate—the personages should be introduced as acting and speaking with fervor; not, in Heaven's name, to become mere musical pictures."

It is in its lyricism that *Elijah* is most inspired. Pages such as Obadiah's aria "If with all your hearts," Elijah's aria "It is enough," the aria of the Angel, "O rest in the Lord," are among the loftiest of Mendelssohn's melodic creations; it is these sections that fill the work with an overpowering humanity. But there can be no denying the dramatic effect of the work as a whole. It begins at once with remarkable theatrical force, with the fiery recitative of Elijah "As God the Lord of Israel liveth, before whom I stand, there shall not be dew nor rain these years but according to my word." Only then does the overture appear. It is like an immense dirge, speaking of the tragedy to come. A wailing figure rises in the lower strings. It is the germ of the entire overture, evolved with culminating power. At length the chorus breaks in with the first of several cries of anguish, "Help Lord, wilt Thou destroy." After that—through stirring recitatives, extended passages of dialogue, choral passages of overpowering effect and at times of barbaric and savage intensity (as in the double chorus "Baal, we cry to thee," and the chorus that follows, "Hear our cry, O Baal"), the building up of impressive climaxes, and the continual accentuation of the human elements—*Elijah* becomes a work whose place, one feels, is more appropriately in a theater than in a house of worship.

The oratorio is divided into two sections. In the first Elijah brings on the drought in Israel because the people have proved false to God and have followed the false Baal. He works miracles, proves victorious over the prophets of Baal, and finally puts them to death. In the second part his enemies try to destroy him. He suffers tribulations at the hands of Jezebel. But he is, at last, protected by the Lord and is conducted to heaven in a flaming chariot.

Orchestral Music. There is more than normal confusion about the numbering of Mendelssohn's symphonies. The one now regarded as his Symphony No. 1 in C minor, Op. 11 (completed when he was fifteen), is actually his thirteenth. Mendelssohn had written twelve symphonies for string orchestra before this one, and they do not appear in the formal listing. To add to the general confusion, the numbering of the symphonies is based upon the order of their publication rather than composition. The choral Symphony No. 2 in B-flat, *Lobgesang,* Op. 52 (1840), was written after the First, Third, and Fourth. The Symphony No. 3, *Scotch,* was written after the Symphony No. 4, the *Italian.*

The Symphony No. 3 in A minor, Op. 56, was completed, performed, and published in 1842. The inspiration for it had come about a dozen years earlier, during Mendelssohn's first visit to Scotland. The symphony not only utilizes melodies and rhythms that have a Scottish personality, but also brings up pictures of the country, the scenery, and the backgrounds.

The slow introduction of the first movement is a tonal representation of the Scottish landscape, made melancholy by mists and rain. The principal melody of this introduction is heard in the wind instruments and low strings without preliminaries. It is lugubrious and grows more mournful as the introduction expands. A vigorous rhythm brings on the main section of the symphony. The principal melody is now brought forth by strings and clarinet and repeated by flutes and clarinets. Other melodic ideas appear episodically, the most important being a plaintive song for the strings. The elegiac quality persists through the restless development (which is so free in form that it resembles a fantasia) and the recapitulation. The movement ends with a return of the melancholy introduction.

The published score specifies that the four movements be played without pause. The second movement, then, comes without any interruption. It begins with calls for woodwinds and brass. There then appears the first main idea, a gay little Scottish dance in the clarinet, set against staccato notes in the strings. The second theme is also light and whimsical; it is a staccato theme for the strings. These two main themes are worked out freely.

An expansive and introspective melody alternates with a brief marchlike subject (first heard in horns, bassoons, and clarinets) in the third movement. The entire movement has placid beauty in the vein of one of Mendelssohn's *Songs Without Words*. This reflective music is followed by the impetuous drive and brilliant colors of the finale. A bright Scottish melody is the first of three principal ideas; it is given by the violins against staccato chords. The second theme appears in the woodwinds in the upper register. The third, which introduces the coda, is stately and martial music for full orchestra with a Scottish identity.

The Symphony No. 4 in A major, Op. 90—the *Italian* Symphony—was germinated during Mendelssohn's first visit to Italy in 1830. But it was not completed until more than two years after that. Except for the closing movement, there is nothing in the symphony to suggest Italian music. But the buoyancy of its spirit might well suggest Mendelssohn's reactions on first seeing Italy, as expressed in the following lines: "Italy, at last! What I have all my life considered as the greatest possible felicity is now begun."

The symphony opens exuberantly. In the second measure a joyous melody for the violins appears against an accompaniment by horns and woodwinds. The melody is evolved fully, the happy mood persists. A rising passage for the violins brings on the second theme in the clarinets and bassoons. Although somewhat more restrained than the first, this theme is still light in heart. A third theme, presented fugally, introduces the development. It begins in the second violins, passes to the first violins, and after that is taken up by violas and basses. After this fugal idea has been worked up with great power into an effective climax, the recapitulation section brings back all the basic melodies.

Several efforts have been made to read a program into the second movement. Sir Donald Francis Tovey interpreted it as a religious process. To Sir George Grove the two opening measures represented "the cry of a muezzin from his minaret." After this brief introduction, the principal melody of the movement is presented by oboe, bassoons, and violas. The violins take it over, while flutes contribute a piquant contrapuntal background. The melody appears with some further variation before the second theme is offered by the clarinet. Both themes are then treated freely, and the movement ends with a return of the first melody.

The third movement is in the three-part form of the scherzo. In the first we have a graceful subject for first violins. The trio section is introduced with a soft subject for bassoons and horns, soon to be developed into a dialogue between brass and strings. The first part is then brought back, and a conclusion is reached with a hasty recollection of the main idea of the trio.

It is in the fourth movement that the symphony becomes Italian. After six introductory measures, the rhythm of a saltarello is given by woodwinds and strings. The saltarello is a carnival dance requiring athletic movements, and its rhythm is characterized by impulsive leaps. Two flutes then offer the dance theme; they are soon supplemented by two clarinets. A second dance melody appears as a dialogue between first and second violins; this too is in the saltarello rhythm. Excitement is generated as this material is elaborated with an outburst of energy. The atmosphere grows more and more frenetic as still a new dance melody arrives in the strings, this time in the feverish rhythms of a tarantella. The rhythms of both Italian dances are soon combined, with the saltarello coming to the fore as the movement comes to dynamic end.

The Symphony No. 5 in D major, Op. 107, completed in 1830, is known as the *Reformation* Symphony because Mendelssohn wrote it to commemorate the tercentenary of the Augsburg Protestant Confession, the creed of the Lutheran Church. The religious element is injected through the use of two pieces of liturgical music. In the first movement there appears a quotation of the "Dresden Amen" which Wagner was later to use in the prelude to *Parsifal*. This appears softly in the strings immediately after the statement of the first majestic theme by brass and woodwinds. It returns toward the end of the development section to inject a sudden feeling of peace into the formerly stormy proceedings. The Lutheran chorale "Ein' feste Burg" is interpolated in the third and fourth movements. It is originally given by the flutes and soon increases in sonority and power. In the closing measures of the fourth movement it reappears with tremendous effect in full orchestra.

The second movement is an ingratiating scherzo, characterized by Mendelssohn's lightness of touch. The first part is built out of a fanciful little theme for woodwinds and lower strings. The main melody of the trio is first heard in the oboes against a background of plucked strings in the basses.

The Concerto in E minor for Violin and Orchestra, Op. 64 (1844), is one of the most melodious and lovable works in the repertory. Mendelssohn designated that the three movements be played without pause, but it has become customary to allow a slight interruption between the first and second movements. There is only a single introductory measure in the orchestra in the first movement, after which the solo violin enters with the principal melody, one of Mendelssohn's happiest lyrical ideas. The countersubject is soon heard in both the orchestra and the solo instrument. After a passage in double-stops for the violin, there appears another melody in clarinets and flutes over a sustained low open-string "G" in the solo instrument. The development appears after the soloist has repeated the second theme. Before the recapitulation is introduced, there is a short cadenza for the solo violin.

An eight-bar orchestral introduction in the second movement brings on, in the violin, another of Mendelssohn's inspired melodies. There is an agitated middle section, first invoked by the orchestra, but the other-worldly beauty of the opening page returns to end the movement in a spiritual glow.

There is a fourteen-bar transition between the slow movement and the concluding rondo. This begins with a gay and fleeting subject in the solo violin. After some passage work, the orchestra enters loudly with the second main theme of the movement. There is still a third lyrical subject, a stately melody first given by the soloist and soon to be combined contrapuntally with the first theme, the orchestra offering the third theme while the soloist concerns himself with the first. A loud restatement of the second theme in the orchestra prefaces the brilliant coda.

The Concerto No. 1 in G minor for Piano and Orchestra, Op. 25, was written in 1831, thirteen years before the Violin Concerto. The first movement is in two sharply contrasted moods. A crescendo passage of seven bars sets the stage for the entrance of the piano, which arrives with dramatic octaves before entering upon the agitated first theme. The stormy atmosphere continues as the orchestra takes over, but tranquillity arrives with the second theme in the piano. A fanfare in horns and trumpets and a brief cadenza lead to the poetic, nocturnal slow movement, the main theme of which is first given by violas and cellos. Still another fanfare is the passage to the fiery presto which ends the concerto with virtuoso brilliance.

Another work for piano and orchestra is the Capriccio brillant in B minor, Op. 22 (1829). This is a two-section composition beginning with a slow introduction featuring a soulful melody. The second part, in quick tempo, opens with a lively tune and progresses toward a sentimental one.

The orchestral suite *A Midsummer Night's Dream* is made up partially of music which was written in early boyhood; but most of it was written in full maturity. The overture, Op. 21, came in 1826 when Mendelssohn was seventeen years old. Seventeen years after that the King of Prussia asked Mendelssohn to write additional music for a projected performance of the Shakespeare play. At that time Mendelssohn produced thirteen more numbers.

Despite the fact that the overture was the work of a boy, it remains the miracle of the entire score. Elfin in mood, diaphanous and graceful in spirit, delicate and fanciful in ideas, and ultrarefined in instrumentation, it is a completely realized and integrated masterpiece. It catches the very essence of the Shakespeare play while transporting us into a magic world of fairies. Four delicate chords in the woodwinds, another in violins and viola, and a fleeting, glistening staccato melody for divided violins—and we are immediately in fairyland. The spell is never broken, not even when other melodic ideas intrude: first a hunting melody for horns; then a warm theme shared by woodwinds and strings; then a jovial, rustic dance for strings. The overture ends as it began, with four delicate chords.

Of the other thirteen numbers from *A Midsummer Night's Dream*, Op. 61, which were written in 1843, only three are frequently heard.

The "Nocturne" is a peaceful, nostalgic melody for horn. There is a more intense middle section for strings and winds, after which the horn melody is brought back. The "Scherzo" is in the rarefied and nimble-footed vein of the overture, another happy evocation of the fairy world. Its two main themes are given by the woodwinds and unison strings, respectively. Finally there is the "Wedding March," the most widely performed and celebrated piece of wedding music. Only Wagner has accompanied more couples at weddings than Mendelssohn! A fanfare for trumpet leads to the stately march music. There are two trios, the march being repeated after each.

Fingal's Cave, or the *Hebrides,* Overture, Op. 26, is one of Mendelssohn's finest landscapes. He visited the famous cavern in the Hebrides during his visit to Scotland in the summer of 1829. The scene made such an impression on him that then and there the opening theme of the overture occurred to him. The overture was completed more than a year later.

The picture of the ocean waves rolling toward the mouth of the cavern is vividly portrayed in the first theme for lower strings and bassoons. There is an extensive enlargement of this melody, with a great variety in the harmony and orchestration. Then the second theme appears, also in the lower register: it is first presented by cellos and bassoons. The picture grows brighter as the melodic material is transferred from the lower to the upper register of the orchestra. The development pays a great deal of attention to the first theme. In the recapitulation the melodies return in the lower register.

The *Ruy Blas* Overture, Op. 95, was written in 1839 for the drama of Victor Hugo, which was set in the court of Charles II of Spain. Hugo himself explained that the philosophical motive of this drama is "a people aspiring to a higher state." After four solemn bars for brass and woodwinds, a hint of the first theme in the strings prefaces the arrival of the first theme in first violins and flutes. The solemn opening bars also precede the second theme, heard in clarinet, bassoon, and cellos.

Piano Music. The *Lieder ohne Worte,* or *Songs Without Words,* forty-eight in number, written between 1830 and 1835, and collected in eight volumes (Op. 19, 30, 38, 53, 62, 67, 85, 102), are bouquets of sentimental or atmospheric or descriptive little thoughts. Mendelssohn here created a new genre: an instrumental piece that has the vocal and lyrical character of a song. In this extensive library of piano pieces we find the most popular piece of music Mendelssohn ever wrote, the "Spring Song," in A major, Op. 62, No. 6. But this slight, almost ingenuous, melody is by no means characteristic. The finest items among these *Songs* are treasurable impressions caught in music of great charm and melodic originality. Among the best are: the "Hunting Song" in A major, Op. 19, No. 3; three "Venetian Boat Songs," in the keys of G minor (Op. 19, No. 6), F-sharp minor (Op. 30, No. 6), and A minor (Op. 62, No. 5); the "Funeral March," in E minor, Op. 62, No. 3; the "Spinning Song" in C major (Op. 67, No. 4); the "Duetto" in A-flat major, Op. 38, No. 6; the "Volkslied" in A minor, Op. 53, No. 5; the "May Breezes" in G major, Op. 62, No. 1; and the "Elegy" in D major, Op. 85, No. 4. (Most of the descriptive titles of these pieces were concocted by the publishers; only "Duetto," "Venetian Boat Songs," and "Volkslied" originated with the composer.) In the "Volkslied" Ernest Hutcheson finds "the anger of an oppressed people clamoring for redress for their wrongs, each verse rising in vehemence to a climax of moving intensity," while the "Duetto" is a love song in which "antiphonal endearments lead to a *unisono* agreement, and a lingering coda tenderly confirms the understanding."

The Rondo capriccioso in E major, Op. 14 (1829), the Variations sérieuses in D minor, Op. 54 (1841), and the six preludes and fugues, Op. 35 (1836–37), are among Mendelssohn's finest works for solo piano. The first consists of a reflective lyrical section contrasted with a capriccio part which, in its lightness and grace, recalls the fairy music of *A Midsummer Night's Dream*. The *Variations sérieuses* is based on a melody of somber but tender beauty. Eighteen variations follow, in which the melody passes from gravity and deep feeling to virtuoso passages of striking pianistic effect. In his six preludes and fugues, in which Mendelssohn pays tribute to Bach, a composer he admired excessively, Romantic attitudes are not abandoned but become integrated within the Baroque structure. Of special interest is the first, in E minor, whose prelude has a melody of recognizable Mendelssohnian elegance, while the fugue is built up to an exciting climax through an exended crescendo and accelerando. In the fourth prelude and fugue, in A-flat major, the two parts are harmonious in that both have sustained lyricism, while in the fifth, in F minor, the two parts are contrasted, the prelude being tender and haunting, and the fugue dramatic and stormy.

Vocal Music. With Mendelssohn's uncommon gift for rich and varied lyricism, it is to be expected that he would make distinguished contributions to song literature. He might never plumb the emotional depths or attain the dramatic heights found in the lieder of Schubert or Schumann; but his sensitive emotion, tenderness, and aristocratic elegance is not of an inferior brand by any means. He strums on more strings than one: pathos in "Schilflied," Op. 71, No. 4 (1842), and "Nachtlied," Op. 71, No. 6 (1847); and exuberant joy in "O Jugend," Op. 57, No. 4 (1834), and "Jagdlied," Op. 84, No. 3 (1834). But he is undoubtedly at his best when he taps his rich melodic vein to permit a sustained flow of fresh and spontaneous lyricism. In such a manner is his most famous song of all, "Auf Flügeln des Gesanges," or "On Wings of Song," Op. 34, No. 2 (1834), poem by Heine, which Liszt transcribed for solo piano, Joseph Achron for violin and piano, and Lionel Tertis for viola and piano.

Gian Carlo Menotti

"Menotti has the whole operatic vocabulary of the Romantic and modern composers at his command."

OLIN DOWNES

BORN: Cadigliano, Italy, July 7, 1911.
MAJOR WORKS: *Ballets*—Sebastian; Errand and the Maze. *Choral Music*—The Death of the Bishop of Brindisi. *Operas* —Amelia Goes to the Ball; The Old Maid and the Thief; The Island God; The Medium; The Telephone; The Consul; Amahl and the Night Visitors; The Saint of Bleecker Street; The Unicorn, the Gorgon, and the Manticore; Maria Golovin; The Last Savage; the Labyrinth; Martin's Lie; Help, Help, the Globolinks; The Most Important Man; Tamu-Tamu. *Orchestral Music*—Piano Concerto; Apocalypse; Violin Concerto; Triple Concerto a Tre.

HIS LIFE

For a long time the difficulty in putting Menotti's career on paper was that no sooner had the story been written and published, than it became incomplete. With each succeeding opera Menotti demonstrated such an advance of technique in composition, artistic self-assurance, understanding of the functions of the operatic theater, imagination and resourcefulness that he gave every promise that—

impressive though his past achievements had been—his best works were yet to come. He was never the man to stand still. In the past he continually entered new avenues of personal and artistic triumph by doing the unexpected, the original, and the unprecedented.

His future may call for additions to, even re-evaluations of, what we say about him here and now. It can never discredit his right to belong in our gallery of important composers. Although he is at an age when Verdi, Wagner, or Puccini were still to produce their greatest works, he has already won a permanent place for himself in contemporary music as perhaps the most successful opera composer since Puccini.

Menotti had the good fortune to be born into an influential and wealthy family. His grandfather had been the mayor of the town, and his father was a highly successful exporter to South America. Menotti's birthplace was in a little town at the edge of Lake Lugano, a pink villa that swarmed with Menottis, since Gian Carlo was the ninth of ten children. The boy found opportunities from the first to indulge his passion for both music and the theater. He was only four when he started piano lessons with his mother and wrote his first composition (a song), and six when he arrived at the decision to become a composer. At that time he wrote a number of pretty tunes to erotic lyrics by Gabriele d'Annunzio. Soon after this he began participating in the little family concerts of chamber music that took place regularly at his home. Partaking of theatrical activity was somewhat more difficult, for he was not much of an actor, as he discovered one day in a school play. However, on his ninth birthday, his mother presented him with a puppet theater. He wrote his own plays, constructed his own sets, designed his own costumes, and contrived his own stage effects.

The family moved on to Milan when Gian Carlo was ten. There the boy attended the academic schools, which held little interest for him. He also attended the Conservatory for several years beginning in 1923, and was often in the audience at La Scala, where his family had a box. In his eleventh year he completed a three-act opera, libretto as well as music. He called it *The Death of Pierrot*—an understatement, to say the least, since in the last act all the characters killed themselves. He soon finished a second opera and was demonstrating an unusual talent at the piano. Handsome, intelligent, and musically gifted, he was proudly exhibited in the most fashionable

Milanese *salons* and was so spoiled that he refused to study as he should have.

Gian Carlo's father died when the boy was fourteen. By that time, following consultations with Toscanini, the mother had come to the wise decision that her son's musical growth was seriously stunted in Milan where he was so pampered and petted. A change of scene seemed in order, and the final decision was made to bring the boy to the United States for further study. But first a trip had to be made to South America to straighten out the father's business affairs.

Menotti and his mother arrived in New York in 1928. There Tullio Serafin, the distinguished conductor of the Metropolitan Opera, provided Gian Carlo with a letter of introduction to Rosario Scalero, teacher of composition at the Curtis Institute in Philadelphia. To Scalero, the boy—for all his apparent gifts—appeared "undisciplined and raw." "Talent," Scalero said sternly, "is not enough. You must learn to work, and work hard, something you have never done before. If you promise me you will make the effort, I will teach you." Menotti promised faithfully. Realizing that her son was now in good hands, his mother returned to Italy, leaving him alone in the new, strange land.

He received a scholarship for the Curtis Institute. It was not an easy period. For the first time in his life he had to subject himself to rigorous discipline; and an inflexibly severe master made him work hard. Besides, he was terribly lonely, and he had to learn a new language at the same time, for he did not know a word of English. He solved the language problem (mostly by going to the movies four times a week) just as he got into the habit of working hard. He was a good, though not particularly brilliant, pupil.

As he progressed with his studies, his musical interests began changing from Brahmsian Romanticism (which influenced him to write Variations on a Theme of Schumann, for piano, recipient of the Lauber Composition Award in 1931) to Baroque polyphony. By the time he was twenty-two he had outgrown polyphony, as well as concert music, and was planning an opera. He got the idea for *Amelia Goes to the Ball* during a summer holiday in Vienna, and while still in Europe completed the libretto (written at first in Italian and then translated into English) and music. It was a one-act *opera buffa* inspired by his boyhood experiences and associations in the rich *salons* of Milan. *Amelia Goes to the Ball* was introduced in Philadelphia on April 1, 1937, in a production by the Curtis Institute under Fritz Reiner's direction. It gave such a pronounced impression of creative freshness and dramatic verve that forthwith Menotti was commissioned by the National Broadcasting Company to write an opera exclusively for the radio. On April 27, 1939, NBC introduced that work: *The Old Maid and the Thief*. Like its predecessor it was in a comic vein, and its libretto was the work of its composer; this time, however, Menotti had written his text directly in English.

Meanwhile, in the summer of 1937, Menotti visited the town of his birth, Cadigliano, which was neither so small nor so remote as not to have learned that its native son had written an opera. One day the local postmistress cycled furiously toward his house waving a telegram as she rode. *"Il Metropolitano! Il Metropolitano!"* she yelled at the top of her voice. She was bearing Menotti the news that the Metropolitan had accepted *Amelia* for performance the following season. That Sunday the news was announced in the church, and later that day the town gave Menotti a party.

Amelia Goes to the Ball was presented by the Metropolitan Opera House on March 3, 1938. (It was played seven times during that and the following season.) One month later the opera was heard (in its original Italian) in the San Remo Opera in Italy. That *Amelia* came to a comparatively obscure Italian opera house instead of to La Scala or some other great theater was due to Menotti's integrity. Dino Alfieri, Italian Minister of Culture under Mussolini, had urged Menotti to join the Fascist party, promising him in return performances throughout Italy by the foremost opera houses. Menotti declined; though still an Italian citizen he refused to identify himself with the regime. Only one small Italian theater, therefore, would perform his work.

Amelia Goes to the Ball was the first Menotti opera to be presented by the Metropolitan Opera House. The second was *The Island God*, seen in 1942. It was a failure with both the critics and the audiences. Menotti's reaction was stoic. "It is good for the soul." Actually Menotti felt that he learned more from that failure than from his successes, and he explains his subsequent triumphs by the fact that he could consciously avoid the mistakes he had made.

His dissatisfaction with *The Island God* led him to abandon opera for a while. He now wrote the score for his first ballet, *Sebastian*, introduced in New York on October 31, 1944. (With new staging and choreography it was revived by the American Ballet Theatre in New York in 1957.) He also wrote a piano concerto for Rudolf Firkusny, who introduced it with the Boston Symphony on November 2, 1945. At the same time he devoted himself to teaching, having been appointed in 1941 to the Department of Composition at the Curtis Institute from which he had been graduaed eight years earlier.

In 1945, Menotti received a $1000 grant from the American Academy and National Institute of Arts and Sciences, and one year later he was given a Guggenheim Fellowship. During this period he returned to opera, the idea for a new stage work having come to him at a séance. He wrote that opera, *The Medium,* specifically on a commission from the Ditson Fund, and it was introduced at Columbia University on May 8, 1946. Convinced that *The Medium* had audience appeal, two young, neophyte theatrical producers—Chandler Cowles and Efrem Zimbalist, Jr.—decided to bring it to Broadway. The advance sale of $47 was a frightening warning that the brave producers refused to heed. They opened their production on May 1, 1947—and to a public long conditioned against operatic entertainment. From a nearby hotel window Menotti would spend the hour before curtain time counting the patrons who came into the theater. He did not require an adding machine. During the first few weeks the public came in scattered handfuls. At last both the finances and the faith of the producers gave out. A closing date was announced. There then took place what to this day is regarded as one of the minor miracles of our present-day theater. A sudden spurt of business at the box office necessitated extending the run for another short period, at which time another closing date was set. And once again business spurted, then boomed. By word of mouth the report had spread that *The Medium* and its slight and amusing one-act companion piece, *The Telephone* (1946), were wonderful shows. By the end of the spring season the production was strong enough to continue its run indefinitely and to establish itself as a hit. After that, *The Medium* was presented throughout the United States and in London and Paris, totaling more than one thousand performances within a few years. It was also made into a motion picture under Menotti's direction.

The Consul, which came to Broadway on March 16, 1950, was an even greater success. Menotti had been apprehensive about the possible audience appeal of his new work. "It is a very gloomy opera," he said. However, launched with overwhelming critical acclaim, *The*

Consul had an immediate advance sale of $100,000 and became one of the season's outstanding theatrical hits. It gathered honor after honor, including the Pulitzer Prize and the New York Drama Critics Circle Award. (The latter award was given to *The Consul* as the best musical play of the year, but three members of the Circle also singled it out as the best dramatic play.) Toscanini saw it at a dress rehearsal and then revisited it several times during its run. At the rehearsal, in the middle of the second act, the Maestro rose, walked over to Menotti, embraced him, and quietly returned to his seat. The general public found that *The Consul* was exciting entertainment. In the New York *Times Magazine,* Howard Taubman quoted a patron who came up to one of the producers and said: "It is touching and beautiful. Gosh, and I was afraid it was going to be an opera!" A hat-check girl insisted on picking up the tab for a round of drinks enjoyed by Menotti and a few friends as her token of gratitude for what she described as an unforgettable theatrical experience. After *The Consul* established itself as one of the season's major successes, the producers presented Menotti with a handpainted tie. The following line was scrawled on it: "It's a very gloomy opera."

Later on, *The Consul* was produced in a dozen countries, in eight different languages including the Flemish and the Turkish. Menotti became a celebrity. His story in *Life* was headed by the caption: "The Wizard of Opera." To this acclaim Menotti's reaction was characteristic: "Now is the time for humility," he told his producers.

In Italy, however, *The Consul* was attacked. It was presented by La Scala in 1950, the first time in its long and hallowed history that an opera written and introduced in America had been performed by that institution. Communists in the audience created a disturbance, interpreting the opera as an indictment against iron-curtain countries. Patriotic Italians denounced it because Menotti—of Italian birth and citizenship—preferred to live and work in the United States.

Having written operas for the radio and the Broadway theater, Menotti was now to experiment with a new technique. Commissioned by the National Broadcasting Company to write an opera expressly for television transmission, Menotti completed the text and music of *Amahl and the Night Visitors.* It was presented on Christmas Eve 1951 and—as the first opera ever written exclusively for television —was an event sufficiently important to warrant front-page treatment on the New York *Times.* "Television, operatically speaking, has come of age," was the verdict of Olin Downes. The broadcast was repeated by the National Broadcasting Company as an annual Christmas feature for many years. The opera was also produced on the stage by notable opera companies including the New York City Opera, and, in 1953, at the Florence May Music Festival.

The Saint of Bleecker Street—introduced in New York on December 27, 1954—won for Menotti the Pulitzer Prize in music a second time, as well as awards from the Drama Critics and Music Critics circles. This grim, realistic play was followed by a work of a strikingly different character and style: a "madrigal fable" entitled *The Unicorn, the Gorgon, and the Manticore,* first performed in Washington, D.C., on October 21, 1955. This is an intimate allegorical chamber opera for a chorus, nine instruments and ten dancers, whose score comprises an introduction, twelve madrigals, and six orchestral interludes. But in *Maria Golovin*—commissioned by NBC for the Brussels World's Fair where it was introduced on August 20, 1958—Menotti reverted successfully to a contemporary scene and realistic writing in a melodramatic style.

Menotti's versatility, so strikingly evident in what he had written up to 1958, continued to characterize his subsequent musicodramatic works. *Labyrinth,* in 1963, was a one-act opera for television commissioned by the NBC Opera Company. Symbolic, and at times even Dadaistic, *Labyrinth* used a hotel as symbol for the world while each of its characters represented some facet of life. *The Last Savage,* in 1963, was an *opera buffa* whose world *première* took place at the Opéra-Comique in Paris on October 21, 1963; its American *première* followed at the Metropolitan Opera on January 23, 1964. *Martin's Lie* was a modest church opera of chamber music dimensions. Though commissioned by the Columbia Broadcasting System, it was first mounted in a cathedral in Bristol, England, on June 3, 1964, during the Bath Festival. This performance was taped and telecast in the United States one year later. *Help, Help, the Globolinks*—which the composer described as "an opera for children and those who love children"—was introduced by the Hamburg Opera on December 18, 1968.

Besides his activity as composer, Menotti has been the producer of Samuel Barber's opera *Vanessa* at the Metropolitan Opera House and the Salzburg Festival. He also wrote the libretto for *Vanessa.* And in the summer of 1958 he became the founder and president of an annual "Festival of the Two Worlds" in the small town of Spoleto, near Assisi, Italy. Running that festival (and raising money for it) absorbed his energies until, in 1967, Menotti finally decided to turn over many of his own duties to a general manager, a newly created post which went to Massimo Bogianckino, former director of the Rome Opera.

When he is not traveling or at Spoleto, Menotti resides in "Capricorn," a rambling eight-room house on seventy acres near Mount Kisco, New York. He shares it with the American composer Samuel Barber and the poet Robert Horan, each of whom has his own studio in a different part of the house. That of Menotti is so constricted and overcrowded that it has room only for himself and his piano. At first this created a problem, as Menotti's habit is to work by fits and starts and then to pace the room nervously while smoking. He solved it by working in his studio and taking strolls in the adjoining room. When he sketches a scene he must shut the door tight. He sings out the entire scene at the top of his voice. As he sings he makes corrections, then starts singing the scene all over again. When quiet has finally been restored his friends know that the scene has been completed.

He has a prodigious capacity for work; he works all day long, often seven days a week, and at times on several projects. But this does not mean he is free of extramusical interests and hobbies, which include bird breeding, collecting paintings and sculpture, playing tennis, reading horror stories, and, in the company of congenial people, exchanging stimulating conversation or plain gossip.

HIS MUSIC

In reviewing *The Consul*, Virgil Thomson made the following observation: "*The Consul* is a music drama of great power in a production remarkably efficient. I doubt if it makes musical history, but the musical elements contribute in a major way to a spectacle that may well have its place in our century's history of the stage."

Menotti's operas are important as theatrical spectacles. Their greatest significance does not lie—as it does with most operas—in the score. His music is frequently more functional than inspired. It has no distinguishable identity. Menotti draws from every available style and idiom to cater to his dramatic need: from the popular to the esoteric, from the lyrical to the dissonant, from the romantic to the realistic. Music is never an end, but a means; the end is the projection of effective theater. Divorced from the theater, his music lacks genuine distinction and originality; for this reason parts of his operas are rarely presented in the concert hall. But within the theater his music has tremendous impact.

Like Wagner, he is a one-man theater. He not only writes his own text and music, but is his own stage director, casting director, and has an important voice in every other phase of production. He has an extraordinary sixth sense for picking out any ingredient that might make up good drama. That sixth sense helped him select from the ranks of comparatively inexperienced and unknown singers performers such as Marie Powers, Patricia Neway, and the twelve-year-old boy soprano Chet Allen, whose brilliant and penetrating characterizations of, respectively, Flora, Magda, and Amahl were important factors in the great success of the productions of *The Medium, The Consul,* and *Amahl and the Night Visitors.* That sixth sense enabled him to find the *mot juste* (either in text, or in the music, or in a piece of stagecraft) for every situation and mood. Even routines that others would discard as phony (the sudden shattering of a windowpane, a spooky séance, a dream dance, hypnotism, legerdemain, and so forth) become vital parts of the artistic whole and heighten the dramatic effect. His sense for good theater never fails him.

Whether Menotti has yet produced a great opera is open to question for the simple reason that he has as yet produced no great operatic score. But there is no doubt that he has succeeded in creating *effective* opera, opera that is a living experience in the theater, capable of dealing with everyday problems and people and holding the fascinated interest of his audience. He has done more than this. By resiliently adapting opera for the radio, theater, cinema, and television —assimilating within opera the individual techniques of each of these media—he has opened up for it new horizons.

ANALYTICAL NOTES

Opera. *Amelia Goes to the Ball* (1937) was Menotti's first success. It is a one-act comic opera in the *buffa* style of Wolf-Ferrari. Book and music are infectiously witty and well integrated. In the traditional style of the *opera buffa,* an inexhaustible flow of melody is combined with piquant harmonies (even polytonality and atonality in moderation), provocative orchestral effects, and leaping rhythms to point up a piece of stage business or to catch a passing mood wittily.

An effervescent little overture sets the gay mood for the coming action. The story concerns Amelia, pampered daughter of the Milanese *salon,* who wants to go to a ball. It looks as if her every attempt to get there is doomed to frustration. Her husband discovers he has a rival for her affection and makes a great fuss. After he leaves the room angrily, the lover comes in through the window to express his great love to Amelia. He is discovered by the returning husband, and they begin to discuss this embarrassing situation much to the despair of Amelia, who fears she will be late for the ball. At length she smashes a vase over her husband's head. Calling the police, she orders the arrest of her lover as a burglar. The husband is dispatched to the hospital and the lover to jail. And now Amelia can at least go to the ball—in the company of the Chief of Police.

The Medium (1945) is, by contrast, a tragedy. Menotti's music, so bright and crisp in *Amelia,* assumes somber hues. With the fullest resources of modern harmony and tonality, and with an expressive song-speech as recitative, Menotti creates the macabre atmosphere of his eerie play with overpowering effect. But he is astute enough to contrast many of the dark pages with lighter moods.

The central character is Flora, a fake medium. During one of her séances she thinks a cold, clammy hand is seizing her throat. Terrified, she is led to confess to her clients that she is a fraud, but they do not believe her. Her suspicions fall on a mute in her employ, Toby, who is in love with her daughter; Flora is convinced that Toby wants to murder her. So upset does she become that she seeks escape in drink. In a drunken stupor she fires a gun through a wooden cabinet in which Toby is hiding and kills him.

The Telephone (1946) a one-act opera, returns to the gaiety of *Amelia.* The text and music are slight. They complement each other in irresponsible gaiety and in indulgence in a delicious tongue-in-cheek absurdity. There is a disarming naïveté about all the proceedings. The telephone is the villain of the piece. Its continual ringing frustrates the attempt of a young lover to propose to his sweetheart. At last he rushes out of her living room to the corner drugstore. Her telephone rings again. It is her lover—proposing by phone!

In *The Consul* (1949) we are in a police state in the Europe of our time; the opera's characters are caught helplessly in the bureaucratic red tape. The scene shifts from a home—darkened by the immense shadow of the omnipresent secret police—to the consulate of a free land, through which the victims of tyranny hope to find escape into freedom. The wait at the consulate is interminable, while doom stands watch just around the corner. One of the victims is Magda, who is trying to get a visa out of the country to join her husband who has already managed to find freedom. While she waits her child dies and her husband returns from his freedom to join her, only to be taken by the police. In the end Magda can find escape through but a single avenue: suicide.

It is a grim and bitter play for which Menotti provided music no less stark. Dissonance, polytonality, song-speech, free rhythms evoke all the terror that so crushes the victims of a dictatorial state. But there is full-blooded lyricism too, ranging from the effete little music-hall tune with which the opera opens to the magnificent and culminating aria of Magda (one of the high moments of the opera), which closes the second act.

Amahl and the Night Visitors is a short Christmas opera commissioned by the National Broadcasting Company for a television broadcast on Christmas Eve 1951. Menotti prepared his own text, the idea for which came to him after seeing *The Adoration of the Magi,* a Flemish painting by Hieronymous Bosch. The book he wrote has the simplicity and poignancy of an age-old folk legend. The Magi, following the star that leads them to the child Jesus in the Manger, come upon the hovel of Amahl, a crippled beggar boy, and his mother. Amahl is awed by the sight of these Three Kings. When he learns of their mission the child unhesitatingly gives them his crutches as a gift to the Holy Child. But when the boy goes forth to present his gift to the Kings he discovers that a miracle has taken place: he is able to walk.

While the score places considerable emphasis on recitatives, most of which are extraordinarily expressive and varied, it is also filled with many passages of lyrical beauty, with powerful choruses, and with tender ensemble numbers in all of which the poetic mood of the opera as a whole prevails without interruption. It is the atmosphere and mood of the opera as a whole, rather than any individual parts, that give the works its emotional force. Although *Amahl and the Night*

Visitors was written for and has been frequently seen on the television screen, it has also been given successful stage presentations.

In *The Saint of Bleecker Street* (1954) and *Maria Golovin* (1958) Menotti reverts to the stark realism and melodrama for which he has become famous. Both operas are built around afflicted people. The heroine of *The Saint of Bleecker Street* is a religious mystic, a sickly girl who dies at the height of the ceremonies in which she is accepted as the Bride of Christ by her Church. In *Maria Golovin* the principal male character is a blind man in love with Maria, the latter an emotionally starved woman whose husband has for several years been a prisoner of war. In both operas, Menotti brings to his eclectic musical style that remarkable capacity to express emotional torment and project dramatic episodes, and that keen feeling for atmosphere and characterization which make for excellent theater as well as excellent music.

The Last Savage (1963) represented a radical change of pace for Menotti, away from harrowing realism on the one hand and broad farce on the other. For *The Last Savage* is a satire on such present-day social and cultural refinements as cocktail parties and beatniks, abstract painters and composers of serial music, Government bureaucracy and trade unions. The plot concerns the efforts of an American woman anthropologist, daughter of a millionaire, to find the legendary Abominable Snowman in India. There she meets and falls in love with the Maharajah's son. Since she refuses to marry until she has accomplished her anthropological mission, the Maharajah arranges to have his stable boy assume the identity of the Snowman. Throughout, the composer-lyricist puts tongue in cheek.

The Most Important Man (1971) touches upon racial problems by having its hero, a black scientist in an apartheid community probably in South Africa, creating a formula able to make its owner the world's most powerful man. He becomes involved in a life-and-death struggle with white scientists for its possession. In the end he is killed and his formula is destroyed.

Tamu-Tamu was written for the ninth International Congress of Anthropological and Ethnological Sciences in Chicago in 1973. It is a two-act chamber opera combining speech with pleasing song. The title is Indonesian for "the guests," and the text dramatizes a clash between the opposing cultures of modern Americans in Indonesia and its war-torn natives.

Giacomo Meyerbeer

"History will point to Meyerbeer's music as one of the most important steps to Wagner's art."

HUGO RIEMANN

BORN: Berlin, September 5, 1791.
DIED: Paris, May 2, 1864.
MAJOR WORKS: *Operas*—Robert le Diable; Les Huguenots; Le Prophète; L'Etoile du nord; Dinorah; L'Africaine.

HIS LIFE

A Jew born in Germany and trained in Italy was the greatest exponent of French grand opera. He was born as Jakob Liebmann Beer, the son of a wealthy Berlin banker. The "Meyer" was prefixed to his last name after he had received a legacy from a wealthy relative of that name; Jakob became Giacomo when he began writing Italian operas. He was a child prodigy. After a period of study with Franz Ignaz Lauska he made a successful concert appearance as pianist playing the Mozart D minor Concerto; he was only seven years old at the time. Repeated appearances during the next two years ensured his position as one of the most gifted and highly acclaimed concert pianists in Berlin.

Muzio Clementi, celebrated teacher of the piano and composer of the *Gradus ad Parnassum,* which to this day is regarded as indispensable to the training of the young pianist, heard Meyerbeer play in 1802. He was so impressed that, though he was in retirement, he offered to teach him without a fee. At the same time Meyerbeer studied theory with Zelter and counterpoint with Anselm Weber. An exercise in fugal writing convinced Weber that his pupil had unusual talent. He sent the fugue on to one of the most distinguished musicians of the day: Abbé Vogler (1749–1814), theorist, teacher, and composer of operas, choral works, and decidedly popular "storm pieces" for organ. Vogler was less impressed with the fugue than Weber had been. He returned it to Meyerbeer extensively corrected and revised, together with a detailed treatise on the writing of fugues. Meyerbeer proceeded to write a new fugue according to the rules set down in Vogler's treatise. The Abbé was now enthusiastic. "Come to me at Darmstadt where you will be my son," he wrote Meyerbeer. "Art opens to you a glorious future."

In 1810 Meyerbeer became Vogler's pupil and household guest. His fellow student and bosom friend was Karl Maria von Weber (later to become the first of the great German Romantic composers in opera). Vogler subjected Meyerbeer to a rigorous schedule: practicing on the piano and organ; doing composition exercises; writing choral pieces and fugues. Under this regimen Meyerbeer thrived. In the two years he studied with Vogler he wrote several large works, including a cantata, *God and Nature,* and his first opera, *Jephtha's Vow.*

The cantata, after being introduced in Darmstadt, was given a major performance in Berlin by the Singakademie on May 8, 1811. A critic writing for one of the Berlin newspapers remarked its "glowing life, genuine loveliness, and above all the perfect power of burning genius." The fact that this critic was Meyerbeer's close friend Karl Maria von Weber (brought to Berlin by Meyerbeer to hear the performance) may have had something to do with the effusive praise.

With Abbé Vogler's words, "there is nothing more I can teach you" ringing pleasantly in his ears, Meyerbeer left Darmstadt in 1812. His first stop was Munich, where his opera *Jephtha's Vow* was performed. It was a disheartening failure. Meyerbeer went on to Vienna intending to renew his long-interrupted career as piano virtuoso. But on his first evening in Vienna he heard a concert by Nepomuk Hummel, then one of the most celebrated pianists, which temporarily thwarted his intention. Eventually Meyerbeer did give a recital and was acclaimed. He also continued composing. A second opera, *Wirt und Gast* (or *Alimelek*), originally seen in Stuttgart on January 6, 1813, was presented in Vienna, but with no greater success than *Jephtha's Vow*. For a brief period Meyerbeer thought of renouncing composition for good. Fortunately he met and was heartened by Antonio Salieri, one of Vienna's most venerable musicians, who convinced him that his failures had been due to an inadequate preparation. On Salieri's advice Meyerbeer went to Italy in 1815 to learn about opera at its source.

In Italy, the German musician was transformed into an Italian. He himself put it this way: "All my feelings became Italian. All my thoughts became Italian. After I had lived a year there it seemed to me that I was an Italian born. I was completely acclimated to the splendid glory of nature, art, and the gay congenial life, and could therefore enter into the thoughts, feelings and sensibilities of the Italians. Of course such a complete re-turning of my spiritual life had an immediate effect upon my methods of composition." In brief, he had become a composer of Italian opera; the influence of Rossini asserted itself. *Romilda e Costanza,* seen in Padua on July 19, 1817, was such a triumph that many different Italian opera houses commissioned him to write new works. The operas yielded by those commissions placed Meyerbeer with the most popular composers in Italy. These operas included *Semiramide riconosciuta* (1819), *Emma di Resburgo* (1819), *Margherita d'Anjou* (1820), and *L'Esule di Granata* (1822). The last of these, following its *première* at La Scala in Milan on March 12, 1822, was widely produced throughout Europe.

He was back in Berlin in 1823. Karl Maria von Weber directed performances of *Wirt und Gast* and *Emma di Resburgo* at the Dresden Opera. In spite of this, Weber was none too happy with Meyerbeer's Italian-made operas. "It makes my heart bleed," he wrote to Meyerbeer, "to see a German composer of creative power stoop to become a mere imitator in order to curry favor with the crowd." Meyerbeer himself was none too satisfied with the kind of operas he was writing. He was soon to refer to them as his "wild oats." And signs of his dissatisfaction could be found in *Il Crociato in Egitto,* successfully introduced in Venice on May 7, 1824. Here we find the penetration of Germanic influences in his work, particularly in his harmonic and orchestral writing, even though his partiality for Italian lyricism had not been abandoned.

Then, in 1826, Meyerbeer came to Paris. For a while he wrote nothing. He listened, studied, and assimilated. The ideals of French opera, which placed so much emphasis on the drama, were clarified to him through personal associations with such eminent French opera composers as Jacques Halévy (1799–1862)—then still in his apprenticeship but soon to produce his masterwork, *La Juive*—and the master of the *opéra comique,* Daniel François Auber (1782–1871). The Gallicized Italian, Luigi Cherubini (1760–1842), already one of the dominant figures in French opera, was also an influence.

When Meyerbeer returned to the writing of opera, it was to be in the French rather than the Italian vein. *Robert le Diable,* on a text by Eugène Scribe, presented at the Opéra on November 21, 1831, was an instantaneous success and a permanent one. It attracted a fortune into the box office of the Opéra: approximately four million francs within twenty-five years. *Les Huguenots,* seen at the Opéra on February 29, 1836, was at first somewhat less successful; but before long it seized the imagination of French opera audiences and inspired enthusiasm from such discriminating musicians as Berlioz and the young Richard Wagner. Still a third triumph followed: *Le Prophète,* its first performance taking place at the Opéra on April 16, 1849.

Meyerbeer had become one of the most celebrated composers in all Europe. France conferred on him membership in the Legion of Honor and subsequently made him Commander; it also elected him to the Institut. From London came an appointment to the Royal Academy; from the Netherlands, the Order of the Oak Crown; from the University of Jena, an honorary degree.

In 1843, Meyerbeer became Kapellmeister to the King of Prussia in Berlin. He wrote numerous choral works for the royal chapel, functional pieces for the court, and a new opera (*Ein Feldlager in Schlesien,* heard on December 7, 1844). He was also active as conductor for many notable operas including Weber's *Euryanthe* and Wagner's *Rienzi.*

He made frequent trips out of Berlin to many different parts of Europe, mostly to Paris to attend performances of his new operas. One of these was *Le Prophète,* already mentioned. Another was a comic opera, *L'Etoile du nord*—the first work of a foreigner to be introduced at the Opéra-Comique, on February 16, 1854. During its first performance there the enthusiasm of the audience was so spontaneous and without bounds that every major number had to be repeated. One hundred performances were given in the first year. His second comic opera, *Le Pardon de Ploërmel,* performed at the Opéra-Comique on April 4, 1859, was also a huge success under its later and more familiar title of *Dinorah.*

Meyerbeer devoted the last years of his life to the opera *L'Africana,* which he had begun in 1838. Conscious that it was his most important work, he brought to it the most painstaking effort, revising continually and making so many demands on his librettist, Scribe, that at one time they parted company. Work was made more difficult by poor health and failing eyesight. But it continued. With the opera in rehearsal, he was still making so many alterations that its performance had to be delayed continually. He died without hearing this opera. (It was seen for the first time one year after his death, on April 28, 1865.)

Morbidly afraid all his life of being buried alive, he instructed his heirs in writing that his body must lie in state in Paris for four days before interment. He also gave specific orders that his face must remain fully visible during that period following his death; that little bells be placed on his hands and feet so that the slightest movement would make them jingle; that two guardians must stand watch at his coffin twenty-four hours a day; that on the fifth day an incision of the brachial artery be made to ensure that no life was left in the body. All these instructions were followed religiously.

To the accompaniment of his own music Meyerbeer's body was taken to the railroad station for transfer to his native city. A hero's funeral took place after which, in striking contrast, Meyerbeer was buried in the humble Jewish Cemetery.

His unpretentious grave was symbolic of his life. A man of wealth and taste, he could have lived in the grand manner had he wished. He preferred the simple. His home in Paris was extremely modest. His table was frugal. He never took a carriage when he could walk. He never drank or smoked. He allowed himself the luxury of only one servant. For all this he was often contemptuously criticized as a miser. But his many generous benefactions to individuals and organizations give the lie to the accusation that he was parsimonious. He himself explained: "I have no desire to stand aloof from my associates and play the rich amateur."

HIS MUSIC

Meyerbeer was the most important composer to place the word "grand" in French grand opera. It was an Italian who had first arrived at the traditions of French opera. He was Jean Baptiste Lully (1632–87). His concern was with stage action, and the emphasis he placed in his music on dramatic effect, particularly in his recitatives and orchestration, set his operas sharply apart from those of the Italians. A Frenchman, Jean Philippe Rameau (1683–1764), went one step further in making music serve the play. This ever growing interest in the play was further reflected in the works of Luigi Cherubini (1760–1842) and Gasparo Spontini (1774–1851), with their elaborate ballets and scenes of great pomp. The "grand manner" was now the accepted style in French opera; and it reached its apotheosis with Meyerbeer.

But had Meyerbeer's operas been the lavish framework for heroic historical plays—that and no more—they would surely have been withdrawn from the opera stage long ago (even as the works of Cherubini and Spontini have been withdrawn). But for all his weakness for superficial veneer, for visual effect, for excessive heroics, and for meretricious writing—there was no question but that he never allowed his eye to stray from his audience—he was, at his best, a creator of originality and importance, even an innovator. His dramatic instinct rarely failed him; he knew the theater and was a master of stage effect. He had, to a marked degree, the gift of melody as well as an unerring hand in ensemble writing. He had an extraordinary orchestral virtuosity. Such a marked advance was made by his operas in merging theater and music that Liszt regarded Meyerbeer as inaugurating a "new epoch in operatic writing."

ANALYTICAL NOTES

Opera. Pageantry within century-old historical settings distinguished the three operas with which Meyerbeer helped establish the French tradition. *Robert le Diable* (1831) takes place in thirteenth-century Palermo. Its hero is a Norman duke whose mother is mortal while his father is a devil disguised as a man. Seeking Isabella's love,

Robert enlists the aid of diabolical powers in return for his soul. But he repents, becomes dissuaded from his aim to abduct Isabella, and denounces his father, who then is consigned to the underworld.

Les Huguenots (1836) and *Le Prophète* (1849) both draw their material from the history book: the former from the massacre in France of the Huguenots at the hands of the Catholics in 1572; the latter, the uprising of the Anabaptists in Holland in the sixteenth century. *Les Huguenots* involves Raoul de Nangis, a Huguenot nobleman, in a stormy romance with Valentine, daughter of Count de Bris; both Raoul and Valentine are murdered by the Catholics soon after their marriage. In *Le Prophète* the love interest engages John of Leyden, leader of the Anabaptists in their rebellion, and Bertha. This romance also ends in violent death.

Though spectacle, stirring choruses, and surging dramatic climaxes distinguish all three operas, the affecting lyricism Meyerbeer had learned to write during his Italian period had not been forgotten. In *Robert le Diable* we find it in the two celebrated romantic arias *"Robert, toi que j'aime"* and *"Nonnes, qui reposez"*; in *Les Huguenots* in Raoul's poignant air *"Pius blanche que la blanche hermine"* and in Marguerite's hymn to the beauty of the Touraine countryside, *"O beau pays de la Touraine;* in *Le Prophète,* in the vocal highlight of the whole opera, a mother's song of gratitude to her son, John, *"Ah, mon fils!"*

In both *Les Huguenots* and *Le Prophète,* a religious melody is prominently used—the Lutheran chorale "Ein' feste Burg" in *Les Huguenots,* and the unison chant "Ad nos, ad salutam" in *Le Prophète*. An orchestral excerpt from *Le Prophète* is probably the most popular single piece of music Meyerbeer ever wrote. It is the "Coronation March" from Act IV, Scene 2, in which John is crowned king outside the Münster Cathedral.

L'Africana, or *L'Africaine* (1864), Meyerbeer's last opera, does not lack those striking theatrical scenes and stirring climaxes for which he was justifiably famous. But it is not for its pageantry that *L'Africana* has maintained its popularity through the years. *L'Africana* is, indeed, one of Meyerbeer's more economical productions. Of his French operas it is the one in which he depended most on Italian style and lyricism for his artistic effect. The impact the opera has always had on audiences is due to its stirring emotional content, dramatic power, and exotic background.

The setting is Portugal and the Island of Madagascar between the fifteenth and sixteenth centuries, and the central character is Vasco da Gama, the famous explorer. Returning from an African expedition Vasco da Gama brings back with him the African queen Selika, who is in love with him, and her servant Nelusko. But da Gama is in love with Inez, whose father demands that she marry Don Pedro. Don Pedro contrives to have da Gama temporarily jailed while he goes forth seeking the new African land which the explorer had discovered; he takes with him both Inez and Selika. Da Gama follows to warn Don Pedro that his ship is to be attacked by Nelusko's men; but his warning is unheeded. Don Pedro's ship is attacked. Selika manages to take da Gama back with her to the beautiful island of Madagascar. But when da Gama learns that Inez is still alive he deserts Selika to find her. Overwhelmed, the African queen commits suicide.

In the first act, the council chamber of the King of Portugal, we hear two splendid arias. The first is by Inez, who, awaiting the return of da Gama from his expedition, rapturously recalls the explorer's tender farewell to her, *"Del Tago sponde addio"* (*"Adieu mon doux rivage"*). After da Gama's return he makes a fiery petition to the councilors for new ships and men with which to continue his explorations and bring new glory to Portugal, *"Io vidi, miei signori"* (*"J'ai vu, nobles seigneurs"*).

Selika's poignant cradle song, *"In grembo a me"* (*"Sur mes genoux"*), and Nelusko's elaborate aria pledging his loyalty to Selika and his native land, *"Figlia dei re"* (*"Fille des rois"*), are among the most impressive pages in the second act, which is set in the prison of the Inquisition.

In the third act, on Don Pedro's ship, Nelusko delivers to the sailors a powerful aria about the sea which, when enraged, destroys those who come into contact with it, *"Adamastor, re dell' onde profonde"* (*"Adamastor, roi des vagues profondes"*). The fourth act, on the island of Madagascar, has the most celebrated aria of the opera. It is Vasco da Gama's ecstatic hymn to the beauty of the new land, *"O Paradiso"* (*"O Paradis"*).

In its original version the fifth act was divided into two scenes, but the first of these (in the Queen's garden) is now usually omitted. The opera ends with the death of Selika on a promontory by the sea, after Vasco da Gama has sailed forth to find Inez. Just before her death

Selika sings a tender aria in which she seeks eternal peace through death, *"O tempio sontuoso"* (*"O Temple magnifigue"*). The opera concludes with a chant of an unseen chorus telling that in the kingdom of love all are equal, *"Questo sol e il soggiorno"* (*"C'est ici le séjour"*).